18th Conference of the European Chapter of the Association for Computational Linguistics (EACL 2024)

System Demonstrations

St. Julian's, Malta
21 - 22 March 2024

ISBN: 978-1-7138-9445-2

Printed from e-media with permission by:

Curran Associates, Inc.
57 Morehouse Lane
Red Hook, NY 12571

Some format issues inherent in the e-media version may also appear in this print version.

Association for Computational Linguistics
209 N. Eighth Street
Stroudsburg, Pennsylvania 18360

Phone: 1-570-476-8006
Fax: 1-570-476-0860

acl@aclweb.org

Additional copies of this publication are available from:

Curran Associates, Inc.
57 Morehouse Lane
Red Hook, NY 12571 USA
Phone: 845-758-0400
Fax: 845-758-2633
Email: curran@proceedings.com
Web: www.proceedings.com

EACL 2024

The 18th Conference of the European Chapter of the Association for Computational Linguistics

Proceedings of System Demonstrations

March 17-22, 2024

The EACL organizers gratefully acknowledge the support from the following sponsors.

Platinum

Megagon Labs

Gold

Bloomberg Engineering

snowflake

Bronze

Adobe

Babelscape

D&I Champion

HITS Heidelberger Institut für Theoretische Studien

Order copies of this and other ACL proceedings from:

Association for Computational Linguistics (ACL)
317 Sidney Baker St. S
Suite 400 - 134
Kerrville, TX 78028
USA
Tel: +1-855-225-1962
acl@aclweb.org

Introduction

Welcome to the proceedings of the system demonstration track of the 18th Conference of the European Chapter of the Association for Computational Linguistics (EACL 2024) on March 17-22, 2024. For the EACL 2024 system demonstration track, we received 58 submissions, of which 24 were selected for inclusion in the program (acceptance rate of 41.3%). We would like to thank the members of the program committee for their timely help in reviewing the submissions. Lastly, we thank the many authors that submitted their work to the demonstrations track. As this year's EACL conference is a hybrid event, the demonstration papers will be presented through virtual presentations and also in person during the poster sessions. We appreciate the efforts made by all authors to showcase their work and contribute to the success of the conference.

Orphée De Clercq, Nikos Aletras
EACL 2024 System Demonstration Chairs

Program Committee

Chairs

Nikolaos Aletras, University of Sheffield and Amazon
Orphee De Clercq, LT3, Ghent University

Program Committee

Rodrigo Agerri, HiTZ Center-Ixa, University of the Basque Country UPV/EHU
Zeynep Akkalyoncu, University of Waterloo
Rafael Anchiêta, Federal Institute of Piauí
Eleftherios Avramidis, German Research Center for Artificial Intelligence (DFKI)
Mohaddeseh Bastan, Stony Brook University
Himanshu Beniwal, Indian Institute of Technology Gandhinagar
Gábor Berend, University Of Szeged
Aljoscha Burchardt, DFKI
Alberto Cetoli, Private
Chung-Chi Chen, National Institute of Advanced Industrial Science and Technology
Guanyi Chen, Central China Normal University
Jhih-Jie Chen, National Tsing Hua University
Yagmur Gizem Cinar, Amazon
Danilo Croce, University of Roma, Tor Vergata
Marina Danilevsky, IBM Research
Ellen De Geyndt, UGent
Michael Desmond, IBM Research
Chenchen Ding, NICT
Carl Edwards, University of Illinois, Urbana-Champaign
Sudeep Gandhe, Google Inc
Xianpei Han, Institute of Software, Chinese Academy of Sciences
Freddy Heppell, The University of Sheffield
Ales Horak, Masaryk University
Claudiu Hromei, Department of Enterprise Engineering University of Rome, Tor Vergata, Italy
Xiaodan Hu, University of Illinois at Urbana-Champaign
Ali Hürriyetoğlu, KNAW
Jeff Jacobs, Columbia University
Sudipta Kar, Amazon Alexa AI
Constantinos Karouzos, University of Sheffield
Philipp Koehn, Johns Hopkins University
Mamoru Komachi, Hitotsubashi University
Valia Kordoni, Humboldt-Universität zu Berlin
Philippe Laban, Salesforce Research
Tuan Lai, University of Illinois at Urbana-Champaign
Mark Last, Ben-Gurion University of the Negev
Xintong Li, Apple
Wolfgang Maier, Mercedes-Benz AG
Stella Markantonatou, ILSP/R.C. Athena
Margot Mieskes, University of Applied Sciences, Darmstadt
Hamdy Mubarak, Qatar Computing Research Institute
Diane Napolitano, The Washington Post

Tae-Gil Noh, OMQ GmbH
Feifei Pan, Amazon
Prokopis Prokopidis, ILSP/Athena RC
Pablo Ruiz Fabo, LiLPa, Université de Strasbourg
Danae Sanchez Villegas, University of Sheffield
Sashank Santhanam, University of North Carolina at Charlotte/ Apple
Sven Schmeier, Researcher
Jaydeep Sen, IBM Research AI
Liang-Hsin Shen, National Taiwan University
Michal Shmueli-Scheuer, IBM Research
Lei Shu, Google Research
Jian Sun, China Mobile Research Institute
Chenkai Sun, University of Illinois at Urbana-Champaign
Natalia Vanetik, Shamoon College of Engineering
Qingyun Wang, University of Illinois at Urbana-Champaign
Rui Wang, Vipshop (China) Co., Ltd.
Zhen Xu, Tencent PCG
Huiyin Xue, The University of Sheffield
Atsuki Yamaguchi, University of Sheffield
Tae Yano, Expedia Group
Seid Muhie Yimam, Universität Hamburg
Qi Zeng, University of Illinois at Urbana-Champaign
Qi Zhang, Fudan University
Chengzhi Zhang, Nanjing University of Science and Technology
Guangyou Zhou, School of Computer Science, Central China Normal University
Cangqi Zhou, Nanjing University of Science and Technology

Table of Contents

TextBI: An Interactive Dashboard for Visualizing Multidimensional NLP Annotations in Social Media Data

Maxime Masson[1,2], Christian Sallaberry[1], Marie-Noelle Bessagnet[1], Annig Le Parc Lacayrelle[1], Philippe Roose[1], and Rodrigo Agerri[2]

[1]LIUPPA, E2S, University of Pau and Pays Adour (UPPA), Pau, France
[2]HiTZ Center - Ixa, University of the Basque Country UPV/EHU

Abstract

In this paper we introduce *TextBI*, a multimodal generic dashboard designed to present multidimensional text annotations on large volumes of multilingual social media data. This tool focuses on four core dimensions: spatial, temporal, thematic, and personal, and also supports additional enrichment data such as sentiment and engagement. Multiple visualization modes are offered, including frequency, movement, and association. This dashboard addresses the challenge of facilitating the interpretation of NLP annotations by visualizing them in a user-friendly, interactive interface catering to two categories of users: (1) domain stakeholders and (2) NLP researchers. We conducted experiments within the domain of tourism leveraging data from X (formerly Twitter) and incorporating requirements from tourism offices. Our approach, *TextBI*, represents a significant advancement in the field of visualizing NLP annotations by integrating and blending features from a variety of Business Intelligence, Geographical Information Systems and NLP tools. A demonstration video is also provided.[1]

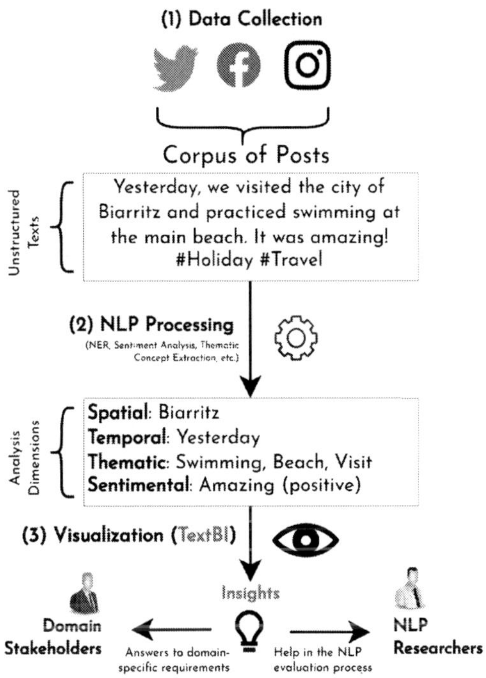

Figure 1: TextBI's role in the interaction with the NLP pipeline

1 Introduction

In today's data-driven era, the ability to quickly analyze, interpret, and make decisions based on vast amounts of data has become crucial (Leung et al., 2013). This is particularly true for social media platforms, which generate extensive amounts of textual data. Natural Language Processing (NLP) plays a crucial role in transforming unstructured text data, like social media posts, into structured knowledge (Souili et al., 2015). However, the enormous quantity of social media information and the wide range of potential automatic annotations can make it challenging to efficiently extract insights from annotated social media data. Consequently, there is a need for tools that can facilitate the interpretation and understanding of automatic annotations within a social media corpus for people who are not necessarily domain-experts. This paper introduces *TextBI*, a generic, multi-modal dashboard that enables comprehensive visualizations of multidimensional annotations extracted from social media (see Fig. 1).

TextBI offers a user-friendly and intuitive interface that presents text annotations visually. *TextBI* goes further than existing NLP visualization tools by incorporating interactions, multidimensional combined filtering, and visual synchronization, commonly found in Business Intelligence (BI) tools. Raw multilingual text annotations are converted into interactive visuals, making them more

[1]https://youtu.be/x714RKvo9Cg

Proceedings of the 18th Conference of the European Chapter of the Association for Computational Linguistics System Demonstrations, pages 1–9
March 17-22, 2024 ©2024 Association for Computational Linguistics

easily understandable thereby facilitating their interpretation. This dashboard operates on four generic dimensions: spatial (*location data*), temporal (*time stamps*), thematic (*data semantics linked with a domain resource*), and personal (*user-related data and profiles*). Furthermore, it supports optional and extensible enrichment data, including sentiment and engagement metrics (e.g., *likes, shares*). *TextBI* also comes with a generic data model (APs Model; Masson et al., 2023b) capable of modeling any annotated corpus from social media along the aforementioned dimensions.

Data collection and NLP must be undertaken before its use to produce an annotated corpus of social media posts. *TextBI* is designed to address the requirements of two distinct categories of users:

- **Domain Stakeholders**: seeking specific insights related to their field. For example, in the tourism industry, tourism offices might find it beneficial to analyze certain types of information. This could include identifying the most popular tourist activities, determining which cities are often visited together, and understanding the emotions or opinions of visitors regarding their experiences. This information can assist them in making informed decisions.

- **NLP Researchers** in need of a tool to evaluate NLP processes and models. This could involve observing the distribution of various types of annotations to better diagnose recurring issues.

Both categories of users may have different end goals, but there might be common interests in terms of what they want to observe. We believe that both groups are likely to share an interest in identifying frequencies, associations, and sequences of annotations. Additionally, they may want to conduct cross-dimensional analyses involving different types of annotations. Thus, *TextBI* could meet the requirements for both categories of end-users.

Previous work on Business Intelligence (BI; Datig and Whiting, 2018; Orlovskyi and Kopp, 2020; Vashisht and Dharia, 2020; Desai et al., 2021), Geographical Information Systems (GIS; Kurt Menke et al., 2016) and NLP tools (Chantrapornchai and Tunsakul, 2021; Rajaonarivo et al., 2022) have addressed the visualization of NLP annotations in an independent manner. In this work we take into account previous approaches while also addressing their respective limitations. From BI tools, we borrow the interactive design, user-friendly interfaces, and visual synchronization, adapting these features for their use with annotated text data as opposed to traditional numerical data. We adopt detailed spatial views of GIS tools, acknowledging that social media data often contains a spatial aspect. However, unlike traditional GIS tools, we aim for a multidimensional approach, not just a spatial one. From NLP tools, we take their analytical strength, such as co-occurrence and frequency analysis, but go beyond their usual focus on text and basic words to include dimensional entities like thematic concepts, locations, and time periods. By merging these elements, TextBI aims to provide an inclusive visualization of NLP annotations that benefits both researchers and domain-specific stakeholders.

Summarizing, we believe that *TextBI* represents a significant advancement in the field of visualizing NLP annotations by integrating and blending features of a variety of tools.

2 Related Work

Geographical Information Systems (GIS) such as QGIS (Kurt Menke et al., 2016) and ArcGIS (Booth et al., 2001) offer a wide variety of functionalities to meet the varying needs of different users. While these systems are useful for visualizing geospatial data in depth, their primary focus is on the spatial aspect of data, which limits their usefulness in non-spatial data contexts. Although GIS tools are capable of displaying thematic data (Murthy et al., 2003), they must be associated with a specific spatial area.

In the realm of **Business Intelligence (BI) tools**, Tableau (Datig and Whiting, 2018), Power BI (Ferrari and Russo, 2016), and QlikView (Shukla and Dhir, 2016) are recognized for their ability to empower decision-making processes (Hansoti, 2010; Orlovskyi and Kopp, 2020) via their interactive data exploration and user-friendly dashboards. However, these tools are primarily designed to handle numerical and well-structured data, resulting in significant challenges when working with text data. While certain efforts have been made to incorporate NLP processes into BI tools (Vashisht and Dharia, 2020; Desai et al., 2021), they struggle to present sequential data (*e.g., trajectories*) and draw connections across text annotations from various dimensions. Additionally, these tools lack comprehensive support for multilingual data.

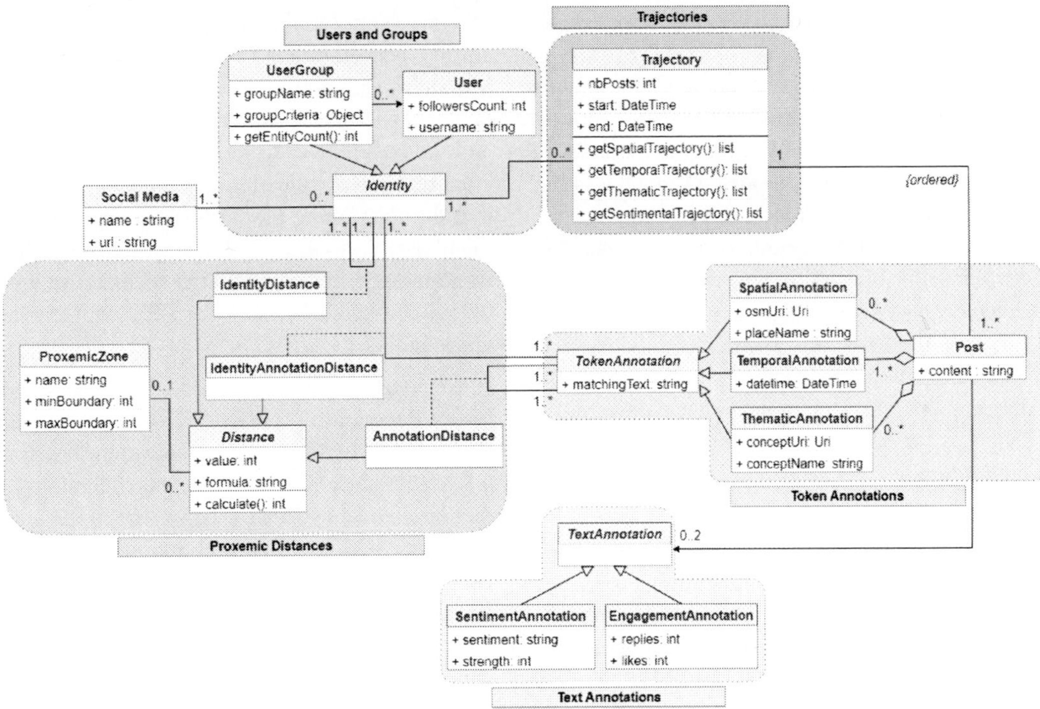

Figure 2: The generic APs data model using proxemics to model social media data (Masson et al., 2023b).

When it comes to **NLP tools**, they can be divided into two main categories. Some of them, such as SpaCy (Chantrapornchai and Tunsakul, 2021), TextRazor (Rajaonarivo et al., 2022), GATE (Maynard et al., 2000), and Gensim (Rehurek and Sojka, 2011), primarily focus on data processing, offering limited visualization capabilities such as word clouds, semantic graphs, and text-based annotation views. Other tools, such as IRaMuTeQ (Loubère and Ratinaud, 2014), Voyant (Welsh, 2014), VOSviewer (Van Eck and Waltman, 2013), and SentimentViz (Healey and Ramaswamy, 2022), offer a broader range of visualization options, but are generally focused on a single dimension (like *sentiment*) or word-based statistical analyses. However, some of these tools can be challenging for non-computer scientists due to their complexity.

3 Generic Data Model

The *TextBI* dashboard is based on a data model called the *APs Model* with the aim of modeling in a generic way any kind of annotated social media corpus. This data model consists of 5 dimensions. The class diagram of the data model is shown in Fig. 2.

The **Users and Groups** dimension allows modeling the studied population: individual users and user groups featuring common characteristics or traits.

The **Trajectory** dimension provides the ordered sequence of posts belonging to a given user. It gives a comprehensive view of an user's activities on the chosen social media and allows linking posts together. It can be broken down into several sub-trajectories (*spatial, thematic, spatio-thematic, etc.*).

The **Token Annotation** dimension models the posts along with their associated *token annotations*. A given post can have several token annotations. Those can be spatial (*toponyms*), temporal (*temporal entities*) or thematic (*domain concepts*). Thematic annotations are resolved according to the studied domain description (domain specific ontology, thesaurus or dictionary). These semantic resources provide additional hierarchy information. When it comes to spatial annotations, those are associated with a unique identifier linked to a spatial database. This allows for places to feature hierarchical relationships (e.g., *a city is within a region, itself within a country*).

The **Text Annotation** dimension contains *Sentiment Annotation* which models the overall sentiment of the associated post and *Engagement Annotation* which models the engagement associated with a given post (*based on the number of replies, likes and quotes*).

The classes for both text and token annotations are designed to be extensible, thereby empowering the end user with the flexibility to incorporate new annotation types as desired. Annotations can be instantiated by running NLP modules on the extracted social media posts (*e.g., NER, concept extraction*) or by parsing post metadata (*e.g., engagement metrics, geotags, etc.*).

Lastly, the **Proxemic Distances** dimension allows calculating and storing distances across spatial, temporal, thematic or individual entities. Such distances can be computed within a unique dimension or through two distinct dimensions.

4 Annotation Setup

The first step (see Fig. 1) in generating our visualization with *TextBI* consists of initializing the data model using an annotated corpus of data tied to a domain-specific knowledge base. In our case, we make use of the *Thesaurus on Tourism and Leisure Activities* (World Tourism Organization, 2002), an extensive multilingual terminology with over 2500 touristic concepts. With respect to the corpus, we collected 3,293 tweets issued by tourists during the summer of 2019 from the social media X (formerly Twitter) [2]. The data collection approach is outlined in Masson et al. (2022). The data model was instantiated using two types of data: metadata and tweet content. Metadata-based instantiation was a straightforward process, encompassing elements like engagement metrics, profile features, timestamps, and geotags, among others. The textual content of the tweets was processed using three deep learning-based NLP modules to generate automatic annotations at the token level for (1) locations and (2) thematic concepts, and at the text level for (3) sentiment. We divided the dataset into three parts with a split of 60% for training, 20% for validation, and 20% for testing, ensuring a uniform distribution of languages and users across these splits. The main objective of these experiments was to establish the optimal method while keeping the amount of manually labelled data to a minimum. This meant testing various few-shot and fine-tuning techniques for each of the three NLP tasks mentioned above (Masson et al., 2023a).

Thus, with respect to sentiment analysis (1), we experimented with various techniques such as using pre-trained models fine-tuned on our tweet corpus, and employing a few-shot method such as Pattern-Exploiting Training (PET; Schick and Schütze, 2020). However, due to space constraints and the paper's focus, we cannot elaborate on a comprehensive evaluation. Ultimately, we found that the fine-tuning the XLM-T model for sentiment (Barbieri et al., 2022) was the most effective approach, achieving a high accuracy value of 0.939, compared to 0.877 for PET with the language model.

We adopted a similar methodology for Named Entity Recognition (NER) (2), which involved a single class (LOC) that encompassed a broad array of 995 place names. Here, the challenge was the low frequency of the label words in the annotated data. Despite this, fine-tuning multilingual BERT (mBERT; Devlin et al., 2018) demonstrated superior performance with an F1-micro (Tjong Kim Sang, 2002) score of 0.848, compared to 0.788 with the few-shot technique for sequence labelling implemented by EntLM (Ma et al., 2021).

Lastly, for the task of thematic concept extraction (3), which included a highly diverse set of classes (315 instantiated touristic concepts from the thesaurus) with few label words, we found that prompt-based few-shot learning with EntLM was significantly more effective, achieving an F1-micro score of 0.840, compared to 0.241 for the fine-tuning approach. For extensive details of the experiments briefly outlined in this section please check Masson et al. (2023a).

In the next section, we will describe how to visualize these automatically generated annotations using *TextBI*.

5 The TextBI Dashboard

The *TextBI* dashboard (Fig. 3) is a web-based tool that allows interactive visualization of NLP annotations for social media data. It is designed to be adaptable to any social media and domain, as long as the data adheres to the specified data model (see Section 3). The dashboard offers a variety of features to facilitate the analysis of multilingual social media data across four dimensions: spatial, temporal, thematic, and personal. In our context, the domain is tourism, implying potential stakeholders could include tourism offices or Destination Marketing Organizations (Gretzel et al., 2006).

[2]https://twitter.com/

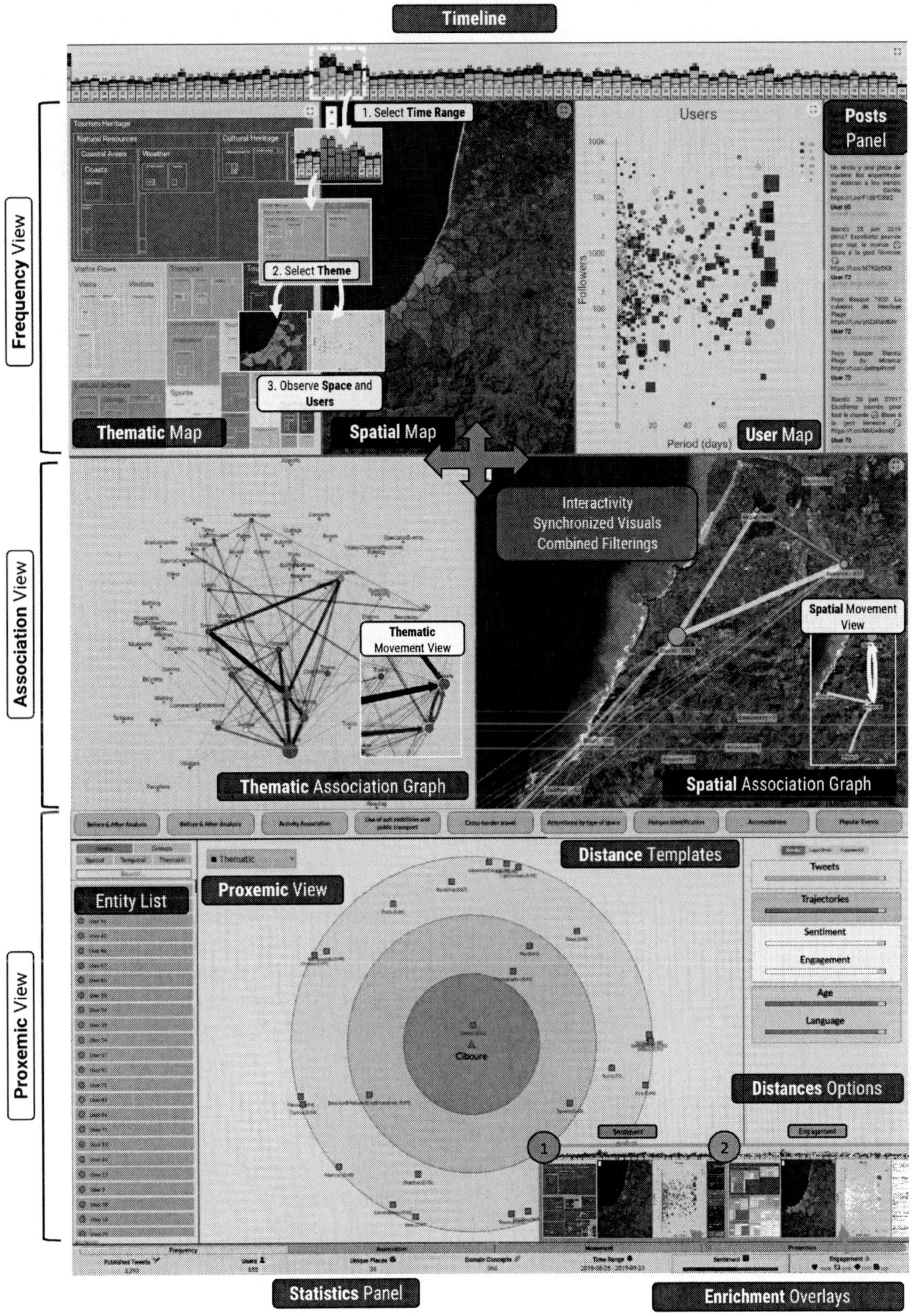

Figure 3: Overview of the TextBI platform. Live demonstration is available: `https://youtu.be/x714RKvo9Cg`

5.1 Frequency View

The **Frequency** view (Fig. 3) acts as the main interface, highlighting spatial, temporal, and thematic frequencies through four major visualizations.

The **Thematic Map** treemap (Fig. 3, *Thematic Map*) visualizes the hierarchical structure and frequency of thematic concepts from a semantic resource, such as a dictionary, thesaurus, or ontology. For instance, mapping tweet concepts to the *Thesaurus on Tourism and Leisure Activities* (World Tourism Organization, 2002), we find tourism heritage-related concepts are most frequent, accounting for roughly 40% of discovered concepts, with many linked to natural resources such as the coast and sea.

The **Spatial Map** (Fig. 3, *Spatial Map*) is another visualization showcasing the frequency of places mentioned in posts. Users can set the spatial granularity, which can range from broad categories such as countries to more specific ones like Points of Interest (POIs). Places are aggregated depending on the chosen granularity. The map uses a linear gradient for representation, with more transparent areas signifying fewer originating posts. Here, we focus on the French Basque Coast region at the city level and observe a hotspot of tweets in 3 cities at the northernmost part of the region. These nearby cities appear to be popular among visitors.

Next, the **User Map** (Fig. 3, *User Map*) is a scatter plot that presents the users' posting frequency on the x-axis against the count of the users' followers on the y-axis. This design helps in the rapid identification of influential users. Each user's language is represented by color and symbol, with the symbol's size corresponding to the number of posts from that user. 655 users are depicted in this example, spanning over 6 languages (*French, Spanish, English, Basque, Italian, and undetermined*).

Lastly, the **Timeline** (Fig. 3, *Timeline*) view offers a visualization of the volume of posts per day across the dataset range, divided into different times of the day such as morning, afternoon, or evening. It provides various temporal granularity options, including days, months, seasons, and years. Here, we use daily granularity for the summer of 2019. We observe a peak of tweets between the 24th and 28th of July.

5.2 Association View

In the **Association** view (Fig. 3, *Association View*), the dashboard presents visual representations that illustrate the connections between entities through their co-occurrences in posts. These connections are depicted using non-directed graphs, where the nodes represent entities such as thematic concepts or places, and the edges indicate the strength of co-occurrence between them. This allows for easy identification of heavily correlated concepts or places. As expected, *Sun, Beach, Surfing, Sea*, and other coastal concepts are heavily linked. This view can also display movements (Fig. 3, *Movement Views*), focusing on the sequencing of entities in user trajectories, for example, the transition from one thematic concept or place to another. This sequencing is visualized through directed graphs where edges indicate the amount of time two concepts or places are sequenced in user trajectories.

5.3 Proxemics View

TextBI's proxemic view (Fig. 3, *Proxemic View*) offers users the ability to analyze datasets via a proxemic approach (Hall et al., 1968; Greenberg et al., 2011), selecting entities such as a user, group, thematic concept, place, or time period as references. For instance, in our demonstration, we selected *Ciboure*, a touristic city, as the reference entity, and compared it with thematic concepts. The interface includes a left panel for selecting references, a central crosshair panel for results, and a right settings panel for customizing distance calculations. The system supports many combinations such as user-to-themes or place-to-users.

While specifics of the distance calculation formula are not covered in this paper, users can customize settings, for example, assigning higher weight to positive or highly-engaged tweets. The interface also features a template panel offering pre-defined distance settings for specific study domains. In the tourism domain, the *Accommodation* template, for example, limits the display to accommodation-related thematic concepts.

5.4 Enrichment Overlays

In *TextBI*, visuals support the superimposition (referred to as **overlays**) of sentiment and engagement enrichment data (Fig. 3, *Enrichment Overlays*). Sentiment is indicated through color coding (*green for positive, red for negative, and orange for mixed sentiment*), enabling a better understanding of aggregate sentiment by themes, places, time or user. Engagement is visualized using a linear gradient (*blue indicating strong engagement, white indicating low engagement*), providing insights into user engagement. We can see that most tourist concepts tend to be associated with a positive sentiment, but some, like *Transport* or *Ecology*, are more mixed.

5.5 Interactions and Visual Synchronization

The *TextBI* platform employs interactions commonly found in Business Intelligence (BI) tools, ensuring a fluid synchronization of visualizations. It accommodates multi-dimensional filtering options such as spatial-temporal, spatial-thematic, and user-temporal. When a user selects a particular location, theme, user, or time range, all subsequent visualizations adjust to display only tweets associated with the chosen filter. The system even allows for combined filtering. Within its proxemic view, users can conveniently drag and drop references onto the center of the crosshair panel.

Consider the example depicted in Fig. 3 highlighted in yellow. If the user chooses the time range of July 24th to 27th, the thematic map updates to display a higher concentration of the *Celebration* thematic concept. Further clicking on the *Celebration* concept leads the spatial map to highlight a hotspot in the city of *Bayonne*. This coincides with the timing of the *Bayonne Celebration*, a local event that attracts over a million attendees.

The dashboard base features a *statistics panel* (Fig. 3, *Statistics Panel*) showing data related to active filters, including post, user, concept, and place counts; current post time range; total engagement level; and prevailing sentiments. Filtered posts are displayed in the *Posts Panel* on the right.

5.6 Technical Aspects and Limitations

TextBI is a web application developed using HTML, CSS, and JavaScript. It runs solely on the client-side, so it does not require a back-end web server and can be run locally. The data model has been implemented using the JSON format.

TextBI serves as a data display and aggregation tool, providing statistical analyses and calculating distances. It does not engage in any data processing tasks of its own. Data collection and transformation, including NLP, need to be completed in advance. Currently, *TextBI* does not support any analytical dimensions beyond those mentioned above. In the future, we aim to make it easily extensible through a plugin system.

6 Conclusion and Future Perspectives

We have introduced a novel dashboard called *TextBI*, designed to facilitate the visualization of automatic NLP annotations on social media data for both domain stakeholders and NLP researchers. It is powered by a generic data model, making it completely adaptable. *TextBI* focuses on four dimensions: space, time, theme, and user, and offers various viewing options. Additional enrichment data is also supported. *TextBI* provides extensive interactivity, including combined filtering, visual synchronization, aggregation, and more. Our future plans include enhancing TextBI with features such as a user interface for granularity selection and enabling it to process live data by integrating with *InfluxDB* (Ahmad and Ansari, 2017). After testing it on other domains and larger datasets to ensure its scalability, we intend to make *TextBI* open-source.

Acknowledgments

This work has been partially supported by the HiTZ center and the Basque Government (Research group funding IT-1805-22). We also acknowledge the funding from the following projects: (i) DeepKnowledge (PID2021-127777OB-C21) MCIN/AEI/10.13039/501100011033 and ERDF A way of making Europe; (ii) Disargue (TED2021-130810B-C21), MCIN/AEI/10.13039/501100011033 and European Union NextGenerationEU/PRTR. Rodrigo Agerri currently holds the RYC-2017-23647 fellowship (MCIN/AEI/10.13039/501100011033 and by ESF Investing in your future). Additionally, this work was also partially supported by the urban community of Pau Béarn Pyrénées.

References

Khaleel Ahmad and Masroor Ansari. 2017. Hands-on influxdb. In *NoSQL: Database for Storage and Retrieval of Data in Cloud*, pages 341–354. Chapman and Hall/CRC.

Francesco Barbieri, Luis Espinosa Anke, and Jose Camacho-Collados. 2022. Xlm-t: Multilingual language models in twitter for sentiment analysis and beyond. In *Proceedings of the Thirteenth Language Resources and Evaluation Conference*, pages 258–266.

Bob Booth, Andy Mitchell, et al. 2001. Getting started with arcgis.

Chantana Chantrapornchai and Aphisit Tunsakul. 2021. Information extraction tasks based on bert and spacy on tourism domain. *ECTI Transactions on Computer and Information Technology (ECTI-CIT)*, 15(1):108–122.

Ilka Datig and Paul Whiting. 2018. Telling your library story: tableau public for data visualization. *Library Hi Tech News*, 35(4):6–8.

Zeel Desai, Karishma Anklesaria, and Harish Balasubramaniam. 2021. Business intelligence visualization using deep learning based sentiment analysis on amazon review data. In *2021 12th International Conference on Computing Communication and Networking Technologies (ICCCNT)*, pages 1–7. IEEE.

Jacob Devlin, Ming-Wei Chang, Kenton Lee, and Kristina Toutanova. 2018. Bert: Pre-training of deep bidirectional transformers for language understanding. *arXiv preprint arXiv:1810.04805*.

Alberto Ferrari and Marco Russo. 2016. *Introducing Microsoft Power BI*. Microsoft Press.

Saul Greenberg, Nicolai Marquardt, Till Ballendat, Rob Diaz-Marino, and Miaosen Wang. 2011. Proxemic interactions: the new ubicomp? *interactions*, 18(1):42–50.

Ulrike Gretzel, Daniel R Fesenmaier, Sandro Formica, and Joseph T O'Leary. 2006. Searching for the future: Challenges faced by destination marketing organizations. *Journal of Travel Research*, 45(2):116–126.

Edward T Hall, Ray L Birdwhistell, Bernhard Bock, Paul Bohannan, A Richard Diebold Jr, Marshall Durbin, Munro S Edmonson, JL Fischer, Dell Hymes, Solon T Kimball, et al. 1968. Proxemics [and comments and replies]. *Current anthropology*, 9(2/3):83–108.

Bhumika Hansoti. 2010. Business intelligence dashboard in decision making. *Purdue University, College of Technology Directed Projects*.

Healey and Ramaswamy. 2022. Twitter sentiment visualization. Accessed: 2023-06-30.

GISP Kurt Menke, Richard Smith Jr, Luigi Pirelli, GISP John Van Hoesen, et al. 2016. *Mastering QGIS*. Packt Publishing Ltd.

Daniel Leung, Rob Law, Hubert Van Hoof, and Dimitrios Buhalis. 2013. Social media in tourism and hospitality: A literature review. *Journal of travel & tourism marketing*, 30(1-2):3–22.

Lucie Loubère and Pierre Ratinaud. 2014. Documentation iramuteq 0.6 alpha 3 version 0.1. *http://www.iramuteq.org*.

Ruotian Ma, Xin Zhou, Tao Gui, Yiding Tan, Linyang Li, Qi Zhang, and Xuanjing Huang. 2021. Template-free prompt tuning for few-shot ner. *arXiv preprint arXiv:2109.13532*.

Maxime Masson, Rodrigo Agerri, Christian Sallaberry, Marie-Noelle Bessagnet, Annig Le Parc Lacayrelle, and Philippe Roose. 2023a. Optimal strategies to perform multilingual analysis of social content for a novel dataset in the tourism domain. *arXiv preprint arXiv:2311.14727*.

Maxime Masson, Philippe Roose, Christian Sallaberry, Rodrigo Agerri, Marie-Noelle Bessagnet, and Annig Le Parc Lacayrelle. 2023b. Aps: A proxemic framework for social media interactions modeling and analysis. In *International Symposium on Intelligent Data Analysis*, pages 287–299. Springer.

Maxime Masson, Christian Sallaberry, Rodrigo Agerri, Marie-Noelle Bessagnet, Philippe Roose, and Annig Le Parc Lacayrelle. 2022. A domain-independent method for thematic dataset building from social media: the case of tourism on twitter. In *International Conference on Web Information Systems Engineering*, pages 11–20. Springer.

Diana Maynard, Hamish Cunningham, Kalina Bontcheva, Roberta Catizone, George Demetriou, Robert Gaizauskas, Oana Hamza, Mark Hepple, Patrick Herring, Brian Mitchell, et al. 2000. A survey of uses of gate. Technical report, Technical Report CS–00–06, Department of Computer Science, University of Sheffield.

KSR Murthy, E Amminedu, and V Venkateswara Rao. 2003. Integration of thematic maps through gis for identification of groundwater potential zones. *Journal of the Indian Society of Remote Sensing*, 31:197–210.

Dmytro Orlovskyi and Andrii Kopp. 2020. A business intelligence dashboard design approach to improve data analytics and decision making. In *Selected Papers of the 7th International Conference "Information Technology and Interactions" (IT&I-2020). Conferece Proceedings, Kyiv, Ukraine, December 02-03, 2020*, volume 2833 of *CEUR Workshop Proceedings*, pages 48–59. CEUR-WS.org.

Landy Rajaonarivo, Tsunenori Mine, and Yutaka Arakawa. 2022. Coupling of semantic and syntactic graphs generated via tweets to detect local events. In *2022 12th International Congress on Advanced Applied Informatics (IIAI-AAI)*, pages 128–133. IEEE.

Radim Rehurek and Petr Sojka. 2011. Gensim—statistical semantics in python. *Retrieved from genism. org*.

Timo Schick and Hinrich Schütze. 2020. Exploiting cloze questions for few shot text classification and natural language inference. *arXiv preprint arXiv:2001.07676*.

Ayushi Shukla and Saru Dhir. 2016. Tools for data visualization in business intelligence: case study using the tool qlikview. In *Information Systems Design and Intelligent Applications: Proceedings of Third International Conference INDIA 2016, Volume 2*, pages 319–326. Springer.

Achille Souili, Denis Cavallucci, and François Rousselot. 2015. Natural language processing (nlp)–a solution for knowledge extraction from patent unstructured data. *Procedia engineering*, 131:635–643.

Erik F. Tjong Kim Sang. 2002. Introduction to the CoNLL-2002 shared task: Language-independent named entity recognition. In *COLING-02: The 6th Conference on Natural Language Learning 2002 (CoNLL-2002)*.

Nees Jan Van Eck and Ludo Waltman. 2013. Vosviewer manual. *Leiden: Univeristeit Leiden*, 1(1):1–53.

Vipul Vashisht and Pankaj Dharia. 2020. Integrating chatbot application with qlik sense business intelligence (bi) tool using natural language processing (nlp). In *Micro-Electronics and Telecommunication Engineering: Proceedings of 3rd ICMETE 2019*, pages 683–692. Springer.

Megan E Welsh. 2014. Review of voyant tools. *Collaborative Librarianship*, 6(2):96–98.

World Tourism Organization. 2002. *Thesaurus on Tourism and Leisure Activities*. World Tourism Organization.

kNN-BOX: A Unified Framework for Nearest Neighbor Generation

Wenhao Zhu*, Qianfeng Zhao*, Yunzhe Lv*,
Shujian Huang, Siheng Zhao, Sizhe Liu, Jiajun Chen
National Key Laboratory for Novel Software Technology, Nanjing University, China
`{zhuwh,qianfeng,lvyz,zhaosh,liusz}@smail.nju.edu.cn`, `{huangsj,chenjj}@nju.edu.cn`

Abstract

Augmenting the base neural model with a token-level symbolic datastore is a novel generation paradigm and has achieved promising results in machine translation (MT). In this paper, we introduce a unified framework kNN-BOX, which enables quick development and visualization for this novel paradigm. kNN-BOX decomposes the datastore-augmentation approach into three modules: datastore, retriever and combiner, thus putting diverse kNN generation methods into a unified way. Currently, kNN-BOX has provided implementation of seven popular kNN-MT variants, covering research from performance enhancement to efficiency optimization. It is easy for users to reproduce these existing work or customize their own models. Besides, users can interact with their kNN generation systems with kNN-BOX to better understand the underlying inference process in a visualized way. In experiment section, we apply kNN-BOX for machine translation and three other seq2seq generation tasks (text simplification, paraphrase generation and question generation). Experiment results show that augmenting the base neural model with kNN-BOX can bring large performance improvement in all these tasks. The code and document of kNN-BOX is available at `https://github.com/NJUNLP/knn-box`. The demo can be accessed at `http://nlp.nju.edu.cn/demo/knn-box/`. The introduction video is available at `https://www.youtube.com/watch?v=m0eJ1dHVR3w`.

1 Introduction

Equipping the base neural model with a symbolic datastore is a novel paradigm for enhancing generation quality. Khandelwal et al. (2021) apply this paradigm in machine translation, known as kNN-MT, and achieves promising results, especially in MT domain adaptation and multilingual MT. Afterwards, the following work keep optimizing this approach, making it a more mature methodology, e.g., dynamically deciding the usage of retrieval results (Zheng et al., 2021), building a light and explainable datastore (Zhu et al., 2023a), injecting kNN knowledge into the neural model (Zhu et al., 2023b).

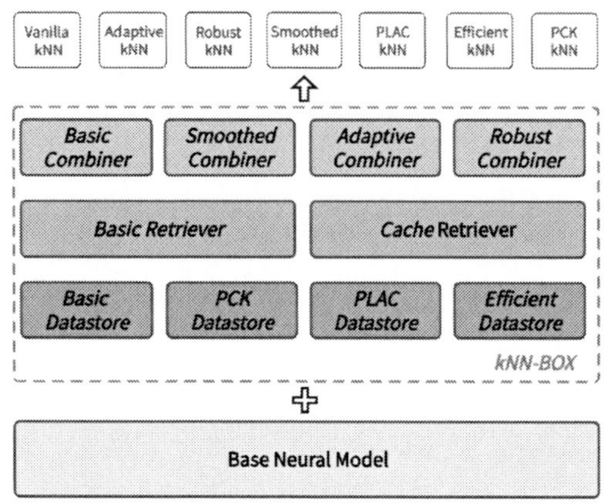

Figure 1: kNN-BOX decomposes the datastore-augmentation approach into three modules, namely, DATASTORE, RETRIEVER and COMBINER, putting diverse kNN generation methods into an unified way.

However, we notice that these kNN generation methods are implemented with diverse codebases, e.g., *Fairseq*[1], *Transformers*[2] and *JoeyNMT*[3], which hinders comparison between these methods and potential fusion of latest research advances. Interpretability is another interesting point in kNN research, as the community is curious why kNN generation works and whether it is reliable.

In this paper, we introduce a unified framework kNN-BOX for nearest neighbor generation, which supports quick development and visualization anal-

*Equal Contributions.

[1] `https://github.com/facebookresearch/fairseq`
[2] `https://github.com/huggingface/transformers`
[3] `https://github.com/joeynmt/joeynmt`

Proceedings of the 18th Conference of the European Chapter of the Association for Computational Linguistics System Demonstrations, pages 10–17
March 17-22, 2024

ysis. Our framework decomposes the datastore-augmentation approach into three modules: DATASTORE, RETRIEVER and COMBINER, thus putting diverse kNN generation methods into a unified way (Figure 1). Up till now, kNN-BOX has released implementation of seven popular kNN-MT models, covering research from performance enhancement (Khandelwal et al., 2021; Jiang et al., 2021; Zheng et al., 2021; Jiang et al., 2022) to efficiency optimization (Martins et al., 2022; Wang et al., 2022; Zhu et al., 2023a), which can help users to quickly reproduce existing works. Moreover, users can easily fuse advanced models with kNN-BOX, for example, jointly using a better combiner and a lighter datastore, to achieve the best of both worlds.

Another useful feature of kNN-BOX is supporting visualized interactive analysis. Via our provided web service, users can interact with their kNN model and observe its inference process, e.g. the content and distribution of its retrieval results (Figure 3). We hope kNN-BOX can help the community to better understand the interpretability of kNN generation.

Experiment results on machine translation datasets show that kNN-BOX is a reliable platform for model reproduction and development. In addition, we apply kNN-BOX for three other seq2seq tasks, i.e., text simplification, paraphrase generation and question generation. Experiment results show that augmenting the base neural model with kNN-BOX is also beneficial in these tasks, showing the great potential of nearest neighbor generation and the wide usage of our kNN-BOX toolkit. At the time of writing, we are happy to see that kNN-BOX has been used as the backbone of this year's ACL paper (Liu et al., 2023) and EMNLP papers (Li et al., 2023; Zhang et al., 2023), and we hope this toolkit to support more valuable research in the future.

2 Background: kNN-MT

Before introducing kNN-BOX, we recap kNN-MT approach in this section. Generally, kNN-MT framework aims at memorizing translation knowledge in parallel corpus $\mathcal{C}$ into a datastore $\mathcal{D}$ and use it to augment the NMT model $\mathcal{M}$ during inference.

Memorizing Knowledge into Datastore To extract translation knowledge, translation pair $(\mathcal{X}, \mathcal{Y})$ is fed into $\mathcal{M}$ for teacher-forcing decoding. At time step t, the continuous representation of the translation context $(\mathcal{X}, \mathcal{Y}_{<t})$, i.e. the hidden state h_t from the last decoder layer, is taken as *key*:

$$h_t = \mathcal{M}(\mathcal{X}, \mathcal{Y}_{<t})$$

and the target token y_t is taken as *value*. Each *key-value* pair explicitly memorizes the translation knowledge: generating the *value* token at the decoder hidden state *key*. With a single forward pass over the entire corpus, the full datastore $\mathcal{D}$ can be constructed:

$$\mathcal{D} = \{(h_t, y_t) \mid \forall y_t \in \mathcal{Y}, (\mathcal{X}, \mathcal{Y}) \in \mathcal{C}\}, \quad (1)$$

Generating with Memorized Knowledge The constructed datastore is then combined with the base NMT model as an augmentation memory. During inference, the NMT model retrieves related knowledge from the datastore to adjust its own translation prediction.

Specifically, the NMT model uses the contextualized representation of the test translation context $(\mathcal{X}, \mathcal{Y}_{<t})$ to query the datastore for nearest neighbor representations and the corresponding target tokens $\mathcal{N}_k = \{(h^j, y^j)\}_{j=1}^{k}$. The retrieved entries are then converted to a distribution over the vocabulary:

$$p_{\text{knn}}(y|\mathcal{X}, \mathcal{Y}_{<t}) \propto \sum_{(h^j, y^j) \in \mathcal{N}_k} \mathbb{1}(y = y^j) \cdot s(h_t, h^j) \quad (2)$$

where s measures the similarity between h_t and h^j:

$$s(h_t, h^j) = \exp[\frac{-d(h_t, h^j)}{T}]$$

Here, d denotes L_2-square distance and T is the temperature. In the end, the output distribution of the NMT model and symbolic datastore are interpolated with the weight λ:

$$\begin{aligned} p(y|\mathcal{X}, \mathcal{Y}_{<t}) = \lambda \cdot \ & p_{\text{knn}}(y|\mathcal{X}, \mathcal{Y}_{<t}) \\ & + (1 - \lambda) \cdot p_{\text{nmt}}(y|\mathcal{X}, \mathcal{Y}_{<t}) \end{aligned} \quad (3)$$

Recent Advances in kNN-MT To make kNN-MT more effective, efficient and explainable, various methods have been devised. Zheng et al. (2021) and Jiang et al. (2022) propose to dynamically decide the usage of retrieval results to exclude potential noise in nearest neighbors. Jiang et al. (2021) explore the setting of multi-domain adaptation and remedy the catastrophic forgetting problem. Inspired by He et al. (2021), Martins et al. (2022)

introduce three ways to improve the efficiency of kNN-MT, i.e. dimension reduction, datastore pruning and adaptive retrieval. Later, Wang et al. (2022) propose to reduce dimension and prune datastore with a learnable network. Recently, Zhu et al. (2023a) explore the interpretability issue in kNN-MT and builds a light and more explainable datastore according to the capability of the NMT model.

3 Unified Framework: kNN-BOX

This section describes how we design and implement kNN-BOX, and introduce how users run kNN-BOX for developing kNN generation models and interacting with the deployed model visually.

3.1 Design and Implementation

We develop kNN-BOX based on the widely-used generation framework *Fairseq*, making it easy to apply kNN-BOX for other generation tasks. The overall workflow of kNN-BOX is illustrated in Figure 2. For better compatibility and extensibility, we decompose the datastore-augmentation approach into three modules: DATASTORE, RETRIEVER and COMBINER, where each module has its own function:

- DATASTORE: saving generation knowledge as *key-values* pairs (Equation 1).
- RETRIEVER: retrieving nearest neighbors from the datastore during inference.
- COMBINER: converting retrieval results to a distribution (Equation 2) and interpolating the output distribution of the neueal model and symbolic datastore (Equation 3).

With this design, diverse kNN models can be implemented in a unified way. For a specific kNN variant, it usually makes a modification on one of the three modules, compared to vanilla kNN generation model. Therefore, users can customize the corresponding module and quickly develop a kNN generation model.

Supporting visual interactive analysis is another useful feature of kNN-MT. By saving intermediate computation results, we enable kNN-BOX to visualize the inference process. We hope this feature will help users to better understand their own model.

3.2 Usage

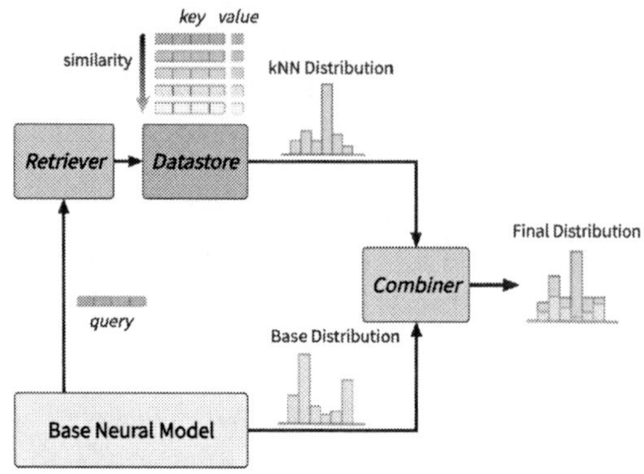

Figure 2: Overall workflow of augmenting the base neural model with kNN-BOX.

Reproducing Existing Work Until now, kNN-BOX has released implementation of seven popular kNN-MT models [4], covering research from performance enhancement to efficiency optimization. Besides, kNN-BOX has also provided the corresponding shell scripts to run them, enabling users to quickly reproduce existing work. Detailed guidance can be found in `README.md`[5].

Developing New Models kNN-BOX is designed not only for reproducing existing work, but also for developing new models on new tasks. For each module, users can pick one of its implementation from kNN-BOX or customize their own version, and combine three modules together to build a new kNN generation model. In this process, only few lines of codes needs to be added, which can save users a lot of time. More importantly, this implementation fashion enables users to easily build a fused model, e.g., combining the most explainable datastore (PLACDATSTORE) with the strongest combiner (ROBUSTCOMBINER). To perform generation tasks other than machine translation, users only need to switch the training corpus to build a task-specific datastore.

Visualizing Generalization Process By running our provided script to launch a web page (shown in Figure 3), users can interact with their kNN general model visually. Users can type in text in the upper

[4]They are vanilla kNN-MT (Khandelwal et al., 2021), Adaptive kNN-MT (Zheng et al., 2021), Smoothed kNN-MT (Jiang et al., 2021), Robust kNN-MT (Jiang et al., 2022), PCK kNN-MT (Wang et al., 2022), Efficient kNN-MT (Martins et al., 2022), PLAC kNN-MT (Zhu et al., 2023a).

[5]`https://github.com/NJUNLP/knn-box/blob/master/README.md`

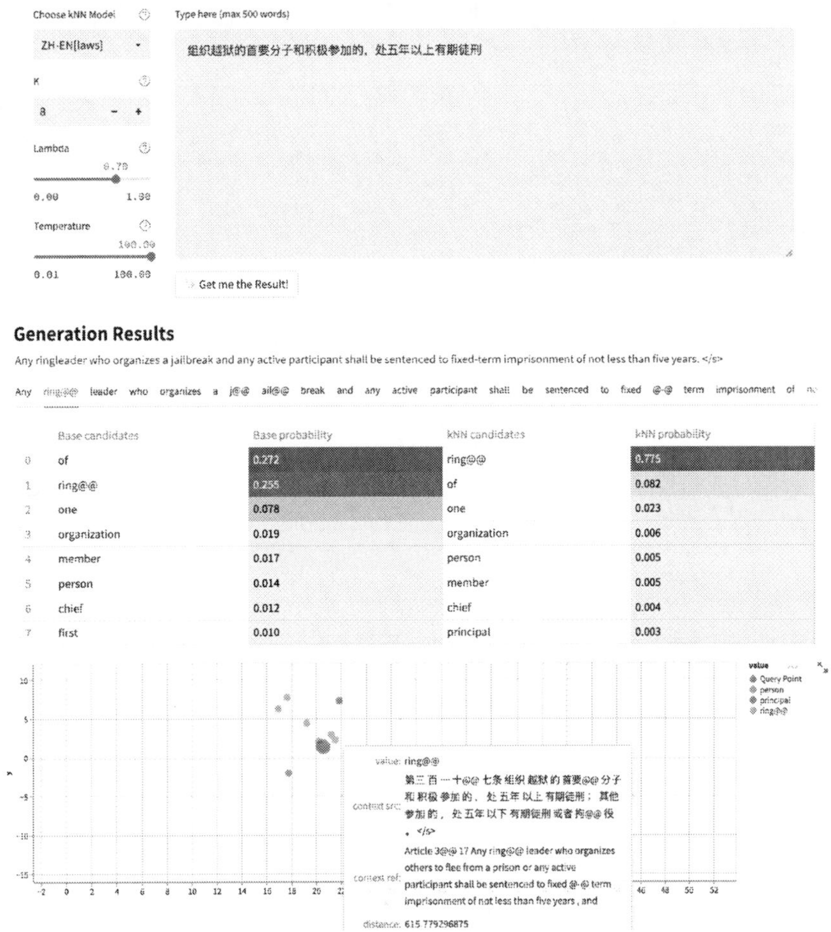

Figure 3: A screenshot of visualization web page provided by kNN-BOX, where users can interact with their own kNN model and analyze its inference process visually. The upper panel allows users to type in text and tune hyperparameters. The middle panel displays the generation result (words with "@@" means that they are generated subwords) and prediction distribution of each decoding step. The bottom panel shows the relative distribution of query and retrieval results, and more detailed information of each nearest neighbor. For example, in this figure, the user moves mouse to one of the nearest entries and check its detailed information.

input window and tune generation hyperparameters in the upper-left panel. The generated results, both detokenized and tokenized, will then be displayed. Taking kNN-MT as an example, after clicking a word in the translation, users can see the translation probability given by both NMT model and kNN-MT model. Moreover, detailed information of the retrieved datastore entries will be displayed in the bottom panel. By selecting on a certain nearest neighbor point, users can see the corresponding value token, translation context and *query-key* distance. Overall, the visualization page can help user to interact with their kNN generation model and explore its inner working process.

4 Experiments

To evaluate the effectiveness of kNN-BOX, we conduct experiments on machine translation and three other seq2seq tasks.

4.1 Experimental Settings

Dataset For machine translation, we adopt four German-English OPUS datasets [6] (Medical, Law, IT and Koran) (Tiedemann, 2012), which are used in almost all kNN-MT work. We use TED dataset [7] (Qi et al., 2018) to evaluate kNN-BOX on multi-

[6] `https://opus.nlpl.eu/`

[7] `https://github.com/neulab/word-embeddings-for-nmt`

Model	Reference	Law		Medical		IT		Koran	
		Scale↓	BLEU↑	Scale↓	BLEU↑	Scale↓	BLEU↑	Scale↓	BLEU↑
Base Neural Model	Ng et al., 2019	-	45.5	100%	40.0	-	38.4	-	16.3
Vanilla kNN-MT	Khandelwal et al., 2021	100%	61.3	100%	54.1	100%	45.6	100%	20.4
Adaptive kNN-MT	Zheng et al., 2021	100%	62.9	100%	56.1	100%	47.2	100%	20.3
Smoothed kNN-MT	Jiang et al., 2021	100%	63.3	100%	56.8	100%	47.7	100%	19.9
Robust kNN-MT	Jiang et al., 2022	100%	63.6	100%	57.1	100%	48.6	100%	20.5
PCK kNN-MT	Wang et al., 2022	90%	62.8	90%	56.4	90%	47.4	90%	19.4
Efficient kNN-MT	Martins et al., 2022	57%	59.9	58%	52.3	63%	44.9	66%	19.9
PLAC kNN-MT	Zhu et al., 2023a	55%	62.8	55%	56.2	60%	47.0	75%	19.9

Table 1: Some works implemented by kNN-BOX. Scale refers to the relative datastore size compared to a full datastore that covers all target language token occurrences in the parallel corpus. Smaller scale means a lighter datastore and higher BLEU means better translation quality.

Directions	Model	Avg.	Cs	Da	De	Es	Fr	It	Nl	Pl	Pt	Sv
En → X	M2M-100	29.1	20.7	36.2	26.7	35.1	33.7	29.8	27.7	15.6	31.9	33.7
	+ kNN-BOX	**32.6**	**22.3**	**40.2**	**29.5**	**39.2**	**38.7**	**33.5**	**31.9**	**17.9**	**37.1**	**36.0**
X → En	M2M-100	33.4	27.5	40.0	31.8	36.6	35.1	33.4	31.9	21.1	38.9	37.3
	+ kNN-BOX	**37.7**	**31.3**	**44.5**	**37.1**	**42.0**	**40.4**	**38.4**	**36.2**	**24.9**	**41.8**	**41.0**

Table 2: Effect of augmenting M2M100 with kNN-BOX (Robust kNN-MT) on multilingual TED dataset. For brevity, we only show the effect of applying Robust kNN with kNN-BOX. "En → X" and "X → En" denotes translating English into other languages and translating other languages into English respectively. Bold text indicates the higher score across two models

lingual machine translation [8]. Moreover, we conduct experiments on two text simplification dataset: NEWSELA-AUTO [9] and WIKI-AUTO [10] (Jiang et al., 2020), a paraphrase generation dataset QQP [11], and a question generation dataset QUASAR-T [12] (Dhingra et al., 2017) to demonstrate effectiveness of kNN-BOX on these generation tasks.

Base Neural Model On OPUS dataset, we follow previous kNN-MT work and use the winner model of WMT'19 De-En news translation task (Ng et al., 2019) as the base model. On multilingual TED dataset, we use M2M100 (Fan et al., 2021) as the base model, which is a many-to-many multilingual translation model. On the rest of dataset, Transformer (Vaswani et al., 2017) is used as the base model.

Metric We use BLEU score calculated by *sacrebleu*[13] to evaluate the generation quality for all tasks except text simplification, where we use SARI score (Xu et al., 2016) calculated by *easse*[14] to evaluate simplification quality.

4.2 Main Results

kNN-BOX can help user to quickly augment the base NMT model with kNN methods. By running our provided shell scripts, users can quickly reproduce existing kNN-MT models. Table 1 show the translation performance of these models on OPUS dataset. We see that augmenting the base neural machine translation model with a datastore brings significant performance enhancement. Among these methods, Robust kNN-MT achieves the highest BLEU scores, and PLAC kNN-MT builds a lightest datastore while maintaining translation performance. Table 2 reports experiment results on TED dataset. We can see that applying kNN-BOX brings large performance improvement on all translation directions.

kNN-BOX is reliable platform for model reproduction We carefully compare the reproduced results with the results produced by the original implementation. We find that two groups of results

[8] We evaluate English-centric translation performance on ten languages: Cs, Da, De, Es, Fr, It, Nl, Pl, Pt and Sv.

[9] `https://newsela.com/data/`

[10] `https://github.com/chaojiang06/wiki-auto/tree/master/wiki-auto/ACL2020/`

[11] `https://www.kaggle.com/c/quora-question-pairs`

[12] `https://github.com/bdhingra/quasar`

[13] `https://github.com/mjpost/sacrebleu`

[14] `https://github.com/feralvam/easse`

Task	Dataset	Metric	Base Model	kNN-BOX
Text Simplification	Wiki-Auto	SARI	38.6	**39.4**
	Newsela-Auto	SARI	35.8	**38.2**
Paraphrase Generation	QQP	BLEU	28.4	**29.5**
Question Generation	Quasar-T	BLEU	9.6	**15.7**

Table 3: The performance of applying kNN-BOX (vanilla kNN-MT) on three other seq2seq tasks: text simplification, paraphrase generation and question generation. Here, we apply the vanilla kNN generation method for augmentation. Bold text indicates the higher score across two models. Augmenting base neural models in these tasks with kNN-BOX also bring large performance improvement.

Datastore	Retriever	Combiner	Scale↓	BLEU↑
BASICDATASTORE	BASICRETRIEVER	BASICCOMBINER	100%	61.3
PCKDATASTORE	BASICRETRIEVER	ADAPTIVECOMBINER	90%	62.8
EFFICIENTDATASTORE	BASICRETRIEVER	ADAPTIVECOMBINER	57%	61.5
EFFICIENTDATASTORE	BASICRETRIEVER	ROBUSTCOMBINER	57%	61.8
PLACDATASTORE	BASICRETRIEVER	ADAPTIVECOMBINER	55%	62.8
PLACDATASTORE	BASICRETRIEVER	ROBUSTCOMBINER	55%	63.7

Table 4: Experiment results of fusing advanced datastore and combiner. Smaller scale means a lighter datastore and higher BLEU means better translation quality.

are well-aligned (shown in Appendix A), demonstrating that kNN-BOX is reliable platform for reproducing kNN-MT models.

kNN-BOX shows great potential in other seq2seq generation tasks as well Apart from machine translation task, we further evaluate kNN-BOX on three other seq2seq tasks: text simplification, paraphrase generation and question generation. Experiment results are shown in Table 3. Augmenting the base neural model with kNN-BOX brings performance enhancement in all three tasks. The performance improvement on three tasks is up to 2.4 SARI, 1.1 BLEU and 6.1 BLEU respectively, which shows the great potential of studying datastore-augmentation in generation tasks and the wide usage of our toolkit.

kNN-BOX accelerates the fusion of lasted research advances A potential drawback of implementing kNN-MT with diverse codebases is hindering the fusion of lasted research advances. With kNN-BOX, research advances on DATASTORE, COMBINER and RETRIEVER can be fused conveniently. Table 4 shows the performance of some mixed models on OPUS-Law dataset, where we jointly use different DATASTORE and COMBINER. We can see that jointly using PLACDATASTORE and ROBUSTCOMBINER achieve strong translation performance with a much smaller datastore.

5 Conclusion and Future Work

This paper introduces kNN-BOX, an open-sourced toolkit for nearest neighbor generation. kNN-BOX decomposes datastore-augmented approach into three decoupled modules: DATASTORE, RETRIEVER and COMBINER, thus putting diverse kNN generation methods into a unified way. kNN-BOX provides implementation of several kNN-MT models, covering research from performance enhancement and efficiency optimization, which can help users to quickly reproduce existing work. kNN-BOX also enjoys great extensibility, which can be used to develop new models and be applied for new generation tasks. More importantly, kNN-BOX supports users to interact with their deployed model in a visualized way, which enables in-depth analysis on the inner working process of the model. In experiment section, we show that kNN-BOX can not only be applied for enhancing neural machine translation model, but also for enhancing neural generation model in other seq2seq tasks.

In the future, we will keep update this toolkit to provide implementation of more retrieve-and-generate methods and optimize the framework to make it more user-friendly, and explore the possibility to apply kNN-BOX for more generation tasks.

Limitation

We discuss two potential limitations of our kNN-BOX toolkit below:

- Inference Latency: The nearest neighbor retrieval system queries the datastore at each timestep, which introduces inference latency.
- Datastore reusability: The datastore is constructed using a specific model, which limits its reusability. This means that the datastore cannot be seamlessly integrated or utilized with other models.

Acknowledgement

Shujian Huang is the corresponding author. This work is supported by National Science Foundation of China (No. 62376116, 62176120), the Liaoning Provincial Research Foundation for Basic Research (No. 2022-KF-26-02).

References

Bhuwan Dhingra, Kathryn Mazaitis, and William W Cohen. 2017. Quasar: Datasets for question answering by search and reading. *arXiv preprint arXiv:1707.03904*.

Angela Fan, Shruti Bhosale, Holger Schwenk, Zhiyi Ma, Ahmed El-Kishky, Siddharth Goyal, Mandeep Baines, Onur Celebi, Guillaume Wenzek, Vishrav Chaudhary, et al. 2021. Beyond english-centric multilingual machine translation. *The Journal of Machine Learning Research*, 22(1):4839–4886.

Junxian He, Graham Neubig, and Taylor Berg-Kirkpatrick. 2021. Efficient nearest neighbor language models. In *Proceedings of the Conference on Empirical Methods in Natural Language Processing (EMNLP)*.

Chao Jiang, Mounica Maddela, Wuwei Lan, Yang Zhong, and Wei Xu. 2020. Neural CRF model for sentence alignment in text simplification. In *Proceedings of the 58th Annual Meeting of the Association for Computational Linguistics*, pages 7943–7960, Online. Association for Computational Linguistics.

Hui Jiang, Ziyao Lu, Fandong Meng, Chulun Zhou, Jie Zhou, Degen Huang, and Jinsong Su. 2022. Towards robust k-nearest-neighbor machine translation. In *Proceedings of the 2022 Conference on Empirical Methods in Natural Language Processing*, pages 5468–5477, Abu Dhabi, United Arab Emirates. Association for Computational Linguistics.

Qingnan Jiang, Mingxuan Wang, Jun Cao, Shanbo Cheng, Shujian Huang, and Lei Li. 2021. Learning kernel-smoothed machine translation with retrieved examples. In *Proceedings of the Conference on Empirical Methods in Natural Language Processing (EMNLP)*.

Urvashi Khandelwal, Angela Fan, Dan Jurafsky, Luke Zettlemoyer, and Mike Lewis. 2021. Nearest neighbor machine translation. In *International Conference on Learning Representations (ICLR)*.

Xuanhong Li, Peng Li, and Po Hu. 2023. Revisiting source context in nearest neighbor machine translation. In *Proceedings of the Conference on Empirical Methods in Natural Language Processing (EMNLP)*.

Shudong Liu, Xuebo Liu, Derek F. Wong, Zhaocong Li, Wenxiang Jiao, Lidia S. Chao, and Min Zhang. 2023. kNN-TL: k-nearest-neighbor transfer learning for low-resource neural machine translation. In *Proceedings of the 61st Annual Meeting of the Association for Computational Linguistics (ACL)*.

Pedro Martins, Zita Marinho, and Andre Martins. 2022. Efficient machine translation domain adaptation. In *Proceedings of the Workshop on Semiparametric Methods in NLP: Decoupling Logic from Knowledge*.

Nathan Ng, Kyra Yee, Alexei Baevski, Myle Ott, Michael Auli, and Sergey Edunov. 2019. Facebook FAIR's WMT19 news translation task submission. In *Proceedings of the Conference on Machine Translation (WMT)*.

Ye Qi, Devendra Sachan, Matthieu Felix, Sarguna Padmanabhan, and Graham Neubig. 2018. When and why are pre-trained word embeddings useful for neural machine translation? In *Proceedings of the 2018 Conference of the North American Chapter of the Association for Computational Linguistics: Human Language Technologies, Volume 2 (Short Papers)*.

Jörg Tiedemann. 2012. Parallel data, tools and interfaces in OPUS. In *Proceedings of the Eighth International Conference on Language Resources and Evaluation (LREC)*.

Ashish Vaswani, Noam Shazeer, Niki Parmar, Jakob Uszkoreit, Llion Jones, Aidan N Gomez, Lukasz Kaiser, and Illia Polosukhin. 2017. Attention is all you need. In *Advances in Neural Information Processing Systems (NeurIPS)*.

Dexin Wang, Kai Fan, Boxing Chen, and Deyi Xiong. 2022. Efficient cluster-based k-nearest-neighbor machine translation. In *Proceedings of the Annual Meeting of the Association for Computational Linguistics (ACL)*.

Wei Xu, Courtney Napoles, Ellie Pavlick, Quanze Chen, and Chris Callison-Burch. 2016. Optimizing statistical machine translation for text simplification. *Transactions of the Association for Computational Linguistics*, 4:401–415.

Xiangyu Zhang, Yu Zhou, Guang Yang, and Taolue Chen. 2023. Syntax-aware retrieval augmented code generation. In *Findings of the Association for Computational Linguistics: EMNLP 2023*.

Xin Zheng, Zhirui Zhang, Junliang Guo, Shujian Huang, Boxing Chen, Weihua Luo, and Jiajun Chen. 2021. Adaptive nearest neighbor machine translation. In *Proceedings of the Annual Meeting of the Association for Computational Linguistics (ACL).*

Wenhao Zhu, Shujian Huang, Yunzhe Lv, Xin Zheng, and Jiajun Chen. 2023a. What knowledge is needed? towards explainable memory for kNN-MT domain adaptation. In *Findings of the Association for Computational Linguistics: ACL 2023.*

Wenhao Zhu, Jingjing Xu, Shujian Huang, Lingpeng Kong, and Jiajun Chen. 2023b. INK: Injecting kNN knowledge in nearest neighbor machine translation. In *Proceedings of the 61st Annual Meeting of the Association for Computational Linguistics (ACL).*

A Performance Alignment between kNN-BOX's implementation and original implementation

Table 5 compares the reproduced results with kNN-BOX and the results produced by the original implementation, where the same base neural model and the same dataset is used. Comparison results show that there is only a minor gap between two groups of results, demonstrating that the reliability of kNN-BOX.

Model	Law	Medical	IT	Koran
Base NMT[15]	45.5	40.0	38.4	16.3
↪ kNN-BOX	45.5	40.0	38.4	16.3
Vanilla kNN-MT [16]	61.3	54.1	45.6	20.4
↪ kNN-BOX	61.3	54.1	45.6	20.4
Adaptive kNN-MT [17]	62.9	56.6	47.6	20.6
↪ kNN-BOX	62.9	56.1	47.2	20.3
PCK kNN-MT [18]	63.1	56.5	47.9	19.7
↪ kNN-BOX	62.8	56.4	47.4	19.4
Robust kNN-MT [19]	63.8	57.0	48.7	20.8
↪ kNN-BOX	63.6	57.1	48.6	20.5

Table 5: BLEU scores of original implementation and kNN-BOX's implementation. "↪ kNN-BOX' denotes the reults reproduced using our framework.

[15]https://github.com/facebookresearch/fairseq

[16]https://github.com/urvashik/knnmt

[17]https://github.com/zhengxxn/adaptive-knn-mt

[18]https://github.com/tjunlp-lab/PCKMT

[19]https://github.com/DeepLearnXMU/Robust-knn-mt

A Human-Centric Evaluation Platform for Explainable Knowledge Graph Completion

Zhao Xu[1], **Wiem Ben Rim**[1], **Kiril Gashteovski**[1,2], **Timo Sztyler**[1], **Carolin Lawrence**[1]
[1]NEC Laboratories Europe, Heidelberg, Germany
[2]CAIR, Ss. Cyril and Methodius University, Skopje, North Macedonia
firstname.lastname@neclab.eu

Abstract

Explanations for AI are expected to help human users understand AI-driven predictions. Evaluating plausibility, the helpfulness of the explanations, is therefore essential for developing eXplainable AI (XAI) that can really aid human users. Here we propose a human-centric evaluation platform[1] to measure plausibility of explanations in the context of eXplainable Knowledge Graph Completion (XKGC). The target audience of the platform are researchers and practitioners who want to 1) investigate real needs and interests of their target users in XKGC, 2) evaluate the plausibility of the XKGC methods. We showcase these two use cases in an experimental setting to illustrate what results can be achieved with our system.

1 Introduction

A Knowledge Graph (KG) is a structured representation of knowledge that captures the relationships between entities. It is composed of triples in the format *(subject, relation, object)*, denoted as $t = (s, r, o)$, where two entities are connected by a specified relation. For example, in the triple *(London, isCapitalOf, UK)*, *London* and *UK* are the entities, and *isCapitalOf* is the relation. These entities can be depicted as nodes in a knowledge graph, while the relation denotes a labeled link connecting the subject to the object. Knowledge graphs are beneficial for many NLP tasks, e.g., fact checking (Hu et al., 2021; Kim et al., 2023), question answering (Hu et al., 2022; Srivastava et al., 2021) and information extraction (Gashteovski et al., 2020).

The applicability of KGs in downstream tasks, however, is often limited by their incompleteness (Saxena et al., 2022): they do not contain exhaustive information about *all* relationships between the defined entities (Destandau and Fekete, 2021). To address this issue, researchers and practitioners have worked on Knowledge Graph Completion (KGC): the task of predicting new relationships between the entities in the knowledge graph. For this, two parts of a triple (i.e., *slots*) are given to a KGC system (Rossi et al. (2021); Lin et al. (2018), *inter alia*) and the third is inferred; e.g., answering the query $t = (s, r, ?)$. Such methods learn low-dimensional representations of entities and relations for predictive inference.

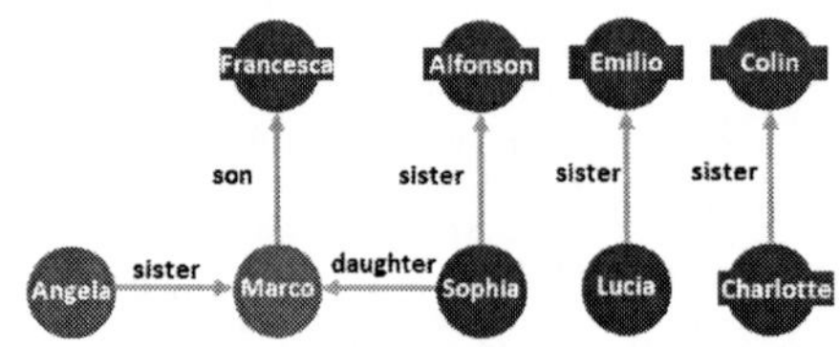

Figure 1: An example explaining a predicted triple (in red) with important training triples (in blue), learned according to gradients by Lawrence et al. (2021). They are faithful, yet not helpful for users to understand the prediction.

The embedding based KGC models, however, are black boxes that do not (and cannot) provide explanations of why the model makes a certain prediction. The lack of transparency significantly hampers users' trust and engagement with KGC systems, especially in the high-risk domains, such as medicine (Han and Liu, 2022; Chaddad et al., 2023). To provide explanations for such embedding-based KGC systems, researchers have proposed explainable KGC (XKGC) methods (Betz et al., 2022; Lawrence et al., 2021; Pezeshkpour et al., 2019). However, it remains unexplored how helpful users find the explanations provided by these methods. For instance, Figure 1 shows an example explanation that would not be helpful for the end user.

We thus target to evaluate what kind of explanations are *helpful* for the users because ultimately,

[1]The video of the demo: https://www.dropbox.com/scl/fi/p2sczcyvqk6zyr9omcf1e/eacl2024EvaXKGC.mp4?rlkey=j2pvz8alqihxmyiv5q7cxkx1z&dl=0.
The live demo website of the human-evaluation platform: https://xai.privacy.nlehd.de/start-evaluation.

Proceedings of the 18th Conference of the European Chapter of the Association for Computational Linguistics System Demonstrations, pages 18–26

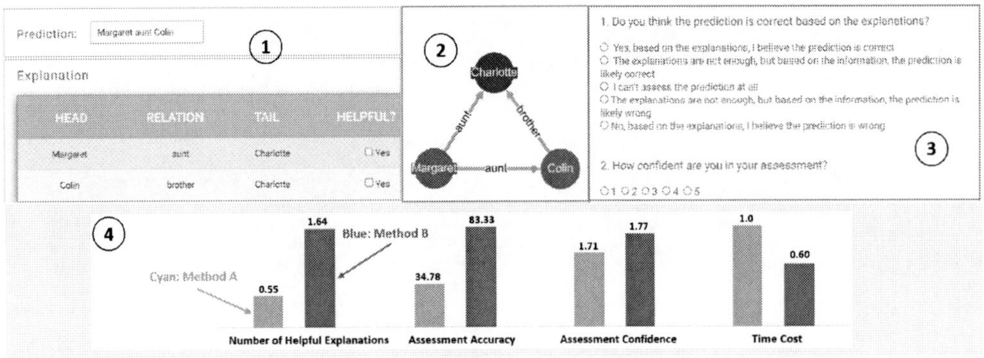

Figure 2: Our evaluation platform to measure plausibility of XKGCs with human-centric evaluation. (1) Shows the prediction and explanations to human testers. (2) Visualizes the prediction and explanations as a graph for the testers to easily comprehend and reason about the relationships. Users can evaluate the helpfulness of the explanations by clicking either the tick boxes in (1) or the edges in the visualized graph (2). (3) Asks the testers to assess the correctness of the prediction based on the explanations. (4) After collecting feedback from N (defined by researchers) testers, plausibility of XKGC is measured with: number of helpful explanations (helpExpl), accuracy (Acc) and confidence of testers assessment, time cost. More details can be found in Sec. 6.

the explanations should directly aid them. Therefore, it is important to measure the *plausibility* of the explanations: the extent to which an explanation generated by XAI is comprehensible and beneficial to human users (Jacovi and Goldberg, 2020; Lage et al., 2019). Thus, to evaluate the plausibility of the explanations, we present a human-centric platform illustrated in Figure 2.

Our evaluation platform offers the following novel contributions. First, it introduces a new evaluation paradigm that assesses how well explanations can assist users in judging the correctness of KGC predictions. In contrast to the prevalent human evaluation paradigm in the literature that requests annotators to simulate AI's behavior (Yin and Neubig, 2022; Hase and Bansal, 2020; Lage et al., 2019; Doshi-Velez and Kim, 2017), the new paradigm aligns better with real human-AI interaction systems, where AIs facilitate humans rather than the other way around. Furthermore, given the growing complexity of AI, it becomes increasingly challenging for annotators to imitate AI's behavior without comprehensive training, especially when utilizing crowdsourcing platforms like Amazon Mechanical Turk (AMT) (Clark et al., 2021). Another notable advantage of our system is its capability to quantify the helpfulness of explanations in an objective manner. Our system suggests metrics, such as the accuracy rate of annotators' judgments, which stems itself from well-defined ground truth to quantitatively measure human feedback.

With these novel contributions, our evaluation platform can effectively measure plausibility of XKGC methods. Considering the diversity of humans, our system also provides various statistical tools to rigorously and comprehensively analyze the collected feedback for reliable conclusions. Additionally, our evaluation platform aids in identifying genuine requirements from users regarding explanations, thereby it can assist in developing and refining XKGC methods to generate explanations that are centered around human needs. Finally, we formulate our study on human-centric evaluation as practical guidelines, which can be replicated to design evaluations for other use cases in the future.

2 Human Centric Evaluation for XKGC

We build an online system to evaluate XKGCs in a human centric manner. Our system considers the real needs and interests of human users in collaboration with AI, allowing us to investigate: *can humans assess correctness of a KGC prediction based on its explanations? Which explanations are helpful for human users?* The answers to these questions provide hints for evaluating the ultimate goal of an XAI method: the generated explanations are expected to assist human users in understanding AI-driven predictions. To this end, our platform has two user views: one for researchers to set up a test and the other for testers to give feedback.

2.1 Researcher

Researchers can prepare the evaluation study by uploading a JSON file that contains both the predic-

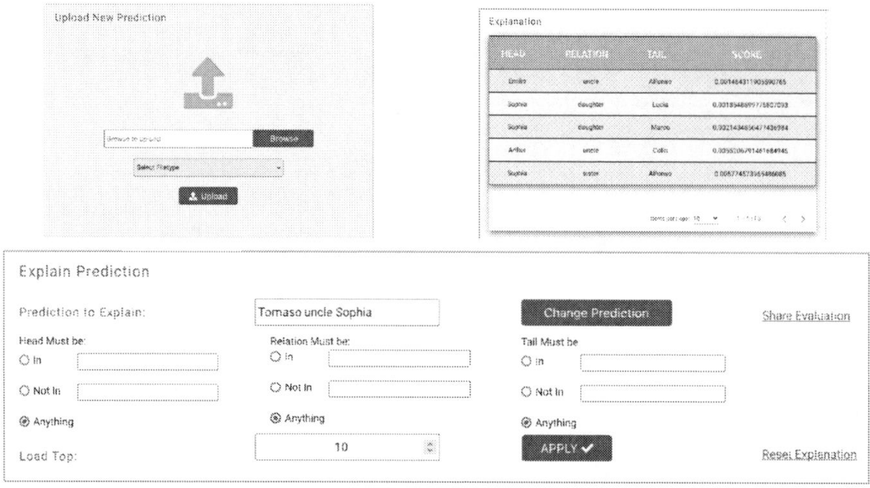

Figure 3: Top-left: the page to load the input JSON file about predictions and explanations to be evaluated. Top-right: the overview of the predictions in the input file for the researchers to check. Bottom: the filter for the researchers to select predictions and explanations to show to testers. The researchers can select any number of predictions they need for user evaluation.

tions and possible explanations. Here is an example JSON file including one prediction and its explanation. If the researchers want to evaluate multiple predictions, then they only need to add these predictions in the json file.

```
"Colin son James": {
    "correct": 1,
    "probability": 0.56884,
    "explanation": [
        [
            [
                "James",
                "father",
                "Colin"
            ],
            0.19817171057308347
        ],
        [
            [
                "Charlotte",
                "sister",
                "Colin"
            ],
            0.217222705276661
        ],
}
```

Each predicted triple is associated with a set of *explanation* triples. Each explanation triple has a score that indicates their importance, which can be used for filtering and ranking the explanations. This score can e.g. come from the XKGC method. In addition, each prediction has the *correct* attribute which indicates whether this prediction is correct or not. The false prediction can be viewed as a control setup, which allows us to test whether users can determine if a prediction is correct based on the given explanations. Additionally, it allows us to assess the engagement of testers (see Sec. 5 for details). The *probability* attribute specifies the likelihood of the predicted triple by the KGC method.

After the JSON is uploaded (top-left panel of Figure 3), the system lists all triples for the researchers to check (top-right panel). Next, the researchers can click on a particular triple to see its explanations as well as a filtering options (bottom panel). With the filtering options, the researcher can choose which predicted triples and explanations they would like to keep for the human evaluation. Finally, the system shows a preview page where the researchers can check the evaluation test that will be displayed for the testers.

2.2 Tester

After the evaluation test has been setup, the researchers can share the link of the online system with the testers to evaluate. The system can work with crowdsourcing websites, e.g. Amazon Mechanical Turk (AMT), to employ testers for human evaluations. Figure 4 illustrates how an evaluation task can be set up with our system on AMT.

The top panels of Figure 2 showcase the interface for testers. For each prediction, the tester can inspect the explanations, which are displayed in two formats (table and graph). Panel (1) shows the prediction and explanations in a format of table. For the testers to easily comprehend and reason about the relationships, the prediction and explanations are also visualized as a graph, shown as Panel (2). Based on the explanations, they can decide on whether they believe a prediction to be correct

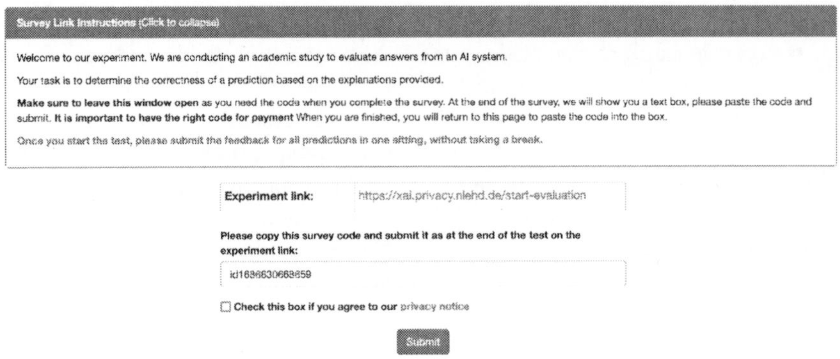

Figure 4: Launch an human evaluation study based on our system in Amazon Mechanical Turk.

or not on a scale from 1 to 5. In addition, they need to specify whether an explanation is *Helpful*. This can either be done by clicking a tick box in the explanation table (see Panel (1)) or by clicking on an edge in the graph to mark the corresponding triple as helpful (see Panel (2)). The selections of the user will be synchronized in both formats.

Once done, the tester can submit the feedback and move on to the next prediction. After the last prediction, we offer the tester an additional form to share any feedback with us. This page can also be used, e.g. to share an identifying code that allows us to utilize the evaluation system with AMT, where the code is used to check completeness and engagement for payment.

3 Architecture of the Evaluation System

The system is as a web application consisting of frontend (HTML5/JavaScript) and backend (Python). We will describe the respective components and the data flow (shown in Figure 5) in detail.

3.1 Backend

The backend is a Python-based software framework (Flask[2]) providing multiple HTTP REST interfaces to enable human-centric data management, evaluation, feedback collection, and analysis. Combining these interfaces essentially leads to an all-in-one solution for conducting a human-centric evaluation. When it comes to data modeling, we ensure flexibility and scalability by using a key-value database (MongoDB[3]). While our solution also encompasses a frontend component, the versatility of the backend allows it to seamlessly integrate with any other application or system.

[2]https://palletsprojects.com/p/flask/

[3]https://www.mongodb.com/

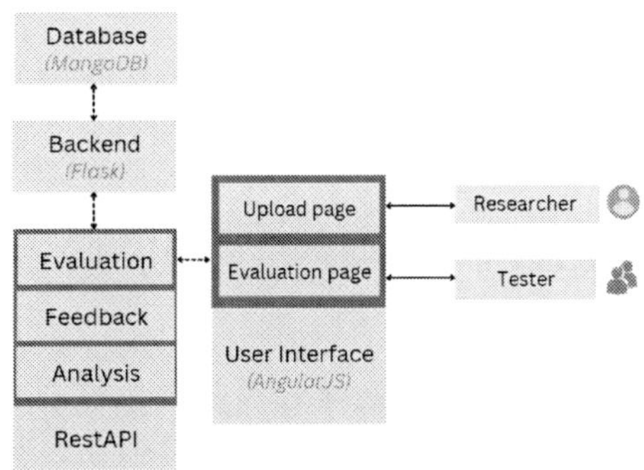

Figure 5: System architecture: the interaction of the researchers and the testers with their respective user interfaces and the overview of the backend and RestAPI.

3.2 Frontend

The frontend is implemented in JavaScript (AngularJS[4]), HTML5 and CSS, and provides user-friendly access to the functionalities provided by the backend. It consists of two environments, separating the evaluation and the data management. The data management includes uploading data, but also to specify filters and related settings to configure the evaluation.

3.3 Data Flow

Figure 5 illustrates an application example of our solution: First, a researcher interacts with the "Upload page" to upload the data (i.e., predictions and explanations) to be used in the evaluation. Then, she is redirected to the configuration page to, e.g., apply filters to the predictions (see Figure 3). Finally, the researcher can generate and share the URL to access the evaluation. When a tester visits the URL, the evaluation page presents the predictions to her one after the other and in a random

[4]https://angularjs.org/

order. The tester submit her feedback on the predictions and the corresponding explanations. The evaluation results will be stored by the backend in our key-value database and can be downloaded as a JSON file.

Our system is deployed on a powerful server with 48 Threads (24 cores), 256 GB memory and 1GB Full-Duplex Internet connection. In theory, it can support more than one thousand testers to visit the evaluation platform.

4 Statistical Analysis of Human Feedback

Due to the complexity and costliness of human evaluation, as well as the diversity among human testers, the collected feedback tends to be both limited in quantity and diverse in quality. Consequently, statistical analysis assumes a critical role to draw reliable conclusions from human feedback. We include the following statistical analysis tools in our platform.

Power analysis. In human evaluation, there is often an important question: How many testers are necessary to draw a solid conclusion? There is no a universally applicable minimum sample size for obtaining statistically significant results (Hogg et al., 2015). Power analysis is commonly used in e.g., social-science and clinical research literature (Cohen, 1988), which determines an adequate sample size for a human evaluation based on a stated effect size that defines the difference level of the compared methods. As the effect size used in power analysis is prospectively anticipated before the evaluation by the researchers, it is good to analyze the post hoc power of an observed effect size derived from the collected human feedback, especially if the findings are non-significant (Onwuegbuzie and Leech, 2004).

Hypothesis testing. Are the observed results in human feedback statistically significant or simply due to chance? Hypothesis testing, e.g. t-tests, Wilcoxon Signed-Rank test, Mann Whitney test and Brunner-Munzel test, can be employed to measure them. With hypothesis tests, we can distinguish between real effects and random variations in a rigorous manner.

Mixed effect analysis. Human feedback is often subject to variability of individual differences, engagement levels, and other random variation. (Linear) mixed effect analysis (Bates et al., 2015) can thus be used to quantify and assess the variability within testers' responses. Specifically, it can measure both fixed effects (differences caused by the compared methods) and random effects (differences due to variation of individuals) quantitatively.

Correlation Analysis. In addition, correlation analysis can also be applicable to analyze the relations among different metrics. For example, we suggest multiple metrics to quantify plausibility, including: accuracy rate of tester's assessment, confidence of testers, number of helpful explanations, and time cost. Correlation analysis can explore relationships between metrics, and may provide insights into the reliability and validity of the results.

5 Guidelines for Human-Centric Evaluation

Human evaluation can be subject to various biases that may affect the reliability of the conclusions (Hase and Bansal, 2020; Chandrasekaran et al., 2018; Gajos and Mamykina, 2022). The following concerns need to be addressed.

Engagement. Testers often exhibit varying levels of engagement and various thinking modes. To mitigate the impact of tester bias, we propose that each tester assesses ≥ 2 XKGC methods, analyzing the feedback with paired tests, especially when the number of available testers is limited. Additionally, testers' engagement tends to decrease over time. Therefore, it is crucial to impose a constraint on the total evaluation time (e.g. one hour per session). Furthermore, to ensure the testers' proper engagement during the evaluation process, we can randomly assign some straightforward predictions as checkpoints for validation.

Equivalency. All testers should evaluate similar set of predictions in a similar order. This is to reduce deviations caused by individual predictions.

Diversity. Testers may have the tendency to retain information from previous predictions, which can result in the earlier assessments influencing the later ones. Consequently, we recommend selecting predictions that are as distinct from each other as possible to mitigate this concern.

Balance. Predictions should be balanced. Specifically, numbers of correct and erroneous predictions should be similar, and the order of predictions should be random, such that testers cannot simply guess prediction results.

Human-understandable benchmark data. The data used in a human evaluation needs to be human understandable, otherwise testers have no clue how to assess predictions and explanations.

While a seemingly obvious statement, in practice we found it difficult to find KGC data that satisfies this constraint. In addition, testers recruited for a human evaluation are often lay people, not professionals of an area, thus plain datasets without domain-specific knowledge (such as biology and healthcare) would be better. If the evaluated XKGCs are domain specific, e.g., disease diagnosis, then specialists should accordingly be employed.

6 Experimental Study

To demonstrate what results and findings can be acquired with the proposed system, we conducted two evaluations.

6.1 Interview Users for Needs on XKGC

XAI is human-centric in nature. There is no one-for-all solution to meet all users' expectations. Our human-centric evaluation platform can help the researchers and practitioners interview their users to find: (1) what the users really need for understanding the KGC predictions in their applications, and (2) whether the generated explanations by their methods make sense for their users.

We conducted a series of interviews with the evaluation system. A human-understandable KGC dataset was selected as benchmark data. We used the kinship dataset (Kok and Domingos, 2007) because it is easily human understandable. Although the dataset is of small size, it involves key challenges of knowledge graphs, such as multiple relations and 1:n relations between entities. We randomly selected a set of KGC predictions and explained them with an XKGC method (Lawrence et al., 2021), denoted as *Method A*. Figure 1 illustrated an example prediction and its explanations.

With the evaluation system, we visualized the predictions and their explanations to the testers and interviewed: *what will be a helpful explanations for them?* and *why do they think an explanation helpful?* The interview is summarized in Table 1. Based on the collected feedback in the interview, we have made the following significant findings.

First, the interviews revealed that the testers often search for "paths" that link the nodes of the predicted triple to the nodes of explanations. See for example the "triangle" explanation in left panel of Figure 6, where two triples as the explanations can connect the two nodes of the predictions with another node in a triangle relationship. In situations where explanations don't connect to the predicted triples users consider the explanations are nonsensical for them.

Second, testers often find a rather small set of explanations helpful (2-3) and remark that a large number of explanations (e.g. >10) create confusion.

Third, often it would be helpful for testers to have additional information from the knowledge graph - but this additional information was not identified by *Method A*. For example, *Method A* cannot create an explanation linking four entities, such as in right panel of Figure 6.

Purpose	Investigate needs of humans on explanations of AI-driven predictions in the context of knowledge graph completion.
Intervie-wees	5 interviewees: 3 with machine learning background, 2 with good understanding about users of their AI system.
Guide	A guide is created, including text- and video-introduction to the evaluation platform.
Ques-tions	1. What will be a helpful explanations for users? 2. Why do users think an explanation helpful?

Table 1: User interview for their needs on XKGC.

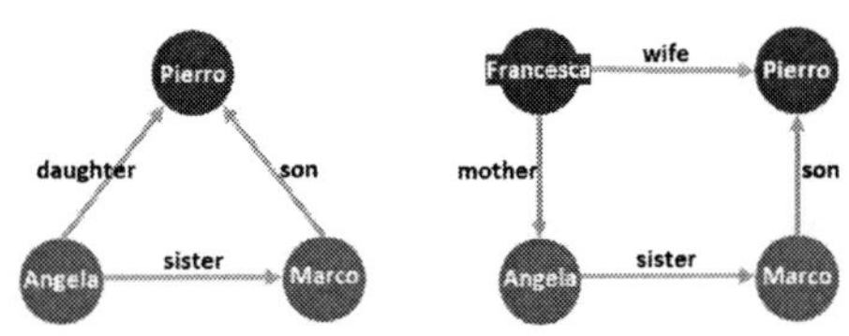

Figure 6: Explanations (in blue) learned with *Method B* for a predicted triple (in red): (a) explanation path of length $\ell = 2$, and (b) length $\ell = 3$. The path based explanations are more meaningful for human users because they create a connection between the entities in the predicted triple.

6.2 Compare Plausibility of XKGCs

We also used the evaluation platform to compare two XKGC methods: which would be more helpful for users. The kinship dataset (Kok and Domingos, 2007) is selected again due to human understandability for lay testers. Figure 1 and Figure 6 illustrate the explanations of the two methods, *method A* and *method B*, respectively. In order to mitigate potential biases introduced by individual testers, we select the predicted triples based on the guidelines in Section 5. The details are presented in Table 2.

1	Each tester evaluates 14 predicted triples to keep their engagement.
2	The first two triples serve as practice to facilitate testers understanding and comfort with the system and the questions. The feedback is not included in statistical analysis.
3	The rest of the triples are different from each other. Each is randomly drawn from a unique relation (12 relation types in total in the dataset).
4	Half of triples are correctly or incorrectly predicted to avoid dummy feedback.
5	Paired test is employed. Half of triples are randomly selected for either XAI method.
6	The predicted triples are randomly shuffled.
7	All testers evaluate the same set of predicted triples in the same order for fairness.

Table 2: Selecting predictions for a human-centric evaluation with the Kinship data.

30 testers are invited to evaluate the predictions, following the steps illustrated in Section 2. We received the feedback from 23 of them. For each tester (anonymous) and each prediction, our platform collected the metrics: accuracy of assessment (denoted as Acc), confidence of assessment, number of helpful explanations (denoted as helpExpl), and time cost. Our platform also provides diverse statistical tools (see Section 4) to analyze the measurements, e.g. the results shown in the bottom panel of Figure 2. One can find that *Method B* outperforms *Method A* in all four metrics. Most notably, *Method B* is attributed more helpful explanations (1.64 vs. 0.55) and leads to enhanced accuracy in testers' assessments (35% vs. 83%). From this we conclude that *Method B* indeed generates more helpful explanations for human testers in the context of kinship predictions.

7 Related Work

Human evaluation has attracted increasing attention in XAI research due to its ultimate goal of aiding human to understand AI predictions. Many evaluation benchmarks are based on simulatability (Doshi-Velez and Kim, 2017): how well human can simulate AI with help of explanations. For instance, Nguyen (2018) employed forward simulation to evaluate attribute-based XAI methods for text classification. Hase and Bansal (2020) extended the simulation test with counterfactual simulation to compare different types of explanations for text and tabular data. Arora et al. (2021) executed in-depth analysis of simulation tests for explanations of review classification. In addition, there are other human evaluations for XAI outside of NLP. For example, Alufaisan et al. (2021) proposed a decision-making based evaluation to measure human performance on decisions given predictions and explanations. More human evaluation tests can be found in the surveys e.g. Zhou et al. (2021). However the literature lacks a human evaluation tool to facilitate researchers on human-centric evaluation of KGC explanations.

Existing KGC evaluation platforms focus on measurement of prediction performance. For instance, Zhou et al. (2022) proposed a reconsideration of the used metrics by creating a "complete" judgement set inspired by evaluation of information retrieval. Rim et al. (2021) proposed the use of unit tests in order to evaluate models in a fine-grained manner by considering different capabilities. Widjaja et al. (2022) provided refined performance evaluation by bucketizing the test set into user-specified chunks. To bridge the gap, our platform provides a tool to measure plausibility of KGC explanations with human evaluation.

8 Conclusion

AI explanations only achieve their goal if the explanation is helpful to the human user. To measure this, we present a human-centric evaluation platform in the context of explainable knowledge graph completion. Distinguishing from the simulatability-based evaluation, our system assesses how well explanations assist users in judging the correctness of KGC predictions, and thus aligns better with human-AI interaction systems, where AI facilities humans rather than the other way around. To alleviate possible biases, we provide a set of guidelines in experiment design, and diverse analysis tools for reliable conclusions. The experiments demonstrate the findings and results that can be acquired with the proposed system.

References

Yasmeen Alufaisan, Laura R. Marusich, Jonathan Z. Bakdash, Yan Zhou, and Murat Kantarcioglu. 2021. Does explainable artificial intelligence improve human decision-making? In *Proceedings of the AAAI Conference on Artificial Intelligence*, pages 6618–6626.

Siddhant Arora, Danish Pruthi, Norman M. Sadeh, William W. Cohen, Zachary C. Lipton, and Graham

Neubig. 2021. Explain, edit, and understand: Rethinking user study design for evaluating model explanations. *CoRR*, abs/2112.09669.

Douglas Bates, Martin Mächler, Ben Bolker, and Steve Walker. 2015. Fitting linear mixed-effects models using lme4. *Journal of Statistical Software*, 67(1).

Patrick Betz, Christian Meilicke, and Heiner Stuckenschmidt. 2022. Adversarial explanations for knowledge graph embeddings. In *Proceedings of the 31st International Joint Conference on Artificial Intelligence (IJCAI-22)*.

Ahmad Chaddad, Jihao Peng, Jian Xu, and Ahmed Bouridane. 2023. Survey of explainable ai techniques in healthcare. *Sensors*, 23(2).

Arjun Chandrasekaran, Viraj Prabhu, Deshraj Yadav, Prithvijit Chattopadhyay, and Devi Parikh. 2018. Do explanations make vqa models more predictable to a human? In *Proceedings of the Conference on Empirical Methods in Natural Language Processing*, pages 1036–1042.

Elizabeth Clark, Tal August, Sofia Serrano, Nikita Haduong, Suchin Gururangan, and Noah A. Smith. 2021. All that's 'human' is not gold: Evaluating human evaluation of generated text. In *Proceedings of the 59th Annual Meeting of the Association for Computational Linguistics and the 11th International Joint Conference on Natural Language Processing (Volume 1: Long Papers)*, pages 7282–7296, Online. Association for Computational Linguistics.

Jacob Cohen. 1988. *Statistical power analysis for the behavioral sciences.* Lawrence Erlbaum Associates.

Marie Destandau and Jean-Daniel Fekete. 2021. The missing path: Analysing incompleteness in knowledge graphs. *Information Visualization*, 20(1):66–82.

Finale Doshi-Velez and Been Kim. 2017. Towards a rigorous science of interpretable machine learning. *arXiv preprint*, arXiv:1702.08608.

Krzysztof Z. Gajos and Lena Mamykina. 2022. Do people engage cognitively with ai? impact of ai assistance on incidental learning. In *Proceedings of the 27th Annual Conference on Intelligent User Interfaces*, pages 794–806.

Kiril Gashteovski, Rainer Gemulla, Bhushan Kotnis, Sven Hertling, and Christian Meilicke. 2020. On Aligning OpenIE Extractions with Knowledge Bases: A Case Study. In *Proceedings of the First Workshop on Evaluation and Comparison of NLP Systems*, pages 143–154, Online. Association for Computational Linguistics.

Henry Han and Xiangrong Liu. 2022. The challenges of explainable ai in biomedical data science. *BMC Bioinformatics*, 22.

Peter Hase and Mohit Bansal. 2020. Evaluating explainable ai: Which algorithmic explanations help users predict model behavior? In *Proceedings of the 58th Annual Meeting of the Association for Computational Linguistics*, pages 5540–5552.

Robert V. Hogg, Elliot A. Tanis, and Dale L. Zimmerman. 2015. *Probability and Statistical Inference.* Pearson.

Linmei Hu, Tianchi Yang, Luhao Zhang, Wanjun Zhong, Duyu Tang, Chuan Shi, Nan Duan, and Ming Zhou. 2021. Compare to the knowledge: Graph neural fake news detection with external knowledge. In *Proceedings of the 59th Annual Meeting of the Association for Computational Linguistics and the 11th International Joint Conference on Natural Language Processing (Volume 1: Long Papers)*, pages 754–763, Online. Association for Computational Linguistics.

Ziniu Hu, Yichong Xu, Wenhao Yu, Shuohang Wang, Ziyi Yang, Chenguang Zhu, Kai-Wei Chang, and Yizhou Sun. 2022. Empowering language models with knowledge graph reasoning for open-domain question answering. In *Proceedings of the 2022 Conference on Empirical Methods in Natural Language Processing*, pages 9562–9581, Abu Dhabi, United Arab Emirates. Association for Computational Linguistics.

Alon Jacovi and Yoav Goldberg. 2020. Towards faithfully interpretable NLP systems: How should we define and evaluate faithfulness? In *Proceedings of the 58th Annual Meeting of the Association for Computational Linguistics, ACL*, page 4198–4205.

Jiho Kim, Sungjin Park, Yeonsu Kwon, Yohan Jo, James Thorne, and Edward Choi. 2023. FactKG: Fact verification via reasoning on knowledge graphs. In *Proceedings of the 61st Annual Meeting of the Association for Computational Linguistics (Volume 1: Long Papers)*, pages 16190–16206, Toronto, Canada. Association for Computational Linguistics.

Stanley Kok and Pedro Domingos. 2007. Statistical predicate invention. In *Proceedings of the International Conference on Machine Learning (ICML)*.

Isaac Lage, Emily Chen, Jeffrey He, Menaka Narayanan, Been Kim, Samuel J. Gershman, and Finale Doshi-Velez. 2019. Human evaluation of models built for interpretability. *Proceedings of the AAAI Conference on Human Computation and Crowdsourcing*, 7(1):59–67.

Carolin Lawrence, Timo Sztyler, and Mathias Niepert. 2021. Explaining neural matrix factorization with gradient rollback. In *35th AAAI Conference on Artificial Intelligence*.

Yankai Lin, Xu Han, Ruobing Xie, Zhiyuan Liu, and Maosong Sun. 2018. Knowledge representation learning: A quantitative review.

Dong Nguyen. 2018. Comparing automatic and human evaluation of local explanations for text classification.

In *Proceedings of the 2018 Conference of the North American Chapter of the Association for Computational Linguistics: Human Language Technologies, Volume 1 (Long Papers)*, pages 1069–1078, New Orleans, Louisiana. Association for Computational Linguistics.

A. J. Onwuegbuzie and N. L. Leech. 2004. Post hoc power: A concept whose time has come. *Understanding Statistics*, 3(4):201–230.

Pouya Pezeshkpour, Yifan Tian, and Sameer Singh. 2019. Investigating robustness and interpretability of link prediction via adversarial modifications. In *Proceedings of the 2019 Conference of the North American Chapter of the Association for Computational Linguistics, NAACL*, pages 3336–3347.

Wiem Ben Rim, Carolin Lawrence, Kiril Gashteovski, Mathias Niepert, and Naoaki Okazaki. 2021. Behavioral testing of knowledge graph embedding models for link prediction. In *3rd Conference on Automated Knowledge Base Construction.*

Andrea Rossi, Denilson Barbosa, Donatella Firmani, Antonio Matinata, and Paolo Merialdo. 2021. Knowledge graph embedding for link prediction: A comparative analysis. *ACM Trans. Knowl. Discov. Data*, 15(2).

Apoorv Saxena, Adrian Kochsiek, and Rainer Gemulla. 2022. Sequence-to-Sequence Knowledge Graph Completion and Question Answering. *ArXiv*, abs/2203.10321.

Saurabh Srivastava, Mayur Patidar, Sudip Chowdhury, Puneet Agarwal, Indrajit Bhattacharya, and Gautam Shroff. 2021. Complex question answering on knowledge graphs using machine translation and multi-task learning. In *Proceedings of the 16th Conference of the European Chapter of the Association for Computational Linguistics: Main Volume*, pages 3428–3439, Online. Association for Computational Linguistics.

Haris Widjaja, Kiril Gashteovski, Wiem Ben Rim, Pengfei Liu, Christopher Malon, Daniel Ruffinelli, Carolin (Haas) Lawrence, and Graham Neubig. 2022. KGxBoard: Explainable and Interactive Leaderboard for Evaluation of Knowledge Graph Completion Models. In *Conference on Empirical Methods in Natural Language Processing.*

Kayo Yin and Graham Neubig. 2022. Interpreting language models with contrastive explanations. In *Proceedings of the Conference on Empirical Methods in Natural Language Processing (EMNLP)*, pages 184–198.

Jianlong Zhou, Amir H. Gandomi, Fang Chen, and Andreas Holzinger. 2021. Evaluating the quality of machine learning explanations: A survey on methods and metrics. *Electronics*, 10(5).

Ying Zhou, Xuanang Chen, Ben He, Zheng Ye, and Le Sun. 2022. Re-thinking knowledge graph completion evaluation from an information retrieval perspective. In *Proceedings of the 45th International ACM SIGIR Conference on Research and Development in Information Retrieval*. ACM.

pyTLEX: A Python Library for TimeLine EXtraction

Akul Singh, Jared Hummer, Mustafa Ocal, & Mark Finlayson
Florida International University
Knight Foundation School of Computing and Information Sciences
CASE Building, 11200 S.W. 8th Street, Miami, FL USA 33199
{asing118,jhumm001,mocal,markaf}@fiu.edu

Abstract

pyTLEX is an implementation of the TimeLine EXtraction algorithm (TLEX; Finlayson et al., 2021) that enables users to work with TimeML annotations and perform advanced temporal analysis, offering a comprehensive suite of features. TimeML is a standardized markup language for temporal information in text. pyTLEX allows users to parse TimeML annotations, construct TimeML graphs, and execute the TLEX algorithm to effect complete timeline extraction. In contrast to previous implementations (i.e., jTLEX for Java), pyTLEX sets itself apart with a range of advanced features. It introduces a React-based visualization system, enhancing the exploration of temporal data and the comprehension of temporal connections within textual information. Furthermore, pyTLEX incorporates an algorithm for increasing connectivity in temporal graphs, which identifies graph disconnectivity and recommends links based on temporal reasoning, thus enhancing the coherence of the graph representation. Additionally, pyTLEX includes a built-in validation algorithm, ensuring compliance with TimeML annotation guidelines, which is essential for maintaining data quality and reliability. pyTLEX equips researchers and developers with an extensive toolkit for temporal analysis, and its testing across various datasets validates its accuracy and reliability.

1 Introduction

Temporal information plays a crucial role in natural language processing and text analysis. TimeML, an SGML-based markup language, allows the annotation of temporal information in texts, including events, temporal expressions, links, and temporal signals (Pustejovsky et al., 2003a) [1]. TimeML annotations can be generated using automatic analyzers (Verhagen et al., 2005), manual annotation (Minard et al., 2016), or some combination of the two. TimeML annotations can be used to build temporal graphs, where nodes are events and temporal expressions, and edges are temporal relations. However, they provide only a partial ordering of events and times. Meanwhile, the global order (i.e., a timeline) is more useful for various NLP applications, including question-answering systems (Radev et al., 2002), text summarization (Mamidala and Sanampudi, 2021), and text visualization (Di Mascio et al., 2010).

To effect the extraction of timelines from TimeML annotations, we previously developed the TLEX algorithm, based on Constraint Satisfaction Problems (CSP), which provides an exact solution to the problem (in contrast to machine-learning-based approaches). TLEX converts TimeML annotations into an exact timeline, and in previous work, we introduced JTLEX, an open-source Java library, which implemented the TLEX algorithm (Ocal et al., 2023). jTLEX not only parsed TimeML annotations but also allowed users to manipulate TimeML graphs.

Like jTLEX, pyTLEX also takes a TimeML annotated file as input, then (1) parses the annotations into TimeML objects, (2) builds a TimeML graph, (3) partitions the TimeML graph into temporally connected graphs to separate real-life events and subordinated events, (4) transforms the temporally connected graphs into point algebra (PA) graphs, and (5) solves the PA graphs to extract a timeline. If a timeline cannot be extracted, meaning the graph is temporally inconsistent, (6) it detects the minimum inconsistent subgraph and returns it to the annotator to fix it. Finally, if the order of events and times are indeterminant (multiple possible ordering), (7) it calculates the temporal indeterminacy.

PyTLEX goes beyond jTLEX and introduces several new features. It includes a React-based application for graph and timeline visualization, making the exploration of temporal data more intuitive and insightful. The library incorporates an

[1] SGML is a markup language for defining the structure of documents in a machine-readable and human-readable format.

Proceedings of the 18th Conference of the European Chapter of the Association for Computational Linguistics
System Demonstrations, pages 27–34

algorithm for automatically increasing connectivity, which detects graph disconnectivity and automatically suggests temporal links. Additionally, pyTLEX offers a rule-based system for validating compliance with the annotation guidelines.

We have tested pyTLEX on the TimeBank corpus (Pustejovsky et al., 2003b), which contains 183 TimeML annotated news articles. In less than 9 minutes on current consumer laptop (3.0 GHz Intel Core i7-1185G7 with 32GB of RAM), pyTLEX validated the annotations, extracted timelines, and visualized them. We release our demonstration system as well as a screencast video showing its operation[2].

2 Library Overview

2.1 User Input

pyTLEX offers comprehensive processing and manipulation capabilities for all the data present within a TimeML annotation. It accommodates various input sources, allowing the incorporation of TimeML annotations from a `.tml` file, a JSON-style TimeML encoding, or plain text. Users can also create TimeML annotations manually, adhering to the TimeML annotation guide (Sauri et al., 2006), or generate annotations automatically using advanced TimeML annotators like TARSQI (Verhagen et al., 2005), ClearTK (Bethard, 2013), CAEVO (Chambers et al., 2014), or CATENA (Mirza and Tonelli, 2016). It is important to note that automatic TimeML annotation tools, while efficient, may introduce limitations such as information loss, temporal inconsistencies, and incorrect annotations (Ocal et al., 2022a). The advantage of pyTLEX lies in its ability to detect and rectify such issues, as described in the subsequent sections.

2.2 TimeML Parser

pyTLEX offers a TimeML parser for transforming TimeML annotations into a collection of TimeML objects or the raw text. pyTLEX also validates annotation compliance with the standard.

2.3 Graph Constructor

In a TimeML graph, nodes correspond to events and times, and edges represent TimeML links, as illustrated in Figure 1. This graph encapsulates a wealth of information that can be programmatically queried, including sets of links and nodes, specific links by their ID, nodes by their ID, and lists of incoming or outgoing links, among other properties.

[2] `https://cognac.cs.fiu.edu/pytlex/`

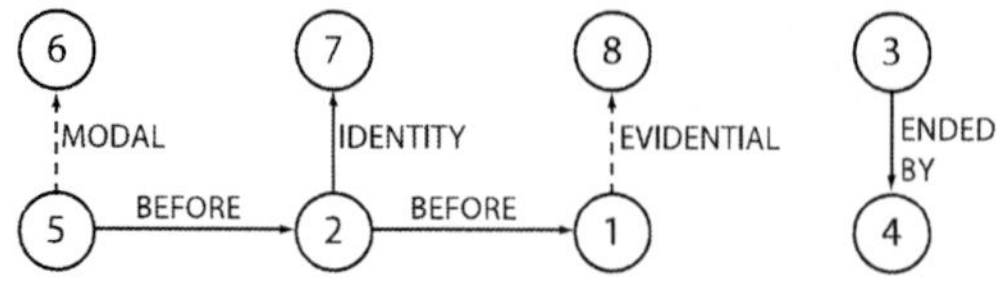

Figure 1: Visualization of the TimeML graph for `wsj_0555.tml` from the TimeBank corpus. SLINKs are given in dashed lines. pyTLEX partitions the TimeML graph into four temporally connected subgraphs.

PyTLEX also allows users to programmatically modify the TimeML graph. Users can introduce or remove links and nodes within the graph, allowing them to create custom graphs. The graph implementation can be exported as JSON, which can later be used for visualization. An example of a TimeML graph is given in Figure 1.

2.4 Partitioner

There are three types of TimeML links: <TLINK> and <ALINK> signify temporal order between events and times, while <SLINK> conveys modal, counterfactual, or conditional relationships between two events, as in the example "Tyler *forgot* to *bring* his wallet." In this instance, a counterfactual relationship exists between the events *forgot* and *bring*. The event *bring* never transpired in the "real world" described in the text. As detailed in the TLEX paper, pyTLEX partitions a TimeML graph into temporally connected subgraphs to identify such distinctions. The subgraph(s) containing "real world" events are called the *main* subgraph(s) and those connected to the main subgraphs via subordination links as *subordinated* subgraphs.

2.5 Transformer

As described in the TLEX algorithm, pyTLEX converts each temporally connected subgraph into a Point Algebra (PA) graph, where nodes are time points, and edges are primitive temporal constraints $<, =$. For example, if we have two events (A and B) with A being *BEFORE* B, this relationship is translated into a PA graph as $A^- < A^+ < B^- < B^+$, with '-' and '+' marking the start and end time points of a node. Figure 2 shows the PA graph for the TimeML graph in Figure 1. The PA graph is necessary for the temporal constraint satisfaction problem (TCSP) that is used to generate the

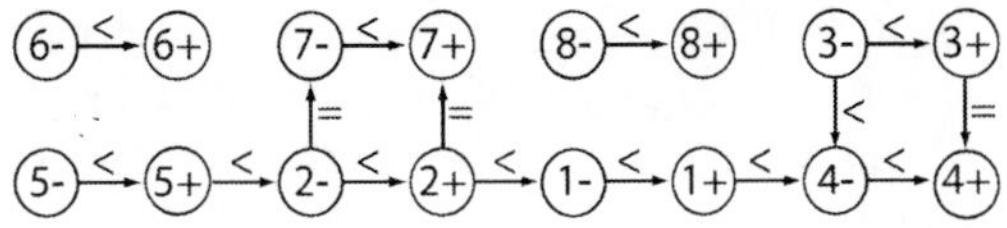

Figure 2: Visualization of the output of the transforming temporally connected subgraphs in Figure 1 into the PA graph after the connectivity increaser added the before link between 1 and 4.

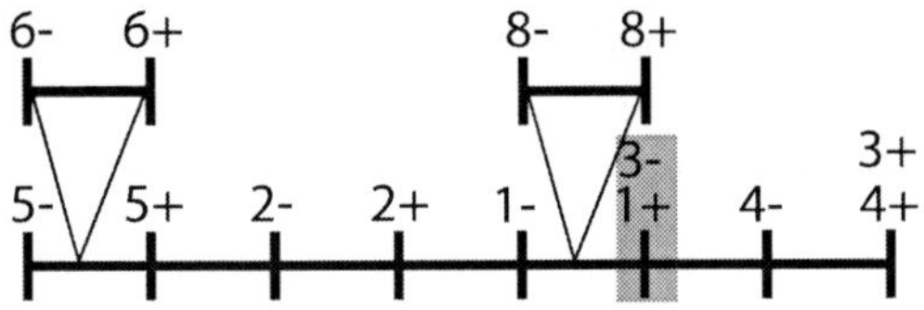

Figure 3: Visualization of the timeline of the TimeML graph in Figure 1. Grey regions indicate indeterminate sections.

timeline, as detailed in Section 2.6.

2.6 Solver

Once each temporally connected subgraph is transformed into a Point Algebra (PA) graph, pyTLEX uses the Z3 Python library for Constraint Satisfaction Problems (CSP) to assign integers to the time points within the graph. The timeline is then obtained by sorting these assigned integers. The Z3 Python library is a theorem prover and solver that is commonly used for solving complex mathematical and logical problems (De Moura and Bjørner, 2008). By default, pyTLEX generates the smallest solution where the first time point is assigned 1 and each subsequent time point the next lowest integer.

When applied to all the PA graphs, pyTLEX generates an exact trunk-and-branch timeline structure, where the trunk corresponds to the main timeline representing the main subgraph, and branches represent subordinated timelines associated with the subordinated subgraphs, as visualized in Figure 3. Therefore, the main timeline conveys the global order of "real world" events and times, while subordinated branches capture subordinated events. Users can extract various details from the timeline, such as its length, the first and last time points, the main timeline, subordinated branches, the count of subordinated branches, the number of time points, and the list of attachment time points where subordinated branches connect to the main timeline.

2.7 Inconsistency Detector

As described in the TLEX paper, the annotation must be consistent for the solver to extract a timeline. pyTLEX incorporates an inconsistency detection mechanism designed to identify inconsistent cycles in the TimeML graph. In such cases, pyTLEX identifies the specific links responsible for the inconsistency, thus enabling users to correct their annotations.

2.8 Indeterminacy Calculator

In many cases, natural language texts lack sufficient information to establish a unique ordering of events and times, resulting in multiple possible global orderings. As illustrated in Figure 2, there is no information regarding the relative order between $1+$ and $3-$. PyTLEX employs the TLEX algorithm to quantify temporal indeterminacy within a timeline. The algorithm explores and compares the shortest timeline with 100 alternative timelines (exhaustive computation of all possible timelines is computationally burdensome). If two adjacent points in the shortest timeline are not adjacent in all the other timelines, their order is indeterminate, and such sections can be marked as depicted in Figure 3.

2.9 Increasing Connectivity

During TimeML annotation, it's not uncommon for annotators to unintentionally overlook the annotation of temporal links. Such omissions can lead to disconnectivity within the TimeML graph, thereby disrupting the integrity of the timeline. pyTLEX integrates an algorithm detailed in (Ocal et al., 2022b) to address this problem. This algorithm leverages temporal reasoning to intelligently propose temporal links between two disconnected subgraphs. In essence, it undertakes a comparison of the temporal expressions within these subgraphs and, based on the evaluation of time values, automatically recommends the addition of temporal links. This not only streamlines the timeline generation process but also ensures the coherence and connectivity of temporal relationships within the annotated text. For example, in Figure 1, the TimeML graph is disconnected. Using the time values of 1 and 4, pyTLEX can suggest that 1 is BEFORE 4; inserting such a link results in a connected timeline, as shown in Figure 3.

2.10 Validation

The TimeML annotation guide (Sauri et al., 2006) establishes a set of rules governing the structure of TimeML annotations. pyTLEX incorporates these as a rule-based system that can scrutinize TimeML annotations and ensure compliance with those defined rules. Our validation system incorporates the algorithm presented in our prior work (Ocal et al., 2022b) to assess adherence to Rules 1 to 6. Furthermore, it adopts the algorithm outlined in (Derczynski and Gaizauskas, 2012) to verify compliance with Rule 7. Additionally, our system performs checks to identify instances of repeating links within the TimeML graph (Rule 8), reinforcing the integrity of the annotation.

2.11 Visualization

To visualize its JSON outputs, pyTLEX provides a React-based application that allows users to visually explore the TimeML graph, its partitions, and the resulting timelines. Additionally, the visualization application harnesses the output from the inconsistency detector to highlight problematic links within the graph. This visual aid empowers users to readily identify issues and undertake necessary corrections. Furthermore, pyTLEX incorporates visual cues to highlight indeterminate sections of the timeline, making it a valuable resource for narrative comprehension and understanding. For pyTLEX visualization, we have provided the demo video on the pyTLEX website [3].

3 Use Cases

A user guide and license information can be found on the pyTLEX website[4]. Here, we illustrate an approach for one of the TimeML annotations of the TimeBank corpus, called `wsj_0555.tml`. This file and the rest of the corpus can be obtained from the LDC website[5]. The following text, shown in the example below, is a snippet of the TimeML-annotated text of `wsj_0555.tml`. The TimeML graph corresponding to the snippet text is shown in Figure 1, where we can see that the nodes of the graph are either events or times, and the edges are TimeML relations. Event instance IDs and timeIDs are given in square brackets (DCT = DOCUMENT CREATION TIME).

[DCT:10/30/89$_{1[t12]}$]: Waxman Industries Inc. **said**$_{2[ei44]}$ holders of \$6,542,000 face amount of its 6 1/4% convertible subordinated debentures, **due**$_{3[ei45]}$ **March** 15, 2007$_{4[t13]}$, have **elected**$_{5[ei46]}$ to **convert**$_{6[ei47]}$ the debt into about 683,000 common shares. The conversion price is \$9.58 a share. The company **said**$_{7[ei48]}$ the holders **represent**$_{8[ei49]}$ 52% of the face amount of the debentures.

Users can read the file and create the TimeML graph as follows:

```
timeML_graph = Graph('wsj_0555.tml');
```

Users can retrieve any information about the graph, such as links (all or one by ID), nodes (all or one by ID), incoming links, outgoing links, JSON output, number of nodes, number of links, number of link types, etc. Listing 1 shows the output of pyTLEX when the user requests the information about the first link of wsj_0555.tml.

Moreover, users can actively manipulate their graph by adding or removing nodes and links or even constructing entirely custom graphs. The following code snippet demonstrates the process of creating a customized graph and adding two new nodes along with a link.

```
node1 = TimeX(1, "FUTURE_REF", True, "
    next wednesday")
node2 = TimeX(2, "FUTURE_REF", True, "
    next thursday")
link1 = Link(1, "TLINK", "BEFORE", node1
    , node2)
timeML_nodes = set()
timeML_nodes.add(node1)
timeML_nodes.add(node2)
timeML_links.add(link1)
timeML_graph = Graph(timeML_nodes,
    timeML_links)
```

After the TimeML graph is created, users can perform timeline extraction. Accessing the graph's partitions can be achieved as follows:

```
timeML_graph.main_partitions
timeML_graph.subordination_partitions
```

As can be seen from Figure 1, this TimeML graph has disconnectivity. PyTLEX can automatically propose a link based on the values of t12 (10/30/1989) and t10 (03/15/2007) through the use of the algorithm for increasing connectivity. Consequently, PyTLEX suggests the link "t12 –BEFORE-> t10" to the user. Users have the option to incorporate this suggested link, thereby achieving a fully connected graph and, by extension, a fully connected timeline:

[3] https://cognac.cs.fiu.edu/pytlex/

[4] https://cognac.cs.fiu.edu/pytlex/

[5] https://catalog.ldc.upenn.edu/LDC2006T08

```
Link: {ID = 1, LinkTag = TLINK, Syntax
    = "", Temporal Relation = BEFORE,
    Origin = null
    Related to time - Timex: {tID =
        t12, Type = DATE, Value =
        1989-10-30 , Mod = null,
        Temporal Function = true,
        Quantity = null, Frequency =
        null}
    Event Instance - Event Instance:
    {ID = eiid44, Tense = PAST, Aspect
        = NONE, Part of Speech = VERB,
        Polarity = POS, Modality = "
        null", Cardinality = "null",
        Signal = null
        EVENT: eid = e1, class =
            REPORTING, stem = say}
    }
```

Listing 1: pyTLEX parser output for printing the information about the first link of the graph.

```
Main Timeline: {
    eiid46- = 1
    eiid46+ = 2
    eiid48- = 3
    eiid44- = 3
    eiid44+ = 4
    eiid48+ = 4
        t12- = 5
        t12+ = 6
    eiid45- = 6
        t10- = 7
    eiid45+ = 8
        t10+ = 8
}
Attachment Points: {eiid46->eiid47,
    eiid48->eiid49}
Subordinated Timelines: {
[eiid47- = 1, eiid47+ = 2],
[eiid48- = 1, eiid48+ = 2]}
```

Listing 2: pyTLEX timeline output for the wsj_0555.tml file.

```
partitions = partition_graph(graph)
links = graph.links
Connectivity_Increaser.
    connect_partitions(partitions,len(
    links))
```

Now that we have the fully connected graph, we can extract the timeline. Users, can retrieve the *exact* trunk-and-branch timeline structure using:

```
timeML_graph.timeline
```

The output will be as shown in Listing 2. As can be seen, pyTLEX returns the *main* timeline, subordinated timelines, and the attachment points for each subordinated timeline.

After extracting the timeline, users can also retrieve the indeterminacy score, as well as the indeterminant time points. For our example, pyTLEX

```
[Graph Type: Main Graph
Nodes Count = 2
Links count = 2
TLinkType: 2
ALinkType: 0
SLinkType: 0
Nodes:
eiid2048, t57
Links: (From -> To)
(t57 BEFORE eiid2048)
(eiid2048 BEFORE t57)
]
```

Listing 3: pyTLEX inconsistent subgraph output for the wsj_1011.tml file.

returns **0.125 indeterminacy score**, and **{t12+, eiid45-}** indeterminant time points after running:

```
IndeterminacyDetector.solve(g)
```

Users can validate annotations, for example, by checking the ALINK replacement rule (Rule 4) and the orphaned node rule (Rule 7):

```
filepath = r"../pytlex_data/
    TimeBankCorpus/wsj_0586.tml"
Sanity_Check.sco_ALINK_rule(filepath)
Sanity_Check.orphaned_node_rule(filepath
    )
```

Since the graph of `wsj_0555.tml` is consistent, pyTLEX's inconsistency detection method yields an empty set, indicating the absence of temporal inconsistencies. To elucidate the mechanics of the inconsistency detection algorithm, we can use `wsj_1011.tml`, which is a temporally inconsistent file from the TimeBank corpus. Following the execution of the graph construction method, users can run the `generate_inconsistent_subgraphs(g)` function to obtain information about the inconsistent cycle. For this specific file, pyTLEX generates an output as shown in Listing 3, presenting both the inconsistent subgraph and relevant subgraph details.

For pyTLEX visualization, we have provided the demo video on the pyTLEX website [6].

4 Related Work

As we discussed in Section 1, TimeML is a standardized temporal markup language. While numerous tools have been created for generating TimeML annotations, including (Verhagen et al., 2005; Saurí et al., 2005; Min et al., 2007; Chang and Manning, 2012; Chambers, 2013; Chambers et al., 2014; Bethard, 2013; Mirza and Tonelli, 2016), there are

[6] https://cognac.cs.fiu.edu/pytlex/

only a small number of tools designed to evaluate TimeML annotations.

Tango, a Java-based TimeML parser tool, can parse TimeML annotated documents and construct TimeML graphs (Verhagen et al., 2006). It offers users the ability to modify the graph and conducts temporal consistency checks using temporal closure. Tango was used in the evaluation of the TimeBank corpus, although it did not flag any inconsistencies within the TimeBank files. Notably, Tango employs <TIMEX> values to depict the graph in a timeline format, where each segment encompasses a <TIMEX> and the associated events. However, it does not furnish the global ordering of events.

Similarly, TBOX (Verhagen, 2007) can create a TimeML graph from TimeML annotations but eliminates temporal closure links. TBOX presents each event in this simplified graph as a box and positions these boxes based on their temporal relations, arranged according to their temporal order. This approach presents challenges with temporally indeterminate annotations.

Boguraev and Ando (2006) evaluated of the initial version of the TimeBank corpus, denoted as TimeBank 1.1. They analyzed the distribution of relations, event classes, Timex types, and TimeML components. Notably, their findings revealed that the annotation tool employed in the construction of TimeBank introduced a consistent shift of a single character. Additionally, they identified discrepancies in the types of Timex tags or instances of missing Timex tags associated with the same Timex signal in TimeBank 1.1. Boguraev et al. (2007) extended their analysis to TimeBank 1.2, enabling a comparative assessment. They selected a random document from both corpora and manually evaluated it to ascertain the number of errors in each version. Their results suggest that TimeBank 1.2 represented a notable improvement over 1.1.

TimeML-strict is a Java-based validation tool for TimeML (Derczynski et al., 2013). It implements a range of criteria, including the identification of any missing document creation time (DCT), the verification of non-linguistic content, and the confirmation that all links reference existing objects.

CAVaT is a Python utility for parsing TimeML annotations and providing quantitative insights, including distributions of TimeML objects (Derczynski and Gaizauskas, 2012). It offers functionality to detect self-loops, orphaned nodes, and disconnectivity within TimeML graphs. CAVaT excludes <SLINK>s from its analysis, which can result in subordinated events being erroneously identified as orphaned objects and subgraphs being marked as disconnected, despite their connectivity through <SLINK>s. CAVaT can identify temporal inconsistencies within the graph using closure. When temporal inconsistencies are present, CAVaT returns the most recently added constraint to the inconsistent cycle, which is important because identifying the complete inconsistent cycle based on a single edge can be particularly challenging for annotators, especially in the context of large graphs.

In addition to these TimeML tools, NLP researchers have used machine learning-based techniques for timeline extraction from TimeML annotations (Mani et al., 2006; Do et al., 2012; Kolomiyets et al., 2012; Leeuwenberg and Moens, 2020). These approaches come with specific constraints, and none of them address all temporal links, covering a maximum of 6 out of the 13 types. Additionally, they fail to distinguish between real-life events and subordinated events, and they may not effectively handle temporal indeterminacy within the annotations.

In contrast to prior work, pyTLEX provides an open-source implementation of TLEX, a technique for extracting exact timelines from TimeML annotations. Like its predecessor, jTLEX, pyTLEX incorporates a TimeML parser and a graph constructor. It distinguishes subordinated events from real-world events, extracts the global order of events and times in a trunk-and-branch timeline structure, automatically identifies and rectifies inconsistencies, and identifies and gauges indeterminacy. However, pyTLEX has a number of extended capabilities. It not only detects and resolves disconnectivities within both graphs and timelines but also integrates a validation system for TimeML annotations. Additionally, it offers a visualization system, enhancing comprehension for users.

5 Conclusion

We present pyTLEX, an open-source Python library that enables the programmatic extraction of exact timelines from TimeML-annotated texts via a standard Python API. PyTLEX provides several capabilities, including TimeML parsing, graph extraction, timeline generation, inconsistency identification, temporal indeterminacy assessment, disconnectivity detection and resolution, corpus validation, and advanced visualization capabilities. We release pyTLEX as an open-source library, freely available for non-commercial usage[7].

References

Steven Bethard. 2013. Cleartk-timeml: A minimalist approach to tempeval 2013. In *Second joint conference on lexical and computational semantics (* SEM), volume 2: proceedings of the seventh international workshop on semantic evaluation (SemEval 2013)*, pages 10–14.

Branimir Boguraev and Rie Kubota Ando. 2006. Analysis of timebank as a resource for timeml parsing. In *LREC*, pages 71–76.

Branimir Boguraev, James Pustejovsky, Rie Ando, and Marc Verhagen. 2007. Timebank evolution as a community resource for timeml parsing. *Language Resources and Evaluation*, 41:91–115.

Nathanael Chambers. 2013. Navytime: Event and time ordering from raw text. Technical report, NAVAL ACADEMY ANNAPOLIS MD.

Nathanael Chambers, Taylor Cassidy, Bill McDowell, and Steven Bethard. 2014. Dense event ordering with a multi-pass architecture. *Transactions of the Association for Computational Linguistics*, 2:273–284.

Angel X Chang and Christopher D Manning. 2012. Sutime: A library for recognizing and normalizing time expressions. In *Lrec*, volume 3735, page 3740.

Leonardo De Moura and Nikolaj Bjørner. 2008. Z3: An efficient smt solver. In *International conference on Tools and Algorithms for the Construction and Analysis of Systems*, pages 337–340. Springer.

Leon Derczynski and Robert Gaizauskas. 2012. Analysing temporally annotated corpora with cavat. *arXiv preprint arXiv:1203.5051*.

Leon Derczynski, Hector Llorens, and Naushad UzZaman. 2013. Timeml-strict: clarifying temporal annotation. *arXiv preprint arXiv:1304.7289*.

T Di Mascio, R Gennari, I Lang, and P Vittorini. 2010. Visual tools for annotating temporal expressions with timeml: a critical overview. Technical Report KRDB10-5, KRDB Research Centre for Knowledge and Data, Free University of Bozen-Bolzano, Bolzano, Italy.

Quang Xuan Do, Wei Lu, and Dan Roth. 2012. Joint inference for event timeline construction. In *Proceedings of the 2012 Joint Conference on Empirical Methods in Natural Language Processing and Computational Natural Language Learning (EMNLP-CoNLL'12)*, pages 677–687.

[7]https://cognac.cs.fiu.edu/pytlex/

Mark A Finlayson, Andres Cremisini, and Mustafa Ocal. 2021. Extracting and aligning timelines. In *Computational Analysis of Storylines: Making Sense of Events*, page 87. Cambridge University Press.

Oleksandr Kolomiyets, Steven Bethard, and Marie-Francine Moens. 2012. Extracting narrative timelines as temporal dependency structures. In *Proceedings of the 50th Annual Meeting of the Association for Computational Linguistics (ACL'12)*, pages 88–97.

Artuur Leeuwenberg and Marie-Francine Moens. 2020. Towards extracting absolute event timelines from english clinical reports. *IEEE/ACM Transactions on Audio, Speech, and Language Processing*, 28:2710–2719.

Kishore Kumar Mamidala and Suresh Kumar Sanampudi. 2021. A novel framework for multi-document temporal summarization (mdts). *Emerging Science Journal*, 5(2):184–190.

Inderjeet Mani, Marc Verhagen, Ben Wellner, Chong Min Lee, and James Pustejovsky. 2006. Machine learning of temporal relations. In *Proceedings of the 21st International Conference on Computational Linguistics and the 44th Annual Meeting of the Association for Computational Linguistics (ICCL-ACL'06)*, pages 753–760. Sydney, Australia.

Congmin Min, Munirathnam Srikanth, and Abraham Fowler. 2007. Lcc-te: a hybrid approach to temporal relation identification in news text. In *Proceedings of the fourth international workshop on semantic evaluations (SemEval-2007)*, pages 219–222.

Anne-Lyse Minard, Manuela Speranza, Ruben Urizar, Begona Altuna, Marieke Van Erp, Anneleen Schoen, and Chantal Van Son. 2016. Meantime, the newsreader multilingual event and time corpus. In *Proceedings of the Tenth International Conference on Language Resources and Evaluation (LREC'16)*, pages 4417–4422.

Paramita Mirza and Sara Tonelli. 2016. Catena: Causal and temporal relation extraction from natural language texts. In *Proceedings of COLING 2016, the 26th International Conference on Computational Linguistics: Technical Papers*, pages 64–75.

Mustafa Ocal, Adrian Perez, Antonela Radas, and Mark Finlayson. 2022a. Holistic evaluation of automatic timeml annotators. In *Proceedings of the Language Resources and Evaluation Conference*, pages 1444–1453, Marseille, France. European Language Resources Association.

Mustafa Ocal, Antonela Radas, Jared Hummer, Karine Megerdoomian, and Mark Finlayson. 2022b. A comprehensive evaluation and correction of the timebank corpus. In *Proceedings of the Language Resources and Evaluation Conference*, pages 2919–2927, Marseille, France. European Language Resources Association.

Mustafa Ocal, Akul Singh, Jared Hummer, Antonela Radas, and Mark Finlayson. 2023. jTLEX: a Java library for TimeLine EXtraction. In *Proceedings of the 17th Conference of the European Chapter of the Association for Computational Linguistics: System Demonstrations*, pages 27–34, Dubrovnik, Croatia. Association for Computational Linguistics.

James Pustejovsky, José Castaño, Robert Ingria, Roser Saurí, Robert Gaizauskas, Andrea Setzer, and Graham Katz. 2003a. TimeML: robust specification of event and temporal expressions in text. In *Fifth International Workshop on Computational Semantics (IWCS-5)*, pages 1–11.

James Pustejovsky, Patrick Hanks, Roser Saurí, Andrew See, Rob Gaizauskas, Andrea Setzer, Dragomir Radev, Beth Sundheim, David Day, Lisa Ferro, and Marcia Lazo. 2003b. The TimeBank corpus. In *Proceedings of Corpus Linguistics Conference*, pages 647–656. Lancaster, UK.

Dragomir Radev, Beth Sundheim, Lisa Ferro, Roser Saurí, Andy See, and James Pustejovsky. 2002. Using timeml in question answering.

Roser Saurí, Robert Knippen, Marc Verhagen, and James Pustejovsky. 2005. Evita: a robust event recognizer for qa systems. In *Proceedings of Human Language Technology Conference and Conference on Empirical Methods in Natural Language Processing*, pages 700–707.

Roser Sauri, Jessica Littman, Robert Gaizauskas, Andrea Setzer, and James Pustejovsky. 2006. TimeML annotation guidelines, version 1.2.1. https://catalog.ldc.upenn.edu/docs/LDC2006T08/timeml_annguide_1.2.1.pdf.

Marc Verhagen. 2007. Drawing timeml relations with tbox. In *Annotating, extracting and reasoning about time and events*, pages 7–28. Springer.

Marc Verhagen, Robert Knippen, Inderjeet Mani, and James Pustejovsky. 2006. Annotation of temporal relations with tango. In *LREC*, pages 2249–2252.

Marc Verhagen, Inderjeet Mani, Roser Saurí, Jessica Littman, Robert Knippen, Seok Bae Jang, Anna Rumshisky, John Phillips, and James Pustejovsky. 2005. Automating temporal annotation with tarsqi. In *ACL*, pages 81–84.

DepressMind: A Depression Surveillance System for Social Media Analysis

Roque Fernández-Iglesias, Marcos Fernández-Pichel,
Mario Ezra Aragón and **David E. Losada**
Centro Singular de Investigación en Tecnoloxias Intelixentes (CiTIUS),
Universidade de Santiago de Compostela, Spain
roque.fernandez.iglesias@rai.usc.es,
{marcosfernandez.pichel,ezra.aragon,david.losada}@usc.es

Abstract

Depression is a pressing global issue that impacts millions of individuals worldwide. This prevailing psychological disorder profoundly influences the thoughts and behavior of those who suffer from it. We have developed DepressMind[1], a versatile screening tool designed to facilitate the analysis of social network data. This automated tool explores multiple psychological dimensions associated with clinical depression and estimates the extent to which these symptoms manifest in language use. Our project comprises two distinct components: one for data extraction and another one for analysis. The data extraction phase is dedicated to harvesting texts and the associated meta-information from social networks and transforming them into a user-friendly format that serves various analytical purposes. For the analysis, the main objective is to conduct an in-depth inspection of the user publications and establish connections between the posted contents and dimensions or traits defined by well-established clinical instruments. Specifically, we aim to associate extracts authored by individuals with symptoms or dimensions of the Beck Depression Inventory (BDI).

1 Introduction

Psychological analysis is a multifaceted discipline dedicated to the study of human behavior and the intricacies of related mental processes. This field holds immense significance as it helps to gain deeper insights into individuals and the functioning of their minds. Such insights are instrumental in both the treatment and prevention of mental health issues. Among the most pressing concerns within psychological analysis is depression, a pervasive mood disorder that affects countless individuals worldwide (World Health Organization, 2023). Depression constitutes a serious affliction that significantly diminishes a person's quality of life and can have profound consequences on his physical and mental well-being. Although there is a wide range of available therapeutic approaches, ranging from psychotherapy to pharmaceutical interventions, the burden of inadequately treated or unrecognized depression is still substantial (Evans-Lacko et al., 2018). Recent years have witnessed a noticeable increase in the global prevalence of depression (World Health Organization, 2022), reflecting the need for further research and design of new screening tools.

The Internet and Social Media (SM) have sparked a revolutionary transformation in the way we communicate. Online sources have also opened up new possibilities in psychological analysis, particularly for extracting behavioral patterns from specific demographic groups. One of the primary advantages is the availability of a large amount of data and multiple pieces of evidence about human behavior. These valuable resources can be exploited to perform observational studies that support mental health research. SM platforms are spaces where individuals can freely express themselves and publicly share their thoughts, feelings, and opinions. Some popular sites and forums have become meeting points for disclosing personal preoccupations. Notably, online communities focused on topics like depression and other mental health issues have emerged, enabling individuals to share their personal experiences and receive support from others who have navigated similar challenges (Skaik and Inkpen, 2020; Ríssola et al., 2021; Crestani et al., 2022).

It is crucial to develop new screening mechanisms to early detect the increasing severity of depressive symptoms and provide explanatory extracts of the evidence found. To that end, we exploit advanced Natural Language Processing (NLP) solutions to analyze patterns and trends of depression. Such automated screening would allow to moni-

[1]A demonstration video of DepressMind is available at: https://youtu.be/rd6ZVWbxYrM

Proceedings of the 18th Conference of the European Chapter of the Association for Computational Linguistics System Demonstrations, pages 35–43

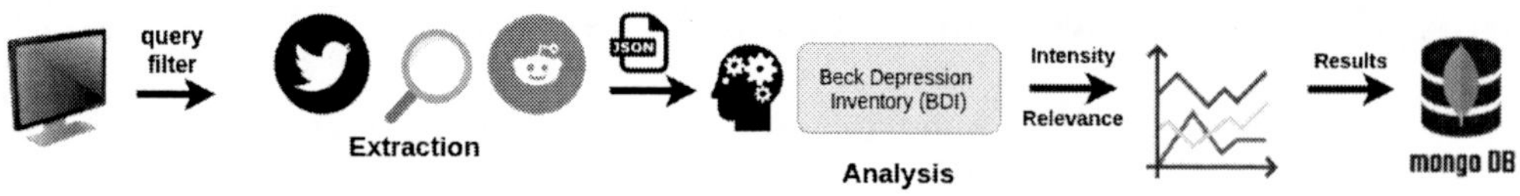

Figure 1: General diagram of DepressMind's architecture. First, it collects data from different sources (social networks), and then, it analyzes the levels of intensity and relevance in depression according to the BDI test.

tor a large number of people and identify those who may be at risk of developing a mental disorder. In practice, this could lead to interventions that provide individuals with the right support in time. Alternatively, the insights gained by our tool could inform preventive measures and help detect risk factors. For example, by understanding the evolution of depressive symptoms in specific segments of the population (e.g. individuals of a certain age) we could instigate the definition of new communication or mitigation measures by relevant health authorities. In any case, this exploitation would have to be done with proper ethical and privacy precautions. The goal of this paper is to exemplify the potential contributions of this technology, while its actual deployment is beyond the scope of the present project. Furthermore, DepressMind is available for research purposes and, thus, those interested in extracting and analyzing online data from a BDI perspective can get access to this new screening tool[2].

DepressMind stands on a retrieval method that supports a semantic representation for each category of the BDI-II questionnaire. BDI (Beck et al., 1961) is a recognized clinical instrument designed to assess the manifestation of 21 depressive symptoms, such as sadness, pessimism, or loss of energy. Given a textual excerpt, DepressMind computes two different metrics, relevance, and intensity, with respect to each BDI symptom. The whole process is depicted in Figure 1. We can summarize our contributions as follows:

- Development of a Reddit and Twitter extraction module designed to compile a comprehensive collection of online publications using specific filtering criteria (e.g., keywords, user accounts, communities, etc.).

- Implementation of an advanced analytical tool capable of assessing psychological dimensions and their temporal evolution. This analysis leverages semantic similarity estimates and linguistic models to provide valuable insights into user-generated content.

- Integration of the above components into a user-friendly web application that streamlines the process of analyzing Beck Depression Inventory (BDI) dimensions over a precompiled dataset of social media posts. This application allows users to visualize results through graphs and statistical representations for a more comprehensive understanding of the data.

2 Related Work

In recent times, the field of digital mental health analysis has experienced significant expansion. Automated NLP techniques have emerged as effective means for identifying traces of mental health disorders from user-generated online publications. For instance, in a pioneering study, Choudhury et al. (2013) conducted initial research on automatically detecting depression. These researchers collected reliable data on depression through crowd-sourcing, employing the CES-D (Center for Epidemiological Studies Depression Scale) inventory to assess depression levels (Radloff, 1977).

Gaur et al. (2018) introduced an unsupervised method aimed at aligning the content from different mental health-related subreddits with the most suitable DSM-5 (Diagnostic and Statistical Manual of Mental Disorders - 5th Edition) categories (Association, 2013). Given the knowledge encoded into the DSM-5 manual and other meticulously curated medical resources, a specialized lexicon was constructed. This language resource included n-grams associated with each mental health disorder listed in the DSM-5. Additionally, the authors enhanced an existing ontology related to drug abuse, incorporating terminology and slang expressions derived from Reddit. The resulting lexicon was exploited to quantify the connection between the content of

[2]https://github.com/roque-fernandez/DepressMind

the subreddits and the DSM-5 categories.

In a study conducted by Perez et al. (Pérez et al., 2022), an innovative approach was introduced to automatically measure the severity of depression among social media users. This research team addressed the challenge of quantifying the intensity of depression indicators and explored the application of neural language models to capture various aspects of the user-generated content. This team presented two alternative methods for evaluating depression symptoms, based on the individual's willingness to openly discuss them. The first method relied on analyzing global language patterns present in the user's posts, while the second method focused on identifying direct mentions of symptom-related concerns. Both approaches resulted in automatic estimates of the overall BDI-II score.

In a related vein, Pérez et al. (2023) introduced a platform designed to assist in the assessment and monitoring of depression symptoms among social media users. The tool aimed at capturing a broad context of the individuals by incorporating user profiling capabilities. The authors claimed that the platform could assist professionals in labeling data and utilizing depression estimators and profiling models.

These initiatives have piqued our interest in exploring the potential of semantic matching between relevant medical questionnaires and user-generated publications. Our system, DepressMind, allows us to extract and visualize BDI-related extracts and we present here a preliminary evaluation that shows its potential to automatically estimate an individual's response to the BDI-II items.

3 Design and Implementation

3.1 Data collection

To facilitate data collection, we developed a dedicated module that allows us to gather information from Twitter and Reddit. This module serves as an intermediary, streamlining the process of parsing user-generated content. The tracking process adapts based on the data source. In the case of Twitter, our module utilizes the free access Twint library[3] to connect with Twitter's API and retrieve a specified number of tweets based on user-defined

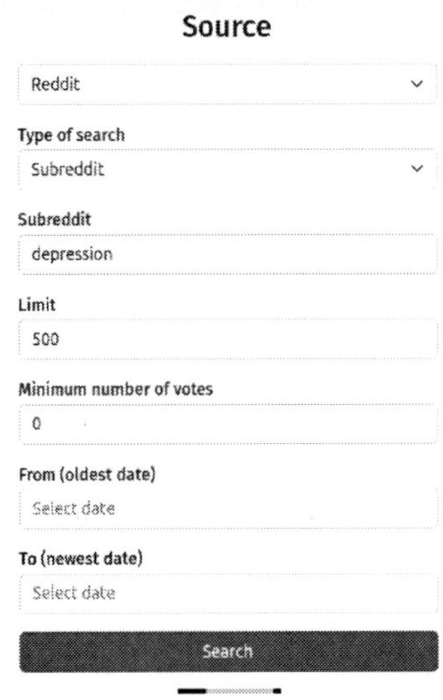

Figure 2: DepressMind's extraction interface.

filters. The collected data is then stored in a JSON file. For Reddit, we have implemented a custom tracker designed specifically for this platform. This tracker retrieves Reddit posts, applies the necessary filters, and stores results in JSON format. Furthermore, our system produces a separate file designed for recording statistics for the resulting collection.

The Reddit crawler parses the HTML code and extracts class patterns and tags associated with Reddit posts. To that end, we employ BeautifulSoup, a Python library that simplifies the parsing and data extraction from XML and HTML documents. Given the evolving nature of Reddit, consistent data extraction has become challenging. Our extraction works from the OldReddit interface. In May 2018, Reddit introduced a new interface and appearance that met with significant disapproval (over 80% of users). Consequently, the site decided to maintain the old interface on a separate domain. To this day, approximately 15% of users continue to access Reddit via the old interface, with no plans to discontinue. This legacy interface provides us with a unique advantage, as its HTML structure is more amenable to automated crawling.

DepressMind supports four extraction possibilities: by subreddit, by user account, by keywords, and a general (unrestricted) extraction. These extraction options share certain parameters, such as the maximum number of posts to be retrieved, and the range of dates of the extracted publications. Figure 2 shows an instance of the subreddit-based

[3]At the time of building DepressMind, Twint allowed free access to publications and downloads. Due to changes in Twitter's policies (now referred to as "X"), this module is temporarily disabled. We are actively monitoring for future updates that may reinstate its functionality.

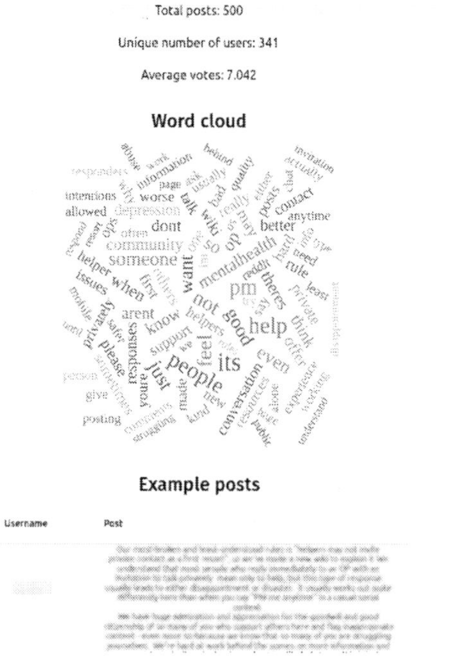

Figure 3: Example of the output after the extraction (the user posts and accounts have been pixelated for privacy reasons).

option. After the extraction, DepressMind displays the number of posts found, a word cloud, some example posts, and other general statistics (see Figure 3).

3.2 Analysis of Psychological Dimensions

The extraction functionalities described above allow any user to produce and download a JSON-formatted dataset and, thus, DepressMind can be employed by researchers or practitioners to build their collections. In any case, our primary goal was to make a depression screening tool and, thus, DepressMind includes a BDI-based analytical module. To that end, DepressMind assesses the semantic proximity between the texts gathered from social media and the textual content of the BDI questionnaire. Each BDI item contains a title (e.g. "Guilty Feelings") and some possible responses (e.g. "0. I don't feel particularly guilty", "1. I feel guilty a good part of the time", "2. I feel quite guilty most of the time", or "3. I feel guilty all the time"). These texts are used to assess the relevance and intensity of each topic, as described below.

3.2.1 Relevance

This analysis aims to address the question: How relevant are individual depression symptoms within

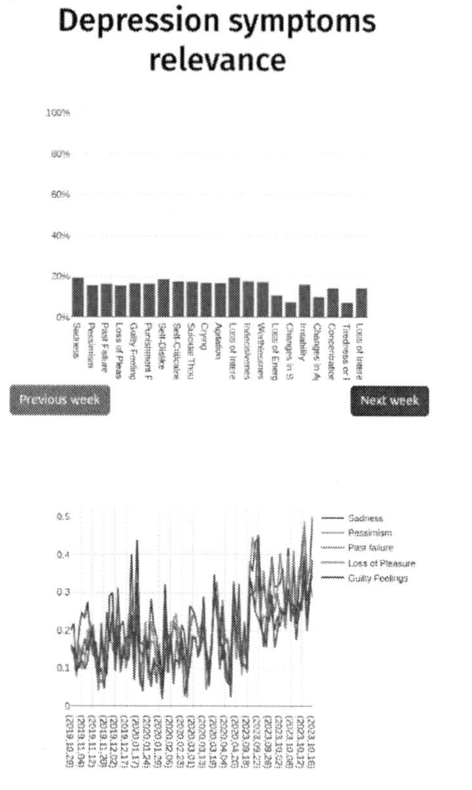

Figure 4: Relevance analysis and evolution over time of each BDI topic.

our collection? Given a collection of posts, DepressMind outputs an array of 21 values, one for each BDI symptom. Each element in the array estimates the topical presence of the BDI item in the corpus. These estimates are produced as follows. First, DepressMind transforms each question from the BDI into an embedding representation utilizing SentenceBERT (Reimers and Gurevych, 2019), an adaptation of the pre-trained BERT model designed to produce semantically meaningful sentence embeddings[4]. For every topic, we generate embedding representations of the title of the corresponding BDI item and each potential response. The similarity between a sentence in the corpus and a BDI item is computed as the maximum similarity (using cosine similarity) between the embedding of the sentence (e_s) and the embeddings of the BDI title and the BDI responses: $score_{rel}(s, BDI_n) = max\{sim(e_s, e_{title_n}), sim(e_s, e_{response1_n}), ...\}$.

The relevance of a BDI item in the corpus (C) is computed as the average relevance computed over the entire set of sentences: $rel(BDI_n, C) =$

[4]More specifically, with the all-MiniLM-L6-v2 model

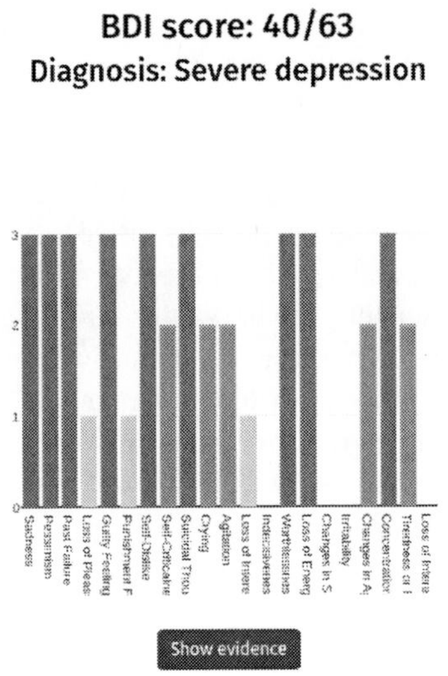

Figure 5: Intensity analysis.

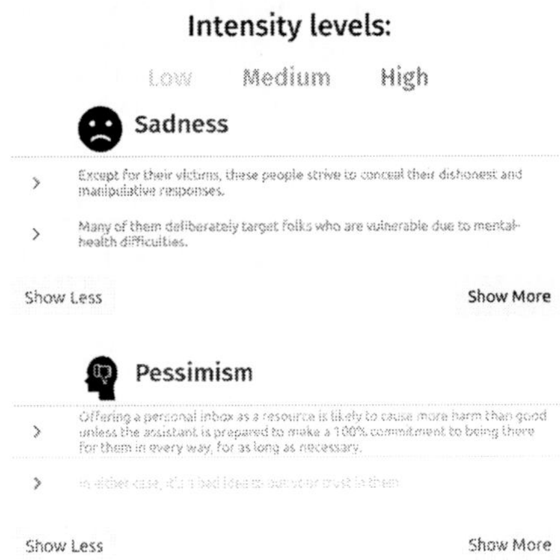

Figure 6: Top scoring sentences for two BDI items (sadness and pessimism). For privacy reasons, texts have been paraphrased.

$avg_{s \in C}\ score_{rel}(s, BDI_n)$. Figure 4 shows an example of this analysis.

3.2.2 Intensity

This metric estimates the intensity of each depression symptom in the input corpus. While the relevance of a symptom informs us about topicality (i.e., the presence of sentences related to the BDI item), intensity provides insight into the level of severity. Many relevant sentences might induce different intensity levels. For instance, "I never sleep" and "I have occasional sleeping problems" are both relevant to the BDI item on sleeping problems but the first one should be assigned a higher intensity score. Given a collection of posts, DepressMind outputs an array of 21 intensity values, one for each BDI symptom. These scores are integer values ranging from 0 to 3. This is the standard ordinal scale of the responses in the BDI questionnaire. These estimates are produced as follows.

For each BDI item, we only consider as candidates the sentences whose relevance $score_{rel}(s, BDI_n)$ is greater than a given threshold. For each candidate sentence, we try to align it with the possible responses of the BDI item. To that end, we employ an entailment model[5] with three possible output categories: *contradiction*, *entailment*, *neutral*. If the candidate sentence does not entail the response (output category is *contradiction* or *neutral*) then the alignment is discarded. Otherwise, we apply a softmax function to the entailment value, which returns the probability that the sentence s supports the response. DepressMind aligns the sentence with the response that has the highest probability of entailment and outputs the response's severity level, $val_{int}(s, BDI_n) \in \{0, 3\}$. For example, for the "Suicidal thoughts" symptom, a sentence such as "I want to kill myself" would be aligned with the response "I would kill myself if I had the chance" and, thus, it would be assigned an intensity value of 3. Finally, the BDI item's intensity score of the entire corpus is computed as the maximum intensity over the available sentences: $int(BDI_n, C) = max_{s \in C}\ val_{int}(s, BDI_n)$. The rationale is that a single severe sentence should be a matter of concern. Figure 5 shows an example of the intensity analysis. DepressMind also shows explanatory evidence, by presenting the sentences that led to the final intensity estimation (see Fig 6).

4 Empirical Evaluation

To validate the tool, we utilized the eRisk evaluation datasets (2019, 2020, and 2021) (Losada et al., 2019, 2020; Parapar et al., 2021). These evaluation tasks aim to estimate the severity of the 21 BDI symptoms for a set of social media users. For each user, the datasets include a self-report BDI questionnaire and the user's history of publications (participants gave their consent for tracking of their public posts). We fed each user's collection to DepressMind, obtained the estimated levels of severity, and compared them with those filled by the users. The next subsection describes the four effectiveness metrics. Further details about them

[5]We used the cross-encoder/nli-deberta-v3-base model.

method	AHR	ACR	ADODL	DHCR
		eRisk 2019		
ours	0.3143	0.6492	0.7476	0.2000
participants	0.3345	0.6416	0.7454	0.2611
		eRisk 2020		
ours	0.3156	0.6574	0.7481	0.2571
participants	0.3432	0.6688	0.7963	0.2807
		eRisk 2021		
ours	0.2601	0.6319	0.7383	0.3375
participants	0.3107	0.6555	0.7586	0.2196

Table 1: Effectiveness results over the three datasets. The lower result reports the mean performance achieved by the participants in the eRisk shared task.

are available at (Losada et al., 2019, 2020; Parapar et al., 2021).

4.1 Metrics

Average Hit Rate (AHR): AHR measures how often the automated questionnaire produces identical responses to the real questionnaire.
Average Closeness Rate (ACR): ACR takes into consideration the ordinal scale and penalizes more the errors where the system's response deviated significantly from the actual user's response.
Average Difference in Overall Depression Levels (ADODL): While the previous metrics focus on effectiveness at the BDI item level, ADODL calculates the total depression level, which is the sum of all responses, for both the real and automated questionnaires, and measures the difference.
Depression Category Hit Rate (DCHR): DCHR considers the four possible overall depression levels (0–13: minimal depression, 14–19: mild depression, 20–28: moderate depression, 29–63: severe depression) and measures the proportion of users for whom DepressMind assigned a depression category that matches the category determined by the real questionnaire.

4.2 Results and Analysis

Table 1 shows the results of DepressMind and compares them with the mean results of the participants in the three evaluation campaigns. In general, our approach yields competitive results in comparison with the systems implemented by the participating teams. Furthermore, the participants' systems employed extensive feature engineering leading to black-box models, while DepressMind visually explains its decisions and presents evidence that can be validated by an expert. We leave the exploration of more complex solutions (e.g., other sentence embedding models) for future work. Regardless, there exists potential for enhancing the structure of our model and integrating further methods to narrow the performance gap between the current version of DepressMind and the most effective eRisk systems. In any case, the challenge is intrinsically difficult, as most users do not publicly disclose information about many BDI topics. From our perspective, the most compelling feature of this screening technology is not its capacity for automatic diagnosis, but rather its proficiency in highlighting the most significant concerns, discerning temporal trends, and providing valuable insights to expert users (e.g., to psychologists).

To further analyze these collections, let us focus on the individual influence of specific BDI items. To this end, Figure 7 plots the percentage of users with relevant evidence for each BDI item (blue bars) and the percentage of intense sentences for each BDI item in the collection (orange bars). This helps to shed light on the BDI items that are more prominently discussed on social media. Topics such as feelings of worthlessness, sadness, agitation, and punishment are the most recurrent and also produce most of the severe sentences. In contrast, topics like crying, self-criticism, and loss of interest in sexual activities have little presence and intensity. Notably, in all the datasets, most topics have less than half of the users with relevant evidence. This underscores how challenging it is to infer depression symptoms from social media evidence. With no relevant information on these topics, a model can hardly provide a reliable assessment. In such cases, DepressMind assumes a score of 0, potentially leading to an underestimation of the individual's state. In the future, it would be worthwhile to explore alternative imputation approaches, such as estimating overall depression scores based on partially completed questionnaires or estimating missing BDI symptoms based on related topics.

5 Conclusion

In this study, we try to contribute to the understanding of a pressing global issue: the prevalence of depression. Our main goal was to make a positive contribution in the area of automated methods for screening depression. To that end, we introduced DepressMind, an analytical tool that extracts social media posts and assesses their relevance and severity concerning the 21 standardized BDI symptoms. An evaluation of several depression datasets has

2019		
% entailments	Dimension	% users with evidence
0.59	Worthlessness	95.00
0.27	Sadness	75.00
0.16	Punishment Feelings	70.00
0.30	Agitation	70.00
0.16	Pessimism	65.00
0.12	Guilty Feelings	60.00
0.07	Suicidal Thoughts or Wishes	55.00
0.08	Changes in Sleeping Pattern	55.00
0.29	Self-Dislike	50.00
0.08	Loss of Energy	50.00
0.03	Loss of Pleasure	40.00
0.03	Loss of Interest	40.00
0.07	Irritability	40.00
0.07	Past Failure	35.00
0.04	Concentration Difficulty	35.00
0.07	Changes in Appetite	25.00
0.03	Tiredness	25.00
0.03	Crying	20.00
0.01	Indecisiveness	20.00
0.01	Self-Criticalness	15.00
0.01	Loss of Interest in Sex	10.00

2020		
% entailments	Dimension	% users with evidence
0.26	Worthlessness	81.43
0.16	Punishment Feelings	80.00
0.22	Agitation	65.71
0.16	Sadness	60.00
0.12	Self-Dislike	45.71
0.08	Changes in Sleeping Pattern	45.71
0.05	Loss of Pleasure	42.86
0.05	Guilty Feelings	42.86
0.05	Irritability	42.86
0.06	Changes in Appetite	42.86
0.04	Tiredness	42.86
0.04	Pessimism	40.00
0.03	Past Failure	40.00
0.03	Suicidal Thoughts or Wishes	40.00
0.04	Loss of Energy	38.57
0.03	Loss of Interest	37.14
0.05	Concentration Difficulty	37.14
0.02	Loss of Interest in Sex	30.00
0.02	Self-Criticalness	25.71
0.01	Indecisiveness	21.43
0.02	Crying	20.00

2021		
% entailments	Dimension	% users with evidence
0.37	Worthlessness	75
0.48	Agitation	73.75
0.20	Punishment Feelings	68.75
0.21	Sadness	65
0.26	Self-Dislike	56.25
0.12	Irritability	53.75
0.15	Loss of Energy	51.25
0.10	Changes in Sleeping Pattern	48.75
0.08	Loss of Pleasure	45
0.06	Changes in Appetite	45
0.15	Concentration Difficulty	45
0.08	Tiredness	45
0.09	Pessimism	43.75
0.04	Past Failure	41.25
0.10	Suicidal Thoughts or Wishes	41.25
0.06	Guilty Feelings	38.75
0.05	Self-Criticalness	37.5
0.02	Loss of Interest in Sex	36.25
0.08	Loss of Interest	33.75
0.02	Indecisiveness	25
0.02	Crying	23.75

Figure 7: Intensity and Relevance of the 21 BDI items.

produced promising results, highlighting the potential to enhance our understanding, assessment, and management of various depression symptoms. This work represents an initial advancement towards harnessing the power of data to address mental health challenges on a broader scale. In our future work, we aim to explore the use of specialized lexical resources for more effective sentence extraction and to exploit clinical data for training more specialized language models. We are also interested in expanding this study to different languages, as most of the research studies on mental disorders have been centered on English.

Ethics Statement and Limitations

This form of analysis aims to support the development of emerging technologies designed to alert about early signs of depression and provide substantial supporting evidence. As highlighted by Neuman et al. (2012), it is important to view these novel screening methods not as "magic replacements for human experts", but rather as computational tools that can significantly alleviate the workload on public health systems, especially in terms of facilitating regional preventive measures. This project did not involve any interaction with social media users, such as interventions to provide health-related recommendations. Instead, it is an observational study focused on publicly accessible data and available research collections. The three evaluation datasets are publicly available and transparent, and our research strictly adhered to ethical guidelines, specifically those related to AI ethics by design. For instance, the data collections are anonymized. Furthermore, we put in place stringent measures to safeguard sensitive information (e.g., the example sentences reported in the paper were paraphrased). Our ultimate goal is to make a positive contribution to society, with a key emphasis on improving our understanding of depression.

Another limitation is that at the time of building the system, Twint allowed free access to Twitter publications and downloads. Due to changes in Twitter's policies (now referred to as "X"), the Twitter feature is temporarily inactive. We are continuously observing for potential revisions that could restore its operation.

Additionally, it is essential to acknowledge that the datasets retrieved using DepressMind or those used to evaluate the tool may exhibit inherent biases typical of social media data. For example, gender, age, or sexual orientation biases. Any researcher or practitioner using DepressMind to collect and analyze data should bear this in mind and apply proper fairness and bias correction measures.

Acknowledgments

The authors thank: i) the financial support supplied by the Consellería de Cultura, Educación, Formación Profesional e Universidades (accreditation 2019-2022 ED431G-2019/04, ED431C 2022/19) and the European Regional Development Fund, which acknowledges the CiTIUS-Research Center in Intelligent Technologies of the University of Santiago de Compostela as a Research Center of the Galician University System, and ii) the financial support supplied by project PID2022-137061OB-C22 (Ministerio de Ciencia e Innovación, Agencia Estatal de Investigación, Proyectos de Generación de Conocimiento; supported by the European Regional Development Fund).

The fourth author thanks the financial support obtained from project SUBV23/00002 (Ministerio de Consumo, Subdirección General de Regulación del Juego).

The authors also thank the funding of project PLEC2021-007662 (MCIN/AEI/10.13039/501100011033, Ministerio de Ciencia e Innovación, Agencia Estatal de Investigación, Plan de Recuperación, Transformación y Resiliencia, Unión Europea-Next Generation EU).

References

American Psychiatric Association. 2013. *Diagnostic and statistical manual of mental disorders*, 5th edition. American Psychiatric Publishing, Washington.

Aaron Beck, C.H. Ward, M. Mendelson, J. Mock, and J. Erbaugh. 1961. An inventory for measuring depression. *Arch Gen Psychiatry*.

Munmun De Choudhury, Michael Gamon, Scott Counts, and Eric Horvitz. 2013. Predicting depression via social media. In *Proceedings of the Seventh International Conference on Weblogs and Social Media, ICWSM 2013, Cambridge, USA*.

Fabio Crestani, David E Losada, and Javier Parapar. 2022. *Early Detection of Mental Health Disorders by Social Media Monitoring: The First Five Years of the ERisk Project*, volume 1018. Springer Nature.

Sara Evans-Lacko, Sergio Aguilar-Gaxiola, Ali Al-Hamzawi, Jordi Alonso, Corina Benjet, Ronny Bruffaerts, Wai-Tat Chiu, and Silvia Florescu. 2018. Socio-economic variations in the mental health treatment gap for people with anxiety, mood, and substance use disorders: Results from the who world mental health (wmh) surveys. *Psychological Medicine*, 48:1560–1571.

Manas Gaur, Ugur Kursuncu, Amanuel Alambo, Amit Sheth, Raminta Daniulaityte, Krishnaprasad Thirunarayan, and Jyotishman Pathak. 2018. "let me tell you about your mental health!": Contextualized classification of reddit posts to dsm-5 for web-based intervention. In *Proceedings of the 27th ACM International Conference on Information and Knowledge Management*, CIKM '18, page 753–762.

David E. Losada, Fabio Crestani, and Javier Parapar. 2019. Overview of erisk 2019 early risk prediction on the internet. In *Experimental IR Meets Multilinguality, Multimodality, and Interaction*, pages 340–357, Cham. Springer International Publishing.

David E. Losada, Fabio Crestani, and Javier Parapar. 2020. Overview of erisk 2020: Early risk prediction on the internet. In *Experimental IR Meets Multilinguality, Multimodality, and Interaction*, pages 272–287, Cham. Springer International Publishing.

Yair Neuman, Yohai Cohen, Dan Assaf, and Gabbi Kedma. 2012. Proactive screening for depression through metaphorical and automatic text analysis. *Artificial Intelligence in Medicine*, 56(1):19–25.

Javier Parapar, Patricia Martín-Rodilla, David E. Losada, and Fabio Crestani. 2021. Overview of erisk 2021: Early risk prediction on the internet. In *Experimental IR Meets Multilinguality, Multimodality, and Interaction*, pages 324–344, Cham. Springer International Publishing.

Anxo Pérez, Marcos Fernández-Pichel, Javier Parapar, and David E. Losada. 2023. Depresym: A depression symptom annotated corpus and the role of llms as assessors of psychological markers. *ArXiv*, abs/2308.10758.

Anxo Pérez, Javier Parapar, and Álvaro Barreiro. 2022. Automatic depression score estimation with word embedding models. *Artificial Intelligence in Medicine*, 132:102380.

Lenore Sawyer Radloff. 1977. The ces-d scale: A self-report depression scale for research in the general population. *Applied Psychological Measurement*, 1(3):385–401.

Nils Reimers and Iryna Gurevych. 2019. Sentence-bert: Sentence embeddings using siamese bert-networks. In *Proceedings of the 2019 Conference on Empirical Methods in Natural Language Processing*. Association for Computational Linguistics.

Esteban A. Ríssola, David E. Losada, and Fabio Crestani. 2021. A survey of computational methods for online mental state assessment on social media. *ACM Trans. Comput. Healthcare*, 2(2).

Ruba Skaik and Diana Inkpen. 2020. Using social media for mental health surveillance: A review. *ACM Comput. Surv.*, 53(6).

WHO World Health Organization. 2022. Covid-19 pandemic triggers 25% increase in prevalence of anxiety and depression worldwide.

WHO World Health Organization. 2023. Depressive disorder (depression).

Check News in One Click: NLP-Empowered Pro-Kremlin Propaganda Detection

Veronika Solopova
Technische Universität Berlin, Germany
veronika.solopova@tu-berlin.de

Viktoriia Herman
Berlin, Germany
gvika739@gmail.com

Christoph Benzmüller
Universität Bamberg, Germany
christoph.benzmueller@uni-bamberg.de

Tim Landgraf
Freie Universität Berlin, Germany
tim.landgraf@fu-berlin.de

Abstract

Many European citizens become targets of the Kremlin propaganda campaigns, aiming to minimise public support for Ukraine, foster a climate of mistrust and disunity, and shape elections (Meister, 2022). To address this challenge, we developed "Check News in 1 Click", the first NLP-empowered pro-Kremlin propaganda detection application available in 7 languages, which provides the lay user with feedback on their news, and explains manipulative linguistic features and keywords. We conducted a user study, analysed user entries and models' behaviour paired with questionnaire answers, and investigated the advantages and disadvantages of the proposed interpretative solution.

1 Introduction

Evidence that we are living through a global crisis of trust in news is substantial, which inspired many a debate concerning the measures needed to rebuild it (Flew et al., 2020; Gaziano, 1988). An increasing number of people are getting their news online, particularly the younger generation, while many have started avoiding the news, first those concerning the COVID-19 pandemic and now those about the Russian war in Ukraine, majorly due to low credibility and negativity.(Coster, 2022). At the same time, digital platforms are viewed more sceptically, than traditional news, especially political ones as they are believed to be agenda-driven and contain propaganda (Mont'Alverne et al., 2022; Flanagin and Metzger, 2000; Kalogeropoulos et al., 2019).
State-sponsored pro-Kremlin propaganda became a major issue, as reports claim that only a small per cent of Russian bots are being uncovered and detected (Menn, 2022). Geissler et al. (2023) showed that Twitter's (now X's) activity supporting Russia generated nearly 1 million likes, about 14.4 million followers and a substantial proportion of pro-Russian messages that went viral.
To address this issue, we created an accessible online user interface to check news in terms of pro-Kremlin propaganda, general manipulation and non-neutrality in 7 languages. It receives users' news and offers the model's verdict, its probability, as well as an explanation of manipulative keywords, linguistic strategies and indicators, shown to be associated with pro-Kremlin news. In addition to the models from our previous study (Solopova et al., 2023), we trained new ones for Italian and German languages, exploring the usefulness of the data-augmentation strategy through translation, as well as multi-language versus language-specific pre-trained transformer models for this task. Here, we present our system architecture and the user study we conducted, quantifying user satisfaction and desirable features and analysing user entries.

1.1 Related Work

Many tools have been developed to warn readers about fake news and "weaponize" them to understand the manipulative news better. An increasing amount of tools are based on automated text analysis and classification, mostly available only for English. **The Factual**[1] is rating the credibility of the news each day using the site's sourcing history, the author's track record, and the diversity of sources in a news article as key features. **ClaimBuster**[2] is an online tool for instant fact-checking, allowing users to check the veracity of their texts, by searching for a fact-checked claim similar to user's input. The **Fake News Graph Analyzer** characterises spreaders in large diffusion graphs (Bodaghi et al., 2021). The **Grover** (Zellers et al., 2019) uses a fake news detection model, which takes on the language of specific publications to detect misinformation more

[1] https://www.thefactual.com
[2] https://idir.uta.edu/claimbuster/

Proceedings of the 18th Conference of the European Chapter of the Association for Computational Linguistics System Demonstrations, pages 44–51
March 17-22, 2024

accurately. **Bad News** (Roozenbeek et al., 2022; Basol et al., 2020) is a gamified platform intended to build user understanding of the techniques and tactics involved in disseminating disinformation. They show that attitudinal resistance against online misinformation through psychological inoculation may reduce cultural susceptibility to misinformation.

Considering propaganda detection as a specific case of disinformation, only a few projects develop comprehensive interfaces accessible to the public. **Proppy** (Barrón-Cedeño et al., 2019) was trained on known propaganda sources using a variety of stylistic features and is constantly clustering news sources. **PROTECT** (Vorakitphan et al., 2022) and **Prta** (Da San Martino et al., 2020) allow users to explore the articles, texts and URLs by highlighting the spans in which propaganda techniques occur through a dedicated interface. **Hamilton 2.0**[3] is a real-time dashboard, created by the project of the Alliance for Securing Democracy, which aggregates analysis of the narratives and topics promoted by Russian, Chinese, and Iranian government officials state-funded and state-linked media accounts and news. **NewsGuard** [4] uses a team of journalists and experienced editors to produce reliable ratings and scores for news and information websites. To the best of our knowledge, no research-based open-source tools using AI to check potential Russian propaganda in a user's specific piece of news and in several languages are currently available.

2 Methods

2.1 Data

In addition to English, Russian, Ukrainian, French and Romanian, from our previous study, we chose to add German and Italian models to our tool. According to the European Union project EUvsDisinfo[5], "no other EU member has been subjected to such a powerful disinformation attack as Germany has been". In its database of fake media pieces accumulated since late 2015, German media holds the 1st place, while Italy is in third.

We used fact-checked and attested pro-Kremlin propaganda articles from Propaganda Diary (VoxCheck, 2020). Around 5% was also added from the press of political parties associated with pro-Kremlin sympathy. This amounted to 963 articles. As an example of trust-worthy media, we used VoxCheck's "white list" including sources such as ZDF, Der Welt, Frankfurter Allgemeine Zeitung, and Spiegel (676 altogether). As an augmentation set, we translated 537 neutral news with BBC and The Guardian translations from English to German using translators python API[6] and 565 RT.ru and Ria.news from Russian to German. Together native news set consists of **1639** texts, while the the augmented one is **2741**.

In Italian, we collected **2229** news from the Propaganda Diary, out of them 922 with attested Russian Propaganda and 1307 ones from the "white list" (e.g. Internazionale, La Repubblica, Corriere). We augmented the 'propaganda' class by 304 samples with translations from Russian to Italian of Sputniknews, resulting in **2533** texts.

Model	F1	MCC	AUC
SVM-de-it	0.82	0.64	0.82
BERT-de-it	0.01	0.51	0.51
SVM-de-w/tr	0.90	0.80	0.90
SVM-de-w/o-tr	0.92	0.83	0.93
BERT-de-w/tr	0.94	0.88	0.99
BERT-de-w/o-tr	0.95	0.92	0.99
SVM-it-w/tr	0.78	0.57	0.78
SVM-it-w/o-tr	0.75	0.49	0.74
BERT-it-w/tr	0.96	0.80	0.96
BERT-it-w/o-tr	0.94	0.73	0.93
SVM-multi	0.88	n/a	n/a
BERT-multi	0.92	n/a	n/a

Table 1: Evaluation of the models used in the study. MCC and AUC results are not given for SVM-multi and BERT-multi as in the previous study Cohen's kappa was used instead. The numbers are rounded to 2 digits after the comma. de- stands for German model, it- for the Italian, w/tr - with augmentation through translation, w/otr- without.

2.2 Models

The models from our initial study included one multilingual SVM model trained on morpho-syntactic features and keywords from the glossary of manipulative terms of Russian propaganda curated by the National Security and Defence Council of Ukraine and a fine-tuned multilingual BERT model (Devlin et al., 2019). We followed a similar scheme for the German and Italian models. We first trained both

[3]https://securingdemocracy.gmfus.org/hamilton-dashboard

[4]https://www.newsguardtech.com/special-reports/russian-disinformation-tracking-center/

[5]https://euvsdisinfo.eu

[6]https://pypi.org/project/translators/

Support Vector Machine (SVM) and BERT multilingual models for both languages together and augmented the data with translated articles. This approach only drew a 0.8 weighted F1-score for SVM and a drastically low 0.51 for the BERT model. Training models separately increased performance in each language, except for the Italian SVM model (0.77 on average, and the highest score was 0.78.). The result for the German SVM increased to 0.87 in 5-fold cross-validation, and 0.9 on the best seed. We used the bert-base-german-cased model and dbmdz pre-trained bert-base-italian-cased model, both implemented through HuggingFace[7] framework. The German model scored 0.94 F1, and 0.99 auroc, with 0.88 mcc, while the Italian one scored 0.90 F1, 0.93 auroc and 0.8 mcc on the best fold, with averages across the folds being 0.88 F1, 0,96 auroc, 0.77 mcc.

We decided to revise our augmentation policies and excluded non-native data. Interestingly, results dropped for both SVM and BERT models in the case of the Italian language (0.73 F1 on average) and drastic to 0.72 mcc, 0.94 auroc and 0.86 F1 averaged over 3 folds, although translations in the training set only accounted for 12% of texts. In contrast, while translations were 40% of the augmented set, the German model's performance slightly increased without them, with SVM achieving 0.91 F1 best and 0.89 on average and the BERT model gaining up to 0.036 in mcc and 0.1 in F1 (see Table 1 for training results).

2.3 System description

The interface is a web app, written with Python Flask framework for the back-end, and HTML, CSS and JavaScript for the front-end. The proposed news is fetched from the input window. The code for the front- and back-end is available under MIT License in our GitHub[8].

First of all, the language is identified using langid.py (Lui and Baldwin, 2012). If the detected language is one of the languages we support the appropriate BERT model (language-specific for Italian and German and multi-language one for the rest of the languages) predicts the probability of propaganda in the text. If the text is longer than 520 tokens, it is divided into several chunks. If at least one contains propaganda, the whole text is classified as such. If the language is not

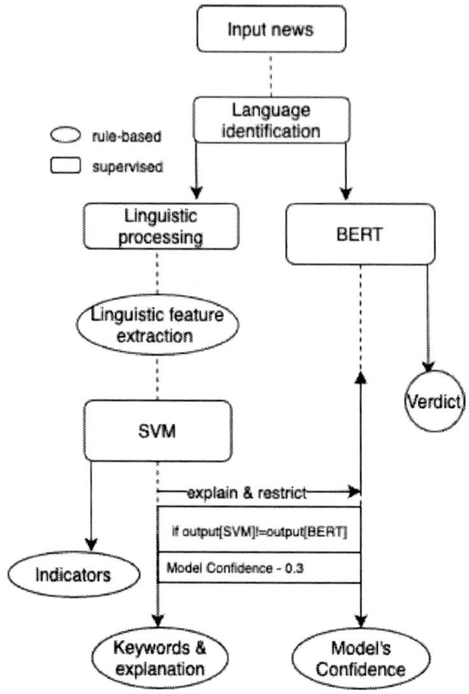

Figure 1: The figure illustrates the system's mock-up. The elliptical elements are rule-based reasoners while squared ones are trained models.

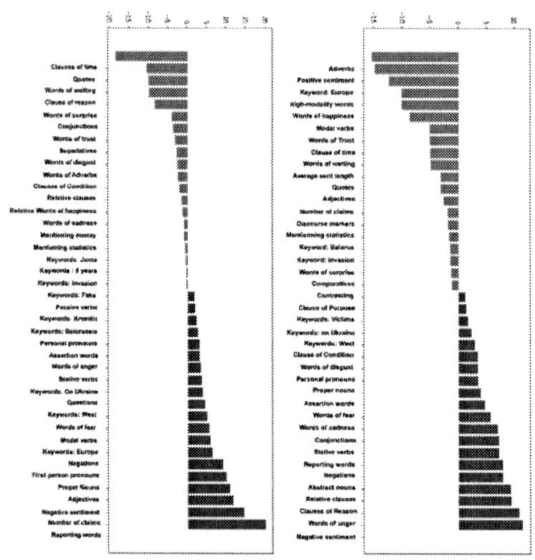

Figure 2: The figure illustrates the distribution of the learnt features according to the stance. The upper red side shows the features with the highest negative coefficients for "Pro-Kremlin propaganda" prediction (hence, more likely in Western, Pro-Ukrainian media), while the lower blue side shows the coefficients indicative of "Pro-Kremlin propaganda".

[7] https://huggingface.co

[8] https://github.com/verosol/propaganda_website

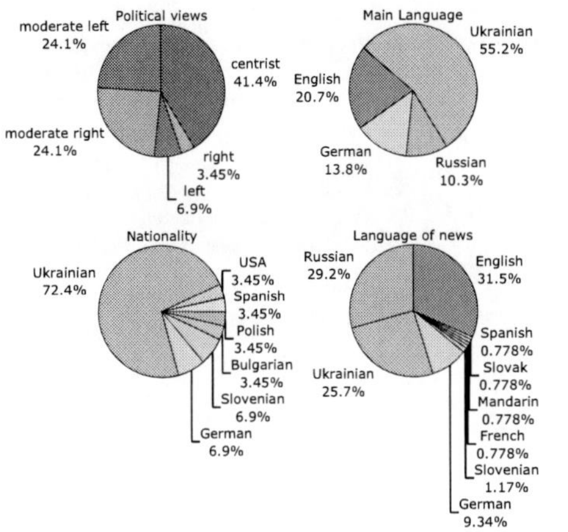

Figure 3: The figure illustrates statistics on the users who took part in the survey and used the application.

supported, the news is translated into English using Traslators API. The program saves both the verdict, 'Propaganda' or 'No propaganda', and the probability of the predicted class. In parallel, the linguistic feature extraction script, using Spacy[9] for lemmatisation and part-of-speech tagging, analyses the whole body of the news and passes the feature and keyword vector to the specific SVM model (Italian, German or multilingual). If SVM predicts an opposite class from the BERT model, we deduct 45% probability from the BERT's probability for the predicted class, and if the probability becomes lower than 30%, we change the prediction to the opposite one. The mock-up can be seen in Figure 1.

For each RBF-kernel SVM model, we also trained a linear one and looked into the coefficients of features and keywords and their association with a particular stance (Figure 2). The top features are then used as linguistic indicators and are shown to the user as warnings of potential manipulative, non-neutral language associated with the stances. Important keywords are presented separately with explanations from the Glossary of the National Security and Defence Council of Ukraine on a click. Comparing the important features and keywords, we discovered, that each language had its patterns of how Pro-Kremlin propaganda manifested itself, so we crafted indicators for each language separately. Some indicators, such as the abundance of negations, clause of purpose and reporting words, appeared to be universally indicative of pro-Russian propaganda in all of the languages we analysed. However, many features from our previous study, indicative of Pro-Kremlin propaganda were found more predictive of the Western stance in the two new languages. For example, frequent discourse markers, which are highly indicative of the pro-Kremlin side for other languages, are not associated with this prediction in German. The same stands for both German and Italian in terms of a high amount of quotes and clauses of time. In contrast, the clause of reason, highly predictive of a pro-Western stance for most languages, has the same tendency in Italian, but the opposite in German.

[9]https://spacy.io

2.4 User study design

Users were asked to check at least three different news in the app [10] and fill out an integrated user questionnaire.

To understand the user profile we asked about the nationality, the language they searched in, their political stance, and how many pieces of news they verified. To quantify their experience, we asked their opinion about every element of the news analysis, its usefulness and accuracy, the preferable form (web application, desktop application, browser extension, chatbot), if they learnt something about propaganda and if they would continue using it, as well as the age group they would recommend this tool to (e.g. elder relatives, peers, teenagers, etc). From the back-end side, we collected the news the users entered, their own label ('propaganda' or not) and the analysis that the model provided.

The invitation to the user study was sent to various platforms on social media: several Italian, French and Ukrainian Facebook groups, subreddits r/EuropeanUnion, r/Samplesize, r/takemysurvey, r/YUROP,r/Ukraine, r/Ukraina; Dou.ua, a website for Ukrainian developers and IT workers, Instagram stories. The user study contained the consent form. A system demonstration video[11] is available.

3 Results

191 users used the app with 257 unique requests, and only 29 out of them participated in the survey. 72% of the users in the survey are of Ukrainian origin, central Europeans (Polish, Bulgarian, Slovenian, Slovak) account for another 15%, 7%

[10]https://checknewsin1.click

[11]https://youtu.be/3dRXF5InGaE

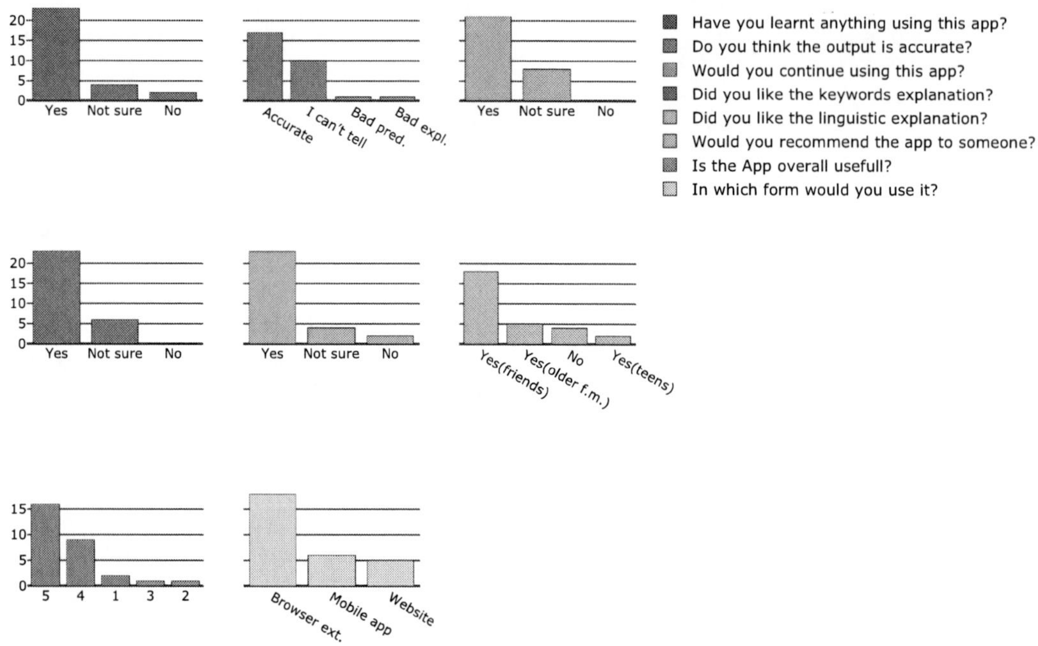

Figure 4: The figure shows the results of the user study questionnaire.

German, with one American and Spanish user. Ukrainian was named as the main language only 55% of the time though, while 20% searched news in English, 13% in German and 10% in Russian. The full pull of users showed further language variety: almost 1/3 of all news entered into the app were actually in English, 1/3 in Russian and a slightly smaller percentage in Ukrainian. Apart from 10 entries detected in German, other languages included French, Spanish, Slovenian and Mandarin. As for the political views of the respondents, 41% self-identified as centrists, 24% as moderate right or left, while only 7% and 3.5% were left or right respectively (see Figure 3).

3.1 Survey results

As illustrated in Figure 4, the majority of users (86%) positively received the tool evaluating its usefulness as four or five on a scale of five, and only four respondents assessed the use as three and below. 79% responded that they learned something new while using the tool. The same per cent liked the keyword explanations and linguistic indicators, whereas 72% said that would continue using this app further. Only 58% of users said that they think the output of the models was accurate while 34% could not tell and 2 users either considered the verdict or the explanation to be wrong. 63% would recommend the tool to their friends, 17% to older relatives and only 7̃% to teenagers, while 13% said they would not recommend it to anyone.

Talking about the potential formats for the tool, 62% chose that browser extension would be the most preferable form, while mobile application is also slightly more preferred than the website option as it is (20% against 17%).

3.2 User and model label comparison

The multilingual BERT model showed an imbalanced prediction rate for different languages. The new German model had almost 50/50% positive/negative prediction rate, similar to the labels provided by the users. At the same time in Russian and Ukrainian language the verdict 'propaganda' was issued by the model only 8% of the time, while in English it was 28%. In contrast, the users labelled almost identical amounts of news as 'propaganda' and 'not propaganda' in English and Ukrainian, while in Russian 73% of submissions were claimed to contain it. Overall, only 21% of verdicts and user labels coincide in German, 36% in Russian, almost 50% in English and 52% in Ukrainian.

Diving deeper into the differences between the proposed and predicted labels, in German, there is an

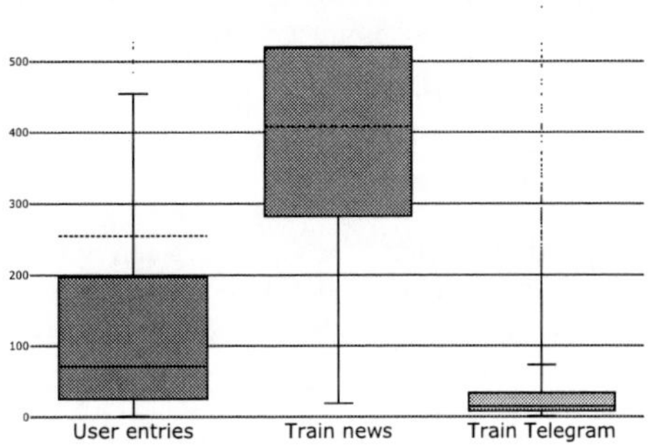

Figure 5: The figure illustrates differences in the text length between the training sub-corpora and the user inputs.

almost equal percentage of mismatch (41% model: 'No', user: 'Yes' and 37% model: 'Yes', user: 'No'). In other languages, the model is majorly predicting 'no propaganda'. In the case of Russian, e.g. the model did not predict 'propaganda' any single time when the user would say otherwise, with a similar result in Ukrainian (1.5%).

4 Discussion and Conclusion

Two major factors could explain the discrepancies between the user labels and the BERT predictions: either the user was wrong or the model, and here both tendencies seem to be present. As illustrated by Figure 5, we compared the distribution of the text lengths of the conventional news (which are rather large ~407 tokens), Telegram news (which are rather short ~32 tokens) in the training set and the news offered by the user (~205). We could see that the latter distribution with all quartiles falls perfectly in between the 2 training set constituents. Generally, the news can be even larger than the ones in our training set. For instance, the average article length of The New York Times is 622 words and 516 for The Washington Post (Menendez-Alarcon, 2012).

A brief qualitative analysis shows that while many inputs are indeed news, they are also majorly Reddit comments, tweets, and user-generated words and sentences. We implemented the opportunity for the user to provide us with the link and not only copy-paste a text, which then we scrape using newspaper library[12]. Some inserted a link to Elon Musk's tweets, and while X cannot be scraped. On very long entries, the model did not once predict 'propaganda' and coincided in this prediction with the user. It had at least 15% better matching with user labels on very short samples, similar to Telegram posts in length, proving that length can indeed be a reason for some miss-classifications, when the user was correct. However, the length is only the surface description of the underlying genre missing from the training material: the users are not as interested in conventional news checking, as in flagging and quick discovery of bots and malicious actors in social media comments and tweets. A high number of Ukrainian participants and a high number of certain responses concerning the tool's accuracy also showed that users predominantly were sure of their ability to recognize propaganda, but were interested in ways of quickly eliminating it from the informational eco-sphere. The indicators and keywords provided an important addition to the main model's verdict. Not only did the constraints we introduced on the main model help mitigate strong language-related biases, but they also appeared to be more reliable, as they do not mismatch as often with user annotations. Only in 16% of cases where there were more pro-Russian propaganda features found and 8%, where no pro-Western features were reported at all, would the user consider it a 'no propaganda' sample. With the user label being 'Russian propaganda', there was only 12% with more pro-western than pro-Kremlin indicators identified, and 7% where no pro-Kremlin associated features were offered to the user. The strong performance of the indicators may have had a positive influence on the overall user evaluation of feedback's accuracy. Users also often underestimate their knowledge of propaganda or are not very attentive when providing the label. While we received a lot of negative labels, the linguistic features indicate that most of the news pieces are not neutral. 37% of the news which was strongly not neutral were attributed to the 'no propaganda' label by the users. Only 6% of truly neutral entries were rightfully annotated as such, and 4% of them were called propaganda.

Overall, the results of the user survey, however limited in number, are positive. Both accuracy, recommendation, and interest in continuing to use the app are majorly high and both keywords and linguistic explanations were appreciated. In the free form, where we asked the users what they would like to change, it was even suggested to put more stress on the explanations and take away the overall verdict, showing the percentage of propaganda present. Apart from minor front-end suggestions,

[12]https://newspaper.readthedocs.io

such as more visual support and instructions, some users were indicating that there was news with a pro-Western stance which were citing the President of Russia, which contained propaganda, and such cases may have to be dealt with separately. For the same reasons, the field of fact-checking is moving from the direct text-to-label classification towards more fine-grained and multi-featured infosphere-based prediction (Grover et al., 2022). The need to introduce many constraints for the main model through other models in our study is also a reflection of this trend. Including the layer user and human moderators in the research should become standard practice, as it helps better understand the needs of the community and tailor future solutions accordingly.

Ethics Statement

The demographics of our study, although include different nationalities, are still predominantly from Ukraine, and young adults (who are the usual users of the platforms we used to market the study), thus excluding younger and more senior groups. We were also not able to attract Romanian and Italian users, despite targeted marketing in their groups. It is also important to state that open-source propaganda research also provides malicious actors with the means to counteract automated tools and adapt the style so that it is even more difficult to detect in the future. We still claim that it is even more crucial to educate the wider public about the instruments to verify the news they consume.

References

Alberto Barrón-Cedeño, Giovanni Da San Martino, Israa Jaradat, and Preslav Nakov. 2019. Proppy: A system to unmask propaganda in online news. In *AAAI Conference on Artificial Intelligence*.

Melisa Basol, Jon Roozenbeek, and Sander van der Linden. 2020. Good news about bad news: Gamified inoculation boosts confidence and cognitive immunity against fake news. *Journal of Cognition*.

Amirhosein Bodaghi, Jonice Oliveira, and Jonathan J.H. Zhu. 2021. The fake news graph analyzer: An open-source software for characterizing spreaders in large diffusion graphs. *Software Impacts*, 10:100182.

Helen Coster. 2022. More people are avoiding the news, and trusting it less, report says. *Reuters*. Accessed on August 28, 2023.

Giovanni Da San Martino, Shaden Shaar, Yifan Zhang, Seunghak Yu, Alberto Barrón-Cedeño, and Preslav Nakov. 2020. Prta: A system to support the analysis of propaganda techniques in the news. In *Proceedings of the 58th Annual Meeting of the Association for Computational Linguistics: System Demonstrations*, pages 287–293, Online. Association for Computational Linguistics.

Jacob Devlin, Ming-Wei Chang, Kenton Lee, and Kristina Toutanova. 2019. BERT: Pre-training of deep bidirectional transformers for language understanding. In *Proceedings of the 2019 Conference of the North American Chapter of the Association for Computational Linguistics: Human Language Technologies, Volume 1 (Long and Short Papers)*, pages 4171–4186, Minneapolis, Minnesota. Association for Computational Linguistics.

Andrew J Flanagin and Miriam J Metzger. 2000. Perceptions of internet information credibility. *Journal. Mass Commun. Q.*, 77(3):515–540.

Terry Flew, Uwe Dulleck, Caroline Fisher, Sora Park, and Ozan Isler. 2020. Trust and mistrust in australian news media. *University of Canberra Research Portal*.

Cecilie Gaziano. 1988. How credible is the credibility crisis? *Journalism Quarterly*, 65(2):267–278.

Dominique Geissler, Dominik Bär, Nicolas Pröllochs, and Stefan Feuerriegel. 2023. Russian propaganda on social media during the 2022 invasion of ukraine.

Karish Grover, Srinivasa Madhava Phaneendra Angara, Md. Shad Akhtar, and Tanmoy Chakraborty. 2022. Public wisdom matters! discourse-aware hyperbolic fourier co-attention for social-text classification. *ArXiv*, abs/2209.13017.

Antonis Kalogeropoulos, Jane Suiter, Linards Udris, and Mark Eisenegger. 2019. News media trust and news consumption: factors related to trust in news in 35 countries. *International Journal of Communication*, 13.

Marco Lui and Timothy Baldwin. 2012. langid.py: An off-the-shelf language identification tool. In *Proceedings of the ACL 2012 System Demonstrations*, pages 25–30, Jeju Island, Korea. Association for Computational Linguistics.

Stefan Meister. 2022. Germany: Target of russian disinformation. *DGAP External Publications*, WP/22/144:211719.

Antonio Menendez-Alarcon. 2012. Newspapers coverage of spain and the united states: A comparative analysis. *Sociology Mind*, 2:67–74.

Joseph Menn. 2022. Russians boasted that just 1 *The Washington Post*.

Camila Mont'Alverne, Amy Ross Arguedas, Benjamin Toff, Richard Fletcher, and Rasmus Kleis Nielsen. 2022. The trust gap: how and why news on digital platforms is viewed more sceptically versus news in general. *The Reuters Institute for the Study of Journalism.* Accessed on August 18, 2023.

Jon Roozenbeek, Cecilie S. Traberg, and Sander van der Linden. 2022. Technique-based inoculation against real-world misinformation. *Royal Society Open Science*, 9(5):211719.

Veronika Solopova, Oana-Iuliana Popescu, Christoph Benzmüller, and Tim Landgraf. 2023. Automated multilingual detection of pro-kremlin propaganda in newspapers and telegram posts. *Datenbank Spektrum.*

Vorakit Vorakitphan, Elena Cabrio, and Serena Villata. 2022. PROTECT – a pipeline for propaganda detection and classification. In *Proceedings of the Eighth Italian Conference on Computational Linguistics CliC-it 2021*, pages 352–358. Accademia University Press.

VoxCheck. 2020. Vox check propaganda diary. Data retrieved from Propaganda Diary, `https://rusdisinfo.voxukraine.org`.

Rowan Zellers, Ari Holtzman, Hannah Rashkin, Yonatan Bisk, Ali Farhadi, Franziska Roesner, and Yejin Choi. 2019. Defending against neural fake news. In *Advances in Neural Information Processing Systems 32.*

NESTLE: a No-Code Tool for Statistical Analysis of Legal Corpus

Kyoungyeon Cho[1,*] **Seungkum Han**[1] **Young Rok Choi**[1] **Wonseok Hwang**[1,2,*,†]

[1]LBox [2]University of Seoul

{kycho, hsk2950, yrchoi, wonseok.hwang}@lbox.kr

Abstract

The statistical analysis of large scale legal corpus can provide valuable legal insights. For such analysis one needs to (1) select a subset of the corpus using document retrieval tools, (2) structure text using information extraction (IE) systems, and (3) visualize the data for the statistical analysis. Each process demands either specialized tools or programming skills whereas no comprehensive unified "no-code" tools have been available. Here we provide NESTLE, a no-code tool for large-scale statistical analysis of legal corpus. Powered by a Large Language Model (LLM) and the internal custom end-to-end IE system, NESTLE can extract any type of information that has not been predefined in the IE system opening up the possibility of unlimited customizable statistical analysis of the corpus without writing a single line of code. We validate our system on 15 Korean precedent IE tasks and 3 legal text classification tasks from LEXGLUE. The comprehensive experiments reveal NESTLE can achieve GPT-4 comparable performance by training the internal IE module with 4 human-labeled, and 192 LLM-labeled examples.

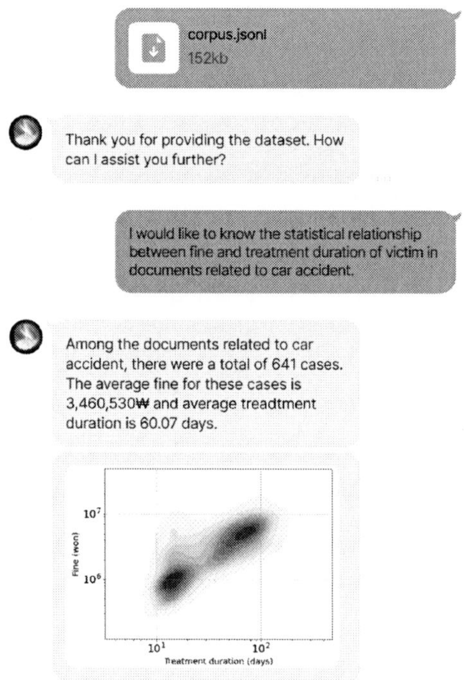

Figure 1: Illustration of NESTLE.

1 Introduction

Legal documents include a variety of semi-structured information stemming from diverse social disputes. For instance, precedents include factual information (such as blood alcohol level in a driving under the influence (DUI) case or loss in an indemnification case) as well as a decision from the court (fine, imprisonment period, money claimed by the plaintiff, money approved by the court, etc). While each document contains detailed information about specific legal events among a few individuals, community-level insights can be derived only by analyzing a substantial collection of these documents. For instance, the consequence of the subtle modification to the statute might only become evident through a comprehensive statistical analysis of the related legal corpus. Indeed a recent study shows that how the revision of the Road Traffic Act has changed the average imprisonment period in drunk driving cases by analyzing 24k Korean precedents (Hwang et al., 2022a).

Conducting a comprehensive statistical analysis on a legal corpus on a large scale may entail following three key steps: (1) choosing a subset of the corpus using retrieval tools, (2) structuralizing the documents using information extraction (IE) systems, and (3) visualizing the data for the statistical analysis. Each step requires either specialized tools or programming knowledge, impeding analysis for the majority of legal practitioners. Particularly dur-

* Equal contribution.
† Corresponding author

Proceedings of the 18th Conference of the European Chapter of the Association for Computational Linguistics System Demonstrations, pages 52–61
March 17-22, 2024

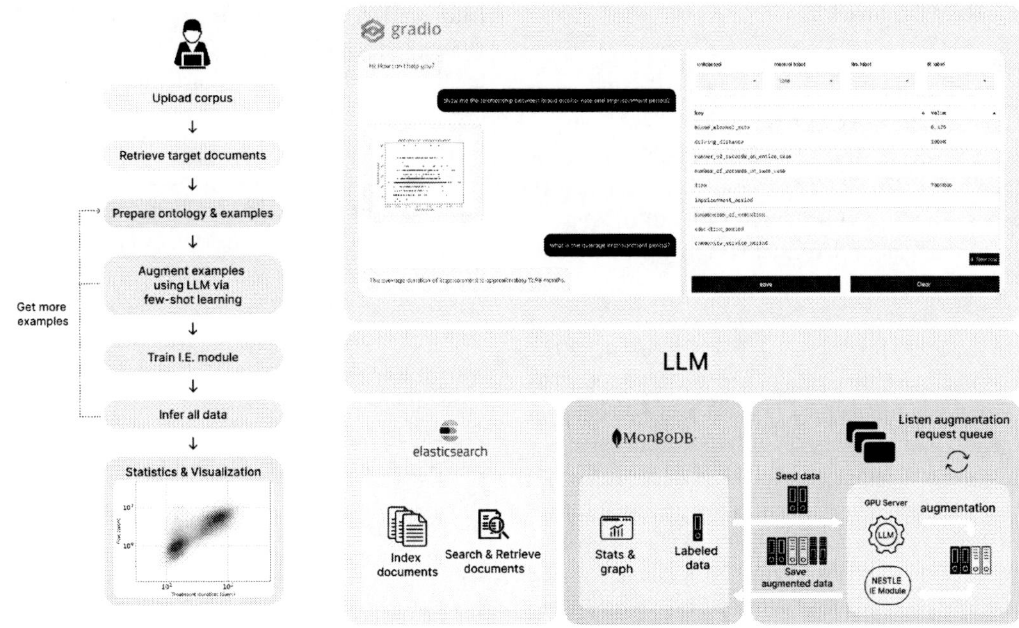

Figure 2: The workflow of NESTLE

ing text structuration, if the target information is not predefined in the ontology of the IE system, one needs to build their own system.

To overcome such limitation, we developed NESTLE[1], a no-code tool for statistical analysis of legal corpus. With NESTLE, users can search target documents, extract information, and visualize statistical information of the structured data via the chat interface, accompanied by an auxiliary GUI for the fine-level controls, such as hyperparameter selection, ontology modification, data labeling, etc. A unique design choice of NESTLE is the combination of LLM and an custom end-to-end IE system (Hwang et al., 2022a) that brings the following merits. First, NESTLE can handle custom ontology provided by users thanks to the end-to-end (generative) property of the IE module. Second, NESTLE can extract target information from the corpus with as few as 4 examples powered by the LLM. For given few examples, LLM builds the training dataset for the IE module under few-shot setting. Finally, the overall cost can be reduced by 200 times, and the inference time can be accelerated by 6 times compared to IE systems that rely exclusively on LLM, like ChatGPT, when analyzing 1 million documents.

We validate NESTLE on three legal AI tasks: (1) 4 Korean Legal IE tasks (Hwang et al., 2022a), (2) 11 new Korean Legal IE tasks derived from LBOX-OPEN dataset (Hwang et al., 2022b), and (3) 3 English legal text classification tasks from LEXGLUE (Chalkidis et al., 2022; Chalkidis, 2023; Tuggener et al., 2020; Lippi et al., 2018). The comprehensive experiments reveal NESTLE can achieves GPT-4 comparable performance with just 4 human-labeled, and 192 LLM-labeled examples. In summary, our contributions are as below.

- We develop NESTLE, a no-code tool that can assist users to perform large scale statistical analysis of legal corpus from a few (4–8) given examples.
- We extensively validate NESTLE on 15 Korean precedent IE tasks and 3 English legal text classification while focusing on three real-world metrics: accuracy, cost, and time[2].
- We show NESTLE can achieve GPT-4 comparable accuracy but with 200 times lower cost and in six times faster inference compared to IE systems that solely rely on commercial LLM like ChatGPT for analyzing 1 million documents.

[1]NO-CODE TOOL FOR STATISTICAL ANALYSIS OF LEGAL CORPUS

[2]The demo is available from `http://nestle-demo.lbox.kr`. The part of the datasets (including 550 manually curated test set for few-shot IE tasks) will be available from `https://github.com/lbox-kr/nestle`

2 Related Works

Large Language Model as an Agent With rapid popularization of LLM (OpenAI, 2023; Touvron et al., 2023a,b; Anil et al., 2023; Anthropic, 2023; Taori et al., 2023; Zheng et al., 2023), many recent studies examine the capability of LLM as an agent that can utilize external tools (Liang et al., 2023; Li et al., 2023; Liu et al., 2023; Wang et al., 2023; Song et al., 2023; Zhuang et al., 2023; Tang et al., 2023; Patil et al., 2023; Qin et al., 2023; Viswanathan et al., 2023). There are few studies focusing on the capability of LLM as a data analysis agent. Zhang et al. develop Data-Copilot that can help users to interact with various data sources via chat interface. Ma et al. examines the capability of GPT-3 (CODEX, `code-davinci-002`) as few-shot information extractor on eight NER and relation extraction tasks and propose using LLM to rerank outputs from small language models. Ding et al. evaluate the capability of GPT-3 as a data annotators on SST2 text classification task and CrossNER tasks reporting that GPT-3 shows good performance on SST2. He et al. propose 'explain-then-annotate' framework to enhance LLM's annotation capability. Under their approach, GPT-3.5 achieves either super-human or human-comparable scores on three binary classification tasks.

Our work is different from these previous works in that we focus on building a no-code tool for "statistical analysis" of "corpus" where efficient, accurate, yet customizable methods of structuralization of large-scale documents are necessary. Our work is also different in that we focus on information extraction tasks from legal texts. Finally, rather than performing all IE via LLM, we focus on hybridization between commercial LLM and open-sourced small language model (SLM) by distilling knowledge of LLM to SLM. In this way, the API cost of using LLM does not increase linearly with the size of corpus enabling NESTLE to be applied to industrial scale corpus.

Viswanathan et al. recently proposes Prompt2Model allowing users to construct an NLP system by providing a few examples. Compared to Prompt2Model, NESTLE is specialized in large-scale IE task in legal domain and provides additional features like chat-based statistical analysis and GUI for fine-level control. Also NESTLE is rigorously validated on a variety of legal IE tasks.

Information Extraction from Legal Texts Previous studies build IE systems for legal texts using tagging-based methods (Cardellino et al., 2017; Mistica et al., 2020; Hendrycks et al., 2021; Habernal et al., 2022; Chen et al., 2020; Pham et al., 2021; Hong et al., 2021; Yao et al., 2022) or generative methods (Pires et al., 2022; Hwang et al., 2022a).

Our system is similar to (Hwang et al., 2022a) in that we use an end-to-end IE system and focus on statistical analysis of legal information. However our work is unique in that we present a no-code tool and explore hybridization of commercial LLM and open-sourced SLM to expand the scope of analysis to a large-scale corpus while focusing on three real-world metrics: accuracy, time, and cost.

3 System

NESTLE consists of three major modules: a search engine for document retrieval, a custom end-to-end IE systems, and LLM to provide chat interface and label data. Through conversations with the LLM, users can search, retrieve, and label data from the corpus. After labeling a few retrieved documents, users can structure entire corpus using the IE module. After that, users can conduct statistical analysis through the chat interface using the LLM. Internally, user queries are converted into executable logical forms to call corresponding tools via the "function calling" capability of ChatGPT. The overall workflow is depicted in Fig. 2.

Search Engine The search engine selects a portion of the corpus for statistical analysis from given user queries. Utilizing LLM like ChatGPT, we first extract potential keywords or sentences from user queries, then forward them to the search engine for further refinement and selection. Elasticsearch is used for handling large volumes of data efficiently.

IE Module To structure documents, users first generate a small set of seed examples via either a chat interface or GUI for fine-level control. Then LLM employs these seed examples to label other documents via few-shot learning. The following prompt is used for the labeling

`You are a helpful assistant for IE tasks. After reading the following text, extract information about` *FIELD-1, FIELD-2, ..., FIELD-n* `in the following JSON format. '`*FIELD-1*`: [value1, value2, ...],` *FIELD-2*`: [value1, value2, ...], ...,` *FIELD-n*`: [value1, value2, ...]'.`

TASK DESCRIPTION

Table 1: Performance of various models on KORPREC-IE task showing the F_1 scores for individual fields: BAC (blood alcohol level), Dist (travel distance), Vehicle (vehicle type), Rec (previous drunk driving record), Loss, Loss-A (aiding and abetting losses), Fine (fine amount), Imp (imprisonment type and period), Susp (execution suspension period), Educ (education period), Comm (community service period). The average scores (AVG) are calculated excluding DRUNK DRIVING task, as all models achieve high scores on it. Scores are based on test sets, each containing 100 examples per task.

Name	LLM module	IE module backbone size	# of training examples	# of LLM-labeled examples	AVG	DRUNK DRIVING			EMBZ	FRAUD		RULING-CRIMINAL				
			(per task)	(per task)	F_1	BAC	Dist	Rec	Loss	Loss	Loss-A	Fine	Imp	Susp	Educ	Comm
mt5-small[a]	-	0.3B	50	-	58.0	95.8	93.0	90.1	72.2	42.9	0	79.4	89.4	85.7	60.4	34.1
mt5-large[a]	-	1.2B	50	-	63.9	98.0	96.4	93.6	87.5	64.8	0	84.7	82.1	96.7	68.1	27.0
NESTLE-S_0	ChatGPT	0.3B	4[b]	92	62.2	98.0	95.3	93.0	70.1	52.2	0.0	71.2	96.5	93.6	76.7	37.5
NESTLE-S	ChatGPT	0.3B	4	192	64.7	98.0	95.3	89.8	77.3	56.5	0.0	77.4	96.5	98.9	57.1	54.2
NESTLE-L_0	ChatGPT	1.2B	4	92	71.8	97.4	94.7	93.0	84.9	65.3	0.0	86.7	97.9	98.9	82.4	57.9
NESTLE-L	ChatGPT	1.2B	4	192	77.3	98.0	95.3	91.7	87.0	68.0	11.8	88.9	97.9	97.8	94.5	72.7
NESTLE-L+	GPT-4	1.2B	4	192	83.6	-	-	-	90.5	71.2	38.1	89.2	95.8	98.9	96.4	88.9
NESTLE-XXL+	GPT-4	12.9B	4	192	80.4	-	-	-	92.5	72.6	28.6	92.3	96.6	96.8	88.9	75.0
ChatGPT	-	-	4	-	79.6	99.0	95.3	95.2	87.5	75.2	34.8	87.1	97.8	96.5	94.7	63.4
ChatGPT + aux. inst.	-	-	4	-	-	-	-	-	-	75.6	41.7	88.5	98.6	98.8	96.4	72.7
GPT-4	-	-	4	-	88.7	98.5	97.8	92.1	93.5	82.3	59.3	93.9	97.1	98.9	92.6	92.3
ISLA[a]	-	1.2B	–1,000	-	90.3	99.5	97.4	99.0	91.7	80.3	69.6	95.5	95.7	98.9	98.2	92.3

a: From (Hwang et al., 2022a).
b: 8 examples are used in RULING-CRIMINAL task.

INPUT TEXT 1, *PARSE 1*

INPUT TEXT 2, *PARSE 2*

...

INPUT TEXT n, *PARSE n*

INPUT TEXT[3]

The generated examples are used to train the IE model. We use open-sourced language model multilingual T5 (mt5) (Xue et al., 2021) as a backbone. mt5 is selected as (1) it provides checkpoints of various scale up to 13B, and (2) previous studies show Transformers with encoder-decoder architecture perform better than decoder-only models in IE tasks (Hwang et al., 2022a,b). The model has also demonstrated effectiveness in distilling knowledge from LLM for QA tasks (Li et al., 2022). The trained model is used to parse remaining documents retrieved from previous step.

4 Demo

In this section, we provide the explanation for our demo. The video is also available at `https://youtu.be/twkpjYJrvI8`

Labeling Interface Users can upload their data (unstructured corpus) using an upload button. Althernatively, they can test the system with examples prepared from 7 legal domains by selecting them through the chat interface. Each dataset comes with approximately 1500 documents and 20 manually labeled examples. After loading the dataset, users can view and perform manual labeling on documents using the dropdown menu where the values of individual fields (such as blood alcohol level, fine amount, etc.) can be labeled or the new fields can be introduced. The changes are automatically saved to the database.

IE Module Interface Users can select options such as model size, number of training epochs, and number of training examples within the IE Module Interface. The training of IE module typically takes from 40 minutes to an hour, depending on the parameters above. The data is automatically augmented by LLM when the number of manually labeled examples is less than the specified number of training examples above.

Statistical Analysis Interface Using the chat interface from the second tab of our demo, users can perform various statistical analyses such as data visualization and calculation of various statistics. Users can also retrieve a target document upon request.

5 Experiments

All experiments are performed on NVIDIA A6000 GPU except the experiments with mt5-xxl where eight A100 GPUs are used. The IE module of NESTLE is fine-tuned with batch size 12 with learning rate 4e-4 using AdamW optimizer. Under this condition, the training sometimes becomes unstable. In this case, we decrease the learning rate to 3e-4. The

[3]The original prompt is written in Korean but shown in English for the clarity.

high learning rate is purposely chosen for the fast training. The training are stopped after 60 epochs (NESTLE-S), or after 80 epochs (NESTLE-L, NESTLE-L+). In case of NESTLE-XXL, the learning rate is set to 2e-4 and the model is trained for 20 epochs with batch size 8 using deepspeed stage 3 offload (Ren et al., 2021). For efficient training, LoRA is employed in all experiments (Hu et al., 2022) using PEFT library from Hugging face (Mangrulkar et al., 2022). In all evaluations, the checkpoint from the last epoch is used.

For the data labeling, we use ChatGPT version `gpt-3.5-turbo-16k-0613` and GPT-4 version `gpt-4-0613`. In all other operations with LLM, we use the same version of ChatGPT except during normalization of numeric strings such as imprisonment period and fines where `gpt-3.5-turbo-0613` is used. We set temperature 0 to minimize the randomness as IE tasks do not require versatile outputs. The default values are used for the other hyperparameters. During the few shot learning, we feed LLM with the examples half of which include all fields defined in the ontology while the remaining half are selected randomly.

6 Results

We validate NESTLE on 15 Korean precedent IE tasks and 3 English legal text classification tasks.

15 Korean precedent IE tasks are further divided into two categories: KORPREC-IE which consists of 4 tasks from criminal cases previously studied in (Hwang et al., 2022a) and LBOXOPEN-IE, which is generated from LBOXOPEN (Hwang et al., 2022b) using the factual descriptions from 7 criminal cases and 4 civil cases. In all tasks, a model needs to extract a legally important information from factual description or ruling of cases such as blood alcohol level, fraud loss, fine, and imprisonment period, the duration of required hospital treatment for injuries, etc.

Three classification tasks are EURLEX, LEDGAR, and UNFAIR-ToS from LEXGLUE (Chalkidis et al., 2022; Tuggener et al., 2020; Lippi et al., 2018). EURLEX dataset consists of a pair of European Union legislation (input) and corresponding legal concepts (output) from the EuroVoc Thesaurus. In LEDGAR task, a model needs to classify the paragraphs from contracts originated from US Securities and Exchange Commission fillings. Similarly, UNFAIR-ToS is a task of predicting 8 types of unfair contractual

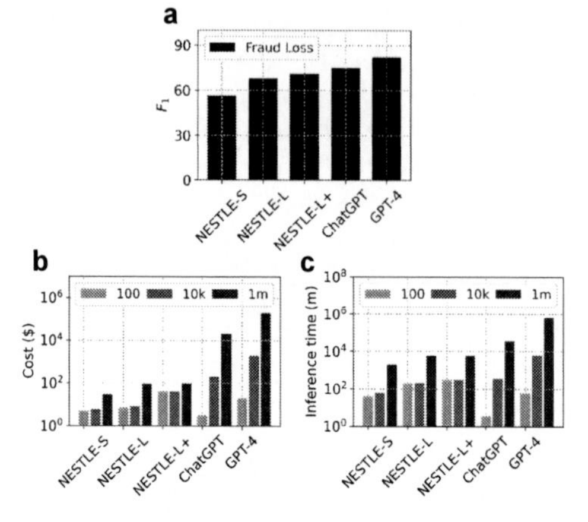

Figure 3: Trade-off analysis on FRAUD task focuses on three real-world metrics: (a) accuracy, (b) cost, and (c) time.

terms for given individual sentences from 50 Terms of Service. These 3 classification tasks are used to demonstrate NESTLE on common (English) legal AI benchmark and also to show NESTLE can be applied to general AI tasks that can be represented in text-to-text format (Raffel et al., 2020).

NESTLE shows competent performance with only four examples We first validate NESTLE on KORPREC-IE that consists of four tasks: DRUNK DRIVING, EMBEZZLEMENT, FRAUD, and RULING-CRIMINAL. With four seed examples and 92 LLM-labeled examples, we train mt5-small (Xue et al., 2021). The result shows that our method already achieves + 4.2 F_1 on average compared to the case trained with 50 manually labeled examples (Table 1, 1st vs 3rd rows, 5th column).

NESTLE can achieve GPT-4 comparable performance To enhance the accuracy of NESTLE, we scale both the quantity of labeled examples by LLM and the size of the backbone of NESTLE's end-to-end IE module. With a greater quantity of LLM-labeled examples (from 92 to 192), NESTLE achieves +2.5 F_1 on average (3rd vs 4th rows) while the labeling time increases (for example, from 2.4 minutes to 10.6 minutes in FRAUD task). With a larger backbone (from mt5-small (0.3B) to mt5-large (1.2B)), NESTLE's shows +9.6 F_1 (3rd vs 5th rows). With both, NESTLE shows +15.1 F_1 (3rd vs 6th rows). However, both the labeling time and the training time increase (for example, from 15 minutes to 170 minutes in FRAUD task).

If the accuracy of teacher model (ChatGPT) is low, the performance of student (mt5) may be

Table 2: Performance of GPT-4 and NESTLE-L on the seven criminal IE tasks from LBOXOPEN-IE. F_1 scores are shown: nRec (the number of identical criminal records), nRec-A (the number of criminal records), Waiver (the victim's intent to waive punishment), Injury (the extent of injuries), and Gender (the victim's gender).

Name	AVG	Indecent Act.[1]			Obstruction[2]		Traffic injuries [3]				Drunk driving [4]				Fraud [5]	Injuries [6]		Violence [7]		
	F_1	nRec	nRec-A	Waiver	nRec	nRec-A	nRec	nRec-A	Waiver	Injury	nRec	nRec-A	BAC	Dist	Loss	Injury	Gender	nRec	nRec-A	Gender
GPT-4	81.1	88.2	85.7	83.1	78.7	82.6	55.6	66.7	68.4	96.0	88.2	88.2	100	99.0	94.9	94.1	81.6	47.1	61.3	81.6
NESTLE-L	78.1	88.9	76.5	52.9	71.8	57.1	73.4	78.0	71.9	95.8	71.8	64.9	100	96.9	81.0	96.9	75.0	64.9	71.8	93.6

1: Indecent act by compulsion (강제추행), 2: Obstruction of performance of official duties (공무집행방해), 3: Bodily injuries from traffic accident (교통사고처리특례법위반(치상), 4: Drunk driving (도로교통법위반(음주운전)), 5: Fraud (사기), 6: Inflicting bodily injuries (상해), 7: Violence (폭행)

Table 3: Performance of GPT-4 and NESTLE-L on the four civil IE tasks from LBOXOPEN-IE. F_1 scores for individual fields are shown: Dom (the event domain such as real estate, fire incident, etc), Ctr (the type of contract), Exp (the amount of money that plaintiffs spent), Loan (the sum of money borrowed by the defendant), and Relat (the relation between plaintiff and defendant).

Name	AVG	Indem[1]			Loan[2]		UFP[3]			LFD[4]		
	F_1	Dom	Ctr	Exp	Loan	Relat	Dom	Ctr	Relat	Dom	Ctr	Relat
GPT-4	83.1	97.0	90.4	95.8	73.2	93.3	93.9	64.9	59.4	92.8	73.9	79.1
NESTLE-L	71.5	73.4	63.9	82.9	59.2	30.5	82.4	78.0	83.7	87.4	64.4	81.0

1: Price of indemnification (구상금), 2: Loan (대여금), 3: Unfair profits (부당이득금), 4: Lawsuit for damages (손해배상(기))

Table 4: F_1 scores of ChatGPT and NESTLE-L on EURLEX, LEDGAR, and UNFAIR-ToS from LEXGLUE were evaluated using 1,000 random samples from their original test sets, following (Chalkidis, 2023). The number of manually labeled examples (n_{train}) and the number of LLM-labeled examples (n_{LLM}) are shown in the 2nd and 3rd columns respectively..

Name	n_{train}	n_{LLM}	EURLEX		LEDGAR		UNFAIR-ToS	
			μ-F$_1$	m-F$_1$	μ-F$_1$	m-F$_1$	μ-F$_1$	m-F$_1$
ChatGPT[a]	8	-	24.8	13.2	62.1	51.1	64.7	32.5
ChatGPT[b]	32	-	33.0	18.3	68.3	55.6	88.3	57.2
NESTLE-L	32	192	34.1	16.7	58.8	41.5	91.5	51.4

a: `gpt-3.5-turbo-0301`. From (Chalkidis, 2023).
b: `gpt-3.5-turbo-16k-0613`.

bounded by it. To check the upper bound of the achievable accuracies, we measure the few-shot performance of ChatGPT. NESTLE-L and ChatGPT shows only 2.3 F_1 difference on average (6th vs 9th rows, 5th column) indicating the student models may approach the upper bound. To improve NESTLE further, we replace ChatGPT with GPT-4. Although the labeling time and cost increase roughly by 10 times, the average scores increase by +6.3 F_1 (Table 1 6th vs 7th rows). Notably, this score is higher than ChatGPT by +4.0 F_1 (7th vs 9th rows).

Next we attempt to scale the backbone of the IE module from mt5-large to mt5-xxl (12.9B). Note that unlike commercial LLMs, the IE module can be trained on multiple GPUs for efficient training and indeed the total training time decreases by 70 minutes even compared to a smaller model (NESTLE-L) by changing GPU from a single A6000 GPU to eight A100 GPUs. However, we could not observe noticeable improvement in F_1.

NESTLE can be generalized to other datasets Although we have validated NESTLE on KORPREC-IE, the dataset mainly consists of numeric fields from criminal cases. For further validation, we build LBOXOPEN-IE from LBOXOPEN (Hwang et al., 2022b). LBOXOPEN-IE consists of 7 tasks from criminal cases (Table 2) and 4 tasks from civil cases (Table 3). Compared to KORPREC-IE, the target fields are more diverse including non-numeric fields such as a contract type, plaintiff and defendant relation, victims' opinion, incident domain, etc as well as numeric fields such as the extent of injury, number of previous criminal records, loan, and more.

We use NESTLE-L and measure the performance on manually curated 550 examples (50 for each task). NESTLE-L achieves a GPT-4 comparable performance in 7 criminal tasks (Table 2, 78.1 vs 81.1) and lower performance in 4 civil tasks (Table 3, 71.5 vs 83.1). This implies NESTLE can be used to glimpse the statistical trend of specific information included in a corpus, but some care must be taken as their accuracies range between ~70 and ~90. To overcome this limitation, NESTLE also offers a GUI for rectifying the LLM-augmented examples and collecting more examples manually. In general, higher accuracy can be achieved by utilizing a specialized backbone in the IE module for the target tasks, alongside a more robust LLM, which is a direction for our future work.

Finally, the further validation on three English legal text classification tasks from LEXGLUE shows NESTLE-L can achieve ChatGPT comparable performance (Table 4, 2nd vs 3rd rows).

7 Analysis

We have shown that NESTLE can extract information with accuracies comparable to GPT-4 on many tasks. In this section, we extend our comparison of NESTLE to commercial LLMs focusing on two additional real-world metrics: cost and time. As a case study, we select FRAUD task from KORPREC-IE where all models struggled (Table 1, 11th and 12th columns, Fig. 3a). We calculate the overall cost by summing up (1) manual labeling cost, (2) API cost, and (3) training and inference cost. The manual labeling cost is estimated from the cost of maintaining our own labeling platform (the cost of employing part-time annotators is considered). The API cost is calculated by counting input and output tokens and using the pricing table from OpenAI. The training and inference cost is calculated by converting the training and inference time to dollars based on Lambdalabs GPU cloud pricing. Note that the API cost increases linearly with the size of the corpus when using commercial LLM. On the other hand, in NESTLE, only the inference cost increases linearly with the size of the corpus. The results show that, for 10k documents, the overall cost of NESTLE-L is only 4% of ChatGPT and 0.4% of GPT-4 (Fig. 3b). For 1 million documents, the overall cost of NESTLE-L is 0.5% of ChatGPT and 0.05% of GPT-4 (Fig. 3b). This highlights the efficiency of NESTLE. Similarly, the estimation of overall inference time for 1 million documents reveals NESTLE-L takes 83% or 99% less time compared to ChatGPT or GPT-4 respectively[4].

8 Conclusion

We develop NESTLE, a no-code tool for statistical analysis of legal corpus. To find target corpus, structure them, and visualize the structured data, we combine a search engine, a custom end-to-end IE module, and LLM. Powered by LLM and the end-to-end IE module, NESTLE enables unrestricted personalized statistical analysis of the corpus. We extensively validate NESTLE on 15 Korean precedent IE tasks and 3 English legal text classification tasks while focusing on three real-world metrics: accuracy, time, and cost. Finally, we want to emphasize that although NESTLE is specialized for legal IE tasks, the tool can be easily generalized to various NLP tasks that can be represented in a text-to-text format.

[4]The further detailed comparison is available from https://github.com/lbox-kr/nestle

9 Ethical Considerations

The application of legal AI in the real world must be approached cautiously. Even the arguably most powerful LLM, GPT-4, still exhibits hallucinations (OpenAI, 2023) and its performance in the real world legal tasks is still limited (Shui et al., 2023; Zhong et al., 2023; Martinez, 2023). This may imply that AI systems offering legal conclusions should undergo thorough evaluation prior to being made accessible to individuals lacking legal expertise.

NESTLE is not designed to offer legal advice to general users; instead, it aims to assist legal practitioners by providing statistical data extracted from legal documents. Furthermore, to demonstrate the extent to which NESTLE can be reliably used for analysis, we conducted extensive validation on 15 IE tasks. While NESTLE shows generally high accuracy, our experiments reveal that NESTLE is not infallible, indicating that the resulting statistics should be interpreted with caution.

All the documents used in this study consist of Korean precedents that are redacted by the Korean government following the official protocol (Hwang et al., 2022b).

Acknowledgements

We thank Gene Lee for his critical reading of the manuscript, Minjoon Seo for his insightful comments, Paul Koo for his assistant in preparing the figures, and Min Choi for her assistant in preparing the demo.

References

Rohan Anil, Andrew M. Dai, Orhan Firat, Melvin Johnson, Dmitry Lepikhin, Alexandre Passos, Siamak Shakeri, Emanuel Taropa, Paige Bailey, Zhifeng Chen, Eric Chu, Jonathan H. Clark, Laurent El Shafey, Yanping Huang, Kathy Meier-Hellstern, Gaurav Mishra, Erica Moreira, Mark Omernick, Kevin Robinson, Sebastian Ruder, Yi Tay, Kefan Xiao, Yuanzhong Xu, Yujing Zhang, Gustavo Hernandez Abrego, Junwhan Ahn, Jacob Austin, Paul Barham, Jan Botha, James Bradbury, Siddhartha Brahma, Kevin Brooks, Michele Catasta, Yong Cheng, Colin Cherry, Christopher A. Choquette-Choo, Aakanksha Chowdhery, Clément Crepy, Shachi Dave, Mostafa Dehghani, Sunipa Dev, Jacob Devlin, Mark Díaz, Nan Du, Ethan Dyer, Vlad Feinberg, Fangxiaoyu Feng, Vlad Fienber, Markus Freitag, Xavier Garcia, Sebastian Gehrmann, Lucas Gonzalez, Guy Gur-Ari, Steven Hand, Hadi Hashemi, Le Hou, Joshua Howland, Andrea Hu, Jeffrey Hui, Jeremy Hurwitz, Michael Isard, Abe Ittycheriah, Matthew Jagielski, Wenhao Jia, Kathleen Kenealy, Maxim Krikun, Sneha Kudugunta, Chang Lan, Katherine Lee, Benjamin Lee, Eric Li, Music Li, Wei Li, YaGuang Li, Jian Li, Hyeontaek Lim, Hanzhao Lin, Zhongtao Liu, Frederick Liu, Marcello Maggioni, Aroma Mahendru, Joshua Maynez, Vedant Misra, Maysam Moussalem, Zachary Nado, John Nham, Eric Ni, Andrew Nystrom, Alicia Parrish, Marie Pellat, Martin Polacek, Alex Polozov, Reiner Pope, Siyuan Qiao, Emily Reif, Bryan Richter, Parker Riley, Alex Castro Ros, Aurko Roy, Brennan Saeta, Rajkumar Samuel, Renee Shelby, Ambrose Slone, Daniel Smilkov, David R. So, Daniel Sohn, Simon Tokumine, Dasha Valter, Vijay Vasudevan, Kiran Vodrahalli, Xuezhi Wang, Pidong Wang, Zirui Wang, Tao Wang, John Wieting, Yuhuai Wu, Kelvin Xu, Yunhan Xu, Linting Xue, Pengcheng Yin, Jiahui Yu, Qiao Zhang, Steven Zheng, Ce Zheng, Weikang Zhou, Denny Zhou, Slav Petrov, and Yonghui Wu. 2023. Palm 2 technical report.

Anthropic. 2023. Introducing claude. `https://www.anthropic.com/index/introducing-claude`.

Cristian Cardellino, Milagro Teruel, Laura Alonso Alemany, and Serena Villata. 2017. Legal NERC with ontologies, Wikipedia and curriculum learning. In *Proceedings of the 15th Conference of the European Chapter of the Association for Computational Linguistics: Volume 2, Short Papers*, pages 254–259, Valencia, Spain. Association for Computational Linguistics.

Ilias Chalkidis. 2023. Chatgpt may pass the bar exam soon, but has a long way to go for the lexglue benchmark. *SSRN*.

Ilias Chalkidis, Abhik Jana, Dirk Hartung, Michael Bommarito, Ion Androutsopoulos, Daniel Katz, and Nikolaos Aletras. 2022. LexGLUE: A benchmark dataset for legal language understanding in English. In *Proceedings of the 60th Annual Meeting of the Association for Computational Linguistics (Volume 1: Long Papers)*, pages 4310–4330, Dublin, Ireland. Association for Computational Linguistics.

Yanguang Chen, Yuanyuan Sun, Zhihao Yang, and Hongfei Lin. 2020. Joint entity and relation extraction for legal documents with legal feature enhancement. In *Proceedings of the 28th International Conference on Computational Linguistics*, pages 1561–1571, Barcelona, Spain (Online). International Committee on Computational Linguistics.

Bosheng Ding, Chengwei Qin, Linlin Liu, Yew Ken Chia, Boyang Li, Shafiq Joty, and Lidong Bing. 2023. Is GPT-3 a good data annotator? In *Proceedings of the 61st Annual Meeting of the Association for Computational Linguistics (Volume 1: Long Papers)*, pages 11173–11195, Toronto, Canada. Association for Computational Linguistics.

Ivan Habernal, Daniel Faber, Nicola Recchia, Sebastian Bretthauer, Iryna Gurevych, Christoph Burchard, et al. 2022. Mining legal arguments in court decisions. *arXiv preprint arXiv:2208.06178*.

Xingwei He, Zhenghao Lin, Yeyun Gong, A-Long Jin, Hang Zhang, Chen Lin, Jian Jiao, Siu Ming Yiu, Nan Duan, and Weizhu Chen. 2023. Annollm: Making large language models to be better crowdsourced annotators.

Dan Hendrycks, Collin Burns, Anya Chen, and Spencer Ball. 2021. Cuad: An expert-annotated nlp dataset for legal contract review. *NeurIPS*.

Jenny Hong, Derek Chong, and Christopher Manning. 2021. Learning from limited labels for long legal dialogue. In *Proceedings of the Natural Legal Language Processing Workshop 2021*, pages 190–204, Punta Cana, Dominican Republic. Association for Computational Linguistics.

Edward J Hu, Yelong Shen, Phillip Wallis, Zeyuan Allen-Zhu, Yuanzhi Li, Shean Wang, Lu Wang, and Weizhu Chen. 2022. LoRA: Low-rank adaptation of large language models. In *International Conference on Learning Representations*.

Wonseok Hwang, Saehee Eom, Hanuhl Lee, Hai Jin Park, and Minjoon Seo. 2022a. Data-efficient end-to-end information extraction for statistical legal analysis. In *Proceedings of the Natural Legal Language Processing Workshop 2022*, pages 143–152, Abu Dhabi, United Arab Emirates (Hybrid). Association for Computational Linguistics.

Wonseok Hwang, Dongjun Lee, Kyoungyeon Cho, Hanuhl Lee, and Minjoon Seo. 2022b. A multi-task benchmark for korean legal language understanding and judgement prediction. In *Thirty-sixth Conference on Neural Information Processing Systems Datasets and Benchmarks Track*.

Minghao Li, Feifan Song, Bowen Yu, Haiyang Yu, Zhoujun Li, Fei Huang, and Yongbin Li. 2023. Api-bank: A benchmark for tool-augmented llms.

Shiyang Li, Jianshu Chen, Yelong Shen, Zhiyu Chen, Xinlu Zhang, Zekun Li, Hong Wang, Jing Qian, Baolin Peng, Yi Mao, Wenhu Chen, and Xifeng Yan. 2022. Explanations from large language models make small reasoners better.

Yaobo Liang, Chenfei Wu, Ting Song, Wenshan Wu, Yan Xia, Yu Liu, Yang Ou, Shuai Lu, Lei Ji, Shaoguang Mao, Yun Wang, Linjun Shou, Ming Gong, and Nan Duan. 2023. Taskmatrix.ai: Completing tasks by connecting foundation models with millions of apis.

Marco Lippi, Przemyslaw Palka, Giuseppe Contissa, Francesca Lagioia, Hans-Wolfgang Micklitz, Giovanni Sartor, and Paolo Torroni. 2018. CLAUDETTE: an automated detector of potentially unfair clauses in online terms of service. *CoRR*, abs/1805.01217.

Xiao Liu, Hao Yu, Hanchen Zhang, Yifan Xu, Xuanyu Lei, Hanyu Lai, Yu Gu, Hangliang Ding, Kaiwen Men, Kejuan Yang, Shudan Zhang, Xiang Deng, Aohan Zeng, Zhengxiao Du, Chenhui Zhang, Sheng Shen, Tianjun Zhang, Yu Su, Huan Sun, Minlie Huang, Yuxiao Dong, and Jie Tang. 2023. Agentbench: Evaluating llms as agents.

Yubo Ma, Yixin Cao, YongChing Hong, and Aixin Sun. 2023. Large language model is not a good few-shot information extractor, but a good reranker for hard samples!

Sourab Mangrulkar, Sylvain Gugger, Lysandre Debut, Younes Belkada, and Sayak Paul. 2022. Peft: State-of-the-art parameter-efficient fine-tuning methods. `https://github.com/huggingface/peft`.

Eric Martinez. 2023. Re-evaluating gpt-4's bar exam performance.

Meladel Mistica, Geordie Z. Zhang, Hui Chia, Kabir Manandhar Shrestha, Rohit Kumar Gupta, Saket Khandelwal, Jeannie Paterson, Timothy Baldwin, and Daniel Beck. 2020. Information extraction from legal documents: A study in the context of common law court judgements. In *Proceedings of the The 18th Annual Workshop of the Australasian Language Technology Association*, pages 98–103, Virtual Workshop. Australasian Language Technology Association.

OpenAI. 2023. Gpt-4 technical report.

Shishir G. Patil, Tianjun Zhang, Xin Wang, and Joseph E. Gonzalez. 2023. Gorilla: Large language model connected with massive apis. *arXiv preprint arXiv:2305.15334*.

Nhi Pham, Lachlan Pham, and Adam L. Meyers. 2021. Legal terminology extraction with the termolator. In *Proceedings of the Natural Legal Language Processing Workshop 2021*, pages 155–162, Punta Cana, Dominican Republic. Association for Computational Linguistics.

Ramon Pires, Fábio C. de Souza, Guilherme Rosa, Roberto A. Lotufo, and Rodrigo Nogueira. 2022. Sequence-to-sequence models for extracting information from registration and legal documents. In *Document Analysis Systems*, pages 83–95, Cham. Springer International Publishing.

Yujia Qin, Shengding Hu, Yankai Lin, Weize Chen, Ning Ding, Ganqu Cui, Zheni Zeng, Yufei Huang, Chaojun Xiao, Chi Han, Yi Ren Fung, Yusheng Su, Huadong Wang, Cheng Qian, Runchu Tian, Kunlun Zhu, Shihao Liang, Xingyu Shen, Bokai Xu, Zhen Zhang, Yining Ye, Bowen Li, Ziwei Tang, Jing Yi, Yuzhang Zhu, Zhenning Dai, Lan Yan, Xin Cong, Yaxi Lu, Weilin Zhao, Yuxiang Huang, Junxi Yan, Xu Han, Xian Sun, Dahai Li, Jason Phang, Cheng Yang, Tongshuang Wu, Heng Ji, Zhiyuan Liu, and Maosong Sun. 2023. Tool learning with foundation models.

Colin Raffel, Noam Shazeer, Adam Roberts, Katherine Lee, Sharan Narang, Michael Matena, Yanqi Zhou, Wei Li, and Peter J. Liu. 2020. Exploring the limits of transfer learning with a unified text-to-text transformer. *Journal of Machine Learning Research*, 21(140):1–67.

Jie Ren, Samyam Rajbhandari, Reza Yazdani Aminabadi, Olatunji Ruwase, Shuangyan Yang, Minjia Zhang, Dong Li, and Yuxiong He. 2021. Zero-offload: Democratizing billion-scale model training.

Ruihao Shui, Yixin Cao, Xiang Wang, and Tat-Seng Chua. 2023. A comprehensive evaluation of large language models on legal judgment prediction. *arXiv preprint arXiv:2310.11761*.

Yifan Song, Weimin Xiong, Dawei Zhu, Cheng Li, Ke Wang, Ye Tian, and Sujian Li. 2023. Restgpt: Connecting large language models with real-world applications via restful apis.

Qiaoyu Tang, Ziliang Deng, Hongyu Lin, Xianpei Han, Qiao Liang, and Le Sun. 2023. Toolalpaca: Generalized tool learning for language models with 3000 simulated cases.

Rohan Taori, Ishaan Gulrajani, Tianyi Zhang, Yann Dubois, Xuechen Li, Carlos Guestrin, Percy Liang, and Tatsunori B. Hashimoto. 2023. Stanford alpaca: An instruction-following llama model. `https://github.com/tatsu-lab/stanford_alpaca`.

Hugo Touvron, Thibaut Lavril, Gautier Izacard, Xavier Martinet, Marie-Anne Lachaux, Timothée Lacroix, Baptiste Rozière, Naman Goyal, Eric Hambro, Faisal Azhar, Aurelien Rodriguez, Armand Joulin, Edouard Grave, and Guillaume Lample. 2023a. Llama: Open and efficient foundation language models.

Hugo Touvron, Louis Martin, Kevin Stone, Peter Albert, Amjad Almahairi, Yasmine Babaei, Nikolay Bashlykov, Soumya Batra, Prajjwal Bhargava, Shruti Bhosale, Dan Bikel, Lukas Blecher, Cristian Canton Ferrer, Moya Chen, Guillem Cucurull, David Esiobu, Jude Fernandes, Jeremy Fu, Wenyin Fu, Brian Fuller, Cynthia Gao, Vedanuj Goswami, Naman Goyal, Anthony Hartshorn, Saghar Hosseini, Rui Hou, Hakan Inan, Marcin Kardas, Viktor Kerkez, Madian Khabsa, Isabel Kloumann, Artem Korenev, Punit Singh Koura, Marie-Anne Lachaux, Thibaut Lavril, Jenya Lee, Diana Liskovich, Yinghai Lu, Yuning Mao, Xavier Martinet, Todor Mihaylov, Pushkar Mishra, Igor Molybog, Yixin Nie, Andrew Poulton, Jeremy Reizenstein, Rashi Rungta, Kalyan Saladi, Alan Schelten, Ruan Silva, Eric Michael Smith, Ranjan Subramanian, Xiaoqing Ellen Tan, Binh Tang, Ross Taylor, Adina Williams, Jian Xiang Kuan, Puxin Xu, Zheng Yan, Iliyan Zarov, Yuchen Zhang, Angela Fan, Melanie Kambadur, Sharan Narang, Aurelien Rodriguez, Robert Stojnic, Sergey Edunov, and Thomas Scialom. 2023b. Llama 2: Open foundation and fine-tuned chat models.

Don Tuggener, Pius von Däniken, Thomas Peetz, and Mark Cieliebak. 2020. LEDGAR: A large-scale multi-label corpus for text classification of legal provisions in contracts. In *Proceedings of the Twelfth Language Resources and Evaluation Conference*, pages 1235–1241, Marseille, France. European Language Resources Association.

Vijay Viswanathan, Chenyang Zhao, Amanda Bertsch, Tongshuang Wu, and Graham Neubig. 2023. Prompt2model: Generating deployable models from natural language instructions.

Guanzhi Wang, Yuqi Xie, Yunfan Jiang, Ajay Mandlekar, Chaowei Xiao, Yuke Zhu, Linxi Fan, and Anima Anandkumar. 2023. Voyager: An open-ended embodied agent with large language models.

Linting Xue, Noah Constant, Adam Roberts, Mihir Kale, Rami Al-Rfou, Aditya Siddhant, Aditya Barua, and Colin Raffel. 2021. mT5: A massively multilingual pre-trained text-to-text transformer. In *Proceedings of the 2021 Conference of the North American Chapter of the Association for Computational Linguistics: Human Language Technologies*, pages 483–498, Online. Association for Computational Linguistics.

Feng Yao, Chaojun Xiao, Xiaozhi Wang, Zhiyuan Liu, Lei Hou, Cunchao Tu, Juanzi Li, Yun Liu, Weixing Shen, and Maosong Sun. 2022. Leven: A large-scale chinese legal event detection dataset. *arXiv preprint arXiv:2203.08556*.

Wenqi Zhang, Yongliang Shen, Weiming Lu, and Yueting Zhuang. 2023. Data-copilot: Bridging billions of data and humans with autonomous workflow.

Lianmin Zheng, Wei-Lin Chiang, Ying Sheng, Siyuan Zhuang, Zhanghao Wu, Yonghao Zhuang, Zi Lin, Zhuohan Li, Dacheng Li, Eric. P Xing, Hao Zhang, Joseph E. Gonzalez, and Ion Stoica. 2023. Judging llm-as-a-judge with mt-bench and chatbot arena.

Wanjun Zhong, Ruixiang Cui, Yiduo Guo, Yaobo Liang, Shuai Lu, Yanlin Wang, Amin Saied, Weizhu Chen, and Nan Duan. 2023. Agieval: A human-centric benchmark for evaluating foundation models.

Yuchen Zhuang, Yue Yu, Kuan Wang, Haotian Sun, and Chao Zhang. 2023. Toolqa: A dataset for llm question answering with external tools.

Multi-party Multimodal Conversations Between Patients, Their Companions, and a Social Robot in a Hospital Memory Clinic

Angus Addlesee, Neeraj Cherakara, Nivan Nelson, Daniel Hernández García
Nancie Gunson, Weronika Sieińska, Christian Dondrup, Oliver Lemon
The Interaction Lab
Heriot-Watt University
Edinburgh, UK

Abstract

We have deployed an LLM-based spoken dialogue system in a real hospital. The ARI social robot embodies our system, which patients and their companions can have multi-party conversations with together. In order to enable this multi-party ability, multimodality is critical. Our system, therefore, receives speech and video as input, and generates both speech and gestures (arm, head, and eye movements). In this paper, we describe our complex setting and the architecture of our dialogue system. Each component is detailed, and a video of the full system is available with the appropriate components highlighted in real-time. Our system decides when it should take its turn, generates human-like clarification requests when the patient pauses mid-utterance, answers in-domain questions (grounding to the in-prompt knowledge), and responds appropriately to out-of-domain requests (like generating jokes or quizzes). This latter feature is particularly remarkable as real patients often utter unexpected sentences that could not be handled previously.

1 Introduction

Both commercial and research spoken dialogue systems (SDSs), conversational agents, and social robots have been designed with a focus on dyadic interactions. That is, a two-party conversation between one individual user and a single system/robot. These are only guaranteed in specific settings, like people interacting with Siri on their own phone, or with Amazon Alexa in single-occupant homes. When Alexa is in a family home, their lack of multi-party capabilities are apparent (Porcheron et al., 2018), but this becomes a critical limitation when deploying social robots in public spaces. Families visit museums and libraries, groups of friends roam shopping malls and bars, and couples travel through airports and support each other at hospital appointments. Social robots are being deployed and tested in all of these settings (Al Moubayed et al., 2012; Keizer et al., 2014; Furhat Robotics, 2015; Foster et al., 2019; Vlachos et al., 2020; Gunson et al., 2022), in which multi-party conversations (MPCs), involving people talking to both the robot and each other, do commonly occur (see Figure 1).

Figure 1: Hospital memory clinic visitors using our SDS on the ARI social robot (Cooper et al., 2020).

Tasks that are typically trivial in the dyadic setting become considerably more complex when conversing with multiple users (Traum, 2004; Gu et al., 2022b): (1) The speaker is no longer simply the other person, so the meaning of the dialogue depends on recognising who said each utterance (see (A) in Table 1); (2) addressee recognition is similarly more complicated (see Sec 3.2) as people address each other, the robot, and groups; and (3) response generation depends on who said what to whom, relying on the semantic content and surrounding multi-party context. To make things even more difficult, MPCs provide additional unique challenges that are underexplored. Dyadic SDSs must identify and answer the user's goals to be practically useful. In MPCs, users can provide another person's goal (see (B) in Table 1), answer

Proceedings of the 18th Conference of the European Chapter of the Association for Computational Linguistics
System Demonstrations, pages 62–70

Example	User	Utterance	Note of Interest
(A)	U1	I think it is London	If turn 2 was U2, it would be agreement,
	U1	Yeah... London	so speaker recognition changes meaning.
(B)	U1	My husband needs the bathroom	Providing other user's goal.
(C)	U1	What time is my appointment?	U2 answers U1's question, but addressee
	U2	It's at 10am	was ambiguous without gaze info.
(D)	U1	We are hungry	Shared goal indicated by 'we', and robot
	ARI	The café is through the door on your left, but you should fast before your visit.	can point to the 'left'. Fasting is in red as it is a world-knowledge hallucination.
(E)	U1	Name a song by...	This is an OOD question that could not
	ARI	By who?	be answered without the LLM-based
	U1	Queen	SDS. The partial utterance is handled
	ARI	Bohemian Rhapsody	naturally which improves accessibility.

Table 1: Utterances and interactions that illustrate behaviours of interest to this paper (referred to where appropriate). Examples B & C from MPCs with hospital memory clinic patients, their companions, and our SDS on the ARI robot. Example A: (Schauer et al., 2023). Examples D & E: (Addlesee, 2024).

each other's goals (see (C) in Table 1), and even share goals (see (D) in Table 1, (Eshghi and Healey, 2016)). We therefore established multi-party goal-tracking in previous work (Addlesee et al., 2023d).

Both dyadic and multi-party human conversations are subtly guided and supported by visual cues (Goodwin, 1981; Bavelas and Gerwing, 2011; Addlesee et al., 2019). Screwing-up of the face, brow furrows, looking up, nodding, smiling, eye-contact, etc... though crucial, are lost completely by current commercial SDSs. Due to the added complexity of MPCs, visual cues are even more crucial (Moujahid et al., 2022). For example, It is ambiguous who U1 is addressing in Example (C) in Table 1 because gaze behaviour is essential (Auer, 2018), yet missing.

In this paper, we present our multi-party multimodal SDS embodied by the ARI social robot (Cooper et al., 2020) that is currently deployed in a hospital, and interacts with memory clinic patients and their companions. It can give directions, provide light entertainment (like quizzes and jokes), and inform people about bus times, the cafe menu, and more. Large language models (LLMs) have revolutionised our field, they are excellent at language understanding, and this includes MPCs (Hu et al., 2019; Gu et al., 2021, 2022a; Zhong et al., 2022) as their pre-training includes scripts and meeting transcripts containing multiple people. They also hold a wealth of general knowledge, enabling abilities like question answering (QA), joke telling, and playing quizzes. Our SDS is therefore LLM-based to provide a state-of-the-art experience for hospital patients. We first describe our setting, and then detail each module of our system's architecture in Figure 2. A demo video of this system is available on YouTube[1].

2 The Hospital Setting

Dementia diagnosis is a stressful process. Patients typically spend entire days at the hospital with a friend or family member for support. The hours are filled with multiple appointments, but a large portion of the day is also spent waiting anxiously for test results or the next appointment. Our goal is to provide a system that is both practically useful, but also entertaining, to provide participants with some light distraction from their otherwise stressful day. The research staff at the hospital are our collaborators on the SPRING project, and they run the experiments with volunteer patients, their companions, and the ARI robot (see Figure 1).

The EU's H2020 SPRING project aims to explore "how to create robots able to move, see, hear and communicate with several actors, in complex and unstructured populated spaces"[2]. We are one of eight project partners, and our focus is the SDS. Other partners work on collision prevention during navigation, route planning, ego-noise suppression, gaze tracking, running live experiments with patients in the hospital, and more.

3 Dialogue System

Our system presented in this paper has been iteratively improved through regular user tests and interviews with patients visiting the hospital memory clinic. The initial system (Gunson et al., 2022) was developed before the recent LLM advance, relying on a 'traditional' modular architecture based upon

[1] https://www.youtube.com/watch?v=xMCpcsLhN_I

[2] https://spring-h2020.eu/

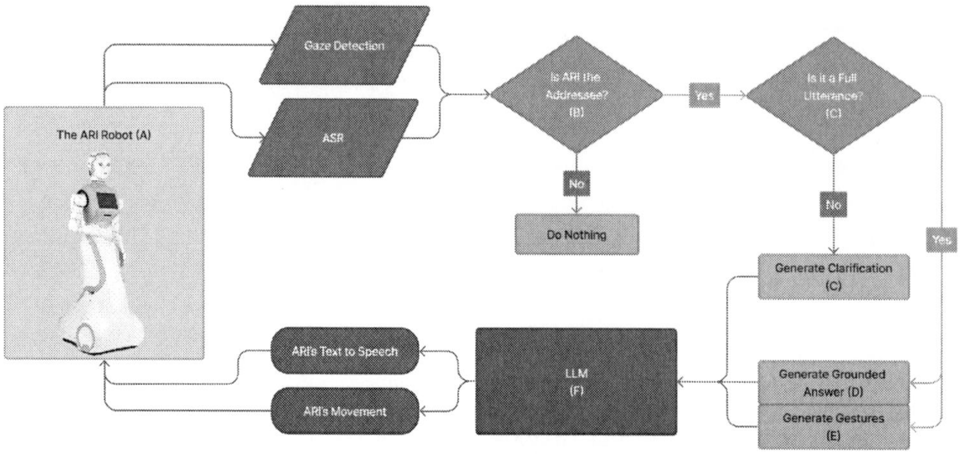

Figure 2: The architecture of our multi-party multimodal dialogue system deployed on the ARI robot.

Alana V2 (Papaioannou et al., 2017; Curry et al., 2018). As patients were usually accompanied by a companion, the lack of multi-party capabilities proved problematic. It interrupted users as it responded to every turn, not allowing them to talk to each other at any point. We therefore designed and ran a multi-party data collection in a wizard-of-oz setup (Addlesee et al., 2023c,d), and have used this data to motivate and evaluate the system we present here. Not only is this new system multi-party and multimodal, it improves QA accuracy, improves accessibility to people with dementia (Addlesee, 2024), and enables added functionality. Where previously, we had to specifically design the system to tell jokes and run entertaining quizzes (Addlesee et al., 2023a; Schauer et al., 2023), LLMs can now handle this inherently due to their world knowledge. Most importantly, both users and the hospital staff have reported that the user experience has improved drastically. In this section, we detail each system component illustrated in Figure 2.

3.1 Robot Platform

Our system is deployed on the ARI humanoid robot, designed for use as a socially assistive companion (Cooper et al., 2020). ARI is 1.65m tall, has a mobile base, a touch-screen on the torso, movable arms to gesture, and a head with LCD eyes that enable gaze behaviour. A photo of ARI can be seen in Figure 1 and component (A) in Figure 2. It is equipped with a ReSpeaker Mic v2.0 array[3], an RGB camera (in the head), and a 180° fish-eye camera (in the chest) allowing us to capture and record the audio and video of the whole interaction from the robot's perspective. The robot verbalises given responses using Acapela Text-To-Speech[4].

3.2 Detecting the User's Addressee

Dyadic SDSs reply to every user turn. As discussed in Section 1, people talk to both the robot and each other in MPCs. If the robot replied to U1 in Example (C), Table 1, then it would have interrupted U2. The addressee of U1's turn is ambiguous given the text alone. Alternatively, if the user said "Do you want to sit down?", it would be clear that ARI is not being addressed from just the text. In order to measure how effective gaze information is to determine the addressee in our specific setting, we annotated real MPCs collected in the hospital. We have video recordings of the interactions with the robot's cameras and an external camera. Using both the video and audio, the gold addressee of each turn was annotated along with whether the user was looking at ARI or not.

Using the Vicuna-13b-v1.5 LLM (Chiang et al., 2023), we created two addressee detectors. In one case, we prompted it with the dialogue history and current user's turn. In the second case, we added whether the user is looking at ARI or not. Both prompts asked the LLM whether the user "is currently addressing the other person or the robot"[5].

Addressee detection accuracy increased from 53.35% to 85.40% when given the gaze information. Reducing interruption of the user is a huge

[3] https://wiki.seeedstudio.com/ReSpeaker_Mic_Array_v2.0

[4] https://www.acapela-group.com/

[5] All the exact prompts can be found on GitHub https://github.com/AddleseeHQ/mp-llm-demo-prompts.

improvement, but we do not want the robot to start ignoring people entirely. That is, we do not want the patient to address the robot and get no response. It is therefore critical to maximise recall, which increased from 31.33% to 91.00% when provided gaze information. A gaze detection model (Tonini et al., 2023) is used to get information on when a speaker is looking at ARI, and this is fed into component (B) in Figure 2.

3.3 Generating Clarification Requests

In a hospital's memory clinic, voice accessibility is critical (Addlesee, 2023), and people with dementia pause more frequently and for longer durations mid-sentence due to word-finding problems (Boschi et al., 2017; Slegers et al., 2018). These pauses are mistaken as end of turn by the ASR, resulting in the user being interrupted with nonsense or a generic response like "I'm sorry, I didn't understand that". The user is forced to repeat their entire turn again, a frustrating and unnatural interaction (Nakano et al., 2007; Jiang et al., 2013; Panfili et al., 2021).

Accessibility settings, in Siri for example (Apple, 2022), allow users to modify how long the ASR waits until it decides that a sentence is complete. This is a wonderful temporary solution for people with more progressed cognitive impairment, but it is not naturally interactive, as the user would then have to wait for long durations between *every* turn. Producing incremental clarification requests (iCRs) is, therefore, important for building naturally interactive SDSs (Chiyah-Garcia et al., 2023).

3.3.1 CR Corpus and Taxonomy

Corpora of interrupted sentences paired with their meaning representations were recently released (Addlesee and Damonte, 2023a,b), finding that interrupted sentence recovery pipelines reliant on CRs were best at recovering the intended meaning of the question. They did not focus on generating natural, human-like iCRs in response to partial sentences. Using a subset of their SLUICE corpus (Addlesee and Damonte, 2023a), we elicited 12 CRs from annotators for 250 interrupted questions. This new corpus SLUICE-CR, therefore, contains a total of 3,000 human CRs (Addlesee, 2024).

All CRs within SLUICE-CR are intended to elicit how the interlocutor would have gone on to complete their turn. Example (E) in Table 1 illustrates this. Each CR in the corpus is classified into one of four distinct categories. First, there are sentential CRs (SentCRs), and these stand on their own as full sentences (e.g. "Who wrote what?"). We can see in Table 2 that humans rarely generated these, but LLMs that were not exposed to SLUICE-CR (the basic prompt) relied predominantly on SentCRs. All other CRs in the corpus are iCRs, fragments that are constructed as a continuation or completion of the truncated turn. iCRs are classified further. Reprise CRs (RCRs) simply retrace some of the words from the end of the truncated turn to localise the point of interruption (Howes et al., 2012), for example, responding "zipcode of?" in response to "What is the zipcode of...". Sluice CRs (SCRs) are similar to RCRs, but they end in a wh-word (who, what, where, etc...). For example, "zipcode of who?" or Example (E) in Table 1.

Table 2: Clarification request generation results. SMA: Sluice Match Accuracy. SentCR: Sentential CR. RCR: Reprise CR. SCR: Sluice CR. Prompt styles = Basic, Annotation, and Reasoning.

Model	Prompt	SMA	SentCR	RCR	SCR
Human	-	-	3.8	39.6	35.2
GPT-4	B	11.7	91.2	0.0	0.0
	A	**98.4**	6.8	1.2	79.6
	R	97.6	0.8	1.2	86.0
Llama-2 13b-chat	B	3.3	91.6	0.4	0.0
	A	0.0	100	0.0	0.0
	R	2.0	99.2	0.0	0.0
Llama-2 70b-chat	B	2.6	99.6	0.0	0.0
	A	91.6	69.2	7.6	8.4
	R	86.0	51.6	20.0	12.0
Vicuna 13b-v1.5	B	11.7	98.4	0.0	0.0
	A	83.9	73.2	0.0	20.4
	R	87.0	66.4	2.4	20.0

3.3.2 CR Results

With that taxonomy in mind, we evaluated LLMs using SLUICE-CR (Addlesee, 2024). The results relevant to the hospital deployment can be found in Table 2. The 'basic' prompt simply passed the truncated turn to each LLM with no context. The 'annotation' prompt contained the task instructions given to the human annotators, which contains CR examples, and the 'reasoning' prompt added a reason for each example (Fu et al., 2022).

Of the models that learned to generate iCRs, GPT-4 and Vicuna-13b-v1.5 both relied more on SCRs. Llama-70b-chat generated more RCRs, opting to commonly forego the sluice entirely. Generating human-like iCRs is practically useless if they are not semantically appropriate. 85.5% of the human CRs contained a sluice, so we devised a new metric called the sluice match accuracy (SMA): measuring the percentage of model generated CRs with a wh-word that is an exact match to at least one of the wh-words in the 12 human CRs for each partial question. SMA thereby preserves semantic type ambiguity captured by the human-annotators.

From these metrics alone, it is clear that GPT-4 is outstanding if data privacy is not a concern. In sensitive settings without hardware limitations, Llama-2-70b-chat is best. Given our sensitive setting with hardware limitations, we use Vicuna-13b-v1.5 as our system's core LLM. In order to handle our user's incomplete sentences, we first ask the LLM whether the turn was a complete sentence. If it is not, we use the 'reasoning' prompt to generate an iCR to create a more accessible and naturally interactive conversational system. This can be seen in the architecture in Figure 2, denoted by (C).

3.4 Generating Responses

Unlike older dialogue systems, we interface with our core LLM using prompts. As mentioned in Section 3.3, we are using Vicuna-13b-v1.5. We provide the hospital information in a prompt with some additional guardrails, like "you are not qualified to give any medical advice or make medical diagnoses" and "you do not have access to individual patient records or schedules". Both patients and hospital staff reported that our new LLM-based system has improved greatly, compared to our previous system (Gunson et al., 2022). In order to measure the improvement in its QA capabilities, we created a set of 100 in-domain questions that were designed to provide broad coverage of the modular system capabilities. These were a mix of hand-crafted and real questions asked by patients in our collected data. In-domain error rates, where incorrect or no information was given in response to the question, improved from 29.2% to 11.5%.

One huge benefit of using LLMs is their inherent ability to perform general chit-chat, tell jokes, and access a wealth of general knowledge. In the original system, we could only respond suitably to utterances that the system was pre-designed to handle – and we would attempt to respond to unexpected utterances with tips, teaching the user what the system can do (e.g. "I'm not sure, but I can help you with directions and menu information."). Many of these unexpected utterances can now be handled directly by the LLM.

3.4.1 Grounding Responses to the Provided In-prompt Knowledge

Certain LLMs, like ChatGPT and Bard, are regularly asked general knowledge questions and expected to understand chit-chat. General LLM evaluation has therefore focused on their world knowledge learned at pre-training. For example, the popular Hugging Face Open LLM benchmark (the de facto standard leaderboard) ranks each model based on their performance across four tasks: (1) The AI2 Reasoning Challenge (Clark et al., 2018), a set of grade-school science questions; (2) MMLU (Hendrycks et al., 2020), a set of elementary level questions covering mathematics, US history, computer science, law, and more; (3) HelloSwag (Zellers et al., 2019), testing whether the model can select "what will happen next?" given a common sense scenario and some options; and (4) TruthfulQA (Lin et al., 2022), a set of 817 questions on various topics, like law and politics.

These corpora highlight the field's effort to reduce model hallucination. It is vital to clarify that they focus on hallucination reduction of outputs generated from the LLM's *static world knowledge*. In fact, this world knowledge can generate harmful hallucinations due to conflicts with the information given in the prompt. The text in red in Example (D) in Table 1 highlights this issue. Our prompt does not state that patients must fast before their appointment, and this response would result in a hospital patient going hungry. Other examples include how long a patient must wait for their medication to wear off before driving (Addlesee, 2024).

To tackle this problem, we must coax the LLM to ground its response to the in-prompt knowledge given at runtime, and not rely on non-domain-specific and potentially out-of-date knowledge learned at pre-training. To measure the impact of in-prompt grounding strategies, we used 50 questions from our project paired with a text passage. We do not always know what an LLM is trained on, and this could potentially include the website of our real hospital, so this passage described a fictitious hospital that no LLM could possibly know. We provide four prompts:

Basic: The passage followed by the question.

Jodie: Our prompt provides the passage as a quote by Jodie W. Jenkins, a fictitious non-celebrity name (according to Google). We then ask the LLM to answer according to Jodie. The exact pattern is this: 'Jodie W. Jenkins said "PASSAGE". Answer according to Jodie W. Jenkins. QUESTION'.

Expert: In order to ensure any prompt-grounding benefit is not simply a result of adding "according to", we again provide the passage as a quote by Jodie W. Jenkins, but add "Answer according to

Table 3: Knowledge grounding results. [light shading] indicates an improvement compared to the 'basic' prompt. [dark shading] indicates a performance drop compared to the 'basic' prompt. **Bold** marks the best scores per model (Addlesee, 2024).

LLM	Basic Prompt		Jodie Prompt		Expert Prompt		Wikipedia Prompt	
	Quip	Acc	Quip	Acc	Quip	Acc	Quip	Acc
Dolly-12b	38.71	36	35.74	**42**	28.08	32	**39.21**	34
GPT-4	41.04	94	**42.92**	**98**	42.61	92	38.66	90
Llama-7b-chat	43.06	56	**44.56**	**84**	41.64	72	40.84	74
Llama-13b-chat	**48.51**	**60**	41.18	**60**	44.04	50	44.29	58
Llama-70b-chat	44.10	64	**58.73**	**82**	52.44	70	53.78	68
Llama-70b-chat (0.95 temp)	44.52	68	**53.18**	**80**	52.01	70	52.82	68
Vicuna-13b-v1.1	64.93	46	**80.95**	**54**	29.17	12	31.93	26
Vicuna-13b-v1.5	40.97	70	**41.14**	**74**	36.30	52	34.17	56

UnitedHealth" instead of Jodie W. Jenkins.
Wikipedia: The Expert prompt with one word replaced. The expert name is set to "Wikipedia".

3.4.2 Response Grounding Results

In related work, Weller et al. (2023) measured LLM grounding to world knowledge. In order to measure how well an LLM's output was grounded to Wikipedia, they devised a metric: QUIP-score. This score is the character n-gram precision of the generated output compared to the source corpus. It is a useful metric in our case too, as we can measure how precisely each LLM's output is grounded in the given in-prompt knowledge. This focus on precision also punishes a model's output when it hallucinates – our goal here too. Using our corpus (Addlesee, 2024), we used this QUIP-score and the answer's accuracy to measure in-prompt grounding performance, as grounding is impractical if it does not preserve QA performance.

Table 3 illustrates the impressive performance of our 'Jodie' prompt. The Quip-score did decrease for two of the models, but the accuracy never deteriorated, and increased by up to 28% (mean: 10%). Even though the 'Expert' and 'Wikipedia' prompts differ from the 'Jodie' prompt by just one name, they generate more text that is not contained in the given prompt (as shown by the lower Quip-scores), and these additional hallucinations result in an accuracy drop.

Our current SDS utilises this 'Jodie' prompt in component (D) in Figure 2 to improve in-prompt grounding, reducing potential user harm.

3.5 Gesture Generation

As discussed in Section 1, MPCs are far more complex than two-party interactions. The SDS must track who said what to whom (Gu et al., 2022b), track the goals of multiple users (Addlesee et al., 2023d), and generate responses *to specific addressees*. As our SDS is embodied by the ARI social robot (Cooper et al., 2020), we can produce helpful gestures with its controllable arms, head, and eyes. While some gestures are charming, like facing the robot's palms upward when welcoming a user to an interaction, other gestures are more functional. The robot can look at the user it is addressing, point when giving directions, and indicate that it is passing the turn to another user with its arm. These functional gestures are what we evaluate here. In component (E) in Figure 2, you can see that we generate gestures using the Vicuna-13b-v1.5 LLM (component (F)) in parallel with the grounded answer generation. In the prompt, we provide some examples of functional gestures, using the gesture tags that the robot expects (Cherakara et al., 2023). The answer text is passed to ARI's text-to-speech, and the generated gesture tags are passed to ARI's movement controls. We do not generate gestures when listening to the user, as the microphones become saturated by ego-noise (motor sounds), and the ASR fails to hear the user's utterance (Addlesee et al., 2023b).

We annotated a set of 110 generated system responses with gold functional gesture tags. Using our gesture generation method, the generated gestures were accurate 86% of the time. Generating an incorrect gesture (e.g. pointing in the wrong direction) is more problematic than missing a gesture, and the gesture generation precision was 0.91.

4 Conclusions and Future Work

We have iteratively developed and deployed a multimodal, multi-party spoken dialogue system in a hospital memory clinic. This SDS is embodied by the ARI social robot, allowing us to generate gestures in addition to speech. Using data collected with real memory clinic patients in this complex setting, our system is able to decide when to take its turn, generate natural clarification requests (improving accessibility for people with memory impairment), answer in-domain questions grounded to our domain specific knowledge, and respond appropriately to out-of-domain requests like generating jokes, quizzes, and general chit-chat.

We are currently running further data collection in the hospital with the LLM-based SDS. Using this data, we will further refine our system and curate corpora that will be released to allow other researchers to work on this complex, yet vital task.

Ethical Considerations

Some LLMs, like ChatGPT, can only be used through an API. This is a huge privacy concern, especially in the healthcare setting. Even if participants were instructed carefully, it is impossible to ensure they would not reveal personally identifiable information – this problem is exacerbated in a memory clinic setting (Addlesee and Albert, 2020). For this reason, we must use more open and transparent LLMs (Liesenfeld et al., 2023). We selected Vicuna-13b-v1.5 as it was the best performing model that could run on our hardware.

In Section 3.4 we detailed our in-prompt hallucination reduction efforts, but these will never reach zero. Hospital staff run the experiments, so they can correct the robot if it ever produces a hospital-related hallucination. This is also why we do not provide the SDS with any personal information like patient appointment schedules – we do not want to cause confusion.

In a real deployment, prompt poisoning could be an issue. A bad actor can manipulate the system to output incorrect responses through dialogue. This is not possible in our data collection, as we reset the system between participants (the patients are also unlikely to be bad actors). If deployed, speaker diarization and dialogue history deletion can mitigate this risk, but it is critical to highlight that LLMs can be manipulated.

Acknowledgements

This research was funded by the EU H2020 program under grant agreement no. 871245 (`https://spring-h2020.eu/`). We would also like to thank our anonymous reviewers for their time and valuable feedback.

References

Angus Addlesee. 2023. Voice assistant accessibility. In *Proceedings of the 13th International Workshop on Spoken Dialogue Systems Technology (IWSDS)*.

Angus Addlesee. 2024. *Incremental Multi-party Conversational AI for People with Dementia*. Ph.D. thesis, Heriot-Watt University.

Angus Addlesee and Pierre Albert. 2020. Ethically collecting multi-modal spontaneous conversations with people that have cognitive impairments. In *LREC 2020 Workshop Language Resources and Evaluation Conference 11–16 May 2020*, page 15.

Angus Addlesee and Marco Damonte. 2023a. Understanding and answering incomplete questions. In *Proceedings of the 5th Conference on Conversational User Interfaces*.

Angus Addlesee and Marco Damonte. 2023b. Understanding disrupted sentences using underspecified abstract meaning representation. In *Proceedings of INTERSPEECH 2023*, pages 1224–1228.

Angus Addlesee, Daniel Denley, Andy Edmondson, Nancie Gunson, Daniel Hernández Garcia, Alexandre Kha, Oliver Lemon, James Ndubuisi, Neil O'Reilly, Lia Perochaud, Raphaël Valeri, and Miebaka Worika. 2023a. Detecting agreement in multi-party dialogue: evaluating speaker diarisation versus a procedural baseline to enhance user engagement. In *Proceedings of the workshop on advancing GROup UNderstanding and robots aDaptive behaviour (GROUND)*.

Angus Addlesee, Arash Eshghi, and Ioannis Konstas. 2019. Current challenges in spoken dialogue systems and why they are critical for those living with dementia. In *Dialogue for Good (DiGo)*.

Angus Addlesee, Ioannis Papaioannou, and Oliver Lemon. 2023b. Building for speech: Designing the next generation of social robots for audio interaction. In *Proceedings of the 2nd Workshop on Working with Trouble and Failures in Conversation Between Humans and Robots (WTF)*.

Angus Addlesee, Weronika Sieińska, Nancie Gunson, Daniel Hernández Garcia, Christian Dondrup, and Oliver Lemon. 2023c. Data collection for multi-party task-based dialogue in social robotics. In *Proceedings of the 13th International Workshop on Spoken Dialogue Systems Technology (IWSDS)*.

Angus Addlesee, Weronika Sieińska, Nancie Gunson, Daniel Hernández García, Christian Dondrup, and Oliver Lemon. 2023d. Multi-party Goal Tracking with LLMs: Comparing Pre-training, Fine-tuning, and Prompt Engineering. In *Proceedings of the 24th Annual Meeting of the Special Interest Group on Discourse and Dialogue*.

Samer Al Moubayed, Jonas Beskow, Gabriel Skantze, and Björn Granström. 2012. Furhat: a back-projected human-like robot head for multiparty human-machine interaction. In *Cognitive Behavioural Systems: COST 2102 International Training School, Dresden, Germany, February 21-26, 2011, Revised Selected Papers*, pages 114–130. Springer.

Apple. 2022. Use accessibility features with siri on iphone. [Online; accessed 14-April-2023].

Peter Auer. 2018. Gaze, addressee selection and turn-taking in three-party interaction. *Eye-tracking in interaction: Studies on the role of eye gaze in dialogue*, pages 197–231.

Janet Beavin Bavelas and Jennifer Gerwing. 2011. The listener as addressee in face-to-face dialogue. *International Journal of Listening*, 25(3):178–198.

Veronica Boschi, Eleonora Catricala, Monica Consonni, Cristiano Chesi, Andrea Moro, and Stefano F Cappa. 2017. Connected speech in neurodegenerative language disorders: a review. *Frontiers in psychology*, 8:269.

Neeraj Cherakara, Finny Varghese, Sheena Shabana, Nivan Nelson, Abhiram Karukayil, Rohith Kulothungan, Mohammed Afil Farhan, Birthe Nesset, Meriam Moujahid, Tanvi Dinkar, Verena Rieser, and Oliver Lemon. 2023. FurChat: An embodied conversational agent using LLMs, combining open and closed-domain dialogue with facial expressions. In *Proceedings of the 24th Meeting of the Special Interest Group on Discourse and Dialogue*, pages 588–592, Prague, Czechia. Association for Computational Linguistics.

Wei-Lin Chiang, Zhuohan Li, Zi Lin, Ying Sheng, Zhanghao Wu, Hao Zhang, Lianmin Zheng, Siyuan Zhuang, Yonghao Zhuang, Joseph E Gonzalez, et al. 2023. Vicuna: An open-source chatbot impressing gpt-4 with 90%* chatgpt quality. *See https://vicuna. lmsys. org (accessed 14 April 2023)*.

Javier Chiyah-Garcia, Alessandro Suglia, Arash Eshghi, and Helen Hastie. 2023. 'what are you referring to?' evaluating the ability of multi-modal dialogue models to process clarificational exchanges. In *Proceedings of the 24th Meeting of the Special Interest Group on Discourse and Dialogue*, pages 175–182, Prague, Czechia. Association for Computational Linguistics.

Peter Clark, Isaac Cowhey, Oren Etzioni, Tushar Khot, Ashish Sabharwal, Carissa Schoenick, and Oyvind Tafjord. 2018. Think you have solved question answering? try arc, the ai2 reasoning challenge. *arXiv preprint arXiv:1803.05457*.

Sara Cooper, Alessandro Di Fava, Carlos Vivas, Luca Marchionni, and Francesco Ferro. 2020. ARI: The Social Assistive Robot and Companion. In *29th IEEE International Conference on Robot and Human Interactive Communication, RO-MAN 2020*, pages 745–751.

Amanda Cercas Curry, Ioannis Papaioannou, Alessandro Suglia, Shubham Agarwal, Igor Shalyminov, Xinnuo Xu, Ondrej Dušek, Arash Eshghi, Ioannis Konstas, Verena Rieser, et al. 2018. Alana v2: Entertaining and informative open-domain social dialogue using ontologies and entity linking. *Alexa Prize Proceedings*.

Arash Eshghi and Patrick GT Healey. 2016. Collective contexts in conversation: Grounding by proxy. *Cognitive science*, 40(2):299–324.

Mary Ellen Foster, Bart Craenen, Amol Deshmukh, Oliver Lemon, Emanuele Bastianelli, Christian Dondrup, Ioannis Papaioannou, Andrea Vanzo, Jean-Marc Odobez, Olivier Canévet, et al. 2019. MuMMER: Socially intelligent human-robot interaction in public spaces. *arXiv preprint arXiv:1909.06749*.

Yao Fu, Hao Peng, Ashish Sabharwal, Peter Clark, and Tushar Khot. 2022. Complexity-based prompting for multi-step reasoning. *arXiv preprint arXiv:2210.00720*.

Press Furhat Robotics. 2015. Franny, frankfurt airport's new multilingual robot concierge can help you in over 35 languages. *Furhat Robotics Press Release*.

Charles. Goodwin. 1981. *Conversational organization: interaction between speakers and hearers*. Academic Press.

Jia-Chen Gu, Chao-Hong Tan, Chongyang Tao, Zhen-Hua Ling, Huang Hu, Xiubo Geng, and Daxin Jiang. 2022a. HeterMPC: A Heterogeneous Graph Neural Network for Response Generation in Multi-Party Conversations. In *Proceedings of the 60th Annual Meeting of the Association for Computational Linguistics (Volume 1: Long Papers)*, pages 5086–5097.

Jia-Chen Gu, Chongyang Tao, and Zhen-Hua Ling. 2022b. WHO Says WHAT to WHOM: A Survey of Multi-Party Conversations. In *Proceedings of the Thirty-First International Joint Conference on Artificial Intelligence (IJCAI-22)*.

Jia-Chen Gu, Chongyang Tao, Zhenhua Ling, Can Xu, Xiubo Geng, and Daxin Jiang. 2021. MPC-BERT: A pre-trained language model for multi-party conversation understanding. In *Proceedings of the 59th Annual Meeting of the Association for Computational Linguistics*, pages 3682–3692.

Nancie Gunson, Daniel Hernández García, Weronika Sieińska, Christian Dondrup, and Oliver Lemon. 2022. Developing a social conversational robot for the hospital waiting room. In *2022 31st IEEE International Conference on Robot and Human Interactive Communication (RO-MAN)*, pages 1352–1357. IEEE.

Dan Hendrycks, Collin Burns, Steven Basart, Andy Zou, Mantas Mazeika, Dawn Song, and Jacob Steinhardt. 2020. Measuring massive multitask language understanding. In *International Conference on Learning Representations*.

Christine Howes, Ptarick GT Healey, Matthew Purver, and Arash Eshghi. 2012. Finishing each other's... responding to incomplete contributions in dialogue. In *Proceedings of the Annual Meeting of the Cognitive Science Society*, volume 34.

Wenpeng Hu, Zhangming Chan, Bing Liu, Dongyan Zhao, Jinwen Ma, and Rui Yan. 2019. GSN: A graph-structured network for multi-party dialogues. In *Proceedings of the Twenty-Eighth International Joint Conference on Artificial Intelligence (IJCAI-19)*.

Jiepu Jiang, Wei Jeng, and Daqing He. 2013. How do users respond to voice input errors? lexical and phonetic query reformulation in voice search. In *Proceedings of the 36th international ACM SIGIR conference on Research and development in information retrieval*, pages 143–152.

Simon Keizer, Mary Ellen Foster, Zhuoran Wang, and Oliver Lemon. 2014. Machine learning for social multiparty human–robot interaction. *ACM transactions on interactive intelligent systems (TIIS)*, 4(3):1–32.

Andreas Liesenfeld, Alianda Lopez, and Mark Dingemanse. 2023. Opening up chatgpt: Tracking openness, transparency, and accountability in instruction-tuned text generators. In *Proceedings of the 5th International Conference on Conversational User Interfaces*, pages 1–6.

Stephanie Lin, Jacob Hilton, and Owain Evans. 2022. Truthfulqa: Measuring how models mimic human falsehoods. In *Proceedings of the 60th Annual Meeting of the Association for Computational Linguistics (Volume 1: Long Papers)*, pages 3214–3252.

Meriam Moujahid, Helen Hastie, and Oliver Lemon. 2022. Multi-party interaction with a robot receptionist. In *2022 17th ACM/IEEE International Conference on Human-Robot Interaction (HRI)*, pages 927–931. IEEE.

Mikio Nakano, Yuka Nagano, Kotaro Funakoshi, Toshihiko Ito, Kenji Araki, Yuji Hasegawa, and Hiroshi Tsujino. 2007. Analysis of user reactions to turn-taking failures in spoken dialogue systems. In *Proceedings of the 8th SIGdial Workshop on Discourse and Dialogue*, pages 120–123.

Laura Panfili, Steve Duman, Andrew Nave, Katherine Phelps Ridgeway, Nathan Eversole, and Ruhi Sarikaya. 2021. Human-ai interactions through a gricean lens. *Proceedings of the Linguistic Society of America*, 6(1):288–302.

Ioannis Papaioannou, Amanda Cercas Curry, Jose L Part, Igor Shalyminov, Xinnuo Xu, Yanchao Yu, Ondrej Dušek, Verena Rieser, and Oliver Lemon. 2017. Alana: Social dialogue using an ensemble model and a ranker trained on user feedback. *Alexa Prize Proceedings*.

Martin Porcheron, Joel E Fischer, Stuart Reeves, and Sarah Sharples. 2018. Voice interfaces in everyday life. In *proceedings of the 2018 CHI conference on human factors in computing systems*, pages 1–12.

Laura Schauer, Jason Sweeny, Charlie Lyttle, Zein Said, Aron Szeles, Cale Clark, Katie McAskill, Xander Wickham, Tom Byars, Daniel Hernández Garcia, Nancie Gunson, Angus Addlesee, and Oliver Lemon. 2023. Detecting agreement in multi-party conversational ai. In *Proceedings of the workshop on advancing GROup UNderstanding and robots aDaptive behaviour (GROUND)*.

Antoine Slegers, Renee-Pier Filiou, Maxime Montembeault, and Simona Maria Brambati. 2018. Connected speech features from picture description in alzheimer's disease: A systematic review. *Journal of Alzheimer's Disease*, 65(2):519–542.

Francesco Tonini, Nicola Dall'Asen, Cigdem Beyan, and Elisa Ricci. 2023. Object-aware gaze target detection. In *Proceedings of the IEEE/CVF International Conference on Computer Vision*, pages 21860–21869.

David Traum. 2004. Issues in multiparty dialogues. In *Advances in Agent Communication: International Workshop on Agent Communication Languages, ACL 2003, Melbourne, Australia, July 14, 2003. Revised and Invited Papers*, pages 201–211. Springer.

Evgenios Vlachos, Anne Faber Hansen, and Jakob Povl Holck. 2020. A robot in the library. In *International conference on human-computer interaction*, pages 312–322. Springer.

Orion Weller, Marc Marone, Nathaniel Weir, Dawn Lawrie, Daniel Khashabi, and Benjamin Van Durme. 2023. " according to..." prompting language models improves quoting from pre-training data. *arXiv preprint arXiv:2305.13252*.

Rowan Zellers, Ari Holtzman, Yonatan Bisk, Ali Farhadi, and Yejin Choi. 2019. Hellaswag: Can a machine really finish your sentence? In *Proceedings of the 57th Annual Meeting of the Association for Computational Linguistics*, pages 4791–4800.

Ming Zhong, Yang Liu, Yichong Xu, Chenguang Zhu, and Michael Zeng. 2022. DialogLM: Pre-trained model for long dialogue understanding and summarization. In *Proceedings of the AAAI Conference on Artificial Intelligence*, volume 36, pages 11765–11773.

ScamSpot: Fighting Financial Fraud in Instagram Comments

Stefan Erben[1,2], Andreas Waldis[1,3]
[1]Lucerne University of Applied Sciences and Arts
[2]University of Applied Sciences Technikum Vienna
[3]Ubiquitous Knowledge Processing Lab (UKP Lab), Department of Computer Science and Hessian Center for AI (hessian.AI), Technical University of Darmstadt

<office@stefanerben.com>

Abstract

The long-standing problem of spam and fraudulent messages in the comment sections of Instagram pages in the financial sector claims new victims every day. Instagram's current spam filter proves inadequate, and existing research approaches are primarily confined to theoretical concepts. Practical implementations with evaluated results are missing. To solve this problem, we propose ScamSpot, a comprehensive system that includes a browser extension, a fine-tuned BERT model and a REST API. This approach ensures public accessibility of our results for Instagram users using the Chrome browser. Furthermore, we conduct a data annotation study, shedding light on the reasons and causes of the problem and evaluate the system through user feedback and comparison with existing models. ScamSpot is an open-source project and is publicly available at https://scamspot.github.io/.

1 Introduction

Financial fraud has switched its medium – from phone calls and emails to social media (Ramli et al., 2023; Soomro & Hussain, 2019). A recent report from the U.S. Federal Trade Commission shows that the number of social media scams has soared in recent years and especially cryptocurrency scams are initiated on Instagram[1].

Last year, the topic also gained political attendance[2], but so far, Instagram users have not seen any improvements (Table 8) and industry experts continue to voice their concerns about the spam and scam problem (Kerr et al., 2023). While spam is defined as unsolicited or unwanted content/comments (Hayati et al., 2010), scam is characterized as deceptive or fraudulent activity resulting in mostly financial loss for the victim (Liebau & Schueffel, 2019). New and inexperienced investors in particular fall victim to targeted attacks, often losing significant sums of money in the process[1].

Instagram's existing spam filter has a precision of 98.36%, but only a recall of 11.51% (Table 6). Existing research mentioned in Section 6 made its first success in theoretical concepts and general spam detection, yet no practical solutions to detect financial spam and scam comments have been published. The problem has not been solved, as 90% of our survey participants expressed their dissatisfaction (Table 8), showcasing the urgency for a solution.

To close this gap, we show a way to efficiently classify comments with high precision and communicate the results to the user in real-time to improve the user experience and reduce the likelihood of fraud incidents. The solution is ScamSpot, a system designed to remove spam and scam comments from Instagram. More specifically, we contribute as follows:

- **Dataset & Data Annotation**: We compile what we believe to be the first large dataset of over 100,000 comments focusing specifically on Instagram comments of the financial space (Sections 2 and 3). We annotate over 3,000 comments as part of a data annotation study, which shows that

[1] https://www.ftc.gov/news-events/data-visualizations/data-spotlight/2022/06/reports-show-scammers-cashing-crypto-craze

[2] https://www.feinstein.senate.gov/public/index.cfm/press-releases?ID=C51E17BC-D39D-4913-AA6C-09AB6B259083

Proceedings of the 18th Conference of the European Chapter of the Association for Computational Linguistics System Demonstrations, pages 71–81
March 17-22, 2024 ©2024 Association for Computational Linguistics

domain-specific knowledge is needed to accurately classify the comments. By making all our data publicly available, we enable further research in this area.

- **ScamSpot System**: Our core solution, encompasses a fine-tuned BERT model (Section 4.1), a user-friendly Chrome browser extension (Section 4.2) and a REST API (Section 4.3). This enables the detection and removal of fraudulent comments on Instagram in real-time.

- **Systematic Evaluation**: We evaluate ScamSpot in two cycles, both quantitatively and qualitatively (Section 5). Our results demonstrate dramatic improvements in usability and increased user satisfaction, emphasising the relevancy of ScamSpot.

The result is an evaluated and deployed application that enables every Instagram user to use the website with a significantly reduced risk of encountering spam and fraud, making the user experience more enjoyable and secure.

2 Dataset & Data Annotation Study

The development of ScamSpot necessitates the creation of a specialized dataset, as existing research lacks robust data samples for Instagram comments, particularly in the financial sector. Recognizing the gap, we embark on a two-fold mission: not only to gather this essential data but also to annotate it meticulously, thereby contributing a valuable resource to the community.

To address this need, we develop a Python script utilizing an existing library[3] to access Instagram's private API. Between February 28th and May 4th 2023, we collected data from 38 Instagram pages related to finance and cryptocurrencies. This effort yields a dataset of over 100,000 comments, which, to our knowledge, represents one of the largest publicly available datasets in this niche. We have made this dataset, along with the scraping script, openly accessible, enabling others to benefit from and expand upon our work. Comment examples can be found in Table 7 in the appendix.

The pivotal aspect of our study was the annotation of 3,445 comments (66.6% genuine, 33.4% spam/scam). We annotate the dataset ourselves using a simple, self-developed web interface. While one of the team members has several years of experience as an owner of multiple large financial Instagram pages, the quality of the annotated comments was validated by continuously checking a subset of comments against the later hand-picked experts' classifications.

To better understand how expertise in the financial sector influences the identification of spam and scams we perform a data annotation study. We divide participants into two groups: 'experts' with substantial industry knowledge and 'amateurs' with less or no such experience. This distinction is critical, as it highlights the challenges faced by non-experts in recognizing fraudulent content, a key factor in the importance of ScamSpot.

While experts reach a Fleiss Kappa agreement of 0.618, amateurs manage only 0.519 (Fleiss, 1971). This disparity underscores the necessity of expert knowledge in accurately classifying such comments. To solidify these results, we conduct a follow-up study with 11 handpicked industry experts, resulting in a near-perfect Fleiss Kappa score of 0.808. These results not only validate our approach but also emphasize the nuanced differences in definitions of spam and scam among professionals.

The insights from this annotation study are instrumental in shaping ScamSpot. They not only inform the training of our models but also highlight the real-world challenge faced by everyday Instagram users, particularly the less experienced ones, in navigating financial fraud. This aspect is later also mirrored in the performance of advanced language models like GPT-3 and GPT-4, which also struggle with categorizing these comments, further accentuating the complexity of the task and the value of our expert-driven approach.

To sum up, our efforts in data collection and annotation are not just preliminary steps but foundational to the development of ScamSpot. By making these resources publicly available, we aim to facilitate further research in this vital area, emphasizing the importance of domain-specific expertise in combating financial fraud on social media platforms.

[3] https://github.com/adw0rd/instagrapi

3 Model Considerations

The next objective is to demonstrate an effective system rather than conduct an exhaustive analysis of various models. Nevertheless, we test a variety of models to identify an effective solution for detecting fraudulent Instagram comments. The selection of models includes traditional statistical models, large language models and BERT as a representative of the transformer models. The following specific models are selected:

- **Statistical Models**: We start with a linear regression, a decision tree and a random forest model which provide us with a baseline and show that they lack the sophistication needed for our complex requirements.
- **Large Language Models (LLMs)**: We assess the advanced natural language processing capabilities of GPT-3 ("`gpt-3.5-turbo`") and GPT-4 ("`gpt-4-1106-preview`"). Their ability to understand and generate human-like text is a key consideration in our analysis. However, the lack of transparency and control over the training data of these models is a major limitation. Despite the adjustment of seed and temperature parameters (Table 5), the results are not deterministic. Three test runs are made for each model and the results can be found in Table 5. The best results are documented in Table 1.
- **Transformer Models**: As a representative, we select BERT ("`bert-base-cased`") and fine-tune it based on the annotated data mentioned in Section 2. Its capability to understand context makes it a strong candidate in our selection.

In this study, we adopt a zero-shot approach with LLMs like GPT-3 and GPT-4, contrasting them with the fine-tuned BERT model. This methodology is chosen to demonstrate the practical usability of general-purpose LLMs in their standard configuration. While models like GPT-3 and GPT-4 show proficiency in general tasks, our findings align with those of Yu et al. (2023), when illustrating their limitations in specific tasks compared to fine-tuned models. This highlights the necessity of model selection tailored to task specificity and resource availability.

	Recall	Precision	F1
IG	0.1151	**0.9836**	0.2061
DT	0.8032	0.7692	0.7859
RF	0.8093	0.9244	0.8631
LR	0.8353	0.9163	0.8740
GPT-3	0.3739	0.3660	0.3699
GPT-4	0.6348	0.5530	0.5911
BERT	**0.9213**	0.9286	**0.9249**

Table 1: Model metrics. IG: Instagram's current spam filter, DT: Decision Tree, RF: Random Forest, LR: Linear Regression, BERT: Fined-tuned BERT model from ScamSpot

Despite the hype around large language models, the results in Table 1 show that even established models like a fine-tuned BERT model can drastically outperform newer models like GPT-4 or GPT-3. While both BERT and LLMs are transformer-based, our research also demonstrates that a fine-tuned BERT model is more successful in specific tasks, which is also shown by Yu et al. (2023).

This leads us to the decision to select a fine-tuned BERT model for ScamSpot. The reasons also include:

- **Promising Results**: Tests show that the fine-tuned BERT model far outperforms the other models in detecting fraudulent Instagram comments (Table 1).
- **Stability and Predictability**: Our fine-tuned BERT model demonstrates stable and predictable performance, a crucial factor for consistent user experience compared to the tested LLMs (Table 5).
- **Local Execution**: Unlike LLMs like GPT-3.5 and GPT-4, which often require external cloud services potentially exposing data to third parties, BERT can be deployed internally, ensuring data privacy. Moreover, BERT's smaller model size leads to lower energy consumption, an important consideration in sustainable AI development.
- **Adaptability to New Data**: BERT's ability to understand context and meanings beyond just keyword matching makes it superior to simpler models like TF-IDF vectors. This adaptability is vital for detecting variations in

spam messages, ensuring our system remains effective in the face of evolving spam tactics.

In conclusion, our comprehensive testing and evaluation process leads us to choose a fine-tuned BERT model. The configuration for fine-tuning the model can be found in Table 3. This decision is informed by a balance of performance, stability, transparency, and futureproofing against evolving spam and scam strategies.

4 ScamSpot

To deliver comment classifications to users in real-time efficiently, we develop a Chrome browser extension, realizing the ScamSpot architecture. This approach is inspired by Rachmat (2018), which demonstrates the effectiveness of presenting classification results through a Chrome extension. Our approach differs by directly displaying the classifications without requiring users to do anything other than use the Instagram website. This approach allows the user to take full advantage of the AI model without compromising the user experience. Our system design consists of 3 main components.

The fine-tuned BERT model enables the classification of Instagram comments. The Chrome browser extension, which is installed by the user and runs on the user's device, allows us to extract the comments, communicate with our API, and manipulate the HTML DOM to display the results in real-time. A REST API acts as the connection between the browser extension and the BERT model.

4.1 BERT Model

One of the most important steps is to fine-tune a pre-trained BERT model for classifying Instagram comments (Devlin et al., 2019). BERT might not be the latest model, but the initial results are promising compared to other models (Table 1) and the process for implementation is straightforward. We also see that several other projects have had success in fine-tuning a BERT model in recent months with similar tasks (Sahmoud & Mikki, 2022; Santoso, 2022; Tida & Hsu, 2022). Figure 2 shows the model architecture and the associated specifications, Table 5 documents the fine-tuning of the BERT model including hyperparameters. We use the "`bert-base-cased`" model, which we train based on our annotated dataset of 3,445 comments (66.6% genuine, 33.4% spam or scam). Annotated comments are split 80:10:10 for training, validation, and testing. Both data as well as the code to fine-tune the model can be found as an open-source repository[4].

4.2 Chrome Browser Extension

To make the results accessible to the end user, we choose a Chrome browser extension. It is important for us to ensure a smooth and easy implementation for the user, which is possible with this approach. Through HTML scraping, comments are extracted locally from the user's browser and sent to our REST API. Based on the response, the comments

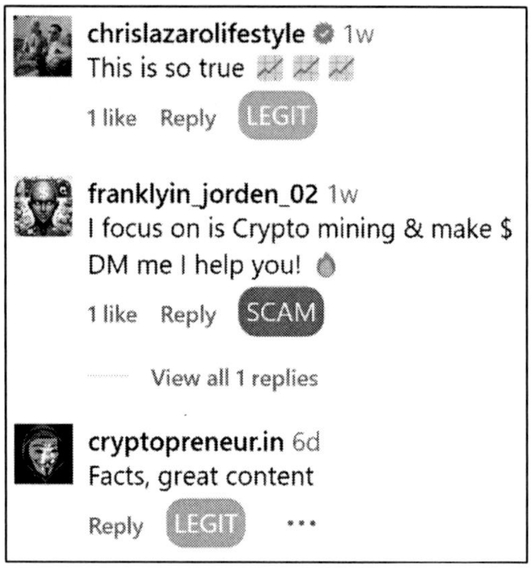

Figure 1: ScamSpot Mode 1, genuine and spam / scam comments are visually marked.

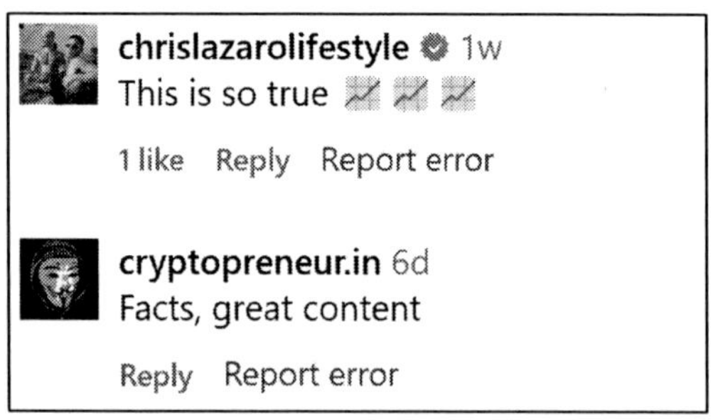

Figure 2: ScamSpot Mode 2, only genuine comments are visible, users can report invalid classifications.

[4] `https://github.com/ScamSpot/scamspot_ml-models/`

in the HTML DOM are modified. The browser extension as well as its code is publicly available[5].

4.3 REST API

The REST API is developed using the Flask web framework and deployed utilizing Gunicorn, a Python Web Server Gateway Interface (WSGI) HTTP server. The server loads the fine-tuned BERT model and classifies the comment received on the `/scam` endpoint. The server's response indicates whether the comment is genuine or not. The code is available as a public repository[6]. Until now, the endpoints of the API have been accessible without user authentication/token access. This allows others to quickly use the API and prevents compliance issues. As usage increases, a user management system is planned, but as little data as possible should be stored.

4.4 Features

To use the application, the users need to install the Chrome browser extension and follow the brief installation guide[5]. After successful installation, the user can choose between two modes.

- **Detecting Fraudulent Comments**: The first mode of the application marks spam/fraud comments with a red label (Figure 1). Users are warned about a potential fraudulent comment, reducing the likelihood of a fraud case. However, the evaluation surveys conducted as part of the research show that users do not want to see spam or scam comments at all (Table 8).

- **Hiding Spam & Scam**: The second mode complies with these requests and hides all comments that are classified as spam or scam (Figure 2). The evaluation survey has clearly shown that users prefer the second mode, resulting in a drastically improved user experience.

- **Dynamic System**: Another valuable feature enables users to report incorrectly classified comments, contributing to model enhancement through subsequent data-driven refinement.

5 System Evaluation

ScamSpot's effectiveness is evaluated in two cycles based on Hevner's Design Science Research Framework (Hevner et al., 2004), which emphasizes the iterative development and refinement of a system through multiple cycles of design, testing, and feedback. In each cycle, both qualitative and quantitative evaluation metrics are considered.

The quantitative results focus on the metrics and the effectiveness of the model itself. As can be seen in Table 1, the model achieves both precision and recall of 92% after the second cycle.

Our model exhibits notable performance compared to other baseline models as well as OpenAI's GPT-3 and GPT-4, justifying its utilization in the project. The F1 scores can be found in Table 1, with the fine-tuned BERT model archiving a considerably higher F1 score.

When comparing the results with Instagram's existing spam filter, the model also performs well. While Instagram's spam filter only achieves a recall of 11.51%, our model achieves 92.13%. However, we must give credit to Instagram's spam filter as its precision was 98.36%, while our model only achieves 92.86%. This shows room for improvement.

Another notable result is that both GPT models fail to correctly categorise comments as spam/scam or genuine. Despite multiple approaches and different prompts, the results are surprisingly disappointing. Results can be found in Table 5.

Not only the quantitative but also the qualitative results improve drastically after the second cycle, in which the feedback from the first evaluation cycle was implemented. 20 ScamSpot users are asked in a questionnaire about their experiences with the system and their feedback.

When using the prototype, almost all test users report that the user experience has improved and that they are more willing to interact with others in the comments section. With the browser extension, users report overall positive feelings of joy and

[5] https://github.com/ScamSpot/scamspot_chrome-extension/

[6] https://github.com/ScamSpot/scamspot_api/

	Method	Sample size	Prototype	Evaluation	F1 score
[1] (Septiandri & Wibisono, 2017)	SVM	24,602 comments	×	×	96.0%
[2] (Rachmat et al., 2018)	Prototype based on [1]		✓	×	-
[3] (Haqimi et al., 2019)	CNB	2,600 comments	×	×	92.4%
[4] (Priyoko & Yaqin, 2019)	NB	1,400 comments	×	×	83.0%
[5] ScamSpot	BERT	3,445 comments	✓	✓	92.5%

Table 2: Qualitative comparison of ScamSpot to previous works. SVM: Support Vector Machine, CNB: Complement Naive Bayes, NB: Naive Bayes

excitement compared to frustration and annoyance without ScamSpot, as shown in Figure 3.

6 Related Work

In recent years, academic steps have already been taken regarding spam detection in social networks (Kaddoura et al., 2022). Most research has focused on Twitter, partly because it is easier to scrape data for training purposes and therefore ignored Instagram. Still, progress has also been made on Instagram, but more around account-based spam detection (Durga & Sudhakar, 2023; Kumar et al., 2023; Saranya Shree et al., 2021). The few comment-based approaches have so far focused on general spam, not financial fraud in Instagram comments.

A qualitative comparison of similar projects and papers can be found in Table 2. The first notable approach was in 2017, focusing on Indonesian comments with a large dataset and resulted in an F1 score of 96.0% (Septiandri & Wibisono, 2017). In 2019 two papers were published using smaller datasets while archiving an F1 score of 92.4% (Haqimi et al., 2019) and 83.0% (Priyoko & Yaqin, 2019).

The idea of using a browser extension and a REST API originated from a research team who based their work on the results of study [1] from Table 2. They constructed a prototype based on this approach (Rachmat et al., 2018).

Their system differentiates itself from ours since it focuses on comments under posts from Indonesian celebrities and users of the prototype still had to manually click on comments to check if they were spam. Our goal was to further improve the concept and ensure people see results directly within the website without having to click anything. Furthermore, a user evaluation also differentiates our work to ensure validated results.

The decision to fine-tune a BERT model (Devlin et al., 2019) was heavily influenced by the papers published shortly before our project which all archived great results in spam detection (Sahmoud & Mikki, 2022; Santoso, 2022; Tida & Hsu, 2022).

However, to our knowledge, there have been no studies looking at spam and fraud in comments under financial-related Instagram content.

7 Conclusion and Further Work

We introduce ScamSpot as an application that enables Instagram users to navigate the social media platform more safely by detecting fraudulent comments and removing unpleasant spam messages from the comment section of Instagram posts. We have shown that the combination of the fine-tuned BERT model and the Chrome browser extension results in a measurably better user experience and can reduce the number of fraud cases during active use.

Our solution is scalable and allows users with no technical background to safely use the application.

This work also contributes a scraped dataset of over 100,000 comments and an annotated dataset of 3,345 comments, which will help future projects and provide the results of our data annotation study. In addition, we evaluate our ScamSpot on both a quantitative and qualitative level and achieve excellent performance and a positive user impact.

To sum up, we show for the first time the viability and effectiveness of a fine-trained BERT for this classification problem, setting a precedent for future research on this issue. We further highlight the importance of combating spam and scams on Instagram, underscoring the need for solutions like ScamSpot.

In future developments, it is crucial to consider implementing more sophisticated machine learning models to enhance classification accuracy. This includes exploring the capabilities of newer variants of BERT and other encoder-only models such as DeBERTa, which have demonstrated superior performance in various classification tasks. Additionally, the potential of models like Mistral, Llama2, and their relatives should be investigated, especially in comparison to GPT models, to understand their effectiveness and efficiency in this context. Future research should also explore the effectiveness of LLMs by employing a non-zero-shot approach, customizing and training them specifically for this use case.

Moreover, further studies could focus on platforms other than Instagram, e.g., Twitter or YouTube, as their comments may be different but the concept is similar. Reducing the computational resources needed and thus reducing the cost and environmental impact is another approach for the future.

Ethical Statement and Limitations

ScamSpot aims to promote a more equitable and inclusive financial system as well as protect new investors from fraudsters. We believe that the choice to take responsibility for one's financial future by starting to invest is a big step and that inexperienced investors should not be afraid of being scammed while they are still inexperienced and maybe a little naive.

All data generated and used in this study is publicly available and used under strict ethical guidelines. Nevertheless, environmental issues arise as we are aware that both the training and the operation of the BERT model mean an increase in CO_2 demand. BERT may not be the latest model, but despite its age, it performed well in our use case and the implementation was easy. Nevertheless, one of the limitations is the model is computationally intensive and requires a lot of resources.

Another limitation was the dependency on Instagram. The goal of the project was to find the best possible way to deliver results to the end user and allow all users to use Instagram more safely. The research team concluded that a Chrome browser extension combined with a REST API is an effective way to ensure results for the average user. However, a major limitation is that it was not possible to embed the results directly into the Instagram app, which is used by most Instagram users. This solution only works on a Chrome browser on a desktop device and major HTML DOM changes on Instagram's website could impact the functionality of our solution.

The problem of false positives is also an important issue for this topic, and the research team concluded that more time should be invested in this matter. Higher precision would further argue for the use of the browser extension.

Acknowledgements

We would like to thank the Lucerne University of Applied Sciences and Arts and the University of Applied Sciences Technikum Vienna for providing us with the opportunity to conduct our research. This work was funded by both InvestmentExplorer and CryptoExplorer GmbH.

References

Jacob Devlin, Ming-Wei Chang, Kenton Lee, and Kristina Toutanova. 2019. BERT: Pre-training of deep bidirectional transformers for language understanding. In *Proceedings of the 2019 Conference of the North American Chapter of the Association for Computational Linguistics (NAACL)*, pages 4171–4186. Association for Computational Linguistics.

Durga, P., and Sudhakar, D. T. 2023. The Use Of Supervised Machine Learning Classifiers For The Detection Of Fake Instagram Accounts. In *Journal of Pharmaceutical Negative Results*, pages 267–279.

Joseph L. Fleiss. 1971. Measuring nominal scale agreement among many raters. In *Psychological Bulletin*, *76*, pages 378–382.

Nur Haqimi, Nur Rokhman, and Sigit Priyanta. 2019. Detection Of Spam Comments On Instagram Using Complementary Naïve Bayes. In *IJCCS (Indonesian Journal of Computing and Cybernetics Systems)*, *13*, pages 263–272.

Pedram Hayati, Vidyasagar Potdar, Alex Talevski, Nazanin Firoozeh, Saeed Sarenche, and Elham A Yeganeh. 2010. Definition of Spam 2.0: New Spamming Boom. In *4th IEEE International Conference on Digital Ecosystems and Technologies*, pages 580–584, Dubai, United Arab Emirates

Alan R. Hevner, Salvatore T. March, Jinsoo Park, and Sudha Ram. 2004. Design Science in Information Systems Research. In *MIS Quarterly*, *28*(1), pages 75–105.

Sanaa Kaddoura, Ganesh Chandrasekaran, Daniela Elena Popescu, and Jude Hemanth Duraisamy. 2022. A systematic literature review on spam content detection and classification. In *PeerJ Computer Science*, *8*, e830.

David S. Kerr, Karen A. Loveland, Katherine Taken Smith, and Lawrence Murphy Smith. 2023.

Cryptocurrency Risks, Fraud Cases, and Financial Performance. Risks, 11(3), Article 3.

Pradeep Kumar Roy and Shivam Chahar. 2023. Fake Profile Detection on Social Networking Websites: A Comprehensive Review. In *IEEE Transactions on Artificial Intelligence, vol. 1, no. 3*, pages 271-285.

Daniel Liebau and Patrick Schueffel. 2019. Crypto-Currencies and ICOs: Are They Scams? An Empirical Study. SSRN Scholarly Paper 3320884.

Beta Priyoko and Ainul Yaqin. 2019. Implementation of Naive Bayes Algorithm for Spam Comments Classification on Instagram. In *2019 International Conference on Information and Communications Technology (ICOIACT)*, pages 508–513.

Antonius Rachmat, Willy Raharjo, and Yuan Lukito. 2018. Integration of REST-Based Web Service and Browser Extension for Instagram Spam Detection. In *International Journal of Advanced Computer Science and Applications, 9*.

Rosniza Ramli, Salwa Muda, Eley Suzana Kasim, Norlaila Md. Zin, Norhidayah Ismail and Hazlina Mohd Padil. 2023. Examining the Relationship between Social Media and Intention to Invest in an Investment Scams among Students. In *Information Management and Business Review, 15(4(SI)I)*, pages 387–393.

Thaer Sahmoud and Dr Mikki. 2022. Spam Detection Using BERT. ArXiv, page arXiv:2206.02443v2.

Irvan Santoso. 2022. Short Message Service Spam Detection Using BERT. In L. C. Tang & H. Wang (Eds.), *Big Data Management and Analysis for Cyber Physical Systems*, pages 37–45. Springer International Publishing.

Saranya Shree, S., Subhiksha, C., & Subhashini, R. (2021). Prediction of Fake Instagram Profiles Using Machine Learning. SSRN Scholarly Paper 3802584.

Ali Akbar Septiandri and Okiriza Wibisono. 2017. Detecting spam comments on Indonesia's Instagram posts. In *Journal of Physics: Conference Series, 801*, 012069.

Tariq Rahim Soomro and Mumtaz Hussain. 2019. Social Media-Related Cybercrimes and Techniques for Their Prevention. In *Applied Computer Systems, 24(1)*, pages 9–17.

Vijay Srinivas Tida and Sonya Hy Hsu. 2022. Universal Spam Detection using Transfer Learning of BERT Model. In *Proceedings of the 55th Hawaii International Conference on System Sciences*, page 7669–7677.

Hao Yu, Zachary Yang, Kellin Pelrine, Jean Francois Godbout and Reihaneh Rabbany 2023. Open, Closed, or Small Language Models for Text Classification? ArXiv page, arXiv:2308.10092

A Model Configurations

All code repositories can be found here: https://scamspot.github.io/.

Configuration Aspect	Details/Settings
Pre-trained Model Name	bert-base-cased
Tokenizer	BertTokenizer from bert-base-cased
Epochs	10
Maximum Length	512
Batch Size	16
Data Split	Train: 80%, Validation: 10%, Test: 10%
Model Class	ScamClassifier
Optimizer	AdamW with learning rate 2e-5, correct_bias=False
Scheduler	Linear schedule without warmup (num_warmup_steps=0)
Loss Function	CrossEntropyLoss

Table 3: BERT Model Configurations

Configuration	Value
Model	GPT-4 (gpt-4-1106-preview) and GPT-3.5 (gpt-3.5-turbo)
Max Tokens	10
Seed	42 *Note: As per OpenAI's API documentation, results are not deterministic, even with a seed value and a temperature of 0.*
Temperature	0
F1 Score	The F1 Score was based on the highest result obtained across three attempts.
System Prompt	You are a comment moderator at Instagram classifying comments.
User Prompt	Classify the following Instagram comment as 'spam', 'scam', or 'genuine'. Reply only with the label for this comment: '[comment]'
Mapping	'spam', 'scam' = 1 'genuine' = 0

Table 4: GPT Model Configurations

B Model & Data Evaluation

Algorithm	F1 Score	Accuracy	Precision	Recall	ROC AUC Score
GPT-3	0.3699	0.5747	0.3660	0.3739	0.5246
GPT-3	0.3557	0.5689	0.3550	0.3565	0.5160
GPT-3	0.3514	0.5660	0.3506	0.3522	0.5127
GPT-4	0.5911	0.7068	0.5530	0.6348	0.6889
GPT-4	0.4889	0.6328	0.4566	0.5261	0.6062
GPT-4	0.3537	0.5704	0.3553	0.3522	0.5160

Table 5: Model evaluation of GPT-4 (gpt-4-1106-preview) and GPT-3.5 (gpt-3.5-turbo)

C Existing Instagram Spam Filter

Instagram already hides potential spam messages, which can be displayed again by the user with one click at the end of the comments section. Based on our evaluation, Instagram's existing spam filter has a precision of 98.36%, but only a recall of 11.51%. Posts were selected randomly (Table 6).

Links & Confusion Matrix
https://www.instagram.com/p/Cr1eVGbtrZq/ Confusion Matrix: 8,0,9,5
https://www.instagram.com/p/CpskFlcouAm/ Confusion Matrix: 0,0,32,6
https://www.instagram.com/p/CrlTySlPSSL/ Confusion Matrix: 8,1,50,43
https://www.instagram.com/p/CsLCoRIvTNO/ Confusion Matrix: 0,0,32,6

Table 6: Instagram Spam Filter Metrics

D Example Comments

entrepreneurship isn't easy just like protesting when you don't have clue of what's going on that's why i encourage people to passively do something spectacular in case you're seeking for an option on how to make money online get in touch with #hāźeł mcẹwən̈
i have tried several platforms they didn t workout but when i did take the risk to invest $1000 in less than week i got $26 000 from her platform i must confess you are truly the best @trade_with_denise_alvina
while waiting for your salary you can earn up to $12 000 in seven working days despite the covid-19 situation you can still make.moremoney without going out @wealthwithmarilynn
if you dream of #dogecoin becoming 1$

E User Evaluation

90% of survey participant [N=20] reported that they don't think that Instagram has done enough to combat the current situation with spam and scam on the platform. All users used the browser extension.

ID	Amount of spam	Has IG done enough	UX Before	Interaction Before	UX After	Interaction After
1	A large amount	No	Annoyed, Frustrated	Not likely	Neutral, I still see the comments	Not likely
2	Almost all of it	No	Worried, It's pretty sad, there are only red comments, nearly all from fraudsters	Unlikely	Interested	Likely
3	A large amount	No	Annoyed, As always, half of the comment section is spam	Unlikely	Annoyed	Unlikely
4	A small amount	I'm not sure	Neutral	Not likely	Neutral	Not likely
5	A large amount	No	Frustrated, Worried	Unlikely	Frustrated	Not likely
6	Almost all of it	No	Worried	Unlikely	Neutral	Likely
7	Almost all of it	No	Annoyed	Unlikely	Interested	Likely
8	A large amount	No	Frustrated, Demotivating	Unlikely	Better, but I want only real comments	Not likely
9	A large amount	No	Annoyed, Frustrated	Unlikely	Neutral	Not likely
10	A large amount	No	Worried	Unlikely	Annoyed	Not likely
11	A large amount	No	Annoyed, Frustrated	Unlikely	Happy, Enthusiastic	Likely
12	A large amount	No	Annoyed, Frustrated, Worried	Unlikely	Happy, Interested	Very likely
13	A small amount	I'm not sure	Neutral	Not likely	Interested	Likely
14	Almost all of it	No	Annoyed	Unlikely	Interested	Likely
15	A large amount	No	Annoyed, Frustrated	Unlikely	Interested	Likely
16	Almost all of it	No	Annoyed, Frustrated, No real human connection pssobile, there are only scammers	Unlikely	Happy, Enthusiastic, It's great, I only see real comments	Very likely
17	Almost all of it	No	Annoyed, Frustrated, I am a page owner myself and I know that this problem has been going on for years, but Instagram does nothing about it.	Unlikely	Happy, Enthusiastic, Love it!	Very likely
18	Almost all of it	No	Annoyed	Unlikely	Happy, Enthusiastic	Likely
19	A large amount	No	Annoyed, Frustrated	Unlikely	Interested	Likely
20	Almost all of it	No	Annoyed, IG doesn't do anything against scams in the crypto space	Unlikely	Enthusiastic, I need this also for Twitter, works great	Very likely

Table 8: Survey responses of the user evaluation; UX = User Experience

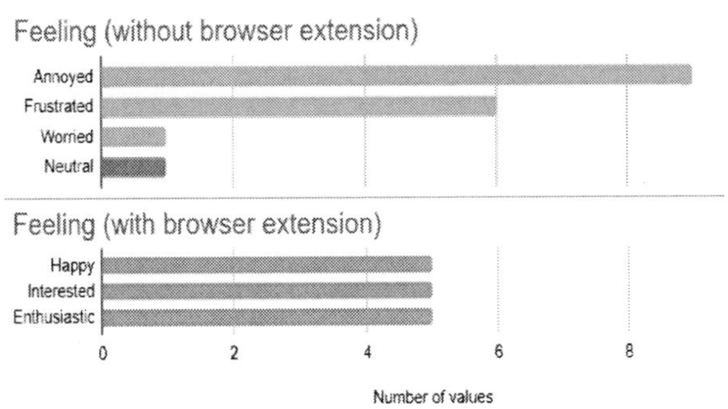

Figure 3: User experience reported without and with the browser extension [N=20]

NarrativePlay: Interactive Narrative Understanding

Runcong Zhao[1*], Wenjia Zhang[1,2*], Jiazheng Li[1*], Lixing Zhu[1], Yanran Li, Yulan He[1,2,3], Lin Gui[1]
[1]King's College London, [2]University of Warwick, [3]The Alan Turing Institute
{runcong.zhao, wenjia.1.zhang, jiazheng.li, lixing.zhu}@kcl.ac.uk
yanranli.summer@gmail.com, {yulan.he, lin.1.gui}@kcl.ac.uk

Abstract

In this paper, we introduce NarrativePlay, a novel system that allows users to role-play a fictional character and interact with other characters in narratives in an immersive environment. We leverage Large Language Models (LLMs) to generate human-like responses, guided by personality traits extracted from narratives. The system incorporates auto-generated visual display of narrative settings, character portraits, and character speech, greatly enhancing the user experience. Our approach eschews predefined sandboxes, focusing instead on main storyline events from the perspective of a user-selected character. NarrativePlay has been evaluated on two types of narratives, detective and adventure stories, where users can either explore the world or increase affinity with other characters through conversations.

1 Introduction

People's experiences and thought processes can be effectively stored in a database, serving as a valuable repository of personality traits. Recent studies (Park et al., 2023; AutoGPT, 2023; Ouyang et al., 2022) have leveraged LLMs to generate human-like responses, which are guided by relevant memories retrieved from such a personality database when prompting LLMs. This significant advancement presents an exciting opportunity for creating an immersive and interactive environment that could enable emulating the dynamic storylines one might encounter while reading books, akin to those featured in the television series "Westworld". However, current LLM-based methods for interactive agents usually focus on specific capabilities in predetermined scenarios (Wang et al., 2023; Xu et al., 2023), often depending on manual settings for characters and environments (Zhu et al., 2023). For instance, Park et al. (2023) used a short narrative to seed each agent's identity, while chen Gao and Emami (2023) tailored non-player character (NPC) characteristics according to game-relevant features. This requires a deep understanding of the task by humans, who then manually craft it. As a result, this demands significant manual inputs and lacks generalisability. We lack a universal framework for designing adaptable AI agents for varied scenarios.

Narratives contain extensive character-centric details, including *Personalities*, *Relationships*, *Appearance*, etc. All these information can be used to craft vivid characters and adapted to generate the portrait and voice for characters. Additionally, narratives offer coherent events experienced by characters, adding depth and richness to each character. While extracting comprehensive character traits from long and complex narratives is challenging and remain largely under-explored (Xu et al., 2022), we show in this paper how to leverage the strong zero-shot learning capability of LLMs to create interactive agents.

Creating interactive and immersive environments for users and agents can be challenging due to two key factors: (1) *Setting Extraction*. Environments or narrative settings are often vaguely defined unless crucial to the plot. Existing research predominantly concentrates on agent behaviours within manually constructed sandboxes (Riedl and Bulitko, 2012; Côté et al., 2018; Hausknecht et al., 2020; Park et al., 2023). We propose an approach focusing on main storyline events from the perspective of a user-selected character, reducing the complexity of identifying narrative settings. (2) *Visual Representations of Setting Elements*. Leveraging stable diffusion models (Koh et al., 2021; Rombach et al., 2022) as external knowledge (Alayrac et al., 2022), we use image generation models to fill in missing details in environments.

We categorise user (or player) behaviours and compile commonly asked questions to evaluate agents' responses. As we design interactive nar-

*Equal contribution.

Proceedings of the 18th Conference of the European Chapter of the Association for Computational Linguistics System Demonstrations, pages 82–93

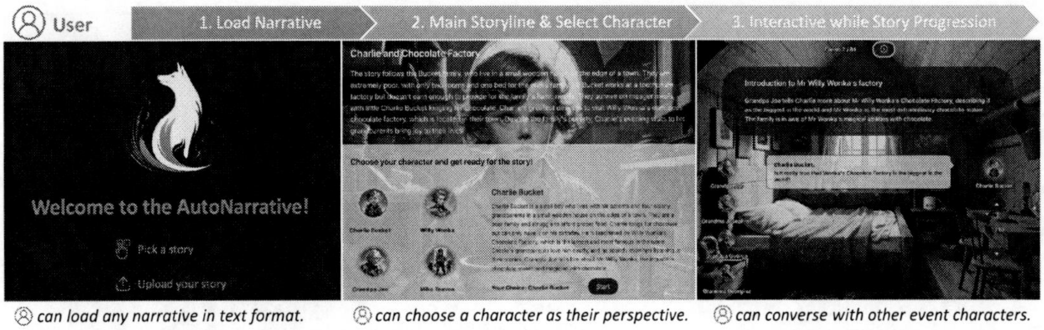

Figure 1: Our system's interactive process begins when a user provides a narrative to the system. They then choose a character as their narrative identity, through whom they can engage with the story. Users can have conversations with other characters, thereby experiencing the story in a more immersive way.

ratives in a novel setting, we have developed approaches which address certain limitations of existing works. NarrativePlay opens up an interesting avenue of interactive narrative understanding.

A screencast video introducing the system[1] and the demo[2] are available online. In summary, the contributions are:

- We have developed NarrativePlay, a novel web-based platform capable of transforming narrative inputs into immersive interactive experiences. Our system synchronises text with visual displays of story settings, character portraits and speech, leveraging advanced multimodal LLMs to enhance user experience.
- We have proposed to extract character traits from narratives for authentic characters that generate human-like responses and adhere to predefined roles, serving as a general framework to design agents for diverse scenarios.
- Instead of using resource-intensive and less versatile predefined sandboxes, our approach focuses on main storyline events from narratives. We simplify the complex world into visuals from a user-chosen perspective, enhancing adaptability.
- We have categorised player behaviours and compiled common questions in interactive narratives to assess the quality of agent responses.

2 Architecture of NarrativePlay

Figure 3 shows an overview of NarrativePlay, including three modules: (1) main storyline extraction; (2) narrative image and speech synthesis; and (3) main storyline progression.

[1]https://youtu.be/Moki-3NDZ78

[2]http://narrative-play.eastus.cloudapp.azure.com/

2.1 Main Storyline Extraction

We utilise the the most recent ChatGPT model `gpt-3.5-turbo` to extract structured information from text. In what follows, we describe how we extract characters, events, conversations, and settings using the ChatGPT API, more details can be found in Appendix §B.

Characters For an input narrative S, our initial step is to solicit a list of the characters involved. Subsequently, for each newly occurred character c, we additionally summarise their defining characteristics, which includes their core traits, appearance, and quotes. These elements are extracted separately because we have observed that the GPT model tends to introduce more formatting errors when tasked with extracting a larger set of defining characteristics at once (Appendix §A).

Events For each event, we extract the description, the characters involved, the location, and the conversation that takes place during the event. This approach allows us to link each event with its corresponding characters and locations, thereby eliminating the need to extract the timeline of the story. If multiple characters are involved in the same event, we will also attempt to get the conversations between those characters in the event. We extract conversations for two reasons: firstly, there is no need to further extract the embedded subevents (if any) as they are captured in conversational content. Secondly, it allows for a smoother transition to new conversations between users (i.e., users' chosen narrative characters) and agents (i.e., other characters in a narrative).

Settings Character locations and event environments, unless vital to the plot, are often vaguely

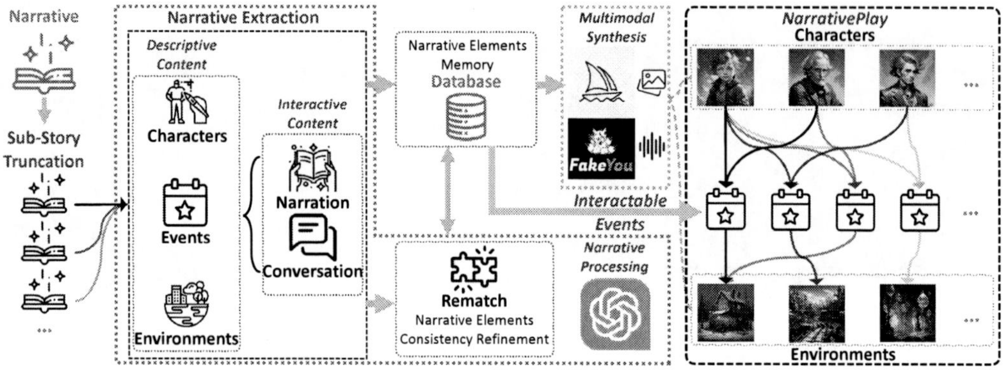

Figure 2: Demonstration of our **NarrativePlay** through a pipeline view.

described in narratives and may thus require clarification. This makes automatic extraction very challenging. To overcome this, we propose focusing on location of main storyline events extracted from narratives and visualising settings rooted in the event descriptions.

It is common to observe multiple mentions of the same location in narratives. For example, "Old people's room", "Grandparents' room" and "Bedroom" all refer to the same place. Additionally, vague descriptions such as "Various locations", "Their house", and "Unknown" are common and further complicate the setting extraction task. Generating images from event environment descriptions partly alleviates the issues of location co-referencing. Moreover, while capturing dynamic changes in location attributes, like the onset of snowfall in winter, is challenging when extracted directly from narratives, such details can be more easily represented in the generated images.

While fostering meaningful interactions among users and agents without traditional sandbox constraints is challenging, our solution reduces the complexities of the world from the user-selected character's perspective. We guide the visibility among agents via shared event participation.

2.2 Narrative Image and Speech Synthesis

Narrative Image Synthesis We leverage the stable diffusion models as external knowledge (Alayrac et al., 2022) to generate scenarios in situations where information is lacking. While creating specialised knowledge bases for specific narrative worldviews (e.g., magical realms, post-apocalyptic wastelands, futuristic settings) remains a challenge, we adapt models trained on specific picture styles, such as fairy tales and oil painting, to auto-complete the intricate details of the location settings.

We utilise character and event features extracted for the text-to-image generative models as we discussed above. Our framework offers two modes of image synthesis: (1) **Local Synthesis**: For users with substantial compute resources, an open-source text-to-image model, `openjourney`, accessible via HuggingFace[3], is used to generate images locally. (2) **Cloud-based Synthesis**: For users with limited compute resources, we have incorporated an API request-based image generation service offered by Hotpot AI[4] into our framework for generating character portraits, which offers a more stable generation style. Additionally, for event image generation, we employ Midjourney[5] as it provides more varieties and detailed pictures.

While advancements in video synthesis have been notable (Singer et al., 2022), the considerable computational resources required, coupled with the subpar quality of the generated video, presently render the user experience suboptimal, thus precluding its implementation at this stage.

Narrative Speech Synthesis Our multimodal synthesis framework also includes the transformation of narrative text into compelling speech, enriching the experience with an auditory dimension. For this crucial task, we primarily employ Text-to-Speech (TTS) models from the FakeYou[6] platform, which offers over three thousand models, allowing each narrative character a unique voice. With the extensive TTS model assortment from FakeYou,

[3]`https://huggingface.co/prompthero/openjourney`
[4]`https://hotpot.ai/`
[5]`https://www.midjourney.com/`
[6]`https://fakeyou.com/`

Model	Personality		Appearance		Environment		Experienced Events	
	Genera -tive	Example	Genera -tive	Example	Genera -tive	Example	Genera -tive	Example
Generative Agents	✗	**John Lin** A pharmacy shopkeeper at the Willow Market and Pharmacy who loves to help people...	✗		✗		✓	1. wake up and complete the morning routine at 8:00 am, 2. go to Oak Hill College to take classes starting 10:00 am, 3. ...
The Turing Quest	✗	**Balgruuf the Greater** Jarl of Whiterun, Loyal, Noble, Blonde... *Goal:* The safety and prosperity of the people of whiterun...	✗		✗		✗	1. Sitting on throne in dragonsreach. 2. Contemplating the war and recent reports of dragons. 3. Give quests to players.
Werewolf	✗	**Villagers** Discuss with all players including your enemies... Objectives: You need to kill all werewolves with your partner...	✗			-	✗	You are playing a game called the Werewolf with some other players. This game is based on text conversations. Here are the game rules...
Avalon's Game of Thoughts	✗	**Merlin** *Background:* Know the identities of evil players ... *Goal:* Win without revealing identity...	✗			-	✗	1. Team Selection: Each round, the leader proposes a team to embark on a quest... 2. Quest Phase: Selected team decide to support or sabotage the quest...
NarrativePlay (Ours)	✓	**Alice** *Background*: Alice is a young and curious girl... *Objective*: To navigate the strange environment ...	✓		✓	 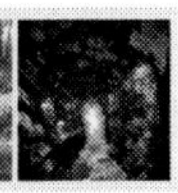	✓	1. Alice is tired of sitting by her sister on the bank... 2. A White Rabbit with pink eyes runs by Alice, exclaiming he's late. This piques Alice's curiosity... 3. ...

Figure 3: Existing LLM-based interactive agents typically specialise in particular capabilities within predetermined scenarios. This often demands significant manual configuration for characters and settings and lacks versatility. Therefore, we have proposed to extract comprehensive character traits from narratives. Narratives inherently contain detailed character-related information, such as *Skills*, *Intents*, and *Relationships*. Narratives also provide details on *Age*, *Gender*, *Wears*, etc., which can be employed to generate the portrait and voice for characters. Additionally, narratives encompass coherent events experienced by characters, adding depth and richness to each character. As shown here, NarrativePlay can be applied to various types of narratives, serving as a general framework for designing agents across diverse scenarios.

our framework facilitates the creation of diverse and captivating narrative experiences.

A noteworthy feature of our approach is real-time text-to-speech conversion, creating an interactive and immersive storytelling environment that sustains user engagement.

2.3 Main Storyline Progression

As shown in Figure 1, we progress the main storyline with three stages:

Narrative Input In the process of creating an interactive narrative with our system, the user begins by selecting or uploading their chosen narrative.

Character Selection Following above, NarrativePlay extracts the main storyline and subsequently presents the information about the background and characters. Users are then asked to select from the listed major characters to begin their adventure (Domínguez et al., 2016), which are defined as those involved in at least 20% of the events. We restrict users' choices to the top major characters in order to have a better story flow. The agent's memory is initialised at this stage, laying the groundwork for future interactions.

Story Progression Once a character is selected, we present events related to the chosen character to the user. The location image is displayed as the background picture and the event description appears as a narration in the black box at the top of the page. Each event displays the involved characters on the left, with the user-selected character on the right. If there are conversations extracted for this event, they will be played first with voice renditions. Then, the user can click on any other character to engage in conversations with them. During this stage, NarrativePlay retrieves the most relevant, recent, and important memories from the agent's past, ensuring continuity and context-awareness (Harrell and Zhu, 2009) in the generated responses. NarrativePlay also updates the agents' memories in accordance with the progression of events, user inputs, and agent responses.

We assign a weight w_m to each memory m to retrieve the top memories for use in the prompt. Consequently, the weight of each memory, given the input x, is defined as: $w_m = \frac{\mathbf{h_m} \cdot \mathbf{h_x}}{\|\mathbf{h_m}\| \|\mathbf{h_x}\|} + c^{(I-i)} + s_m$, where $\mathbf{h_m}$ is the embedding for memory m, $\mathbf{h_x}$ is the embedding for input x, c is the decay factor set to 0.99, $i \in \{0, 1, ...I\}$ is the event index (with I being the current event index), and s_m is the importance score given by GPT-3.5 based on the character and the memory. In summary, this equation denotes: `Retrieval Weight` $=$ `Relevance` $+$ `Recency` $+$ `Importance`.

We generate responses using the character information, the current events, the user input, and the retrieved memory using prompt in B.5. When a user selects a character to interact with, we assume the user's character is approaching the chosen character. There is a chance p, dependent on the relationship between the two characters, that the chosen character might initiate a conversation.

3 Evaluation

Evaluating such a system is challenging due to the lack of gold-standard responses, especially about events and environments. Human assessment demands deep narrative understanding, making it costly, and subjective interpretations may cause low inter-annotator agreement.

We instead recruit three annotators to read whole narratives and rate responses to our specifically designed questions. We also explore automatic evaluation methods using LLaMA-2-70B (Touvron et al., 2023). We did not use GPT-4 for this purpose, as it shares a significant amount of training data with GPT-3.5, which could lead to an unfair evaluation. For each evaluation aspect, we provide detailed instruction, including the corresponding rubric and evaluation examples, to help both human annotator and LLaMA to understand our scoring instruction.

Evaluations are conducted on two distinct narrative types: the adventure story *Charlie and the Chocolate Factory* (CCF) and the detective novel *Murder on the Orient Express* (MOE).

3.1 Evaluation Schema

Player Questions We categorise player behaviours and outline questions that might be commonly asked by players in interactive narratives into the following types: (1) *Character*: Questions related to the characters themselves, which could be about their background explicitly stated in the story or traits that can only be implied from the story, such as "What is your favourite colour?". (2) *Clarification*: Questions arise when a player is confused or requires more information. They might ask for explanations of story elements, reminders of intents, or clarifications about confusing events or instructions. This requires the capability to accurately recall specific events or dialogues from their memory. (3) *Relationships*: Queries concern the relationships between characters, such as their current status, history, or potential developments.(4) *Strategy*: Queries to seek guidance on narrative progress, requiring the agent to recall their short-term or long-term intents. This type of question various depending on a particular story, such as "Which path should I take to reach [destination] fastest?" in an adventure novel, and "What is the best way to approach this puzzle?" in a detective novel. (5) *Hypothetical*: Queries explore "what-if" scenarios, asking how the characters might respond under different conditions or actions.

Evaluation Aspects To evaluate our system's performance, we employ the controlled assessment method used by Park et al. (2023) to examine the responses from each individual agent. Inspired by the previous work in chat-oriented dialogue system evaluation (Finch et al., 2023), we chose the following evaluation aspects, which are important under our interactive narrative setting: *Consistency*, *Relevance*, *Empathy*, *Commonsense*.
Further details on evaluation can be found in §C.

3.2 Evaluation Results

Extracted Information We first present the information extraction results in Table 1. 'Incorrect' refers to the percentage of extracted characters that do not correspond to specific characters, such as "unknown", "somebody", or "people worldwide". Such incorrect identifications commonly appear for characters who are not central to the main plot and might be encountered briefly without a significant role. Therefore, these errors typically have a minimal impact on the main storyline. For correctly extracted characters, we assess the accuracy of their extracted summaries, intents, appearances, and speeches, ensuring they accurately correspond to the target character. We also evaluate the percentage of duplications (e.g., "Mrs Caroline Hubbard", "elderly American lady", and "Linda Arden"). Duplicated characters could detrimentally affect the memories, as the memories for the same character are saved as separate entities.

Story	Incorrect ↓	Duplicate ↓	Summary↑	Intent↑	Appearance ↑	Voice ↑
CCF	0.191	0.211	0.868	0.816	0.921	0.868
MOE	0.272	0.407	0.898	0.576	0.915	0.780

Table 1: Extracted Information Evaluation.

Table 1 indicates that detective narrative poses more significant challenges. Unlike in *CCF*, where characters are introduced the first time they appeared in the story, in *MOE*, characters often attempt to hide their true identities, and clues are left for readers to discover. Consequently, they often begin with an appearance description from the main character's perspective, such as "elderly American lady", or "a middle-aged woman dressed in black with a broad, expressionless face. German or Scandinavian". As the story progresses, more information about the character, including their name, experiences, and intents, is revealed. This can confuse the model, leading it to identify descriptions at different stages as separate characters. Furthermore, intents are challenging to identify when characters first appeared in the narrative.

Agent Responses We carried out a comprehensive human evaluation on the quality of agent responses on four aspects: We use 1-3 to represent {Inconsistent, Partially consistent, Consistent} for consistency, {Irrelevant, Partially relevant, relevant} for relevance, and {Non-empathetic, No clue, Empathetic} for empathy. Additionally, we use 1-2 to represent {Opposing, Conforming} for Commonsense. As shown in Table 2, we observed that while the agent performed well in terms of *relevance* and *commonsense*, it fell short in *consistency* and *empathy* for both narratives. For instance, agents maintained a cheerful demeanour and expressed enthusiasm for travel even after a murder. Besides, agents often divulged everything they knew from memory, which works for stories like *CCF*, but is unsuitable for detective narratives where characters may lie to serve their interests.

Category	Consistency		Relevance		Empathy		Commonsense	
	w/o	w/	w/o	w/	w/o	w/	w/o	w/
Charlie and the Chocolate Factory								
Overall	1.915	2.085	2.970	2.967	2.252	2.444	2.000	2.000
Major Characters	1.900	2.117	2.972	2.950	2.222	2.483	2.000	2.000
Minor Character	1.944	2.022	2.967	3.000	2.311	2.387	2.000	2.000
Fleiss' kappa	0.486		0.317		0.337		1.000	
Murder on the Orient Express								
Overall	2.267	2.400	3.000	3.000	2.157	2.219	2.000	2.000
Major Characters	2.011	2.367	3.000	3.000	2.033	2.222	2.000	2.000
Minor Character	2.458	2.425	3.000	3.000	2.250	2.217	2.000	2.000
Fleiss' kappa	0.404		1.000		-0.003		1.000	

Table 2: Human evaluation on the quality of agent responses w/ and w/o the retrieved memory, as well as the response quality between major and minor characters.

Equipped with memories, NarrativePlay surpasses the baseline that lacks memory. In *CCF*, major characters perform better than minor ones, likely due to their more detailed narratives guiding LLMs to better understand the characters and predict their behaviours. However, in *MOE*, minor characters outperform major ones. This is likely because the more complex responses required for major characters are only minimally supported by their memories, which are saved as separate entities due to the difficulty of LLMs in dealing with multiple mentions of the same character.

Category	Consistency		Relevance		Empathy		Commonsense	
	w/o	w/	w/o	w/	w/o	w/	w/o	w/
Charlie and the Chocolate Factory								
Overall	1.433	1.333	1.633	1.547	1.587	1.507	0.613	0.567
Major Characters	1.467	1.500	1.567	1.700	1.433	1.467	0.600	0.617
Minor Character	1.411	1.222	1.656	1.444	1.667	1.533	0.400	0.411
Murder on the Orient Express								
Overall	1.000	0.960	0.933	0.753	1.213	1.107	0.640	0.640
Major Characters	1.367	1.367	1.000	1.100	1.333	1.333	0.733	0.733
Minor Character	0.822	0.689	0.767	0.522	1.056	0.956	0.489	0.489

Table 3: Automatic Evaluation using LLaMa-2-70B. LLaMa evaluates responses from major characters higher than those from minor characters and rates responses without memory usage higher than those with memory. We found there are still gaps between human understanding and LLaMa.

While prior studies (Park et al., 2023; AutoGPT, 2023) have maxed out the context window at 4,096 tokens for each ChatGPT API call to enhance reasoning and prompting, we found that a longer prompt does not necessarily yield improved performance. In fact, it may potentially distract the model from focusing on the core information. Despite our efforts to automatically adjust weights of the relevant memories, their significance diminishes when being incorporated into the prompt.

4 Conclusions and Future Work

NarrativePlay, a novel platform, transforms narratives into interactive experiences, addressing challenges of storyline extraction, authentic character creation, and versatile environment design. By focusing on the main events and leveraging advanced LLMs, it aligns text, image, and speech, marking a step forward in immersive interactive narratives. Furthermore, we categorise player behaviours and design commonly asked questions to evaluate the system's performance, and provide an evaluation framework for interactive narratives. With a potential for wider applications like game generation, NarrativePlay paves the way for future advancements in narrative understanding.

Our current work has the following limitations. First, due to the lack of an API from Midjourney, manual input of GPT-generated prompts is necessary. Although we provide HotPot API as an alternative, the quality of its generated pictures is inferior to those from Midjourney. Second, the prolonged waiting time for the FakeYou API adversely affects real-time generation, potentially impairing user experience. Third, we assume a linear event timeline in the input narrative, excluding time jumps or flashbacks. Future work needs to explore dealing with more complex narrative structures. Fourth, human evaluation is expensive. For future work, we plan to gather user activities to collect data for evaluating our system's performance.

Ethics

Although we have not identified any harmful outputs from ChatGPT in our study, it is worth noting that previous research has observed instances where ChatGPT produced unexpected results. We encourage other researchers to utilise this framework to scrutinise the output generated from specific prompts in ChatGPT that may have the potential to generate harmful information.

Acknowledgements

This work was supported in part by the UK Engineering and Physical Sciences Research Council (grant no. EP/T017112/2, EP/V048597/1, EP/X019063/1). YH is supported by a Turing AI Fellowship funded by the UK Research and Innovation (grant no. EP/V020579/2).

References

Jean-Baptiste Alayrac, Jeff Donahue, Pauline Luc, Antoine Miech, Iain Barr, Yana Hasson, Karel Lenc, Arthur Mensch, Katherine Millican, Malcolm Reynolds, Roman Ring, Eliza Rutherford, Serkan Cabi, Tengda Han, Zhitao Gong, Sina Samangooei, Marianne Monteiro, Jacob Menick, Sebastian Borgeaud, Andrew Brock, Aida Nematzadeh, Sahand Sharifzadeh, Mikolaj Binkowski, Ricardo Barreira, Oriol Vinyals, Andrew Zisserman, and Karen Simonyan. 2022. Flamingo: a visual language model for few-shot learning. In *Proc. of NeurIPS*.

AutoGPT. 2023. Auto-GPT: An autonomous GPT-4 experiment.

Qi chen Gao and Ali Emami. 2023. The turing quest: Can transformers make good npcs? In *Proc. of ACL - Student Research Workshop*, Toronto, Canada.

Marc-Alexandre Côté, Ákos Kádár, Xingdi Yuan, Ben Kybartas, Tavian Barnes, Emery Fine, James Moore, Ruo Yu Tao, Matthew Hausknecht, Layla El Asri, Mahmoud Adada, Wendy Tay, and Adam Trischler. 2018. Textworld: A learning environment for text-based games.

Ignacio X Domínguez, Rogelio E Cardona-Rivera, James K Vance, and David L Roberts. 2016. The mimesis effect: The effect of roles on player choice in interactive narrative role-playing games. In *Proc. of the CHI conference on human factors in computing systems*.

Sarah E. Finch, James D. Finch, and Jinho D. Choi. 2023. Don't forget your abc's: Evaluating the state-of-the-art in chat-oriented dialogue systems. In *Proc. of ACL - Student Research Workshop*.

D. Fox Harrell and Jichen Zhu. 2009. Agency play: Dimensions of agency for interactive narrative design. In *Proc. of the AAAI Spring Symposium: Intelligent Narrative Technologies II*.

Matthew Hausknecht, Prithviraj Ammanabrolu, Marc-Alexandre Côté, and Xingdi Yuan. 2020. Interactive fiction games: A colossal adventure. In *Proc. of AAAI*.

Jing Yu Koh, Jason Baldridge, Honglak Lee, and Yinfei Yang. 2021. Text-to-image generation grounded by fine-grained user attention. In *Proc. of WACV*.

Jiazheng Li, Runcong Zhao, Yulan He, and Lin Gui. 2023. Overprompt: Enhancing chatgpt capabilities through an efficient in-context learning approach. In *NeurIPS R0-FoMo Workshop*.

Long Ouyang, Jeff Wu, Xu Jiang, Diogo Almeida, Carroll L. Wainwright, Pamela Mishkin, Chong Zhang, Sandhini Agarwal, Katarina Slama, Alex Ray, John Schulman, Jacob Hilton, Fraser Kelton, Luke E. Miller, Maddie Simens, Amanda Askell, Peter Welinder, Paul Francis Christiano, Jan Leike, and Ryan J. Lowe. 2022. Training language models to follow instructions with human feedback. In *Proc. of NeurIPS*.

Joon Sung Park, Joseph C. O'Brien, Carrie J. Cai, Meredith Ringel Morris, Percy Liang, and Michael S. Bernstein. 2023. Generative agents: Interactive simulacra of human behavior.

Mark Owen Riedl and Vadim Bulitko. 2012. Interactive narrative: An intelligent systems approach. *AI Magazine*.

Robin Rombach, Andreas Blattmann, Dominik Lorenz, Patrick Esser, and Björn Ommer. 2022. High-resolution image synthesis with latent diffusion models. In *Proc. of CVPR*.

Uriel Singer, Adam Polyak, Thomas Hayes, Xi Yin, Jie An, Songyang Zhang, Qiyuan Hu, Harry Yang, Oron Ashual, Oran Gafni, Devi Parikh, Sonal Gupta, and Yaniv Taigman. 2022. Make-a-video: Text-to-video generation without text-video data.

Hugo Touvron, Louis Martin, Kevin Stone, Peter Albert, Amjad Almahairi, Yasmine Babaei, Nikolay Bashlykov, Soumya Batra, Prajjwal Bhargava, Shruti Bhosale, Dan Bikel, Lukas Blecher, Cristian Canton Ferrer, Moya Chen, Guillem Cucurull, David Esiobu, Jude Fernandes, Jeremy Fu, Wenyin Fu, Brian Fuller, Cynthia Gao, Vedanuj Goswami, Naman Goyal, Anthony Hartshorn, Saghar Hosseini, Rui Hou, Hakan Inan, Marcin Kardas, Viktor Kerkez, Madian Khabsa, Isabel Kloumann, Artem Korenev, Punit Singh Koura, Marie-Anne Lachaux, Thibaut Lavril, Jenya Lee, Diana Liskovich, Yinghai Lu, Yuning Mao, Xavier Martinet, Todor Mihaylov, Pushkar Mishra, Igor Molybog, Yixin Nie, Andrew Poulton, Jeremy Reizenstein, Rashi Rungta, Kalyan Saladi, Alan Schelten, Ruan Silva, Eric Michael Smith, Ranjan Subramanian, Xiaoqing Ellen Tan, Binh Tang, Ross Taylor, Adina Williams, Jian Xiang Kuan, Puxin Xu, Zheng Yan, Iliyan Zarov, Yuchen Zhang, Angela Fan, Melanie Kambadur, Sharan Narang, Aurelien Rodriguez, Robert Stojnic, Sergey Edunov, and Thomas Scialom. 2023. Llama 2: Open foundation and fine-tuned chat models.

Shenzhi Wang, Chang Liu, Zilong Zheng, Siyuan Qi, Shuo Chen, Qisen Yang, Andrew Zhao, Chaofei Wang, Shiji Song, and Gao Huang. 2023. Avalon's game of thoughts: Battle against deception through recursive contemplation.

Ying Xu, Dakuo Wang, Mo Yu, Daniel Ritchie, Bingsheng Yao, Tongshuang Wu, Zheng Zhang, Toby Li, Nora Bradford, Branda Sun, Tran Hoang, Yisi Sang, Yufang Hou, Xiaojuan Ma, Diyi Yang, Nanyun Peng, Zhou Yu, and Mark Warschauer. 2022. Fantastic questions and where to find them: FairytaleQA – an authentic dataset for narrative comprehension. In *Proc. of ACL*.

Yuzhuang Xu, Shuo Wang, Peng Li, Fuwen Luo, Xiaolong Wang, Weidong Liu, and Yang Liu. 2023. Exploring large language models for communication games: An empirical study on werewolf.

Lixing Zhu, Runcong Zhao, Lin Gui, and Yulan He. 2023. Are nlp models good at tracing thoughts: An overview of narrative understanding. In *Proc. of EMNLP Findings*.

A Response Format Errors

Unwanted Output GPT is trained as a chatbot, so it tends to provide an explanation before generating the required output, often leading to the inclusion of non-essential content. An example is shown below:

```
In the given list, there are a few
characters that can be considered
duplicates based on certain keywords or
names:
```

Significantly, adopting a JSON format mitigates this issue.(Li et al., 2023)

Incomplete Response However, when all tasks are assigned to GPT in one go, the complexity often results in omissions of required content. Therefore, we divide the task into several steps, such as extracting characters, events, and settings, as discussed in Section 2.1.

Additionally, there are cases where the model generates incomplete outputs, and this is not due to a maximum token limit. The cause remains unknown due to the opaque nature of the GPT model. In such scenario, NarrativePlay outputs either null results or some predefined values, depending on whether there will be a potential disruption to the narrative flow.

Syntax Error When GPT is tasked with generating text with specific structures, it might not always do so correctly due to its limitations in understanding complex formatting rules. Syntax errors can cause challenges in parsing JSON. Here are some examples of common errors:

1. Missing commas. We implement post-processing to address issues such as missing syntax, and, if errors persist, we instruct the GPT model to rectify them.

```
{“keywords”: [“town”, “chocolate factory
”, “small”, “impoverished”, “mysterious”]
␣“description’: “The town is a small and
impoverished place with dull and dreary
surroundings. Most of the residents live
 in humble conditions, struggling to
make ends meet.’}
```

2. Mixed double quotes and single quotes. JSON need double quote on string to be parsed. We found that, in most cases, this issue can be addressed by using examples with double quotes in the prompt, guiding GPT to adhere to our preferred format.

```
{‘keywords’: [‘town’, ‘chocolate factory
’, ‘small’, ‘impoverished’, ‘mysterious
’], ‘description’: ‘The town is a small
and impoverished place with dull and
dreary surroundings. Most of the
residents live in humble conditions,
struggling to make ends meet.’}
```

3. Quotation marks within the value of a dictionary. A similar correction can be achieved in most cases by adding a backslash before double quotes in the prompt examples to guide GPT to use the escape character.

```
{“speaker”: “Grandpa Joe”, “content”:
“And then Mr Slugworth’s factory began
making sugar balloons that you could
blow up to huge sizes before you popped
them with a pin and gobbled them up. And
```

```
so on, and so on. And Mr Willy Wonka
tore his beard and shouted, "This is
terrible! I shall be ruined! There are
spies everywhere!"}
```

B Main Storyline Extraction

Because of the input limitation, we first divide an input narrative into smaller chunks, ensuring that individual sentences are kept intact.

A notable challenge when utilising LLMs for Information Extraction (IE) is that the LLM-generated outputs do not always follow our desirable format, as shown in §A. In our context, we employ the JSON formatting, system prompts, and example outputs to mitigate such errors. Additionally, we implement post-processing to address issues such as missing punctuation, and, if errors persist, we instruct the GPT model to rectify them. Despite these attempts, we can only reduce, not completely eliminate, the output formatting errors. In scenarios where the output format remains incorrect, NarrativePlay outputs either null results or some predefined values, depending on whether there will be a potential disruption to the narrative flow. For instance, if the intent of a character can not be extracted, the system will leave this field empty. Conversely, for character appearance, we randomly choose a hair colour and an eye colour as the default. Leaving the character appearance field blank may lead to inconsistent attributes, for example, the character's eye colour may change from blue to brown in the middle of a narrative.

We employ the most recent ChatGPT model `gpt-3.5-turbo` for main storyline extraction and example outputs obtained from the story using GPT-4 to boost performance. In what follows, we describe in details how we extract various narrative elements using ChatGPT. We highlighted the prompt and variable(s) in blue in our designed prompt template below:

B.1 Prompt for Personality Extraction

For an input narrative S, our initial step is to solicit a list of the characters involved:

```
Find all characters in the given story, return in
JSON format
Extract characters in the story, here is
 the format example: [{"name": "Charlie
Bucket"}, {"name": "Grandpa Joe"}]
Here is the story: S
```

To establish the personality for each character as an interactive agent, we extract their core traits using the following prompt:

```
Derive details pertaining to the specified
character from the provided text. If the
text lacks adequate details, make an inference.
Present the output in JSON format
Generate the character background
summary, keywords, and the intent of c.
The output format is {"summary": "here is
 the background", "keywords":
"personality keywords", "intent":
"character's intent"}.
Here is the story: S
```

In order to generate picture for each character, we extract their appearance using the prompt:

```
Imagine the appearance of the specified character
from the provided text. Present the output in
JSON format.
Generate the appearance, gender and age
of c. {character description} The output
format is {"appearance": "brown hair,
blue eyes, poor", "gender": "male", "age
": "middle age"}.
```

In order to match the voice of each character, we classify their gender and age using the prompt:

```
Identify the character's gender and age. Present
the output in JSON format.
Identify the gender and age of c.
{character description} For gender, choose
from 'male' or 'female'. For age, choose
 from 'child', 'yongth', 'middle age', '
old age'. The output format is {"gender
": "male", "age": "child"}.
```

B.2 Prompt for Event Extraction

To eliminate the need to extract the timeline of the story, we link each event with its corresponding characters and locations. This strategy is particularly useful for narratives where multiple events could be described simultaneously, making it difficult to disentangle them. We assume that a character cannot be present in multiple events simultaneously. Though this assumption may not hold all the time, we found that it works well in our evaluated scenarios. We leave the extraction of more complex events as our future work.

To extract events, we employ the following prompt:

```
Identify all events in the given story, return in
JSON format.
Extract a list of main events. Each
event should include the event name,
characters involved in the event,
location, and a detailed description.
Here is a format example: [{"event":
"Grandpa Joe telling story about Prince
Pondicherry", "character": "Grandpa Joe,
Charlie", "location": "Grandparents' room
", " description": "Grandpa Joe recounts
```

```
the story of Prince Pondicherry, an
Indian prince who commissioned Mr Willy
Wonka to build a colossal palace
entirely out of chocolate. The palace
had one hundred rooms, and everything,
from the bricks to the furniture, was
made of chocolate. Despite Mr Wonka's
warning that the palace wouldn't last
long, the prince refused to eat it and
intended to live in it. However, on a
hot day, the palace melted, leaving the
prince swimming in a lake of chocolate.
The family finds the story amusing,
highlighting Mr Wonka's incredible
creations."}]
Here is the story: S
```

B.3 Prompt for Conversation Extraction

To extract conversations that occur within the event, we employ the following prompt:

```
Find all conversation, their speakers and content
in the given story, return in JSON format.
Extract the conversation link to the
given event as a list: {event description}
Here is a format example: [{"speaker":
"Grandpa Joe", "content": "Not people,
Charlie. Not ordinary people, anyway."},
 {"speaker": "Charlie Bucket", "content":
 "Then who?"}, {"speaker": "Grandpa Joe",
 "content": "Ah-ha . . . That's it, you
see . . . That's another of Mr Willy
Wonka's clevernesses."}]
Here is the story: S
```

B.4 Prompt for Setting Extraction

Existing research predominantly concentrates on agent behaviours within manually constructed sandboxes, where environments, agents, and actions are pre-defined (Côté et al., 2018; Hausknecht et al., 2020). However, constructing sandboxes for narratives with diverse backgrounds and settings is resource-intensive and lacks generalisability.

To visualise the settings, we extract the description of the location using the following prompt:

```
Generate keywords and descriptions for the given
locations in the story. The description should
only describe the environment and NOT include
people. The output should be in JSON format.
For the location: l
Extract keywords and description of the
location looking. For example, with
location "small wooden house", output {
"keyword": "Cozy, cramped, inadequate
space", "description": "The small wooden
house with its wooden exterior has
limited space, and there was only one
bed."}. With location "town", output {
"keyword": "chocolate factory, small,
impoverished, mysterious", "description":
 "Most residents live in humble,
impoverished conditions, with dull and
dreary surroundings. The town\'s
ordinary and monotonous appearance
starkly contrasts the wonder and magic
that unfolds within the walls of the
famous chocolate factory."}
Here is the story: S
```

B.5 Prompt for Conversation Response

To initialise a conversation with the user, we employ the following prompt:

```
As {character}, engage in a dialogue with the
intent of {intent}. Respond to the
conversation using the given context or memories
and limit your response to under 50 words. Please
submit your response in JSON format.
YOU are: {character}
{event description}
Initiates a conversation with {user's
character}.
Here is your memory: {memory}
Give your response in format {"response
": "here is the response"}.
```

To generate response for the user input, we employ the following prompt:

```
As {character}, engage in a dialogue with the
intent of {intent}. Respond to the
conversation using the given context or memories
and limit your response to under 50 words. Please
submit your response in JSON format.
YOU are: {character}
{event description}
Here is your memory: {memory}
Response according to what SAYS to you:
{user input} Give your response in format
{"response": "here is the response"}.
```

C Further Evaluation Details

C.1 Evaluation Instruction

For each evaluation aspect, we provide rubric and evaluation examples to both human annotator and LLaMA for scoring. For example, in the event where Mr Wonka gives Charlie and Grandpa Joe mugs of chocolate from the river remarking on their seemingly hungry appearance, we ask Charlie Bucket "If you were to spend time with someone, who would it be, and why?". Then Charlie's response will be scored from the following four aspects.

(1) ***Consistency*** Assessing if the response conflicts with prior settings. We give inconsistent, partially consistent and consistent example responses as follows:

- Inconsistent Response from Charlie: *"I want to spend time with Mr. Salt, because we share a love for chocolate."* It contradicts Charlie's character. Mr. Salt is Veruca Salt's father,

Category	Question
Character	Who are you? What is your purpose?
Clarification	Who is [name], and why do we need to locate him?
Relationships	Do you recognise that lady? Are you acquainted with her?
Strategy	What is the most effective way to solve this puzzle?
Hypothetical (CCF)	If you owned this factory, what would you do?
Hypothetical (MOE)	If your friend were to be killed and the legal system could not bring the perpetrator to justice, what would you do?

Table 4: Evaluation Questions

not known for loving chocolate, and Charlie's relationship with him is not portrayed as particularly close.

- Partially Consistent Response from Charlie: *"Look, Mother, look! I've found the last Golden Ticket! It's mine! I bought two bars of chocolate and one of them had the Golden Ticket! It's the fifth one, Mother!"* The response is in line with Charlie's character but contradicts recent events: Charlie has already had the ticket for a while, and is currently visiting the factory.

- Consistent Response from Charlie: *"If I could spend time with anyone, it would be Mr. Willy Wonka. I am fascinated by his chocolate factory and the magic he creates with chocolate. I would love to learn from him and see the wonders of his factory firsthand."* The answer is in line with Charlie's character, as depicted in the narrative. Charlie is known to admire Willy Wonka and his magical chocolate factory. The response, while not directly mentioning the event of receiving a chocolate mug from Mr. Wonka, remains consistent with the established context and Charlie's fascination with Mr. Wonka and his factory.

We utilise the following prompt to generate consistent evaluation from LLaMA:

```
Evaluate the consistency of the agent's response
based on the given setup, which includes the
context event, the question asked, and the agent
who is answering the question. The output should
be in JSON format.
Consistency evaluates if the response
conflicts with prior settings. Based on
the consistency of the agent's response,
category it into "Inconsistent",
"Partially Consistent", or "Consistent".
```

(2) ***Relevance*** Evaluating if the response disregards the player's recent inquiry. Here are some example responses identified as inrelevant, partially relevant and relevant:

- Inrelevant Response from Charlie: *"Look, Mother, look! I've found the last Golden Ticket! It's mine! I bought two bars of chocolate and one of them had the Golden Ticket! It's the fifth one, Mother!"* It totally ignores the question.

- Partially Relevant Response from Charlie: *"I enjoy reading books in my free time. My favourite author is Roald Dahl."* The response tries to answer the question but end up being off-topic.

- Relevant Response from Charlie: *"If I could spend time with anyone, it would be Mr. Willy Wonka. I am fascinated by his chocolate factory and the magic he creates with chocolate. I would love to learn from him and see the wonders of his factory firsthand."* The answer directly responds to and answers the question.

To acquire relevance evaluation from LLaMA, we utilize the following prompt:

```
Evaluate the relevance of the agent's response
based on the given setup, which includes the
context event, the question asked, and the agent
who is answering the question. The output should
be in JSON format.
Relevance evaluates whether the response
 ignores what the player just said.
Based on the relevance of the agent's
response, category it into "Inrelevant",
 "Partially Relevant", or "Relevant".
```

(3) ***Empathy***: Evaluates whether the response showcases suitable emotional reactions and accurate understanding of emotions as a human would. For instance, if Charlie asks Grandpa Joe, "who are you", a human-like response would include an emotional reaction such as anger or sadness, which is often missed in agents' responses. We category response empathy into non-empathetic, no clue, and empathetic, and list three corresponding instances:

- Non-empathetic Response from Charlie: *"Grandpa Joe is my grandpa. The last time*

I met him, I jumped into the camera and disappeared! It was awesome!" He was likely shocked or scared due to the physical transformation after jumping into the camera, so the emotion here is incorrect.

- No Clue Response from Charlie: *"Grandpa Joe is Charlie's grandfather. Last time, he was helping Charlie out of the chocolate river."* No clear sentiment is shown in this response.

- Empathetic Response from Charlie: *"Grandpa Joe is one of my boring, old grandparents. The last time I met him, he tried to stop me from watching TV and made me go outside to play. It was so annoying!"* Even this is incoherent, it shows correct emotion of the character.

To generate empathy evaluation from LLaMA, we employ the following prompt:

```
Evaluate the empathy of the agent's response
based on the given setup, which includes the
context event, the question asked, and the agent
who is answering the question. The output should
be in JSON format.
Empathy evaluates whether the response
showcases suitable emotional reactions
and accurate understanding of emotions
as a human would.
Based on the empathy of the agent's
response, category it into "Non-
empathetic", "No Clue", or "Empathetic.
```

(4) ***Commonsense*** Evaluates how much the response fits the narrative world. Followings are two example responses identified as opposing or conforming in commonsense:

- Opposing Response from Charlie: *"Grandpa Joe is a giraffe, and the last time I saw him, he was flying in the sky."* This statement defies common sense in two ways. First, Grandpa Joe is a human, not a giraffe. Second, neither humans nor giraffes can fly in the context given.

- Conforming Response from Charlie: *"Grandpa Joe is Charlie Bucket's grandfather. The last time I met him, we were both inside Willy Wonka's Chocolate Factory. He was accompanying Charlie during the tour."* It accurately identifies who Grandpa Joe is and provides a reasonable recounting of their last meeting according to the narrative.

We employ the following prompt, in order to generate commonsense evaluation from LLaMA:

```
Evaluate the commonsense of the agent's response
based on the given setup, which includes the
context event, the question asked, and the agent
who is answering the question. The output should
be in JSON format.
Commonsense evaluates how much the
response fits the narrative world.
Based on the commonsense of the agent's
response, category it into "Opposing",
or "Conforming".
```

C.2 Setting

For major characters, we further assessed their answers across different turns. This distinction is critical since narratives typically depict major characters as dynamic, undergoing change, whereas minor characters remain static. We used the prompt without any memory as our baseline.

C.3 Annotators

For the evaluation process, we enlisted the expertise of three PhD students from computer science backgrounds. These annotators have read and comprehended the two narratives provided. Prior to the tasks, they underwent training on evaluation schema. They were compensated at an hourly rate of $31.92, and each task was estimated to take about 8 hours to complete.

DP-NMT: Scalable Differentially-Private Machine Translation

Timour Igamberdiev[1] **Doan Nam Long Vu**[1] **Felix Künnecke**[1]
Zhuo Yu[1] **Jannik Holmer**[1] **Ivan Habernal**[2]
Trustworthy Human Language Technologies
[1] Department of Computer Science, Technical University of Darmstadt
[2] Department of Computer Science, Paderborn University
timour.igamberdiev@tu-darmstadt.de
www.trusthlt.org

Abstract

Neural machine translation (NMT) is a widely popular text generation task, yet there is a considerable research gap in the development of privacy-preserving NMT models, despite significant data privacy concerns for NMT systems. Differentially private stochastic gradient descent (DP-SGD) is a popular method for training machine learning models with concrete privacy guarantees; however, the implementation specifics of training a model with DP-SGD are not always clarified in existing models, with differing software libraries used and code bases not always being public, leading to reproducibility issues. To tackle this, we introduce `DP-NMT`, an open-source framework for carrying out research on privacy-preserving NMT with DP-SGD, bringing together numerous models, datasets, and evaluation metrics in one systematic software package. Our goal is to provide a platform for researchers to advance the development of privacy-preserving NMT systems, keeping the specific details of the DP-SGD algorithm transparent and intuitive to implement. We run a set of experiments on datasets from both general and privacy-related domains to demonstrate our framework in use. We make our framework publicly available and welcome feedback from the community.[1]

1 Introduction

Privacy-preserving natural language processing (NLP) has been a recently growing field, in large part due to an increasing amount of concern regarding data privacy. This is especially a concern in the context of modern neural networks memorizing training data that may contain sensitive information (Carlini et al., 2021). While there has been a body of research investigating privacy for text classification tasks (Senge et al., 2022) and language models (Hoory et al., 2021; Anil et al., 2022), there has not been as much focus on text generation tasks, in particular neural machine translation (NMT). However, NMT is particularly worrying from a privacy perspective, due to a variety of machine translation services available online that users send their personal data to. This includes built-in NMT services to existing websites, e-mail clients, and search engines. After data has been sent to these systems, it may be further processed and used in the development of the NMT system (Kamocki and O'Regan, 2016), which has a significant risk of being memorized if trained in a non-private manner.

One of the most popular methods for tackling this privacy issue is differential privacy (DP), being a formal framework which provides probabilistic guarantees that the contribution of any single data point to some analysis is bounded. In the case of NLP and machine learning (ML), this means that a data point associated with some individual which is included in the model's training data cannot stand out 'too much' in the learning process of the model.

The DP-SGD algorithm (Abadi et al., 2016b) is one of the most standard methods to achieve this for ML systems, yet implementations of DP-SGD often lack some technical details on the specifics of the algorithm. In particular, this includes the privacy amplification method assumed for calculating the privacy budget ε when composed over all training iterations of the model. This means that the exact *strength of the privacy protection* that the resulting systems provide is not clear, with the 'standard' **random shuffling** method for iterating over batches providing a weaker privacy guarantee for the training data than **Poisson sampling**. With different implementations using different software libraries, the community currently does not have a consistent platform for conducting experiments for scalable differentially private systems, such as NMT.

To tackle this problem, we develop a modular framework for conducting research on private NMT in a transparent and reproducible manner. Our pri-

[1] `https://github.com/trusthlt/dp-nmt`

Proceedings of the 18th Conference of the European Chapter of the Association for Computational Linguistics
System Demonstrations, pages 94–105
March 17-22, 2024 ©2024 Association for Computational Linguistics

mary goal is to allow for a deeper investigation into the applications of DP for NMT, all while ensuring that important theoretical details of the DP-SGD methodology are properly reflected in the implementation. Following previous work on DP-SGD (Subramani et al., 2021; Anil et al., 2022), we implement our framework in the JAX library (Bradbury et al., 2018), which provides powerful tools that help to reduce the significant computational overhead of DP-SGD, allowing for scalability in implementing larger systems and more extended training regimes.

Our primary contributions are as follows. First, we present `DP-NMT`, a framework developed in JAX for leading research on NMT with DP-SGD. It includes a growing list of available NMT models, different evaluation schemes, as well as numerous datasets available out of the box, including standard datasets used for NMT research and more specific privacy-related domains. Second, we demonstrate our framework by running experiments on these NMT datasets, providing one of the first investigations into privacy-preserving NMT. Importantly, we compare the random shuffling and Poisson sampling methods for iterating over training data when using DP-SGD. We demonstrate that, in addition to the theoretical privacy guarantee, there may indeed be differences in the model performance when utilizing each of the two settings.

2 DP-SGD and subsampling

We describe the main ideas of differential privacy (DP) and DP-SGD in Appendix A. We refer to Abadi et al. (2016b); Igamberdiev and Habernal (2022); Habernal (2021, 2022); Hu et al. (2024) for a more comprehensive explanation.

A key aspect of the DP-SGD algorithm (see Alg. 1 in the Appendix) is **privacy amplification by subsampling**, in which a stronger privacy guarantee can be obtained for a given dataset x when a subset of this dataset is first randomly sampled (Kasiviswanathan et al., 2011; Beimel et al., 2014). If the sampling probability is q, then the overall privacy guarantee can be analyzed as being approximately $q\varepsilon$.

A key point here is the nature of this sampling procedure and the resulting privacy guarantee. The moments accountant of Abadi et al. (2016b), which is an improvement on the strong composition theorem (Dwork et al., 2010) for composing multiple DP mechanisms, assumes Poisson sampling. Under this procedure, *each data point* is included in a mini-batch with probability $q = L/N$, with L being the *lot size* and N the size of the dataset. An alternative method to Poisson sampling is uniform sampling, in which mini-batches of a fixed size are independently drawn at each training iteration (Wang et al., 2019; Balle et al., 2018).

In practice, however, many modern implementations of DP-SGD utilize **random shuffling**, with the dataset split into fixed-size mini-batches. Several training iterations thus form an epoch, in which each training data point appears exactly once, in contrast to Poisson sampling for which the original notion of 'epoch' is not quite suitable, since each data point can appear in any training iteration and there is no "single passing of the training data through the model". In Abadi et al. (2016b), the term *epoch* is redefined as $\frac{N}{L}$ lots, being essentially an expectation of the number of batches when utilizing N data points for training the model. While simply shuffling the dataset can indeed result in privacy amplification (Erlingsson et al., 2019; Feldman et al., 2022), the nature of the corresponding privacy guarantee is **not the same** as the guarantee achieved by Poisson sampling, generally being weaker. We refer to Ponomareva et al. (2023, Section 4.3) for further details.

3 Related work

3.1 Applications of DP-SGD to NLP

The application of DP-SGD to the field of NLP has seen an increasing amount of attention in recent years. A large part of these studies focus on differentially private pre-training or fine-tuning of language models (Hoory et al., 2021; Yu et al., 2021; Basu et al., 2021; Xu et al., 2021; Anil et al., 2022; Ponomareva et al., 2022; Shi et al., 2022; Wu et al., 2022; Li et al., 2022; Yin and Habernal, 2022; Mattern et al., 2022; Hansen et al., 2022; Senge et al., 2022). A primary goal is to reach the best possible privacy/utility trade-off for the trained models, in which the highest performance is achieved with the strictest privacy guarantees.

In the general machine learning setting, the exact sampling method that is used for selecting batches at each training iteration is often omitted, since this is generally not a core detail of the training methodology. Possibly for this reason, in the case of privately training a model with DP-SGD, the sampling method is also often not mentioned. However, in contrast to the non-private setting, here **sampling**

is actually a core detail of the algorithm, which has an **impact on the privacy accounting procedure**. In the case that experimental descriptions with DP-SGD include mentions of *epochs* without further clarification, this in fact suggests the use of the random shuffling scheme, as opposed to Poisson sampling, as described in Section 2. In addition, sometimes the code base is not publicly available, in which case it is not possible to validate the sampling scheme used.

Finally, standard implementations of DP-SGD in the Opacus (Yousefpour et al., 2021) and TensorFlow Privacy (Abadi et al., 2016a) libraries often include descriptions of DP-SGD implementations with randomly shuffled fixed-size batches. For instance, while Opacus currently has a `DPDataLoader` class which by default uses their `UniformWithReplacementSampler` class for facilitating the use of Poisson sampling, some of the tutorials currently offered appear to also use static batches instead.[2] A similar situation is true for TensorFlow Privacy.[3] While these libraries support per-example gradients as well, several core features of JAX make it the fastest and most scalable option for implementing DP-SGD (Subramani et al., 2021), described in more detail below in Section 4.

We therefore stress the importance of clarifying implementation details that may not be as vital in the general machine learning setting, but are very relevant in the private setting. As described by Ponomareva et al. (2023), it is an open theoretical question as to how random shuffling and Poisson sampling differ with respect to privacy amplification gains, with known privacy guarantees being weaker for the former.

3.2 Private neural machine translation

The task of private neural machine translation remains largely unexplored, with currently no studies we could find that incorporate DP-SGD to an NMT system. Wang et al. (2021) investigate NMT in a federated learning setup (McMahan et al., 2017), with differential privacy included in the aggregation of parameters from each local model, adding Laplace noise to these parameters. Several other studies explore NMT with federated learning, but do not incorporate differential privacy in the methodology (Roosta et al., 2021; Passban et al., 2022; Du et al., 2022). Hisamoto et al. (2020), applied a membership inference attack (Shokri et al., 2017) on a 6-layer Transformer (Vaswani et al., 2017) model in the scenario of NMT as a service, with the goal of clients being able to verify whether their data was used to train an NMT model. Finally, Kamocki and O'Regan (2016) address the general topic of privacy issues for machine translation as a service. The authors examine how these MT services fit European data protection laws, noting the legal nature of various types of data processing that can occur by both the provider of such a service, as well as by the users themselves.

4 Description of software

The aim of our system is to offer a reliable and scalable approach to achieve differentially private machine translation. Figure 1 illustrates the central structure of our system. The user can upload a translation dataset that is either accessible on the HuggingFace Datasets Hub[4] or is provided by us out of the box, and integrate it seamlessly for both training and efficient privacy accounting, utilizing HuggingFace's Datasets library (Lhoest et al., 2021).

Accelerated DP-SGD with JAX and Flax Our goal is to accelerate DP-SGD training through the use of a Transformer model implemented with JAX and Flax (Bradbury et al., 2018; Heek et al., 2023). The speed of training DP-SGD in the framework can be considerably enhanced through vectorization, just-in-time (JIT) compilation, and static graph optimization (Subramani et al., 2021). JIT compilation and automatic differentiation are defined and established on the XLA compiler. JAX's main transformation methods of interest for fast DP-SGD are `grad`, `vmap`, and `pmap`, offering the ability to mix these operations as needed (Yin and Habernal, 2022). In the DP-SGD scenario, combining `grad` and `vmap` facilitates efficient computation of per-example gradients by vectorizing the gradient calculation along the batch dimension (Anil et al., 2022). Additionally, our training step is decorated by `pmap` to leverage the XLA compiler on multiple GPUs, significantly accelerating training speed. The framework offers to conduct experiments with multiple encoder-decoder models

[2] `https://opacus.ai/tutorials/building_image_classifier`.

[3] `https://www.tensorflow.org/responsible_ai/privacy/tutorials/classification_privacy`.

[4] `https://huggingface.co/datasets`

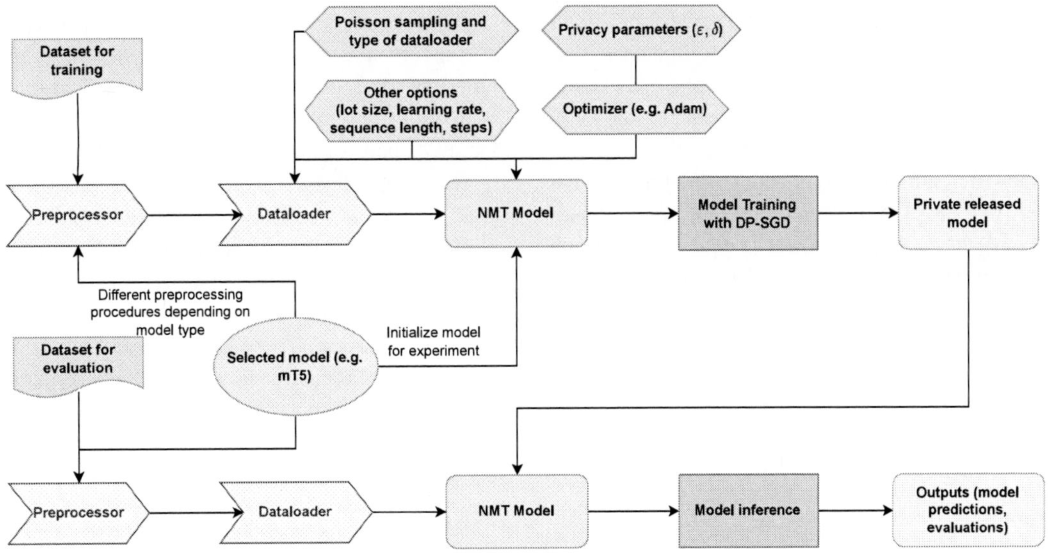

Figure 1: Framework Pipeline. Similar components are represented with different colors. Green: Dataset selection. Blue: Experimental configurations (including privacy settings). Grey: Dataset preparation. Orange: Model-specific elements. Red: Model training. Purple: Model inference. Yellow: Output of experiments.

and integrate new seq2seq models, in addition to existing ones, such as mBART (Liu et al., 2020), T5 (Raffel et al., 2020), and mT5 (Xue et al., 2021). When selecting a model, the corresponding preprocessor will prepare the dataset accordingly. This allows the software to be flexible and modular, enabling researchers to exchange models and datasets to perform a range of private NMT experiments.

Model training and inference The experimental workflow of our framework works in two phases, namely model training and model inference. For both phases, the process begins with a data loader that can be either a framework-provided dataset or a user-specified dataset. Subsequently, the loaded dataset is prepared based on user-defined parameters, including standard options (e.g. sequence length), as well as parameters relating to DP-SGD (e.g. data loader type, sampling method, and batch size). After selecting the model, the user separates it into different procedures according to the model type. Subsequently, the model is initiated, optionally from a checkpoint that has already been trained. Then, the primary experiment is carried out based on the specified mode, which includes (1) fine-tuning on an existing dataset, (2) using an existing fine-tuned checkpoint to continue fine-tuning on the dataset, or (3) inference without teacher forcing.

Integrating `DPDataloader` from Opacus One notable improvement in our software is the incorporation of the `DPDataloader` from Opacus (Yousefpour et al., 2021) for out-of-the-box Poisson sampling. This is different from the existing approaches in JAX used by Yin and Habernal (2022); Subramani et al. (2021); Ponomareva et al. (2022), who employ iteration over a randomly shuffled dataset, which theoretically provides weaker DP bounds. Evaluation metrics such as BLEU (Papineni et al., 2002) and BERTScore (Zhang et al., 2020) are available for each mode. We incorporate the differential privacy component during the training phase of the systems.

Engineering challenges for LLMs Throughout development, we encountered multiple engineering challenges. Initially, our academic budget limitations made it difficult to train a larger model due to the significant memory consumption during per-example gradient calculations. Consequently, we anticipated a relatively small physical batch size on each GPU. We attempted to freeze parts of the model for faster training and improved memory efficiency, as Senge et al. (2022) noted. However, in Flax, the freezing mechanism only occurs during the optimization step and does not affect per-example gradient computation. Therefore, it does not solve the issue of limited physical batch sizes. Multiple reports suggest that increasing the lot size leads to better DP-SGD performance due to an improved gradient signal-to-noise ratio and an increased likelihood of non-duplicated example sampling across the entire dataset (Hoory et al., 2021; Yin and Habernal, 2022; Anil et al., 2022). However, compared to previous work on large models that mostly relied on dataset iteration (Yin and Habernal, 2022; Ponomareva et al., 2022), implementing the original DP-SGD with large lots using Poisson sampling, a large language model (LLM) with millions of parameters, and on multiple GPUs presents a challenge that makes comparison difficult. To address this issue, we first conduct a sampling process on a large dataset, then divide it into smaller subsets that the GPU can handle. We then build up the large lot using gradient accumulation. It is crucial that we refrain from implementing any additional normalization operations that might change the gradient sensitivity (Ponomareva et al., 2023; Hoory et al., 2021), prior to the noise addition step.

5 Experiments

To demonstrate our framework in use, fill the gaps on current knowledge of the privacy/utility trade-off for the task of NMT, as well as examine the effects of using random shuffling vs. Poisson sampling, we run a series of experiments with DP-SGD on several NMT datasets, using a variety of privacy budgets.

5.1 Datasets

We utilize datasets comprising two main types of settings. The first is the general NMT setting for comparing our models with previous work and investigating the effectiveness of DP-SGD on a common NMT dataset. For this we utilize WMT-16 (Bojar et al., 2016), using the German-English (DE-EN) language pair as the focus of our experiments.

The second setting is the more specific target domain of private texts that we are aiming to protect with differentially private NMT. For the sake of reproducibility and ethical considerations, we utilize datasets that *imitate* the actual private setting of processing sensitive information, namely business communications and medical notes, but are themselves publicly available. The first dataset is the Business Scene Dialogue corpus (BSD) (Rikters et al., 2019), which is a collection of fictional business conversations in various scenarios (e.g. "face-to-face", "phone call", "meeting"), with parallel data for Japanese and English. While the original corpus consists of half English $\rightarrow$ Japanese and half Japanese $\rightarrow$ English scenarios, we combine both into a single Japanese $\rightarrow$ English (JA-EN) language pair for our experiments.

The second dataset is ClinSPEn-CC (Neves et al., 2022), which is a collection of parallel COVID-19 clinical cases in English and Spanish, originally part of the biomedical translation task of WMT-22. We utilize this corpus in the Spanish $\rightarrow$ English (ES-EN) direction. These latter two datasets simulate a realistic scenario where a company or public authority may train an NMT model on private data, for later public use. We present overall statistics for each dataset in Table 1.

Dataset	Lang. Pair	# Trn.+Vld.	# Test
WMT-16	DE-EN	4,551,054	2,999
BSD	JA-EN	22,051	2,120
ClinSPEn-CC	ES-EN	1,065	2,870

Table 1: Dataset statistics. Trn.: Train, Vld.: Validation.

5.2 Experimental setup

For each of the above three datasets, we fine-tune a pre-trained mT5 model (Xue et al., 2021), opting for the `mT5-small`[5] version due to computational capacity limitations described in Section 4. We compare ε values of ∞, 1000, 5, and 1, representing the non-private, weakly private, moderately private, and very private scenarios, respectively (see Lee and Clifton (2011); Hsu et al. (2014); Weiss et al. (2023) for a more detailed discussion on selecting the 'right' ε value). We fix the value of δ to 10^{-8} for all experiments, staying well below the recommended $\delta \ll \frac{1}{N}$ condition (Abadi et al., 2016b).

For all of the above configurations, we compare two methods of selecting batches of data points from the dataset for our DP-SGD configurations, namely **random shuffling** and **Poisson sampling**. Following previous work (Hoory et al., 2021; Anil et al., 2022; Yin and Habernal, 2022), we utilize very large batch sizes for both of these methods, setting L to a large value and building up the resulting drawn batches with gradient accumulation for the latter method, as described in Section 4. We refer to Appendix B for a more detailed description of our hyperparameter search. We evaluate our

[5] `https://huggingface.co/google/mt5-small`

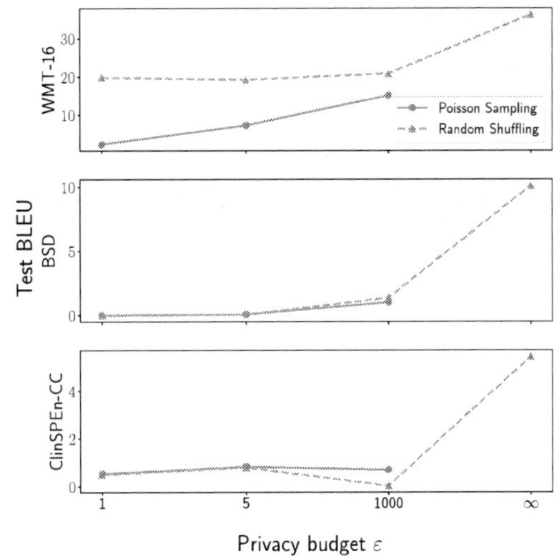

Figure 2: Test BLEU scores for each of the three datasets using varying privacy budgets, comparing the random shuffling and Poisson sampling methods to iterate over the dataset. Non-private results are additionally shown for each dataset ($\varepsilon = \infty$) with random shuffling. Lower ε corresponds to a stronger privacy guarantee.

model outputs using BLEU (Papineni et al., 2002), and BERTScore (Zhang et al., 2020) metrics.

5.3 Results and Discussion

Figure 2 shows the results of our experiments, reporting BLEU scores on the test partition of each dataset.

Privacy/utility trade-off We verify the soundness of our models in the non-private setting ($\varepsilon = \infty$) by comparing with past non-private results, particularly for the commonly used WMT-16 dataset. For WMT-16 DE-EN, we reach a BLEU score of 36.2, being similar to past models (e.g. Wei et al. (2021) obtain a BLEU score of 38.6 using their 137B parameter FLAN model). In the case of BSD and ClinSPEn-CC, these datasets are not as 'standard' within the NMT community, and therefore have a more limited chance for comparison.

For private results, we can see a clear difference between the drop in WMT-16 performance vs. that of BSD and ClinSPEn-CC. This is not at all surprising, given that the latter two datasets are vastly smaller in comparison to WMT-16, making it far more difficult to train an NMT model, particularly in the noisy setting of DP-SGD. In addition, ClinSPEn-CC contains a large amount of complicated medical terminology that adds an extra layer of difficulty for a model. We therefore need to conduct further investigations into applications of DP-SGD to very small datasets in order to reach more meaningful ε values.

Method of dataset iteration When comparing random shuffling with Poisson sampling, we can see practically no difference for BSD and ClinSPEn-CC, most likely due to the low DP-SGD results for these two datasets. The differences are more notable for WMT-16, where there is a clear gap between the two sets of configurations. For instance, at $\varepsilon = 1$, WMT-16 shows a BLEU score of 19.83 when using random shuffling, in contrast to 2.35 with Poisson sampling. The latter method therefore shows a far greater drop from the non-private setting, improving more gradually as ε is increased.

There are several possible explanations for this. With Poisson sampling, while each data point has an equal probability of being drawn to make up a particular batch, it is possible that some data points end up being drawn more frequently than others for several training iterations. This may have an impact on the model learning process, possibly missing out on the signal from certain useful data points at various stages of training. Another reason may be that we simply require additional hyperparameter optimization with Poisson sampling, expanding the search space further.

6 Conclusion

We have introduced `DP-NMT`, a modular framework developed using the JAX library, with the goal of leading research on neural machine translation with DP-SGD. To demonstrate our framework in use, we have presented several experiments on both general and privacy-related NMT datasets, comparing two separate approaches for iterating over training data with DP-SGD, and facilitating in filling the research gap on the privacy/utility trade-off in this task. We are continuing to actively expand the framework, including the integration of new models and NMT datasets. We hope that our framework will help to expand research into privacy-preserving NMT and welcome feedback from the community.

Ethics and Limitations

An important ethical consideration with regards to our framework is its intended use. We strive to further the field of private NMT and improve the current knowledge on how to effectively apply differential privacy to data used in NMT systems. However, applications of differential privacy to textual data are still at an early research stage, and **should not currently be used in actual services that handle real sensitive data of individuals.**

The primary reason for this is that our understanding of what is *private information* in textual data is still very limited. Applications of differential privacy in the machine learning setting provide a privacy guarantee to each individual *data point*. In the context of DP-SGD, this means that if any single data point is removed from the dataset, the impact on the resulting model parameter update is bounded by the provided multiplicative guarantee in Eqn. 1. In other words, it does not stand out 'too much' in its contribution to training the model.

For textual data, a single data point will often be a sentence or document. However, this does not mean that there is a one-to-one mapping from *individuals* to sentences and documents. For instance, multiple documents could potentially refer to the same individual, or contain the same piece of sensitive information that would break the assumption of each data point being independent and identically distributed (i.i.d.) in the DP setting. Thus, we require further research on how to properly apply a privacy guarantee to individuals represented within a textual dataset. We refer to Klymenko et al. (2022); Brown et al. (2022); Igamberdiev and Habernal (2023) for a more comprehensive discussion on this.

Acknowledgements

This project was supported by the PrivaLingo research grant (Hessisches Ministerium des Innern und für Sport). The independent research group TrustHLT is supported by the Hessian Ministry of Higher Education, Research, Science and the Arts. Thanks to Luke Bates for helpful feedback on a preliminary draft.

References

Martin Abadi, Paul Barham, Jianmin Chen, Zhifeng Chen, Andy Davis, Jeffrey Dean, Matthieu Devin, Sanjay Ghemawat, Geoffrey Irving, Michael Isard, Manjunath Kudlur, Josh Levenberg, Rajat Monga, Sherry Moore, Derek G. Murray, Benoit Steiner, Paul Tucker, Vijay Vasudevan, Pete Warden, Martin Wicke, Yuan Yu, and Xiaoqiang Zheng. 2016a. Tensorflow: A system for large-scale machine learning. In *Proceedings of the 12th USENIX Conference on Operating Systems Design and Implementation*, OSDI'16, page 265–283, USA. USENIX Association.

Martin Abadi, Andy Chu, Ian Goodfellow, H Brendan McMahan, Ilya Mironov, Kunal Talwar, and Li Zhang. 2016b. Deep learning with differential privacy. In *Proceedings of the 2016 ACM SIGSAC conference on computer and communications security*, pages 308–318.

Rohan Anil, Badih Ghazi, Vineet Gupta, Ravi Kumar, and Pasin Manurangsi. 2022. Large-scale differentially private BERT. In *Findings of the Association for Computational Linguistics: EMNLP 2022*, pages 6481–6491, Abu Dhabi, United Arab Emirates. Association for Computational Linguistics.

Borja Balle, Gilles Barthe, and Marco Gaboardi. 2018. Privacy amplification by subsampling: Tight analyses via couplings and divergences. *Advances in neural information processing systems*, 31.

Priyam Basu, Tiasa Singha Roy, Rakshit Naidu, and Zumrut Muftuoglu. 2021. Privacy enabled financial text classification using differential privacy and federated learning. In *Proceedings of the Third Workshop on Economics and Natural Language Processing*, pages 50–55, Punta Cana, Dominican Republic. Association for Computational Linguistics.

Amos Beimel, Hai Brenner, Shiva Prasad Kasiviswanathan, and Kobbi Nissim. 2014. Bounds on the sample complexity for private learning and private data release. *Machine learning*, 94:401–437.

Ondrej Bojar, Rajen Chatterjee, Christian Federmann, Yvette Graham, Barry Haddow, Matthias Huck, Antonio Jimeno Yepes, Philipp Koehn, Varvara Logacheva, Christof Monz, et al. 2016. Findings of the 2016 conference on machine translation (wmt16). In *First conference on machine translation*, pages 131–198. Association for Computational Linguistics.

James Bradbury, Roy Frostig, Peter Hawkins, Matthew James Johnson, Chris Leary, Dougal Maclaurin, George Necula, Adam Paszke, Jake VanderPlas, Skye Wanderman-Milne, and Qiao Zhang. 2018. JAX: composable transformations of Python+NumPy programs. `http://github.com/google/jax`.

Hannah Brown, Katherine Lee, Fatemehsadat Mireshghallah, Reza Shokri, and Florian Tramèr. 2022. What does it mean for a language model to preserve privacy? In *Proceedings of the 2022 ACM Conference on Fairness, Accountability, and Transparency*, pages 2280–2292.

Nicholas Carlini, Florian Tramer, Eric Wallace, Matthew Jagielski, Ariel Herbert-Voss, Katherine Lee, Adam Roberts, Tom Brown, Dawn Song, Ulfar Erlingsson, et al. 2021. Extracting training data from large language models. In *30th USENIX Security Symposium (USENIX Security 21)*, pages 2633–2650.

Yichao Du, Zhirui Zhang, Bingzhe Wu, Lemao Liu, Tong Xu, and Enhong Chen. 2022. Federated nearest neighbor machine translation. In *The Eleventh International Conference on Learning Representations*.

Cynthia Dwork and Aaron Roth. 2013. The Algorithmic Foundations of Differential Privacy. *Foundations and Trends® in Theoretical Computer Science*, 9(3-4):211–407.

Cynthia Dwork, Guy N Rothblum, and Salil Vadhan. 2010. Boosting and differential privacy. In *2010 IEEE 51st Annual Symposium on Foundations of Computer Science*, pages 51–60. IEEE.

Úlfar Erlingsson, Vitaly Feldman, Ilya Mironov, Ananth Raghunathan, Kunal Talwar, and Abhradeep Thakurta. 2019. Amplification by shuffling: From local to central differential privacy via anonymity. In *Proceedings of the Thirtieth Annual ACM-SIAM Symposium on Discrete Algorithms*, pages 2468–2479. SIAM.

Vitaly Feldman, Audra McMillan, and Kunal Talwar. 2022. Hiding among the clones: A simple and nearly optimal analysis of privacy amplification by shuffling. In *2021 IEEE 62nd Annual Symposium on Foundations of Computer Science (FOCS)*, pages 954–964. IEEE.

Ivan Habernal. 2021. When differential privacy meets NLP: The devil is in the detail. In *Proceedings of the 2021 Conference on Empirical Methods in Natural Language Processing*, pages 1522–1528, Punta Cana, Dominican Republic. Association for Computational Linguistics.

Ivan Habernal. 2022. How reparametrization trick broke differentially-private text representation learning. In *Proceedings of the 60th Annual Meeting of the Association for Computational Linguistics (Volume 2: Short Papers)*, pages 771–777, Dublin, Ireland. Association for Computational Linguistics.

Victor Petrén Bach Hansen, Atula Tejaswi Neerkaje, Ramit Sawhney, Lucie Flek, and Anders Søgaard. 2022. The impact of differential privacy on group disparity mitigation. In *Proceedings of the Fourth Workshop on Privacy in Natural Language Processing*, pages 12–12.

Jonathan Heek, Anselm Levskaya, Avital Oliver, Marvin Ritter, Bertrand Rondepierre, Andreas Steiner, and Marc van Zee. 2023. Flax: A neural network library and ecosystem for JAX. `http://github.com/google/flax`.

Sorami Hisamoto, Matt Post, and Kevin Duh. 2020. Membership inference attacks on sequence-to-sequence models: Is my data in your machine translation system? *Transactions of the Association for Computational Linguistics*, 8:49–63.

Shlomo Hoory, Amir Feder, Avichai Tendler, Sofia Erell, Alon Peled-Cohen, Itay Laish, Hootan Nakhost, Uri Stemmer, Ayelet Benjamini, Avinatan Hassidim, and Yossi Matias. 2021. Learning and Evaluating a Differentially Private Pre-trained Language Model. In *Findings of the Association for Computational Linguistics: EMNLP 2021*, pages 1178–1189, Punta Cana, Dominican Republic. Association for Computational Linguistics.

Justin Hsu, Marco Gaboardi, Andreas Haeberlen, Sanjeev Khanna, Arjun Narayan, Benjamin C Pierce, and Aaron Roth. 2014. Differential privacy: An economic method for choosing epsilon. In *2014 IEEE 27th Computer Security Foundations Symposium*, pages 398–410. IEEE.

Lijie Hu, Ivan Habernal, Lei Shen, and Di Wang. 2024. Differentially Private Natural Language Models: Recent Advances and Future Directions. In *Proceedings of the 18th Conference of the European Chapter of the Association for Computational Linguistics*, page (to appear), Malta. Association for Computational Linguistics.

Timour Igamberdiev and Ivan Habernal. 2022. Privacy-Preserving Graph Convolutional Networks for Text Classification. In *Proceedings of the Language Resources and Evaluation Conference*, pages 338–350, Marseille, France. European Language Resources Association.

Timour Igamberdiev and Ivan Habernal. 2023. DP-BART for privatized text rewriting under local differential privacy. In *Findings of the Association for Computational Linguistics: ACL 2023*, pages 13914–13934, Toronto, Canada. Association for Computational Linguistics.

Paweł Kamocki and Jim O'Regan. 2016. Privacy issues in online machine translation services-european perspective. In *Proceedings of the Tenth International Conference on Language Resources and Evaluation (LREC'16)*, pages 4458–4462.

Shiva Prasad Kasiviswanathan, Homin K Lee, Kobbi Nissim, Sofya Raskhodnikova, and Adam Smith. 2011. What can we learn privately? *SIAM Journal on Computing*, 40(3):793–826.

Oleksandra Klymenko, Stephen Meisenbacher, and Florian Matthes. 2022. Differential privacy in natural language processing the story so far. In *Proceedings of the Fourth Workshop on Privacy in Natural Language Processing*, pages 1–11, Seattle, United States. Association for Computational Linguistics.

Jaewoo Lee and Chris Clifton. 2011. How Much Is Enough? Choosing ϵ for Differential Privacy. In *Proceedings of the 14th Information Security Conference (ISC 2011)*, pages 325–340, Xi'an, China. Springer Berlin / Heidelberg.

Quentin Lhoest, Albert Villanova del Moral, Yacine Jernite, Abhishek Thakur, Patrick von Platen, Suraj Patil, Julien Chaumond, Mariama Drame, Julien Plu, Lewis Tunstall, Joe Davison, Mario Šaško, Gunjan Chhablani, Bhavitvya Malik, Simon Brandeis,

Teven Le Scao, Victor Sanh, Canwen Xu, Nicolas Patry, Angelina McMillan-Major, Philipp Schmid, Sylvain Gugger, Clément Delangue, Théo Matussière, Lysandre Debut, Stas Bekman, Pierric Cistac, Thibault Goehringer, Victor Mustar, François Lagunas, Alexander Rush, and Thomas Wolf. 2021. Datasets: A community library for natural language processing. In *Proceedings of the 2021 Conference on Empirical Methods in Natural Language Processing: System Demonstrations*, pages 175–184, Online and Punta Cana, Dominican Republic. Association for Computational Linguistics.

Xuechen Li, Florian Tramer, Percy Liang, and Tatsunori Hashimoto. 2022. Large language models can be strong differentially private learners. In *International Conference on Learning Representations*.

Yinhan Liu, Jiatao Gu, Naman Goyal, Xian Li, Sergey Edunov, Marjan Ghazvininejad, Mike Lewis, and Luke Zettlemoyer. 2020. Multilingual denoising pre-training for neural machine translation. *Transactions of the Association for Computational Linguistics*, 8:726–742.

Justus Mattern, Zhijing Jin, Benjamin Weggenmann, Bernhard Schoelkopf, and Mrinmaya Sachan. 2022. Differentially private language models for secure data sharing. In *Proceedings of the 2022 Conference on Empirical Methods in Natural Language Processing*, pages 4860–4873, Abu Dhabi, United Arab Emirates. Association for Computational Linguistics.

Brendan McMahan, Eider Moore, Daniel Ramage, Seth Hampson, and Blaise Aguera y Arcas. 2017. Communication-efficient learning of deep networks from decentralized data. In *Artificial intelligence and statistics*, pages 1273–1282. PMLR.

Mariana Neves, Antonio Jimeno Yepes, Amy Siu, Roland Roller, Philippe Thomas, Maika Vicente Navarro, Lana Yeganova, Dina Wiemann, Giorgio Maria Di Nunzio, Federica Vezzani, et al. 2022. Findings of the wmt 2022 biomedical translation shared task: Monolingual clinical case reports. In *WMT22-Seventh Conference on Machine Translation*, pages 694–723.

Kishore Papineni, Salim Roukos, Todd Ward, and Wei-Jing Zhu. 2002. Bleu: a method for automatic evaluation of machine translation. In *Proceedings of the 40th Annual Meeting of the Association for Computational Linguistics*, pages 311–318, Philadelphia, Pennsylvania, USA. Association for Computational Linguistics.

Peyman Passban, Tanya Roosta, Rahul Gupta, Ankit Chadha, and Clement Chung. 2022. Training mixed-domain translation models via federated learning. In *Proceedings of the 2022 Conference of the North American Chapter of the Association for Computational Linguistics: Human Language Technologies*, pages 2576–2586.

Natalia Ponomareva, Jasmijn Bastings, and Sergei Vassilvitskii. 2022. Training text-to-text transformers with privacy guarantees. In *Findings of the Association for Computational Linguistics: ACL 2022*, pages 2182–2193, Dublin, Ireland. Association for Computational Linguistics.

Natalia Ponomareva, Hussein Hazimeh, Alex Kurakin, Zheng Xu, Carson Denison, H Brendan McMahan, Sergei Vassilvitskii, Steve Chien, and Abhradeep Guha Thakurta. 2023. How to dp-fy ml: A practical guide to machine learning with differential privacy. *Journal of Artificial Intelligence Research*, 77:1113–1201.

Colin Raffel, Noam Shazeer, Adam Roberts, Katherine Lee, Sharan Narang, Michael Matena, Yanqi Zhou, Wei Li, and Peter J. Liu. 2020. Exploring the limits of transfer learning with a unified text-to-text transformer. *Journal of Machine Learning Research*, 21(140):1–67.

Matīss Rikters, Ryokan Ri, Tong Li, and Toshiaki Nakazawa. 2019. Designing the business conversation corpus. In *Proceedings of the 6th Workshop on Asian Translation*, pages 54–61, Hong Kong, China. Association for Computational Linguistics.

Tanya Roosta, Peyman Passban, and Ankit Chadha. 2021. Communication-efficient federated learning for neural machine translation. *arXiv preprint arXiv:2112.06135*.

Manuel Senge, Timour Igamberdiev, and Ivan Habernal. 2022. One size does not fit all: Investigating strategies for differentially-private learning across NLP tasks. In *Proceedings of the 2022 Conference on Empirical Methods in Natural Language Processing*, pages 7340–7353, Abu Dhabi, UAE.

Weiyan Shi, Aiqi Cui, Evan Li, Ruoxi Jia, and Zhou Yu. 2022. Selective differential privacy for language modeling. In *Proceedings of the 2022 Conference of the North American Chapter of the Association for Computational Linguistics: Human Language Technologies*, pages 2848–2859, Seattle, United States. Association for Computational Linguistics.

Reza Shokri, Marco Stronati, Congzheng Song, and Vitaly Shmatikov. 2017. Membership inference attacks against machine learning models. In *2017 IEEE symposium on security and privacy (SP)*, pages 3–18. IEEE.

Pranav Subramani, Nicholas Vadivelu, and Gautam Kamath. 2021. Enabling Fast Differentially Private SGD via Just-in-Time Compilation and Vectorization. In *Advances in Neural Information Processing Systems*, volume 34, pages 26409–26421. Curran Associates, Inc.

Ashish Vaswani, Noam Shazeer, Niki Parmar, Jakob Uszkoreit, Llion Jones, Aidan N. Gomez, Lukasz Kaiser, and Illia Polosukhin. 2017. Attention Is All You Need. In *Advances in Neural Information Processing Systems 30*, pages 5998–6008, Long Beach, CA, USA. Curran Associates, Inc.

Jianzong Wang, Zhangcheng Huang, Lingwei Kong, Denghao Li, and Jing Xiao. 2021. Modeling without sharing privacy: Federated neural machine translation. In *Web Information Systems Engineering–WISE 2021: 22nd International Conference on Web Information Systems Engineering, WISE 2021, Melbourne, VIC, Australia, October 26–29, 2021, Proceedings, Part I 22*, pages 216–223. Springer.

Yu-Xiang Wang, Borja Balle, and Shiva Prasad Kasiviswanathan. 2019. Subsampled rényi differential privacy and analytical moments accountant. In *The 22nd International Conference on Artificial Intelligence and Statistics*, pages 1226–1235. PMLR.

Jason Wei, Maarten Bosma, Vincent Zhao, Kelvin Guu, Adams Wei Yu, Brian Lester, Nan Du, Andrew M Dai, and Quoc V Le. 2021. Finetuned language models are zero-shot learners. In *International Conference on Learning Representations*.

Christopher Weiss, Frauke Kreuter, and Ivan Habernal. 2023. To share or not to share: What risks would laypeople accept to give sensitive data to differentially-private NLP systems? *arXiv preprint*.

Xinwei Wu, Li Gong, and Deyi Xiong. 2022. Adaptive differential privacy for language model training. In *Proceedings of the First Workshop on Federated Learning for Natural Language Processing (FL4NLP 2022)*, pages 21–26, Dublin, Ireland. Association for Computational Linguistics.

Chang Xu, Jun Wang, Francisco Guzmán, Benjamin Rubinstein, and Trevor Cohn. 2021. Mitigating data poisoning in text classification with differential privacy. In *Findings of the Association for Computational Linguistics: EMNLP 2021*, pages 4348–4356, Punta Cana, Dominican Republic. Association for Computational Linguistics.

Linting Xue, Noah Constant, Adam Roberts, Mihir Kale, Rami Al-Rfou, Aditya Siddhant, Aditya Barua, and Colin Raffel. 2021. mT5: A massively multilingual pre-trained text-to-text transformer. In *Proceedings of the 2021 Conference of the North American Chapter of the Association for Computational Linguistics: Human Language Technologies*, pages 483–498, Online. Association for Computational Linguistics.

Ying Yin and Ivan Habernal. 2022. Privacy-preserving models for legal natural language processing. In *Proceedings of the Natural Legal Language Processing Workshop 2022*, pages 172–183, Abu Dhabi, United Arab Emirates (Hybrid). Association for Computational Linguistics.

Ashkan Yousefpour, Igor Shilov, Alexandre Sablayrolles, Davide Testuggine, Karthik Prasad, Mani Malek, John Nguyen, Sayan Ghosh, Akash Bharadwaj, Jessica Zhao, Graham Cormode, and Ilya Mironov. 2021. Opacus: User-Friendly Differential Privacy Library in PyTorch. *arXiv preprint*.

Da Yu, Saurabh Naik, Arturs Backurs, Sivakanth Gopi, Huseyin A Inan, Gautam Kamath, Janardhan Kulkarni, Yin Tat Lee, Andre Manoel, Lukas Wutschitz, et al. 2021. Differentially private fine-tuning of language models. In *International Conference on Learning Representations*.

Tianyi Zhang, Varsha Kishore, Felix Wu, Kilian Q Weinberger, and Yoav Artzi. 2020. BERTScore: Evaluating Text Generation with BERT. In *International Conference on Learning Representations*.

A Background on Differential Privacy and DP-SGD

Differential Privacy Differential privacy (DP) is a mathematical framework which formally guarantees that the output of a randomized algorithm $\mathcal{M} : \mathcal{X} \rightarrow \mathcal{Y}$ abides by the following inequality in Eqn. 1, for all *neighboring* datasets $x, x' \in \mathcal{X}$, i.e. datasets which are identical to one another, with the exception of one data point (Dwork and Roth, 2013)

$$\Pr[\mathcal{M}(x) \in S] \leq e^{\varepsilon} \Pr[\mathcal{M}(x') \in S] + \delta, \quad (1)$$

for all $S \subseteq \mathcal{Y}$.

We refer to the algorithm $\mathcal{M}$ as being (ε, δ)-differentially private, where $\varepsilon \in [0, \infty)$, also known as the *privacy budget*, represents the strength of the privacy guarantee. A lower ε value represents an exponentially stronger privacy protection. $\delta \in [0, 1]$ is a very small constant which relaxes the pure differential privacy of $(\varepsilon, 0)$-DP, providing better composition when iteratively applying multiple DP mechanisms to a given dataset.

In order to transform a non-private algorithm $f : \mathcal{X} \rightarrow \mathcal{Y}$ into one satisfying an (ε, δ)-DP guarantee, we generally add Gaussian noise to the output of f. Overall, the whole process restricts the degree to which any single data point can stand out when applying algorithm $\mathcal{M}$ on a dataset.

DP-SGD A popular method for applying DP to the domain of machine learning is through differentially private stochastic gradient descent (DP-SGD) (Abadi et al., 2016b). The core of the methodology relies on adding two extra steps to the original stochastic gradient descent algorithm. For any input data point x_i, we first calculate the gradient of the loss function for a model with parameters θ, $\mathcal{L}(\theta)$, at training iteration t. Hence, $g_t(x_i) = \nabla_{\theta_t} \mathcal{L}(\theta_t, x_i)$.

We then incorporate a *clipping* step, in which the ℓ_2-norm of $g_t(x_i)$ is clipped with clipping constant

C, as in Eqn. 2, in order to constrain the range of possible values. This is followed by a *perturbation* step, adding Gaussian noise to the clipped gradients, as in Eqn. 3.

$$\bar{g}_t(x_i) = \frac{g_t(x_i)}{\max\left(1, \frac{\|g_t(x_i)\|_2}{C}\right)} \tag{2}$$

$$\hat{g}_t = \frac{1}{L}\sum_{i \in L} \left(\bar{g}_t(x_i) + \mathcal{N}(0, \sigma^2 C^2 \mathbf{I})\right) \tag{3}$$

Importantly, L represents the *lot size*, being a group of data points that are randomly drawn from the full training dataset at each iteration. The final gradient descent step is then taken with respect to this noisy gradient $\hat{g}_t$. We outline the DP-SGD algorithm in more detail in Algorithm 1.

Algorithm 1 DP-SGD

function DP-SGD($f(\boldsymbol{x};\Theta)$, $(\boldsymbol{x}_1,\ldots,\boldsymbol{x}_n)$, $|L|$ — 'lot' size, T — # of steps)
  for $t \in (1, 2, \ldots, T)$ **do**
    Add each training example to a 'lot' L_t with probability $|L|/N$
    for each example in the 'lot' $\boldsymbol{x}_i \in L_t$ **do**
      $\boldsymbol{g}(\boldsymbol{x}_i) \leftarrow \nabla\mathcal{L}(\theta_t, \boldsymbol{x}_i)$ ▷ Compute gradient
      $\bar{\boldsymbol{g}}(\boldsymbol{x}_i) \leftarrow \boldsymbol{g}(\boldsymbol{x}_i)/\max(1, \|\boldsymbol{g}(\boldsymbol{x}_i)\|/C)$ ▷ Clip gradient
      $\tilde{\boldsymbol{g}}(\boldsymbol{x}_i) \leftarrow \bar{\boldsymbol{g}}(\boldsymbol{x}_i) + \mathcal{N}(0, \sigma^2 C^2 \boldsymbol{I})$ ▷ Add noise
    $\hat{\boldsymbol{g}} \leftarrow \frac{1}{|L|}\sum_{k=1}^{|L|} \tilde{\boldsymbol{g}}(\boldsymbol{x}_k)$ ▷ Gradient estimate of 'lot' by averaging
    $\Theta_{t+1} \leftarrow \Theta_t - \eta_t \hat{\boldsymbol{g}}$ ▷ Update parameters by gradient descent
  return Θ

B Hyperparameters

We present our hyperparameter search space as follows. We experiment with learning rates in the range $[10^{-5}, 0.01]$ and maximum sequence lengths in $[8, 64]$. Following previous work, we utilize large batch and lot sizes for our experiments, finding $1,048,576$ to be the best for WMT-16, $2,048$ for BSD, and 256 for ClinSPEn-CC. We build up these batch sizes using gradient accumulation with a physical batch size of 16. In the case of Poisson sampling, we first sample using large lot sizes and build the resulting drawn batch using gradient accumulation, as described in Section 4. We train models for up to 25 epochs, using the same definition for *epochs* as in Abadi et al. (2016b) in the Poisson sampling setting, being $\frac{N}{L}$. We take the ceiling in case of L not cleanly dividing into N. Each configuration is run using 5 seeds for the BSD and ClinSPEn-CC datasets and 3 seeds for WMT-16, reporting the mean and standard deviation of results.

We additionally present our computational runtimes in Table 2. All experiments are run on up to two 80GB NVIDIA A100 Tensor Core GPUs.

Dataset	ε	Iteration Method	Epoch Time
WMT-16	∞	Random shuffling	2 h 45 m 08 s
WMT-16	1000	Random shuffling	2 h 59 m 15 s
WMT-16	1000	Poisson sampling	4 h 08 m 01 s
WMT-16	5	Random shuffling	1 h 30 m 03 s
WMT-16	5	Poisson sampling	4 h 02 m 35 s
WMT-16	1	Random shuffling	1 h 29 m 49 s
WMT-16	1	Poisson sampling	4 h 09 m 02 s
BSD	∞	Random shuffling	0 h 01 m 17 s
BSD	1000	Random shuffling	0 h 01 m 59 s
BSD	1000	Poisson sampling	0 h 01 m 49 s
BSD	5	Random shuffling	0 h 00 m 52 s
BSD	5	Poisson sampling	0 h 01 m 49 s
BSD	1	Random shuffling	0 h 01 m 09 s
BSD	1	Poisson sampling	0 h 02 m 15 s
ClinSPEn-CC	∞	Random shuffling	0 h 00 m 09 s
ClinSPEn-CC	1000	Random shuffling	0 h 00 m 05 s
ClinSPEn-CC	1000	Poisson sampling	0 h 00 m 28 s
ClinSPEn-CC	5	Random shuffling	0 h 00 m 10 s
ClinSPEn-CC	5	Poisson sampling	0 h 00 m 27 s
ClinSPEn-CC	1	Random shuffling	0 h 00 m 15 s
ClinSPEn-CC	1	Poisson sampling	0 h 00 m 27 s

Table 2: Sample epoch runtimes for each configuration. Some differences between configurations arise due to different optimal hyperparameters, with larger sequence lengths leading to longer epoch times.

C Detailed Results

Dataset	ε	Iteration Method	Test BLEU	Test BERTScore
WMT-16	∞	Random shuffling	36.19 (0.13)	0.95 (0.00)
WMT-16	1000	Random shuffling	20.86 (0.56)	0.92 (0.00)
WMT-16	1000	Poisson sampling	15.12 (0.08)	0.91 (0.00)
WMT-16	5	Random shuffling	19.24 (0.52)	0.92 (0.00)
WMT-16	5	Poisson sampling	7.23 (0.21)	0.89 (0.00)
WMT-16	1	Random shuffling	19.83 (0.64)	0.92 (0.00)
WMT-16	1	Poisson sampling	2.35 (0.07)	0.84 (0.00)
BSD	∞	Random shuffling	10.09 (2.75)	0.90 (0.01)
BSD	1000	Random shuffling	1.36 (0.67)	0.87 (0.01)
BSD	1000	Poisson sampling	1.01 (0.07)	0.87 (0.00)
BSD	5	Random shuffling	0.06 (0.05)	0.85 (0.01)
BSD	5	Poisson sampling	0.06 (0.06)	0.84 (0.02)
BSD	1	Random shuffling	0.00 (0.01)	0.45 (0.22)
BSD	1	Poisson sampling	0.00 (0.00)	0.65 (0.15)
ClinSPEn-CC	∞	Random shuffling	5.42 (2.41)	0.86 (0.02)
ClinSPEn-CC	1000	Random shuffling	0.03 (0.02)	0.75 (0.01)
ClinSPEn-CC	1000	Poisson sampling	0.70 (0.19)	0.78 (0.00)
ClinSPEn-CC	5	Random shuffling	0.80 (0.56)	0.79 (0.00)
ClinSPEn-CC	5	Poisson sampling	0.83 (0.27)	0.79 (0.00)
ClinSPEn-CC	1	Random shuffling	0.50 (0.20)	0.78 (0.00)
ClinSPEn-CC	1	Poisson sampling	0.54 (0.22)	0.78 (0.00)

Table 3: Detailed results of each experimental configuration. Scores shown as "mean (standard deviation)". Results show the average over 3 seeds for the WMT-16 dataset, and 5 seeds for BSD and ClinSPEn-CC.

AnnoPlot: Interactive Visualizations of Text Annotations

Elisabeth Fittschen[†], **Daniel Bruehl**[†], **Julia Spahr**[†]
Phuoc Thang Le[‡], **Yuliia Lysa**[†], **Tim Fischer**[‡]
Language Technology Group, Department of Informatics, Universität Hamburg, Germany
[†] {firstname.lastname}@studium.uni-hamburg.de,
[‡] {firstname.lastname}@uni-hamburg.de

Abstract

This paper presents AnnoPlot, a web application designed to analyze, manage, and visualize annotated text data. Users can configure projects, upload datasets, and explore their data through interactive visualization of span annotations with scatter plots, clusters, and statistics. AnnoPlot supports various transformer models to compute high-dimensional embeddings of text annotations and utilizes dimensionality reduction algorithms to offer users a novel 2D view of their datasets. A dynamic approach to dimensionality reduction allows users to adjust visualizations in real-time, facilitating category reorganization and error identification. The proposed application is open-source, promoting transparency and user control. Especially suited for the Digital Humanities, AnnoPlot offers a novel solution to address challenges in dynamic annotation datasets, empowering users to enhance data integrity and adapt to evolving categorizations.

1 Introduction

Within the context of NLP, sequence annotation is the practice of tagging sections of text with appropriate labels. For example, this could involve classifying the phrase "Finding Nemo" as a "movie" in the sentence "I love Finding Nemo."

Annotation projects, such as the creation of annotated datasets, face a variety of challenges, one of which is data quality and validity. As data is added and use cases evolve, prior category definitions might be insufficient and need to be updated or reorganized. As datasets grow and evolve, achieving a good overview becomes increasingly complex, which is necessary to revise labeling strategy and category definition (Payan et al., 2021).

AnnoPlot addresses this issue by offering comprehensive two-dimensional views of the provided dataset without any prior training or classification model necessary. Such views of span annotations and category systems enable users to:

- quickly gain an overview of large datasets and their overarching category structure
- reorganize categories within the dataset
- interactively adjust the visualization to fit the intended category definition better
- better identify and fix potential erroneous annotations

Many of these functionalities are valuable for applications in NLP and especially for the management of Named Entity Recognition datasets. However, they are also of great interest to domains and disciplines beyond those. In the digital humanities, annotating datasets, building complex category systems, and the refinement of such are typical workflows of qualitative, hermeneutic research processes.

AnnoPlot generates two-dimensional representations akin to systems such as BERTopic (Grootendorst, 2022). First, the span annotations are encoded with a pre-trained transformer model, yielding large embeddings, typically of 512 up to 1024 dimensions. In this work, we use BERT-based transformer encoders since BERT (Devlin et al., 2019) embeddings have proven to be very information-rich, meaning a large variety of data is encoded in the high-dimension embeddings.

Next, dimensionality reduction techniques are implemented to generate a two-dimensional representation for visualization purposes.

Our proposed tool offers an interactive dimension reduction algorithm based on the well-known UMAP (McInnes et al., 2020) algorithm and its parametric neural network implementation (Sainburg et al., 2021). The user can remotely train the small reduction algorithm network to fit annotated text passages to the categories. In case of further customization necessity, dots or clusters representing annotations can be dragged in the interactive view to inform the model about the desired changes for the subsequent training iterations. This training happens in real-time; the user can see updates or

Proceedings of the 18th Conference of the European Chapter of the Association for Computational Linguistics
System Demonstrations, pages 106–114
March 17-22, 2024 ©2024 Association for Computational Linguistics

stop the process in case of mistakes or overfitting.

AnnoPlot provides a customizable and dynamic application for the analysis of annotated datasets that stands apart from expensive commercial solutions like MAXQDA or Galileo. Our application lets users interactively modify annotations, hierarchical category systems, and visualizations in real-time without requiring pre-trained, category-specific models. By bridging the gap between advanced data visualization techniques and user-friendly applications, AnnoPlot makes a noteworthy addition to current annotation tools. AnnoPlot is an open source project; the code can be found in its github repository[1] together with a short video demonstrating its core functions. A live demonstration of AnnoPlot can be found here[2].

2 Related Work

AnnoPlot offers an interactive user interface for data visualization of annotated texts and classification category management. In the context of category structuring and reorganization, AnnoPlot can be compared with MAXQDA's *Creative Coding* feature. MAXQDA[3], a qualitative data analysis software, facilitates the organization and hierarchical structuring of codes through its *Creative Coding* functionality. This process involves generating, sorting, and organizing codes, defining relationships between them, and creating a hierarchical structure. However, *Creative Coding* primarily focuses on manual categorization and organization and does not offer any automation. In contrast, AnnoPlot leverages embedding representations to offer an initial starting point while offering similar category management functionality.

Examining general visualization, AnnoPlot's 2D visualization of annotated text passages can be contrasted with tools like the embedding view functionality of Galileo[4]. Galileo is a platform that provides tools and modules to evaluate machine learning classifiers, including NLP classifiers for sequence annotation. The Embedding view utilizes embeddings and a parametric UMAP reduction to visualize classifier results. However, its primary focus is on showcasing classifier performance, and potential areas of uncertainty, rather than facilitating dataset analysis or category reorganization. AnnoPlot, on the other hand, is designed for quick and interactive analysis of annotated text datasets, enabling users to gain insights into the overarching structure and quality of their annotations. The absence of a classifier in AnnoPlot makes its interactive dimension reduction feature particularly valuable, allowing for real-time adjustments and customization based on user input.

In terms of visualization techniques that utilize a processing pipeline of embedding and dimensionality reduction, AnnoPlot shares similarities with many applications such as BERTopic (Grootendorst, 2022) and the TensorFlow embedding projector (Smilkov et al., 2016).

In regards to user interactions, research analysis of interactive dimension reducing tools (Sacha et al., 2017) identified seven distinct categories of interactive dimensionality reduction algorithms, three of which apply to AnnoPlot:

- Annotation & Labeling: the visualization can leverage user given/changeable annotation data when fitting visualization to correspond to categories.
- Parameter Tuning: the user can alter the visualization by tuning UMAP hyperparameters and choosing which transformer model computes the embeddings.
- Data Manipulation: the user can move data points in the dynamic view, and get feedback on how other points move in response.

A notably similar approach to interactive data visualization is taken by Zexplorer (González Martínez et al., 2020) an extension of the bibliography system Zotero. Zexplorer maps selected features of research papers, including a BERT embedding of the paper's abstract, to two dimensions utilizing a neural network approximation of UMAP. Similar to AnnoPlot it offers interactive training of this network through draggable data points.

The development of AnnoPlot was motivated by the absence of interactive features for the visual analysis of annotations in the most popular (Neves and Ševa, 2019) open-source annotation tools such as WebAnno (Yimam et al., 2014), brat (Stenetorp et al., 2012), CATMA (Gius et al., 2023), and INCEpTION (Klie et al., 2018). AnnoPlot combines contextualized embedding representations of annotations with interactive visualizations for analyzing annotated datasets and category structuring.

[1] https://github.com/uhh-lt/anno-plot

[2] https://anno-plot.ltdemos.informatik.uni-hamburg.de/

[3] https://www.maxqda.com/

[4] https://www.rungalileo.io/

3 System Architecture

The application is designed to visualize annotated text segments within the provided datasets and facilitate the modification of existing annotations. Further, it computes and assigns clusters to text segments, helping users to identify annotation errors. It allows users to create projects to manage datasets within it and the flexibility to import data in standard data formats such as CoNLL (Tjong Kim Sang and De Meulder, 2003). When exporting the data, datasets within a project are merged. The tool includes a search function to navigate the dataset and the clusters. Finally, the tool offers detailed statistics for projects, codes, and clusters.

AnnoPlot offers two views: one dedicated to presenting annotated text segments and the other focused on hierarchical category systems. Users can create, delete, and rename data points in both views. Furthermore, users can merge categories and train the existing embeddings further. The views are rendered using the D3.js library. In general, the frontend implementation of the application is realized through React/Next.js.

The backend was implemented in Python using FastAPI and PostgreSQL for data storage. The data processing pipeline to compute 2D representations of annotated text passages consists of a BERT-based transformer model, UMAP, and HDBSCAN. The Hugging Face library is employed to load models and allows for flexibility in which model to use in the pipeline.

The hardware requirements for running AnnoPlot are largely dependent on the embedding model chosen. For development and testing, we used the "bert-base" model with a 3080 RTX GPU (10 GB). The backend uses transformer/BERT-based models for inference and, at most, trains a small (4 layer) dynamic umap model. While a GPU is not strictly required it is highly recommended for UX performance. Annoplot is deployed using Docker. Every System component i.e., the database, frontend, and backend is deployed in a separate docker container, which are orchestrated in a docker compose file.

3.1 Visualization of Annotated Text Segments

The Plot View (see Figure 1), visualizes the uploaded annotated data. Each dot corresponds to an annotated text passage, for example, the annotated named entity "Finding Nemo" in the sentence "My favorite movie is Finding Nemo"; the color indicates the user-given category, i.e., "Movie".

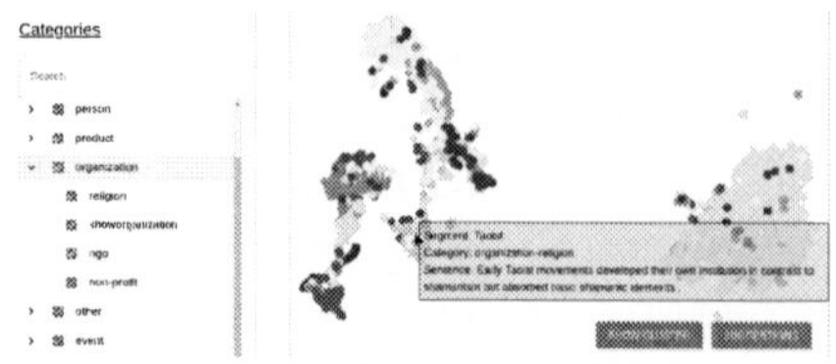

Figure 1: The Plot View, generated using the static UMAP dimension reduction. Left is an overview of the hierarchical category system for filtering the annotations. A tool-tip shows related information about the hovered annotation, including the context sentence.

Dots corresponding to similar entities tend to cluster together. Ideally, this clustering occurs according to the pre-defined categories.

User Interaction Overview

Dots are the product of embeddings of corresponding annotations and a reduction function. These two processes can be customized in the Configurations tab. The user can choose which embedding model to use by linking to a corresponding Huggingface repository; any BERT or RoBERTa-based (Zhuang et al., 2021) model is compatible. This also allows the user to use their own fine-tuned models. The user can also choose between a static and dynamic UMAP model to be used for dimensionality reduction, of which the "n components" hyperparameter can be adjusted.

The main features of this view are the overview of the dataset and functionalities to revise annotations and category choices. For example, the plot can indicate that two categories are not clearly separated or overlap significantly; this might suggest sub-optimal category choice or inconsistent annotation. Further, the plot can reveal that annotations of the same category group in different regions; this might suggest introducing a new (sub-) category.

To the plot's left is an overview of all categories. These can be selected and de-selected to filter for those of current interest. Hovering over dots allows the user to see the respective entity data. Upon right-clicking, a context menu allows the user to re-categorize or delete the corresponding named entity.

If the dynamic UMAP model was selected, the user has two more options, as shown in Figure 2.

The user can train the model according to categories by pressing the train button. This option uses the annotated data for semi-supervised training of the dynamic UMAP model. It will be trained for ten epochs; after each epoch, the model updates,

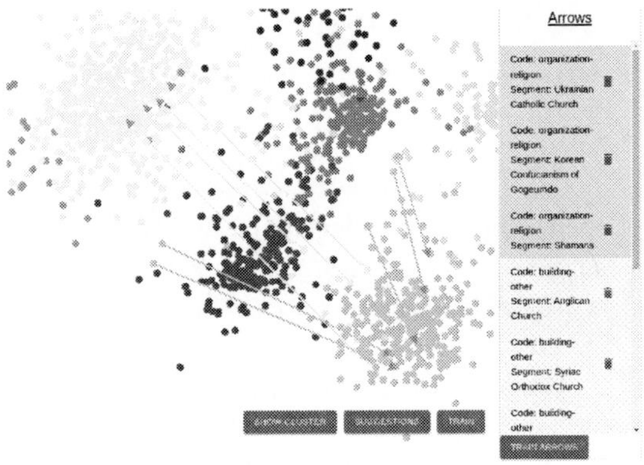

Figure 2: The Plot View, generated using the dynamic UMAP dimension reduction. Arrows have been manually drawn to denote the desired position for multiple points. Pressing the "Train Arrows" button will rearrange the visualization accordingly.

and the dots move to their new positions. The user can choose to preemptively terminate the training steps by pressing stop. Training will stop after the current epoch has finished.

The user can also move data points to a desired position. When dragging points, an arrow will appear, following the cursor, indicating the direction the dot should move. The user can do this for multiple dots appearing on the right. When the user is done, clicking the train button will trigger the model to train for these new dot positions.

When using the dynamic model, the user can go through all dots not within their intended cluster and either fix their annotation or move them, thereby fine-tuning the UMAP reduction.

Implementation Details

Dot coordinates are generated in two steps. First, a context-rich, high-dimensional embedding (depending on the model typically 512-1024) is created from the entity data (entity and its surrounding text). Then, the embeddings of all data points are reduced to two dimensions using a dimension reduction algorithm.

There are dozens of combinations of embedding models and dimension reduction algorithms. In this paper, we focus on a BERT-based embedding model and UMAP-based reduction algorithms.

Embeddings are generated by passing the annotated text passage, e.g. a named entity, and surrounding sentences (limited by the model's input size) into a transformer-based encoder. This results in high dimensional embeddings per input tokens.

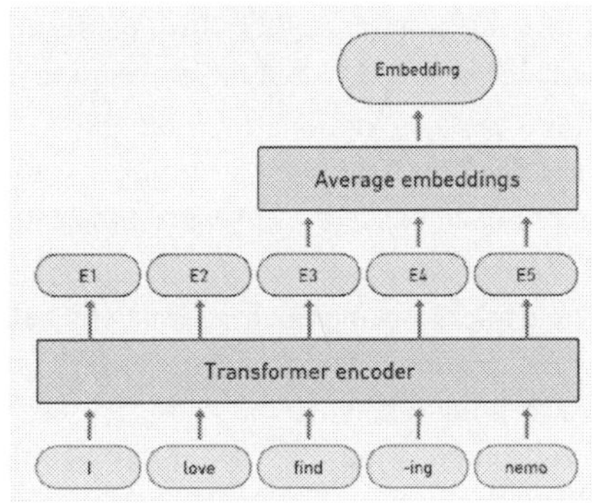

Figure 3: Visualization of the Embedding process. The sentences surrounding a span annotation are embedded by a transformer encoder. Tokens of the annotated entity are averaged to compute the final entity embedding.

The token embeddings, part of the named entity, are averaged to create the entity embedding (see Figure 3). Input token sequences are embedded in batches to enhance the processing efficiency.

Next, the embeddings of all annotated text segments within one dataset are passed to UMAP, which maps the data to two dimensions according to their structure in high-dimensional space.

In the process described, the 2D representation of an annotated text passage is created independent of its category, as the category is not passed to the embedding model. This results in a deterministic mapping from an annotation to two dimensions for a specific annotated dataset. This is a significant disadvantage of the proposed process, as such representation cannot possibly accurately capture the wide variety of classification schemas possible. The named entity *Finding Nemo* in "I love Finding Nemo" could, for instance, be categorized by type (Movie/TV series), company (Disney/Pixar), or release decade (the 2000s/2010s). However, with the current approach, it would be mapped to the same 2D coordinates, which is not desired.

For this reason, the tool also implements a dynamic UMAP solution for dimensionality reduction. Here, the user can interactively train a parametric neural network UMAP (Sainburg et al., 2021) to fit the user's category system and interpretation. The network employs a comparatively modest architecture, consisting of a single input layer that dynamically adjusts to the input size, followed by three hidden layers, each comprising 200 neurons, and a final output layer with a size determined by the number of components (defaulting to 2). This relatively small model reduces the risk of overfitting and, therefore, of diluting the knowledge encoded within the embeddings.

There are two options to train the reduction model. The first option utilizes triplet loss to adjust the representations to better separate the categories from each other.

The triplet loss approach operates by selecting anchors, positives, and negatives to form triplets for each unique label in the data. The loss function used here is the TripletMarginLoss, defined mathematically as

$$L = \sum \max \left(d(a,p) - d(a,n) + margin, 0\right),$$

where $d(x,y)$ represents the distance between two points and a, p, n denotes the anchor, positive, and negative samples, respectively. In our case, the margin was set to 1.0.

The second approach allows for a more direct, interactive manipulation of the data points. Users can 'move' dots, and the model is trained to optimize for the new positions of these dots. This retraining uses Mean Squared Error (MSE) loss, with the positions of other dots being held in place using a moving average.

Both training methods utilize the Adam optimizer. The learning rate was set to 2×10^{-4} for the triplet loss method and to 5×10^{-5} for the direct dot movement method.

3.2 Visualization of the Category System

In the Category View (see Figure 4), categories are visualized in a bubble chart, mirroring the presentation style of the Plot View. It provides an overview of all categories within the imported datasets.

Figure 4: Category View, corresponding to the data seen in Figure 1. Notably, person, scholar (right two points) and location, building, library (top three points) cluster together.

User Interaction Overview

The Category View helps the user reorganize and refine the categories by merging, deleting, and changing their hierarchical structure.

Like in the Visualization for Annotated Text Segments (Figure 1), a legend on the left side shows all possible categories and sub-categories within a project, allowing the user to search or filter for specific categories.

The colors and positions of categories are in sync with the Annotated Text Segments View. The number and position of annotated text segments within a category determine the size of the bubble, providing users with a quick overview of the distribution of annotations across different categories.

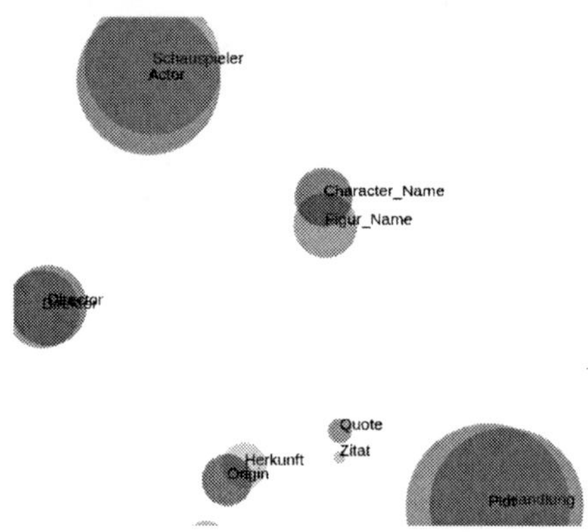

Figure 5: Visualization of MITMovieCorpus(eng, ger). Notably, the German categories like "Schauspieler", "Direktor" and "Figur Name" are very close to their English counterparts (Actor, Director, Character Name).

The user can use these spatial relations to get a quick insight into their data. In Figure 5, for instance, the categories of two datasets can be seen; one is part of the MIT Movie Corpus (Liu et al., 2013) annotated using German labels, the other using English labels. The categories containing semantically similar data are easily identifiable, often wholly overlapping. Even without understanding German, it is straightforward to determine which categories can be merged.

By right-clicking a category, the category or subcategory can be renamed, deleted, or merged with another category. At the bottom of the view, additional options allow the creation, removal, or merging of categories.

Visualizing category positions, sizes, and colors offers users an intuitive and comprehensive tool for managing and understanding the structure of their annotated datasets.

Implementation Details

The position and size of categories are calculated using the underlying annotated text segments and their position in 2D (see Section 3.1). A category's position is the average of all its entities' positions, whereas its radius corresponds to its number of entities, whereas a category's radius corresponds to its number of entities.

3.3 Automatic Error Detection

In the annotated text segment view discussed in Section 3.1, the user is also supported in finding categorization errors. The identification of annotation errors is achieved through clustering and outlier detection.

User Interaction Overview

AnnoPlot aids in finding potential annotation errors through the HDBSCAN (Campello et al., 2013) clustering algorithm. Similarly to the embedding and dimensionality reduction functions, this algorithm can also be configured in the Configurations tab. Here, the user can adjust the "min cluster size", "metric", and the "cluster selection method."

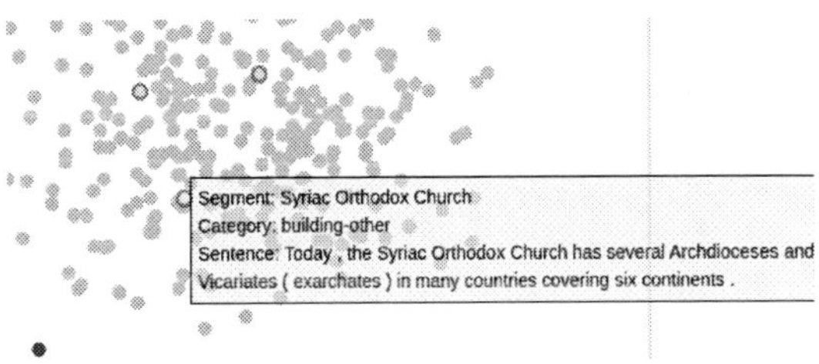

Figure 6: Error identification. The light blue dots are a cluster of religious organizations. A user must now decide if this annotation is correct or incorrect.

The user can choose to show automatically detected errors. All found inconsistent annotations are marked by a red circle and brought to the forefront of the scatter plot, allowing the user to see otherwise obstructed dots (see Figure 6).

The user can also view the raw cluster algorithm result when pressing the "show clusters" button. The result of this can be seen in Figure 7. This can help to understand the error suggestion and allows for transparency. Found annotation errors can be fixed by deleting or re-categorizing annotations that correspond to the dots. Users using the Dynamic UMAP model can additionally choose to move the dot to the category of choice and train the reduction model.

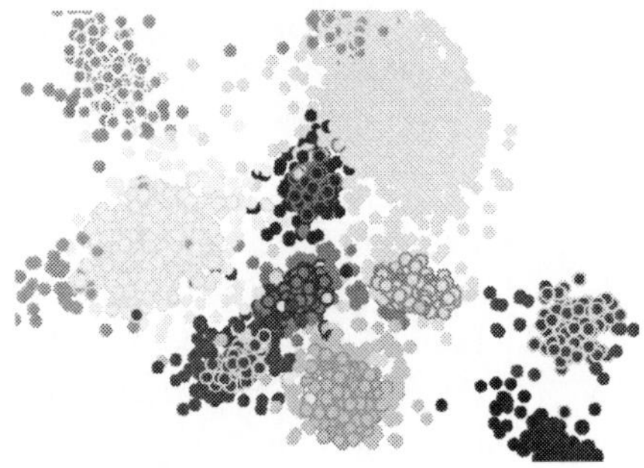

Figure 7: Visualization of calculated clusters as shown in the Plot View. Each cluster is marked by a distinct dot outline color.

Implementation Details

The HDBSCAN clustering algorithm is executed upon each data modification. For every identified cluster, the predominant category label is computed. We employ a simple heuristic to detect annotation errors: A cluster is designated as belonging to a specific category if over 70% of its data points fall within that category. Any data points within these clusters that do not align with the dominant category are flagged as errors. These erroneous points are sent to the frontend and visualized accordingly.

4 Evaluation

To evaluate the effectiveness of error detection and overall clustering validity, errors were intentionally introduced to a dataset. The tool was then monitored on its ability to identify these via its 'error detection' feature.

Dataset Preparation

The CoNLL-2003 (Sang and Meulder, 2003) dataset was chosen as a base, it has 23 thousand annotated segments and four categories "ORG", "MISC", "LOC" and "PER". Errors were uniformly introduced across all categories by selecting and modifying a proportional subset of segments. Labels of selected segments were randomly reassigned to alternative labels. Datasets with error rates of 1%, 5%, and 10% were generated.

Methodology

The datasets were uploaded to AnnoPlot and evaluated using both static and dynamic UMAP reduction. The dynamic UMAP reduction was evaluated for 50 (category) training epochs. The transformer model used for embedding was 'bert-base-uncased', a model without previous training on this task or dataset.

Table 1: The results of the error detection evaluation. True positives (TP), false positives (FP), precision (P%), and recall (R%) are reported for the three different error rates. Both approaches, static UMAP and dynamic UMAP (at epochs 2, 5, 10, 20, 50) were evaluated. The best precision and recall scores are highlighted.

	1% (229 errors)				5% (1163 errors)				10% (2328 errors)			
# epochs	TP	FP	P%	R%	TP	FP	P%	R%	TP	FP	P%	R%
static	60	966	5.85	26.2	284	789	26.47	24.4	573	682	45.66	24.6
2	188	736	20.35	82.1	938	711	56.88	80.7	1779	694	71.94	76.4
5	199	367	35.16	**86.9**	1020	501	67.06	87.7	1969	445	81.57	84.6
10	195	225	46.43	85.2	1039	312	76.91	**89.3**	1983	244	89.04	**85.2**
20	136	42	76.40	59.4	755	52	93.56	64.9	1443	69	**95.44**	62.0
50	42	2	**95.45**	18.3	201	8	**96.17**	17.3	491	24	95.34	21.1

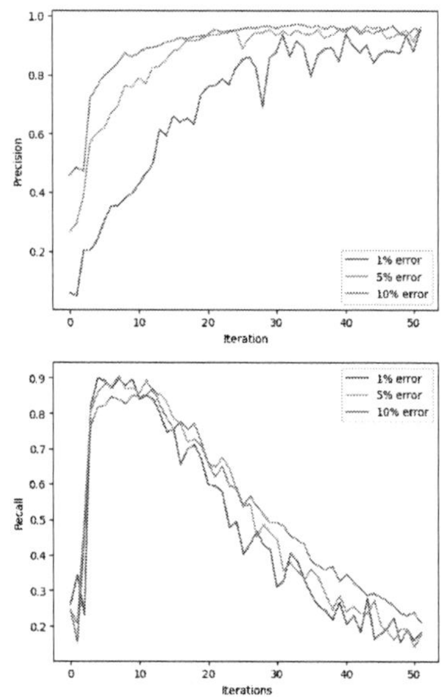

Figure 8: Precision (top) and recall (bottom) of the dynamic UMAP error detection over 50 epochs

Results

Table 1 shows a representative subset of the results. Notably, the dynamic UMAP approach consistently reached higher precision and recall scores than static UMAP. As training progresses, the model seems to overfit, reducing the total amount of errors detected (see Figure 8). However, precision increases at the same time, i.e. only "clear" errors are detected. Optimal F1 scores of 0.705, 0.841, and 0.881 were attained for the datasets (1%, 5%, 10% error) at iterations 13, 11, and 10, respectively. It should be noted that the error detection method only detects points situated within incorrect category clusters. Points outside of or on the periphery of clusters will not be detected.

5 Conclusion & Future Work

In this paper, we presented AnnoPlot, a web application that allows users to easily visualize, manage, and analyze annotated datasets. The proposed tool offers an efficient and streamlined solution for working with span annotations and their category system in a novel way on a 2D canvas. It enables users to upload datasets, add configurations, and manage them as projects, with different data extracted and presented across separate pages. The category and plot views are the main features, displaying categories and annotations clustered together. Users can perform tasks like merging, deleting, and rearranging annotated text passages directly within the view. The plot view also enables the training of dynamic UMAP to optimize the visualization and identify any errors or outliers in the clusters. Statistics are available for categories, clusters, and projects.

This work focused on the visualization, management, and analysis of annotated text datasets. However, extending the proposed approach and interface to support annotated data of other modalities is straightforward. In a future iteration of this tool, we will support image annotations by switching the embedding model with appropriate visual transformers and adapting the software to handle image datasets. This broadens our tool's analytical scope to encompass a large variety of data types.

Further, AnnoPlot will offer more varied dimensionality reduction algorithms, including t-SNE and Principal Component Analysis.

Finally, it is planned to integrate AnnoPlot into a more comprehensive open-source annotation software as an interactive visual analysis feature.

Limitations

The tool, especially the embedding process, relies on transformer models imported from the Hugging Face website. The tool is unable to download new models in case of Hugging Face unavailability.

The embedding process currently relies on large transformer models with a time complexity of $O(n^2)$, limiting the context data available for the embedding generation to about 512-1024 tokens. In our experiments, we limited the context of an annotated text passage to the surrounding sentences and did not run into the context limitation of 1024 tokens.

The visualization of annotated text segments is rendered using D3.js. Currently, up to 10.000 data points can be rendered reliably. To compensate for this, AnnoPlot offers filtering by categories to limit the amount of rendered annotations and allow the analysis of large annotated datasets.

Ethics Statement

AnnoPlot is designed with ethical considerations in mind, prioritizing user privacy, transparency, and control. Several key points highlight the ethical stance of the software:

1. **Open Source and Local Execution:** AnnoPlot is an open-source project, and users have the option to run it locally. This ensures transparency in the codebase and provides users with control over their data.

2. **No Collection of Private Data:** AnnoPlot respects the confidentiality and integrity of user data. The tool does not engage in any unauthorized sharing or transmission of data, and users maintain complete control over their datasets.

3. **Human in the Loop:** AnnoPlot adopts a human-in-the-loop approach, where users actively participate in the annotation and correction process. The tool serves as an assistant to users, allowing them to visualize and manage annotated data effectively.

4. **Potential for Bias Control:** The interactive nature of AnnoPlot, especially in the dynamic UMAP training, allows users to identify and rectify potential biases or errors in categorization. This empowers users to ensure fairness and accuracy in their annotated datasets.

In summary, AnnoPlot is designed to be a responsible and ethical tool, prioritizing user privacy and autonomy.

References

Ricardo Campello, Davoud Moulavi, and Joerg Sander. 2013. Density-Based Clustering Based on Hierarchical Density Estimates. In *Pacific-Asia conference on knowledge discovery and data mining*, volume 7819, pages 160–172, Gold Coast, Australia. Springer.

Jacob Devlin, Ming-Wei Chang, Kenton Lee, and Kristina Toutanova. 2019. BERT: Pre-training of deep bidirectional transformers for language understanding. In *Proceedings of the 2019 Conference of the North American Chapter of the Association for Computational Linguistics: Human Language Technologies, Volume 1*, pages 4171–4186, Minneapolis, Minnesota. Association for Computational Linguistics.

Evelyn Gius, Jan Christoph Meister, Malte Meister, Marco Petris, Mareike Schumacher, and Dominik Gerstorfer. 2023. *CATMA 7 (Version 7.0)*. Zenodo.

Alberto González Martínez, Billy Troy Wooton, Nurit Kirshenbaum, Dylan Kobayashi, and Jason Leigh. 2020. Exploring collections of research publications with human steerable ai. In *Practice and Experience in Advanced Research Computing*, PEARC '20, page 339–348, New York, NY, USA. Association for Computing Machinery.

Maarten Grootendorst. 2022. BERTopic: Neural topic modeling with a class-based TF-IDF procedure. *arXiv preprint arXiv:2203.05794*.

Jan-Christoph Klie, Michael Bugert, Beto Boullosa, Richard Eckart de Castilho, and Iryna Gurevych. 2018. The INCEpTION Platform: Machine-Assisted and Knowledge-Oriented Interactive Annotation. In *Proceedings of the 27th International Conference on Computational Linguistics: System Demonstrations*, pages 5–9, Santa Fe, New Mexico. Association for Computational Linguistics.

Jingjing Liu, Panupong Pasupat, Yining Wang, Scott Cyphers, and Jim Glass. 2013. Query understanding enhanced by hierarchical parsing structures. In *IEEE Workshop on Automatic Speech Recognition and Understanding*, pages 72–77, Olomouc, Czech Republic. IEEE.

Leland McInnes, John Healy, and James Melville. 2020. UMAP: Uniform Manifold Approximation and Projection for Dimension Reduction. *arXiv preprint arXiv:1802.03426*.

Mariana Neves and Jurica Ševa. 2019. An extensive review of tools for manual annotation of documents. *Briefings in Bioinformatics*, 22(1):146–163.

Justin Payan, Yuval Merhav, He Xie, Satyapriya Krishna, Anil Ramakrishna, Mukund Sridhar, and Rahul Gupta. 2021. Towards Realistic Single-Task Continuous Learning Research for NER. In *Findings of the Association for Computational Linguistics: EMNLP 2021*, pages 3773–3783, Punta Cana, Dominican Republic. Association for Computational Linguistics.

Dominik Sacha, Leishi Zhang, Michael Sedlmair, John A. Lee, Jaakko Peltonen, Daniel Weiskopf, Stephen C. North, and Daniel A. Keim. 2017. Visual Interaction with Dimensionality Reduction: A Structured Literature Analysis. *IEEE Transactions on Visualization and Computer Graphics*, 23(1):241–250.

Tim Sainburg, Leland McInnes, and Timothy Q Gentner. 2021. Parametric UMAP embeddings for representation and semi-supervised learning. *arXiv preprint arXiv:2009.12981*.

Erik F. Tjong Kim Sang and Fien De Meulder. 2003. Introduction to the conll-2003 shared task: Language-independent named entity recognition. *CoRR*, cs.CL/0306050.

Daniel Smilkov, Nikhil Thorat, Charles Nicholson, Emily Reif, Fernanda B. Viégas, and Martin Wattenberg. 2016. Embedding Projector: Interactive Visualization and Interpretation of Embeddings. *arXiv preprint arXiv:1611.05469*.

Pontus Stenetorp, Sampo Pyysalo, Goran Topić, Tomoko Ohta, Sophia Ananiadou, and Jun'ichi Tsujii. 2012. brat: a Web-based Tool for NLP-Assisted Text Annotation. In *Proceedings of the Demonstrations at the 13th Conference of the European Chapter of the Association for Computational Linguistics*, pages 102–107, Avignon, France. Association for Computational Linguistics.

Erik F. Tjong Kim Sang and Fien De Meulder. 2003. Introduction to the CoNLL-2003 Shared Task: Language-Independent Named Entity Recognition. In *Proceedings of the Seventh Conference on Natural Language Learning at HLT-NAACL 2003*, pages 142–147, Edmonton, Canada. Association for Computational Linguistics.

Seid Muhie Yimam, Chris Biemann, Richard Eckart de Castilho, and Iryna Gurevych. 2014. Automatic Annotation Suggestions and Custom Annotation Layers in WebAnno. In *Proceedings of 52nd Annual Meeting of the Association for Computational Linguistics: System Demonstrations*, pages 91–96, Baltimore, Maryland. Association for Computational Linguistics.

Liu Zhuang, Lin Wayne, Shi Ya, and Zhao Jun. 2021. A robustly optimized BERT pre-training approach with post-training. In *Proceedings of the 20th Chinese National Conference on Computational Linguistics*, pages 1218–1227, Huhhot, China. Chinese Information Processing Society of China.

GeospaCy: A tool for extraction and geographical referencing of spatial expressions in textual data

Mehtab Alam SYED
CIRAD, Montpellier, France
mehtab-alam.syed@cirad.fr

Elena ARSEVSKA
CIRAD, Montpellier, France
elena.arsevska@cirad.fr

Mathieu ROCHE
CIRAD, Montpellier, France
mathieu.roche@cirad.fr

Maguelonne TEISSEIRE
INRAE, Montpellier, France
maguelonne.teisseire@inrae.fr

Abstract

Spatial information in text enables to understand the geographical context and relationships within text for better decision-making across various domains such as disease surveillance, disaster management and other location-based services. Therefore, it is crucial to understand the precise geographical context for location-sensitive applications. In response to this necessity, we introduce the *GeospaCy* software tool, designed for the extraction and georeferencing of spatial information present in textual data. *GeospaCy* fulfils two primary objectives: 1) Geoparsing, which involves extracting spatial expressions, encompassing place names and associated spatial relations within the text data, and 2) Geocoding, which facilitates the assignment of geographical coordinates to the spatial expressions extracted during the Geoparsing task. Geoparsing is evaluated with a disease news article dataset consisting of event information, whereas a qualitative evaluation of geographical coordinates (polygons/geometries) of spatial expressions is performed by end-users for Geocoding task.

keywords: Geoparsing, Geocoding, Spatial Expressions, Natural Language Processing

1 Introduction

In recent years, spatial information recognition from textual data has gained more attention in the natural language processing (NLP) field. The importance and relevance of the work can be strengthened by highlighting the potential impact and benefits of accurate spatial information extraction in various domains, i.e., disaster management, disease surveillance. For instance, in disease surveillance, a disease outbreak in `'central Paris'` is not the same as one in the `'southern part of Paris'`. Moreover, the extraction and georeferencing of spatial information have significant implications in various domains, including healthcare, financial markets, and e-learning (Hassani et al., 2020). Therefore, the extraction and interpretation of spatial information from textual data play a fundamental role in understanding geographical contexts.

The spatial information can be expressed in the textual documents in both simple and complex ways, depending on the syntax and semantic of expression. This geospatial information is available in the form of absolute spatial information (precise location names, e.g., Milan) and relative spatial information (spatial relations associated with the location name, e.g., North Milan). Both absolute and relative spatial information are essential in providing accurate context for locations in the text, ensuring precision in understanding and responding specific to geographical sensitive applications. While absolute spatial data offers concrete locations, relative spatial information provides contextual references that help to refine and to detail the specific area of interest, resulting into more accurate geographical reference in the text. Therefore, a possible research question is: "Can we develop an efficient and accurate algorithm for extracting spatial relations from textual data and transforming them into valid geospatial representations"?

Traditional methods of text mining often overlook important geographical details by ignoring the complex spatial information found within the text. The motivation behind the development of **GeospaCy** is to overcome this limitation and provide a robust tool specifically tailored to identify and georeference spatial expressions in textual data. The main purpose of *GeospaCy* software tool is to address the demand of precise geographical insights, which are essential for making informed decisions in various domains such as disease surveillance, disaster management, and other location-based services. *GeospaCy* performs two main tasks, i.e., 1) Geoparsing and 2) Geocoding. Geoparsing within the context of the GeospaCy tool involves

Proceedings of the 18th Conference of the European Chapter of the Association for Computational Linguistics System Demonstrations, pages 115–126

the identification and extraction of spatial expressions embedded within unstructured textual data. This task primarily revolves around recognizing spatial expressions such as place names, and spatial relations associated with the place names from the text. Geoparsing task provide a foundation for subsequent geocoding to understand the geographical context of the textual data. In contrast, Geocoding within the GeospaCy tool represents the process of assigning precise geographical coordinates to the spatial expressions identified during the geoparsing task. After the spatial information such as place names or locations have been extracted, geocoding works to convert these textual references into geographical coordinates.

The remainder of this article is structured as follows: Section 2 provides the related work associated to *GeospaCy*. Subsequently, Section 3 describes the software overview, Section 4 briefly details the methodology, Section 5.2 explains the real world use cases and Section 6 presents the conclusion.

2 Related Work

Different research studies have been carried out for both Geoparsing and Geocoding process. The details of the related work are discussed in subsequent sections.

2.1 Geoparsing

Numerous research studies have been carried out with diverse approaches enhancing Geoparsing that revolves around the extraction of spatial information from unstructured text. These Geoparsing approaches include i.e., rule-based approaches, machine learning, ontology-based reasoning, geographical databases and transformer-based language models (Kokla and Guilbert, 2020; Alonso Casero, 2021). In a research study carried out, a rule-based named-entity recognition method was proposed to address specific cases involving spatial named entities in textual data. This approach was validated using historical corpora (McDonough et al., 2019). However, the proposed approach did not address the complex relationship that involves other linguistic features, i.e. part-of-speech (POS), dependency parsing, word vectors etc. In another research (Chen et al., 2017), a best-matched approach is proposed to extract geospatial relations that are referred to anchor places, gazetteered places, and non-gazetteered places. However, it is not defined in the coordinate system to be represented in geographical systems. A further research proposed a voting approach (SPENS) to extract place names through five different system including Stanford NER, Polyglot NER, Edinburgh Geoparser, NER-Tagger, and spaCy (Won et al., 2018). Another research combine multiple features that capture the similarity between candidate disambiguations, the place references, and the context where the place references occurs, in order to disambiguate place among a set of places around the world (Santos et al., 2015). Furthermore, another research (Medad et al., 2020) proposed an approach that is the combination of transfer learning and supervised learning algorithm for the identification of spatial nominal entities. However, the scope of the work was limited to the spatial entities without proper nouns e.g. conferences, bridge at the west, summit, etc. Afterwards, another research (Wu et al., 2022) proposed deep learning models i.e., CasREL and PURE in order to extract geospatial relations in the text. The proposed models were validated with two main approaches, i.e., 1) spatial entities and relations were dealt separately and joint approach. The quantitative results demonstrated that pipeline approach performed better than joint approach using deep learning models. Another research (Zheng et al., 2022) proposed a knowledge-based system (GeoKG) that described geographic concepts, entities, and their relations in order to search through queries.The system is used for geological problem solution and their decision-making. However, the solution is only limited to the geological domain that contains information about geographical events, geographical relationships and concepts. Another research proposed an approach for extracting place names from tweets, named GazPNE2 by combining global gazetteers (i.e., OpenStreetMap and GeoNames) to train deep learning, and pretrained transformer models i.e. BERT (Hu et al., 2022). The extracted place names taken coarse (e.g., city) along with fine-grained (e.g., street and POI) levels and place names with abbreviations. Moreover, recent advancements have introduced the UniversalNER model with more entity types, demonstrating remarkable NER accuracy across various domains, including healthcare, biomedicine, and others (Zhou et al., 2023).

2.2 Geocoding

Diverse research studies have been carried out about geocoding methodologies with the primary objective of transforming toponyms, which are place names or location references in text, into precise geographical coordinates (Gritta et al., 2018). Mostly, geocoding methods rely on address matching, where textual toponyms are compared to a database of known addresses to retrieve latitude and longitude information (Behr, 2010). In a research study carried out, an unsupervised geocoding algorithm is proposed by taking leverage of clustering techniques to disambiguate toponyms extracted from gazetteers and estimate the spatial footprints of fine-grain toponyms that are not present in gazetteers (Moncla, 2015). A further research proposed a system that extracts place names from text, resolves them to their correct entries in a gazetteer, and returns structured geographic information for the resolved place name (Halterman, 2017). The system can be used for various tasks including media monitoring, improved information extraction, document annotation, and geolocating text-derived events. Further research proposed a geotagging algorithm constructed a model in which they used DBpedia-based entity recognition for places disambiguation, and Geonames gazetteer and Google Geocoder API for resolution of geographical coordinates of locations (Middleton et al., 2018). One more research introduced a deep neural network that incorporates Long Short-Term Memory (LSTM) units (Fize et al., 2021). The approach was focused on modelling pairs of toponyms, where the first input toponym is geocoded based on the context provided by the second toponym. The approach effectively reduced contextual ambiguities and generates precise geographical coordinates as output. A further research proposed a representational framework that employed rules, semantic approximations, background knowledge, and fuzzy linguistic variables to geocode imprecise and ad-hoc location referents in terms of fuzzy spatial extents as opposite to atomic gazetteer toponyms (Al-Olimat et al., 2019). Additionally, geocoding services and APIs offered by technology companies and government agencies have become increasingly accessible, providing convenient and efficient solutions for geocoding tasks (Longley and Cheshire, 2017). However, there is no existing Geocoding service or method to convert the extracted toponyms associated with spatial relations into geographical coordinates.

3 GeospaCy Overview

GeospaCy have the capabilities to precisely extract and reference spatial information within unstructured textual data. The main purpose of this software tool is to provide a comprehensive understanding of geographical contexts within textual information. This software tool has a set of features and functionalities which are as follows:

3.1 Geoparsing

In GeospaCy, we extract three kinds of spatial entities, i.e., 1) Geopolitical entities (`GPE`) i.e., place names e.g., Paris, Lyon etc, 2) location entities (`LOC`) i.e., physical locations e.g. Alpe d'Huez and 3) spatial relation entity (`RSE`) i.e., spatial relations associated with place names e.g., nearby Paris, south of Montpellier etc. `'GPE'` and `'LOC'` are extracted through state-of-the-art NER approach, whereas `'RSE'` extraction is the main contribution of this software tool. We further categorized RSE into four main categories i.e., Level-1, Level-2, Level-3 and Compound RSE. *Level-1 RSE* is cardinal/ordinal associated with place names, *Level-2 RSE* is spatial keywords (nearby, border, neighbourhood) associated with place names, *Level-3 RSE* is distance keywords (1 km radius, 2 miles) associated with place name and compound is the combination of Level-1, Level-2 and Level-3 combination.

3.2 Geocoding

The geocoding process, to identify the specific geographic locations of entities, is acquired using the Nominatim API (Clemens, 2015). The coordinates of the `GPE` and `LOC` are directly obtained through this API. Nevertheless, the coordinates of RSE are determined differently. An algorithm developed for establishing spatial relationships processes place name coordinates, retrieved from the Nominatim API, to compute the coordinates of RSE entities. The main contribution of geocoding process is the computation of geographical coordinates of RSE. The output coordinates after geocoding is visualized on OpenStreetMap (OpenStreetMap contributors, 2017) leaflet or downloaded as `GeoJson` format. Figure 1 shows the overview of the GeospaCy software tool.

4 Methodology & Implementation

Our methodology (Syed et al., 2023) is divided into two main phases: 1) Extraction phase (Geoparsing), 2) Geocoding phase respectively. The process

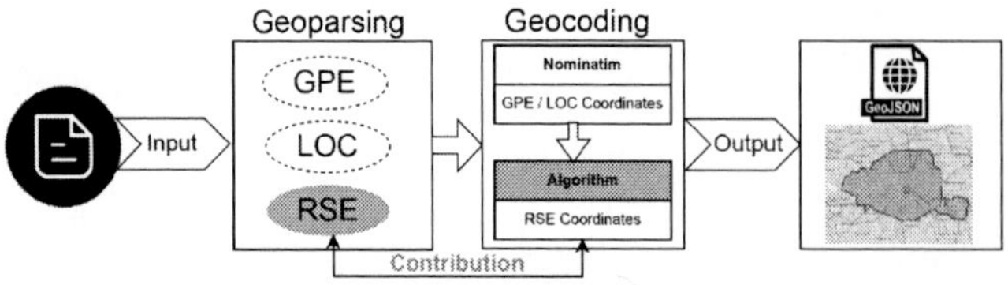

Figure 1: GeospaCy Overview

workflow of extraction of RSE and its georeferencing is shown in Figure 2. The details of the two phases of are explained in the subsequent sections.

4.1 Extraction Phase

In the first phase, RSE are extracted from the text data. We selected state-of-the-art natural language processing (NLP) library *spaCy* (Honnibal and Montani, 2017) for python. *spaCy* has a better performance for NER tasks as compared to other NLP libraries (Vajjala and Balasubramaniam, 2022). The spaCy NER pipeline is customized for recognition of `RSE` label entity types. The steps for the customization of spaCy NER pipeline to recognize `RSE` are as follows:

Model Selection: *GeospaCy* offers three linguistic models, i.e., `en_core_web_sm`, `en_core_web_md`, `en_core_web_lg` and `en_core_web_trf`. The `en_core_web_trf` model is computationally expensive compared to smaller models, and requires significant computational resources to run. However, its high performance and accuracy make it a popular choice for a wide range of NLP applications. After the selection of a linguistic model, the environment is set up for the NLP NER task.

Apply NER: The next step in extraction phase is to apply NER on the textual data. We recognized spatial entities from the textual data with the labels `'GPE'` e.g., Paris and `'LOC'` e.g., Safari Desert respectively. To identify the `RSE`, we extract the clauses that contain the spatial entities in the text.

Clause Extraction: We split the sentence into clauses and save the clause that contains the spatial entity (`GPE` or `LOC`) and ignore the rest of the clauses in the sentence.

Spatial Relations Identification: We extract spatial relations from the candidate clauses. Candidate clauses are identified in the text document as the clauses that contain `GPE/LOC`. In order to extract `RSE` in the clauses, we defined regular expressions for Level-1, Level-2, Level-3 RSE. The regular expressions of these geospatial relations are defined using *Python* regex *re* with the help of Python library *quantities*. *quantities* library is used to get the different quantity units, its abbreviations and their interconversions. If spatial relations are identified in the clause that contained the `GPE/LOC`, then we adjust the span offset according to the spatial relation. The span offset is either adjusted from the end or in the start according to the occurrence of spatial relation relative to `GPE/LOC`.

RSE Spans Extraction: We further identify the spatial relations clauses and made the compatible span having in the NER linguistic pipeline.

RSE Injection: The `GPE/LOC` having spatial relation in the clause is replaced with RSE span in the 'DOC' (the element that contains linguistic feature information) element of spaCy NER pipeline. The label of the `RSE` are injected in the 'DOC' element as `'RSE'`.

4.2 Geocoding Phase

In this phase, the translation of geographical coordinates is derived either by slicing the polygon or by deriving using geospatial operations. The steps involved to extract the geographical coordinates of RSE are as follows:

Acquire coordinates from Nominatim: Nominatim API (Clemens, 2015) provides search by place name, feature description or free text search in OpenStreetMap (OpenStreetMap contributors, 2017) database and return its geographical coordinates based on search queries. The API provides the *GeoJSON* which contains the geometry along with their feature attributes. The coordinates of `RSE` are further determined from the place name (`GPE/LOC`) coordinates.

Derive/Slice RSE Coordinates: The next step is to derive the coordinates of the RSE. Slicing depends on the type of RSE. Level-1 (cardinal/ordinal) RSE coordinates are acquired by slicing the main geometry of the place into **9** RSE geometries.

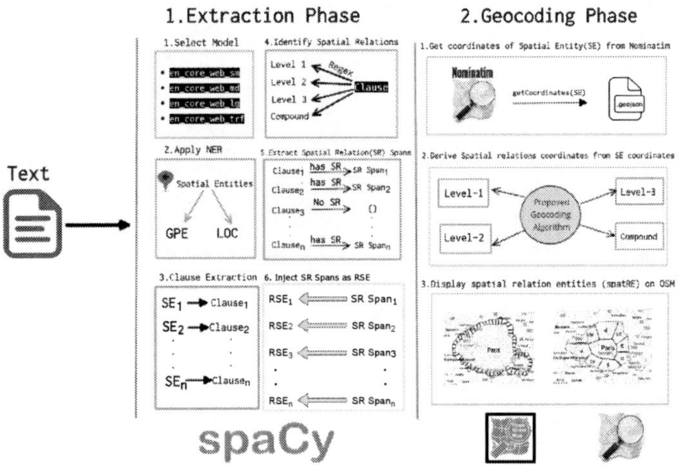

Figure 2: GeospaCy: RSE Extraction and Georeferencing Pipeline

For instance, The Level-1 slicing of Paris can be sliced into 9 geographical shapes: 'Northern Paris', 'Southern Paris', 'Eastern Paris' etc. In contrast to Level-1 RSE, Level-2, Level-3 and compound RSE are derived by applying spatial operations i.e. spatial joins, spatial unions, intersections by using *GeoPandas* (Jordahl et al., 2020) and *Shapely* (Gillies et al., 2007) Python libraries.

RSE output: The RSE output coordinates can be downloaded as `GeoJson` file or visualize on OpenStreetMap leaflet.

5 Experiments

GeospaCy results are evaluated for each phase of the software. These two main phases are: 1) Geoparsing i.e., the extraction of RSE from text and 2) Geocoding i.e., the computed geographical coordinates for RSE. The evaluation of these phases are as follows:

5.1 Extraction and Geocoding Evaluation

The *extraction phase* focused on extraction of RSE in unstructured text, which is then evaluated using a dataset related to disease surveillance. The dataset contains the news extracted by PADI-web[1], which is an event-based surveillance system related to animal health events. The dataset contains the news articles of different diseases i.e., 1) *Antimicrobial Resistance (AMR)* 2) *COVID-19*, 3) *Avian-Influenza*, 4) *Lyme* and 5) *Tick-borne Encephalitis (TBE)* with manually annotated RSE. Precision, recall and F-Score are calculated for the RSE. The RSE recognition task have a precision of ***0.9***, recall of ***0.88*** and F-Score of ***0.88***. The detail of the evaluation are available in Table 1 of the Section A.

GeospaCy calculated the geographical coordinates of RSE. These coordinates were computed and evaluated for cities such as Paris, London, Milan, Madrid, Zagreb, Utrecht, Delft, Lyon, and Florence. For each city, 19 RSE shapes were assessed through qualitative evaluation by end-users, resulting in an average accuracy of **75%**. The detail of the evaluation are available in Table 2 of the Section A.

5.2 Use Cases

GeospaCy can be a useful tool in different use cases, including disease Surveillance, disaster Response management, environmental geographical analysis and other geographical sensitive applications etc. The detail of some use cases associated with disease surveillance are as follows:

Disease Surveillance: In the field of public health (PH) and animal health (AH), health professionals often deal with unstructured textual data from various sources, such as reports, articles, or social media, containing vital information about disease outbreaks, symptoms, and affected areas. *GeospaCy* can parse and extract spatial expressions from these texts, identifying affected regions, hotspots, and areas prone to outbreaks. An example of African Swine Fever (ASF) outbreak with RSE location by

[1] https://padi-web.cirad.fr/en/

(a) Geospacy detected outbreak RSE in the text: **South-east of Fagersta**

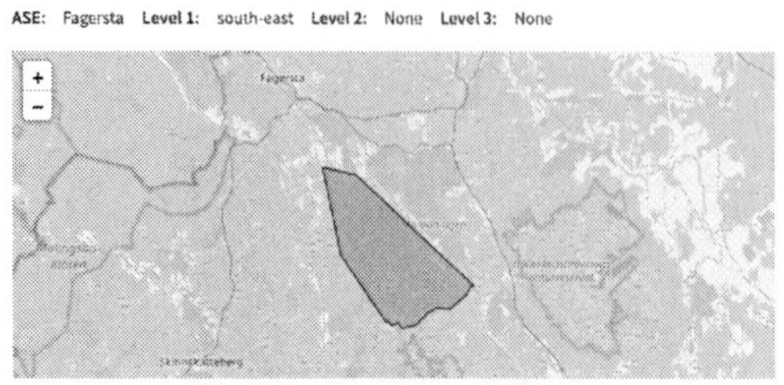

(b) Geospacy detected outbreak location coordinates of **South-east of Fagersta**

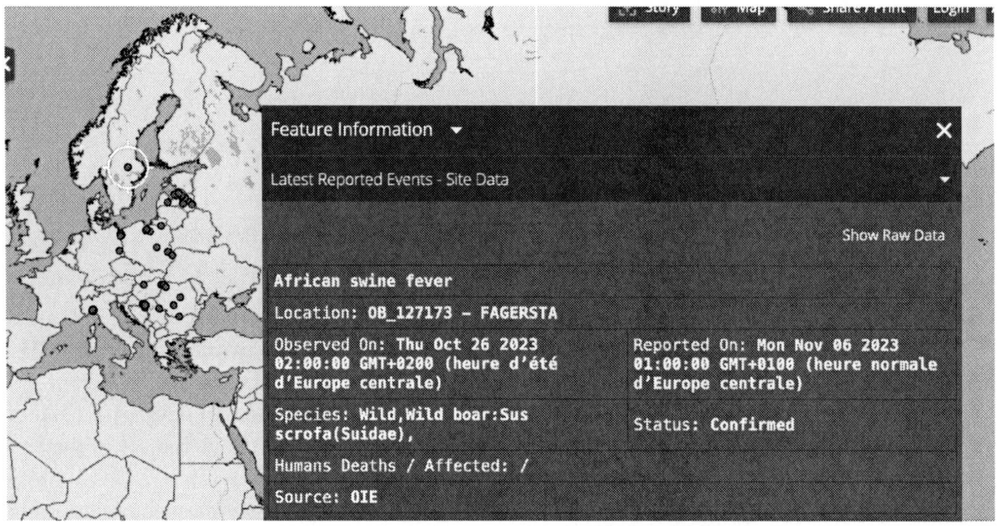

(c) Official Outbreak detected by Empress-i/OIE with location **Fagersta**

Figure 3: An African Swine Fever (ASF) outbreak in South-east of Fagersta, Sweden

GeospaCy and official outbreak by Empress-i are as follows:

`ASF: African Swine Fever (ASF) has been detected in a sample from 7 wild boar found just south-east of Fagersta`[2]

The provided text highlights about "an African Swine Fever (ASF) outbreak occurring in the south-east region of Fagersta, Sweden, with suspected involvement of wild boars on October 26, 2023". The geographical identification of this outbreak was conducted using the GeospaCy tool in conjunction with the official source, Empress-i, as depicted in Figure 3. Figure 3a illustrates how GeospaCy extracted the location information, denoted as *(RSE: South-east of Fagersta)*, from the text. Following this, Figure 3b demonstrates the subsequent step where GeospaCy computed the precise coordinates of the identified RSE, forming a polygon that accurately corresponds to the south-eastern vicinity of Fagersta. For comparison, Figure 3c displays the official source location of the ASF outbreak, pinpointing it to the center of Fagersta. Notably, this example clarifies that GeospaCy provides a more granular and precise region of the outbreak compared to the location indicated by the official source. This indicates the tool potential in offering enhanced spatial precision in identifying outbreak locations.

6 Conclusion

GeospaCy focused on extracting spatial expressions such as `GPE`, `LOC` and the primary contribution of RSE extraction from text, subsequently translating the geographic coordinates of the identified RSE. We proposed a combination of NLP techniques to extract RSE from unstructured text. The results of the RSE extraction are evaluated with news article disease dataset having a precision of *0.9*, recall of *0.88* and micro F-Score of *0.88*. Sub-

[2] https://www.pigprogress.net/health-nutrition/health/asf-sweden-first-outbreak-found-in-wild-boar/

sequently, we conducted a qualitative assessment of RSE geographical coordinates (shapes) with an observed accuracy of 75%.

Short Video

The short video of the GeospaCy tool is available on YouTube for EACL 2024 demonstration on the following link : https://youtu.be/sZb1aUkcRcs.

Software Availability Statement

The code support the findings in this article are openly available in GitHub repositories dedicated to GeospaCy tool[3].

Acknowledgements

GeospaCy tool is partially funded by EU grant 874850 MOOD and is catalogued as MOODXXX. The contents of this publication are the sole responsibility of the authors and do not necessarily reflect the views of the European Commission.

References

Hussein S. Al-Olimat, Valerie L. Shalin, Krishnaprasad Thirunarayan, and Joy Prakash Sain. 2019. Towards geocoding spatial expressions (vision paper). In *Proceedings of the 27th ACM SIGSPATIAL International Conference on Advances in Geographic Information Systems*, SIGSPATIAL '19, page 75–78, New York, NY, USA. Association for Computing Machinery.

Álvaro Alonso Casero. 2021. *Named entity recognition and normalization in biomedical literature: a practical case in SARS-CoV-2 literature*. Ph.D. thesis, ETSI_Informatica.

Franz-Josef Behr. 2010. Geocoding: Fundamentals, techniques, commercial and open services. *AGSE 2010*, page 111.

Hao Chen, Maria Vasardani, and Stephan Winter. 2017. Geo-referencing place from everyday natural language descriptions. *arXiv preprint arXiv:1710.03346*.

Konstantin Clemens. 2015. Geocoding with openstreetmap data. *GEOProcessing 2015*, page 10.

Jacques Fize, Ludovic Moncla, and Bruno Martins. 2021. Deep learning for toponym resolution: Geocoding based on pairs of toponyms. *ISPRS International Journal of Geo-Information*, 10(12):818.

Sean Gillies et al. 2007. Shapely: manipulation and analysis of geometric objects.

[3]https://github.com/mehtab-alam/GeospaCy

Milan Gritta, Mohammad Taher Pilehvar, Nut Limsopatham, and Nigel Collier. 2018. What's missing in geographical parsing? *Language Resources and Evaluation*, 52:603–623.

Andrew Halterman. 2017. Mordecai: Full text geoparsing and event geocoding. *J. Open Source Softw.*, 2(9):91.

Hossein Hassani, Christina Beneki, Stephan Unger, Maedeh Taj Mazinani, and Mohammad Reza Yeganegi. 2020. Text mining in big data analytics. *Big Data and Cognitive Computing*, 4(1):1.

Matthew Honnibal and Ines Montani. 2017. spaCy 2: Natural language understanding with Bloom embeddings, convolutional neural networks and incremental parsing.

Xuke Hu, Zhiyong Zhou, Yeran Sun, Jens Kersten, Friederike Klan, Hongchao Fan, and Matti Wiegmann. 2022. Gazpne2: A general place name extractor for microblogs fusing gazetteers and pretrained transformer models. *IEEE Internet of Things Journal*, 9(17):16259–16271.

Kelsey Jordahl, Joris Van den Bossche, Martin Fleischmann, Jacob Wasserman, James McBride, Jeffrey Gerard, Jeff Tratner, Matthew Perry, Adrian Garcia Badaracco, Carson Farmer, Geir Arne Hjelle, Alan D. Snow, Micah Cochran, Sean Gillies, Lucas Culbertson, Matt Bartos, Nick Eubank, maxalbert, Aleksey Bilogur, Sergio Rey, Christopher Ren, Dani Arribas-Bel, Leah Wasser, Levi John Wolf, Martin Journois, Joshua Wilson, Adam Greenhall, Chris Holdgraf, Filipe, and François Leblanc. 2020. geopandas/geopandas: v0.8.1.

Margarita Kokla and Eric Guilbert. 2020. A review of geospatial semantic information modeling and elicitation approaches. *ISPRS International Journal of Geo-Information*, 9(3):146.

Paul A Longley and James A Cheshire. 2017. Geographical information systems. In *The Routledge Handbook of Mapping and Cartography*, pages 251–258. Routledge.

Katherine McDonough, Ludovic Moncla, and Matje van de Camp. 2019. Named entity recognition goes to old regime france: geographic text analysis for early modern french corpora. *International Journal of Geographical Information Science*, 33(12):2498–2522.

Amine Medad, Mauro Gaio, Ludovic Moncla, Sébastien Mustière, and Yannick Le Nir. 2020. Comparing supervised learning algorithms for spatial nominal entity recognition. *AGILE: GIScience Series*, 1:1–18.

Stuart E Middleton, Giorgos Kordopatis-Zilos, Symeon Papadopoulos, and Yiannis Kompatsiaris. 2018. Location extraction from social media: Geoparsing, location disambiguation, and geotagging. *ACM Transactions on Information Systems (TOIS)*, 36(4):1–27.

Ludovic Moncla. 2015. *Automatic reconstruction of itineraries from descriptive texts.* Ph.D. thesis, Pau.

OpenStreetMap contributors. 2017. Planet dump retrieved from https://planet.osm.org . `https://www.openstreetmap.org`.

João Santos, Ivo Anastácio, and Bruno Martins. 2015. Using machine learning methods for disambiguating place references in textual documents. *GeoJournal*, 80:375–392.

Mehtab Alam Syed, Elena Arsevska, Mathieu Roche, and Maguelonne Teisseire. 2023. Geospatre: extraction and geocoding of spatial relation entities in textual documents. *Cartography and Geographic Information Science*, 0(0):1–17.

Sowmya Vajjala and Ramya Balasubramaniam. 2022. What do we really know about state of the art ner? In *Proceedings of the Thirteenth Language Resources and Evaluation Conference, LREC 2022, Marseille, France, 20-25 June 2022*, pages 5983–5993. European Language Resources Association.

Miguel Won, Patricia Murrieta-Flores, and Bruno Martins. 2018. ensemble named entity recognition (ner): evaluating ner tools in the identification of place names in historical corpora. *Frontiers in Digital Humanities*, 5:2.

Kehan Wu, Xueying Zhang, Yulong Dang, and Peng Ye. 2022. Deep learning models for spatial relation extraction in text. *Geo-spatial Information Science*, 0(0):1–13.

Kun Zheng, Ming Hui Xie, Jin Biao Zhang, Juan Xie, and Shu Hao Xia. 2022. A knowledge representation model based on the geographic spatiotemporal process. *International Journal of Geographical Information Science*, 36(4):674–691.

Wenxuan Zhou, Sheng Zhang, Yu Gu, Muhao Chen, and Hoifung Poon. 2023. Universalner: Targeted distillation from large language models for open named entity recognition. *arXiv preprint arXiv:2308.03279*.

A Appendices

The appendix contains the software demonstration, some example use cases and evaluation of GeospaCy tool. The details of these are as follows:

A.1 Software Demonstration

Figure 4 shows the GeospaCy user interface for spatial entity extraction.

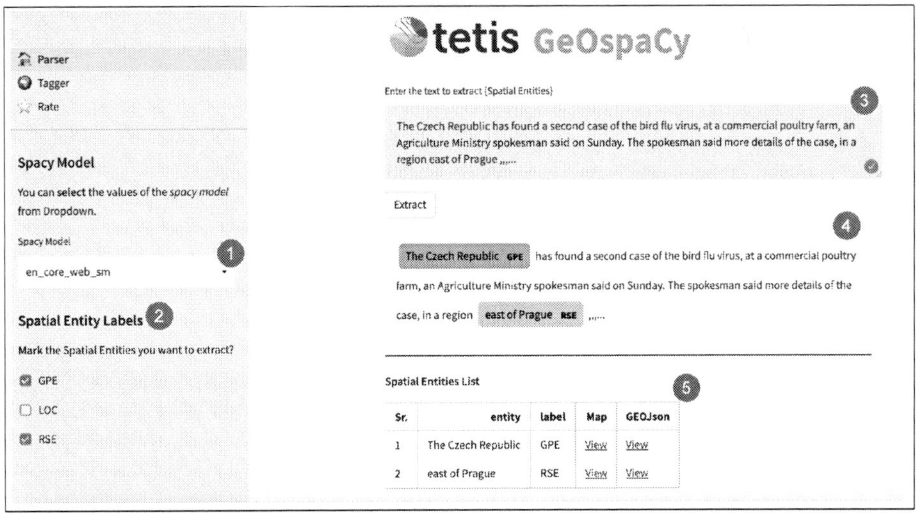

Figure 4: Geoparsing: **1:** selection of spaCy language model for NER (GPE and LOC) recognition, **2:** selection of spatial entity type user wish to extract from text, **3:** input text, **4:** text with highlighted selected spatial entity types and **5:** Table with list of spatial entities with option to view coordinates as GEOJson or on Map

Figure 5 shows the GeospaCy user interface for RSE geographical coordinates visualization.

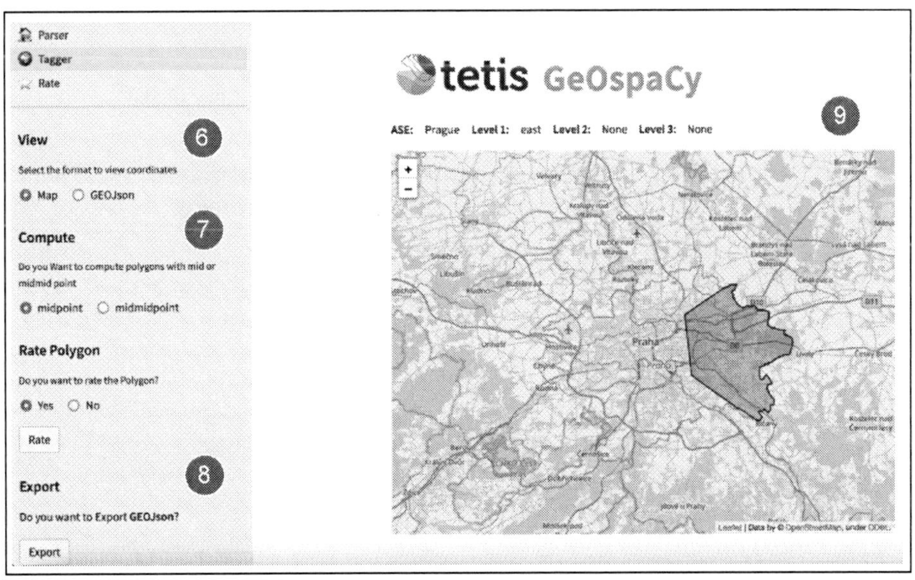

Figure 5: Geocoding: **6:** view geographical coordinates as GEOJson or on Map, **7:** Compute level-1 corrdinates using midpoint(less area inside polygon) or midmidpoint (more area inside polygon), **8:** Export GEOJson on local device and **9:** This region shows the coordinates as Map or GEOJson

A.2 Disease Surveillance Use cases Scenarios

We discuss here some more disease outbreaks detected by PADI-web [4] with improvement of precise location information using GeospaCy tool. The examples are as follows:

`AI: The Czech Republic has found a second case of the bird flu virus, at a commercial poultry farm, an Agriculture Ministry spokesman said on Sunday. The spokesman said more details of the case, in a region east of Prague,.`[5]

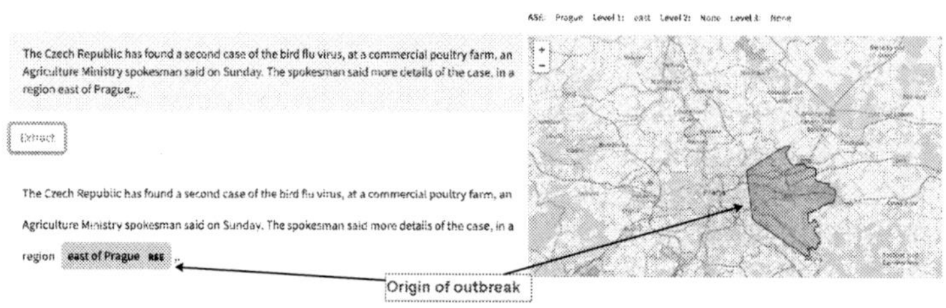

Figure 6: Region of outbreak: east of Prague (RSE)

`AI: The outbreak recorded in poultry and captive birds near Melton, Mowbray, Leicestershire, and the outbreak in captive birds at a wetland centre near Stroud, Gloucestershire have both been confirmed as highly pathogenic.`[6]

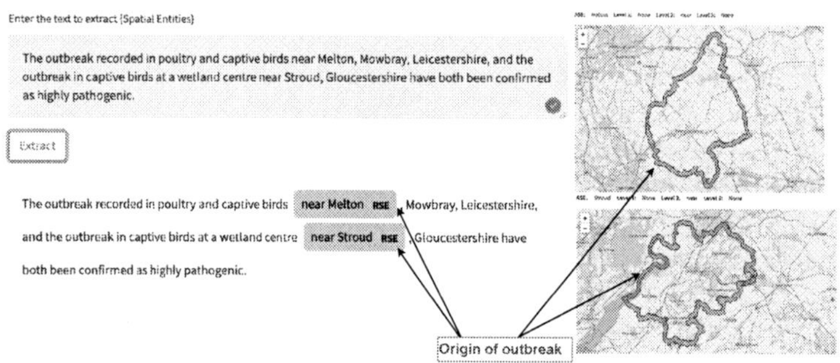

Figure 7: Region of outbreak: near Melton (RSE), near Stroud (RSE)

`AI: France has detected a highly pathogenic strain of bird flu in a pet shop in the Yvelines region near Paris, days after an identical outbreak in one of Corsica's main cities.`[7]

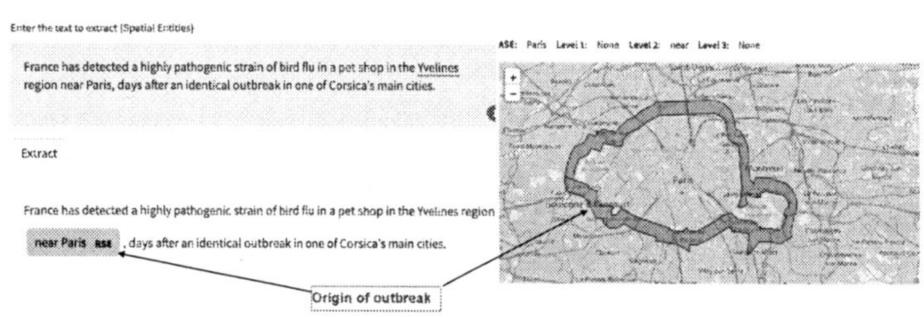

Figure 8: Region of outbreak: near Paris (RSE)

[4] https://padi-web.cirad.fr/en/

[5] https://www.agriculture.com/markets/newswire/czech-republic-reports-second-bird-flu-case

[6] https://www.thepoultrysite.com/news/2020/11/2-bird-flu-clusters-in-the-uk-confirmed-as-highly-pathogenic

[7] https://www.reuters.com/article/us-health-birdflu-france-idUSKBN27Z35D

AI: In less than a week after bird flu was detected in two poultry farms in Vengeri and west Kodiyathoor in Kozhikode district.[8]

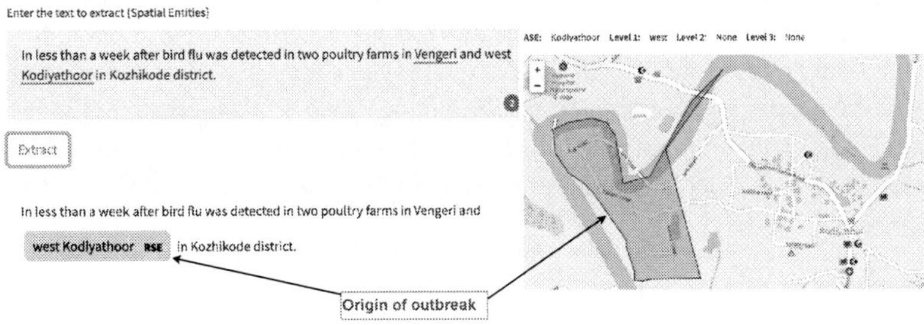

Figure 9: Region of outbreak: west Kodiyathoor (RSE)

AI: The Taipei Times reports that Taiwan has moved to block imports of live poultry after cases of highly pathogenic bird flu were detected at a farm near Cheshire, England.[9]

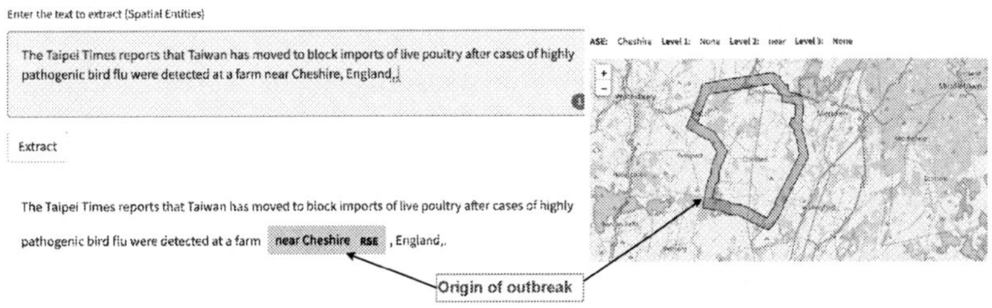

Figure 10: Region of outbreak: near Cheshire (RSE)

[8]https://english.manoramaonline.com/news/kerala/2020/03/12/bird-flu-kozhikode-malappuram.html

[9]https://www.thepoultrysite.com/news/2020/11/south-korea-and-taiwan-ban-uk-poultry-imports-on-bird-flu-fears

A.3 Evaluation: Extraction Phase

We evaluated RSE extraction through state-of-the-art evaluation protocol. For that, we had Named-entity recognition (NER) RSE annotated dataset to evaluate RSE extraction through standardized evaluation scores i.e., precision, recall and F-score. Table 1 shows the precision, recall and F-Score for RSE extraction task. For instance, in the first row of Table 1, the data reveals that 25 news articles were processed for AMR disease. The GeospaCy tool extracted 4 RSE, while 5 RSE were annotated. The evaluation results with precision, recall, and F-score of 1.0, 0.8, and 0.88, respectively. The overall score for all the RSE annotated disease dataset is calculated with precision of **0.9**, recall of **0.88** and F-Score of **0.88**.

Disease Name	No. of Articles	spatRE Extracted	spatRE Actual	Precision	Recall	F-Score
Antimicrobial resistance (AMR)	25	4	5	1	0.80	0.88
COVID-19	100	100	92	0.87	0.94	0.90
Avian-Influenza	150	57	68	0.87	0.83	0.84
Lyme	29	10	10	0.83	1	0.90
Tick-borne Encephalitis (TBE)	73	73	81	0.93	0.83	0.87
Average	377	244	256	**0.9**	**0.88**	**0.88**

Table 1: Extraction Phase Results (RSE Extraction)

A.4 Evaluation: Geocoding Phase

In order to evaluate the Geocoding phase, there is no state-ofthe- art mechanism to evaluate the geographical coordinates of RSE. Therefore, we applied a qualitative assessment to evaluate the geometry of the geographical coordinates of RSE. The criteria of the geometry evaluation are 1) how well the geometry of the RSE geographical coordinates are represented, 2) how well the geometry shows the real geographical region of RSE. The geometries were being evaluated by geographical information system (GIS) end users. For instance, in Table 2, in first row the total score was computed for the 19 spatial relations associated with Paris, including N, S, E, and W, using evaluations provided by end users. The score 19 RSE of Paris evaluated by end user is 136 with the accuracy of 89.5%, with an average score of 3.6 out of 4. Overall, the accuracy of geometries of geographical coordinates of RSE computed by GeospaCy tool for London, Zagreb, Delft and Florence is better as compared to the other mentioned cities.

City	Obtained Score	Total Score	Accuracy(100%)	Mean(4)	Remarks
Paris	136	152	**89.5**	3.6	**Excellent**
London	142	152	**93.4**	3.7	**Excellent**
Milan	106	152	69.7	2.8	Good
Madrid	77	152	50.7	2	Weak
Zagreb	116	152	**76.3**	3.1	**Excellent**
Utrecht	105	152	69.1	2.8	Good
Delft	121	152	**79.6**	3.2	**Excellent**
Lyon	114	152	75	3	Good
Florence	477	608	**78.5**	3.1	**Excellent**

Table 2: Qualitative Evaluation of Spatial Relation by City

MAMMOTH
Massively Multilingual Modular Open Translation @ Helsinki

Timothee Mickus **Stig-Arne Grönroos** **Joseph Attieh** **Michele Boggia**
Ona De Gibert **Shaoxiong Ji** **Niki Andreas Loppi**
Alessandro Raganato **Raúl Vázquez** **Jörg Tiedemann**

University of Helsinki Silo AI
University of Milano-Bicocca NVIDIA

Equal contribution Alphabetical order

Abstract

NLP in the age of monolithic large language models is approaching its limits in terms of size and information that can be handled. The trend goes to modularization, a necessary step into the direction of designing smaller sub-networks and components with specialized functionality. In this paper, we present the MAMMOTH toolkit: a framework designed for training massively multilingual modular machine translation systems at scale, initially derived from OpenNMT-py and then adapted to ensure efficient training across computation clusters. We showcase its efficiency across clusters of A100 and V100 NVIDIA GPUs, and discuss our design philosophy and plans for future information. The toolkit is publicly available online.

`github.com/Helsinki-NLP/mammoth`

1 Introduction

The field of NLP has recently witnessed a hastened transition towards ever-larger monolithic neural networks, exposed to gargantuan amounts of data so as to properly fit their humongous number of parameters. There is also a growing consensus that this is not a sustainable trend: This approach falters whenever data is scarce, and leads to costs—both financial and ecological—that cannot be disregarded.

The problems of scalability are especially prominent in the field of multilingual NLP. Scaling a multilingual model to a high number of languages is prone to suffer from interference, also known as the curse of multilinguality, leading to degradation in per-language performance, mainly due to the limited model capacity (Conneau et al., 2020; Wang et al., 2020). Increasing the overall model size, on the other hand, hits the ceiling in terms of trainability limited by hardware, data and training algorithms. Modularity is one approach attempting to answer the challenges of scalability.

What is modularity? Modularity can be viewed in two complementary ways: as sparsity or as conditional computation. In the former, modularity enforces a principled sparsity of the network, so as to allow a model to be large at training time, but small during inference. In the latter, a modular approach entails routing the information flow to a module in order to select specific model parameters to be used in specific circumstances.

A canonical example is the use of language-specific encoders and decoders for machine translation: For the translation direction going from a source language L_S to a target language L_T, one would use an encoder trained on on the data from the L_S source language, and a decoder trained to handle any and all inference to the L_T target language. Note, that the encoder will typically have seen data with L_S as source language but other languages than L_T as target languages, and mutatis mutandis for the decoder. This dynamic selection of modules entails a principled sparse activation: In this translation scenario, any encoder or decoder linked to some third language L_Z would not contribute to the computation, as if was set at zero.

This design can therefore lead to more efficient inference, since we can avoid computations for a large proportion of the parameters. The modularity also aids in the interpretability of parameters, as it is easy to determine which tasks a parameter contributes to. It also fosters the design of reusable neural network components: Modules can in principle be combined to allow for zero-shot adaptations to novel tasks and situations (Pfeiffer et al., 2021).

What we provide. One of the challenges that come with the study of modularity is the lack of a consensual, broadly available framework for de-

Proceedings of the 18th Conference of the European Chapter of the Association for Computational Linguistics System Demonstrations, pages 127–136

signing and handling such models. The MAMMOTH toolkit is meant to address this gap in the current NLP ecosystem. We build upon the OpenNMT-py library (Klein et al., 2018) and provide a set of utilities to effectively train modular encoder-decoder systems. The MAMMOTH toolkit is tailored toward efficient computation across clusters of compute nodes, and covers a broad range of architectures and use-cases. We also inherit the user-centric concerns of Klein et al. (2018): The design of MAMMOTH include *transforms*, externalized computation steps providing users with means to include arbitrary preprocessing to better suit their experimental needs; moreover we provide utilities to assist users with designing configuration files for massive and complex experiments semi-automatically. The MAMMOTH toolkit is available publicly under a CC-BY license and warmly welcomes prospective developers and researchers wishing to contribute or request the implementation of specific features.

2 Related work

While there exist many open-source frameworks for training NMT systems that have been used for experiments in modular NMT, such as fairseq (Ott et al., 2019), to the best of our knowledge none of them is specifically targeted at modularity. MAMMOTH is the first open-source toolkit to jointly address the issues of scalability, multilinguality and modularity.

The most relevant point of comparison would be the AdapterHub of Pfeiffer et al. (2020): It extends the `transformers` library (Wolf et al., 2020; an NLP-centric model sharing platform and training library) so as to enable training of adapter modules for pre-trained state-of-the-art systems. We base our MAMMOTH modular toolkit on the widely used OpenNMT-py (Klein et al., 2018), a customizable library for training NMT and NLG models with a focus on efficiency based on PyTorch: The more thorough documentation and more systematic organization of OpenNMT-py proved a better starting point for MAMMOTH than the fairseq or transformers libraries.

Another motivation behind MAMMOTH is the lack of a standard for the different architectures of existing works on modular systems. Modularity in multilingual NMT has been addressed in a wide range of custom implementations. One common approach is to train language-specific encoders and decoders. Vázquez et al. (2020) introduce the attention bridge, an intermediate cross-lingual shared layer in between the encoder and decoder. Similarly, Escolano et al. (2021) train language-specific encoders-decoders without sharing any parameters at all. Purason and Tättar (2022) also exploit this method and explore different sharing strategies for the decoder while keeping the decoder language or language-group-specific. Yuan et al. (2023) experiment with massive multilingual MT and propose a plug-and-play approach with detachable modules per language. Other methods investigate the use of language-specific transformer layers (Pires et al., 2023), by keeping some layers source or target language-specific in the encoder. MAMMOTH supports all of the above, and provides a new unifying standard framework for training and testing modular NMT at scale.

3 Toolkit design

We now turn to a description of our toolkit. This section first details the requirements for the toolkit Section 3.1, before moving to the design philosophy we adopted in response to the practical needs outlined in Section 3.2. Finally, we list and describe all major components of our toolkit in Section 3.3.

3.1 Required functionalities

Broad architecture coverage. We aim at a toolkit that covers the major modular architectures proposed in related work (see Section 2) in order to allow systematic studies over a range of implementations in a single all-encompassing framework, ruling out cross-framework variation that prevents a fair comparison of approaches.

In practice, the MAMMOTH toolkit focuses on architectures where modular components can be defined *a priori* and operate as *separable units*. The goal is to allow efficient training of large-scale modular systems from scratch with the possibility of a flexible asymmetric distribution of components across large compute clusters. Furthermore, we aim for efficient inference with a decomposable network where only necessary components need to be loaded for specific tasks. This leaves out sub-network selection approaches, such as the Language Specific Sub-network architecture (LASS; Lin et al., 2021) where a unified multilingual network is split down into language-specific parameters. This also removes dynamic routing approaches, such as the Mixture-of-Experts (MoE;

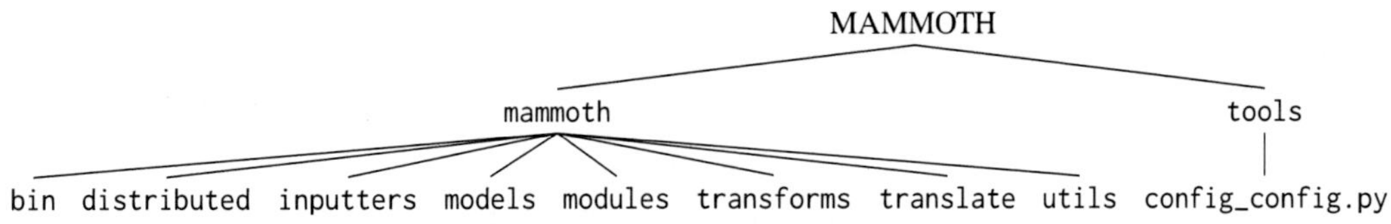

Figure 1: Code repository structure overview

Shazeer et al., 2017) architecture, where a model learns a gating function that activates modules in the network. In such architectures, it is not possible to determine in advance which parameters will be active—and thus all parameters need to be loaded into memory. In contrast, the component-level modularity used in MAMMOTH allows loading only the necessary parameters.

Efficient Training. An important challenge that modular approaches are faced with is owed to their principled sparsity: It is not necessarily feasible—and most often not desirable—to host a copy of all modules on every available computation device. As such, modules have to be assigned to specific devices, which in turn entails that a massively modular system must also be able to handle communication between any two devices that both host a copy of the same module. Minimizing the necessary communication across devices through optimal device assignments of modules becomes a critical aspect for efficient modular training. A practical reality of multilingual and multitask settings is that often data is not equally available for all languages and tasks. Natively handling skewed datasets and ensuring that no computation device is ever idle is also crucial to efficiency.

3.2 Design principles

The MAMMOTH toolkit is designed around the concept of a *task*. A task is the conjunction of three elements, kept constant during the whole of training:

(i) a set of modules;

(ii) a set of preprocessing steps; and

(iii) a single dataset (typically a parallel corpus).

In short, a task corresponds to a specific model behavior. In translation settings, a task will therefore correspond to a specific translation direction (say translating from Swahili to Catalan): All training datapoints for this direction (i) must involve the same modules (pertaining to Swahili encoding and Catalan decoding); (ii) must be preprocessed with the same tokenizers; and (iii) can be grouped into a single bitext.

We furthermore enforce that a task is tied to a specific compute node and device; in other words, we associate each task with an available GPU, and host a copy of all modules relevant to that task on said GPU. This greatly simplifies questions of device allocation and communication efficiency, since we can examine how allocating specific tasks to specific GPUs will impact communication across devices. In short, we can aim to minimize communication by associating tasks that involve the same components on the same computation device, thereby limiting the number of module copies for which gradient would need to be synchronized.

In Figure 2, we showcase a few examples of configurations file snippets to illustrate how tasks can be defined. In essence, the configuration file expects the `tasks` key to be a mapping of task identifiers (e.g., "`train_bg-en`") to task definitions. Each task definition must explicitly state the sequence of modules to be used for the encoders and decoders (or "sharing groups"). This allows for a highly flexible modular configuration, ranging from systems that only involve task-specific modules to non-modular systems. The current main limitations we impose are that (i) all tasks must involve the same number of modules,[1] and (ii) module definitions are specific to a given sequential position. In other words, defining two tasks with encoder sharing groups `[x, y]` and `[y, x]` entails defining four modules, not two. These limitations however allow us to factor out the number of layers each module has, by means of the `enc_layers` and

[1]Note that this does not entail that all tasks involve the same degree of sharing: By setting up task-specific modular components, one can easily define a pipeline that formally contains the same number of modules (so as to satisfy this requirement) and that is only applied to a given task. To take a concrete example, we could define an NMT system where encoders would be comprised of one language-specific module and one language family-specific module: Isolated languages such as Basque would therefore not share any of their encoder parameters with any other languages.

```
tasks:
  train_bg-en:
    src_tgt: bg-en
    enc_sharing_group: [bg]
    dec_sharing_group: [en]
    node_gpu: "0:0"
    path_src: /path/to/train.bg-en.bg
    path_tgt: /path/to/train.bg-en.en
  train_cs-en:
    src_tgt: cs-en
    enc_sharing_group: [cs]
    dec_sharing_group: [en]
    node_gpu: "0:1"
    path_src: /path/to/train.cs-en.cs
    path_tgt: /path/to/train.cs-en.en
  train_en-cs:
    src_tgt: en-cs
    enc_sharing_group: [en]
    dec_sharing_group: [cs]
    node_gpu: "0:1"
    path_src: /path/to/train.cs-en.en
    path_tgt: /path/to/train.cs-en.cs

enc_layers: [6]
dec_layers: [6]
```

(a) Example configuration for task-specific encoders and decoders

```
tasks:
  train_bg-en:
    src_tgt: bg-en
    enc_sharing_group: [bg, all]
    dec_sharing_group: [en]
    node_gpu: "0:0"
    path_src: /path/to/train.bg-en.bg
    path_tgt: /path/to/train.bg-en.en
  train_cs-en:
    src_tgt: cs-en
    enc_sharing_group: [cs, all]
    dec_sharing_group: [en]
    node_gpu: "0:1"
    path_src: /path/to/train.cs-en.cs
    path_tgt: /path/to/train.cs-en.en
  train_en-cs:
    src_tgt: en-cs
    enc_sharing_group: [en, all]
    dec_sharing_group: [cs]
    node_gpu: "0:1"
    path_src: /path/to/train.cs-en.en
    path_tgt: /path/to/train.cs-en.cs

enc_layers: [4, 4]
dec_layers: [4]
```

(b) Example configuration for arbitrarily shared layers in encoders, and task-specific decoders

```
tasks:
  train_bg-en:
    src_tgt: all-all
    enc_sharing_group: [all]
    dec_sharing_group: [all]
    node_gpu: "0:0"
    path_src: /path/to/train.bg-en.bg
    path_tgt: /path/to/train.bg-en.en
    transforms: [prefix]
    src_prefix: "<to_en>"
  train_cs-en:
    src_tgt: all-all
    enc_sharing_group: [all]
    dec_sharing_group: [all]
    node_gpu: "0:1"
    path_src: /path/to/train.cs-en.cs
    path_tgt: /path/to/train.cs-en.en
    transforms: [prefix]
    src_prefix: "<to_en>"
  train_en-cs:
    src_tgt: all-all
    enc_sharing_group: [all]
    dec_sharing_group: [all]
    node_gpu: "0:1"
    path_src: /path/to/train.cs-en.en
    path_tgt: /path/to/train.cs-en.cs
    transforms: [prefix]
    src_prefix: "<to_cs>"

enc_layers: [6]
dec_layers: [6]
```

(c) Example configuration for a non-modular multilingual system. A lack of target language specific parameters necessitates adding a language token using a prefix transform.

Figure 2: Snippets from example configurations

`dec_layers` keys.

3.3 Implementation

Our code-base is historically based on the OpenNMT-py library (Klein et al., 2018). Although the changes accrued to convert it to a modular framework have proven significant enough to require deep refactoring and restructuring, readers may find referring to Klein et al. (2018) a useful addition to the present description to cover the basic aspects of the NMT toolkit. Some practical implementation choices we inherit from OpenNMT-py include the fact that our framework is based on PyTorch (Paszke et al., 2019) as well as the presence of *transforms* and YAML-based configuration files.

Figure 1 provides an overview of the major elements included in the MAMMOTH toolkit. Utilities listed in the `tools` are intended to facilitate setting up training, conducting experiments, or evaluating models. The core source-code itself is filed under the `mammoth` directory. The source files are grouped in eight python submodules.

The `bin` submodule. The `bin` submodule contains utilities for training modular systems and translating using MAMMOTH systems.

The `transforms` submodule. The `transforms` submodule contains a list of default transforms that toolkit users can easily expand to suit their preprocessing needs. Currently, the MAMMOTH toolkit contains transforms for: external tokenization (e.g., using SentencePiece, Kudo and Richardson, 2018) and subword regularization (Kudo, 2018); denoising auto-encoding task, using a BART-style (Lewis et al., 2020) or a MASS-style (Song et al., 2019) objective; filtering low-quality parallel sentences on the fly; and injecting prefixes, such as control and language tokens or decoder-side prompts.

The `distributed` submodule. The `distributed` submodule contains the core implementation of the conceptual tasks we outlined in Section 3.2. It also defines routines for efficient communication in modular settings. In particular, we define an algorithm for broadcasting and synchronizing gradients across all tasks shown in Algorithm 1: The gist of it is that we are able to use the a priori structure to omit communication of parameters that are not on the device at all. For the modules on the device, we signal in how many tasks it has been used, and therefore has a gradient, and rely on this information to sum and renormalize gradients appropriately. The `distributed` submodule also contains explicit implementations for computation contexts (distributed vs. single-GPU vs. CPU-bound training), as well as logic to handle uneven task distributions.

Algorithm 1 Gradient accumulation and communication for one datapoint of task $\mathcal{T}$

Require: set of modules in the complete model, $C = \{C_1, \dots, C_u\}$
Require: set of modules on the device, $D = \{D_1, \dots, D_v\} \subseteq C$
Require: ordered set of modules used in task $\mathcal{T}$, $T = \{T_1, \dots, T_w\} \subseteq D$
Require: inputs and labels, $\langle \mathbf{x}, \mathbf{y} \rangle \in \mathcal{D}_\mathcal{T}$

▷ *forward pass*

$\mathbf{h}_0 \leftarrow \mathbf{x}$
for $i \in \{1, \dots, w\}$ **do**
  $\mathbf{h}_i \leftarrow T_i(\mathbf{h}_{i-1})$
end for

▷ *communicate modules used*

$\text{ready}_T \leftarrow (\mathbf{1}_T(D_1), \ \dots, \ \mathbf{1}_T(D_v))$
$\mathbf{n} \leftarrow$ broadcast ready_T, reduce by sum

▷ *backward pass*

for $j \in \{1, \dots, v\}$ **do**
  $\Delta D_j \leftarrow \begin{cases} -\nabla_{\mathbf{h}_i} D_j & D_j \in T \\ 0 & D_j \notin T \end{cases}$
  $\Delta D_j \leftarrow$ broadcast ΔD_j, reduce by sum
  $\Delta D_j \leftarrow \Delta D_j / \mathbf{n}_j$
end for

The `inputters` submodule. The `inputters` submodule contains all code logic for handling data: It provides objects for representing parallel corpora, handling batching through reservoir sampling, and multiplexing batch streams from multiple tasks whenever more than one task is allocated to a given device.

The `modules` and `models` submodule. These two python submodules contain code logic for defining specific PyTorch components and grouping them together in coherent models.

The `translate` submodule. The `translate` submodule contains all code logic for handling inference.

The `utils` submodule. The `utils` submodule regroups all remaining code logic, including optimizers, loss computation, early stopping and tensorboard reporting.

The `config-config` tool. We prefer explicit over implicit when it comes to the configuration yaml file, even though the configuration can become verbose and repetitive. The `config-config` tool makes configuring MAMMOTH more user friendly. When given a simple meta-configuration file (see Appendix C for an example), it can perform the following operations to generate the complete configuration:

- Path templating for massively multilingual corpora with various directory structures (See Appendix A for details),
- Find which tasks have data in the corpus,
- Determine task weighting and curriculum,
- Determine language groups by clustering,
- Configure the layerwise parameter sharing groups of tasks (See Appendix B for details),
- Ensure that the correct *transforms* are set for translation and denoising autoencoder tasks,
- Allocate tasks to nodes and GPUs. A local search procedure is used, taking into account parameter sharing groups and tasks delayed by curriculum weighting.
- Determine the adapter configuration for each task.

4 Performances

We utilize the Europarl dataset (Koehn, 2005) - a multilingual resource extracted from European Parliament proceedings containing texts in 21 European languages - for model training to showcase the efficiency of our toolkit. We report performances on the Europarl dataset across various parameter-sharing schemes and computing clusters.

Modeling. We use a SentencePiece model trained on OPUS Tatoeba Challenge data with 64k vocabulary size.[2] We adopt three sharing schemes: 1) a language-specific one that uses a balanced architecture with a 6-layer transformer encoder and a 6-layer decoder for each language, 2) a partially shared one that has eight layers of encoders (4 shared and language-specific layers) and four layers of decoders, and 3) a fully shared one with 9-layer encoder and 4-layer decoder for all languages. For the transformer network, we enable position encoding and use a dimension of 512 and 8 attention heads. The feed-forward dimension within the transformer is 2048.

Setup. We utilize two types of GPUs: NVIDIA V100 and A100. We run the toolkit with Python 3.9.16 and PyTorch 2.1.0. We use a maximum sequence length for source and target languages

[2]`https://object.pouta.csc.fi/Tatoeba-MT-spm/opusTC.mul.64k.spm`

of 200, and a batch size of 4096 tokens. The detailed setup guide for the experiment is available in our documentation,[3] including data processing, configurations, and launching scripts.

Benchmarking results. We studied the performance of MAMMOTH on CSC's NVIDIA V100 and A100 clusters, where each node contains four NVIDIA V100/A100 GPUs connected via NVLink and nodes are interconnected via InfiniBand. Scaling benchmarks were undertaken such that the number of tasks increases proportional to the number of allocated GPUs as we are interested in the ability to scale to larger problems with similar load per GPU.

In practice, we train one task on each available GPU for this benchmark. For benchmarking purposes, this task is defined over synthetic data derived from the Europarl dataset (Koehn, 2005): We concatenate bi-texts for all available translation directions, and then randomly split it into 20 subcorpora. While individual data-points remain coherent, this shuffling process allows us to sidestep concerns about variation in linguistic factors, such as sentence length, that were found to be a concern in an earlier iteration of this benchmark.

Moreover, we studied task scaling with three different approaches. Firstly, an approach where all source languages use language-specific encoders and decoders, denoted by "independent." Secondly, an approach where all source languages use the same shared encoder but decoders are target language specific, denoted by "shared." Finally, an approach denoted as "partially shared", where the encoder begins with a stack of language-specific layers, followed by a stack of shared encoder layers, finally passing information to language-specific decoders, similar to the setup discussed in Figure 2b.

Figure 3 shows task scaling benchmarks from a single node up to 5 nodes using the synthetic dataset. We achieve nearly ideal scaling in all of the scenarios: Drops in performance compared to our ideal reference are limited to 5% at most.

To give more context to the benchmarks, we measured the memory footprint and utilizations independently on each GPU. The mean utilization percentage with the five nodes run with language-specific encoders and decoders was 85%, and the device memory footprint was 7.7G out of 32G. Furthermore, we also did performance profiling

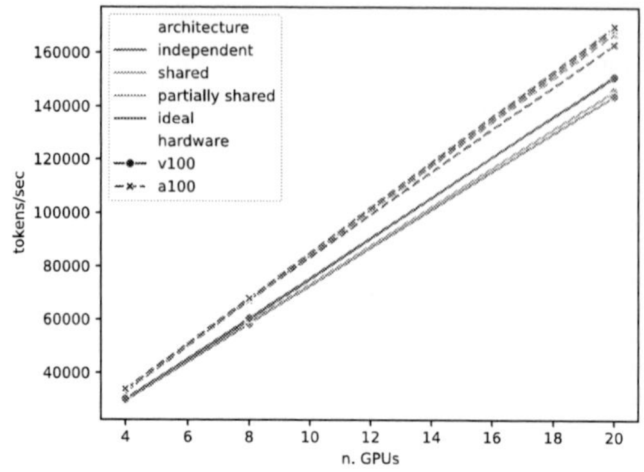

Figure 3: Scaling on V100 and A100 clusters

using NVIDIA Nsight Systems tool to better understand the communication, using the 2-node setup. All communication in the code is outsourced to the NVIDIA Collective Communications Library (NCCL) and at present, it appears that approximately 28 % of the GPU-kernel execution time is spent on NCCL Allreduce. Further communication studies and optimizations with different architectures and setups remain subject to future work. Nevertheless, as we are able to achieve linear scaling beyond a single node, it suggests that the communication overheads are alleviated at scale (relative to tokens processed per second).

Environmental costs. We run the benchmarking experiments on CSC's carbon-neutral data center powered by hydropower. We measure our carbon footprint using the direct eq. CO2 of 0kg/kWh and indirect of 0.024kg/kWh as the carbon efficiency.[4] Each benchmarking experiment runs for around one hour. Our total carbon footprint is 0.11 kg eq. CO2. The estimated carbon footprint for training a model over 24 hours is 0.14 kg eq. CO2.

5 Conclusions and next developments

In this paper, we have introduced MAMMOTH, a toolkit for training modular encoder-decoder neural networks at scale. The toolkit is publicly available under a CC-BY license, and we warmly welcome the help of new developers and researchers wishing to extend it.

Further planned development of the MAMMOTH toolkit will specifically focus on the following elements:

[3] https://helsinki-nlp.github.io/mammoth/examples/train_mammoth_101.html

[4] https://www.syke.fi/fi-FI/Tutkimus__kehittaminen/Kiertotalous/Laskurit/YHiilari

- Interfacing our toolkit with the popular HuggingFace framework, to allow a wider diffusion of MAMMOTH-based modules and reusing existing foundation models for the initialization of modular systems
- Interfacing the MAMMOTH toolkit with the OPUS ecosystem (Tiedemann, 2012), and in particular the OpusFilter tools (Aulamo et al., 2020) so as to delegate data selection to a dedicated third party.
- Providing support for partially frozen modular systems, which would enable adapter-style parameter-efficient fine-tuning.
- Continuing our work of including modular approaches, in particular continuous prefixes.

Acknowledgments

This work is part of the FoTran project, funded by the European Research Council (ERC) under the EU's Horizon 2020 research and innovation program (agreement № 771113). We also thank the CSC-IT Center for Science Ltd., for computational resources.

References

Mikko Aulamo, Sami Virpioja, and Jörg Tiedemann. 2020. OpusFilter: A configurable parallel corpus filtering toolbox. In *Proceedings of the 58th Annual Meeting of the Association for Computational Linguistics: System Demonstrations*, pages 150–156, Online. Association for Computational Linguistics.

Alexis Conneau, Kartikay Khandelwal, Naman Goyal, Vishrav Chaudhary, Guillaume Wenzek, Francisco Guzmán, Edouard Grave, Myle Ott, Luke Zettlemoyer, and Veselin Stoyanov. 2020. Unsupervised cross-lingual representation learning at scale. In *Proceedings of the 58th Annual Meeting of the Association for Computational Linguistics*, pages 8440–8451, Online. Association for Computational Linguistics.

Carlos Escolano, Marta R. Costa-jussà, José A. R. Fonollosa, and Mikel Artetxe. 2021. Multilingual machine translation: Closing the gap between shared and language-specific encoder-decoders. In *Proceedings of the 16th Conference of the European Chapter of the Association for Computational Linguistics: Main Volume*, pages 944–948, Online. Association for Computational Linguistics.

Guillaume Klein, Yoon Kim, Yuntian Deng, Vincent Nguyen, Jean Senellart, and Alexander M. Rush. 2018. OpenNMT: Neural machine translation toolkit.

Philipp Koehn. 2005. Europarl: A parallel corpus for statistical machine translation. In *Proceedings of Machine Translation Summit X: Papers*, pages 79–86, Phuket, Thailand.

Taku Kudo. 2018. Subword regularization: Improving neural network translation models with multiple subword candidates. In *Proceedings of the 56th Annual Meeting of the Association for Computational Linguistics (Volume 1: Long Papers)*, pages 66–75, Melbourne, Australia. Association for Computational Linguistics.

Taku Kudo and John Richardson. 2018. SentencePiece: A simple and language independent subword tokenizer and detokenizer for neural text processing. In *Proceedings of the 2018 Conference on Empirical Methods in Natural Language Processing: System Demonstrations*, pages 66–71, Brussels, Belgium. Association for Computational Linguistics.

Mike Lewis, Yinhan Liu, Naman Goyal, Marjan Ghazvininejad, Abdelrahman Mohamed, Omer Levy, Veselin Stoyanov, and Luke Zettlemoyer. 2020. BART: Denoising sequence-to-sequence pre-training for natural language generation, translation, and comprehension. In *Proceedings of the 58th Annual Meeting of the Association for Computational Linguistics*, pages 7871–7880, Online. Association for Computational Linguistics.

Zehui Lin, Liwei Wu, Mingxuan Wang, and Lei Li. 2021. Learning language specific sub-network for multilingual machine translation. In *Proceedings of the 59th Annual Meeting of the Association for Computational Linguistics and the 11th International Joint Conference on Natural Language Processing (Volume 1: Long Papers)*, pages 293–305, Online. Association for Computational Linguistics.

Myle Ott, Sergey Edunov, Alexei Baevski, Angela Fan, Sam Gross, Nathan Ng, David Grangier, and Michael Auli. 2019. fairseq: A fast, extensible toolkit for sequence modeling. In *Proceedings of the 2019 Conference of the North*. Association for Computational Linguistics.

Adam Paszke, Sam Gross, Francisco Massa, Adam Lerer, James Bradbury, Gregory Chanan, Trevor Killeen, Zeming Lin, Natalia Gimelshein, Luca Antiga, Alban Desmaison, Andreas Kopf, Edward Yang, Zachary DeVito, Martin Raison, Alykhan Tejani, Sasank Chilamkurthy, Benoit Steiner, Lu Fang, Junjie Bai, and Soumith Chintala. 2019. PyTorch: An imperative style, high-performance deep learning library. In *Advances in Neural Information Processing Systems*, volume 32. Curran Associates, Inc.

Jonas Pfeiffer, Aishwarya Kamath, Andreas Rücklé, Kyunghyun Cho, and Iryna Gurevych. 2021. AdapterFusion: Non-destructive task composition for transfer learning. In *Proceedings of the 16th Conference of the European Chapter of the Association for Computational Linguistics: Main Volume*, pages 487–503, Online. Association for Computational Linguistics.

Jonas Pfeiffer, Andreas Rücklé, Clifton Poth, Aishwarya Kamath, Ivan Vulić, Sebastian Ruder, Kyunghyun Cho, and Iryna Gurevych. 2020. AdapterHub: A framework for adapting transformers.

Telmo Pires, Robin Schmidt, Yi-Hsiu Liao, and Stephan Peitz. 2023. Learning language-specific layers for multilingual machine translation. In *Proceedings of the 61st Annual Meeting of the Association for Computational Linguistics (Volume 1: Long Papers)*, pages 14767–14783, Toronto, Canada. Association for Computational Linguistics.

Taido Purason and Andre Tättar. 2022. Multilingual neural machine translation with the right amount of sharing. In *Proceedings of the 23rd Annual Conference of the European Association for Machine Translation*, pages 91–100, Ghent, Belgium. European Association for Machine Translation.

Noam Shazeer, Azalia Mirhoseini, Krzysztof Maziarz, Andy Davis, Quoc Le, Geoffrey Hinton, and Jeff Dean. 2017. Outrageously large neural networks: The sparsely-gated mixture-of-experts layer. *arXiv preprint arXiv:1701.06538*.

Kaitao Song, Xu Tan, Tao Qin, Jianfeng Lu, and Tie-Yan Liu. 2019. MASS: Masked sequence to sequence pre-training for language generation. In *Proceedings of the 36th International Conference on Machine Learning*, volume 97 of *Proceedings of Machine Learning Research*, pages 5926–5936. PMLR.

Jörg Tiedemann. 2012. Parallel data, tools and interfaces in OPUS. In *Lrec*, volume 2012, pages 2214–2218. Citeseer.

Raúl Vázquez, Alessandro Raganato, Mathias Creutz, and Jörg Tiedemann. 2020. A systematic study of inner-attention-based sentence representations in multilingual neural machine translation. *Computational Linguistics*, 46(2):387–424.

Zirui Wang, Zachary C. Lipton, and Yulia Tsvetkov. 2020. On negative interference in multilingual models: Findings and a meta-learning treatment. In *Proceedings of the 2020 Conference on Empirical Methods in Natural Language Processing (EMNLP)*, pages 4438–4450, Online. Association for Computational Linguistics.

Thomas Wolf, Lysandre Debut, Victor Sanh, Julien Chaumond, Clement Delangue, Anthony Moi, Pierric Cistac, Tim Rault, Rémi Louf, Morgan Funtowicz, Joe Davison, Sam Shleifer, Patrick von Platen, Clara Ma, Yacine Jernite, Julien Plu, Canwen Xu, Teven Le Scao, Sylvain Gugger, Mariama Drame, Quentin Lhoest, and Alexander M. Rush. 2020. HuggingFace's transformers: State-of-the-art natural language processing.

Fei Yuan, Yinquan Lu, Wenhao Zhu, Lingpeng Kong, Lei Li, Yu Qiao, and Jingjing Xu. 2023. Lego-MT: Learning detachable models for massively multilingual machine translation. In *Findings of the Association for Computational Linguistics: ACL 2023*, pages 11518–11533.

A Corpus path templating

Paths to corpora are specified using path templates, which can contain variables that will be substituted by the `config-config` tool.

Directional corpus mode. For corpora where the two translation directions of a language pair are distinguished from each other.

src_lang The source language of the task.

tgt_lang The target language of the task.

lang_pair `src_lang-tgt_lang` for convenience.

Symmetric corpus mode. For corpora where a language pair uses the same files for both translation directions.

lang_a The alphabetically first language.

lang_b The alphabetically second language.

side_a 'src' if the language pair is used in the "forward" direction, otherwise 'trg'. Note that the abbreviation for target is 'trg', not 'tgt'.

side_b 'trg' if the language pair is used in the "forward" direction, otherwise 'src'.

sorted_pair the source and target languages in alphabetical order, separated by a hyphen.

As an example, let's say that the corpus contains two files `eng-ben/train.src.gz` (English side) and `eng-ben/train.trg.gz` (Bengali side). The data should be used symmetrically for both Bengali-to-English and English-to-Bengali directions. For the first, `lang_pair` and `sorted_pair` are the same. For the second, `lang_pair` is "eng-ben", but `sorted_pair` is "ben-eng".

Thus, in order to use the files in the correct order, you should use the source path template `{sorted_pair}/train.{side_a}.gz`, and `{sorted_pair}/train.{side_b}.gz` as the target path template.

B Layerwise parameter sharing

The parameter sharing architecture is defined as two concatenations of modules, one for the encoder and one for the decoder. Each module has a specified number of layers, and a parameter sharing pattern. The following parameter sharing patterns are available in `config-config`. Note that arbitrary sharing patterns are possible when generating the configuration file by other means.

FULL fully shared parameters. Will be named using the constant "full".

SRC_GROUP groupwise shared parameters. Will be named according to the cluster id of the source language.

TGT_GROUP groupwise shared parameters. Will be named according to the cluster id of the target language.

GROUP groupwise shared parameters. Same as SRC_GROUP for encoder and TGT_GROUP for decoder. For convenience.

SRC_LANGUAGE language specific parameters. Will be named according to the source language code.

TGT_LANGUAGE language specific parameters. Will be named according to the target language code.

LANGUAGE language specific parameters. Same as SRC_LANGUAGE for encoder and TGT_LANGUAGE for decoder. For convenience.

Note that it is possible to have target-language-dependent modules in the encoder, by using TGT_LANGUAGE or TGT_GROUP in the definition of the encoder sharing patterns[5].

C Example meta-config

We include a practical example of a meta-configuration file in Figure 4.

Note that the number of GPU devices per node (`n_gpus_per_node`) and the maximum number of tasks to allocate per GPU (`n_slots_per_gpu`) should be configured according to the cluster hardware.

[5]Source-language dependent modules in the decoder are possible as well.

```
config_config:
  src_path: "/data/Tatoeba-Challenge/{sorted_pair}/train.src.gz"
  tgt_path: "/data/Tatoeba-Challenge/{sorted_pair}/train.trg.gz"
  ae_path: "/data/Tatoeba-Challenge/monolingual_filtered/{tgt_lang}.txt.gz
  valid_src_path: "/data/Tatoeba-Challenge/dev/dev.{sorted_pair}.{src_lang
  valid_tgt_path: "/data/Tatoeba-Challenge/dev/dev.{sorted_pair}.{tgt_lang
  autoencoder: True
  n_groups: 1
  keep_lc_cache: True
  use_weight: True
  use_introduce_at_training_step: False
  split_large_language_pairs: 0.25
  temperature: 0.2
  ae_weight: 0.1
  zero_shot: True
  transforms:
    - filtertoolong
    - sentencepiece
    - prefix
    - filtertoolong
  ae_transforms:
    - filtertoolong
    - sentencepiece
    - denoising
    - prefix
    - filtertoolong
  enc_sharing_groups:
    - FULL
    - SRC_LANGUAGE
    - FULL
    - TGT_LANGUAGE
    - FULL
  dec_sharing_groups:
    - TGT_LANGUAGE
  translation_config_dir: config/translation/tatoeba.pires23
  n_gpus_per_node: 8
  n_slots_per_gpu: 6
  groups:
    afr: "all"
    asm: "all"
    # omitted for brevity: more languages
    vie: "all"
    zho: "all"

src_vocab:
    afr: "/sentencepiece/opusTC.afr.32k.spm.vocab"
    asm: "/sentencepiece/opusTC.asm.32k.spm.vocab"
    # omitted for brevity: more languages
    vie: "/sentencepiece/opusTC.vie.32k.spm.vocab"
    zho: "/sentencepiece/opusTC.zho.32k.spm.vocab"
tgt_vocab:
    # omitted for brevity: same as src_vocab
overwrite: False

src_subword_model: "/sentencepiece/opusTC.{src_lang}.32k.spm"
tgt_subword_model: "/sentencepiece/opusTC.{tgt_lang}.32k.spm"
enc_layers: [2, 2, 8, 3, 1]
dec_layers: [3]
#### Tuned in HPO
learning_rate: 1e-4
adam_beta1: 0.9
adam_beta2: 0.98
dropout: 0.01
weight_decay: 0.001
label_smoothing:  0.1
accum_count: 16

#### Constant
model_dim: 512
transformer_ff: 2048
heads: 8
warmup_steps: 10000
decay_method: linear_warmup
train_steps: 150000
valid_steps: 5000
save_checkpoint_steps: 5000
optim: adamw
max_grad_norm: 5.0
batch_size: 14000
batch_type: tokens
normalization: tokens
valid_batch_size: 256
max_generator_batches: 2
bridge: false
encoder_type: transformer
decoder_type: transformer
param_init: 0.0
param_init_glorot: true
position_encoding: true
report_every: 100
keep_checkpoint: 3
seed: 3435
model_type: text

#### Sentencepiece
src_subword_nbest: 5
tgt_subword_nbest: 5

#### Filter
src_seq_length: 200
tgt_seq_length: 200

#### Bart
denoising_objective: bart
mask_length: span-poisson
poisson_lambda: 3.5
mask_ratio: 0.5
random_ratio: 0.1
replace_length: 1

structured_log_file: "logs/tatoeba.pires23.jsonl"
save_model: models/tatoeba.pires23
```

Figure 4: Example meta-config

The DURel Annotation Tool: Human and Computational Measurement of Semantic Proximity, Sense Clusters and Semantic Change

Dominik Schlechtweg[1], Shafqat Mumtaz Virk[2], Pauline Sander[1], Emma Sköldberg[2], Lukas Theuer Linke[1], Tuo Zhang[1], Nina Tahmasebi[2], Jonas Kuhn[1], Sabine Schulte im Walde[1]
[1]University of Stuttgart, [2]University of Gothenburg

Abstract

We present the DURel tool that implements the annotation of semantic proximity between uses of words into an online, open source interface. The tool supports standardized human annotation as well as computational annotation, building on recent advances with Word-in-Context models. Annotator judgments are clustered with automatic graph clustering techniques and visualized for analysis. This allows to measure word senses with simple and intuitive micro-task judgments between use pairs, requiring minimal preparation efforts. The tool offers additional functionalities to compare the agreement between annotators to guarantee the inter-subjectivity of the obtained judgments and to calculate summary statistics giving insights into sense frequency distributions, semantic variation or changes of senses over time.

1 Introduction

The concept of **semantic proximity** between word uses has a rather long tradition in Cognitive Semantics (Blank, 1997) and is also acknowledged by notable lexicographers (Kilgarriff, 1997). Semantic proximity quantifies how much the meanings of two word uses "have in common" (Schlechtweg, 2023, cf. p. 25). The concept serves as (often vague) criterion in the lexicographic **clustering** process (Kilgarriff, 2007) and is thus essential to the process of creating dictionary entries of **word senses**. Being essential to the identification of word senses, semantic proximity has further relevance to research building on senses such as lexical semantic change or semantic variation (Schlechtweg, 2023).

In lexical semantics, multiple approaches operationalized semantic proximity in **human annotation** studies, showing that the concept can be practically implemented with reasonable agreement between annotators and correspondence to alternative annotation procedures (Soares da Silva, 1992; Erk et al., 2013; Schlechtweg et al., 2018).

Recently, there has been an upsurge on research in computational modeling of semantic proximity between word uses under the name of **Word-in-Context** models (Pilehvar and Camacho-Collados, 2019; Armendariz et al., 2020), resulting from advances in modeling the meaning of word uses with contextualized embeddings (Peters et al., 2018; Devlin et al., 2019). These models reach high performance (He et al., 2020; Raffel et al., 2020) and thus serve as an excellent starting point for any practical task building on semantic proximity like creating dictionary entries, finding novel/non-recorded senses or identifying words that change their meaning.

We present the **DURel tool** combining the above-described lines of research into a user-friendly, online annotation interface with open source code.[1] The basic annotation data gathered in the system are judgments of semantic proximity between word uses (Blank, 1997; Erk et al., 2013) from multiple human or computational annotators. The tool facilitates the annotation task by providing a data inspection interface and automatic data validation for researchers, an intuitive task interface for annotators, guidelines in multiple languages for annotator training as well as tutorial data for annotator testing. Computational annotators are provided by optimized Word-in-Context models (Pilehvar and Camacho-Collados, 2019; Arefyev et al., 2021) trained on human semantic proximity judgments (i.a. Schlechtweg et al., 2021; Kutuzov and Pivovarova, 2021b; Zamora-Reina et al., 2022). Semantic proximity judgments are represented in a graph (McCarthy et al., 2016), clustered with an automatic **graph clustering** technique (Schlechtweg et al., 2020, 2021) and visualized for analysis (Theuer Linke, 2023). This allows to measure word senses from **simple** and **intuitive** semantic proximity judgments between use

[1]`https://www.ims.uni-stuttgart.de/data/durel-tool`

Proceedings of the 18th Conference of the European Chapter of the Association for Computational Linguistics System Demonstrations, pages 137–149
March 17-22, 2024 ©2024 Association for Computational Linguistics

pairs. The tool offers functionalities to compare the agreement between annotators to guarantee the **inter-subjectivity** of the obtained judgments. It provides further functionalities to calculate summary statistics over the annotated data giving insights into sense frequency distributions, semantic variation or changes of senses over time. The computational annotator component allows to generate word sense clusters for large sets of words and word uses, making it possible, for instance, to analyze large amounts of data or to search unlabelled data systematically for new senses.

2 Related Work

We now compare DURel to existing text annotation tools and related tools from electronic lexicography. There is a number of general-purpose text annotation tools such as CATMA (Gius et al., 2022), INCEpTION (Klie et al., 2018), MTURK[2], PhiTag[3], POTATO (Pei et al., 2022) or Toloka[4]. Many of these allow to define a wide range of custom tasks and can in principle cover use pair annotation (cf. e.g. Giulianelli et al., 2020; Kutuzov and Pivovarova, 2021a). However, this often requires preparation efforts including the writing of small programs as well as the formulation of guidelines and data for annotator training. The aim of the DURel tool is to minimize such additional efforts around organizing a use pair annotation study. DURel achieves this by focusing on this particular task, implementing standardized procedures which have proven to work well in previous studies (i.a. Schlechtweg et al., 2018; Hätty et al., 2019; Schlechtweg et al., 2020; Baldissin et al., 2022). Further unique features of the tool are the task-specific data analysis (see Section 4.2.5) and computational annotators (see Section 4.2.2). Other tools, while offering annotation for a range of tasks, cannot offer these specific possibilities.

With its focus on a semantic annotation task (semantic proximity) and the sense inference functionality (see Section 4.2.4), the DURel tool is relevant to lexicography. The most widely used lexicographic tool is Sketch Engine.[5] The DURel tool differs from Sketch Engine by focusing primarily on crowdsourcing human annotations and offering computational annotation models, whereas Sketch Engine offers frequency-based corpus analysis and manual dictionary making. The two tools could be integrated to provide improved analysis of word meaning.

4: Identical	Identity
↑ 3: Closely Related	↑ Context Variance
2: Distantly Related	Polysemy
1: Unrelated	Homonymy

Table 1: The DURel relatedness scale (Schlechtweg et al., 2018) on the left and its interpretation from Schlechtweg (2023, p. 33) on the right.

3 Background

The DURel tool implements the word sense annotation scheme developed in Schlechtweg et al. (2018, 2020, 2021) and described in detail in Schlechtweg (2023, pp. 31ff.). The scheme builds on use pair proximity annotation on a relatedness scale combined with a graph clustering procedure. Annotators are asked to judge the semantic relatedness of use pairs, such as the two uses of *arm* in (1) and (2), on the scale in Table 1.

(1) [. . .] she opened a vein in her little **arm**, and dipping a feather in the blood [. . .]

(2) [. . .] he saw her within reach of his **arm**, yet the light of her eyes seemed as far off [. . .]

The annotated data of a word is then represented in a graph, which we call Word Usage Graph (WUG), where vertices represent word uses, and weights on edges represent the (median) semantic relatedness judgment of a use pair. The final WUGs are clustered with Correlation Clustering (Bansal et al., 2004; Schlechtweg et al., 2020).

Consider the example in Figure 1 to understand how senses and semantic change can be inferred with the DURel annotation procedure: Assume that WUG G represents the semantic proximity structure annotated for the set of word uses U of the English word *arm* displayed in Table 2. The uses $U_1 = \{A, B, C\}$ and $U_2 = \{D, E, F\}$ were sampled from the two time periods 1820–1860 and 1950–1990 respectively (t_1, t_2). We derive sense clusters on G by building three clusters of uses with high semantic proximity and low semantic proximity to other clusters: $C_1 = \{A, C, F\}$ (blue),

[2]https://www.mturk.com/
[3]https://www.ims.uni-stuttgart.de/data/phitag
[4]https://toloka.ai/en/docs/
[5]https://www.sketchengine.eu

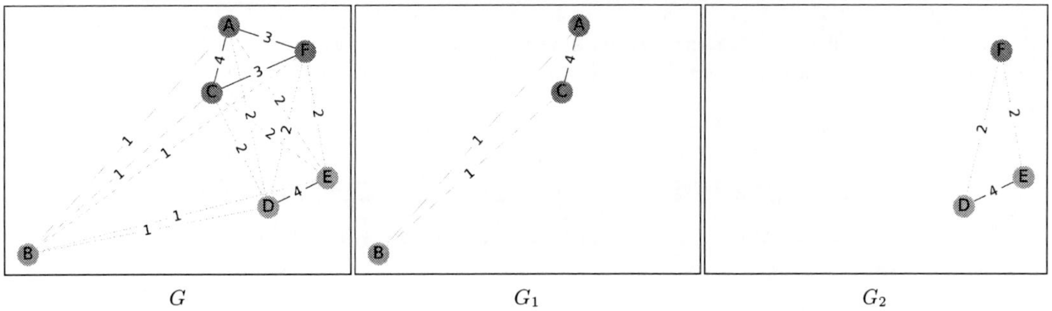

Figure 1: Clustered WUG G of *arm* (left), subgraph for 1st time period G_1 (middle) and subgraph for 2nd time period G_2 (right). **black**/gray lines for **high** (≥ 2.5)/low (< 2.5) edge weights. Spatial proximity of nodes loosely corresponds to their semantic proximity annotation. Visualization taken from Schlechtweg (2023, p. 40).

$C_2 = \{D, E\}$ (orange), $C_3 = \{B\}$ (green). We then build the time-specific subgraphs G_1 and G_2 and are now able to compare the clusters between time periods. For instance, C_3 only exists in the first time period while C_2 only exists in the second time period.

4 Tool description

DURel is a web application supporting user interaction by browser (Mozilla Firefox is recommended).[6] It was created on an architecture incorporating Java Spring for backend, PostgreSQL for the database, HTML/CSS/JavaScript plus Thymeleaf for frontend, and a CSV format for transferring annotations. The source code of the tool is publicly available under a Creative Commons Attribution-NonCommercial-ShareAlike 4.0 International License.[7]

4.1 Data format

Sets of a word uses as in Table 2 are the basic data type that DURel works with. These can be sampled from any corpus by the user and then uploaded to the tool (after registration) as one CSV per word through an interface. The files should contain at least one use context per line along with the target word and target sentence character indices. Additionally, they can contain meta-information such as the target word's POS, the date of the use or a user-specified grouping tag for uses, which can be used later for statistics and visualization.

[6] Find a demo video at `https://www2.ims.uni-stuttgart.de/video/durel-tool/231121-durel-tool-demo.mp4`.

[7] `https://github.com/ChangeIsKey/durel_tool`

4.2 Features

We now describe the central features of the DURel tool.

4.2.1 Project management

By clicking on the tab "Upload Project" the user can create an annotation project. He has to specify the project language and choose a set of CSV files containing word uses to upload. He has then two options options to create annotation instances (use pairs): (i) Let the system generate random sequences per annotator of all possible combinations of use pairs per word. (ii) Upload a user-defined sequence of annotation pairs, which will be presented to each annotator in randomized order. In both cases, the sequence within use pairs is swapped with a 0.5 probability. Alternatively, the user can upload his own gold annotations as annotation project.

Under the tab "My Projects", users can manage, download or delete their projects, as well as assign specific users to projects or make a project entirely public (see Figure 4). A user that has been granted access can annotate for that project.

4.2.2 Use pair annotation

Use pairs are judged on the semantic proximity scale shown in Table 1. An annotator has the option of assigning a label between 1 (unrelated) and 4 (identical), or to assign no label (Cannot decide).

Human annotation When an annotator registers to the DURel tool, they first need to successfully complete an annotation tutorial. Before starting the tutorial, the annotator is asked to read the guidelines page, which explains how to make semantic proximity judgments. In the tutorial, the annotator annotates only a few use pairs of different words.

1824	and taking a knife from her pocket, she opened a vein in her little **arm**,
1842	And those who remained at home had been heavily taxed to pay for the **arms**, ammunition;
1860	and though he saw her within reach of his **arm**, yet the light of her eyes seemed as far off
	...
1953	overlooking an **arm** of the sea which, at low tide, was a black and stinking mud-flat
1975	twelve miles of coastline lies in the southwest on the Gulf of Aqaba, an **arm** of the Red Sea.
1985	when the disembodied **arm** of the Statue of Liberty jets spectacularly out of the

Table 2: Sample of diachronic corpus taken from Schlechtweg (2023, p. 41).

These judgments are then checked against a hidden gold standard. The annotator only passes the tutorial if he reaches a certain level of agreement.

After passing the tutorial, annotators can annotate for projects to which they have been assigned by clicking on the "Annotate" tab (see Figure 6 in Appendix). Each project is divided into several words. Annotators can decide which word they annotate and the annotation can be paused at any time.

For each annotation instance, the tool records the judgment label, an optional comment, the annotator name and the timestamp of the judgment.

Computational annotation We use optimized, multi-lingual Word-in-Context (WiC) models as computational annotators. These are treated analogous to human annotators in the DURel system. They appear as users/annotators in the project management and can be assigned to an annotation project or an individual word by the user through clicking on the "Tasks" tab. Creating a task with a computational annotator will trigger an automatic annotation pipeline in the DURel backend retrieving annotation labels with the respective model and storing them in the DURel database. This allows large-scale data labeling for uploaded projects. The currently available computational annotators are:

- **Random** samples a random integer between 1 and 4 with uniform probability (as baseline).
- **XLMR+MLP+Binary**: XLMR (Conneau et al., 2020) vectorizer with multi-layer perception and binary classification head on concatenated vectors; trained on WiC dataset; predicts either value 1 or 4.
- **XL-Lexeme**: bi-encoder that vectorizes the input sequences using a XLMR-based Siamese Network (Cassotti et al., 2023); trained to minimize the contrastive loss with cosine distance on several WiC datasets; predicts either value 1 or 4 based on thresholding cosine similarity between vectors at 0.5.

4.2.3 Use Analysis

By clicking on the "Data" tab the user can (i) inspect uses or (ii) annotator judgments for each word in their projects (see Figure 5 in Appendix). Uses are displayed in concordance tables showing the aligned target words with additional context. The table offers sorting functions according to multiple criteria. Annotator judgments are displayed in a table with additional information such as the contexts of both uses, the data IDs, annotator name and annotator comment.

4.2.4 Annotation statistics

On the "Statistics" tab the user can calculate a range of summary statistics over the annotated data for analysis. These include (i) various measures of annotator agreement, (ii) label averages for words, groupings and annotators, (iii) comparisons between human and computational annotation. Further, the system allows to infer various meta-measures from the basic semantic proximity annotations. These include (i) word sense clustering, (ii) semantic variation measures, (iii) semantic change measures.

4.2.5 Annotation visualization

The visualization takes the form of a clustered network graph, calculated with Python in the backend, which the Pyvis visualization library, an interface for Vis.js, connects to a HTML, JavaScript and CSS frontend.[8] Nodes in the graph represent word uses and edge weights represent the annotations of use pairs (see Figure 7 in Appendix). Each edge's proximity score is calculated by taking the median between annotator judgments. When all of the annotators have given a score of "Cannot decide", the edge is marked with "NaN". If a node has at least half of its judgments as "Cannot decide", it is excluded from the clustering process. The plotted graph can be filtered according to annotation group, date, edge weight, annotator and noise

[8] https://www.ims.uni-stuttgart.de/data/wugs

nodes or edges. The visualization also includes additional information, such as sense frequency and probability distributions, metainformation on uses, the clustering method and the node positioning method. Users can explore detailed information in additional "Stats" dropdowns. The main goal of the graph visualization is to make it easier to find information on word uses. In contrast to a large text document or table with hundreds of uses, in a clustered graph different meanings can be found quickly.

4.3 Frontend

The user interface of DURel is designed with HTML, CSS, JavaScript and the Thymeleaf template engine. Thymeleaf is a natural choice for an application with Java Spring Boot as it provides full Spring Framework integration.

4.4 Backend

The DURel backend is built with the Spring framework and a PostgreSQL database, both of which are open-source and widely used in industry. It is responsible for user and project management, transferring project data (upload, download), handling the annotation process, and data analysis (use analysis, statistics). The backend runs the WUG visualization pipeline as a subprocess (see Section 4.2.5).

The computational annotation pipeline is implemented as a separate component, built in Python with PyTorch[9] and Hugging Face[10]: It retrieves annotation tasks users create on the DURel website, automatically generates annotations and sends them back to the DURel backend. We deploy the two components on different servers and let them interact with each other by sending REST API requests. The separation gives us the possibility to use the computational annotation pipeline independently from DURel with other annotation tools. It also allows us to deploy the computational annotation pipeline on any server, depending on computational workload, and to run multiple instances of the pipeline to spread the workload to multiple servers.

5 Case Studies and Evaluation

In this section, we describe two case studies to show the usefulness of the tool and to evaluate the computational annotators: (i) The *arm* example is a small scale study on a chosen test word for which we selected word uses from a corpus. (ii) The lexicographer case study conducted on a set of 18 Swedish words is related to an ongoing lexicographic project.

5.1 The *arm* example

For various senses of the word *arm*, Schlechtweg (2023, p. 41) selected the sentences (i.e. word uses) displayed in Table 2 from the online interface of COHA corpus (Davies, 2012). We uploaded these uses to the DURel tool, which combined each sentence with every other sentence into use pairs. These pairs were then annotated with the XL-Lexeme annotator (see Section 4.2.2) and clustered using the correlation clustering algorithm. The resulting cluster structures were then visualized via the system's visualization function (see Figure 8 in Appendix). The generated cluster structures are very similar to the manual annotations: both clusterings distinguish the metaphorical sense 'arm of the sea' (recall Section 3). However, the computational annotator merges the 'body part' and the 'weapon' sense. Hence, while the computational annotator is not perfect, it works reasonably well for this example. We hope that this annotator will prove useful to discover meaning structures in various meaning-related study areas. One such application is given in the next subsection. (We also provide a video demonstration of this example.[11])

5.2 The lexicographer case study

To test DURel in a practical application, we used it in a small study on revealing semantic variation in Swedish. The study is closely related to the work of revising the comprehensive Swedish dictionary published by the Swedish Academy ('The Contemporary Dictionary of the Swedish Academy'; in short SO[12]), a general language definition dictionary with about 65,000 headwords. An important part of the revision work within the dictionary project is to examine whether the meanings of the headwords in SO have developed in some way since the last edition was published. However, the lexicographic team of SO currently do not, in a systematic way, use any formal computational methods for discovering semantic change

[9] https://pytorch.org/

[10] https://huggingface.co

[11] https://www2.ims.uni-stuttgart.de/video/durel-tool/230623-durel-tool-demo.mp4.

[12] https://svenska.se/

Word	ARI	Word	ARI
ofantlig	1.0	klimat	0.083
enkelspårig	1.0	vansinnig	0.0
baksida	0.912	lirka	0.0
bagage	0.785	kapitulera	0.0
fasad	0.652	hemmaplan	0.0
vissen	0.645	hagla	0.0
skör	0.507	fotavtryck	0.0
rutten	0.333	tvärnita	-0.019
ventilera	0.303	kriga	-0.025
Average	**0.343**		

Table 3: Cluster evaluation based on ARI.

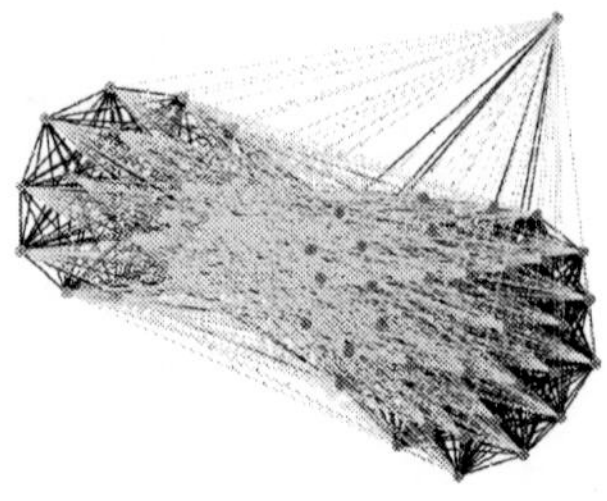

Figure 2: Clusters for *bagage*.

on the lexical level. Hence, the lexicographic challenge is finding relatively new meanings not already recorded. The question is whether the DURel tool can point out meaning variation (as an indicator of change) by clustering different meanings of a word. For that purpose, as a first round of experiments, we selected a set of 18 established Swedish words that are already in SO. These words were thoughtfully selected based on their semantic characteristics: all of them have a main sense and one or more subsenses. For each word, we automatically extracted a collection of 50 random sentences from the SVT (Swedish Television) corpus available through Korp (Borin et al., 2012). These sentences were then uploaded into the tool, automatically paired and annotated with XL-Lexeme, and finally clustered using the correlation algorithm. The resulting clusters were evaluated against lexicographer judgments for sense clusters (gold data).

Table 3 displays the evaluation results using the Adjusted Rand Index (ARI, Hubert and Arabie, 1985) to compare automatically generated clusters with manually curated gold clusters. Each row represents a specific word used to form the clusters, with the corresponding ARI value indicating the similarity between the automatic and gold clusters generated by DURel and the lexicographer respectively. ARI generally ranges from -0.5 to 1, where higher values closer to 1 signify better agreement between the gold clusters and the derived clusters. A value of 0 suggests a random clustering. As can be noted words like *ofantlig*, *enkelspårig*, *baksida*, and *bagage* demonstrate relatively high ARI values, indicating stronger alignment between their respective clusters and the gold clusters. In contrast *tvärnita*, *hemmaplan* and *vansinnig* show ARI values of 0 or slightly negative. The 'Average' row provides an overall assessment by presenting the average ARI across all words. The moderately positive average value suggests that the automatically derived clusters generally encode meaningful semantic information which could be useful for lexicographic work.

In addition to automatic evaluation using ARI, the clusters were analyzed qualitatively by a lexicographer, which provided useful insights. For example consider Figure 2 which shows the clusters produced for the word *bagage* (Eng: 'luggage'). As can be seen, the uses were clustered into three main clusters (colored blue, orange, and green). The blue and orange colored represent the literal and figurative usage of the word respectively while one of the uses was wrongly put into the third, green cluster. A discrepancy between the number of clusters identified by DURel and the number of senses recorded in SO dictionary for the candidate word can be used as an indicator that the description in the dictionary is outdated. Such words can be prioritized for manual inspection in order to update the dictionary entry or otherwise to improve the computational model. An examination of the figurative examples (the orange cluster) revealed that some of the uses can be classified as different variants of the same Swedish idiomatic expression (e.g. *ha något i bagaget*, ENG: 'to have something in the luggage'). This particular idiom, and similar others, is not treated in SO 2021 and will be included in the next edition. Further, the text examples from the corpora form also a good basis to include more language examples in the SO dictionary. In summary, the DURel tool was evaluated by the lexicographer to be helpful in revising the SO dictionary, who otherwise has relied completely on manual cumbersome methodology.

6 Conclusion

We presented the DURel, an online, open-source annotation tool for annotating semantic proximity between word uses. The tool supports human as well as computational annotation, building on recent advances with WiC models. Annotator judgments are automatically clustered and visualized for analysis. This allows to capture word senses with simple and intuitive micro-task judgments between use pairs, requiring minimal preparation efforts. Additionally, DURel can compare the agreement between annotators to guarantee the intersubjectivity of the obtained judgments and to calculate summary statistics over the annotated data giving insights into sense frequency distributions, semantic variation or changes of senses over time. The computational annotator component allows to generate word sense clusters for large sets of words and word uses, making it possible, for instance, to analyze large amounts of data or to search systematically for new senses.

A number of different research groups around the world have used the system to annotate data (e.g. Zamora-Reina et al., 2022; Kutuzov et al., 2022; Aksenova et al., 2022; Chen et al., 2023) and continue to do so: Currently, the tool is being used to annotate an Italian dataset.

6.1 Limitations

DURel provides a range of functionalities feasible only because it focuses on a single task but with the disadvantage of a more narrow application range and low customization. This also binds users to the four-level annotation scale hard-coded into the system. While this scale is motivated by theory (Schlechtweg et al., 2018), there exist valid alternatives (e.g. Erk et al., 2013; Brown, 2008). For users who want to use such an alternative scale, we recommend to conduct the annotation study within a more customizable annotation system like PhiTag. The annotated data can then be uploaded to DURel with the "Upload Judgments" functionality, and clustering and analysis can be applied within DURel.

The tool currently allows to specify a continuous substring of any length as target string in each uploaded word use. Discontinuous target strings, as needed e.g. for discontinuous multi-word expressions such as particle verbs in German, are currently not allowed.

The computational annotators are currently restricted to predict binary labels. In the future, we will provide WiC models optimized for ordinal predictions on all levels of the annotation scale (Zhang, 2023).

Acknowledgments

The development of the tool has been funded by the project 'Towards Computational Lexical Semantic Change Detection' supported by the Swedish Research Council (2019–2022; contract 2018-01184), the research program 'Change is Key!' supported by Riksbankens Jubileumsfond (under reference number M21-0021) and the CRETA center funded by the German Ministry for Education and Research (BMBF). We thank Anne Reuter, Annalena Streichert, Enrique Medina Waldo Castaneda, Sinan Kurtyigit, Serge Kotchourko, Pedro G. Bascoy, Francesco Periti and Jing Chen for contributions to this project.

References

Anna Aksenova, Ekaterina Gavrishina, Elisey Rykov, and Andrey Kutuzov. 2022. Rudsi: graph-based word sense induction dataset for russian.

Nikolay Arefyev, Maksim Fedoseev, Vitaly Protasov, Daniil Homskiy, Adis Davletov, and Alexander Panchenko. 2021. Deepmistake: Which senses are hard to distinguish for a word-in-context model. volume 2021-June, pages 16–30.

Carlos Santos Armendariz, Matthew Purver, Matej Ulčar, Senja Pollak, Nikola Ljubešić, and Mark Granroth-Wilding. 2020. CoSimLex: A resource for evaluating graded word similarity in context. In *Proceedings of the Twelfth Language Resources and Evaluation Conference*, pages 5878–5886, Marseille, France. European Language Resources Association.

Gioia Baldissin, Dominik Schlechtweg, and Sabine Schulte im Walde. 2022. DiaWUG: A Dataset for Diatopic Lexical Semantic Variation in Spanish. In *Proceedings of the 13th Language Resources and Evaluation Conference*, Marseille, France. European Language Resources Association.

Nikhil Bansal, Avrim Blum, and Shuchi Chawla. 2004. Correlation clustering. *Machine Learning*, 56(1-3):89–113.

Andreas Blank. 1997. *Prinzipien des lexikalischen Bedeutungswandels am Beispiel der romanischen Sprachen*. Niemeyer, Tübingen.

Lars Borin, Markus Forsberg, and Johan Roxendal. 2012. Korp – the corpus infrastructure of språkbanken. In *Proceedings of LREC 2012. Istanbul: ELRA*, volume Accepted, page 474–478.

Susan Windisch Brown. 2008. Choosing sense distinctions for WSD: Psycholinguistic evidence. In *Proceedings of the 46th Annual Meeting of the Association for Computational Linguistics on Human Language Technologies: Short Papers*, pages 249–252, Stroudsburg, PA, USA.

Pierluigi Cassotti, Lucia Siciliani, Marco de Gemmis, Giovanni Semeraro, and Pierpaolo Basile. 2023. Xl-lexeme: Wic pretrained model for cross-lingual lexical semantic change. In *Proceedings of the 61th Annual Meeting of the Association for Computational Linguistics*, Online. Association for Computational Linguistics.

Jing Chen, Emmanuele Chersoni, Dominik Schlechtweg, Jelena Prokic, and Chu-Ren Huang. 2023. ChiWUG: A graph-based evaluation dataset for chinese lexical semantic change detection. In *Proceedings of the 4th International Workshop on Computational Approaches to Historical Language Change*, Singapore. Association for Computational Linguistics.

Alexis Conneau, Kartikay Khandelwal, Naman Goyal, Vishrav Chaudhary, Guillaume Wenzek, Francisco Guzmán, Edouard Grave, Myle Ott, Luke Zettlemoyer, and Veselin Stoyanov. 2020. Unsupervised cross-lingual representation learning at scale. In *Proceedings of the 58th Annual Meeting of the Association for Computational Linguistics*, pages 8440–8451, Online. Association for Computational Linguistics.

Mark Davies. 2012. Expanding Horizons in Historical Linguistics with the 400-Million Word Corpus of Historical American English. *Corpora*, 7(2):121–157.

Jacob Devlin, Ming-Wei Chang, Kenton Lee, and Kristina Toutanova. 2019. BERT: Pre-training of deep bidirectional transformers for language understanding. In *Proceedings of the 2019 Conference of the North American Chapter of the Association for Computational Linguistics: Human Language Technologies, Volume 1 (Long and Short Papers)*, pages 4171–4186, Minneapolis, Minnesota. Association for Computational Linguistics.

Katrin Erk, Diana McCarthy, and Nicholas Gaylord. 2013. Measuring word meaning in context. *Computational Linguistics*, 39(3):511–554.

Mario Giulianelli, Marco del Tredici, and Raquel Fernández. 2020. Analysing lexical semantic change with contextualised word representations. In *Proceedings of the 58th Annual Meeting of the Association for Computational Linguistics*, pages 3960–3973, Online. Association for Computational Linguistics.

Evelyn Gius, Jan Christoph Meister, Malte Meister, Marco Petris, Christian Bruck, Janina Jacke, Mareike Schumacher, Dominik Gerstorfer, Marie Flüh, and Jan Horstmann. 2022. Catma.

Anna Hätty, Dominik Schlechtweg, and Sabine Schulte im Walde. 2019. SURel: A gold standard for incorporating meaning shifts into term extraction. In *Proceedings of the 8th Joint Conference on Lexical and Computational Semantics*, pages 1–8, Minneapolis, MN, USA.

Pengcheng He, Xiaodong Liu, Jianfeng Gao, and Weizhu Chen. 2020. Deberta: Decoding-enhanced bert with disentangled attention. *arXiv preprint arXiv:2006.03654*.

Lawrence Hubert and Phipps Arabie. 1985. Comparing partitions. *Journal of Classification*, 2:193–218.

Adam Kilgarriff. 1997. "I don't believe in word senses". *Computers and the Humanities*, 31(2).

Adam Kilgarriff. 2007. *Word Senses*, chapter 2. Springer.

Jan-Christoph Klie, Michael Bugert, Beto Boullosa, Richard Eckart de Castilho, and Iryna Gurevych. 2018. The inception platform: Machine-assisted and knowledge-oriented interactive annotation. In *Proceedings of the 27th International Conference on Computational Linguistics: System Demonstrations*, pages 5–9. Association for Computational Linguistics. Event Title: The 27th International Conference on Computational Linguistics (COLING 2018).

Andrey Kutuzov and Lidia Pivovarova. 2021a. Rushifteval: a shared task on semantic shift detection for russian. *Komp'yuternaya Lingvistika i Intellektual'nye Tekhnologii: Dialog conference*.

Andrey Kutuzov and Lidia Pivovarova. 2021b. Three-part diachronic semantic change dataset for russian.

Andrey Kutuzov, Samia Touileb, Petter Mæhlum, Tita Enstad, and Alexandra Wittemann. 2022. NorDiaChange: Diachronic semantic change dataset for Norwegian. In *Proceedings of the Thirteenth Language Resources and Evaluation Conference*, pages 2563–2572, Marseille, France. European Language Resources Association.

Diana McCarthy, Marianna Apidianaki, and Katrin Erk. 2016. Word sense clustering and clusterability. *Computational Linguistics*, 42(2):245–275.

Jiaxin Pei, Aparna Ananthasubramaniam, Xingyao Wang, Naitian Zhou, Apostolos Dedeloudis, Jackson Sargent, and David Jurgens. 2022. Potato: The portable text annotation tool. In *Proceedings of the 2022 Conference on Empirical Methods in Natural Language Processing: System Demonstrations*.

Matthew Peters, Mark Neumann, Mohit Iyyer, Matt Gardner, Christopher Clark, Kenton Lee, and Luke Zettlemoyer. 2018. Deep contextualized word representations. In *Proceedings of the 2018 Conference of the North American Chapter of the Association for Computational Linguistics: Human Language Technologies*, pages 2227–2237, New Orleans, LA, USA.

Mohammad Taher Pilehvar and Jose Camacho-Collados. 2019. WiC: the word-in-context dataset for evaluating context-sensitive meaning representations. In *Proceedings of the 2019 Conference of the North American Chapter of the Association for Computational Linguistics: Human Language Technologies, Volume 1 (Long and Short Papers)*, pages 1267–1273, Minneapolis, Minnesota. Association for Computational Linguistics.

Colin Raffel, Noam Shazeer, Adam Roberts, Katherine Lee, Sharan Narang, Michael Matena, Yanqi Zhou, Wei Li, Peter J Liu, et al. 2020. Exploring the limits of transfer learning with a unified text-to-text transformer. *J. Mach. Learn. Res.*, 21(140):1–67.

Dominik Schlechtweg. 2023. *Human and Computational Measurement of Lexical Semantic Change*. Ph.D. thesis, University of Stuttgart, Stuttgart, Germany.

Dominik Schlechtweg, Barbara McGillivray, Simon Hengchen, Haim Dubossarsky, and Nina Tahmasebi. 2020. SemEval-2020 Task 1: Unsupervised Lexical Semantic Change Detection. In *Proceedings of the 14th International Workshop on Semantic Evaluation*, Barcelona, Spain. Association for Computational Linguistics.

Dominik Schlechtweg, Sabine Schulte im Walde, and Stefanie Eckmann. 2018. Diachronic Usage Relatedness (DURel): A framework for the annotation of lexical semantic change. In *Proceedings of the 2018 Conference of the North American Chapter of the Association for Computational Linguistics: Human Language Technologies*, pages 169–174, New Orleans, Louisiana.

Dominik Schlechtweg, Nina Tahmasebi, Simon Hengchen, Haim Dubossarsky, and Barbara McGillivray. 2021. DWUG: A large Resource of Diachronic Word Usage Graphs in Four Languages. In *Proceedings of the 2021 Conference on Empirical Methods in Natural Language Processing*, pages 7079–7091, Online and Punta Cana, Dominican Republic. Association for Computational Linguistics.

A. Soares da Silva. 1992. Homonímia e polissemia: Análise sémica e teoria do campoléxico. In *Actas do XIX Congreso Internacional de Lingüística e Filoloxía Románicas*, volume 2 of *Lexicoloxía e Metalexicografía*, pages 257–287, La Coruña. Fundación Pedro Barrié de la Maza.

Lukas Theuer Linke. 2023. Testing the effect of using crowdsourced semantic proximity judgments in the process of human lexicographical word sense clustering. Bachelor thesis, University of Stuttgart.

Frank D. Zamora-Reina, Felipe Bravo-Marquez, and Dominik Schlechtweg. 2022. LSCDiscovery: A shared task on semantic change discovery and detection in Spanish. In *Proceedings of the 3rd International Workshop on Computational Approaches to Historical Language Change*, Dublin, Ireland. Association for Computational Linguistics.

Tuo Zhang. 2023. An ordinal formulation of the graded word-in-context task. Master thesis, University of Stuttgart.

A Appendix

We have included some screenshots of the DURel application below.

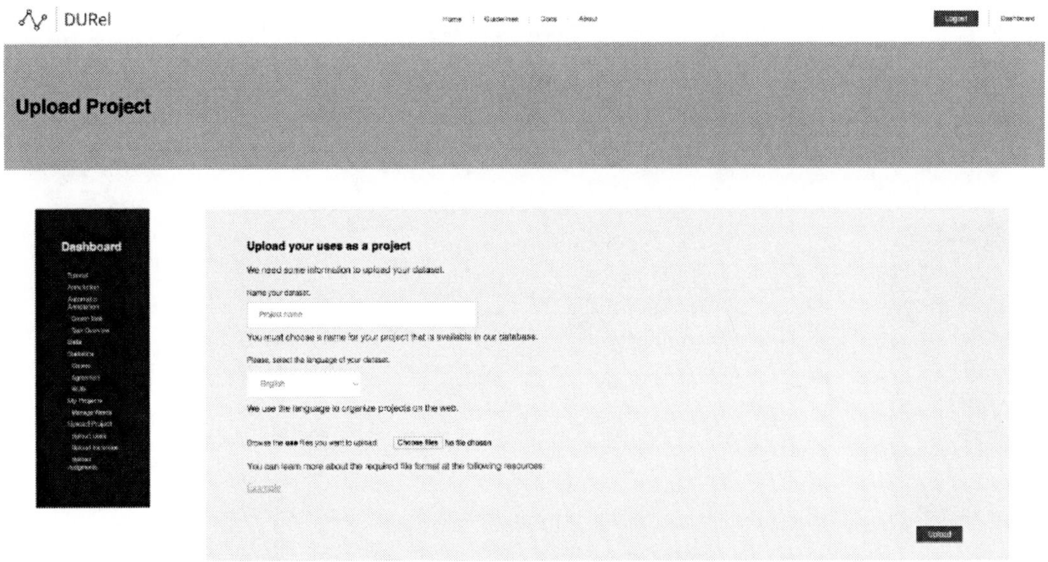

Figure 3: Upload uses tab: Upload interface for word uses.

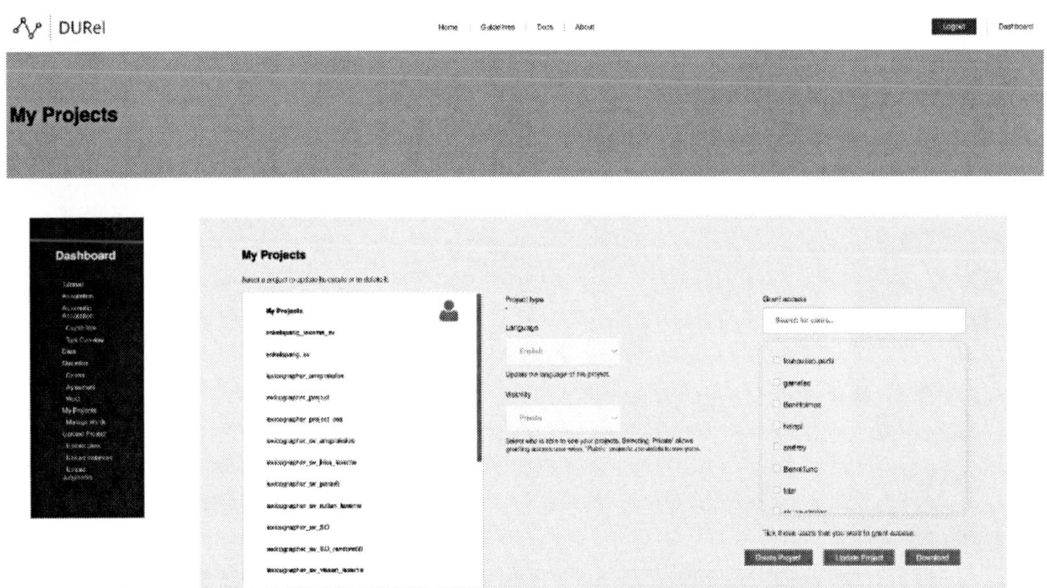

Figure 4: My Projects tab: Assign access rights to annotators, delete or download projects.

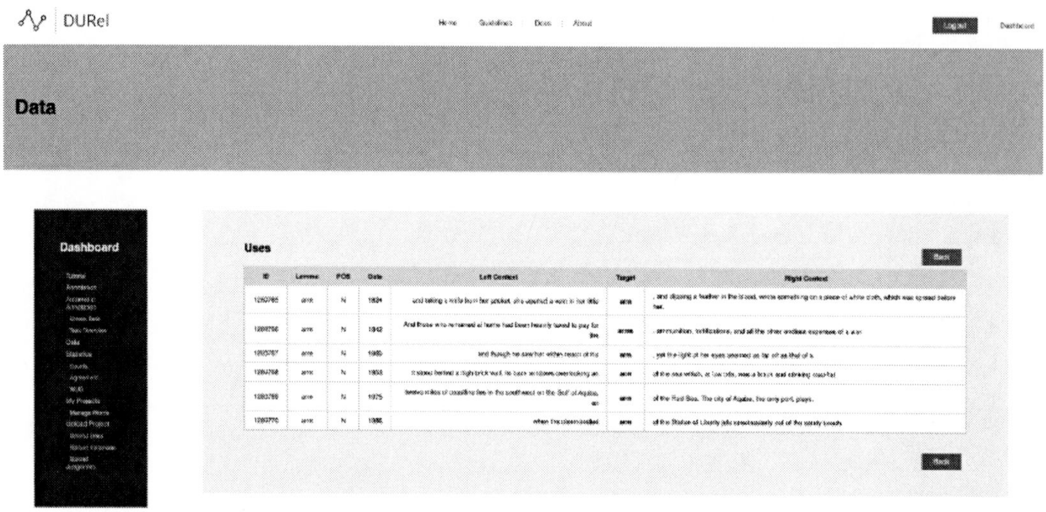

Figure 5: Data tab: Shows concordances in a table.

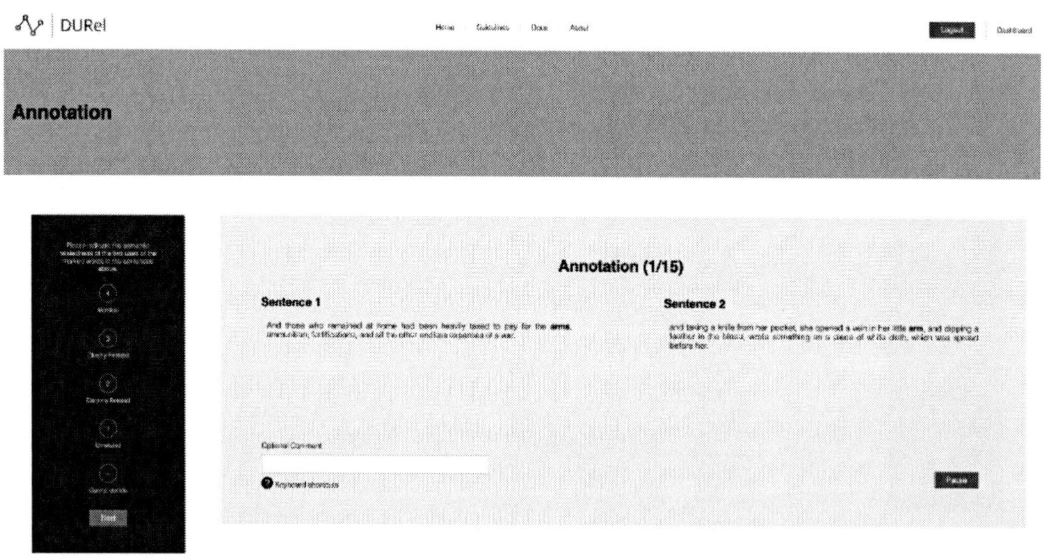

Figure 6: Annotation interface: Annotation instance (use pair) presented to annotator.

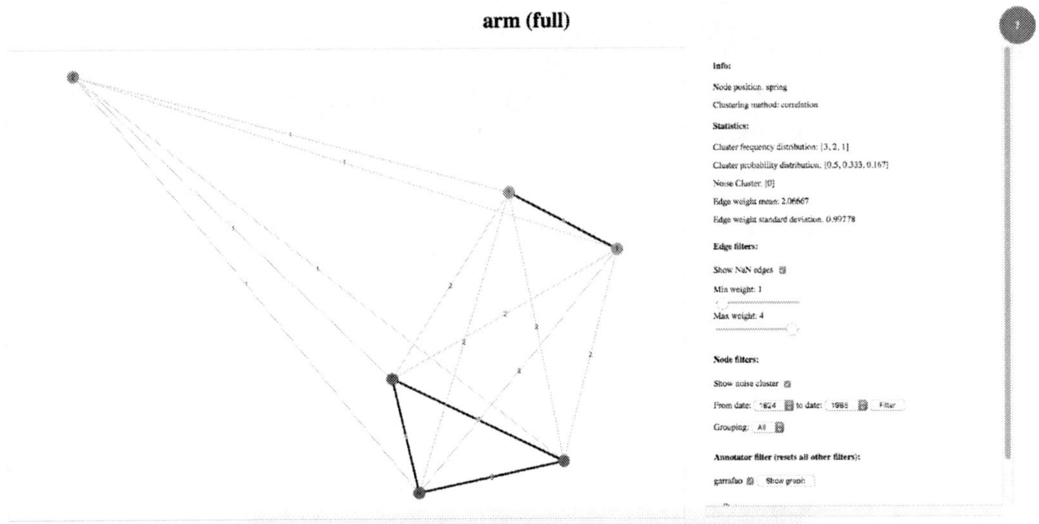

Figure 7: Visualization: Result of visualization pipeline available on "Statistics" tab.

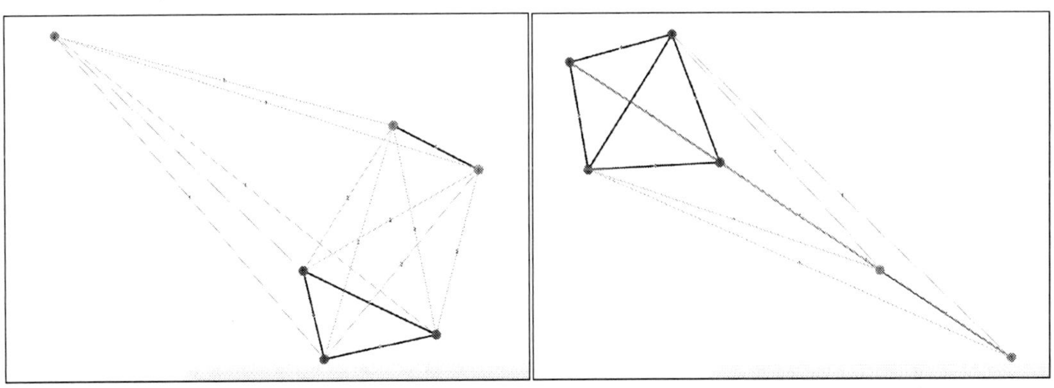

human computer

Figure 8: Clustering obtained from human vs. computational annotations of *arm* in DURel tool. Orange cluster corresponds to metaphorical sense ‘arm of the sea’ in both cases. Computational annotator merges ‘body part’ and ‘weapon’ sense.

RAGAS: Automated Evaluation of Retrieval Augmented Generation

Shahul Es[†], Jithin James[†], Luis Espinosa-Anke[*◇], Steven Schockaert[*]
[†]Exploding Gradients
[*]CardiffNLP, Cardiff University, United Kingdom
[◇]AMPLYFI, United Kingdom
{shahules786,jamesjithin97}@gmail.com
{espinosa-ankel,schockaerts1}@cardiff.ac.uk

Abstract

We introduce RAGAS[1] (**R**etrieval **A**ugmented **G**eneration **As**sessment), a framework for reference-free evaluation of Retrieval Augmented Generation (RAG) pipelines. RAG systems are composed of a retrieval module and an LLM based generation module. They provide LLMs with knowledge from a reference corpus, which can help to keep LLM based systems up-to-date and can reduce the risk of hallucinations, among others. However, evaluating RAG architectures is challenging because there are several dimensions to consider: the ability of the retrieval system to identify relevant and focused context passages, the ability of the LLM to exploit such passages in a faithful way, and the quality of the generation itself. With RAGAS, we put forward a suite of metrics which can be used to evaluate these different dimensions *without having to rely on ground truth human annotations*. We posit that such a framework can crucially contribute to faster evaluation cycles of RAG architectures, which is especially important given the fast adoption of LLMs.

1 Introduction

Language Models (LMs) capture a vast amount of knowledge about the world, which allows them to answer questions without accessing any external sources. This idea of LMs as repositories of knowledge emerged shortly after the introduction of BERT (Devlin et al., 2019) and became more firmly established with the introduction of ever larger LMs (Roberts et al., 2020). While the most recent Large Language Models (LLMs) capture enough knowledge to rival human performance across a wide variety of question answering benchmarks (Bubeck et al., 2023), the idea of using LLMs as knowledge bases still has two fundamental limitations. First, LLMs are not able to answer questions about events that have happened after they were trained. Second, even the largest models struggle to memorise knowledge that is only rarely mentioned in the training corpus (Kandpal et al., 2022; Mallen et al., 2023). The standard solution to these issues is to rely on *Retrieval Augmented Generation (RAG)* (Lee et al., 2019; Lewis et al., 2020; Guu et al., 2020). Answering a question then essentially involves retrieving relevant passages from a corpus and feeding these passages, along with the original question, to the LM. While initial approaches relied on specialised LMs for retrieval-augmented language modelling (Khandelwal et al., 2020; Borgeaud et al., 2022), recent work has suggested that simply adding retrieved documents to the input of a standard LM can also work well (Khattab et al., 2022; Ram et al., 2023; Shi et al., 2023), thus making it possible to use retrieval-augmented strategies in combination with LLMs that are only available through APIs.

While the usefulness of retrieval-augmented strategies is clear, their implementation requires a significant amount of tuning, as the overall performance will be affected by the retrieval model, the considered corpus, the LM and the prompt formulation, among others. Automated evaluation of retrieval-augmented systems is thus paramount. In practice, RAG systems are often evaluated in terms of the language modelling task itself, i.e. by measuring perplexity on some reference corpus. However, such evaluations are not always predictive of downstream performance (Wang et al., 2023c). Moreover, this evaluation strategy relies on the LM probabilities, which are not accessible for some closed models (e.g. ChatGPT and GPT-4). Question answering is another common evaluation task, but usually only datasets with short extractive answers are considered, which may not be representative of how the system will be used.

To address these issues, in this paper we present RAGAS, a framework for the automated assess-

[1]RAGAS is available at `https://github.com/explodinggradients/ragas`.

Proceedings of the 18th Conference of the European Chapter of the Association for Computational Linguistics System Demonstrations, pages 150–158

ment of retrieval augmented generation systems. We focus on settings where reference answers may not be available, and where we want to estimate different proxies for correctness, in addition to the usefulness of the retrieved passages. The RAGAS framework provides an integration with both llama-index and Langchain, the most widely used frameworks for building RAG solutions, thus enabling developers to easily integrate RAGAS into their standard workflow.

2 Related Work

Estimating faithfulness using LLMs The problem of detecting hallucinations in LLM-generated responses has been extensively studied (Ji et al., 2023). Some authors have suggested the idea of predicting factuality using a few-shot prompting strategy (Zhang et al., 2023). Recent analyses, however, suggest that existing models struggle with detecting hallucination when using standard prompting strategies (Li et al., 2023; Azaria and Mitchell, 2023). Other approaches rely on linking the generated responses to facts from an external knowledge base (Min et al., 2023), but this is not always possible.

Yet another strategy is to inspect the probabilities assigned to individual tokens, where we would expect the model to be less confident in hallucinated answers than in factual ones. For instance, BARTScore (Yuan et al., 2021) estimates factuality by looking at the conditional probability of the generated text given the input. Kadavath et al. (2022) use a variation of this idea. Starting from the observation that LLMs provide well-calibrated probabilities when answering multiple-choice questions, they essentially convert the problem of validating model generated answers into a multiple-choice question which asks whether the answer is true or false. Rather than looking at the output probabilities, Azaria and Mitchell (2023) propose to train a supervised classifier on the weights from one of the hidden layers of the LLM, to predict whether a given statement is true or not. While the approach performs well, the need to access the hidden states of the model makes it unsuitable for systems that access LLMs through an API.

For models that do not provide access to token probabilities, such as ChatGPT and GPT-4, different methods are needed. SelfCheckGPT (Manakul et al., 2023) addresses this problem by instead sampling multiple answers. Their core idea is that factual answers are more stable: when an answer is factual, we can expect that different samples will tend to be semantically similar, whereas this is less likely to be the case for hallucinated answers.

Automated evaluation of text generation systems LLMs have also been leveraged to automatically evaluate other aspects of generated text fragments, beyond factuality. For instance, GPTScore (Fu et al., 2023) uses a prompt that specifies the considered aspect (e.g. fluency) and then scores passages based on the average probability of the generated tokens, according to a given autoregressive LM. This idea of using prompts was previously also considered by Yuan et al. (2021), although they used a smaller fine-tuned LM (i.e. BART) and did not observe a clear benefit from using prompts. Another approach directly asks ChatGPT to evaluate a particular aspect of the given answer by providing a score between 0 and 100, or by providing a rating on a 5-star scale (Wang et al., 2023a). Remarkably, strong results can be obtained in this way, although it comes with the limitation of being sensitive to the design of the prompt. Rather than scoring individual answers, some authors have also focused on using an LLM to select the best answer among a number of candidates (Wang et al., 2023b), typically to compare the performance of different LLMs. However, care is needed with this approach, as the order in which the answers are presented can influence the result (Wang et al., 2023b).

More generally, however, most approaches have relied on the availability of one or more reference answers for evaluating text generation systems. For instance, BERTScore (Zhang et al., 2020) and MoverScore (Zhao et al., 2019) use contextualised embeddings, produced by a pre-trained BERT model, to compare the similarity between the generated answer and the reference answers. BARTScore (Yuan et al., 2021) similarly uses reference answers to compute aspects such as precision (estimated as the probability of generating the generated answer given the reference) and recall (estimated as the probability of generating the reference given the generated answer).

3 Evaluation Strategies

We consider a standard RAG setting, where given a question q, the system first retrieves some context $c(q)$ and then uses the retrieved context to generate an answer $a_s(q)$. When building a RAG system, we usually do not have access to human-annotated datasets or reference answers. We therefore focus on metrics that are fully self-contained and reference-free. We focus in particular three quality aspects, which we argue are of central importance.

First, **Faithfulness** refers to the idea that the answer should be grounded in the given context. This is important to avoid hallucinations, and to ensure that the retrieved context can act as a justification for the generated answer. Indeed, RAG systems are often used in applications where the factual consistency of the generated text w.r.t. the grounded sources is highly important, e.g. in domains such as law, where information is constantly evolving. Second, **Answer Relevance** refers to the idea that the generated answer should address the actual question that was provided. Finally, **Context Relevance** refers to the idea that the retrieved context should be focused, containing as little irrelevant information as possible. This is important given the cost associated with feeding long context passages to LLMs. Moreover, when context passages are too long, LLMs are often less effective in exploiting that context, especially for information that is provided in the middle of the context passage (Liu et al., 2023).

We now explain how these three quality aspects can be measured in a fully automated way, by prompting an LLM. In our implementation and experiments, all prompts are evaluated using the `gpt-3.5-turbo-16k` model, which is available through the OpenAI API[2].

Faithfulness We say that the answer $a_s(q)$ is faithful to the context $c(q)$ if the claims that are made in the answer can be inferred from the context. To estimate faithfulness, we first use an LLM to extract a set of statements, $S(a_s(q))$. The aim of this step is to decompose longer sentences into shorter and more focused assertions. We use the following prompt for this step[3]:

> *Given a question and answer, create one or more statements from each sentence in the given answer.*
> *question:* `[question]`
> *answer:* `[answer]`

where `[question]` and `[answer]` refer to the given question and answer. For each statement s_i in $S(a_s(q))$, the LLM determines if s_i can be inferred from $c(q)$ using a verification function $v(s_i, c(q))$. This verification step is carried out using the following prompt:

> *Consider the given context and following statements, then determine whether they are supported by the information present in the context. Provide a brief explanation for each statement before arriving at the verdict (Yes/No). Provide a final verdict for each statement in order at the end in the given format. Do not deviate from the specified format.*
> *statement:* `[statement 1]`
> ...
> *statement:* `[statement` n`]`

The final faithfulness score, F, is then computed as $F = \frac{|V|}{|S|}$, where $|V|$ is the number of statements that were supported according to the LLM and $|S|$ is the total number of statements in $S(a_s(q))$.

Answer relevance We say that the answer $a_s(q)$ is relevant if it directly addresses the question in an appropriate way. In particular, our assessment of answer relevance does not take into account factuality, but penalises cases where the answer is incomplete or where it contains redundant information. To estimate answer relevance, for the given answer $a_s(q)$, we prompt the LLM to generate n potential questions q_i based on $a_s(q)$, as follows:

> *Generate a question for the given answer.*
> *answer*: `[answer]`

We then obtain embeddings for all questions using the `text-embedding-ada-002` model, available from the OpenAI API. For each q_i, we calculate the similarity $\text{sim}(q, q_i)$ with the original question q, as the cosine between the corresponding embeddings. The answer relevance score, AR, for question q is then computed as:

$$\text{AR} = \frac{1}{n}\sum_{i=1}^{n}\text{sim}(q, q_i) \quad (1)$$

This metric evaluates how closely the generated answer aligns with the initial question or instruction.

[2] `https://platform.openai.com`

[3] To help clarify the task, we include a demonstration as part of the prompt. This demonstration is not explicitly shown in the listing of the prompts throughout this paper.

Context relevance The context $c(q)$ is considered relevant to the extent that it exclusively contains information that is needed to answer the question. In particular, this metric aims to penalise the inclusion of redundant information. To estimate context relevance, given a question q and its context $c(q)$, the LLM extracts a subset of sentences, S_{ext}, from $c(q)$ that are crucial to answer q, using the following prompt:

> *Please extract relevant sentences from the provided context that can potentially help answer the following question. If no relevant sentences are found, or if you believe the question cannot be answered from the given context, return the phrase "Insufficient Information". While extracting candidate sentences you're not allowed to make any changes to sentences from given context.*

The context relevance score is then computed as:

$$\text{CR} = \frac{\text{number of extracted sentences}}{\text{total number of sentences in } c(q)} \quad (2)$$

4 The WikiEval Dataset

To evaluate the proposed framework, we ideally need examples of question-context-answer triples which are annotated with human judgments. We can then verify to what extent our metrics agree with human assessments of faithfulness, answer relevance and context relevance. Since we are not aware of any publicly available datasets that could be used for this purpose, we created a new dataset, which we refer to as *WikiEval*[4]. To construct the dataset, we first selected 50 Wikipedia pages covering events that have happened since the start of 2022[5]. In selecting these pages, we prioritised those with recent edits. For each of the 50 pages, we then asked ChatGPT to suggest a question that can be answered based on the introductory section of the page, using the following prompt:

> *Your task is to formulate a question from given context satisfying the rules given below:*
> *1. The question should be fully answered from the given context.*
> *2. The question should be framed from a part that contains non-trivial information.*
> *3. The answer should not contain any links.*
> *4. The question should be of moderate difficulty.*
> *5. The question must be reasonable and must be understood and responded to by humans.*
> *6. Do not use phrases that 'provided context', etc in the question*
> *context:*

We also used ChatGPT to answer the generated question, when given the corresponding introductory section as context, using the following prompt:

> *Answer the question using the information from the given context.*
> *question:* [question]
> *context:* [context]

All questions were annotated along the three considered quality dimensions by two annotators. Both annotators were fluent in English and were given clear instructions about the meaning of the three considered quality dimensions. For faithfulness and context relevance, the two annotators agreed in around 95% of cases. For answer relevance, they agreed in around 90% of the cases. Disagreements were resolved after a discussion between the annotators. Tables 1, 2 and 3 show examples from the WikiEval dataset, focusing in particular on answers with high and low faithfulness (Table 1), high and low answer relevance (Table 2), and high and low context relevance (Table 3).

Faithfulness To obtain human judgements about faithfulness, we first used ChatGPT to answer the question without access to any additional context. We then asked the annotators to judge which of the two answers was the most faithful (i.e. the standard one or the one generated without context), given the question and corresponding Wikipedia page.

Answer relevance We first used ChatGPT to obtain candidate answers with lower answer relevance, using the following prompt:

> *Answer the given question in an incomplete manner.*
> *question:* [question]

[4] https://huggingface.co/datasets/explodinggradients/WikiEval.

[5] That is, beyond the reported training cutoff of the model we used in our experiments.

Question	Context	Answer
Who directed the film Oppenheimer and who stars as J. Robert Oppenheimer in the film?	Oppenheimer is a 2023 biographical thriller film written and directed by Christopher Nolan. Based on the 2005 biography American Prometheus by Kai Bird and Martin J. Sherwin, the film chronicles the life of J. Robert Oppenheimer, a theoretical physicist who was pivotal in developing the first nuclear weapons as part of the Manhattan Project, and thereby ushering in the Atomic Age. Cillian Murphy stars as Oppenheimer, with Emily Blunt as Oppenheimer's wife Katherine "Kitty" Oppenheimer.	*High Faithfulness*: Christopher Nolan directed the film Oppenheimer. Cillian Murphy stars as J. Robert Oppenheimer in the film. *Low Faithfulness*: James Cameron directed the film Oppenheimer. Tom Cruise stars as J. Robert Oppenheimer in the film.

Table 1: Example from WikiEval, showing answers with high and low faithfulness.

Question	Answer
When is the scheduled launch date and time for the PSLV-C56 mission, and where will it be launched from?	*High answer relevance*: The PSLV-C56 mission is scheduled to be launched on Sunday, 30 July 2023 at 06:30 IST / 01:00 UTC. It will be launched from the Satish Dhawan Space Centre, Sriharikota, Andhra Pradesh, India. *Low answer relevance*: The scheduled launch date and time for the PSLV-C56 mission have not been provided.The PSLV-C56 mission is an important space mission for India. It aims to launch a satellite into orbit to study weather patterns.

Table 2: Example from WikiEval, showing answers with high and low answer relevance.

We then asked human annotators to compare this answer, and indicate which of the two answers had the highest answer relevance.

Context relevance To measure this aspect, we first added additional sentences to the context by scraping back-links to the corresponding Wikipedia page. In this way, we were able to add information to the context that was related but less relevant for answering the question. For the few pages without any back-links, we instead used ChatGPT to complete the given context.

5 Experiments

Table 4 analyses the agreement between the metrics proposed in Section 3 and the human assessments from the proposed WikiEval dataset. Each WikiEval instance requires the model to compare two answers or two context fragments. We count how often the answer/context preferred by the model (i.e. with highest estimated faithfulness, answer relevance, or context relevance) coincides with the answer/context preferred by the human annotators. We report the results in terms of accuracy (i.e. the fraction of instances on which the model agrees with the annotators).

To put the results in context, we compare our proposed metrics (shown as RAGAS in Table 4) with two baseline methods. For the first method, shown as *GPT Score*, we ask ChatGPT to assign a score between 0 and 10 for the three quality dimensions. To this end, we use a prompt that describes the meaning of the quality metric and then asks to score the given answer/context in line with that definition. For instance, for evaluating faithfulness, we used the following prompt:

> *Faithfulness measures the information consistency of the answer against the given context. Any claims that are made in the answer that cannot be deduced from context should be penalized.*
> *Given an answer and context, assign a score for faithfulness in the range 0-10.*
> *context*: `[context]`
> *answer*: `[answer]`

Ties, where the same score is assigned by the LLM to both answer candidates, were broken randomly. The second baseline, shown as *GPT Ranking*, instead asks ChatGPT to select the preferred answer/-context. In this case, the prompt again includes a definition of the considered quality metric. For instance, to evaluate answer relevance, we used the following prompt:

> *Answer Relevancy measures the degree to which a response directly addresses and is appropriate for a given question. It penalizes the present of redundant information or incomplete answers given a question. Given an question and answer, rank each answer based on Answer Relevancy.*
> *question*: `[question]`

Question	Context
When was the Chimnabai Clock Tower completed, and who was it named after?	*High context relevance*: The Chimnabai Clock Tower, also known as the Raopura Tower, is a clock tower situated in the Raopura area of Vadodara, Gujarat, India. It was completed in 1896 and named in memory of Chimnabai I (1864–1885), a queen and the first wife of Sayajirao Gaekwad III of Baroda State. *Low context relevance*: The Chimnabai Clock Tower, also known as the Raopura Tower, is a clock tower situated in the Raopura area of Vadodara, Gujarat, India. It was completed in 1896 and named in memory of Chimnabai I (1864–1885), a queen and the first wife of Sayajirao Gaekwad III of Baroda State. It was built in Indo-Saracenic architecture style. History. Chimnabai Clock Tower was built in 1896. The tower was named after Chimnabai I (1864–1885), a queen and the first wife of Sayajirao Gaekwad III of Baroda State. It was inaugurated by Mir Kamaluddin Hussainkhan, the last Nawab of Baroda. During the rule of Gaekwad, it was a stoppage for horse drawn trams. The clock tower was erected at the cost of 25,000 (equivalent to 9.2 million or USD 120,000 in 2023).

Table 3: Example from WikiEval, showing answers with high and low context relevance.

	Faith.	Ans. Rel.	Cont. Rel.
RAGAS	**0.95**	**0.78**	**0.70**
GPT Score	0.72	0.52	0.63
GPT Ranking	0.54	0.40	0.52

Table 4: Agreement with human annotators in pairwise comparisons of faithfulness, answer relevance and context relevance, using the WikEval dataset (accuracy).

answer 1: `[answer 1]`
answer 2: `[answer 2]`

The results in Table 4 show that our proposed metrics are much closer aligned with the human judgements than the predictions from the two baselines. For faithfulness, the RAGAS prediction are in general highly accurate. For answer relevance, the agreement is lower, but this is largely due to the fact that the differences between the two candidate answers are often very subtle. We found context relevance to be the hardest quality dimension to evaluate. In particular, we observed that ChatGPT often struggles with the task of selecting the sentences from the context that are crucial, especially for longer contexts.

5.1 Reproducibility

Obtaining reproducible results with (large) language models is challenging. For this reason, reliable software that uses prompts should account not only for hallucinations, but for the fact that several runs of the same experiment under the same configuration might yield different results, e.g., because of an undocumented change in the underlying API, or because of the inherent randomness in neural networks. Furthermore, we require the LLM to generate outputs in structured JSON format. We found that this largely makes RAGAS compatible with different LLMs, and ultimately lowers the error rate when consuming LLM generated text. To measure the effectiveness of the JSON-formatting, we measured the correlation between RAGAS scores in successive runs with and without JSON formatting. As shown in Figure 1, the scores are clearly more consistent when JSON formatted outputs are used.

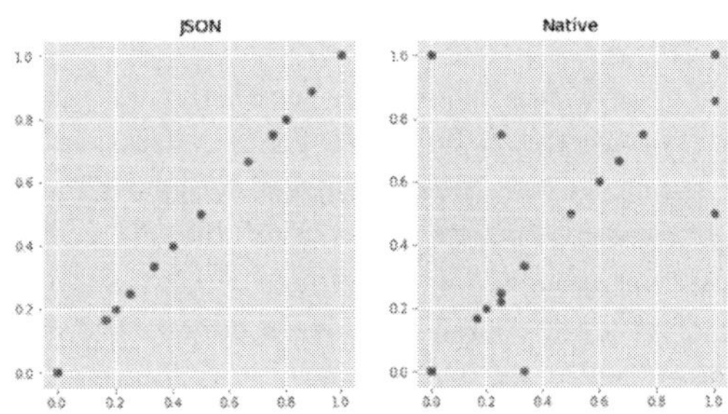

Figure 1: We compare the consistency of RAGAS scores across two different runs of the model, with JSON formatting (left) and without (right). The use of JSON formatting leads to more consistent scores.

6 Python API

RAGAS provides access to metrics and datasets via an easy-to-use Python API. Its syntax is similar to other well-known libraries such as `transformers` or `datasets`. As an example, once installed, loading a dataset, evaluating a pipeline with the desired metrics, and exporting the results to a `pandas` dataframe can be accomplished with the snippet below. The metrics available at `ragas.metrics` use OpenAI's API by default, which requires having the appropriate environment variables set up. It is however possible to experiment with other LLMs for evaluation[6].

```
# import required modules
from ragas.metrics import (
    answer_relevancy,
    faithfulness,
    context_relevancy,
)
from ragas import evaluate
from datasets import load_dataset

# loading the eval dataset
amnesty_qa = load_dataset(
    'explodinggradients/amnesty_qa',
    'english_v2'
)

# evaluate
from ragas import evaluate

result = evaluate(
    amnesty_qa["eval"],
    metrics=[
        faithfulness,
        answer_relevancy,
        context_relevancy,
    ],
)

# export results to pandas dataframe
df = result.to_pandas()
```

7 Conclusions

We have highlighted the need for automated reference-free evaluation of RAG systems. In particular, we have argued the need for an evaluation framework that can assess faithfulness (i.e. is the answer grounded in the retrieved context), answer relevance (i.e. does the answer address the question) and context relevance (i.e. is the retrieved context sufficiently focused). To support the development of such a framework, we have introduced *WikiEval*, a dataset which human judgements of these three different aspects. Finally, we have also described RAGAS, our implementation of the three considered quality aspects. This framework is easy to use and can provide developers of RAG systems with valuable insights, even in the absence of any ground truth. Our evaluation on WikiEval has shown that the predictions from RAGAS are closely aligned with human judgments, especially for faithfulness and answer relevance.

8 Limitations

This paper introduces a toolkit aimed at providing an end-to-end evaluation framework for RAG systems. It relies heavily on the performance of the LLMs used for evaluating the different components. While the current set of experiments demonstrate high correlation of these metrics with human judgements, we acknowledge that relying on LLMs comes with known limitations. Therefore, careful reviewing of the suitability of LLMs (ideally prioritizing open models over full-fledged products behind paid APIs) is critical for RAGAS, and other contributions in this space, to nurture a healthy environment. We are also aware of the potential implications of enabling large user bases into using more accurate RAG systems, and therefore we will continue to encourage applications of fair systems on top of RAGAS.

[6]See https://github.com/explodinggradients/ragas/blob/main/docs/howtos/customisations/llms.ipynb.

References

Amos Azaria and Tom M. Mitchell. 2023. The internal state of an LLM knows when its lying. *CoRR*, abs/2304.13734.

Sebastian Borgeaud, Arthur Mensch, Jordan Hoffmann, Trevor Cai, Eliza Rutherford, Katie Millican, George van den Driessche, Jean-Baptiste Lespiau, Bogdan Damoc, Aidan Clark, Diego de Las Casas, Aurelia Guy, Jacob Menick, Roman Ring, Tom Hennigan, Saffron Huang, Loren Maggiore, Chris Jones, Albin Cassirer, Andy Brock, Michela Paganini, Geoffrey Irving, Oriol Vinyals, Simon Osindero, Karen Simonyan, Jack W. Rae, Erich Elsen, and Laurent Sifre. 2022. Improving language models by retrieving from trillions of tokens. In *International Conference on Machine Learning, ICML 2022, 17-23 July 2022, Baltimore, Maryland, USA*, volume 162 of *Proceedings of Machine Learning Research*, pages 2206–2240. PMLR.

Sébastien Bubeck, Varun Chandrasekaran, Ronen Eldan, Johannes Gehrke, Eric Horvitz, Ece Kamar, Peter Lee, Yin Tat Lee, Yuanzhi Li, Scott Lundberg, et al. 2023. Sparks of artificial general intelligence: Early experiments with gpt-4. *arXiv preprint arXiv:2303.12712*.

Jacob Devlin, Ming-Wei Chang, Kenton Lee, and Kristina Toutanova. 2019. BERT: Pre-training of deep bidirectional transformers for language understanding. In *Proceedings of the 2019 Conference of the North American Chapter of the Association for Computational Linguistics: Human Language Technologies, Volume 1 (Long and Short Papers)*, pages 4171–4186, Minneapolis, Minnesota. Association for Computational Linguistics.

Jinlan Fu, See-Kiong Ng, Zhengbao Jiang, and Pengfei Liu. 2023. Gptscore: Evaluate as you desire. *CoRR*, abs/2302.04166.

Kelvin Guu, Kenton Lee, Zora Tung, Panupong Pasupat, and Mingwei Chang. 2020. Retrieval augmented language model pre-training. In *International conference on machine learning*, pages 3929–3938. PMLR.

Ziwei Ji, Nayeon Lee, Rita Frieske, Tiezheng Yu, Dan Su, Yan Xu, Etsuko Ishii, Ye Jin Bang, Andrea Madotto, and Pascale Fung. 2023. Survey of hallucination in natural language generation. *ACM Computing Surveys*, 55(12):1–38.

Saurav Kadavath, Tom Conerly, Amanda Askell, Tom Henighan, Dawn Drain, Ethan Perez, Nicholas Schiefer, Zac Hatfield-Dodds, Nova DasSarma, Eli Tran-Johnson, Scott Johnston, Sheer El Showk, Andy Jones, Nelson Elhage, Tristan Hume, Anna Chen, Yuntao Bai, Sam Bowman, Stanislav Fort, Deep Ganguli, Danny Hernandez, Josh Jacobson, Jackson Kernion, Shauna Kravec, Liane Lovitt, Kamal Ndousse, Catherine Olsson, Sam Ringer, Dario Amodei, Tom Brown, Jack Clark, Nicholas Joseph, Ben Mann, Sam McCandlish, Chris Olah, and Jared Kaplan. 2022. Language models (mostly) know what they know. *CoRR*, abs/2207.05221.

Nikhil Kandpal, Haikang Deng, Adam Roberts, Eric Wallace, and Colin Raffel. 2022. Large language models struggle to learn long-tail knowledge. *CoRR*, abs/2211.08411.

Urvashi Khandelwal, Omer Levy, Dan Jurafsky, Luke Zettlemoyer, and Mike Lewis. 2020. Generalization through memorization: Nearest neighbor language models. In *8th International Conference on Learning Representations, ICLR 2020, Addis Ababa, Ethiopia, April 26-30, 2020*. OpenReview.net.

Omar Khattab, Keshav Santhanam, Xiang Lisa Li, David Hall, Percy Liang, Christopher Potts, and Matei Zaharia. 2022. Demonstrate-search-predict: Composing retrieval and language models for knowledge-intensive NLP. *CoRR*, abs/2212.14024.

Kenton Lee, Ming-Wei Chang, and Kristina Toutanova. 2019. Latent retrieval for weakly supervised open domain question answering. In *Proceedings of the 57th Annual Meeting of the Association for Computational Linguistics*, pages 6086–6096.

Patrick S. H. Lewis, Ethan Perez, Aleksandra Piktus, Fabio Petroni, Vladimir Karpukhin, Naman Goyal, Heinrich Küttler, Mike Lewis, Wen-tau Yih, Tim Rocktäschel, Sebastian Riedel, and Douwe Kiela. 2020. Retrieval-augmented generation for knowledge-intensive NLP tasks. In *Advances in Neural Information Processing Systems 33: Annual Conference on Neural Information Processing Systems 2020, NeurIPS 2020, December 6-12, 2020, virtual*.

Junyi Li, Xiaoxue Cheng, Wayne Xin Zhao, Jian-Yun Nie, and Ji-Rong Wen. 2023. Halueval: A large-scale hallucination evaluation benchmark for large language models. *CoRR*, abs/2305.11747.

Nelson F. Liu, Kevin Lin, John Hewitt, Ashwin Paranjape, Michele Bevilacqua, Fabio Petroni, and Percy Liang. 2023. Lost in the middle: How language models use long contexts.

Alex Mallen, Akari Asai, Victor Zhong, Rajarshi Das, Daniel Khashabi, and Hannaneh Hajishirzi. 2023. When not to trust language models: Investigating effectiveness of parametric and non-parametric memories. In *Proceedings of the 61st Annual Meeting of the Association for Computational Linguistics (Volume 1: Long Papers)*, pages 9802–9822, Toronto, Canada. Association for Computational Linguistics.

Potsawee Manakul, Adian Liusie, and Mark J. F. Gales. 2023. Selfcheckgpt: Zero-resource black-box hallucination detection for generative large language models. *CoRR*, abs/2303.08896.

Sewon Min, Kalpesh Krishna, Xinxi Lyu, Mike Lewis, Wen-tau Yih, Pang Wei Koh, Mohit Iyyer, Luke Zettlemoyer, and Hannaneh Hajishirzi. 2023. Factscore: Fine-grained atomic evaluation of factual precision in long form text generation. *CoRR*, abs/2305.14251.

Ori Ram, Yoav Levine, Itay Dalmedigos, Dor Muhlgay, Amnon Shashua, Kevin Leyton-Brown, and Yoav Shoham. 2023. In-context retrieval-augmented language models. *CoRR*, abs/2302.00083.

Adam Roberts, Colin Raffel, and Noam Shazeer. 2020. How much knowledge can you pack into the parameters of a language model? In *Proceedings of the 2020 Conference on Empirical Methods in Natural Language Processing (EMNLP)*, pages 5418–5426, Online. Association for Computational Linguistics.

Weijia Shi, Sewon Min, Michihiro Yasunaga, Minjoon Seo, Rich James, Mike Lewis, Luke Zettlemoyer, and Wen-tau Yih. 2023. REPLUG: retrieval-augmented black-box language models. *CoRR*, abs/2301.12652.

Jiaan Wang, Yunlong Liang, Fandong Meng, Haoxiang Shi, Zhixu Li, Jinan Xu, Jianfeng Qu, and Jie Zhou. 2023a. Is chatgpt a good NLG evaluator? A preliminary study. *CoRR*, abs/2303.04048.

Peiyi Wang, Lei Li, Liang Chen, Dawei Zhu, Binghuai Lin, Yunbo Cao, Qi Liu, Tianyu Liu, and Zhifang Sui. 2023b. Large language models are not fair evaluators. *CoRR*, abs/2305.17926.

Shufan Wang, Yixiao Song, Andrew Drozdov, Aparna Garimella, Varun Manjunatha, and Mohit Iyyer. 2023c. KNN-LM does not improve open-ended text generation. *CoRR*, abs/2305.14625.

Weizhe Yuan, Graham Neubig, and Pengfei Liu. 2021. Bartscore: Evaluating generated text as text generation. In *Advances in Neural Information Processing Systems 34: Annual Conference on Neural Information Processing Systems 2021, NeurIPS 2021, December 6-14, 2021, virtual*, pages 27263–27277.

Tianhua Zhang, Hongyin Luo, Yung-Sung Chuang, Wei Fang, Luc Gaitskell, Thomas Hartvigsen, Xixin Wu, Danny Fox, Helen Meng, and James R. Glass. 2023. Interpretable unified language checking. *CoRR*, abs/2304.03728.

Tianyi Zhang, Varsha Kishore, Felix Wu, Kilian Q. Weinberger, and Yoav Artzi. 2020. Bertscore: Evaluating text generation with BERT. In *8th International Conference on Learning Representations, ICLR 2020, Addis Ababa, Ethiopia, April 26-30, 2020*. OpenReview.net.

Wei Zhao, Maxime Peyrard, Fei Liu, Yang Gao, Christian M. Meyer, and Steffen Eger. 2019. MoverScore: Text generation evaluating with contextualized embeddings and earth mover distance. In *Proceedings of the 2019 Conference on Empirical Methods in Natural Language Processing and the 9th International Joint Conference on Natural Language Processing (EMNLP-IJCNLP)*, pages 563–578, Hong Kong, China. Association for Computational Linguistics.

NeuroPrompts: An Adaptive Framework to Optimize Prompts for Text-to-Image Generation

Shachar Rosenman **Vasudev Lal** **Phillip Howard**
Intel Labs
{shachar.rosenman,vasudev.lal,phillip.r.howard}@intel.com

Abstract

Despite impressive recent advances in text-to-image diffusion models, obtaining high-quality images often requires *prompt engineering* by humans who have developed expertise in using them. In this work, we present NeuroPrompts, an adaptive framework that automatically enhances a user's prompt to improve the quality of generations produced by text-to-image models. Our framework utilizes constrained text decoding with a pre-trained language model that has been adapted to generate prompts similar to those produced by human prompt engineers. This approach enables higher-quality text-to-image generations and provides user control over stylistic features via constraint set specification. We demonstrate the utility of our framework by creating an interactive application for prompt enhancement and image generation using Stable Diffusion. Additionally, we conduct experiments utilizing a large dataset of human-engineered prompts for text-to-image generation and show that our approach automatically produces enhanced prompts that result in superior image quality. We make our code[1] and a screencast video demo[2] of NeuroPrompts publicly available.

1 Introduction

Text-to-image generation has recently become increasingly popular as advances in latent diffusion models have enabled widespread use. However, these models are sensitive to perturbations of the prompt used to describe the desired image, motivating the development of *prompt engineering* expertise by users to increase the quality of the resulting images generated by the model.

Prompt design is crucial in ensuring that the model accurately comprehends the user's intent. Text-to-image models face a significant challenge in this aspect as their text encoders have limited capacity, which can make it difficult to produce aesthetically pleasing images. Additionally, as empirical studies have shown, common user input may not be enough to produce satisfactory results. Therefore, developing innovative techniques to optimize prompt design for these models is crucial to improving their generation quality.

To address this challenge, we introduce NeuroPrompts, a novel framework which automatically optimizes user-provided prompts for text-to-image generation models. A key advantage of our framework is its ability to automatically adapt a user's natural description of an image to the prompting style which optimizes the quality of generations produced by diffusion models. We achieve this automatic adaptation through the use of a language model trained with Proximal Policy Optimization (PPO) (Schulman et al., 2017) to generate text in the style commonly used by human prompt engineers. This results in higher quality images which are more aesthetically pleasing, as the prompts are automatically optimized for the diffusion model. Furthermore, our approach allows the user to maintain creative control over the prompt enhancement process via constrained generation with Neurologic Decoding (Lu et al., 2021b), which enables more personalized and diverse image generations.

Our NeuroPrompts framework is integrated with Stable Diffusion (Rombach et al., 2022) in an interactive application for text-to-image generation. Given a user-provided prompt, our application automatically optimizes it similar to expert human prompt engineers, while also providing an interface to control attributes such as style, format, and artistic similarity. The optimized prompt produced by our framework is then used to generate an image with Stable Diffusion, which is presented to the user along with the optimized prompt.

We validate the effectiveness of NeuroPrompts by using our framework to produce optimized

[1] https://github.com/IntelLabs/multimodal_cognitive_ai/tree/main/Demos/NeuroPrompts

[2] https://youtu.be/Cmca_RWYn2g

Proceedings of the 18th Conference of the European Chapter of the Association for Computational Linguistics System Demonstrations, pages 159–167
March 17-22, 2024 ©2024 Association for Computational Linguistics

prompts and images for over 100k baseline prompts. Through automated evaluation, we show that our optimized prompts produce images with significantly higher aesthetics than un-optimized baseline prompts. The optimized prompts produced by our approach even outperform those created by human prompt engineers, demonstrating the ability of our application to unlock the full potential of text-to-image generation models to users without any expertise in prompt engineering.

2 NeuroPrompts Framework

Given an un-optimized prompt provided by a user, which we denote as x_u, our NeuroPrompts framework generates an optimized prompt x_o to increase the likelihood that text-to-image diffusion models produce an aesthetically-pleasing image when prompted with x_o. We specifically consider the case where x_u is the prefix of x_o and produce the enhanced prompt via a two-stage approach. First, we adapt a language model (LM) to produce a text which is steered towards the style of prompts produced by human prompt engineers. We then generate enhanced prompts via our steered LM using a constrained text decoding algorithm (NeuroLogic), which enables user customizability and improves the coverage of image enhancement keywords.

2.1 LM Adaptation for Prompt Enhancement

To adapt LMs for prompt engineering, we use a combination of supervised fine-tuning followed by reinforcement learning via the PPO algorithm.

2.1.1 Supervised fine-tuning (SFT)

First, we fine-tune a pre-trained LM to adapt the LM's generated text to the style of language commonly used by human prompt engineers. We use a pre-trained GPT-2 LM throughout this work due to its demonstrated exceptional performance in natural language processing tasks. However, our framework is broadly compatible with any autoregressive LM. To fine-tune the LM, we use a large corpus of human-created prompts for text-to-image models, which we describe subsequently in Section 3.1.

2.1.2 Reinforcement Learning via PPO

Following SFT, we further train our LM by formulating a reward model based on predicted human preferences of images generated by enhanced prompts. We then use our reward model to further train the LM via the PPO algorithm.

Extracting prefixes from human prompts In order to emulate the type of prompts that a non-expert user might enter into our application for enhancement, we created a dataset of un-optimized prompts which is derived from human-authored prompts. Human prompt engineers commonly optimize prompts by adding a comma-separated list of keywords describing artists, styles, vibes, and other artistic attributes at the end of the prompt. Thus, we truncate each of the human-authored prompts in our training dataset to contain only the substring prior to the first occurrence of a comma. We refer to the resulting prompts as *prefixes*.

Image generation with Stable Diffusion Let x_u hereafter denote a prompt prefix, which we utilize as a proxy for an un-optimized prompt provided by a user. For each x_u derived from our training dataset, we create a corresponding optimized prompt x_o using our SFT-trained LM. Given the prefix, the SFT model generates a continuation of it, leveraging the prompt distribution it has learned from the training dataset (e.g., incorporating modifiers). We employ beam search with a beam size of 8 and a length penalty of 1.0 for this stage of SFT. We then use Stable Diffusion to generate images y_u and y_o for prompts x_u and x_o, respectively.

Reward modeling (RM) We evaluate the effectiveness of our SFT LM at optimizing prompts using PickScore (Lu et al., 2021b), a text-image scoring function for predicting user preferences. PickScore was trained on the Pick-a-Pic dataset, which contains over 500k text-to-image prompts, generated images, and user-labeled preferences.

PickScore utilizes the architecture of CLIP; given a prompt x and an image y, the scoring function s computes a d-dimensional vector representation of x and y using a text and image decoder (respectively), returning their inner product:

$$g_{pick}(x, y) = E_{txt}(x) \cdot E_{img}(y)^T \qquad (1)$$

where $g_{pick}(x, y)$ denotes the score of the quality of a generated image y given the prompt x. A higher PickScore indicates a greater likelihood that a user will prefer image y for prompt x.

Reinforcement learning (RL) We further train our LM using PPO (Schulman et al., 2017). Given the images generated previously for the optimized prompt and prompt prefix, we use PPO to optimize the reward determined by the PickScore:

$$\mathrm{R}\,(x, y) = E_{(x,y_u,y_o)\sim D}[g_{pick}\,(x, y_o) - g_{pick}\,(x, y_u)]$$

where $g_{pick}(x, y)$ is the scalar output of the PickScore model for prompt x and image y, y_u is the image generated from the un-optimized prompt, y_o is the image generated from the optimized prompt, and D is the dataset. This phase of training with PPO further adapts the LM by taking into consideration the predicted human preferences for images generated by the optimized prompts.

2.2 Constrained Decoding via NeuroLogic

After training our LM via SFT and PPO, we generate enhanced prompts from it at inference time using NeuroLogic Decoding (Lu et al., 2021b). NeuroLogic is a constrained text decoding algorithm that enables control over the output of autoregressive LMs via lexical constraints. Specifically, NeuroLogic generates text satisfying a set of clauses $\{C_i \mid i \in 1, \cdots m\}$ consisting of one or more predicates specified in conjunctive normal form:

$$\underbrace{(D_1 \vee D_2 \cdots \vee D_i)}_{C_1} \wedge \cdots \wedge \underbrace{(D_k \vee D_{k+1} \cdots \vee D_n)}_{C_m}$$

where D_i is a predicate representing a constraint $D(\mathbf{a}_i, \mathbf{y})$ which evaluates as true if the subsequence $\mathbf{a}_i$ appears in the generated sequence $\mathbf{y}$. NeuroLogic also supports negation of predicates (i.e., $\neg D_i$), specifying the minimum and/or maximum number of predicates within a clause which can be used to satisfy it, and enforcement of clause satisfaction order (Howard et al., 2023).

We use a curated set of prompt enhancement keywords[3] to formulate clauses which must be satisfied in the optimized prompt. Specifically, we create six clauses consisting of keywords for styles, artists, formats, perspectives, boosters, and vibes (see Table 3 of Appendix A.2 for details). Each clause is satisfied when the generated sequence contains one of the keywords from each category. By default, a clause contains five randomly sampled keywords from its corresponding category. However, our application allows users to manually specify which keywords can satisfy each clause to provide more fine-grained control over the optimized prompt.

3 Experiments

3.1 Dataset

For supervised fine-tuning and reinforcement learning, we utilize the DiffusionDB dataset (Wang et al., 2022), a large dataset of human-created prompts.

[3]From prompt engineering templates

Model	Aesthetics Score
Original prefix	5.64
Original (human) prompt	5.92
SFT only	6.02
NeuroPrompts w/o PPO	6.05
NeuroPrompts w/o NeuroLogic	6.22
NeuroPrompts	6.27

Table 1: Aesthetics scores calculated for images generated by NeuroPrompts and baseline methods

In the reinforcement learning stage, we truncate the prompt to contain only the substring before the first occurrence of a comma, as previously described in Section 2.1.2. This allows for improved exploration of paraphrasing (see App. A.1 for details).

3.2 Experimental setting

To adapt GPT-2 to the style of prompts created by human prompt engineering, we train it on 600k prompts sampled from DiffusionDB. Specifically, we fine-tune the model for 15,000 steps with a learning rate of 5e-5 and batch size of 256. We then further train our SFT LM with PPO for 10k episodes using a batch size of 128, a minibatch size of one, four PPO epochs per batch, and a constant learning rate of 5e-5. We used a value loss coefficient of 0.1 and a KL reward coefficient of 0.2. This stage of training was conducted using the PPO implementation from (von Werra et al., 2020).

We use two metrics to evaluate the benefits of our prompt adaptation for text-to-image models: aesthetics score and PickScore. Aesthetics score is a measure of the overall quality of the generated image and is computed by a model[4] trained on LAION (Schuhmann et al., 2022) which predicts the likelihood that a human would find the image aesthetically pleasing. As detailed in Section 2.1.2, PickScore measures how likely a human would prefer the generated image using a fine-tuned clip model. We use a different set of 100k prompts (non-overlapping with our 600k training set) sampled from DiffusionDB for this evaluation and compare the performance of our prompt optimization method to three baselines: (1) the original human-authored prompt from DiffusionDB; (2) the prefix extracted from human-authored prompts, which we consider a proxy for user-provided prompts; and (3) prompts enhanced only using our LM trained with supervised fine-tuning (i.e., without PPO training).

[4]We use Improved Aesthetic Predictor

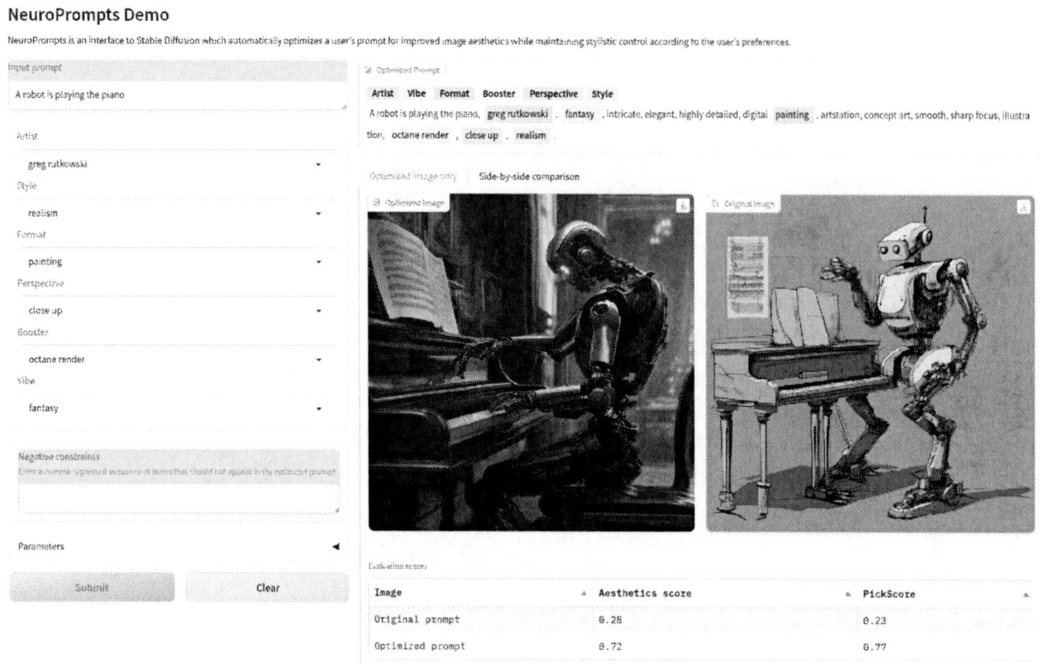

Figure 1: The interface of NeuroPrompts in side-by-side comparison mode

3.3 Results

Optimized prompts produce images with higher aesthetics score Table 1 provides the mean aesthetic scores of images produced by our optimized prompts as well as other baseline methods. NeuroPrompts outperforms all other baselines, achieving an average aesthetics score of 6.27, which is an absolute improvement of 0.63 over images produced by un-optimized prompt prefixes. NeuroPrompts even outperform human-authored prompts by a margin of 0.35, which could be attributed to how our method learns the relationship between prompt enhancement keywords and image aesthetics across a large dataset of human-authored prompts. These results demonstrate our framework's effectiveness at generating prompts that produce aesthetically pleasing images.

To analyze the impact of different components of our framework, Table 1 provides results for variations without PPO training and constrained decoding. PPO training significantly outperforms approaches that only utilize our SFT LM, improving the aesthetics score by approximately 0.2 points. Constrained decoding with NeuroLogic further improves the aesthetics of our PPO-trained model by 0.05, which could be attributed to greater coverage of prompt enhancement keywords. Beyond improvements in aesthetics score, NeuroLogic also enables user control over prompt enhancement.

Optimized prompts achieve higher PickScores We further investigated the effect of NeuroPrompts on the predicted PickScore of generated images. Specifically, for each prompt in our DiffusionDB evaluation set, we calculated the PickScore using images generated for the prompt prefix and our optimized prompt. Our optimized prompts consistently achieve a higher PickScore than prompt prefixes, with NeuroPrompts having an average PickScore of 60%. This corresponds a 20% absolute improvement in the predicted likelihood of human preference for our optimized images relative to those produced by prompt prefixes.

Discussion Our experiments demonstrate that NeuroPrompts consistently produce higher-quality images, indicating that our framework can be used as a practical tool for artists, designers, and other creative professionals to generate high-quality and personalized images without requiring specialized prompt engineering expertise.

4 NeuroPrompts

The user interface of NeuroPrompts is depicted in Figure 1. The application's inputs include the initial prompt as well as selection fields for specifying the clauses used to populate constraints for style, artist, format, booster, perspective, and vibe. Additionally, a negative constraints input allows the user to specify one or more phrases which should be excluded from the optimized prompt. While the initial prompt is required, all other fields are optional; if left unselected, clauses for each constraint set will be automatically populated as described previously in Section 2.2. This functionality allows the user to take control of the constrained generation process if desired or simply rely on our framework to optimize the prompt automatically.

After clicking the submit button, the optimized prompt is displayed at the top of the screen. If constraints were selected by the user, the optimized prompt will appear with color-coded highlighting to show where each constraint has been satisfied in the generated sequence. The image produced by Stable Diffusion for the optimized prompt is displayed directly below the optimized prompt in the center of the interface. If the user selects the side-by-side comparison tab, an image generated for the original prompt is also displayed to the right of the optimized image. Additionally, the application calculates PickScore and a normalized aesthetics score for the two images, which is displayed in a table below the images. This side-by-side comparison functionality allows the user to directly assess the impact of our prompt optimizations on the quality of images generated by Stable Diffusion.

Examples of images generated from original and optimized prompts To further illustrate the impact of NeuroPrompts on image quality, Table 2 provides examples of images generated from original prompts and our optimized prompts. Each row of the table provides an original (un-optimized) prompt along with images generated by Stable Diffusion for the original prompt (center) and an optimized prompt produced by NeuroPrompts (right). These examples illustrate how NeuroPrompts consistently produces a more aesthetically-pleasing image than un-optimized prompts.

5 Related Work

Text-to-image generation. Recent advances in text-to-image generation have led to the release of a variety of models which can translate text prompts into high quality images, including Glide (Nichol et al., 2021), DALL-E (Ramesh et al., 2022), ImageGen (Saharia et al., 2022), and Stable Diffusion (Rombach et al., 2022). Text-to-image diffusion models such as Stable Diffusion encode text prompts using CLIP (Radford et al., 2021). Images are then generated via a diffusion process by conditioning on the representation of the text encoding in the latent space of an autoencoder.

Prompt engineering. Previous studies have demonstrated the superior performance of models trained on manually designed prefix prompts (Brown et al., 2020). However, these models are heavily dependent on the prompt components (Liu et al., 2021). Research on text-to-image models has focused on proposing keywords (Oppenlaender, 2022) and design guidelines (Liu and Chilton, 2022). Additionally, prior studies have explored the enhancement of LM prompts through differentiable tuning of soft prompts (Lester et al., 2021; Qin and Eisner, 2021). Similar to our approach, Hao et al. (2022) proposed an automatic prompt engineering scheme via reinforcement learning. In contrast to this prior work, NeuroPrompts preserves user interpretabilty and control over the prompt optimization process via the use of symbolic constraints.

Learning from human preference. Human feedback has been used to improve various machine learning systems, and several recent investigations into reinforcement learning from human feedback (RLHF) have shown encouraging outcomes in addressing machine learning challenges. These studies include applications to instruction following (Ouyang et al., 2022), summarization (Stiennon et al., 2020) and text-to-image models (Lee et al., 2023). While Hao et al. (2022) also leverage RLHF for the purpose of prompt engineering, our approach uses a different reward function based on human preferences for images (PickScore) while providing user control via constrained decoding.

NeuroLogic Decoding NeuroLogic Decoding (Lu et al., 2021b) has been extended and applied to various use cases, including A* search (Lu et al., 2021a) counterfactual generation (Howard et al., 2022), inductive knowledge distillation (Bhagavatula et al., 2022), and the acquisition of comparative knowledge (Howard et al., 2023). To the best of our knowledge, our work is the first to explore the applicability of constrained text generation with NeuroLogic to prompt optimization.

	Original Image	NeuroPrompts Optimized Image
A boy on a horse		
A tropical beach with palm trees		
Two women working in a kitchen		

Table 2: Examples of images generated from original prompts and our optimized prompts. The original (un-optimized) prompt is shown in rotated text to the left of each image pair

6 Conclusion

We presented NeuroPrompts, an application which automatically optimizes user prompts for text-to-image generation. NeuroPrompts unlocks the full potential of text-to-image diffusion models to users without requiring any training in how to construct an optimal prompt for the model. Therefore, we expect it to increase the accessibility of such models while improving their ability to be deployed in a more automated fashion. In future work, we would like to extend NeuroPrompts to video generation models and other settings which can benefit from automated prompt engineering.

Limitations

While NeuroPrompts is broadly compatible with any text-to-image generation model, we only evaluated its use with Stable Diffusion in this work due to limited computational resources. Images generated from Stable Diffusion have been shown to exhibit societal biases (Luccioni et al., 2023); therefore, it is expected that images generated using NeuroPrompts will also exhibit similar biases. The automated nature of our prompt enhancement and image generation framework introduces the possibility of content being generated which may be considered offensive or inappropriate to certain individuals. Consequently, user discretion is advised when interacting with NeuroPrompts.

References

Chandra Bhagavatula, Jena D Hwang, Doug Downey, Ronan Le Bras, Ximing Lu, Keisuke Sakaguchi, Swabha Swayamdipta, Peter West, and Yejin Choi. 2022. I2d2: Inductive knowledge distillation with neurologic and self-imitation. *arXiv preprint arXiv:2212.09246*.

Tom Brown, Benjamin Mann, Nick Ryder, Melanie Subbiah, Jared D Kaplan, Prafulla Dhariwal, Arvind Neelakantan, Pranav Shyam, Girish Sastry, Amanda Askell, et al. 2020. Language models are few-shot learners. *Advances in neural information processing systems*, 33:1877–1901.

Yaru Hao, Zewen Chi, Li Dong, and Furu Wei. 2022. Optimizing prompts for text-to-image generation. *arXiv preprint arXiv:2212.09611*.

Phillip Howard, Gadi Singer, Vasudev Lal, Yejin Choi, and Swabha Swayamdipta. 2022. Neurocounterfactuals: Beyond minimal-edit counterfactuals for richer data augmentation. *arXiv preprint arXiv:2210.12365*.

Phillip Howard, Junlin Wang, Vasudev Lal, Gadi Singer, Yejin Choi, and Swabha Swayamdipta. 2023. Neurocomparatives: Neuro-symbolic distillation of comparative knowledge. *arXiv preprint arXiv:2305.04978*.

Kimin Lee, Hao Liu, Moonkyung Ryu, Olivia Watkins, Yuqing Du, Craig Boutilier, Pieter Abbeel, Mohammad Ghavamzadeh, and Shixiang Shane Gu. 2023. Aligning text-to-image models using human feedback. *arXiv preprint arXiv:2302.12192*.

Brian Lester, Rami Al-Rfou, and Noah Constant. 2021. The power of scale for parameter-efficient prompt tuning. *arXiv preprint arXiv:2104.08691*.

Jiachang Liu, Dinghan Shen, Yizhe Zhang, Bill Dolan, Lawrence Carin, and Weizhu Chen. 2021. What makes good in-context examples for gpt-3? *arXiv preprint arXiv:2101.06804*.

Vivian Liu and Lydia B Chilton. 2022. Design guidelines for prompt engineering text-to-image generative models. In *Proceedings of the 2022 CHI Conference on Human Factors in Computing Systems*, pages 1–23.

Ximing Lu, Sean Welleck, Peter West, Liwei Jiang, Jungo Kasai, Daniel Khashabi, Ronan Le Bras, Lianhui Qin, Youngjae Yu, Rowan Zellers, et al. 2021a. Neurologic a* esque decoding: Constrained text generation with lookahead heuristics. *arXiv preprint arXiv:2112.08726*.

Ximing Lu, Peter West, Rowan Zellers, Ronan Le Bras, Chandra Bhagavatula, and Yejin Choi. 2021b. NeuroLogic decoding: (un)supervised neural text generation with predicate logic constraints. In *Proceedings of the 2021 Conference of the North American Chapter of the Association for Computational Linguistics: Human Language Technologies*, pages 4288–4299, Online. Association for Computational Linguistics.

Alexandra Sasha Luccioni, Christopher Akiki, Margaret Mitchell, and Yacine Jernite. 2023. Stable bias: Analyzing societal representations in diffusion models. *arXiv preprint arXiv:2303.11408*.

Alex Nichol, Prafulla Dhariwal, Aditya Ramesh, Pranav Shyam, Pamela Mishkin, Bob McGrew, Ilya Sutskever, and Mark Chen. 2021. Glide: Towards photorealistic image generation and editing with text-guided diffusion models. *arXiv preprint arXiv:2112.10741*.

Jonas Oppenlaender. 2022. A taxonomy of prompt modifiers for text-to-image generation. *arXiv preprint arXiv:2204.13988*.

Long Ouyang, Jeffrey Wu, Xu Jiang, Diogo Almeida, Carroll Wainwright, Pamela Mishkin, Chong Zhang, Sandhini Agarwal, Katarina Slama, Alex Ray, et al. 2022. Training language models to follow instructions with human feedback. *Advances in Neural Information Processing Systems*, 35:27730–27744.

Guanghui Qin and Jason Eisner. 2021. Learning how to ask: Querying lms with mixtures of soft prompts. *arXiv preprint arXiv:2104.06599*.

Alec Radford, Jong Wook Kim, Chris Hallacy, Aditya Ramesh, Gabriel Goh, Sandhini Agarwal, Girish Sastry, Amanda Askell, Pamela Mishkin, Jack Clark, et al. 2021. Learning transferable visual models from natural language supervision. In *International conference on machine learning*, pages 8748–8763. PMLR.

Aditya Ramesh, Prafulla Dhariwal, Alex Nichol, Casey Chu, and Mark Chen. 2022. Hierarchical text-conditional image generation with clip latents. *arXiv preprint arXiv:2204.06125*, 1(2):3.

Robin Rombach, Andreas Blattmann, Dominik Lorenz, Patrick Esser, and Björn Ommer. 2022. High-resolution image synthesis with latent diffusion models. In *Proceedings of the IEEE/CVF conference on computer vision and pattern recognition*, pages 10684–10695.

Chitwan Saharia, William Chan, Saurabh Saxena, Lala Li, Jay Whang, Emily L Denton, Kamyar Ghasemipour, Raphael Gontijo Lopes, Burcu Karagol Ayan, Tim Salimans, et al. 2022. Photorealistic text-to-image diffusion models with deep language understanding. *Advances in Neural Information Processing Systems*, 35:36479–36494.

Christoph Schuhmann, Romain Beaumont, Richard Vencu, Cade Gordon, Ross Wightman, Mehdi Cherti, Theo Coombes, Aarush Katta, Clayton Mullis, Mitchell Wortsman, Patrick Schramowski, Srivatsa Kundurthy, Katherine Crowson, Ludwig Schmidt, Robert Kaczmarczyk, and Jenia Jitsev. 2022. Laion-5b: An open large-scale dataset for training next generation image-text models.

John Schulman, Filip Wolski, Prafulla Dhariwal, Alec Radford, and Oleg Klimov. 2017. Proximal policy optimization algorithms. *arXiv preprint arXiv:1707.06347*.

Nisan Stiennon, Long Ouyang, Jeffrey Wu, Daniel Ziegler, Ryan Lowe, Chelsea Voss, Alec Radford, Dario Amodei, and Paul F Christiano. 2020. Learning to summarize with human feedback. *Advances in Neural Information Processing Systems*, 33:3008–3021.

Leandro von Werra, Younes Belkada, Lewis Tunstall, Edward Beeching, Tristan Thrush, and Nathan Lambert. 2020. Trl: Transformer reinforcement learning. `https://github.com/lvwerra/trl`.

Zijie J Wang, Evan Montoya, David Munechika, Haoyang Yang, Benjamin Hoover, and Duen Horng Chau. 2022. Diffusiondb: A large-scale prompt gallery dataset for text-to-image generative models. *arXiv preprint arXiv:2210.14896*.

A Appendix

A.1 Dataset

To train and evaluate our adaptive framework for prompt enhancement in text-to-image generation, we utilized the DiffusionDB dataset (Wang et al., 2022), a large dataset of human-created prompts. We use a subset of 600k prompts from this dataset to conduct supervised fine-tuning of our LM. For the reinforcement learning stage of training, we use a different subset of 400k prompts from DiffusionDB. For each of the 400k prompts, we truncate the prompt to contain only the substring before the first occurrence of a comma, assuming that modifiers generally appear after the first comma. This approach allows for improved exploration of paraphrasing by our policy. We filtered examples with a significant overlap between the prefix and the entire prompt. To achieve this, we used a sentence similarity threshold of 0.6 overlap and excluded cases which exceeded this threshold.

A.2 Prompt enhancement keywords

Table 3 provides the complete set of prompt enhancement keywords utilized in our constraint sets.

Style	Artist	Format	Boosters	Vibes	Perspective
expressionism	pablo picasso	watercolor painting	trending on artstation	control the soul	long shot
suminagashi	edvard munch	crayon drawing	octane render	futuristic	plain background
surrealism	henri matisse	US patent	ultra high poly	utopian	isometric
anime	thomas cole	kindergartener drawing	extremely detailed	dystopian	panoramic
art deco	mark rothko	cartoon	very beautiful	blade runner	wide angle
photorealism	alphonse mucha	in Mario Kart	studio lighting	cinematic	hard lighting
cyberpunk	leonardo da vinci	pixel art	fantastic	fantasy	knolling
synthwave	claude monet	diagram	postprocessing	elegant	shallow depth of field
realism	james gurney	album art cover	well preserved	magnificent	extreme wide shot
pop art	toshi yoshida	under an electron microscope	4k	retrofuturistic	drone
pixar movies	zdzislaw beksinski	photograph	arnold render	awesome	from behind
abstract organic	gustave doré	pencil sketch	detailed	transhumanist	landscape
dadaism	georges braque	stained glass window	hyperrealistic	bright	1/1000 sec shutter
neoclassicism	bill watterson	advertising poster	rendering	wormhole	from below
ancient art	michelangelo	mugshot	vfx	eclectic	head-and-shoulders shot
baroque	greg rutkowski	cross-stitched sampler	high detail	epic	from above
art nouveau	vincent van gogh	illustration	zbrush	tasteful	oversaturated filter
impressionist	caravaggio	pencil and watercolor drawing	70mm	gorgeous	aerial view
symbolism	diego rivera	in Fortnite	hyper realistic	opaque	telephoto
hudson river school	dean cornwell	line art	8k	old	motion blur
suprematism	ralph mcquarrie	product photography	professional	lsd trip	85mm
rococo	rené magritte	in GTA San Andreas	beautiful	lo-fi	viewed from behind
pointillism	john constable	news crew reporting live	trending on artstation	emo	through a porthole
vaporwave	gustave dore	line drawing	stunning	lucid	dark background
futurism	jackson pollock	courtroom sketch	contest winner	moody	fisheye lens
skeumorphism	hayao miyazaki	on Sesame Street	wondrous	crystal	through a periscope
ukiyo-e	lucian freud	wikiHow	look at that detail	melancholy	white background
medieval art	johannes vermeer	daguerreotype	highly detailed	cosmos	on canvas
corporate memphis	hieronymus bosch	3d render	4k resolution	faded	tilted frame
minimalism	hatsune miku	modeling photoshoot	rendered in unreal engine	uplight	framed
fauvism	utagawa kuniyoshi	one-line drawing	photorealistic	concept art	low angle
renaissance	roy lichtenstein	charcoal drawing	blender 3d	atmospheric	lens flare
constructivism	yoji shinkawa	captured on CCTV	digital art	dust	close face
cubism	craig mullins	painting	vivid	particulate	over-the-shoulder shot
memphis design	claude lorrain	macro 35mm photograph	wow	cute	close up
romanticism	funko pop	on America's Got Talent	high poly	stormy	extreme close-up shot
hieroglyphics	katsushika hokusai	pastel drawing	unreal engine	magical	midshot

Table 3: Prompt enhancement keywords utilized in constraint sets

MEGAnno+: A Human-LLM Collaborative Annotation System

Hannah Kim, Kushan Mitra, Rafael Li Chen, Sajjadur Rahman, Dan Zhang
Megagon Labs
{hannah, kushan, rafael, sajjadur, dan_z}@megagon.ai

Abstract

Large language models (LLMs) can label data faster and cheaper than humans for various NLP tasks. Despite their prowess, LLMs may fall short in understanding of complex, socio-cultural, or domain-specific context, potentially leading to incorrect annotations. Therefore, we advocate a collaborative approach where humans and LLMs work together to produce reliable and high-quality labels. We present MEGAnno+, a human-LLM collaborative annotation system that offers effective LLM agent and annotation management, convenient and robust LLM annotation, and exploratory verification of LLM labels by humans. [1]

1 Introduction

Data annotation has long been an essential step in training machine learning (ML) models. Accurate and abundant annotations significantly contribute to improved model performance. Despite the recent advancements of pre-trained Large Language Models (LLM), high-quality labeled data remains crucial in various use cases requiring retraining. For instance, distilled models are often deployed in scenarios where repeated usage of LLMs for inference can be too costly (e.g., API calls) or time-consuming (e.g., hosting on-premise). In specialized domains like medical and human resources, organizations often need customized models to meet heightened accuracy requirements and ensure the privacy of sensitive customer data. In addition to the training step, accurate labeled data is also necessary for evaluating and understanding of model performance.

Recent explorations (Wang et al., 2021; Ding et al., 2023) have showcased the potential of LLMs in automating the data annotation process. Unlike previous task-specific machine learning models, LLMs exhibit remarkable flexibility to handle any textual labeling task as long as suitable prompts are provided. Besides, compared to traditional annotation relying solely on human labor, LLMs can usually generate labels faster and at a lower cost. For example, hiring crowd workers for labeling may encounter problems such as delays, higher cost, difficulty in quality control (Douglas et al., 2023; Sheehan, 2018; Litman et al., 2021; Garcia-Molina et al., 2016). Studies (Gilardi et al., 2023) show that LLMs can achieve near-human or even better-than-human accuracy in some tasks. Furthermore, downstream models trained with LLM-generated labels may outperform directly using an LLM for inference (Wang et al., 2021).

Despite these advancements, it is essential to acknowledge that LLMs have limitations, necessitating human intervention in the data annotation process. One challenge is that the performance of LLMs varies extensively across different tasks, datasets, and labels (Zhu et al., 2023; Ziems et al., 2023). LLMs often struggle to comprehend subtle nuances or contexts in natural language, making involvement of humans with social and cultural understanding or domain expertise crucial. Additionally, LLMs may produce biased labels due to potentially biased training data (Abid et al., 2021; Sheng et al., 2021). In such cases, humans can recognize potential biases and make ethical judgements to correct them.

In this work, we present MEGAnno+, an annotation system facilitating human-LLM collaboration through efficient LLM annotation and selective human verification. While LLM annotations are gaining interest rapidly, a comprehensive investigation on how to onboard LLMs as annotators within a human-in-the-loop framework in labeling tools has not been conducted yet. For example, supporting LLM annotation requires not only user-friendly communications with LLMs, but also a unified backend capable of storing and managing LLM models, labels, and additional artifacts. Efficient

[1] Demo & video: https://meganno.github.io

Proceedings of the 18th Conference of the European Chapter of the Association for Computational Linguistics System Demonstrations, pages 168–176

human verification calls for a flexible search and recommendation feature to steer human efforts towards problematic LLM labels, along with a mechanism for humans to review and rectify LLM labels. Throughout the paper, we explain how we achieve this in our system, showcase a use case, and discuss our findings.

We summarize our contributions as below:

- A human-LLM collaborative annotation system that offers 1) effective management of LLM agents, annotations, and artifacts, 2) convenient and robust interfacing with LLMs to obtain labels, and 3) selective, exploratory verification of LLM labels by humans.
- A use case demonstrating the effectiveness of our system.
- Practical considerations and discussion on adopting LLMs as annotators.

2 Related Work

LLMs as annotators There is growing interest in utilizing LLMs as general-purpose annotators for natural language tasks (Kuzman et al., 2023; Zhu et al., 2023; Ziems et al., 2023). Wang et al. (2021) find that GPT-3 can reduce labeling cost by up to 96% for classification and generation tasks. Similarly, Ding et al. (2023) evaluate GPT-3 for labeling and augmenting data in classification and token-level tasks. Other studies show that for some classification tasks, LLMs can even outperform crowdsourced annotators (Gilardi et al., 2023; He et al., 2023; Törnberg, 2023).

Verification of LLM responses To detect and correct erroneous responses from LLMs, approaches to rank or filter LLM outputs have been explored. The most common method is using model logits to measure model uncertainty (Wang et al., 2021). More recently, Wang et al. (2024) propose training a verifier model using various signals from LLMs' input, labels, and explanations. Alternative methods include asking LLMs to verbalize confidence scores (Lin et al., 2022) and calculating consistency over prompt perturbations (Wang et al., 2023; Xiong et al., 2023). Other line of works investigate self-verification, i.e., LLMs give feedback on their own outputs and use them to refine themselves (Madaan et al., 2023; Cheng et al., 2023). In our system, we focus on human verification of LLM-generated labels and leave model verification and self-verification as future work.

Annotation tools with AI/ML assistance Machine learning models have proven effective in assisting humans in various steps of the training data collection pipeline. Annotation tools and frameworks such as Prodigy (Montani and Honnibal, 2018), HumanLoop (hum), Label Studio (Tkachenko et al., 2020-2022), and Label Sleuth (Shnarch et al., 2022) all aim to enhance the subset selection step with active learning approaches. ML models are also naturally used to make predictions, serving as pre-labels. For instance, INCEpTION (Klie et al., 2018) provides annotation suggestions generated by ML models. HumanLoop (hum) and Autolabel (aut) support the annotation or augmentation of datasets using either commercial or open-source LLMs. In this work, we go beyond using LLMs to assist annotation for human annotators or to replace human annotators. Rather, MEGAnno+ advocates for a *collaboration* between humans and LLMs with our dedicated system design and annotation-verification workflows.

3 Design Considerations

Let us start with a motivating example of Moana, a Data Scientist working at a popular newspaper. Moana is tasked with training a model to analyze the degree of agreement between user comments and political opinion pieces — e.g., whether the comments entail the opinion. Moana opts for LLM annotation, but she encounters various challenges in the process. Firstly, without any guidance for prompting, she resorts to trial-and-error to eventually identify a suitable prompt for the task. Even so, she must perform additional validations to ensure that the annotated labels are within the space of pre-defined labels. Moreover, the API calls to the LLM can be unreliable, throwing exceptions such as timing out and rate limit violations, requiring her to handle such errors manually. Next, Moana lacks the confidence to train a downstream model without verifying the LLM annotations. However, without any assistance in reviewing potential annotation candidates for verification, she has to go through all the annotations, which can be time-consuming. Finally, she has to manually save used model configurations to reuse the model for additional datasets.

From Moana's example, we summarize our design requirements for a human-LLM collaborative annotation system as follows:

1. LLM annotation

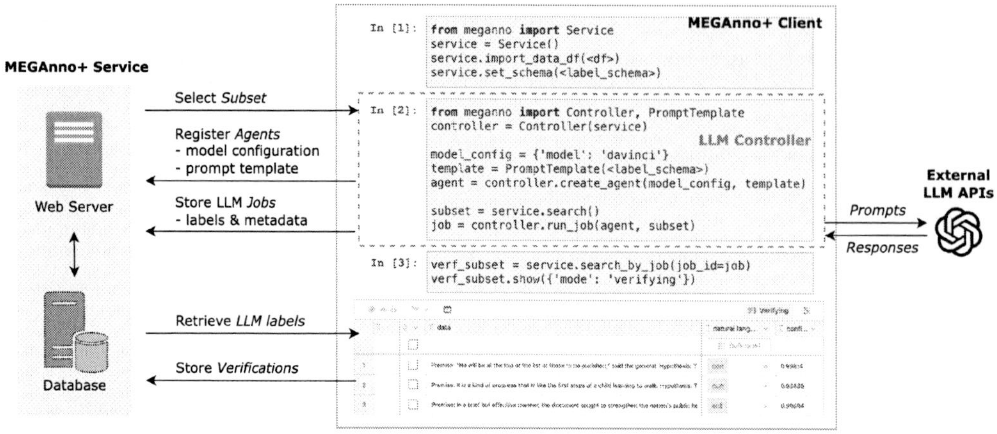

Figure 1: MEGAnno+ system architecture and LLM-integrated workflow. With MEGAnno+ client, users can interact with the back-end service that consists of web and database servers through programmatic interfaces and UI widgets. The middle notebook shows our workflow where cell [2] is LLM annotation and cell [3] is human verification.

   (a) **[Convenient]** Annotation workflow including pre-processing, API calling, and post-processing is automated.
   (b) **[Customizable]** Flexibly modify model configuration and prompt templates.
   (c) **[Robust]** Resolvable errors are handled by the system.
   (d) **[Reusable]** Store used LLM models and prompt templates for reuse.
   (e) **[Metadata]** LLM artifacts are captured and stored as annotation metadata.
2. Human verification
   (a) **[Selective]** Select verification candidates by search query or recommendation.
   (b) **[Exploratory]** Filter, sort, and search by labels and available metadata programmatically and in a UI.

To satisfy these design requirements, we implement our system as an extension to MEGAnno (Zhang et al., 2022), an in-notebook exploratory annotation tool. Its flexible search and intelligent recommendations enable efficient allocation of human and LLM resources toward crucial data points (R 2a,2b). Additionally, MEGAnno provides a cohesive backend for the storage of data, annotations, and auxiliary information (R 1d,1e).

4 System

4.1 System Overview

MEGAnno+ is designed to provide a convenient and robust workflow for users to utilize LLMs in text annotation. To use our tool, users operate within their Jupyter notebook (Kluyver et al., 2016) with the MEGAnno+ client installed.

Our human-LLM collaborative workflow (Fig. 1) starts with LLM annotation. This step involves compiling a subset and using an LLM to annotate it by interacting with the programmatic LLM controller. The LLM controller takes care of 1) agent registration and management (e.g., model selection and validation) and 2) running annotation jobs (e.g., input data pre-processing, initiating LLM calls, post-processing and storing responses), satisfying R 1a,1c. Once LLM annotation is completed, users can verify LLM labels. Users can select a subset of LLM labels to verify by search queries (R 2a), and inspect and correct them in a verification widget in the same notebook (R 2b).

Data Model MEGAnno+ extends MEGAnno's data model where data `Record`, `Label`, `Annotation`, `Metadata` (e.g., text embedding or confidence score) are persisted in the service database along with the task `Schema`.[2] Annotations are organized around `Subsets`, which are slices of the data created from user-defined searches or recommendations. To effectively integrate LLM into the workflow, we introduce new concepts: `Agent`, `Job`, and `Verification`. An `Agent` is defined by the configuration of the LLM (e.g., model's name, version, and hyper-parameters) and a prompt template. When an agent

[2]MEGAnno+ only supports full LLM-integrated workflows for record-level tasks.

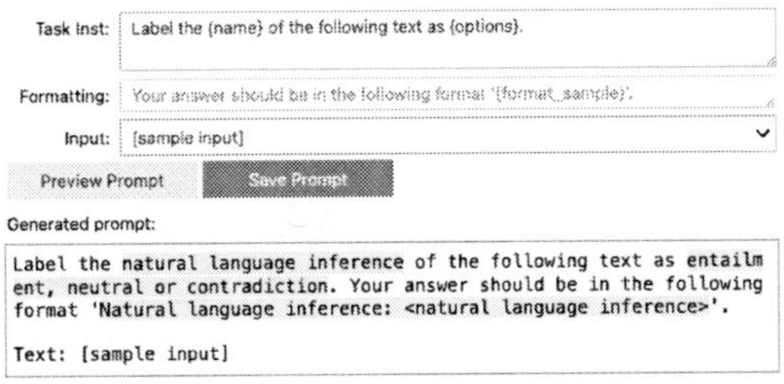

Figure 2: UI for customizing a prompt template and previewing generated prompts. Prompt is generated based on the name and options of label schema.

is employed to annotate a selected data subset, the execution is referred to as a `Job` (see Section 4.3.1). `Verification` captures annotations from human users that confirm or update LLM labels (see Section 4.4).

4.2 Agents: Model and Prompt Management

Since variation in either model configuration or prompt may result in a variable output from an LLM, we define an annotation `Agent` to be a combination of a user-selected configuration and prompt template. Used agents are stored in our database[3] and can be queried based on model configuration. This allows users to reuse agents and even compare the performance of different LLMs on a particular dataset (R 1d).

Model configuration MEGAnno+ enables users to choose an LLM from a list of available models, configure model parameters, and also provide a validation mechanism to ensure the selected model and parameters conform to the LLM API definition and limitations. While MEGAnno+ is designed to support any open-source LLM or commercial LLM APIs, in this work, we only demonstrate OpenAI Completion models for clarity and brevity.

Prompt template To utilize LLMs as annotators, an input record has to be transformed into a prompt text. With MEGAnno+, prompts can be automatically generated based on a labeling schema and a prompt template for users' convenience. We offer a default template that contains annotation instruction, output formatting instruction, and input slot, which can be edited programmatically. We also provide a UI widget to interactively customize the prompt template and preview the generated prompts for selected data samples (Fig. 2, R 1b).

[3]Note that for an agent, we store its prompt template (a rule to build prompt text), not prompts (generated prompts for a set of data records) to save storage.

4.3 LLM Annotation

Unlike human annotation, LLM annotation goes through a multi-step process to collect labels from input data records. We execute this process as an annotation `Job` using the LLM controller.

4.3.1 Initiating LLM Jobs

To start a job, users need to select a data subset to annotate and an agent, i.e., an LLM model and a prompt template. Users can utilize MEGAnno's sophisticated subset selection techniques, including filtering by keywords or regular expressions, or receiving suggestions of similar data records. One can create a new agent or reuse one of previously registered agents. By reusing subsets and agents for new jobs, users can easily compare annotation performance between different models or for different data slices.

4.3.2 Pre-processing

The first step within a job is pre-processing. Using the prompt template of a selected agent, a data subset is converted into a list of prompts. All prompts are validated (e.g., within max token limit) before calling LLM APIs.

4.3.3 LLM API Calls: Error Handling

MEGAnno+ handles the calls to the external LLM APIs to facilitate a smooth, robust, and fault-tolerant experience for users, without having to worry about making any explicit API calls or handling error cases themselves. In order to ensure a fault-tolerant procedure, errors encountered during API calls are handled in two ways: *handle within our system* or *delegate to users*. We handle known LLM API errors that can be solved by user-side intervention. This would be in cases such as a `Timeout` or `RateLimitError` in OpenAI models, or other similar errors which require the user themselves to call to the LLM API again. On encountering such errors, MEGAnno+ retries the call to the LLM API itself. Delegated errors are the ones that require interventions by external service providers and are beyond our scope. For instance, errors such as `APIConnectionError` in OpenAI models occur because of an issue with the LLM API server itself and requires intervention from OpenAI. In this case, MEGAnno+ simply notifies the user and relays the error message.

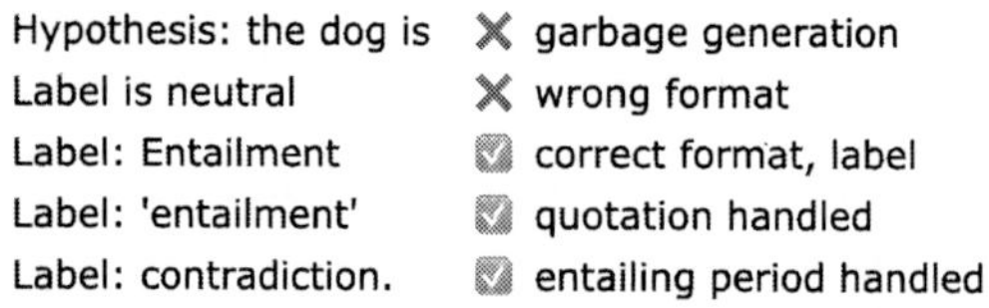

Figure 3: Example LLM responses and extraction results. Minor violations are processed as valid labels.

4.3.4 Post-processing LLM Responses and Storing Labels and Metadata

Label extraction LLM outputs are typically unstructured (i.e., free-text) and can be noisy and unusable for downstream applications, even when prompted to adhere to a specific format. This necessitates careful post-processing of LLM-generated content, converting them into valid labels (Fig. 3). MEGAnno+ conducts an automated post-processing step on LLM responses, handling errors in cases of syntax or formatting violations (i.e., not adhering to the format specified in prompt instructions). Additionally, our tool checks for semantic violations, ensuring that the generated label is valid within the existing schema for the task.

Metadata extraction MEGAnno+ can collect model artifacts and store them as label metadata (R 1e). Examples include model logits, costs associated with inference, used random seed, and so on. They can be useful for further analyses on LLM annotation and human verification. By default, our system only stores token logits to estimate the used LLM's confidence for generated labels. Calculated confidence scores serve as additional signals for decision-making in the human verification step.

Storing in database Following the post-processing step, extracted valid labels and metadata are sent to the backend service for persistence in the database. Invalid labels are not stored in the database to prevent label contamination, but frequent invalid ones are still shown to the user to guide the next iteration (e.g., update labeling schema, improve instruction in prompts).

4.3.5 Monitoring Annotation Jobs

When running a job, we display the progress and statistics of each step of the job for monitoring (Fig. 4). These include 1) agent details such as the selected model and prompt template, 2) input summary such as sample prompts generated using

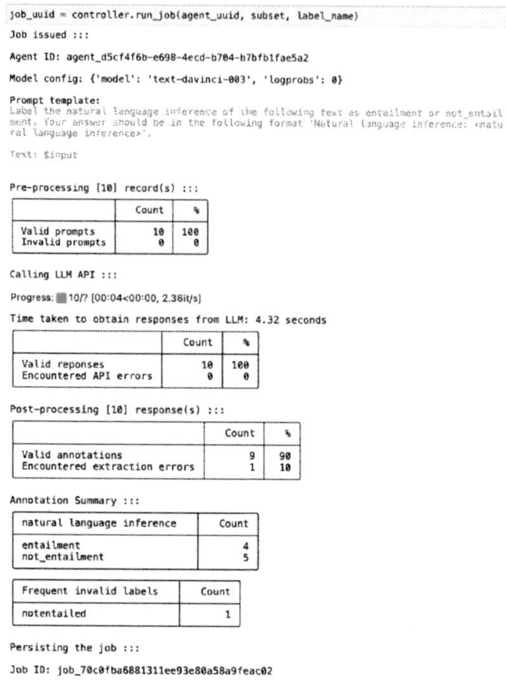

Figure 4: Annotation progress and summary.

the template along with how many prompts are valid or invalid, 3) API call progress such as the time taken to retrieve responses from the API calls, and 4) output summary such as the numbers of valid and invalid responses from API and label distribution of valid responses.

4.4 Verification

LLM labels can be unreliable, requiring human verification to ensure the quality of the collected labeled data.

In-notebook verification widget MEGAnno+ provides a verification widget to complete the LLM annotation workflow in the same notebook. Leveraging MEGAnno+'s robust and customizable search functionality, users can retrieve a subset of LLM labels based on keywords, regular expressions, assigned labels, or metadata. Then utilizing the verification widget (as illustrated in Fig. 5), users can explore the selected subset and decide whether to confirm or correct their LLM-generated labels. The verification UI includes both a table view for exploratory and batch verification, as well as a single view.

Verification priority Human verification, while less expensive than direct annotation, can still be time- and cost-consuming. Therefore, it is crucial

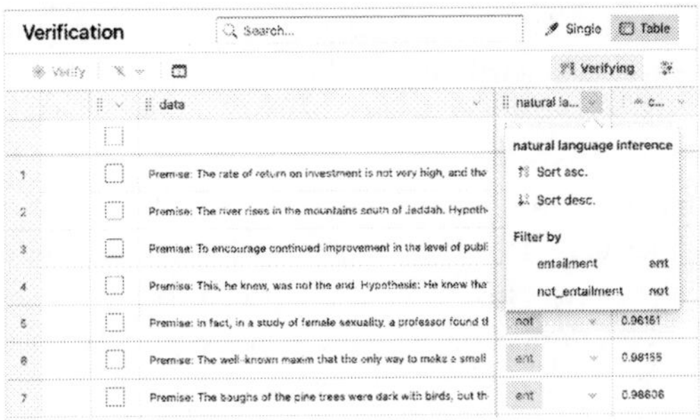

Figure 5: The table view in verification UI. Users can explore LLM annotations via filtering by labels, sorting by confidence scores, or keyword search on text input.

to prioritize and direct human efforts toward more "suspicious" outputs from LLMs. Our widget facilitates this process by presenting metadata, such as model confidence or token logit scores, in a separate column. Users can freely sort and filter rows based on labels or metadata, enabling them to prioritize or focus on labels with low confidence.

Query and export verified labels MEGAnno+ offers flexible query interfaces, allowing users to search for verification by LLM agents (i.e., model and prompt config), as well as jobs. Both the original LLM-generated labels and any potential human corrections are stored in the database, enabling users to filter and retrieve labels "confirmed" or "corrected" by human verifiers. These features establish a foundation for easy in-notebook model and prompt comparison. Ultimately, the query results serve as a view of the labeling project, ready to be exported to downstream applications.

5 Use Case: Natural Language Inference

Moana, the aforementioned data scientist who needs to collect training data quickly, decides to use MEGAnno+ to leverage LLM-powered annotation. First, she imports her unlabeled data and sets the labeling schema as entailment or not entailment. She selects a GPT-3 davinci model with the default parameters and prompt template. To test this setting, she runs the model on 10 samples.

```
c = Controller(<service>, <auth>)
model_config = {'model': 'davinci'}
template = PromptTemplate(label_schema)
agent = c.create_agent(model_config,
    template)
subset = <service>.search(limit=10)
job = c.run_job(agent, subset)
```

After the job is finished, the annotation summary (Fig. 4) shows that all samples are successfully annotated by GPT-3 and 40% are entailment. Also, one response is annotated with 'notentailed', exemplifying the instability of LLMs even with clear instructions. With MEGAnno+'s table view widget, she examines data and labels (Fig. 5). She realizes that some of the records labeled as 'not entailment' are contradictory whereas the rest are neutral. She updates the labeling schema to contain entailment, neutral, and contradiction. Next, she wonders if changing the model's temperature would improve the accuracy of annotation. She creates another agent, GPT-3 with temperature with zero and re-runs annotation on the same subset.

```
model_config2 = {'model': 'davinci', '
    temperature': 0}
agent2 = c.create_agent(model_config2,
    template)
job2 = c.run_job(agent2, subset)
```

She exports the annotations from both jobs and compares them. She concludes that the second model is good enough for her project. She imports her entire data and uses the agent to label them. Since the size of the data is huge, she has to wait till the annotations are done. Fortunately, with MEGAnno+, she can track the progress in the output cell while the job is running. To review the annotations, she sorts the annotations in an ascending order of confidence and manually verifies low confidence ($< 95\%$) annotations.

6 Discussion

How to design an annotation task? Based on our experience, we find that designing an annotation task and a prompt similar to more widely used and standardized NLP tasks is beneficial. For example, framing Moana's problem as a natural language inference task is more effective than framing it as a binary classification of agreement and disagreement. Also, the selection of label options may work better if it is similar to common options for given tasks, such as [positive, neutral, negative] > [super positive, positive, ..., negative] for sentiment classification. Lastly, it is recommended that the format of a prompt be similar to the one used in training as some LLMs have different prompt format than the others. We plan to conduct more systematic test to discover reasonable default prompts for different models.

Are LLMs consistent and reliable annotators? We expect human annotators to maintain a consistent mental model. In other words, when humans are presented with the same question rephrased, we anticipate consistent answers. However, LLMs are known to be sensitive to semantic-preserving perturbations in prompts. For instance, changes in prompt design, the selection and order of demonstrations, and the order of answer options can result in different outputs (Zhao et al., 2021; Pezeshkpour and Hruschka, 2023). Moreover, commercial LLMs can undergo real-time fine-tuning, meaning that prompting with the same setup today may yield different results than prompting yesterday (Chen et al., 2023). Therefore, LLM annotators and human annotators should not be treated the same, and annotation tools should carefully design their data models and workflows to accommodate both types of annotators.

Limitations Our system has several limitations. Our post-processing mechanism may not be robust to cover all tasks and prompts entered by the user. Furthermore, MEGAnno+'s ability to capture metadata is contingent on the LLM model used. For example, `GPT-4` models do not yet provide any form of token logprobs or other metadata which can be captured.

7 Conclusion

MEGAnno+ is a text annotation system for human-LLM collaborative data labeling. With our LLM annotation → Human verification workflow, reliable and high-quality labels can be collected efficiently. Our tool supports robust LLM annotation, selective human verification, and effective management of LLMs, labels, and metadata.

As future work, we are currently working on adding more LLM agents (e.g., open-source LLMs), supporting customized extraction of metadata (e.g., custom uncertainty metric), and improving prompt template UI for data-aware in-context learning. Additionally, we plan to incorporate diverse annotation workflows such as Multi-agent LLM annotation → LLM label aggregation → Human verification; and LLM augmentation → Human verification.

Ethics Statement

First, labels generated by LLMs can exhibit bias or inaccuracy. These models are pre-trained on vast amount of data, which are typically not accessible to the public. Biases present in the training data can be transferred to LLM labels. Also, if the training data lacks relevant or up-to-date knowledge, the model may produce incorrect annotation. Since we cannot access models' inner workings or their training data, it is difficult to identify and understand how and why LLMs make biased or inaccurate labeling decisions. Second, the use of commercial LLMs for labeling data containing sensitive information or intellectual property may pose risks. Data shared with commercial LLMs, such as ChatGPT, may be collected and utilized for retraining these models. To prevent potential data leakage and mitigate associated legal consequences, it is advisable to either mask any confidential information or only use in-house LLMs.

Acknowledgements

We would like to thank Pouya Pezeshkpour and Estevam Hruschka for their helpful comments.

References

Autolabel. Github.com/refuel-ai/autolabel.

Humanloop.com. Humanloop.com.

Abubakar Abid, Maheen Farooqi, and James Zou. 2021. Persistent anti-muslim bias in large language models. In *Proceedings of the 2021 AAAI/ACM Conference on AI, Ethics, and Society*, AIES '21, page 298–306, New York, NY, USA. Association for Computing Machinery.

Lingjiao Chen, Matei Zaharia, and James Zou. 2023. How is chatgpt's behavior changing over time?

Jiale Cheng, Xiao Liu, Kehan Zheng, Pei Ke, Hongning Wang, Yuxiao Dong, Jie Tang, and Minlie Huang. 2023. Black-box prompt optimization: Aligning large language models without model training.

Bosheng Ding, Chengwei Qin, Linlin Liu, Yew Ken Chia, Boyang Li, Shafiq Joty, and Lidong Bing. 2023. Is GPT-3 a good data annotator? In *Proceedings of the 61st Annual Meeting of the Association for Computational Linguistics (Volume 1: Long Papers)*, pages 11173–11195, Toronto, Canada. Association for Computational Linguistics.

Benjamin D Douglas, Patrick J Ewell, and Markus Brauer. 2023. Data quality in online human-subjects research: Comparisons between mturk, prolific, cloudresearch, qualtrics, and sona. *Plos one*, 18(3):e0279720.

Hector Garcia-Molina, Manas Joglekar, Adam Marcus, Aditya Parameswaran, and Vasilis Verroios. 2016. Challenges in data crowdsourcing. *IEEE Transactions on Knowledge and Data Engineering*, 28(4):901–911.

Fabrizio Gilardi, Meysam Alizadeh, and Maël Kubli. 2023. Chatgpt outperforms crowd workers for text-annotation tasks. *Proceedings of the National Academy of Sciences*, 120(30).

Xingwei He, Zhenghao Lin, Yeyun Gong, A-Long Jin, Hang Zhang, Chen Lin, Jian Jiao, Siu Ming Yiu, Nan Duan, and Weizhu Chen. 2023. AnnoLLM: Making large language models to be better crowdsourced annotators.

Jan-Christoph Klie, Michael Bugert, Beto Boullosa, Richard Eckart de Castilho, and Iryna Gurevych. 2018. The INCEpTION platform: Machine-assisted and knowledge-oriented interactive annotation. In *Proceedings of the 27th International Conference on Computational Linguistics: System Demonstrations*, pages 5–9, Santa Fe, New Mexico. Association for Computational Linguistics.

Thomas Kluyver, Benjamin Ragan-Kelley, Fernando Pérez, Brian Granger, Matthias Bussonnier, Jonathan Frederic, Kyle Kelley, Jessica Hamrick, Jason Grout, Sylvain Corlay, Paul Ivanov, Damián Avila, Safia Abdalla, and Carol Willing. 2016. Jupyter notebooks – a publishing format for reproducible computational workflows. In *Positioning and Power in Academic Publishing: Players, Agents and Agendas*, pages 87 – 90. IOS Press.

Taja Kuzman, Igor Mozetič, and Nikola Ljubešić. 2023. Chatgpt: Beginning of an end of manual linguistic data annotation? use case of automatic genre identification.

Stephanie Lin, Jacob Hilton, and Owain Evans. 2022. Teaching models to express their uncertainty in words. *Transactions on Machine Learning Research*.

Leib Litman, Aaron Moss, Cheskie Rosenzweig, and Jonathan Robinson. 2021. Reply to mturk, prolific or panels? choosing the right audience for online research. *SSRN Electronic Journal*.

Aman Madaan, Niket Tandon, Prakhar Gupta, Skyler Hallinan, Luyu Gao, Sarah Wiegreffe, Uri Alon, Nouha Dziri, Shrimai Prabhumoye, Yiming Yang, Shashank Gupta, Bodhisattwa Prasad Majumder, Katherine Hermann, Sean Welleck, Amir Yazdanbakhsh, and Peter Clark. 2023. Self-refine: Iterative refinement with self-feedback.

Ines Montani and Matthew Honnibal. 2018. Prodigy: A new annotation tool for radically efficient machine teaching. *Artificial Intelligence to appear*.

Pouya Pezeshkpour and Estevam Hruschka. 2023. Large language models sensitivity to the order of options in multiple-choice questions.

Kim Bartel Sheehan. 2018. Crowdsourcing research: data collection with amazon's mechanical turk. *Communication Monographs*, 85(1):140–156.

Emily Sheng, Kai-Wei Chang, Prem Natarajan, and Nanyun Peng. 2021. Societal biases in language generation: Progress and challenges. In *Proceedings of the 59th Annual Meeting of the Association for Computational Linguistics and the 11th International Joint Conference on Natural Language Processing (Volume 1: Long Papers)*, pages 4275–4293, Online. Association for Computational Linguistics.

Eyal Shnarch, Alon Halfon, Ariel Gera, Marina Danilevsky, Yannis Katsis, Leshem Choshen, Martin Santillan Cooper, Dina Epelboim, Zheng Zhang, and Dakuo Wang. 2022. Label sleuth: From unlabeled text to a classifier in a few hours. In *Proceedings of the 2022 Conference on Empirical Methods in Natural Language Processing: System Demonstrations*, pages 159–168, Abu Dhabi, UAE. Association for Computational Linguistics.

Maxim Tkachenko, Mikhail Malyuk, Andrey Holmanyuk, and Nikolai Liubimov. 2020-2022. Label Studio: Data labeling software. Open source software available from https://github.com/heartexlabs/label-studio.

Petter Törnberg. 2023. Chatgpt-4 outperforms experts and crowd workers in annotating political twitter messages with zero-shot learning.

Shuohang Wang, Yang Liu, Yichong Xu, Chenguang Zhu, and Michael Zeng. 2021. Want to reduce labeling cost? GPT-3 can help. In *Findings of the Association for Computational Linguistics: EMNLP 2021*, pages 4195–4205, Punta Cana, Dominican Republic. Association for Computational Linguistics.

Xinru Wang, Hannah Kim, Sajjadur Rahman, Kushan Mitra, and Zhengjie Miao. 2024. Human-LLM collaborative annotation through effective verification of LLM labels. In *Proceedings of the 2024 CHI Conference on Human Factors in Computing Systems*, CHI '24, New York, NY, USA. Association for Computing Machinery.

Xuezhi Wang, Jason Wei, Dale Schuurmans, Quoc V Le, Ed H. Chi, Sharan Narang, Aakanksha Chowdhery, and Denny Zhou. 2023. Self-consistency improves chain of thought reasoning in language models. In *The Eleventh International Conference on Learning Representations*.

Miao Xiong, Zhiyuan Hu, Xinyang Lu, Yifei Li, Jie Fu, Junxian He, and Bryan Hooi. 2023. Can llms express their uncertainty? an empirical evaluation of confidence elicitation in llms.

Dan Zhang, Hannah Kim, Rafael Li Chen, Eser Kandogan, and Estevam Hruschka. 2022. MEGAnno: Exploratory labeling for NLP in computational notebooks. In *Proceedings of the Fourth Workshop on Data Science with Human-in-the-Loop (Language Advances)*, pages 1–7, Abu Dhabi, United Arab Emirates (Hybrid). Association for Computational Linguistics.

Zihao Zhao, Eric Wallace, Shi Feng, Dan Klein, and Sameer Singh. 2021. Calibrate before use: Improving few-shot performance of language models. In *Proceedings of the 38th International Conference on Machine Learning*, volume 139 of *Proceedings of Machine Learning Research*, pages 12697–12706. PMLR.

Yiming Zhu, Peixian Zhang, Ehsan-Ul Haq, Pan Hui, and Gareth Tyson. 2023. Can chatgpt reproduce human-generated labels? a study of social computing tasks. *arXiv preprint arXiv:2304.10145*.

Caleb Ziems, William Held, Omar Shaikh, Jiaao Chen, Zhehao Zhang, and Diyi Yang. 2023. Can Large Language Models Transform Computational Social Science? *Computational Linguistics*, pages 1–53.

X-AMR Annotation Tool

Shafiuddin Rehan Ahmed **Jon Z. Cai** **Martha Palmer** **James H. Martin**
University of Colorado, Boulder, USA
{shah7567, jon.z.cai}@colorado.edu

Abstract

This paper presents a novel **Cross**-document **A**bstract **M**eaning **R**epresentation (X-AMR) annotation tool designed for annotating key corpus-level event semantics. Leveraging machine assistance through the Prodigy Annotation Tool, we enhance the user experience, ensuring ease and efficiency in the annotation process. Through empirical analyses, we demonstrate the effectiveness of our tool in augmenting an existing event corpus, highlighting its advantages when integrated with GPT-4. Code and annotations: github.com/ahmeshaf/gpt_coref[1] [2]

1 Introduction

Semantic representations of events play a pivotal role in natural language processing (NLP) tasks, facilitating the understanding and extraction of meaningful information from text. Among the various approaches to represent events, Semantic Role Labeling (SRL; Palmer et al. (2005)) and Abstract Meaning Representation (AMR; Banarescu et al. (2013)) have gained significant attention. In this paper, we delve into the realm of semantic event representations, with a particular focus on a method for expanding AMR.

AMR, a graph-based semantic representation, aims to capture the underlying meaning of sentences by breaking them down into atomic concepts and their semantic relationships. Each concept in AMR is associated with a unique identifier, and the relationships between concepts are represented as labeled edges in a graph. AMR has proven to be versatile, serving as a valuable resource for a wide range of NLP tasks such as machine translation, question answering (Fu et al., 2021), and summarization (Liao et al., 2018). Its ability to provide a structured, language-independent representation of textual content makes it an essential tool in the NLP toolkit.

However, despite its many merits, current AMR techniques are not without limitations. One of the primary challenges lies in linking temporal relations and entity coreference across sentences and documents. This limitation hinders the comprehensive understanding of text, as it often fails to capture the intricate interplay between events and entities that span multiple contexts. This issue becomes particularly pronounced in scenarios involving cross-document event coreference, where events mentioned in one document need to be linked to events in other documents for a coherent understanding of a larger narrative.

To illustrate the challenge of coreference across documents, consider the following example: Two news articles discuss a corporate acquisition. In one article, the event is described as "Company A's purchase of Company B on July 1st, 2008" while in another article, it is referred to as "In 7/08 Company B was acquired by Company A." Establishing the coreference relationship between these two descriptions is non-trivial, yet crucial for creating a comprehensive representation of the acquisition event.

To specifically address the intricate challenges of cross-document event coreference resolution, our research introduces two significant contributions. Firstly, we propose a novel framework X-AMR. This framework is an enhancement of the existing AMR, specifically designed to overcome the challenges inherent in linking events and entities across different documents. X-AMR effectively combines the strengths of AMR with the ability to create a more comprehensive and coherent depiction of narratives that span multiple sources.

Secondly, the development of a specialized interface is another key contribution of our work. Utilizing the model-in-the-loop annotation methodology, we have leveraged the customized Prodigy

[1] Demo: https://youtu.be/TuirftxciNE
[2] Live Link: eacldemo.acl-lawpaper34-demo.site/

Proceedings of the 18th Conference of the European Chapter of the Association for Computational Linguistics
System Demonstrations, pages 177–186
March 17-22, 2024

annotation tool to augment an existing event coreference dataset, the Event Coref Bank plus (ECB+; Cybulska and Vossen (2014)). This development has facilitaed the annotation of X-AMR representations, focusing on the annotation interface and the enhanced X-AMR dataset. Additionaly, we present an evaluation showcasing the accuracy and efficiency of our approach. Our research endeavors to demonstrate the effectiveness of X-AMR in addressing the limitations of current sentence level AMR, especially in linking temporal relations and entity coreference across sentences and documents.

2 Related Work

AMR is a formalism meticulously crafted to capture the semantic nuances of natural language expressions with versatile and expressive power. In the field of Natural Language Processing (NLP), automatic AMR parsing transforms natural language inputs into formal AMR representations, which have demonstrated utility in a diverse array of downstream applications (Liao et al., 2018; Bonial et al., 2020; Kapanipathi et al., 2021; Bai et al., 2021; Li and Flanigan, 2022; Bai et al., 2022; Ribeiro et al., 2022; Rao, 2022).

Formally, AMR are structured as labeled, rooted, directed acyclic graphs, which capture abstract concepts, predicate-argument relationships, and entities found in sentences or utterances. They integrate the semantic content addressed by different representation schemes such as SRL, named entities recognition (NER; Wang et al. (2022)), and coreference resolution into a unified representation. For example, for sentence "HP acquired EYPMCS.", the corresponding AMR is:

```
(d / acquire-01
    :ARG0 (c / company
        :name (n / name
            :op1 "HP"))
    :ARG1 (c2 / company
        :name (n2 / name
            :op1 "EYPMCS"))
```

The above AMR graph captures concepts such as events such as "acquire", named entities such as the HP company, and properties of the entity such as their names as graph nodes and subgraphs. Their interrelations between concepts and events are then depicted through labeled edges. Events are denoted using Propbank rolesets, and semantics relations of the entities and events are specified through numbered arguments and non-core relations from AMR's role inventory. For example, in the above acquisition event, the `ARG0` typically specifies the stereotypical agent of an event and `ARG1` typically specifies the stereotypical patient of an event. Additionaly, AMR graphs formalize local temporal information, as shown in the provided example.

In the preceding disucssion, we highlighted the expressiveness of AMR. However, the expressiveness of AMR introduces complexities in AMR annotation, historically a significant bottleneck for NLP community. The challenge has been to provide a substantial volume of AMR annotations to the data hunger statistical machine learning models given the limitations of available tools. The ISI editor, serving as the first AMR editor, has supported the AMR community for over a decade. Despite the efficacy of the ISI editor, its learning curve is notably steep for annotators. To make AMR annotation more accessible, Cai et al. (2023) developed a new annotation approach. They introduced an AMR editor based on coding, complemented by a neural network parser model, to streamline the annotation process.

The remarkable progress in large language model-based coding assistance, pioneered by OpenAI and Microsoft, is transforming the landscape of program synthesis in software engineering. These models, trained in both natural language and programming languages, excel at completing programs by intelligently integrating code history and human instructions. In a similar vein, CAMRA leverages these large language models (LLMs) to enhance AMR annotation. We are pioneering the extension of LLMs' capabilities, broadening their application to include more complex tasks such as cross-sentential and cross-document coreference and event linking. This initiative represents a significant step forward in harnessing the power of LLMs for even more sophisticated and long-distance dependent language processing tasks.

3 Annotation Methodology

The annotation workflow, as depicted in Figure 1, comprises of two phases. In the first phase we annotate the roleset IDs of the event triggers. Then we specify the arguments of the event incrementally. During these two phases, we maintain an arguments store and a model-in-the-loop that queries the store and suggests annotators with the most likely arguments. This store and the model are updated when new events are annotated.

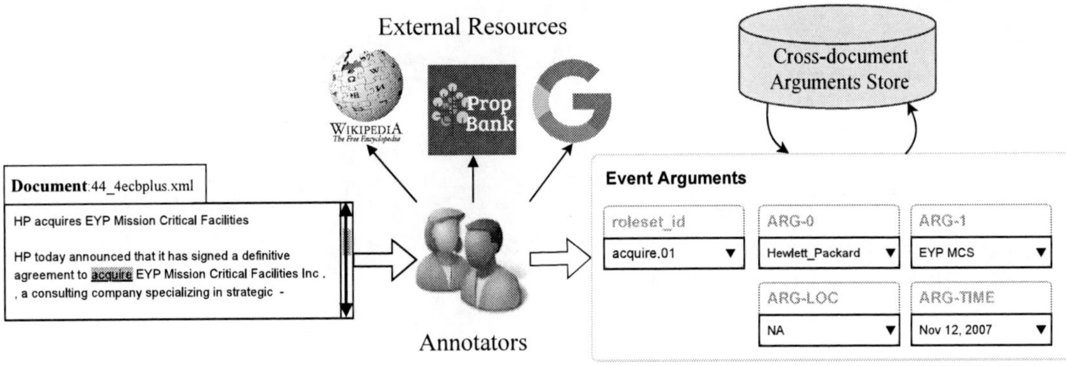

Figure 1: The Annotation Methodology of X-AMR. The annotators are presented with PropBank and are allowed to use external resources, such as Wikipedia and Google News, during the annotations.

Next, we discuss the annotation guidelines, the interface, and the model-in-the-loop in the annotation workflow.

3.1 Annotation Guidelines for X-AMR

We aim to annotate key event semantics with four arguments, ARG-0, ARG-1, ARG-Loc, and ARG-Time, capturing agent, patient (and theme), location, and temporal information. The selection of these arguments is to circumscribe an event by its *minimal participants* (Lombard, 2019; Guarino et al., 2022). We use the guidelines presented in the next section to hand annotate the roleset and argument information for the ECB+ train, development, and test sets using the standardized split of Cybulska and Vossen (2014). Following the annotation guidelines, we provide the enriched annotations of the ECB+ corpus by two Linguistic students. We use a model-in-the-loop annotation methodology with the prodi.gy annotation tool.

3.1.1 PropBank & AMR

Semantic role labeling (SRL) centers on the task of assigning the same semantic role to an argument across various syntactic constructions. For example, *the window* can be the (prototypical) Patient, or thing broken, whether expressed as syntactic object (*The storm broke the window*) or syntactic subject (*The window broke in the storm*).

The Proposition Bank (PropBank; Palmer et al. (2005); Pradhan et al. (2022)) has over 11,000 Frame Files providing valency information (arguments and their descriptions) for fine-grained senses of English verbs, eventive nouns, and adjectives. Figure 2 gives an example Frame File for *agree* as well as an instantiated frame for *HP has an agreement to acquire EYP.*

```
agree.01 - agree     agree.01
 ARG-0: Agreer        ARG-0: HP
 ARG-1: Proposition  ARG-1: acquire.01
                        ARG-1: EYP
```

Figure 2: The PropBank roleset definitions of agree.01 and the expected annotations in X-AMR.

The resulting nested predicate-argument structures from PropBank style-SRL also form the backbones of AMRs, which in addition includes Named Entity (NE) tags and Wikipedia links (for 'HP' and 'EYP' in our example). AMRs also include explicit variables for each entity and event, consistent with Neo-Davidsonian event semantics, as well as inter- and intra-sentential coreference links to form directed, (largely) acyclic graphs that represent the meaning of an utterance or set of utterances.

Our enhanced X-AMR representation follows AMR closely with respect to NE and coreference, but stops short of AMR's additional structuring of noun phrase modifiers (especially with respect to dates, quantities and organizational relations), the discourse connectives and the partial treatment of negation and modality. However, we go further than AMR by allowing for cross-document coreference as well as multi-sentence coreference. X-AMR thus provides us with a flexible and expressive event representation with much broader coverage than standard event annotation datasets such as ACE[3] or Maven (Wang et al., 2020).

3.1.2 Roleset Sense Annotation

The first step in the annotation process involves identifying the roleset sense for the target event

[3]https://www.ldc.upenn.edu/collaborations/past-projects/ace

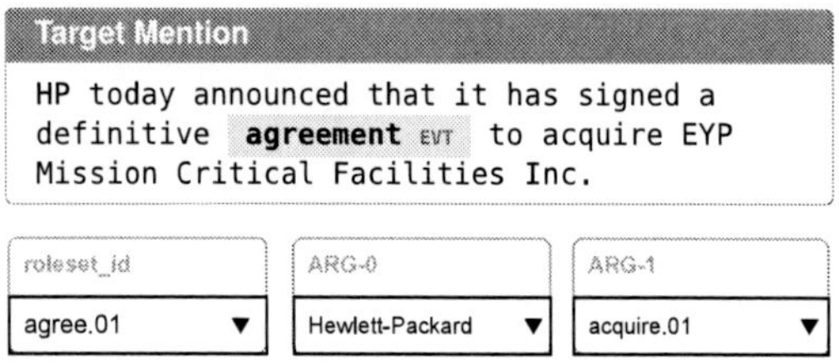

Figure 3: Eventive ARG-1 in the roleset agree.01. The ARG-1 clause is annotated as the connecting event with roleset ID acquire.01

trigger in the given text. Annotators, using an embedded PropBank website and the assistance of the tool's model, select the most appropriate sense by comparing senses across frame files.

Handling Triggers with No Suitable Roleset: If there is no appropriate roleset that specifies the event trigger, particularly in cases when the trigger is a pronoun (it) or proper noun (e.g., Academy Awards), the annotator must then search for a roleset that defines the appropriate predicate.

3.1.3 Document-level Arguments Identification

Next, we identify the document and corpus-level ARG-0 and ARG-1 of the selected roleset. Annotators use the embedded PropBank website as a reference for the roleset's definition, ensuring that the ARG-0 (usually the agent) and ARG-1 (typically the patient) are consistent with the roleset's constraints. For arguments that cannot be inferred, the annotators leave those fields empty.

Within- and Cross-Document Entity Coreference Annotation: Annotators perform within- and cross-document entity coreference using a dropdown box of argument suggestions (suggested by the model-in-the-loop), simplifying coreference link establishment.

Nested ARG-1: In many cases, the ARG-1 may itself be an event. In such cases, the annotator is tasked with identifying the head predicate of the ARG-1 role and providing its corresponding roleset ID. We then search for the annotations for such an ARG-1 and connect it to the target event. Fig 3 has an example of a mention with an eventive ARG-1. For this, the annotator needs to provide the roleset for the predicate of the ARG-1 clause (agree.01) as the ARG-1 in this annotation process.

ARG-Loc & ARG-Time Identification Annotators may also utilize external resources, such as

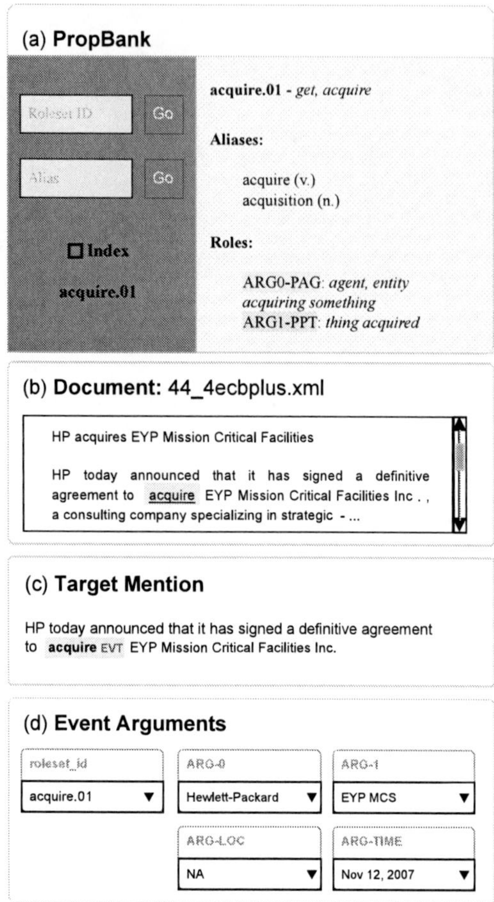

Figure 4: The Annotation Interface Using prodi.gy Annotation Tool

Wikipedia[4], or Google-News, for the accurate identification of temporal and spatial arguments. This is required when the document does not explicitly mention the location and time of the event.

3.2 Annotation Interface

The annotation interface, as depicted in Figure 4, comprises four distinct components: (a) the integrated PropBank website, (b) the document view, (c) the sentence view, and (d) the event argument forms. This interface is hosted on a server using Prodigy, with links distributed to individual annotators.

PropBank Website: We adapt the publicly available PropBank website builder[5] to ensure compat-

[4]Although we add this in the guidelines, the annotators do not wikify. Our choice is to use Wikipedia over the more commonly used KB-wikidata because of GPT-friendly identifiers of the pages. Check out Appendix B.

[5]https://github.com/propbank/propbank-frames

ibility within an embedded environment. This interactive website hosts an indexed list of roleset definitions that annotators refer to.

Target Mention Document: The document containing the current mention is fully displayed in a scrollable view with the event trigger highlighted upon interface loading, facilitating easy access to additional context for annotators.

Target Mention Sentence: This section displays the sentence encompassing the mention, with the event trigger highlighted in Prodigy's named entity recognition (NER) style. Typically, a sentence alone is sufficient to identify the arguments, and therefore, it is in the field of focus first.

Event Arguments Forms: The event argument forms are located in this section, enabling annotators to manually input corpus-level arguments for the events. Each form is equipped with a dropdown list containing previously annotated arguments, facilitating the annotation process. Figure 5 shows the different kinds of arguments stored in each of the argument forms. The `roleset_id` form stores all the rolesets in PropBank, `ARG-0` and `ARG-1` the identified agents and patients up til then, `ARG-LOC` the locations, and `ARG-Time` the dates.

3.3 Model-in-the-loop

Incorporating a model-in-the-loop approach, our annotation framework utilizes a straightforward Word2Vec classifier implemented using spaCy. This classifier ranks sentences containing previously seen arguments in relation to the target sentence. The dynamic ranking of these sentences is reflected in the dropdown list, with the highest-ranked sentence positioned at the top. The annotator is presented with the option to either accept or reject the top-ranked arguments.

Argument Ranking and Selection: Upon loading the annotation interface, the system ranks the arguments from previously annotated sentences alongside the target sentence. The highest-ranked argument is selected by default and presented as the initial choice to the annotator. This ranking is based on the similarity or relevance of the sentences as determined by the Word2Vec classifier.

Acceptance and Integration: Should the annotator choose to accept the top-ranked sentence, it is seamlessly integrated into the set of previous arguments. This integration enhances the corpus-level annotation by incorporating contextually relevant information from the selected sentence.

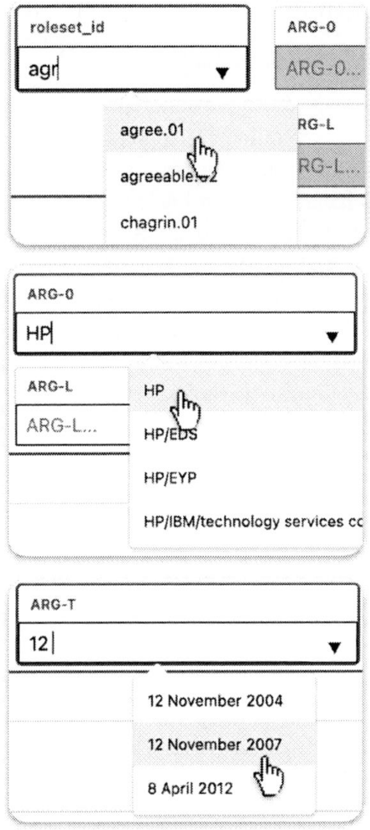

Figure 5: Screenshots

Rejection and New Argument Creation: In the event of rejection, the system generates new arguments, leveraging the embedding of the rejected sentence. This adaptive mechanism ensures that even when an annotator rejects the top-ranked sentence, valuable information is not lost. Instead, it is used to generate potentially relevant arguments for further annotation.

GPT-in-the-loop: Finally, yet importantly, we employ a GPT-based methodology to streamline the extraction of cross-document arguments through a two-step Retrieval Augmented Generation process. A comprehensive breakdown of our prompt engineering techniques is provided in Appendix B. The primary objective of this approach is to establish cross-document entity coreference.

Because of budget constraints, we have limited the execution of this experiment to a subset of the Dev dataset (Dev-small), encompassing a total of 120 mentions. Corpus statistics and annotation analysis are detailed in Appendix A.

4 Analysis

4.1 Model-in-the-loop

We collect X-AMR annotations on the ECB+ dataset, as detailed in Appendix A (refer to the appendix for specific numerical data and human annotation analysis). During the annotation process, we collect human annotations along with predicted rolesets and arguments generated by our model. We assess the model's performance by comparing its predictions to human annotations. We carefully recorded the instances in which annotators made modifications to the predicted text provided by the model. We count the acceptance ratio of the predictions, which not only signifies the model's effectiveness but also represents the amount of effort saved by annotators.

Our analysis on the train, dev, and test sets of ECB+, as illustrated in Figure 7, reveals several noteworthy observations: the correct roleset ID prediction consistently exceeded 80% for both annotators, denoted as A1 and A2. A1 appeared to be more inclined to accept the model's argument predictions compared to A2. This experiment serves as a foundation for future research, and one potential avenue is to incorporate these findings into downstream tasks, such as Event Coreference Resolution, to evaluate the quality of annotations and explore further implications of using model-in-the-loop for X-AMR annotations.

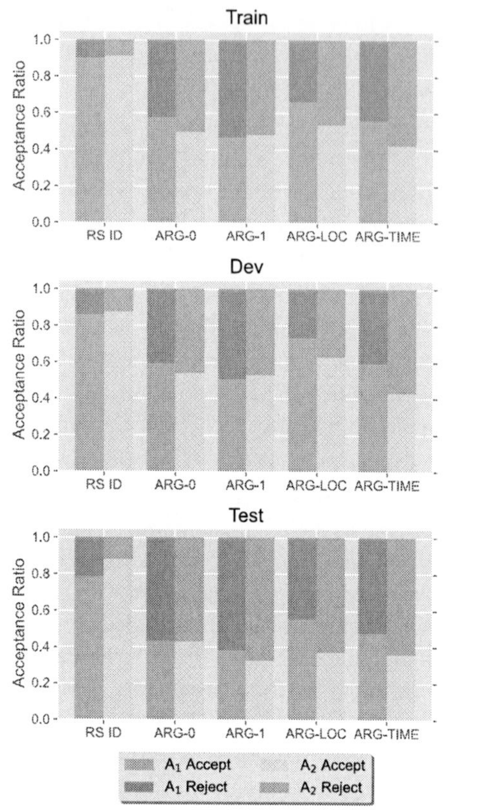

Figure 7: Roleset and ARG Analysis for A_1 and A_2: "A_x Accept" represents the acceptance rate of the model suggestions according to Annotator x; "A_x Reject" represents the rejection rate of the model suggestions according to Annotator x;

4.2 GPT-in-the-loop

In our GPT experiment on Dev-small, we had an adjudicator review 120 mentions and note when they had to adjust GPT's predictions. The outcomes of this evaluation are visually represented in Figure 6, which illustrates the ratio of mentions requiring modification. The main takeaway here is that GPT performed well in generating Location and Time arguments but struggled with predicting roleset IDs and ARG-0, ARG-1 arguments. We believe that integrating the model-in-the-loop approach could help improve performance compared to just using GPT.

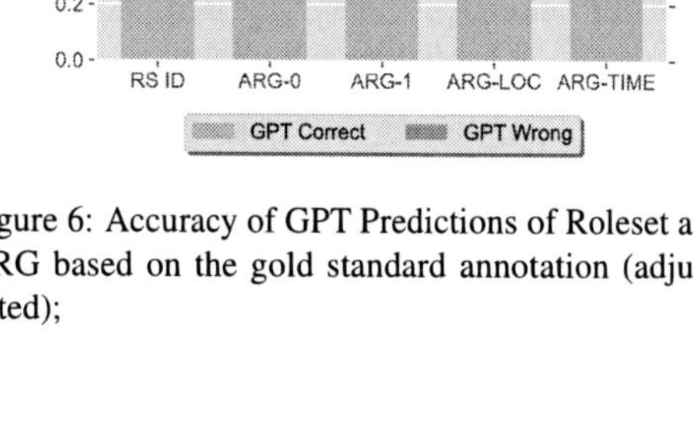

Figure 6: Accuracy of GPT Predictions of Roleset and ARG based on the gold standard annotation (adjudicated);

5 Future Work

The next steps include leveraging the X-AMR structures in creating efficient methods for neuro-symbolic event coreference resolution (ECR). For example, the X-AMR annotations could help in filtering the most pertinent event pairs that can be used with more resource intensive methods for estimating coreference (Ahmed et al., 2023a). Another important direction is in the estimation of the quality and cost savings of our methodology in doing ECR annotations. Quality measured by the number of ECR links that can be found with the least amount of pairwise event mention comparisons (Ahmed et al., 2023b).

6 Conclusion

In this paper, we have introduced a novel approach for cross-document, corpus-level semantic event extraction utilizing the X-AMR framework. To facilitate this process, we have developed a model-in-the-loop annotation tool tailored for X-AMR annotation, seamlessly integrated with Prodigy. This tool has been employed to curate X-AMR annotations by enriching an existing event coreference dataset, with contributions from two annotators. To evaluate the effectiveness of our approach, we have introduced a comprehensive assessment of the predictions, incorporating both the model's output and the assistance of GPT.

Limitations

This work has several limitations. Firstly, the annotation tool used is a one-time paid software, which may restrict its accessibility to some researchers, although we have made the annotation recipe freely available. Secondly, the study relies on gold mentions rather than predicted ones, suggesting a need for future research to incorporate an additional annotation process to identify event triggers. Lastly, the non-reproducibility of GPT is acknowledged, and it may have been pre-trained on the corpus. However, we provide GPT-generated outputs and use them primarily for information generation rather than prediction, especially in event description generation. Future work may focus on distilling information into smaller, reproducible models to address these limitations and enhance the robustness of our approach.

Ethics Statement

Recognizing the rigor and tediousness of the annotation process, our research ensured that all annotators were fairly compensated, given reasonable work hours, and provided with regular breaks to maintain consistency and quality. Comprehensive training and clear guidelines were offered, and a robust communication channel was established to address concerns, ambiguities, and to encourage feedback. Our team made efforts to involve a diverse group of annotators to minimize biases.

To alleviate the monotonous nature of the task, we employed user-friendly tools, rotated tasks, and supported peer discussions. We also acknowledged the crucial role of annotators in our research, ensuring their contributions were recognized and valued. Post-task, a summary of our findings was shared with the annotators, incorporating their feedback into the final manuscript, underlining our commitment to an inclusive and ethical research approach.

By adhering to the EACL guidelines, we aim to emphasize the ethical considerations surrounding the involvement of annotators in research projects. We believe that a humane, respectful, and inclusive approach to data annotation not only results in superior-quality datasets but also upholds the dignity and rights of all involved.

References

Shafiuddin Rehan Ahmed, Abhijnan Nath, James H. Martin, and Nikhil Krishnaswamy. 2023a. $2 * n$ is better than n^2: Decomposing event coreference resolution into two tractable problems. In *Findings of the Association for Computational Linguistics: ACL 2023*, pages 1569–1583, Toronto, Canada. Association for Computational Linguistics.

Shafiuddin Rehan Ahmed, Abhijnan Nath, Michael Regan, Adam Pollins, Nikhil Krishnaswamy, and James H. Martin. 2023b. How good is the model in model-in-the-loop event coreference resolution annotation? In *Proceedings of the 17th Linguistic Annotation Workshop (LAW-XVII)*, pages 136–145, Toronto, Canada. Association for Computational Linguistics.

Xuefeng Bai, Yulong Chen, Linfeng Song, and Yue Zhang. 2021. Semantic representation for dialogue modeling. In *Proceedings of the 59th Annual Meeting of the Association for Computational Linguistics and the 11th International Joint Conference on Natural Language Processing (Volume 1: Long Papers)*, pages 4430–4445, Online. Association for Computational Linguistics.

Xuefeng Bai, Yulong Chen, and Yue Zhang. 2022. Graph pre-training for AMR parsing and generation. In *Proceedings of the 60th Annual Meeting of the Association for Computational Linguistics (Volume 1: Long Papers)*, pages 6001–6015, Dublin, Ireland. Association for Computational Linguistics.

Laura Banarescu, Claire Bonial, Shu Cai, Madalina Georgescu, Kira Griffitt, Ulf Hermjakob, Kevin Knight, Philipp Koehn, Martha Palmer, and Nathan Schneider. 2013. Abstract Meaning Representation for sembanking. In *Proceedings of the 7th Linguistic Annotation Workshop and Interoperability with Discourse*, pages 178–186, Sofia, Bulgaria. Association for Computational Linguistics.

Cosmin Bejan and Sanda Harabagiu. 2010. Unsupervised event coreference resolution with rich linguistic features. In *Proceedings of the 48th Annual Meeting of the Association for Computational Linguistics*, pages 1412–1422, Uppsala, Sweden. Association for Computational Linguistics.

Claire Bonial, Lucia Donatelli, Mitchell Abrams, Stephanie M. Lukin, Stephen Tratz, Matthew Marge, Ron Artstein, David Traum, and Clare Voss. 2020. Dialogue-AMR: Abstract Meaning Representation for dialogue. In *Proceedings of the 12th Language Resources and Evaluation Conference*, pages 684–695, Marseille, France. European Language Resources Association.

Jon Cai, Shafiuddin Rehan Ahmed, Julia Bonn, Kristin Wright-Bettner, Martha Palmer, and James H. Martin. 2023. CAMRA: Copilot for AMR annotation. In *Proceedings of the 2023 Conference on Empirical Methods in Natural Language Processing: System Demonstrations*, pages 381–388, Singapore. Association for Computational Linguistics.

Agata Cybulska and Piek Vossen. 2014. Using a sledgehammer to crack a nut? lexical diversity and event coreference resolution. In *Proceedings of the Ninth International Conference on Language Resources and Evaluation (LREC'14)*, pages 4545–4552, Reykjavik, Iceland. European Language Resources Association (ELRA).

Ruiliu Fu, Han Wang, Xuejun Zhang, Jun Zhou, and Yonghong Yan. 2021. Decomposing complex questions makes multi-hop QA easier and more interpretable. In *Findings of the Association for Computational Linguistics: EMNLP 2021*, pages 169–180, Punta Cana, Dominican Republic. Association for Computational Linguistics.

Nicola Guarino, Riccardo Baratella, and Giancarlo Guizzardi. 2022. Events, their names, and their synchronic structure. *Applied ontology*, 17(2):249–283.

Pavan Kapanipathi, Ibrahim Abdelaziz, Srinivas Ravishankar, Salim Roukos, Alexander Gray, Ramón Fernandez Astudillo, Maria Chang, Cristina Cornelio, Saswati Dana, Achille Fokoue, Dinesh Garg, Alfio Gliozzo, Sairam Gurajada, Hima Karanam, Naweed Khan, Dinesh Khandelwal, Young-Suk Lee, Yunyao Li, Francois Luus, Ndivhuwo Makondo, Nandana Mihindukulasooriya, Tahira Naseem, Sumit Neelam, Lucian Popa, Revanth Gangi Reddy, Ryan Riegel, Gaetano Rossiello, Udit Sharma, G P Shrivatsa Bhargav, and Mo Yu. 2021. Leveraging Abstract Meaning Representation for knowledge base question answering. In *Findings of the Association for Computational Linguistics: ACL-IJCNLP 2021*, pages 3884–3894, Online. Association for Computational Linguistics.

Changmao Li and Jeffrey Flanigan. 2022. Improving neural machine translation with the Abstract Meaning Representation by combining graph and sequence transformers. In *Proceedings of the 2nd Workshop on Deep Learning on Graphs for Natural Language Processing (DLG4NLP 2022)*, pages 12–21, Seattle, Washington. Association for Computational Linguistics.

Kexin Liao, Logan Lebanoff, and Fei Liu. 2018. Abstract Meaning Representation for multi-document summarization. In *Proceedings of the 27th International Conference on Computational Linguistics*, pages 1178–1190, Santa Fe, New Mexico, USA. Association for Computational Linguistics.

Lawrence Brian Lombard. 2019. *Events: A metaphysical study*. Routledge.

Martha Palmer, Daniel Gildea, and Paul Kingsbury. 2005. The Proposition Bank: An annotated corpus of semantic roles. *Computational Linguistics*, 31(1):71–106.

Sameer Pradhan, Julia Bonn, Skatje Myers, Kathryn Conger, Tim O'gorman, James Gung, Kristin Wright-bettner, and Martha Palmer. 2022. PropBank comes of Age—Larger, smarter, and more diverse. In *Proceedings of the 11th Joint Conference on Lexical and Computational Semantics*, pages 278–288, Seattle, Washington. Association for Computational Linguistics.

Ailneni Rakshitha Rao. 2022. ASRtrans at SemEval-2022 task 4: Ensemble of tuned transformer-based models for PCL detection. In *Proceedings of the 16th International Workshop on Semantic Evaluation (SemEval-2022)*, pages 344–351, Seattle, United States. Association for Computational Linguistics.

Leonardo F. R. Ribeiro, Mengwen Liu, Iryna Gurevych, Markus Dreyer, and Mohit Bansal. 2022. FactGraph: Evaluating factuality in summarization with semantic graph representations. In *Proceedings of the 2022 Conference of the North American Chapter of the Association for Computational Linguistics: Human Language Technologies*, pages 3238–3253, Seattle, United States. Association for Computational Linguistics.

Xiaozhi Wang, Ziqi Wang, Xu Han, Wangyi Jiang, Rong Han, Zhiyuan Liu, Juanzi Li, Peng Li, Yankai Lin, and Jie Zhou. 2020. MAVEN: A Massive General Domain Event Detection Dataset. In *Proceedings of the 2020 Conference on Empirical Methods in Natural Language Processing (EMNLP)*, pages 1652–1671, Online. Association for Computational Linguistics.

Yu Wang, Hanghang Tong, Ziye Zhu, and Yun Li. 2022. Nested named entity recognition: A survey. *ACM Trans. Knowl. Discov. Data*, 16(6).

A Dataset Details

The ECB+ corpus is a popular English corpus used to train and evaluate systems for event coreference resolution. It extends the Event Coref Bank corpus (ECB; Bejan and Harabagiu (2010)), with annotations from around 500 additional documents. The corpus includes annotations of text spans that represent events, as well as information about how those events are related through coreference. We divide the documents from topics 1 to 35 into the training and validation sets2 , and those from 36 to 45 into the test set, following the approach of Cybulska and Vossen (2014).

A.1 Annotation Analysis

We have currently annotated all the mentions in the corpus with their Roleset IDs and 5,287 out of the 6,833 with X-AMR. In the three splits, only the Dev set has been fully annotated. We calculate the inter-annotator agreement (IAA) on the common Roleset predictions. The IAA is highest for the Dev set at 0.91, as depicted in Table 1.

	Train	Dev	Test	Dev small
Documents	594	196	206	91
Mentions	3808	1245	1780	120
Roleset ID Agreement	0.84	**0.91**	0.80	–
w/ X-AMR	3195*	1245	847*	120
w/ Nested ARG-1	1081	325	220	24
w/ ARG-Loc	2949	1243	707	120
w/ ARG-Time	3192	1244	805	120

Table 1: ECB+ Corpus statistics for event mentions in ECB+ and the mentions annotated with X-AMR (*Annotation in Progress). Inter-annotator agreement for the Roleset ID is highest for the Dev set.

Arguments: Our analysis reveals a significant presence of mentions with nested ARG-1 annotations, as highlighted in Table 1 (w/ Nested ARG-1). This underscores the importance of capturing nested event relationships effectively. Additionally, our annotations for location and time modifiers successfully capture this information for nearly all mentions (w/ X-AMR), thanks to the assistance provided by drop-down options and the model-in-the-loop approach. These tools are particularly valuable in cases where date references are not explicitly mentioned in the document.

B Prompt Engineering

Our approach for X-AMR extraction with GPT involves a two-step process. In the initial step, we extract the Event Description along with the document-level arguments of the event by utilizing prompts such as `Instructions A`, `JSON Labels A`, and `Inputs A`. Following the generation of individual event descriptions through this step, we employ another prompt-based technique to generate corpus-level arguments.

In this secondary method, we introduce an additional instruction into `Instructions A`, forming `Instructions B`. This instruction directs GPT to identify the most informative Event Description that is coreferent with the current Event. Subsequently, we provide this identified Event Description (`JSON Labels B`) within the context and task GPT with generating missing information, such as date and location, pertaining to the target event. We provide the list of informative event descriptions in the topic of the target event in `Inputs B`.

The estimated cost of running this experiment is about $15.

Instructions A

```
You are a concise annotator that follows
these instructions:

1. Identify the target event trigger
   lemma and its correct roleset sense in
   the given text.
2. Annotate the document-level ARG-0 and
   ARG-1 roles using the PropBank website
   for the roleset definitions.
3. If the ARG-1 role is an event,
   identify the head predicate and
   provide its roleset ID.
4. Perform within-document and
   cross-document anaphora resolution of
   the ARG-0 and ARG-1 using Wikipedia.
5. Use external resources, such as
   Wikipedia, to annotate ARG-Loc and
   ARG-Time.
```

JSON Labels A

```
Here are the definitions of the keys in
the JSON output:

Roleset ID: The PropBank Roleset ID
corresponding to the event trigger
ARG-0: The text in the Document
corresponding to the typical agent
ARG-0 Coreference: The reference to
the ARG-0 in Wikipedia in the format
/wiki/Wikipedia_ID
:
ARG-1 Roleset ID: If the Event is Nested,
provide the Roleset ID for the head event
in ARG-1 clause
ARG-Location: The reference to the event
location in Wikipedia
ARG-Time: The event time in the format
of Month-Day-Year in your knowledge of
the world or the document
Event Description: In a single sentence,
summarize the event capturing the
Roleset_ID and the names and wiki links
of the Participants, Location and Time
```

Inputs A

Target Mention Document: Entire document with the marked event trigger

Target Mention Sentence: Sentence with the marked event trigger

Instructions B

Instructions A

6. Identify the most informative (having Wikipedia and complete dates) and best matching Event Description from the provided list of descriptions.

JSON Labels B

JSON Labels A

Most Informative Event Description: Pick the most informative event description from the Event Description List. Choose by selecting the one that has complete date and Wikipedia links for the arguments and also is coreferent with the target Event. Hint: choose the one starts starts with "On DATE"

Inputs B

Event Description List: Event descriptions of the three most informative and similar events in the corpus.

Target Event Description: Event description of the target event

Target Mention Sentence: Sentence with the marked event trigger

DocChecker: Bootstrapping Code Large Language Model for Detecting and Resolving Code-Comment Inconsistencies

Anh T. V. Dau
FPT Software AI Center
Vietnam
anhdtv7@fpt.com

Jin L.C. Guo
McGill University
Canada
jguo@cs.mcgill.ca

Nghi D. Q. Bui
Fulbright University
Vietnam
nghi.bui@fulbright.edu.vn

Abstract

Comments in source code are crucial for developers to understand the purpose of the code and to use it correctly. However, keeping comments aligned with the evolving codebase poses a significant challenge. With increasing interest in automated solutions to identify and rectify discrepancies between code and its associated comments, most existing methods rely heavily on heuristic rules. This paper introduces **DocChecker**, a language model-based framework adept at detecting inconsistencies between code and comments and capable of generating synthetic comments. This functionality allows **DocChecker** to identify and rectify cases where comments do not accurately represent the code they describe. The efficacy of **DocChecker** is demonstrated using the Just-In-Time and CodeXGlue datasets in various scenarios. Notably, **DocChecker** sets a new benchmark in the Inconsistency Code-Comment Detection (ICCD) task, achieving 72.3% accuracy, and scoring 33.64 in BLEU-4 on the code summarization task. These results surpass other Large Language Models (LLMs), including GPT 3.5 and CodeLlama.

DocChecker is available for use and evaluation. It is available on `https://github.com/FSoft-AI4Code/DocChecker`GitHub and as an Online Tool. A demonstration video of its functionality can be found on YouTube.

1 Introduction

Code summarization is a significant issue in software engineering due to its ability to produce explanatory comments for source code, which is essential for ensuring software quality. Identifying and resolving discrepancies between the source code and its corresponding comments is an essential obstacle. Inconsistencies resulting from code changes not being accurately reflected in comments or from initially imprecise descriptions can cause substantial problems in comprehending and managing software. An illustrative example of this inconsistency, sourced from the CodeSearchNet dataset, is depicted in Figure 1 (Husain et al., 2019). These disparities can cause software defects, degrade software quality, and lower developer productivity, as highlighted in recent studies (Wen et al., 2019; Tan et al., 2012; Panthaplackel et al., 2021; Steiner and Zhang, 2022). Moreover, the prevalent issue of code-comment conflicts in widely used datasets impacts the efficacy of code language models trained on them (Sun et al., 2022; Shi et al., 2022; Manh et al., 2023). Recent large models trained specifically for code understanding and generation tasks may be able to address these challenges (Wang et al., 2021; Nijkamp et al., 2022; Wang et al., 2023; Di Grazia and Pradel, 2023). However, these models' efficacy depends on the quality of the training data, emphasizing the importance of accurate and consistent code-comment pairs.

Code Function

```
func (s *storageZfs) ContainerMount(c container)
                (bool, error) {
        return s.doContainerMount(c.Project(),
                c.Name(), c.IsPrivileged())
}
```

Comment

```
Things we don't need to care about
```

Figure 1: An example of code-comment inconsistency from the CodeSearchNet dataset.

To address these issues, we introduce DocChecker, a framework designed specifically for detecting inconsistencies between code and comments (**ICCD**)). Leveraging the capabilities of AI4SE and insights gained from advancements in code LLMs, DocChecker addresses the critical need for high-quality, consistent documentation in software development. The key idea is to leverage an encoder-decoder backbone network and then

Proceedings of the 18th Conference of the European Chapter of the Association for Computational Linguistics
System Demonstrations, pages 187–194

pre-train code-text pairs. This pre-training process employs a multi-faceted approach, including contrastive learning to *bootstrap* code and text features, binary classification to discern consistent from inconsistent pairs, and text generation to create coherent comments. The backbone of this system is UniXcoder (Guo et al., 2022), chosen for its effectiveness and efficiency in handling multi-modal content. DocChecker is specifically designed not only to detect but also to resolve inconsistencies between code and comments by generating replacement comments that accurately reflect the current state of codebase. Furthermore, compared to state-of-the-art CodeLLMs, our method excels significantly on ICCD and code summarization tasks. DocChecker outperforms StarCoder by 30% and surpasses GPT-3.5 and CodeLlama by 10% in terms of accuracy, even though such models are pre-trained on larger-scale datasets. In summary, the key contributions of DocChecker are:

- We propose DocChecker, a framework built on a code language model, jointly pre-trained with three objectives: contrastive learning between code and text, binary classification, and comment generation.
- The experiments show that DocChecker achieves state-of-the-art results on ICCD and code summarization, compared to existing methods and LLMs such as StarCoder, GPT-3.5, and CodeLlama.
- DockChecker is released as an easy-to-use package that can be deployed and installed on a local machine, facilitating its adoption in real-world software development scenarios.

2 Related Work

2.1 Pre-trained Code Language Models

Large language models have demonstrated remarkable success in code understanding and generation, giving rise to code models such as several notable ones, each specializing in different aspects of code processing. Encoder-decoder models like UniXCoder (Guo et al., 2022), CodeT5 (Wang et al., 2021), CodeT5+(Wang et al., 2023) excel in both understanding and generating code. Encoder-only models, such as CuBERT (Kanade et al., 2020) and CodeBERT (Feng et al., 2020), are adept at code-understanding tasks, with CuBERT focusing on Python and CodeBERT extending to six languages. Meanwhile, decoder-only models such as CodeLlama (Roziere et al., 2023), StarCoder (Li et al., 2023), and Magicoder (Wei et al., 2023), CodeGen(Nijkamp et al., 2022, 2023), and DeepSeek-Coder (Guo et al., 2024) specialize in code generation. Other models are trained based on additional structural features of source code, such as InferCoder (Bui et al., 2021a) and Corder (Bui et al., 2021b). These models are typically trained on large-scale datasets from Github (Kocetkov et al., 2022; Lu et al., 2021), with heuristic rules (Manh et al., 2023) used to select only high-quality parts for training

2.2 Detect Inconsistency Between Code and Comment

Source code comments are important in understanding the meaning of the code function. The significance of comments aligning with source code is divided into two categories: inconsistent code-comment detection and comment updates. Rabbi and Siddik (2020) measures the similarity between code functions and comments, identifying inconsistency when the score falls below a set threshold. Panthaplackel et al. (2021) develops a deep learning-based approach to comprehend and establish relationships between comments and code changes. Instead of using machine learning approaches, others propose rule-based methods for analysis. Ratol and Robillard (2017) introduces Fraco, an Eclipse plugin for fragile comment detection during identifier renaming, while Shi et al. (2022) develops an automated code-comment cleaning tool for accurate noise detection in the CodeSearchNet dataset Husain et al. (2019). Although rule-based methods are clear and straightforward, they struggle with new datasets and lack semantic understanding. Recent research explores automatic comment updating, with tools like CUP (Liu et al., 2021) and HebCUP (Lin et al., 2021) effective for simple changes (a single token change) but not for complex ones. In contrast, our framework excels at detecting and updating inconsistent code-comment pairs.

3 Overview of DocChecker

In this section, we describe DocChecker as a Python package and demonstrate its user interface. For full customization and detailed documentation of DocChecker, users can reference our GitHub repository.

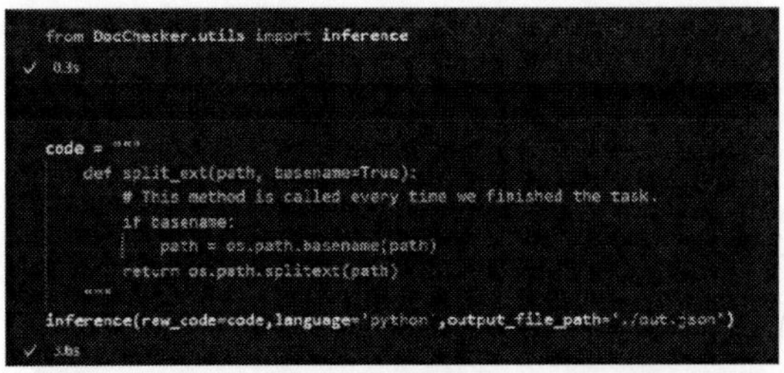

Figure 2: Screenshot for the Input Example.

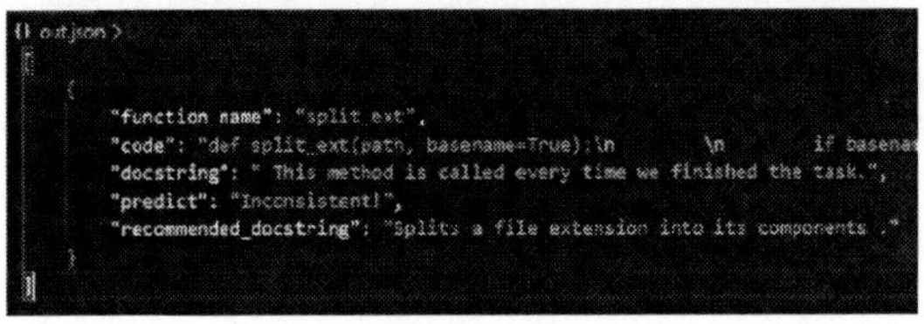

Figure 3: Screenshot for the Output file Example.

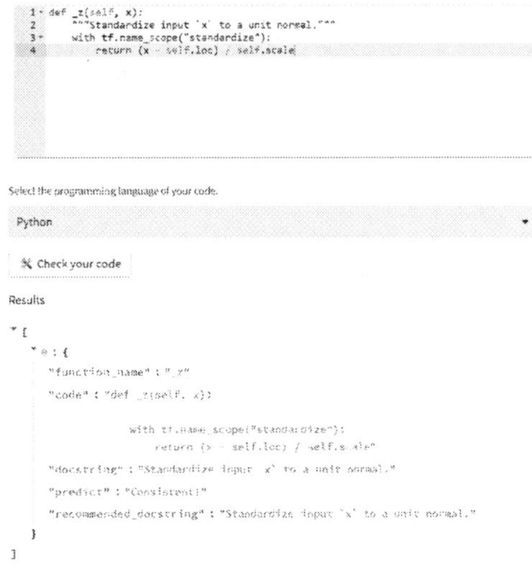

Figure 4: Screenshot for the user interface.

3.1 Python Package

We bundle DocChecker into an easy-to-use library that can be installed via Pypi.

Input: User must provide their source code file as well as the corresponding programming language. DocChecker is able to extract all code functions and their metadata (e.g. function name) by using the AST parser [1]. An example of how to use DocChecker is illustrated in Figure 2.

Output: DocChecker returns in the form of a list of dictionaries corresponding in number to input code functions, including the name of each function in raw code, code snippet, associated docstring, as well as its prediction, and the recommended docstring. If a code-text pair is considered as *"Inconsistent!"*, DocChecker will generate a complete docstring to replace the old ones; otherwise, it will keep the original version. Figure 3 is a screenshot that shows the result of DocChecker's prediction.

3.2 User Interface

We show a demo interface of DocChecker as depicted in Figure 4. It consists of a coding field for directly entering source code or uploading existing code files, a select widget specifying the programming language used for their code, and a button that triggers the query process. When the front-end receives the query result, it displays the previously mentioned list of dictionaries.

[1]We use tree-sitter as the parser `https://github.com/tree-sitter/tree-sitter`.

4 Building Blocks of DocChecker

This section outlines the architecture of DocChecker (see Section 4.1), the objectives guiding its pre-training (Section 4.2), and the specific setup used during pre-training (Section 4.3). Initially, the model undergoes pre-training focusing on contrastive learning and code-to-text generation, followed by fine-tuning for the specific Inconsistency Code-Comment Detection (ICCD) task.

4.1 Architecture

DocChecker's design is influenced by the effectiveness of pre-trained models. Instead of building from scratch, it utilizes existing pre-trained encoder-decoder models. For this project, we selected UniXcoder, an encoder-decoder model (Guo et al., 2022), as our backbone network due to its customizable nature and efficient performance with relatively fewer parameters (details in Section 6.3).

4.2 Pre-training Objectives

DocChecker's pre-training involves three primary objectives:

Code-Text Contrastive Learning (CTC): This aims to align the feature spaces of code and text encoders. We enhance model accuracy by emphasizing similarities in positive code-text pairs and differentiating them from negative pairs. Negative samples are generated following the methodology in (Li et al., 2021), focusing on hard negative pairs based on contrastive similarity.

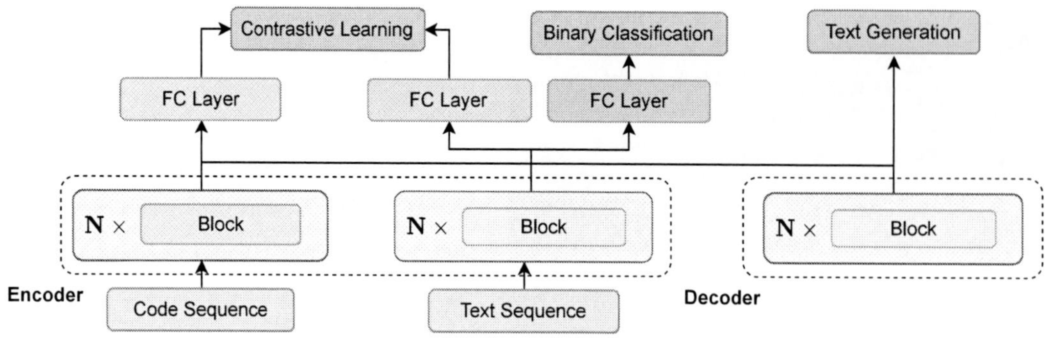

Figure 5: Overview of the DocChecker framework.

Binary Classification (BC): This objective assesses the alignment between code and text. The model distinguishes between consistent (positive) and inconsistent (negative) code-text pairs, enhancing its ability to detect inconsistencies.

Comment Generation (CG): This objective focuses on creating comments that explain a specific code snippet. Training the model to optimize cross-entropy loss in an autoregressive manner improves the model's ability to generate coherent comments.

In addition to these objectives, DocChecker benefits from multi-task learning, sharing the weights between the text encoder and decoder to improve text representation. Separate, fully-connected layers are utilized to capture task-specific differences and minimize task interference.

4.3 Pre-training Setup

DocChecker uses UniXcoder (Guo et al., 2022), which excels at multi-modal contexts and unified cross-modal models. Our goal is to make Dockchecker lightweight and easy to install on a local machine. With 12 hidden layers, 768 hidden sizes, and 3072 intermediate sizes, UniXcoder's architecture of 124M parameters meets our requirements. UniXCoder is also pre-trained on CodeXGLUE, which includes a variety of programming languages. This diverse dataset is critical to ensuring the model's performance in a wide range of software engineering scenarios.

5 Experiment Setup

In this section, we first present the tasks and the datasets used to assess the performance of DocChecker. Then, we describe the baselines and metrics used for evaluation.

5.1 Evaluation Tasks

DocChecker is evaluated for two tasks: ICCD and Code Summarization.

ICCD: For this task, given a comment C with a corresponding code method M, determine whether comment C is semantically out of sync with code function M. To address this challenge, we utilize the post-hoc setting in (Panthaplackel et al., 2021), where code changes that resulted in the mismatch are unknown; Only the current version of the code snippet and old comment are available. This setting is similar to our work, where we want to detect inconsistency for code-text pairs.

Code Summarization: This task aims to generate a natural language summary to explain a given piece of code. By summarizing key concepts and features into a concise format, code summarization addresses the challenge of comprehending programming constructs, especially as codebases continue to grow in complexity.

5.2 Datasets

As we assess the performance of DocChecker across two distinct tasks, we rely on two datasets: the Just-In-Time dataset for the ICCD task and the CodeXGLUE dataset for the code summarization task.

Just-In-Time Dataset ((Panthaplackel et al., 2021)): In this dataset, each sample is the comment-method pair from 2 versions: before and after updating (C_1, M_1) and (C_2, M_2) . In the post-hoc setting, $C = C_1$ and $M = M_2$. They assume that developers updated the comment because it became inconsistent as a result of code changes; they take C_1 to be inconsistent with M_2, consequently leading to a negative example. For positive examples, they additionally examine cases in which $C_1 = C_2$ and assume that the existing comment has been revised to align consistently with the corresponding code snippet. For a more reliable evaluation, they manually check to get 300 clean examples from the test set and note it as the cleaned test set.

CodeXGLUE dataset (Lu et al. (2021)): This dataset comprises six programming languages: Python, Java, JavaScript, Ruby, Go, and PHP. They come from publicly available open source non-fork GitHub repositories, with each documentation representing the first paragraph.

5.3 Baselines:

Baselines for ICCD task: We select the following existing work to compare against DocChecker for its effectiveness on the ICCD task:

- **SVM (Corazza et al., 2018)**: This bag-of-words approach classifies whether a comment is coherent with the method using an SVM with TF-IDF vectors corresponding to the comment and method;
- **Deep-JIT**: (Panthaplackel et al., 2021) presents a method for detecting inconsistencies between natural language comments and source code. With different ways of encoding, they consider three types and note them as *SEQ, GRAPH, HYBRID*. Deep-JIT is the existing SOTA method on the Just-In-Time dataset.
- **Pretrained Language Models of Code**: We evaluate a range of language models specifically designed for code. Firstly, we focus on three prominent and powerful CodeLLMs: **GPT-3.5-Turbo**, **StarCoder** (15B) (Li et al., 2023), and **CodeLlama** (34B) (Roziere et al., 2023). These models are assessed using both zero-shot (0-shot) and few-shot (3-shot) prompting approaches. In the zero-shot setup, no examples from the Just-In-Time dataset are provided, while the few-shot experiment incorporates three code-text pairs with correct labels from the dataset in each prompt. These prompts are then applied to all selected LLMs. Additionally, we also incorporate a comparative analysis with two established pre-trained models: **CodeBERT** (Feng et al., 2020) and **CodeT5** (Wang et al., 2021).

Baselines for Code Summarization task: In this experiment, we focus on the fine-tuning setting and compare our method with smaller-scale LMs, including RoBERTa (Liu et al., 2019), CodeBERT (Feng et al., 2020) trained with masked language modeling; PLBART (Ahmad et al., 2021) is based on BART and pre-trained using denoising objective; CodeT5 (Wang et al., 2021), adapted from T5, takes into account important token-type information in identifiers; and the variant of UniXcoder (Guo et al., 2022) since we utilize UniXcoder as the backbone network.

Method	Cleaned Test set		Full Test Set	
	F1	Acc	F1	Acc
SVM	53.9	60.7	54.6	60.3
Deep-JIT$_{SEQ}$	63.0	60.3	66.3	62.8
Deep-JIT$_{GRAPH}$	65.0	62.2	67.2	64.6
Deep-JIT$_{HYBRID}$	63.3	55.2	66.3	58.9
CodeBERT	67.9	66.9	70.7	69.8
CodeT5	69.5	68.8	70.2	70.1
GPT-3.5 $_{0\text{-shot}}$	60.9	65.1	62.5	64.6
StarCoder $_{0\text{-shot}}$	43.7	43.1	45.2	43.9
CodeLlama $_{0\text{-shot}}$	70.2	68.7	62.6	61.8
GPT-3.5 $_{3\text{-shot}}$	66.4	67.0	66.1	61.4
StarCoder $_{3\text{-shot}}$	44.2	43.6	42.8	42.2
CodeLlama $_{3\text{-shot}}$	70.5	69.2	62.3	62.1
DocChecker	**73.1**	**70.7**	**74.3**	**72.3**

Table 1: Results for post hoc settings on the Just-In-Time dataset

5.4 Evaluation Metrics

Metrics for ICCD: We use two common classification metrics: F1 score (w.r.t. the positive label) and Accuracy (Acc) to report the performance of methods.

Metrics for Code Summarization: For this task, we use the smoothed BLEU-4 (Lin and Och, 2004) as the evaluation metric and report the overall score of six programming languages.

6 Evaluation Results

6.1 Effectiveness of DocChecker on ICCD

Table 1 presents results for all baselines under the post-hoc setting and LLMs. In general, we find that our model can significantly outperform all of the baselines. Despite CodeBERT and CodeT5 being pre-trained models with more parameters and showcasing efficiency in numerous downstream tasks, their performance is behind ours. DocChecker achieves a new SoTA of 72.3% accuracy and 74.3% F1 score on the full test set of Just-In-Time. On the other hand, although previous literature has empirically explored various capabil-

Method	Summarization
	BLEU-4
RoBERTa	16.57
CodeBERT	17.83
PLBART	18.32
CodeT5-small	19.14
CodeT5-base	19.55
UniXcoder	19.30
-w/o contras	19.20
-w/o cross-gen	19.27
-w/o comment	18.97
-w/o AST	19.33
-using BFS	19.24
-using DFS	19.25
DocChecker	**33.64**

Table 2: Results on the code summarization task.

ities of LLMs in diverse natural language processing and code generation tasks, billion-parameter LLMs such as StarCoder, GPT 3.5, and CodeLlama still struggle with ICCD, even with the construction of various types of prompts. In particular, DocChecker produces significant improvements of +10% accuracy and F1 score compared to the selected LLMs.

The experiment results suggest that DocChecker benefits from using a pre-trained language model with our novel pre-training objectives. It supports that our method effectively detects inconsistent samples in the code corpus.

6.2 The effectiveness of DocChecker on Code Summarization

Our results on this task are shown in Table 2. DocChecker is compared to a number of pre-trained code language models during our evaluation. Following DocChecker's pre-training for three aforementioned objectives, our method outperforms others significantly. DocChecker's BLEU-4 score is twice that of RoBERTa and CodeBERT. Furthermore, despite the fact that CodeT5-base uses a 12-layer encoder and a 12-layer decoder, which are twice as powerful as our architecture, its performance is significantly lower. DocChecker outperforms CodeT5 and the backbone network UniXcoder by +13 BLEU-4 scores.

6.3 Influence of the backbone network on DocChecker

DocChecker functions as a framework, so choosing an encoder-decoder model for the backbone network is flexible. This section demonstrates the effect of several pre-trained models on DocChecker's effectiveness. We use CodeBERT, CodeT5, and

Backbone Network	Cleaned test set		Full test set	
	F1	Acc	F1	Acc
CodeBERT	68.2	67.1	71.5	70.4
CodeT5	70.1	69.5	71.9	71.5
UniXcoder	73.1	70.7	74.3	72.3

Table 3: Results of DocChecker pre-trained with different backbone networks on the Just-In-Time dataset.

Code Function

```
public <R> sendAndReceive(final Function
    <HttpResponse, R> responseHandler){
  return responseHandler.apply(send());
}
```

Original Comment

```
Syntax sugar.
```

Recommended comment from DocChecker

```
Send and Receive the response.
```

Code Function

```
Path renameToFinalName(FileSystem fs, Path tempPath)
    throws IOException, StageException {
  return fsHelper.renameAndGetPath(fs, tempPath);
}
```

Original Comment

```
This method should be called every time we finish writing
into a file and consider it done .
```

Recommended comment from DocChecker

```
Renames the given path to the final name .
```

Figure 6: Some inconsistent code-comment examples were collected from the CodeXGlue dataset and our recommended comment to replace.

UniXcoder as the backbone network for DocChecker. Each chosen backbone is pre-trained in the DocChecker framework and fine-tuned using the Just-In-Time dataset. The results in Table 3 show that the pre-trained models perform better after re-pre-training compared to their original versions. However, UniXcoder emerges as the most effective backbone model for this task, so we use it for all of our experiments.

6.4 Practical Application

Aside from demonstrating DocChecker's performance, we highlight its effectiveness in real-world scenarios. We consider the popular CodeXGlue dataset, which extracts functions and paired comments from Github repositories. Although this benchmark dataset is expected to be of high quality, noise is unavoidable due to variations in coding conventions and assumptions used in modern programming languages and IDEs. Using Doc-

Checker, we can filter the dataset's inconsistent code-comment samples and create new comprehensive summary sentences for them.

Figure 6 shows an example of an inconsistent sample identified by DocChecker in the CodeSearchNet dataset. The comment associated with the code snippet is misaligned and needs to be updated. Beyond detection, our method generates a detailed summary sentence for each sample, which replaces the outdated ones.

7 Conclusion

In this paper, we present DocChecker, a framework to filter and generate replacement comments for inconsistent code-comment pairs. The experimental results demonstrate the effectiveness of this method compared to SoTA existing methods and LLMs, showcasing its applicability in both academic and practical contexts. We have released DocChecker as an easy-to-use library, complemented by a user-friendly interface to enhance user interaction.

References

Wasi Uddin Ahmad, Saikat Chakraborty, Baishakhi Ray, and Kai-Wei Chang. 2021. Unified pre-training for program understanding and generation. *arXiv preprint arXiv:2103.06333*.

Nghi DQ Bui, Yijun Yu, and Lingxiao Jiang. 2021a. Infercode: Self-supervised learning of code representations by predicting subtrees. In *2021 IEEE/ACM 43rd International Conference on Software Engineering (ICSE)*, pages 1186–1197. IEEE.

Nghi DQ Bui, Yijun Yu, and Lingxiao Jiang. 2021b. Self-supervised contrastive learning for code retrieval and summarization via semantic-preserving transformations. In *Proceedings of the 44th International ACM SIGIR Conference on Research and Development in Information Retrieval*, pages 511–521.

Anna Corazza, Valerio Maggio, and Giuseppe Scanniello. 2018. Coherence of comments and method implementations: a dataset and an empirical investigation. *Software Quality Journal*, 26:751–777.

Luca Di Grazia and Michael Pradel. 2023. Code search: A survey of techniques for finding code. *ACM Comput. Surv.*, 55(11).

Zhangyin Feng, Daya Guo, Duyu Tang, Nan Duan, Xiaocheng Feng, Ming Gong, Linjun Shou, Bing Qin, Ting Liu, Daxin Jiang, and Ming Zhou. 2020. Codebert: A pre-trained model for programming and natural languages.

Daya Guo, Shuai Lu, Nan Duan, Yanlin Wang, Ming Zhou, and Jian Yin. 2022. Unixcoder: Unified cross-modal pre-training for code representation. pages 7212–7225.

Daya Guo, Qihao Zhu, Dejian Yang, Zhenda Xie, Kai Dong, Wentao Zhang, Guanting Chen, Xiao Bi, Y Wu, YK Li, et al. 2024. Deepseek-coder: When the large language model meets programming–the rise of code intelligence. *arXiv preprint arXiv:2401.14196*.

Hamel Husain, Ho-Hsiang Wu, Tiferet Gazit, Miltiadis Allamanis, and Marc Brockschmidt. 2019. Codesearchnet challenge: Evaluating the state of semantic code search. *CoRR*, abs/1909.09436.

Aditya Kanade, Petros Maniatis, Gogul Balakrishnan, and Kensen Shi. 2020. Learning and evaluating contextual embedding of source code. In *Proceedings of the 37th International Conference on Machine Learning*, ICML'20. JMLR.org.

Denis Kocetkov, Raymond Li, Loubna Ben Allal, Jia Li, Chenghao Mou, Carlos Muñoz Ferrandis, Yacine Jernite, Margaret Mitchell, Sean Hughes, Thomas Wolf, et al. 2022. The stack: 3 tb of permissively licensed source code. *arXiv preprint arXiv:2211.15533*.

Junnan Li, Ramprasaath Selvaraju, Akhilesh Gotmare, Shafiq Joty, Caiming Xiong, and Steven Chu Hong Hoi. 2021. Align before fuse: Vision and language representation learning with momentum distillation. *Advances in neural information processing systems*, 34:9694–9705.

Raymond Li, Loubna Ben Allal, Yangtian Zi, Niklas Muennighoff, Denis Kocetkov, Chenghao Mou, Marc Marone, Christopher Akiki, Jia Li, Jenny Chim, et al. 2023. Starcoder: may the source be with you! *arXiv preprint arXiv:2305.06161*.

Bo Lin, Shangwen Wang, Kui Liu, Xiaoguang Mao, and Tegawendé F. Bissyandé. 2021. Automated comment update: How far are we? In *2021 IEEE/ACM 29th International Conference on Program Comprehension (ICPC)*, pages 36–46.

Chin-Yew Lin and Franz Josef Och. 2004. Orange: a method for evaluating automatic evaluation metrics for machine translation. In *COLING 2004: Proceedings of the 20th International Conference on Computational Linguistics*, pages 501–507.

Yinhan Liu, Myle Ott, Naman Goyal, Jingfei Du, Mandar Joshi, Danqi Chen, Omer Levy, Mike Lewis, Luke Zettlemoyer, and Veselin Stoyanov. 2019. Roberta: A robustly optimized BERT pretraining approach. *CoRR*, abs/1907.11692.

Zhongxin Liu, Xin Xia, David Lo, Meng Yan, and Shanping Li. 2021. Just-in-time obsolete comment detection and update. *IEEE Transactions on Software Engineering*, pages 1–1.

Shuai Lu, Daya Guo, Shuo Ren, Junjie Huang, Alexey Svyatkovskiy, Ambrosio Blanco, Colin Clement, Dawn Drain, Daxin Jiang, Duyu Tang, Ge Li, Lidong Zhou, Linjun Shou, Long Zhou, Michele Tufano, MING GONG, Ming Zhou, Nan Duan, Neel Sundaresan, Shao Kun Deng, Shengyu Fu, and Shujie LIU. 2021. CodeXGLUE: A machine learning benchmark dataset for code understanding and generation. In *Thirty-fifth Conference on Neural Information Processing Systems Datasets and Benchmarks Track (Round 1)*.

Dung Nguyen Manh, Nam Le Hai, Anh T. V. Dau, Anh Minh Nguyen, Khanh Nghiem, Jin Guo, and Nghi D. Q. Bui. 2023. The vault: A comprehensive multilingual dataset for advancing code understanding and generation.

Erik Nijkamp, Hiroaki Hayashi, Caiming Xiong, Silvio Savarese, and Yingbo Zhou. 2023. Codegen2: Lessons for training llms on programming and natural languages. *arXiv preprint arXiv:2305.02309*.

Erik Nijkamp, Bo Pang, Hiroaki Hayashi, Lifu Tu, Huan Wang, Yingbo Zhou, Silvio Savarese, and Caiming Xiong. 2022. Codegen: An open large language model for code with multi-turn program synthesis. *arXiv preprint arXiv:2203.13474*.

Sheena Panthaplackel, Junyi Jessy Li, Milos Gligoric, and Raymond J Mooney. 2021. Deep just-in-time inconsistency detection between comments and source code. In *Proceedings of the AAAI Conference on Artificial Intelligence*, volume 35, pages 427–435.

Fazle Rabbi and Md Saeed Siddik. 2020. Detecting code comment inconsistency using siamese recurrent network. In *Proceedings of the 28th International Conference on Program Comprehension*, ICPC '20, page 371–375. Association for Computing Machinery.

Inderjot Kaur Ratol and Martin P Robillard. 2017. Detecting fragile comments. In *2017 32nd IEEE/ACM International Conference on Automated Software Engineering (ASE)*, pages 112–122. IEEE.

Baptiste Roziere, Jonas Gehring, Fabian Gloeckle, Sten Sootla, Itai Gat, Xiaoqing Ellen Tan, Yossi Adi, Jingyu Liu, Tal Remez, Jérémy Rapin, et al. 2023. Code llama: Open foundation models for code. *arXiv preprint arXiv:2308.12950*.

Lin Shi, Fangwen Mu, Xiao Chen, Song Wang, Junjie Wang, Ye Yang, Ge Li, Xin Xia, and Qing Wang. 2022. Are we building on the rock? on the importance of data preprocessing for code summarization. In *Proceedings of the 30th ACM Joint European Software Engineering Conference and Symposium on the Foundations of Software Engineering*, pages 107–119.

Theo Steiner and Rui Zhang. 2022. Code comment inconsistency detection with bert and longformer. *arXiv preprint arXiv:2207.14444*.

Zhensu Sun, Li Li, Yan Liu, Xiaoning Du, and Li Li. 2022. On the importance of building high-quality training datasets for neural code search. In *Proceedings of the 44th International Conference on Software Engineering*, pages 1609–1620.

Shin Hwei Tan, Darko Marinov, Lin Tan, and Gary T. Leavens. 2012. @tcomment: Testing javadoc comments to detect comment-code inconsistencies. In *2012 IEEE Fifth International Conference on Software Testing, Verification and Validation*, pages 260–269.

Yue Wang, Hung Le, Akhilesh Deepak Gotmare, Nghi DQ Bui, Junnan Li, and Steven CH Hoi. 2023. Codet5+: Open code large language models for code understanding and generation. *arXiv preprint arXiv:2305.07922*.

Yue Wang, Weishi Wang, Shafiq Joty, and Steven C. H. Hoi. 2021. Codet5: Identifier-aware unified pre-trained encoder-decoder models for code understanding and generation.

Yuxiang Wei, Zhe Wang, Jiawei Liu, Yifeng Ding, and Lingming Zhang. 2023. Magicoder: Source code is all you need. *arXiv preprint arXiv:2312.02120*.

Fengcai Wen, Csaba Nagy, Gabriele Bavota, and Michele Lanza. 2019. A large-scale empirical study on code-comment inconsistencies. In *2019 IEEE/ACM 27th International Conference on Program Comprehension (ICPC)*, pages 53–64. IEEE.

TL;DR PROGRESS: Multi-faceted Literature Exploration in Text Summarization

Shahbaz Syed [†] **Khalid Al-Khatib** [‡] **Martin Potthast** [†§]

[†]Leipzig University [‡]University of Groningen [§]ScaDS.AI

shahbaz.syed@uni-leipzig.de

Abstract

This paper presents TL;DR PROGRESS, a new tool for exploring the literature on neural text summarization. It organizes 514 papers based on a comprehensive annotation scheme for text summarization approaches and enables fine-grained, faceted search. Each paper was manually annotated to capture aspects such as evaluation metrics, quality dimensions, learning paradigms, challenges addressed, datasets, and document domains. In addition, a succinct indicative summary is provided for each paper, consisting of automatically extracted contextual factors, issues, and proposed solutions. The tool is available online at https://www.tldr-progress.de, a demo video at https://youtu.be/uCVRGFvXUj8.

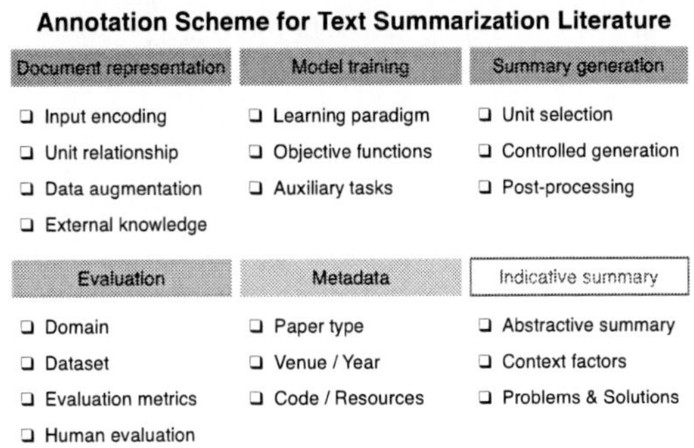

Figure 1: Our annotation scheme is based on a summarization literature analysis. Its four components and their respective facets enable a fine-grained unified analysis of relevant papers. The indicative summary is automatically generated.

1 Introduction

Research in the field of neural text summarization has evolved rapidly from the introduction of sequence-to-sequence (Sutskever et al., 2014; Rush et al., 2015) models to the era of transformers (Vaswani et al., 2017), greatly improving our ability to produce high-quality summaries in line with human preferences (Huang et al., 2020a; Goyal et al., 2022). As a result, the original focus of summarization research on the news domain has broadened to various other domains such as meetings, scientific papers, scripts and opinions.

To keep abreast of current advances, especially researchers new to the field must perform various tasks, including assimilating, organizing, annotating, and reviewing papers across multiple venues. Although search engines tailored to scholarly documents, such as Google Scholar, Semantic Scholar, DBLP, and the ACL anthology, provide access to a vast collection of articles, they merely support the discovery of relevant papers from within a multi-domain collection and do not (strongly) support an in-depth comparative paper analysis.

This paper introduces TL;DR PROGRESS, a literature explorer designed specifically for the text summarization literature. It contributes an intuitive annotation scheme designed to streamline fine-grained, facet-based systematic reviews (Figure 1 and Section 3). To demonstrate the capabilities of our tool, we manually analyze a collection of 514 summarization papers and cover various important aspects for an efficient literature search (Section 4). As part of its goal to organize summarization research, TL;DR PROGRESS provides an indicative summary for each paper, seamlessly integrating automatically extracted contextual information with manually annotated facets (Section 5). This includes identifying for what practical purpose a summarization approach is intended, the current challenges associated with summary generation, and a paper's contributions. Our tool also demonstrates the practical application of large language models (LLMs) in automatic terminology acquisition, involving the extraction of technical terms from papers, including glossary definitions for general concepts and acronym–expansion pairs to improve researchers' recall of specific papers (Section 6).[1]

TL;DR PROGRESS has a dual function: it provides insights into current research and serves as a basis for future automation. In particular, our literature explorer shows a way forward for future research on large-scale systematic reviews of the NLP literature by extensively leveraging LLMs.

[1]https://github.com/webis-de/eacl24-tldr-progress/

Proceedings of the 18th Conference of the European Chapter of the Association for Computational Linguistics System Demonstrations, pages 195–206
March 17-22, 2024

2 Related Work

Paper aggregators such as Google Scholar, Semantic Scholar, DBLP, and the ACL Anthology provide access to a large number of papers from different disciplines and, most importantly, facilitate their discovery. However, these platforms lack solid support for in-depth comparative analysis. PersLEARN (Shi et al., 2023) introduces a perspective-based approach to exploring scientific literature. It empowers early career researchers to develop their viewpoints by interacting with a prompt-based model. The tool identifies evidence from relevant papers that relate to the given seed perspectives and summarizes them to make new connections. In contrast, TL;DR PROGRESS focuses on summarization and provides fine-grained facets for each paper to enhance understanding of their contributions and content, along with indicative summaries, a feature not present in PersLEARN.

As for annotating papers, Autodive (Du et al., 2023) automates the in-place annotation of entities and relationships in PDFs, using external domain-specific NER models. In contrast, our approach includes a domain-specific annotation scheme and manual annotation for quality assurance. In addition, our tool facilitates unsupervised automatic terminology acquisition using LLMs. SciLit (Gu and Hahnloser, 2023) recommends relevant articles based on keywords entered by the user and generates citation sets with extracted highlights. While our tool supports keyword-based lexical search, it is less reliant on user-defined keywords due to its facet-based retrieval system.

Paperswithcode[2] is a platform that links papers with their code implementations. It provides an overview of the state-of-the-art in various NLP tasks. TL;DR PROGRESS complements Paperswithcode (for the summarization task) by providing an interactive dashboard presenting relevant statistics (Section 7) for a comprehensive understanding of the state-of-the-art.

3 Annotation Scheme

To create a comprehensive annotation scheme for summarization papers, we performed an in-depth analysis of the recent relevant literature. As shown in Figure 1, this scheme encapsulates the basic components of a neural summarization architecture, laying the foundation for a fine-grained annotation tailored to individual contributions. Its underlying principle is to categorize contributions according to their main focus, as papers often address one or more components within the summarization pipeline. The annotation scheme distinguishes four components:

1. **Document representation.** Conversion of a source document into a vector representation to model relationships between document units (words, sentences, paragraphs). This may include input data enrichment with user or style-specific information and model augmentation using external knowledge bases.

2. **Model training.** Training of a model with suitable data under a user-defined objective (or reward) function. This may include using pre-trained models for tasks, such as missing text prediction, paraphrasing, and detecting textual entailment.

3. **Summary generation.** Generation of a summary based on the representation of its source document using a trained model. This may include selecting explicit units for inclusion, restricting the summary to a particular style, conditioning the generation process on certain aspects of the source document, and post-processing steps such as length normalization and redundancy removal.

4. **Evaluation.** Evaluation setup such as the document domains and datasets used for testing, automatic evaluation metrics reported, and the human evaluation criteria for qualitative assessment of the generated summaries.

These components encompass different facets. For example, document representation includes "input encoding", "unit relationship", "data augmentation", and "external knowledge". Definitions for each facet are given in Table 1. These facets are not mutually exclusive, i.e., a paper can contribute to several facets simultaneously. For example, a paper may present a novel input encoding scheme that explicitly models unit relationships in the source document. In such cases, we annotate the paper with multiple facets. The annotation scheme also includes metadata for each paper. Overall, our scheme enables a fine-grained retrieval of relevant summarization papers, a feature that is currently not available in other paper aggregators.

[2]https://paperswithcode.com/

Facet	Description / Examples
Document representation	
Input encoding	The paper presents methods to improve the encoding of source documents (e.g., hierarchical/graphical attention, inclusion of discourse structure, etc.)
Unit relationship	The paper investigates methods that explicitly model the relationship between units in the source document, such as words, sentences, or passages.
Data augmentation	The paper introduces methods that use data augmentation techniques, e.g., to extract aspects, to create contrasting examples of robustness, or to overcome data scarcity in low-resource domains.
External knowledge	The paper investigates methods for integrating external knowledge using resources such as knowledge graphs, domain-specific vocabularies, or information from pre-trained language models.
Model training	
Learning Paradigm	Supervised, unsupervised, or reinforcement learning.
Objective Function	The paper introduces methods that incorporate new objective functions that emphasize diversity, faithfulness, or custom objectives appropriate to the task of summarization.
Auxiliary Tasks	The paper explores methods such as multi-task learning or pre-training on related tasks (e.g., textual entailment, paraphrasing, gap sentence prediction) to improve the summarization task.
Summary generation	
Unit Selection	The paper presents methods that explicitly select relevant units, such as words, sentences, or passages, for summarization, addressing the information loss associated with generating fixed-length summaries through techniques such as copying or pointing.
Controlled Generation	The paper presents methods that encourage the model to generate summaries with certain attributes (e.g., style, length, tone), for example, by providing additional textual guidance or limiting the model's vocabulary to a specific domain.
Post Processing	The paper explores methods for post-processing generated summaries to improve their quality. This includes re-ranking, re-writing or swapping certain text spans to achieve the desired goals.
Evaluation	
Domain	The domain of the source documents (e.g., opinions, screenplays, papers, etc.)
Dataset	The datasets used for training/evaluation (e.g., CNN/DailyMail, XSum, etc.)
Evaluation metric	The metrics used for automatic evaluation (e.g., ROUGE, BLEU, etc.)
Human evaluation	The summary quality criteria that were evaluated manually (e.g., informativeness, fluency, etc.)
Metadata	
Paper type	A new method, analysis (evaluation), metric, dataset, or theory.
Venue / Year	Venue and year in which the work was published.
Code / Resources	Artifacts relevant to reproduce the paper's contribution.

Table 1: Description of the annotation scheme shown in Figure 1. Pipeline components correspond to the three major components of the scheme, Document Representation, Model Training, and Summary Generation.

4 Webis Summarization Papers Corpus

To create TL;DR PROGRESS, we compiled a corpus of research papers on neural text summarization, annotated it according to our scheme, and analyzed the distribution of the papers across different dimensions.

4.1 Corpus Construction

To collect summarization papers, we conducted a keyword search ("summ") in the proceedings of the most important venues, including AAAI, AACL, ACL, CHIIR, CIKM, COLING, CONLL, EACL, ECIR, EMNLP, ICLR, IJCAI, IJCNLP, NAACL, NEURIPS, SIGIR, and TACL. The initial collection of 801 papers was refined through a careful review of titles and abstracts to identify papers that were directly relevant to single-document summarization of English texts. These included papers that evaluated or analyzed existing approaches and proposed new metrics, human assessment methodologies, meta-evaluations, datasets, and new model architectures. To extract textual content from the PDFs, we used Science Parse.[3] Papers that could not be automatically extracted or were duplicates were excluded, so that we ended up processing 514 papers. For each of the 514 papers, we performed a thorough manual annotation, focusing on the facets of our annotation scheme. The annotation was performed by one of the authors of this paper. The annotation process was iterative, with the annotator revisiting the previously annotated sections to ensure consistency. Another author reviewed the annotations to ensure their quality.

[3] https://github.com/allenai/science-parse

Venue	Count	Venue	Count	Venue	Count
EMNLP	184	EACL	13	IJCNLP	4
ACL	115	TACL	12	ICLR	2
NAACL	60	CIKM	12	ECIR	2
COLING	34	AACL	11	NEURIPS	2
AAAI	29	IJCAI	9		
SIGIR	17	CONLL	8		

Table 2: Number of papers published per venue. Unsurprisingly, EMNLP and ACL are the most popular venues for summarization research.

Challenges in Text Summarization
Controlled and Tailored Summarization
Efficient Encoding of Long Documents
Exploiting the Structure of Long Documents
Hallucinations in the Generated Summaries
Identifying Important Contents from the Document
Information Loss / Incoherence in Extractive Summarization
Lack of Suitable Training Data
Pretraining and Sample Efficiency
Robust Evaluation Methods

Table 3: Manually annotated labels for problem statement clusters extracted from all papers, highlighting the prevalent challenges in text summarization.

4.2 Corpus Statistics

Table 2 shows the distribution of papers across venues, with EMNLP and ACL emerging as the top venues for summarization research. Among the 514 papers, we observed the following distribution of paper types: 353 dealt with methods, 79 with analysis (including meta-evaluation and quality/model analysis), 73 were corpus-related, 61 focused on metrics and one on theory. The majority of the proposed models were trained using supervised learning (73%), compared to unsupervised (17%) and reinforcement learning (10%). The different paper types were not mutually exclusive, so there were cases where a paper proposed a new dataset and applied methods to it at the same time. In terms of automatic evaluation, the ROUGE metric was used in 71.6% of papers, highlighting its widespread use for evaluating the quality of generated summaries in the field of single-document summarization of English texts. Only 39.5% of the papers included some form of manual evaluation. In terms of reproducibility, we found that 58% of the papers published their code, indicating a slow but growing trend of code availability in this area compared to previous years.

5 Indicative Summaries of Papers

In contrast to informative summaries that aim to replace the entire paper, our tool provides indicative summaries that help users quickly decide if a paper is relevant to their information need. Our indicative summaries are unique in that they encompass an abstractive summary of the paper as well as multiple facets such as datasets, domains, evaluation metrics alongside other information.

5.1 Beyond Abstract as a Summary

Traditionally, the paper abstract serves the purpose of an informative summary (Luhn, 1958) or an ultra-short abstractive summary (Cachola et al., 2020) that outlines the major contributions. Yet, when dealing with a large collection of documents, these summaries fall short, as they do not enable fine-grained retrieval of relevant papers. Moreover, studies have shown that abstracts can introduce bias and may not offer a comprehensive representation of the paper's contents (Elkiss et al., 2008).

In contrast to informative summaries, which essentially substitute the source, indicative summaries serve as a roadmap for the contents of the source document (Mani, 2001). They aid readers in deciding whether they want to explore the source document in greater detail. Particularly in the context of literature reviews, indicative summaries provide an exploratory overview of papers, allowing researchers to quickly navigate and comprehend their contributions. TL;DR PROGRESS introduces a novel indicative summary that integrates manually annotated facets with automatically extracted contextual information. Motivated by the significance of considering contextual factors in summarization (Jones et al., 1999), we extract information related to: (1) the purpose of the generated summaries, (2) the target audience for the summaries, (3) the downstream application of the generated summaries, and (4) the problems and corresponding solutions presented in the paper. Figure 2 (Appendix) exemplifies an indicative summary generated by our tool. This summary distinctly outlines all the pertinent information that a reader would need to determine whether they wish to delve into the paper in more detail.

5.2 Contextual Information Extraction

We demonstrate the utilization of LLMs for the task of indicative summarization by extracting the contextual information described above through

Context Factors Prompt (GPT3.5)

You are a helpful assistant that can read and analyze scientific papers. You are given the following paper: {*Introduction*} Answer the following three questions: (1) Why are the authors generating the summaries of the documents? (2) Who are they for? (3) How will they be used? You must not include the proposed approach by the authors for generating the summaries. You will output a list of the question-answer pairs where each question is prefixed by the token QUESTION: and each answer is prefixed by the ANSWER: token. Each pair is separated by two lines.

Problems and Solutions Prompt (GPT3.5)

You are a helpful assistant that can read and analyze scientific papers. You are given the following paper: {*Introduction*} Can you give me a list of the main problems tackled by the authors and their proposed solutions? In this list, each problem is described followed by a solution proposed by the authors. Each problem starts with the token PROBLEM and each solution starts with the token SOLUTION.
Here is the list:

Table 4: Prompts for extracting contextual information from the introduction of a paper. This information is used to compose indicative summaries of papers. The specific instructions for controlling output format may not be required with newer models.

generative question-answering. To extract this information, we input the introduction section of the paper into the prompt. We devised two prompts corresponding to the *context factors* and *problems and solutions* (see Table 4). Each prompt poses specific questions related to the context, necessitating the generation of answers in a specific format using the relevant content from the paper. We employed GPT-3.5 for our experiments.[4]

We conducted additional analysis of this contextual information to identify the frequently addressed challenges in text summarization. In particular, we employed a soft clustering approach (HDBSCAN (Campello et al., 2013)) on the set of problem statements.[5] This process yielded 9 clusters, which we manually labeled with their respective challenges, as illustrated in Table 3.

6 Automatic Terminology Acquisition

Scientific terminology plays a vital role in research, requiring researchers to recall papers related to specific concepts or acronyms representing models/metrics. Moreover, previously defined terminology might be directly referenced in subsequent papers without detailed explanation (Ball et al., 2002) or even inaccurately paraphrased, compelling researchers to trace back through multiple papers to find the original definitions. The task of automatic terminology acquisition (Judea et al., 2014) aims to tackle this issue by extracting various concepts defined in a paper along with their definitions. In our exploration of this task, we opted for LLMs instead of supervised methods that necessitate labeled data.

We utilized prompt engineering, leveraging GPT-3.5, with the introduction section of the paper as input for automatic terminology acquisition. We formulated two prompts specifically for extracting *glossary definitions* and *acronym-expansion pairs*. Examples of extracted glossary terms and acronym-expansion pairs are provided in Table 6. The prompts are shown in Table 5.

Glossary Prompt (GPT3.5)

You are a scientist who can read and summarize scientific papers. You are given the following paper: {*Introduction*}. Your task is to extract a list of key concepts along with correct definitions like a glossary of the paper. Follow the format [*Concept*: *Definition*].

Acronyms Prompt (GPT3.5)

You are a scientist who can read and summarize scientific papers. You are given the following paper: {*Introduction*}. Your task is to extract a list of acronyms that the authors use along with correct expansions from the paper.
For example (1) EDU: Elementary Discourse Unit, (2) SEHY: Simple Yet Effective Hybrid Model, (3) PLM: Pretrained Language Model. Exclude acronyms for which no expansion is explicitly provided by the authors. Follow the format [*Acronym*: *Expansion*].

Table 5: Prompts for automatic terminology acquisition from the introduction of a paper. We extract glossary as well as acronym-expansion pairs. For the latter, we provide examples of the expected output format.

7 Dashboard and Figure Browser

TL;DR PROGRESS includes an interactive dashboard that provides real-time visualizations of key statistics gathered from the annotated documents. The dashboard displays: (1) the number of papers annotated per year, (2) the distribution of publicly released code and resources per year, (3) the popular datasets and document domains for training/evaluation, (4) the commonly emphasized quality criteria of summary (5) the dominant components targeted from the annotation scheme, and (6) the distribution of addressed challenges.

This extensive dashboard delivers a quantitative overview of the text summarization landscape, in line with the detailed facets and additional metadata

[4] https://platform.openai.com/docs/models/gpt-3-5

[5] We clustered the contextual embeddings (Reimers and Gurevych, 2019) combined with dimensionality reduction using UMAP (McInnes and Healy, 2018).

in our annotation scheme. Key findings from the dashboard include:

1. Authors consistently practice releasing code for reproducibility and adoption.
2. News (54.2%) and scholarly documents (13.3%) dominate as the most studied domains, calling for more diverse investigations.
3. The top three evaluated dimensions for summary quality are informativeness (17%), fluency (10%), and coherence (8.1%).
4. The majority of papers propose new objective functions and input encoding approaches.
5. Predominant challenges include controlled summarization, comprehensive evaluation, insufficient datasets, and risks of hallucinations.

The tool also incorporates a dedicated figure browser (Appendix, Figure 3) hosting **1524** figures and tables (with captions) linked to their sources. This resource streamlines navigation and serves as a handy reference for researchers exploring standard illustrations depicting model architectures or layouts for presenting evaluation results.[6]

8 Evaluation

We conducted an empirical evaluation of the tool's efficacy in supporting systematic literature reviews for text summarization. The study involved presenting targeted inquiries relevant to beginners in the field and instructing participants to leverage both TL;DR PROGRESS and Semantic Scholar for retrieving relevant papers. Additionally, we systematically gathered feedback on the tool's usability and utility for understanding the effectiveness of its features.

8.1 Purpose-driven User Study

We conducted a study with five participants (3 PhDs, 2 PostDocs) specializing in natural language processing or information retrieval, but unfamiliar with text summarization research. Their task was to find up to five relevant papers for each of the ten research questions, covering various aspects of summarization research using both TL;DR PROGRESS and Semantic Scholar.[7] The following research questions were crafted in reference to the New-Summ Workshop's Call for Papers.[8]

[6]We used `PDFFigures 2.0` (Clark and Divvala, 2016).

[7]https://www.semanticscholar.org/

[8]https://newsumm.github.io/2023/

Term	Definition / Expansion
Glossary	
Co-Decoding	An algorithm that takes two review sets as input to compare and contrast the token probability distributions of the models to generate more distinctive summaries (Iso et al., 2021).
Concept-Pruning	An approach to reduce the number of concepts in a model to find optimal solutions efficiently (Boudin et al., 2015).
Drop-Prompt Mechanism	An approach to drop out hallucinated entities from a predicted content plan and to prompt the decoder with the modified plan to generate faithful summaries (Narayan et al., 2021).
Facet Bias Problem	The problem of centrality-based models tending to select sentences from one facet of a document, rather than important sentences from different facets (Liang et al., 2021).
Indegree Centrality	A measure of centrality that assumes a word receiving more relevance score from others is more likely to be important (Xu et al., 2020).
Acronyms	
ADAQSUM	Adapter-based query-focused abstractive summarization (Brazinskas et al., 2022).
COLO	Contrastive learning based re-ranking framework for one-stage summarization (An et al., 2022).
PLATE	Pseudo-labeling with larger attention temperature (Zhang et al., 2022).
ASGARD	Abstractive summarization with graph-augmentation and semantic-driven reward (Huang et al., 2020b).
ASAS	Answer selection and abstractive summarization (Deng et al., 2020).

Table 6: Examples of automatically extracted glossary and acronym–expansion pairs from the papers.

1. How do neural text summarization models address hallucination challenges in abstractive summarization?
2. What are the efficient encoding strategies for handling long documents in neural text summarization?
3. How do neural text summarization models control/tailor the generated summaries to user preferences/aspects/facets?
4. How can pretrained language models be leveraged for improving text summarization?
5. How can additional sources of external knowledge be integrated into the text summarization pipeline?
6. What are the annotation strategies for evaluating hallucination, faithfulness, and factuality in summarization?

7. List at least five corpora that can be used to train scientific document summarization models?
8. List at least five diverse text domains studied in text summarization?
9. What reward functions are proposed to improve summarization via reinforcement learning?
10. What are the various summary quality criteria evaluated via human assessment?

The participants were instructed to evaluate paper relevance using the summaries from the tools, rating them on a scale from 1 (least relevant) to 5 (most relevant). Alongside this, they were requested to share feedback on the usability, the utility of certain features of TL;DR PROGRESS, and its strengths and limitations. This evaluation provides both a comparative analysis and a qualitative understanding of the tool's practicality.

8.2 Results

Our tool effectively narrowed down the large collection of papers to a set of relevant results. The multi-faceted search, in particular, facilitated quick paper filtering without keyword use. Three out of five participants favored our tool for literature review. However, Semantic Scholar offers a more "familiar" search experience and more recent results, albeit requiring extra effort for relevance filtering. Both tools received a score of 4 for the relevance of results. Users also rated the usefulness of features on a scale of 1 (least useful) to 5 (most useful). The advanced search (combining facets) was highly useful (mean score of 4.5), allowing users to easily adapt searches to the research question at hand. This underscores the utility of our annotation scheme (Table 1). Indicative summaries and the list of challenges were sufficiently useful (mean score of 3.6) for quickly skimming paper contents and finding papers addressing specific problems, respectively. Results are visualized in the Appendix, Figure 4.

8.3 Feedback

Users found the tool intuitive and easy to use, appreciating the multi-faceted search and indicative summaries. The dashboard was viewed as a useful resource for obtaining a quantitative overview of the text summarization field. Users offered constructive feedback, suggesting incorporating a more sophisticated search mechanism and integrating it with facet-based filtering. They pointed out that searching only by conceptual components was insufficient, as the resulting set of papers was still large and required further filtering. These insights will be considered for future improvements to the tool.

9 Conclusion

In summary, TL;DR PROGRESS offers an interactive platform for nuanced exploration of over 500 neural text summarization papers from top venues. Utilizing a tailored annotation scheme, the tool guides users through multifaceted retrieval, provides insightful indicative summaries, outlines challenges, and presents a quantitative overview, easing the entry for newcomers into the field.

Limitations

The tool leverages LLMs for automated summarization, extracting contextual factors like summary purpose, issues, solutions, and scientific terminology from papers. While we conducted a random accuracy check, a comprehensive assessment of hallucinations or faithfulness in the extracted information was not performed. We anticipate that with more advanced models, such as GPT-4, we can enhance the assurance of quality and structure the extracted content more effectively. Currently confined to summarization, the tool's annotation scheme can be readily extended to other domains, bootstrapped by experts accordingly. However, existing facets like datasets, domains, metrics, qualitative evaluation, and learning paradigms can be directly annotated for new domains. Additionally, a forthcoming feature is the tool's capability to incorporate new papers, automating the annotation process—a feature we plan to implement in future updates to the tool.

References

Chenxin An, Ming Zhong, Zhiyong Wu, Qin Zhu, Xuanjing Huang, and Xipeng Qiu. 2022. Colo: A contrastive learning based re-ranking framework for one-stage summarization. In *Proceedings of the 29th International Conference on Computational Linguistics, COLING 2022, Gyeongju, Republic of Korea, October 12-17, 2022*, pages 5783–5793. International Committee on Computational Linguistics.

Philip Ball et al. 2002. Paper trail reveals references go unread by citing authors. *Nature*, 420(6916):594–594.

Florian Boudin, Hugo Mougard, and Benoît Favre. 2015. Concept-based summarization using integer linear programming: From concept pruning to multiple optimal solutions. In *Proceedings of the 2015 Conference on Empirical Methods in Natural Language Processing, EMNLP 2015, Lisbon, Portugal, September 17-21, 2015*, pages 1914–1918. The Association for Computational Linguistics.

Arthur Brazinskas, Ramesh Nallapati, Mohit Bansal, and Markus Dreyer. 2022. Efficient few-shot fine-tuning for opinion summarization. In *Findings of the Association for Computational Linguistics: NAACL 2022, Seattle, WA, United States, July 10-15, 2022*, pages 1509–1523. Association for Computational Linguistics.

Isabel Cachola, Kyle Lo, Arman Cohan, and Daniel S. Weld. 2020. TLDR: extreme summarization of scientific documents. In *Findings of the Association for Computational Linguistics: EMNLP 2020, Online Event, 16-20 November 2020*, volume EMNLP 2020 of *Findings of ACL*, pages 4766–4777. Association for Computational Linguistics.

Ricardo J. G. B. Campello, Davoud Moulavi, and Jörg Sander. 2013. Density-based clustering based on hierarchical density estimates. In *Advances in Knowledge Discovery and Data Mining, 17th Pacific-Asia Conference, PAKDD 2013, Gold Coast, Australia, April 14-17, 2013, Proceedings, Part II*, volume 7819 of *Lecture Notes in Computer Science*, pages 160–172. Springer.

Christopher Andreas Clark and Santosh Kumar Divvala. 2016. Pdffigures 2.0: Mining figures from research papers. In *Proceedings of the 16th ACM/IEEE-CS on Joint Conference on Digital Libraries, JCDL 2016, Newark, NJ, USA, June 19 - 23, 2016*, pages 143–152. ACM.

Yang Deng, Wai Lam, Yuexiang Xie, Daoyuan Chen, Yaliang Li, Min Yang, and Ying Shen. 2020. Joint learning of answer selection and answer summary generation in community question answering. In *The Thirty-Fourth AAAI Conference on Artificial Intelligence, AAAI 2020, The Thirty-Second Innovative Applications of Artificial Intelligence Conference, IAAI 2020, The Tenth AAAI Symposium on Educational Advances in Artificial Intelligence, EAAI 2020, New York, NY, USA, February 7-12, 2020*, pages 7651–7658. AAAI Press.

Yi Du, Ludi Wang, Mengyi Huang, Dongze Song, Wenjuan Cui, and Yuanchun Zhou. 2023. Autodive: An integrated onsite scientific literature annotation tool. In *Proceedings of the 61st Annual Meeting of the Association for Computational Linguistics: System Demonstrations, ACL 2023, Toronto, Canada, July 10-12, 2023*, pages 76–85. Association for Computational Linguistics.

Aaron Elkiss, Siwei Shen, Anthony Fader, Günes Erkan, David J. States, and Dragomir R. Radev. 2008. Blind men and elephants: What do citation summaries tell us about a research article? *J. Assoc. Inf. Sci. Technol.*, 59(1):51–62.

Tanya Goyal, Junyi Jessy Li, and Greg Durrett. 2022. News summarization and evaluation in the era of GPT-3. *CoRR*, abs/2209.12356.

Nianlong Gu and Richard H. R. Hahnloser. 2023. Scilit: A platform for joint scientific literature discovery, summarization and citation generation. In *Proceedings of the 61st Annual Meeting of the Association for Computational Linguistics: System Demonstrations, ACL 2023, Toronto, Canada, July 10-12, 2023*, pages 235–246. Association for Computational Linguistics.

Dandan Huang, Leyang Cui, Sen Yang, Guangsheng Bao, Kun Wang, Jun Xie, and Yue Zhang. 2020a. What have we achieved on text summarization? In *Proceedings of the 2020 Conference on Empirical Methods in Natural Language Processing, EMNLP 2020, Online, November 16-20, 2020*, pages 446–469. Association for Computational Linguistics.

Luyang Huang, Lingfei Wu, and Lu Wang. 2020b. Knowledge graph-augmented abstractive summarization with semantic-driven cloze reward. In *Proceedings of the 58th Annual Meeting of the Association for Computational Linguistics, ACL 2020, Online, July 5-10, 2020*, pages 5094–5107. Association for Computational Linguistics.

Hayate Iso, Xiaolan Wang, Yoshihiko Suhara, Stefanos Angelidis, and Wang-Chiew Tan. 2021. Convex aggregation for opinion summarization. In *Findings of the Association for Computational Linguistics: EMNLP 2021, Virtual Event / Punta Cana, Dominican Republic, 16-20 November, 2021*, pages 3885–3903. Association for Computational Linguistics.

K Sparck Jones et al. 1999. Automatic summarizing: factors and directions. *Advances in automatic text summarization*, pages 1–12.

Alex Judea, Hinrich Schütze, and Soeren Bruegmann. 2014. Unsupervised training set generation for automatic acquisition of technical terminology in patents. In *COLING 2014, 25th International Conference on Computational Linguistics, Proceedings of the Conference: Technical Papers, August 23-29, 2014, Dublin, Ireland*, pages 290–300. ACL.

Xinnian Liang, Shuangzhi Wu, Mu Li, and Zhoujun Li. 2021. Improving unsupervised extractive summarization with facet-aware modeling. In *Findings of the Association for Computational Linguistics: ACL/IJCNLP 2021, Online Event, August 1-6, 2021*, volume ACL/IJCNLP 2021 of *Findings of ACL*, pages 1685–1697. Association for Computational Linguistics.

Hans Peter Luhn. 1958. The automatic creation of literature abstracts. *IBM Journal of Reseach and Devopment*, 2(2):159–165.

Inderjeet Mani. 2001. Summarization evaluation: An overview.

Leland McInnes and John Healy. 2018. UMAP: uniform manifold approximation and projection for dimension reduction. *CoRR*, abs/1802.03426.

Shashi Narayan, Yao Zhao, Joshua Maynez, Gonçalo Simões, Vitaly Nikolaev, and Ryan T. McDonald. 2021. Planning with learned entity prompts for abstractive summarization. *Trans. Assoc. Comput. Linguistics*, 9:1475–1492.

Nils Reimers and Iryna Gurevych. 2019. Sentence-bert: Sentence embeddings using siamese bert-networks. In *Proceedings of the 2019 Conference on Empirical Methods in Natural Language Processing and the 9th International Joint Conference on Natural Language Processing, EMNLP-IJCNLP 2019, Hong Kong, China, November 3-7, 2019*, pages 3980–3990. Association for Computational Linguistics.

Alexander M. Rush, Sumit Chopra, and Jason Weston. 2015. A neural attention model for abstractive sentence summarization. In *Proceedings of the 2015 Conference on Empirical Methods in Natural Language Processing, EMNLP 2015, Lisbon, Portugal, September 17-21, 2015*, pages 379–389. The Association for Computational Linguistics.

Yu-Zhe Shi, Shiqian Li, Xinyi Niu, Qiao Xu, Jiawen Liu, Yifan Xu, Shiyu Gu, Bingru He, Xinyang Li, Xinyu Zhao, Zijian Zhao, Yidong Lyu, Zhen Li, Sijia Liu, Lin Qiu, Jinhao Ji, Lecheng Ruan, Yuxi Ma, Wenjuan Han, and Yixin Zhu. 2023. Perslearn: Research training through the lens of perspective cultivation. In *Proceedings of the 61st Annual Meeting of the Association for Computational Linguistics: System Demonstrations, ACL 2023, Toronto, Canada, July 10-12, 2023*, pages 11–30. Association for Computational Linguistics.

Ilya Sutskever, Oriol Vinyals, and Quoc V. Le. 2014. Sequence to sequence learning with neural networks. In *Advances in Neural Information Processing Systems 27: Annual Conference on Neural Information Processing Systems 2014, December 8-13 2014, Montreal, Quebec, Canada*, pages 3104–3112.

Ashish Vaswani, Noam Shazeer, Niki Parmar, Jakob Uszkoreit, Llion Jones, Aidan N. Gomez, Lukasz Kaiser, and Illia Polosukhin. 2017. Attention is all you need. In *Advances in Neural Information Processing Systems 30: Annual Conference on Neural Information Processing Systems 2017, December 4-9, 2017, Long Beach, CA, USA*, pages 5998–6008.

Song Xu, Haoran Li, Peng Yuan, Youzheng Wu, Xiaodong He, and Bowen Zhou. 2020. Self-attention guided copy mechanism for abstractive summarization. In *Proceedings of the 58th Annual Meeting of the Association for Computational Linguistics, ACL 2020, Online, July 5-10, 2020*, pages 1355–1362. Association for Computational Linguistics.

Shengqiang Zhang, Xingxing Zhang, Hangbo Bao, and Furu Wei. 2022. Attention temperature matters in abstractive summarization distillation. In *Proceedings of the 60th Annual Meeting of the Association for Computational Linguistics (Volume 1: Long Papers), ACL 2022, Dublin, Ireland, May 22-27, 2022*, pages 127–141. Association for Computational Linguistics.

A Illustrations

This section shows the indicative summaries of a paper and the figure browser. For indicative summary, we combined automatically extracted contextual information using prompts.

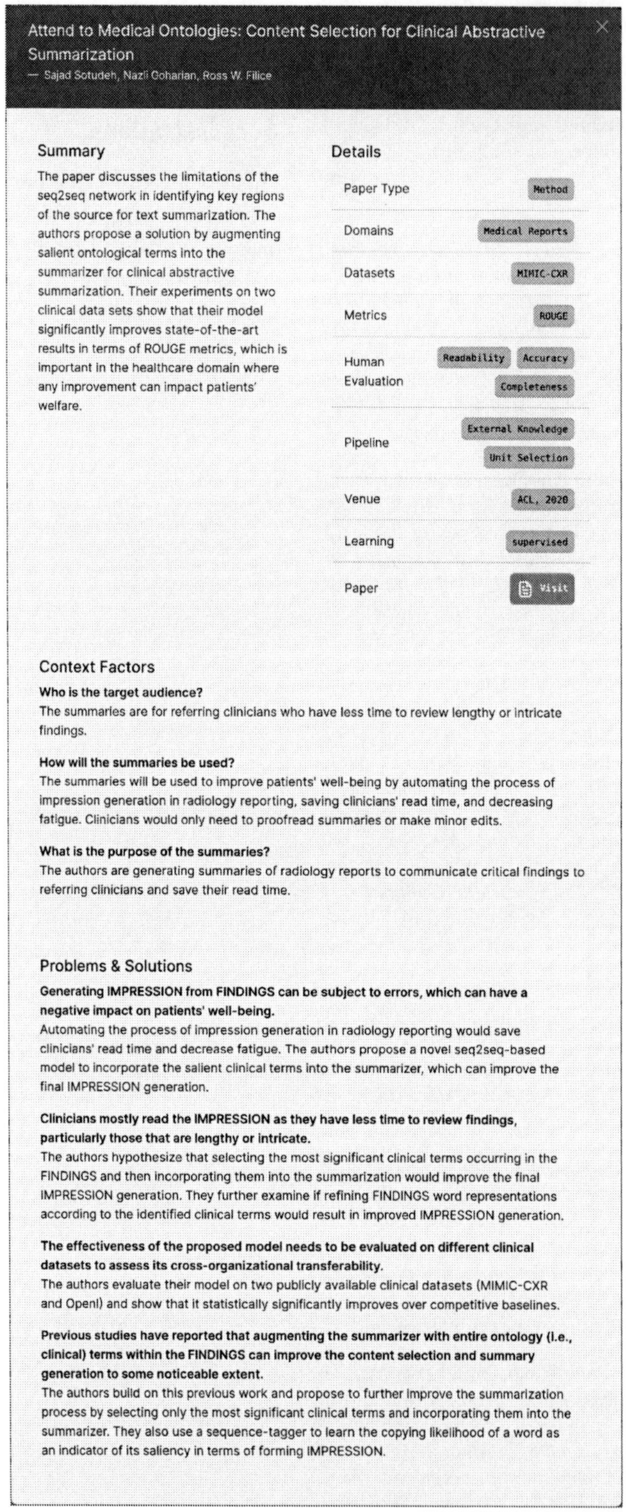

Figure 2: Indicative summary of a paper containing (1) an abstractive summary of the introduction, (2) manually annotated metadata attributes (details), (3) purpose of the summary encompassing the target audience, the downstream use, and the purpose, (4) claims and contributions of the paper.

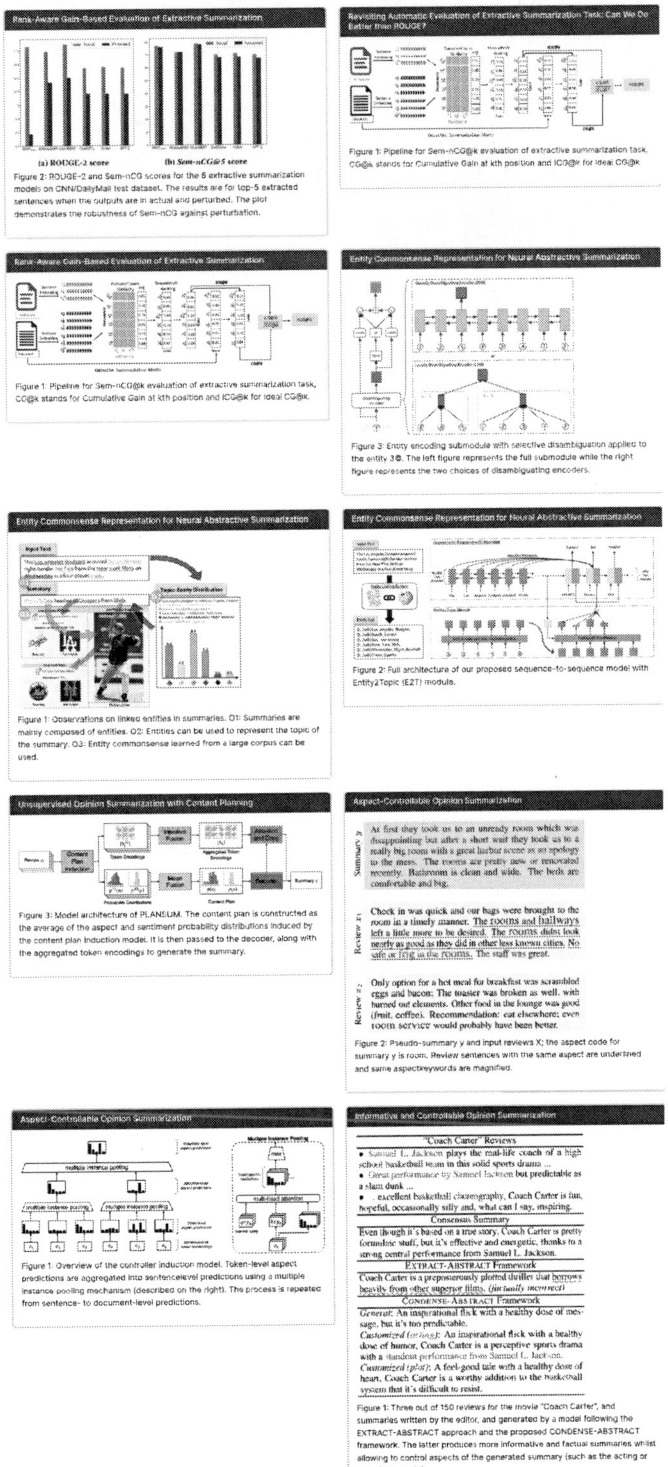

Figure 3: An overview of the figure browser which contains all the tables and figures pulled from the papers, accompanied by their captions.

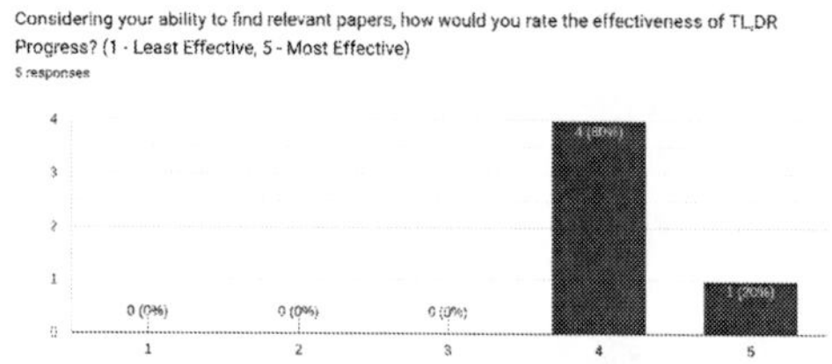

(a) Retrieval effectiveness of TL;DR PROGRESS.

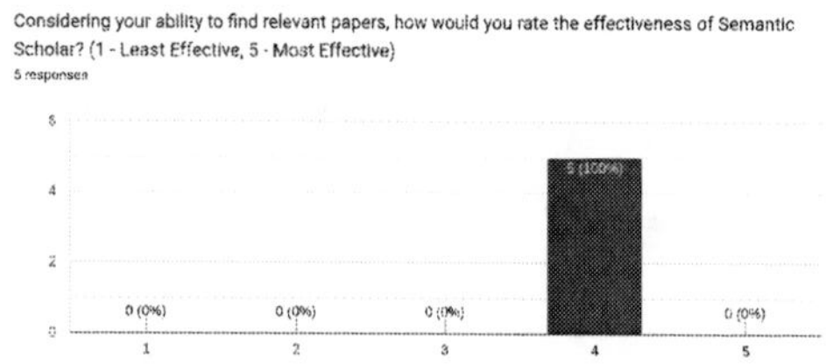

(b) Retrieval effectiveness of Semantic Scholar.

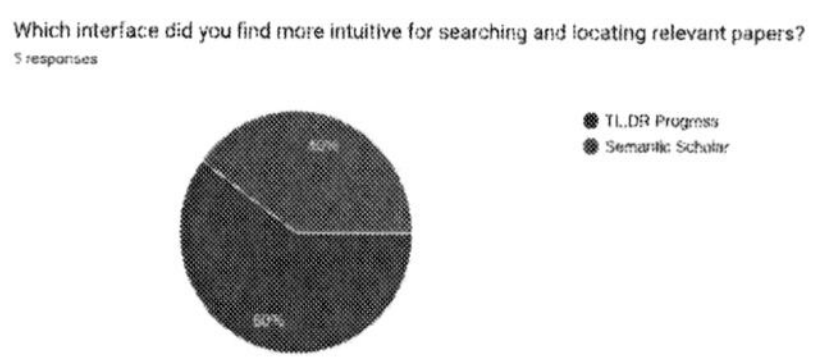

(c) Preference of TL;DR PROGRESS over Semantic Scholar for literature review.

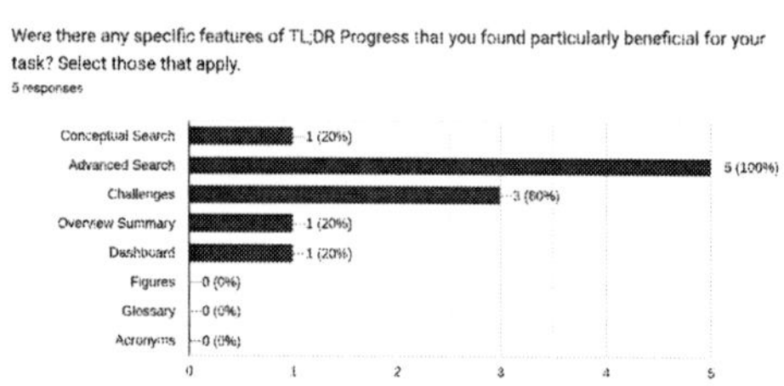

(d) Usefulness of features in TL;DR PROGRESS. Advanced search which allows for combining multiple facets for filtering papers is the most useful feature, followed by the enumerated list of challenges.

Figure 4: Evaluation results of the effectiveness and usefulness of TL;DR PROGRESS compared to Semantic Scholar.

FRAPPE: FRAming, Persuasion, and Propaganda Explorer

Ahmed Sajwani[1,5*], Alaa El Setohy[10,5*], Ali Mekky[2,5*], Diana Turmakhan[3,5*],
Lara Hassan[2,5*], Mohamed El Zeftawy[2,5*], Omar El Herraoui[4,5*],
Osama Mohammed Afzal[5], Qisheng Liao[5], Tarek Mahmoud[5,8],
Zain Muhammad Mujahid[5], Muhammad Umar Salman[5], Muhammad Arslan Manzoor[5],
Massa Baali [5], Jakub Piskorski[6], Nicolas Stefanovitch[9], Giovanni Da San Martino[7], Preslav Nakov[5]
[1]Khalifa University of Science and Technology, [2]Alexandria University, [3]Nazarbayev University, [4]NYU Abu Dhabi,
[5]MBZUAI, [6]Polish Academy of Sciences, [7]University of Padova, [8]Presight
[9]European Commission Joint Research Centre, [10]Egypt Japan University of Science and Technology

Abstract

The abundance of news sources and the urgent demand for reliable information have led to serious concerns about the threat of misleading information. In this paper, we present FRAPPE, a Framing, Persuasion, and Propaganda Explorer system. FRAPPE goes beyond conventional news analysis of articles and unveils the intricate linguistic techniques used to shape readers' opinions and emotions. Our system allows users not only to analyze individual articles for their genre, framings, and use of persuasion techniques, but also to draw comparisons between the strategies of persuasion and framing adopted by a diverse pool of news outlets and countries across multiple languages for different topics, thus providing a comprehensive understanding of how information is presented and manipulated. FRAPPE[1] is publicly accessible at `https://frappe.streamlit.app/` and a video explaining our system is available at `https://www.youtube.com/watch?v=3RlTfSVnZmk`

1 Introduction

As the digital age ushers in an era of unparalleled connectivity and information dissemination, the transition towards online news media has brought several changes in the way the news is produced, consumed, and distributed. Although online news offers advantages such as increased accessibility and reduced cost of publishing, it has also brought several challenges such as the potential reinforcement of biases and propaganda. Consequently, analyzing news articles and offering an in-depth understanding beyond surface-level text has become pivotal for addressing these challenges. To get a global picture, there is also a need to analyze and to compare entire news media as well as the news landscape in different countries around a given topic.

A number of manual fact-checking initiatives have been launched. For example, Media Bias/Fact Check[2] and NewsGuard[3] offer assessments of the biases and the factuality of reporting of entire news outlets. There have also been a number of initiatives for fact-checking individual claims such as FactCheck,[4] PolitiFact,[5] and Snopes,[6] among many others. However, they all require tedious manual work by human fact-checkers, which does not scale and cannot cope with the volume of disinformation online. Thus, automation has been proposed as a possible alternative. Recently, it has been further realized that it is important to focus not only on factuality, but also on the way the message is conveyed, e.g., using subjectivity/humor, framing, and persuasion techniques.

As a parallel research line, a variety of research systems have been developed for the purpose of news analysis across several dimensions. For example, the Prta system (Da San Martino et al., 2020) allows users to explore the use of 18 propaganda techniques in news articles. Another tool, NewsLens (Laban and Hearst, 2017), focuses on constructing cohesive narrative threads that span several years and articles from approximately 20 news sources. Yet another system, Tanbih (Zhang et al., 2019), offers a profiling mechanism that covers a substantial yet confined collection of a few thousand media sources, which it profiles for factuality and bias of reporting. We can also mention NewsScan (Kevin et al., 2018), which is a plugin to profile news articles on the basis of specific labels providing information about the lexical properties (ease of reading), as well as some intrinsic properties (sentiment score, political bias), referred to as *nutrition labels*.

*Equal contribution.

[1]This work was done during a summer internship at the NLP department, MBZUAI.

[2]`https://mediabiasfactcheck.com/`

[3]`https://www.newsguardtech.com/`

[4]`https://www.factcheck.org/`

[5]`https://www.politifact.com/`

[6]`https://www.snopes.com/`

Proceedings of the 18th Conference of the European Chapter of the Association for Computational Linguistics
System Demonstrations, pages 207–213
March 17-22, 2024 ©2024 Association for Computational Linguistics

However, there is a lack of publicly accessible tools with the capability not only to analyze articles, but also to systematically explore and to draw comparisons between the strategies of persuasion and framing adopted by a diverse pool of news outlets and countries across many languages for a specific topic. With the aim to bridge this gap, we developed FRAPPE (FRAming, Persuasion, and Propaganda Explorer), an online news analysis platform that operates in a multilingual setup and provides two main functionalities: on-the-fly analysis for individual articles, and a user-friendly, interactive, and insightful Web interface for analyzing a database of 2M+ articles from 8k+ different media sources around the globe, in a variety of languages, covering two main topics: (*i*) the Russia–Ukraine conflict and (*ii*) climate change. This enables users to gather insights about framing, persuasion, and propaganda at an aggregate level, by news outlet and by country, and also to compare different news outlets and different countries.

2 Data and Models

2.1 Data

Our models were trained on a multilingual multi-faceted dataset of news articles from SemEval-2023 task 3 on "Detecting the Genre, the Framing, and the Persuasion Techniques in Online News in a Multi-Lingual Setup" (Piskorski et al., 2023b). The dataset consists of 1,612 articles covering news on current topics of public interest in six European languages (English, French, German, Italian, Polish, and Russian), with more than 37k annotated spans. Each news article was annotated for genre, framings, and persuasion techniques.

2.2 Model

Our system has trained on models for the three subtasks of SemEval-2023 task 3, which we briefly describe below.

2.2.1 Genre

For genre classification, our objective is to define the intended nature of an article, distinguishing between opinion pieces, objective news reporting, and satire. This categorization follows a multi-class annotation scheme applied at the article level.

We used an advanced transformer-based pre-trained multilingual language model, XLM-RoBERTa (Conneau et al., 2020), and in particular its base-sized model, which has 279M parameters.

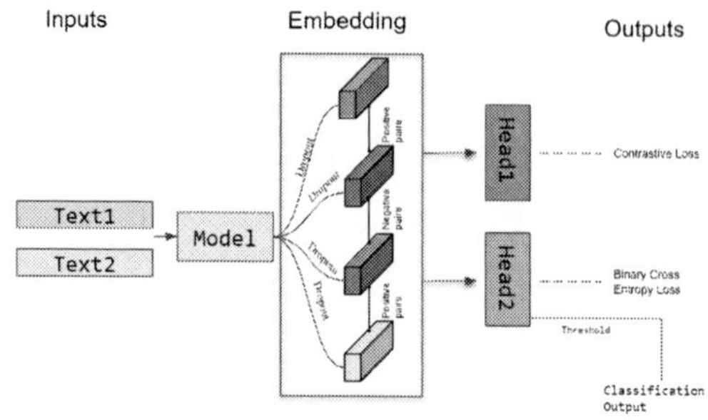

Figure 1: **The architecture of our system for framing and propaganda.** Each input generates two views of representations using dropout. The representations generated by the same text are positive pairs. The contrastive loss and the binary cross entropy loss are calculated separately by two heads and the classification result is calculated after applying a threshold.

This model has excellent transfer learning capabilities. To tailor it specifically to our genre classification task, we fine-tuned the model's last layer by adding a fully connected linear layer with three units (representing the three classes) and applying a softmax activation function.

The training dataset exhibits class imbalance, wherein the presence of satire articles is significantly limited in comparison to the abundance of opinion ones. Consequently, this introduced bias in the model's performance. To mitigate this issue, we used a focal loss function (Mukhoti et al., 2020), a specialized variant of the standard cross-entropy loss, which assigns higher weights to misclassified minority class examples, thereby emphasizing their significance during training and improving the model's ability to handle class imbalance.

Table 1 shows the performance of our model on the test sets for the six languages, with comparison against the baselines and the best systems at SemEval-2023 task 3 subtask A.

Language	Baseline	Our Sys	Best Sys
English	0.288	0.533	0.784
French	0.568	0.686	0.835
German	0.630	0.726	0.819
Italian	0.389	0.621	0.768
Polish	0.490	0.682	0.785
Russian	0.398	0.641	0.755

Table 1: **Genre analysis:** Performance (macro-F1 score) of our system compared to the baselines and to the best systems for the six languages on the test data of SemEval-2023 task 3 subtask A.

Language	Baseline	Our Sys	Best Sys
English	0.349	0.562	0.578
French	0.328	**0.552**	0.552
German	0.487	**0.711**	0.711
Italian	0.485	**0.617**	0.617
Polish	0.593	**0.673**	0.673
Russian	0.229	**0.449**	0.449

Table 2: **Framing analysis:** Performance (macro-F1 score) of our system compared to the baselines and to the best systems for the six languages on the test data of SemEval-2023 task 3 subtask B.

Language	Baseline	Our Sys	Best Sys
English	0.195	0.329	0.375
French	0.240	0.436	0.468
German	0.316	**0.529**	0.529
Italian	0.397	0.548	0.550
Polish	0.179	0.406	0.430
Russian	0.207	**0.395**	0.395

Table 3: **Propaganda analysis:** Performance (macro-F1 score) for our system compared to the baselines and the best systems for the six languages on the test data of SemEval-2023 task 3 subtask C.

2.2.2 Framing

For news framing, we trained our models on the data from SemEval-2023 task 3 subtask B (Piskorski et al., 2023a). This is a challenging task and it is more nuanced than mere topic classification (Card et al., 2015), e.g., while the topic of a news article may be COVID-19, the framing could be from an economic, political, or/and health perspective(s). The task can be formulated as a multilabel text classification problem with fourteen possible labels: *Economic; Capacity and Resources; Morality; Fairness and Equality; Legality, Constitutionality, and Jurisprudence; Policy Prescription and Evaluation; Crime and Punishment; Security and Defense; Health and Safety; Quality of Life; Cultural Identity; Public Opinion; Political; External Regulation and Reputation*. The performance of our model on the test data is shown in Table 2.

Our model's architecture (Liao et al., 2023) is illustrated in Figure 1, featuring two heads: one for contrastive loss and another one for binary entropy loss. During training, the focus is on optimizing the contrastive loss, which is achieved by creating two positive examples from each training example using dropout. Despite the dropout module altering the embeddings of the same training sample, they are still considered positive examples, and their distances are brought closer together. In the context of being a multi-label classification model, any other examples within the same batch are deemed positive only if they have exactly the same target classes. Otherwise, they are treated as negative examples, and the distance between them is pushed apart. Moreover, the loss of the negative examples is weighted, with higher weights assigned to examples containing more diverse classes. Finally, we transform the multi-label classification task into 14 binary classification ones: one for each frame label.

As a result, for each input, there are multiple logits corresponding to each target class. The classification decision is made by predicting that a given example belongs to a target class if the value of the corresponding logit exceeds a specific threshold.

2.2.3 Propaganda

In our propaganda model training, we used data from SemEval-2023 task 3 subtask C and the same model as before. The setup is comparable to the second subtask, with the distinction that the predictions are made for each sentence of the article, rather than for the entire article as a whole. Thus, the model generates predictions at the sentence level. After obtaining predictions for each individual sentence of the article, we combined these predictions to form the final multi-label prediction. This allows us to make comprehensive predictions that take into account the information from each sentence within the article, leading to a more nuanced and context-aware classification of propaganda elements in the text. There are 23 persuasion techniques in total: *appeal to authority; appeal to popularity; appeal to values; appeal to fear/prejudices; flag waving; causal oversimplification; false dilemma or no choice; consequential oversimplification; straw man; red herring; whataboutism; slogans; appeal to time; conversation killer; loaded language; repetition; exaggeration or minimisation' obfuscation - vagueness or confusion; name calling or labeling; doubt; guilt by association; appeal to hypocrisy; and questioning the reputation*. These 23 techniques are grouped into 6 coarse-grained categories: *Attack on Reputation, Justification, Simplification, Distraction, Calls, Manipulative Wording*. The performance of our model on the test data is shown in Table 3.

3 System Architecture

FRAPPE is a comprehensive system with two subsystems. The first one enables users to analyze differences in framings and propaganda techniques across countries and media sources. The second one allows users to explore the genre, the framings, and the propaganda techniques used in an individual custom article, which can be analyzed on the fly. We implemented both subsystems using Streamlit, a free and open-source framework for building and sharing machine learning and data science Web applications.

News Media Explorer We applied our custom-developed models, focusing on framing and persuasion techniques, to a dataset of 2,281,254 articles about the Russia-Ukraine conflict, sourced from 8,318 media outlets across 196 countries. These articles were processed and indexed on our platform, utilizing the models converted to ONNX format and deployed on NVIDIA Triton for enhanced inference speed, powered by two NVIDIA RTX 4090 GPUs. The aggregated results can be explored using the demo, enabling users to conduct customized analysis based on their preferences.

Custom Article Analyzer Inference is done using the models uploaded on the server, and the user is prompted to enter either a news article's URL or the text of an article. In the former case, we use Trafilatura, a Python package and command-line tool, to gather and to extract the article text from the URL (Barbaresi, 2021). After the predictions are done, the genre of the article is displayed, as well as the distribution of the framings and the propaganda techniques it uses.

4 Interface

Our system interface is designed with user friendliness and accessibility in mind, and it offers an immersive journey into the analysis of the two collections of articles we currently have loaded. The interface is divided into two engaging subsections. The News Media Explorer allows the user to explore the analysis of a collection of articles conveniently aggregated both by their source and country of origin, while the Custom Article Analysis offers real-time processing capability for an individual article.

4.1 The News Media Explorer

Setting sail on this analytical journey, users are welcomed by five interactive pages. Each page offers a unique perspective visualizing the following:

1. Framings and persuasion techniques for countries;
2. Framings for countries and sources;
3. Persuasion techniques for countries and sources;
4. Coarse-grained persuasion techniques for countries and sources;
5. Rhetorical propaganda techniques (ethos, pathos, logos) for countries and sources.

The user can choose a country from a list of 186 countries, which are shown sorted by total number of articles. From here, she is guided through a series of visualizations, each revealing detailed insights into the distribution of framings and persuasion techniques across countries and sources.

Figures 2 and 3 are the first landmarks on this journey, visualizing the distribution of framings by country and by source, respectively. The y-axis lists the countries/sources in descending order of articles, while the x-axis gives the percentage of each framing in each country/source. The legend, a colorful tapestry of framings, aids in understanding the chart.

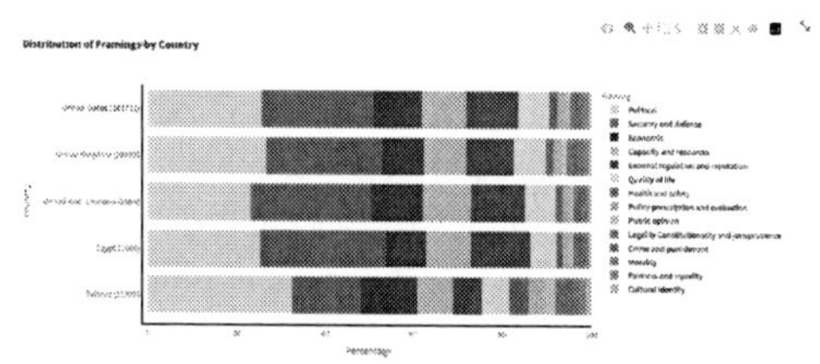

Figure 2: Visualization of framings by country.

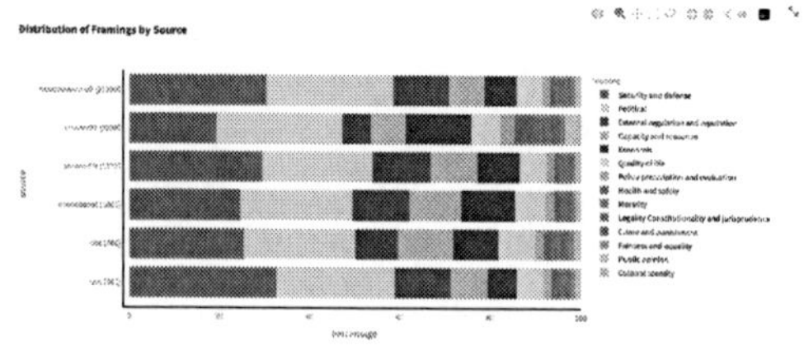

Figure 3: Visualization of framings by source.

The percentage of framings in each country/source (F) is calculated using the following formula:

$$F = \frac{f_{s,c}}{f_{T,c}} \times 100 \quad (1)$$

where $f_{s,c}$ is the frequency of a specific framing within all the articles in a given country/source, and $f_{T,c}$ is the total number of articles for that country/source.

Next, Figures 4 and 5 unfold the story of persuasion techniques by country and source, respectively. Note that we detect the persuasion techniques at the sentence level, considering multiple instances within a single article. Thus, the percentage of each persuasion technique (P) in each country is calculated as follows:

$$P = \frac{F_{t,c}}{F_{T,c}} \times 100 \quad (2)$$

where $F_{t,c}$ is the frequency of a specific persuasion technique in all articles for a given country/news source, and $F_{T,c}$ is the total frequency of all persuasion techniques in all articles from that country/source in our collection.

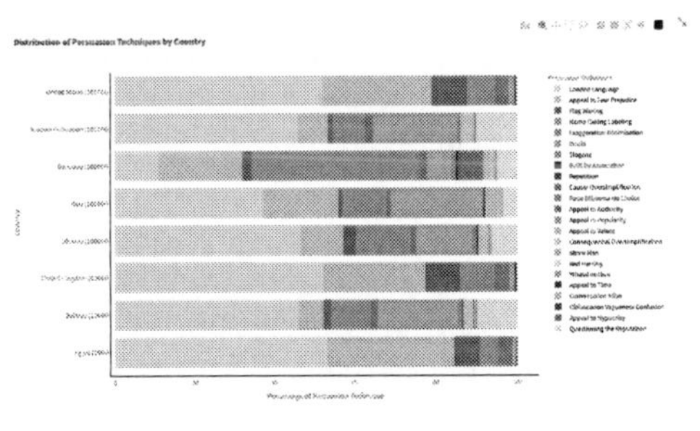

Figure 4: Visualization of persuasion techniques by country.

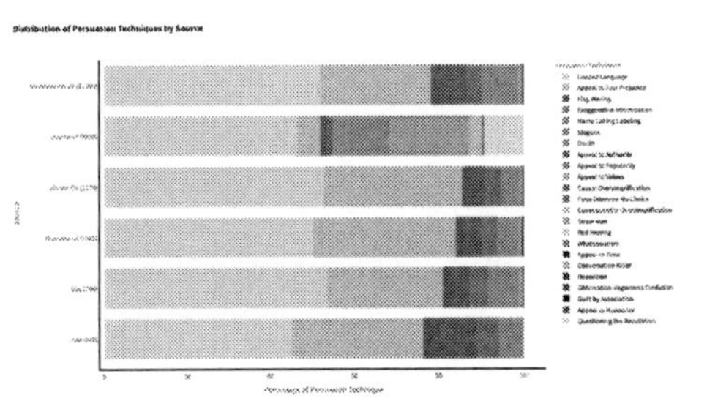

Figure 5: Visualization of persuasion techniques by news medium.

As the journey progresses, a graph displaying the number of articles over time for each country/source emerges, as shown in Figure 6, shedding light on the evolution of media trends.

The final stop within this subsection is an interactive pie chart that presents a global view of all framings in all the selected countries and their respective continents, as shown in Figure 7. This interactive feature invites users to click on parts of the pie chart to collapse or to expand sections, offering an exploratory experience.

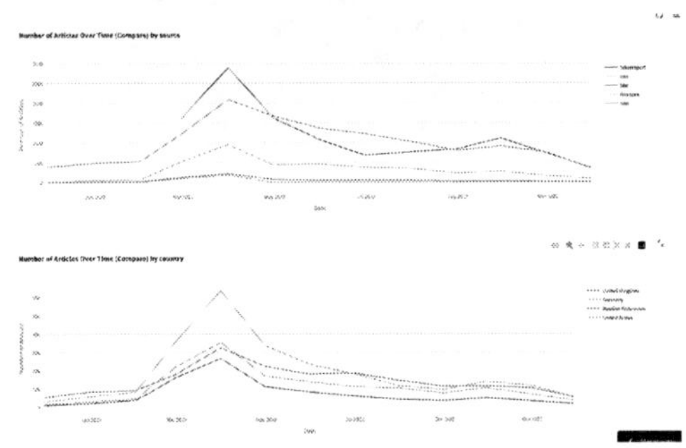

Figure 6: Visualization of the number of articles over time by country and by media source.

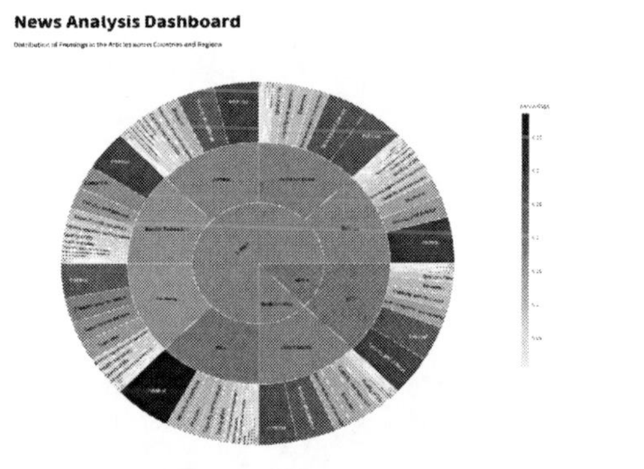

Figure 7: Pie chart of framings by country and continent.

The user can choose to explore the persuasion techniques at two coursers level (as opposed to the original 23 fine-grained techniques) by media and by country. Figure 8 shows the distribution of coarse-grained persuasion techniques across countries, allowing for a higher-level understanding of the prominent persuasion styles used. Figure 9 presents the use of rhetorical techniques such as ethos, pathos, and logos by country, highlighting the variations in strategy and deepening our comprehension of the media persuasion dynamics.

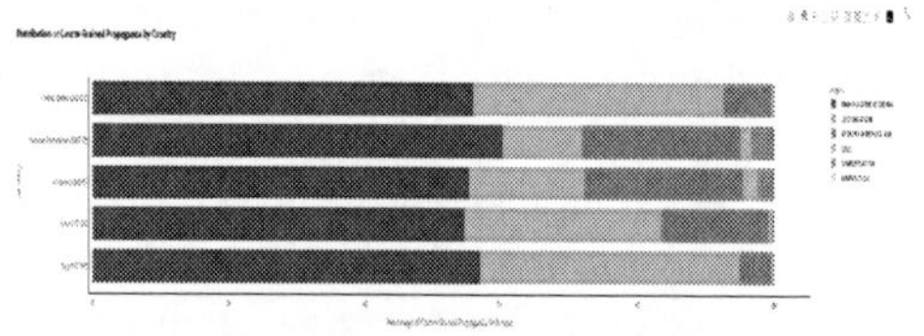

Figure 8: Visualization of coarse-grained persuasion techniques by country.

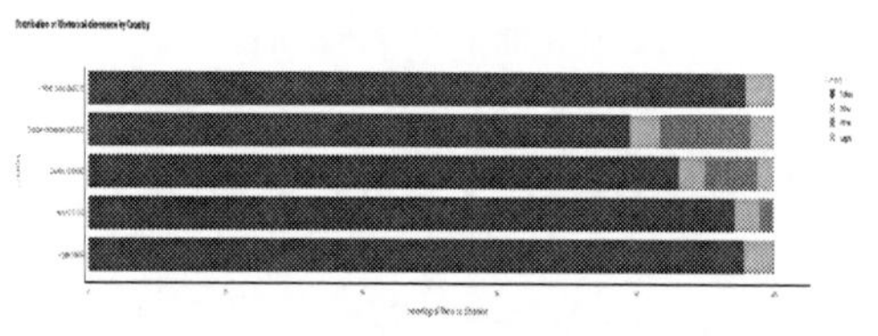

Figure 9: Visualization of rhetorical persuasion techniques by country.

4.2 Custom Article Analysis

The second part of the system, Custom Article Analysis, allows users to delve into a single article of their choice. Users can input their custom article either by entering its URL or by pasting its text into a text box. Upon submission, the system presents three enlightening visualizations, as shown in Figures 10, 11, and 12:

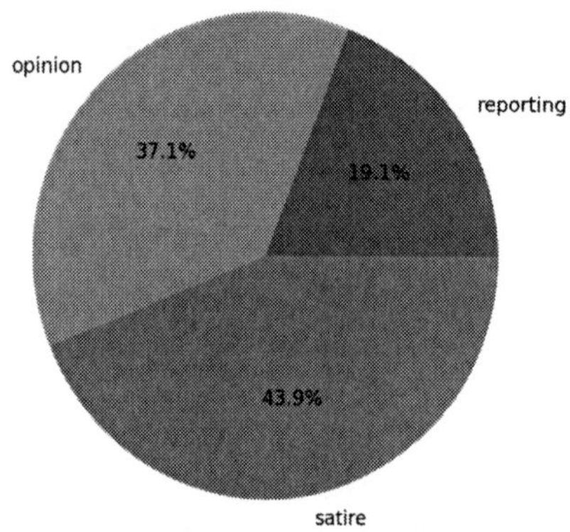

Figure 10: Classification of a custom article as reporting, opinion, or satire.

1. A pie chart unveiling the article's classification as satire, reporting, or opinion. This offers clarity about the article's genre, as shown in Figure 10.

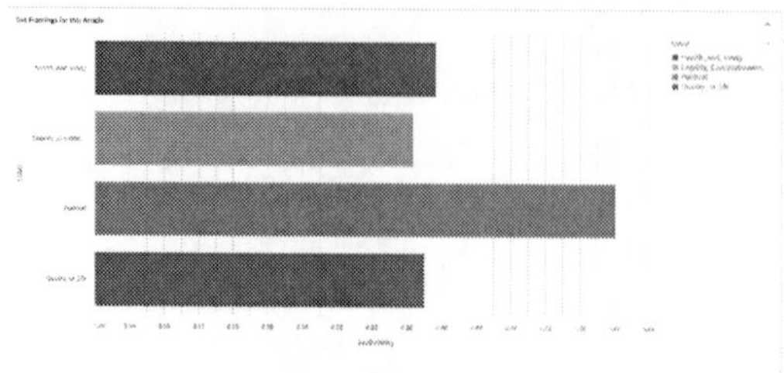

Figure 11: Framings graph for a custom article.

2. A bar chart revealing the framings in the article, offering a deeper understanding of the article's perspectives, as shown in Figure 11.

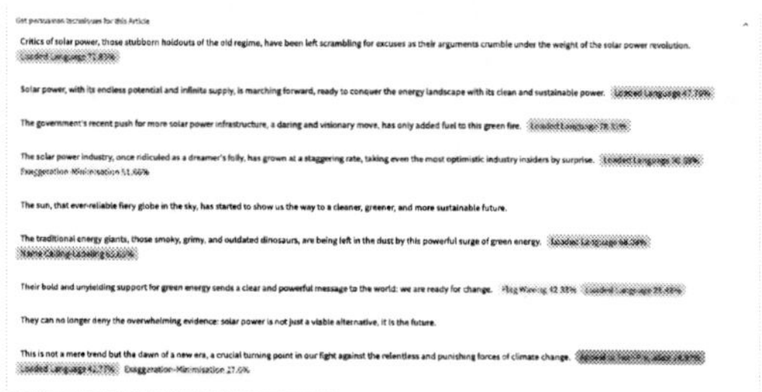

Figure 12: Persuasion techniques for a custom article.

3. A visualization of the persuasion techniques in the article, offering granular insight into the article's rhetoric. This tool is a valuable asset for anyone studying or practicing journalism, as shown in Figure 12.

5 Conclusion and Future Work

We presented FRAPPE, a system for analysis of the news in terms of framing, persuasion, and propaganda techniques, which can be used to tackle the challenge of misleading information in news articles and news outlets. It provides a deep understanding of news articles, allowing users to gain insights into genre, framing, and propaganda techniques, and to perform comparison of media and countries.

In future work, we aim to gather more data, to extend the analysis to other globally discussed topics, and to update our visualizations with more in-depth analysis that goes down to the individual article level. We further plan to create a database that will automatically save every article that was analyzed on the fly (in a separate collection). Finally, we aim to improve our models' accuracy, and to add additional models and analysis.

6 Limitations

We acknowledge certain limitations that we plan to address in future work. First, we need to expand the training data to cover more languages as part of training, in order to improve our models' accuracy when analyzing articles written in these languages (even though, thanks to the multilingual XLM-RoBERTa, we already cover 100 languages). Second, our system does not cover all aspects of analysis that an article can undergo; it currently only unveils genre, framings, and persuasion techniques. Finally, our database is currently limited to our 2M+ articles, and does not automatically reflect future events. We plan continuous data addition covering more topics and languages.

7 Ethics and Broader Impact

One of the foremost ethical considerations is ensuring the transparency and the unbiased analysis in FRAPPE. Users should be aware that our models use neural networks, and as such, they lack explainability. Another warning is that, despite our intent, due to article selection biases, FRAPPE might be favoring some political or social standpoints.

Finally, FRAPPE has the potential to influence the way news articles are perceived and consumed, and journalists may become more aware of the language they use and its potential impact on readers.

References

Adrien Barbaresi. 2021. Trafilatura: A web scraping library and command-line tool for text discovery and extraction. In *Proceedings of the Joint Conference of the 59th Annual Meeting of the Association for Computational Linguistics and the 11th International Joint Conference on Natural Language Processing: System Demonstrations*, ACL-IJCNLP '21, pages 122–131.

Dallas Card, Amber E. Boydstun, Justin H. Gross, Philip Resnik, and Noah A. Smith. 2015. The media frames corpus: Annotations of frames across issues. In *Proceedings of the 53rd Annual Meeting of the Association for Computational Linguistics and the 7th International Joint Conference on Natural Language Processing*, NAACL-HLT'15, pages 438–444, Beijing, China.

Alexis Conneau, Kartikay Khandelwal, Naman Goyal, Vishrav Chaudhary, Guillaume Wenzek, Francisco Guzmán, Edouard Grave, Myle Ott, Luke Zettlemoyer, and Veselin Stoyanov. 2020. Unsupervised cross-lingual representation learning at scale. In *Proceedings of the 58th Annual Meeting of the Association for Computational Linguistics*, ACL '20, pages 8440–8451.

Giovanni Da San Martino, Shaden Shaar, Yifan Zhang, Seunghak Yu, Alberto Barrón-Cedeño, and Preslav Nakov. 2020. Prta: A system to support the analysis of propaganda techniques in the news. In *Proceedings of the 58th Annual Meeting of the Association for Computational Linguistics: System Demonstrations*, ACL '20, pages 287–293.

Vincentius Kevin, Birte Högden, Claudia Schwenger, Ali Şahan, Neelu Madan, Piush Aggarwal, Anusha Bangaru, Farid Muradov, and Ahmet Aker. 2018. Information nutrition labels: A plugin for online news evaluation. In *Proceedings of the First Workshop on Fact Extraction and VERification*, FEVER '18, pages 28–33, Brussels, Belgium.

Philippe Laban and Marti Hearst. 2017. newsLens: building and visualizing long-ranging news stories. In *Proceedings of the Events and Stories in the News Workshop*, pages 1–9, Vancouver, Canada.

Qisheng Liao, Meiting Lai, and Preslav Nakov. 2023. MarsEclipse at SemEval-2023 task 3: Multi-lingual and multi-label framing detection with contrastive learning. In *Proceedings of the the 17th International Workshop on Semantic Evaluation*, SemEval '23, pages 83–87, Toronto, Canada.

Jishnu Mukhoti, Viveka Kulharia, Amartya Sanyal, Stuart Golodetz, Philip Torr, and Puneet Dokania. 2020. Calibrating deep neural networks using focal loss. *Advances in Neural Information Processing Systems*, 33:15288–15299.

Jakub Piskorski, Nicolas Stefanovitch, Giovanni Da San Martino, and Preslav Nakov. 2023a. SemEval-2023 task 3: Detecting the category, the framing, and the persuasion techniques in online news in a multi-lingual setup. In *Proceedings of the 17th International Workshop on Semantic Evaluation*, SemEval'23, pages 2343–2361, Toronto, Canada.

Jakub Piskorski, Nicolas Stefanovitch, Nikolaos Nikolaidis, Giovanni Da San Martino, and Preslav Nakov. 2023b. Multilingual multifaceted understanding of online news in terms of genre, framing, and persuasion techniques. In *Proceedings of the 61st Annual Meeting of the Association for Computational Linguistics*, ACL '23, pages 3001–3022. Association for Computational Linguistics.

Yifan Zhang, Giovanni Da San Martino, Alberto Barrón-Cedeño, Salvatore Romeo, Jisun An, Haewoon Kwak, Todor Staykovski, Israa Jaradat, Georgi Karadzhov, Ramy Baly, Kareem Darwish, James Glass, and Preslav Nakov. 2019. Tanbih: Get to know what you are reading. In *Proceedings of the 2019 Conference on Empirical Methods in Natural Language Processing and the 9th International Joint Conference on Natural Language Processing: System Demonstrations*, EMNLP-IJCNLP '19, pages 223–228, Hong Kong, China.

LLMeBench: A Flexible Framework for Accelerating LLMs Benchmarking

Fahim Dalvi, Maram Hasanain, Sabri Boughorbel, Basel Mousi, Samir Abdaljalil, Nizi Nazar, Ahmed Abdelali*, Shammur Absar Chowdhury, Hamdy Mubarak, Ahmed Ali, Majd Hawasly, Nadir Durrani, Firoj Alam
Qatar Computing Research Institute, HBKU, Qatar
{faimaduddin,fialam}@hbku.edu.qa

Abstract

The recent development and success of Large Language Models (LLMs) necessitate an evaluation of their performance across diverse NLP tasks in different languages. Although several frameworks have been developed and made publicly available, their customization capabilities for specific tasks and datasets are often complex for different users. In this study, we introduce the LLMeBench[1] framework, which can be seamlessly customized to evaluate LLMs for any NLP task, *regardless of language*. The framework features generic dataset loaders, several model providers, and pre-implements most standard evaluation metrics. It supports in-context learning with zero- and few-shot settings. A specific dataset and task can be evaluated for a given LLM in less than 20 lines of code while allowing full flexibility to extend the framework for custom datasets, models, or tasks. The framework has been tested on 31 unique NLP tasks using 53 publicly available datasets within 90 experimental setups, involving approximately 296K data points. We open-sourced LLMeBench for the community[2] and a video demonstrating the framework is available online.[3]

1 Introduction

The rapid advancement of sophisticated large language models (LLMs), supported by in-context learning (ICL) (Dong et al., 2023), has gained unprecedented popularity among both the research and development communities. The emergence of such large models facilitated diverse applications such as solving mathematical reasoning problems (Wei et al., 2022). Given their success, a systematic evaluation and comparison against state-of-the-art is important to accurately gauge the potential of LLMs. A comprehensive evaluation allows understanding of the strengths and weaknesses of these models; guides us towards better human-LLMs interactions through prompting; and facilitates their broader applicability in different scenarios, especially in domains where safety and security are paramount concerns (e.g., healthcare, financial institutes) (Chang et al., 2023; Zhao et al., 2023; Zhu et al., 2023).

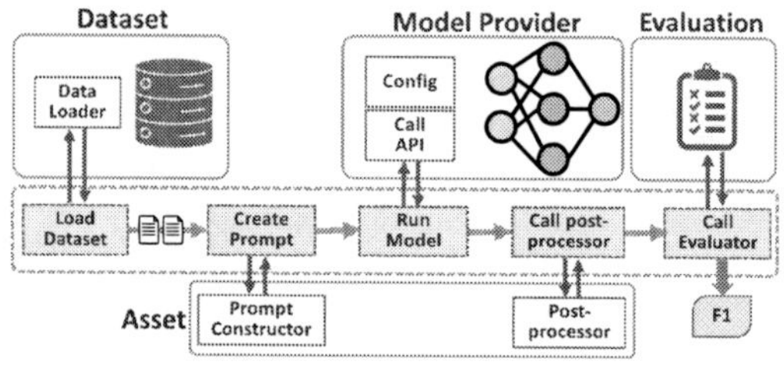

Figure 1: The architecture of the LLMeBench framework. The dotted boxes represent the core implemented modules of the architecture. Customization for new tasks, datasets, and models can be done on `Dataset`, `Model Provider`, `Evaluation`, and `Asset` modules.

Numerous initiatives were launched to comprehensively assess the performance of LLMs on standard NLP tasks. The HELM project (Liang et al., 2022) conducted a thorough evaluation of LLMs for English, spanning various metrics and scenarios. Additionally, the BIG-Bench initiative (Srivastava et al., 2023) introduced an extensive evaluation of 214 tasks, even encompassing languages with limited resources. Notably, evaluations have been carried out on models like GPT2.5 (Radford et al., 2019), ChatGPT (OpenAI, 2023), and BLOOM (Scao et al., 2022) within multitask, multilingual, and multimodal settings. These evaluations were further extended to low-resource languages (Bang et al., 2023; Ahuja et al., 2023; Hendy et al., 2023; Khondaker et al., 2023).

* The contribution was made while the author was at the Qatar Computing Research Institute.

[1]**LLM** effectiveness **Bench**marking. Can be pronounced as "lemme bench".

[2]`https://github.com/qcri/LLMeBench/`

[3]`https://youtu.be/9cC2m_abk3A`

Proceedings of the 18th Conference of the European Chapter of the Association for Computational Linguistics System Demonstrations, pages 214–222
March 17-22, 2024

Evaluating LLMs across diverse tasks often entails challenges related to costs, effort, and time due to complexities like handling API calls, task integration, dataset inclusion, evaluation measures, and potentially hosting datasets on public platforms (e.g., Hugging Face (HF)). To overcome these limitations, in this study, we introduce "LLMeBench", which facilitates a comprehensive evaluation of these LLMs through a seamless and flexible implementation. The proposed framework, as depicted in Figure 1, empowers users to assess various LLMs while simplifying the integration of custom tasks, datasets, and evaluation metrics.

A few evaluation frameworks have emerged to facilitate extensive benchmarking of LLMs. Among these are OpenAI evals,[4] LM Harness (Gao et al., 2021), and OpenICL (Wu et al., 2023). Each framework offers functionalities tailored to specific requirements. For instance, OpenICL focuses on few-shot learning techniques. Our contribution, LLMeBench, stands out by emphasizing a user-friendly, plug-and-play design, that can seamlessly integrate into existing experimental workflows, setting it apart from other alternatives. LLMeBench's uniqueness lies in the following features:

- Supports several generic data loaders (e.g., HF datasets), pre-implements several model providers (such as OpenAI and HF inference APIs for remote execution, and FastChat (Zheng et al., 2023) and Petals (Borzunov et al., 2023) for local deployments), and supports all standard tasks and evaluations, such as classification, regression, etc. Evaluating a new task/dataset/model can be done in as few as 20 lines.
- Allows the user to create their own data loader, connecting to their local server, ensuring data privacy and security.
- Provides users with the flexibility to design diverse tasks, allowing customization of data input/output formats and evaluation criteria.
- Supports zero- and few-shot learning paradigms with ~300 zero-/few-shot prompts serving as a valuable community resource.
- Enables automatic selection of few-shot examples from a user-defined train/dev set using a maximal marginal relevance-based approach.
- Implements an efficient caching mechanism to prevent repeated API calls, resulting in cost savings and resolution of time-out issues.

[4]`https://github.com/openai/evals`

```
class ModelBase(object):
    @abstractmethod
    def prompt(self, **kwargs):
        ''' Call to model API '''
        pass
    @abstractmethod
    def summarize_response(self, response):
        '''Extract response from model output'''
        pass
```

Listing 1: Abstract class for implementing a new `Model`.

- Offers extensive logging and caching capabilities, allowing iterative model outputs post-processing.
- Provides an auto-download mechanism for public datasets, accelerating experimentation.
- Includes 31 tasks recipes featuring different model providers. Rigorously tested with 53 datasets associated with 12 languages.

Furthermore, LLMeBench is an open-source, user-friendly, and adaptable comprehensive benchmarking framework for LLMs. It empowers both experts and non-experts to assess conventional and unique NLP tasks, enhancing comprehension of the models' capabilities and their applicability across standard and novel tasks.

2 LLMeBench

In Figure 1, we provide the architecture of the LLMeBench framework. To ease the burden on users in implementing common elements across experimental setups, which are not specific to a task, the architecture was designed to support a uniform format for both input and intermediate outputs. This was achieved by employing a pipeline that utilizes key-value dictionaries to seamlessly pass data. The framework incorporates *four* fundamental modules, discussed below. The process starts with a `Dataset`, where each input sample S_i is routed to the `Asset` module. Within this module, a prompt is created and then passed to the `Model Provider` for processing. The model's response is then funneled back to the `Asset` module for post-processing. As the processing of all input samples and the generation of corresponding responses conclude, the `Evaluation` module takes on the task of computing evaluation metrics. The whole process of intercommunication is overseen by a `Benchmark Driver`. Throughout these processes, the inputs, processed data, and the intermediate outputs are cached for re-use and quick experimentation.

```python
class DatasetBase(ABC):
    @abstractmethod
    def metadata(self):
        ''' Returns metadata for the dataset. '''
        pass
    @abstractmethod
    def get_data_sample(self):
        ''' Returns a single dictionary, with
            at least the following keys:
            'input': <input-instance>
            'label': <label> '''
        pass
    @abstractmethod
    def load_data(self, data_path):
        ''' Returns a list of dictionaries, with
            at least the following keys:
            'input': <input-instance>
            'label': <label> '''
        pass
```

Listing 2: Abstract class for implementing a new Dataset.

```python
class TaskBase(ABC):
    @abstractmethod
    def evaluate(self, true_labels,
                 predicted_labels):
        pass
```

Listing 3: Abstract class for implementing a new Evaluation.

2.1 Model Provider module

A Model Provider abstracts away all model-specific communication and aims to set the defaults for maximum reproducibility (for instance assign temperature value to zero by default). The framework currently supports OpenAI's API, the HF Inference API, as well as FastChat and Petals for local deployments. Defining a new LLM model is straightforward by extending the ModelBase class. The initial process entails configuring essential parameters for the model setup, including factors like temperature, top_p, etc. Furthermore, it requires the implementation of two abstract methods (shown in Listing 1): prompt – manages the invocation of the model API based on the input prompt; and summarize_response – extracts a summary of the response from raw model output.

2.2 Dataset module

Similar to a Model provider, a Dataset implementation aims to abstract dataset-specific code, such as loading, pre-processing, and formatting of samples. The framework comes with four generic data loaders, including Hugging Face, CSV, and JSON datasets. A custom dataset can be easily implemented by extending the DatasetBase class. When defining a new dataset, the user is required to implement at least three methods (depicted in Listing 2). The first, metadata, is designed to provide comprehensive metadata such as a citation or reference to the source of the dataset, its download link, and the languages it covers. The second function to be implemented in this module is load_data, which should define a data loader capable of returning a list S comprising the samples from the dataset, given the user-specified dataset path. Lastly, get_data_sample should be defined to return a Python dictionary representing a single sample S_i extracted from the dataset.

```python
def config():
    return {
        'dataset':ExampleDataset,'dataset_args':{},
        'task':ExampleTask,'task_args':{},
        'model':OpenAIModel,'model_args':{},
        'general_args':{}}
def prompt(input_sample):
    ''' Construct and return the prompt following
        the model's corrsponding template'''
def post_process(response):
    ''' Apply custom post-processing on response
        and return extracted model predicition'''
```

Listing 4: Methods to implement in the Asset module.

2.3 Evaluation module

The Evaluation module aims to compute metrics and consolidate the results for a task. The framework comes with built-in support for popular task types such as Classification and Regression and is easily extendible to any custom metric by inheriting from the TaskBase class. A custom implementation can define an evaluate function for a task with specific evaluation code and metrics (see Listing 3). The function is passed two lists: the predicted labels, and true or gold labels. Its primary objective is to yield a user-defined Python dictionary comprising key-value pairs representing the outcomes of the evaluation (e.g., {"Accuracy": accuracy value}).

2.4 Benchmarking Asset module

The Asset module represents a benchmarking experiment, utilizing all the modules defined in LLMeBench as can be seen in code snippet Listing 4. Within this module, the user should provide full configuration for the experiment, which includes specifying the Dataset, Model, and Evaluation modules. The module also enables passing model and dataset parameters.

The Asset module must also implement the prompt function, which constructs the actual prompt to pass to the Model, based on the input sample. For scenarios involving few-shot learning, the Asset module is provided with k examples to use in prompt construction. These examples are chosen by the framework from a training dataset specified by the user, where k is a parameter controlled by the user.

Finally, the post_process function is required to be implemented to post-process response from the model. This step is crucial because the output produced by the Model is tailored to the particular model and the prompt used, leading to potential variations across benchmarking experiments.

2.5 Interaction

Once the aforementioned modules are implemented, running a benchmarking experiment becomes a straightforward task, accomplished through a single command that provides access to various adjustable parameters. The package automatically identifies the Asset to run based on wildcard search using the provided asset name. Additionally, the package determines whether to activate the few-shot setup when the number of shots is specified as a parameter (--n_shots <k>). Furthermore, the package supports swift testing of the benchmarking asset by executing it on a small number of n (--limit <n>) samples, which limits the run to the first n samples from the dataset. An example of the command is provided below.

```
$ python -m llmebench --filter '*AssetName*'
--n_shots k --limit n --ignore_cache
<benchmark-dir> <results-dir>
```

3 Features

LLMeBench features a generic framework that serves a broad range of tasks and models in different learning settings (zero-/few-shot) to evaluate model performance. It enables scalable and rigorous evaluation across diverse tasks and languages while offering simplicity of implementation and flexibility in customization.

3.1 Modularity

The LLMeBench framework, as shown in Figure 1, follows loosely-coupled design principles, effectively separating the data loader, models, and evaluation components. These components interact through a Benchmark Driver, ensuring a modular and flexible architecture.

3.2 Generality

The framework is designed to offer generality, with effortless customization of tasks, data, and models. The framework comes with several generic data loaders such as Hugging Face datasets. Additionally, since users have the ability to create their own data loaders, the framework can support any standard data format. At the time of writing this paper, we have conducted tests with different formats including *TSV*, *CSV*, *JSON*, and *JSONL*.

In terms of tasks, the framework demonstrates the capability to handle a diverse array of token and sequence classification tasks. Figure 2 displays the implemented task types, with built-in support for all standard generic tasks. Additionally, any new custom task can be seamlessly incorporated.

The framework also accommodates various types of models, encompassing both open and closed models, each with its own API-based options. For closed models, users can acquire API keys and endpoints from hosting providers. Meanwhile, open models can be hosted on in-house infrastructure or any accessible hosting service through APIs. We evaluated such an integration using BLOOMZ 176B 8bit version and Jais-13b (32 bit) (Sengupta et al., 2023), hosting it within our in-house infrastructure using Petals (Borzunov et al., 2023) and FastChat. Overall, the framework offers a high level of generality and can be readily applied and adapted to a wide range of use cases and research scenarios.

3.3 Prompts

LLMeBench is designed to support both zero- and few-shot learning setups. The instructions in prompts can be written in any language of interest.

Zero-shot prompts provide natural language instructions describing the task and expected output.

Few-shot prompts embed a small number of examples to the natural language instructions for the particular task. The framework utilizes user-defined, task-specific training set to automatically select few-shot examples. Various strategies exist for examples selection. Among these, we have implemented maximal marginal relevance-based (MMR) (Carbonell and Goldstein, 1998) selection, which has demonstrated success in previous work by Ye et al. (2023). The approach computes the similarity between a test example and the example pool (e.g., training dataset) and selects

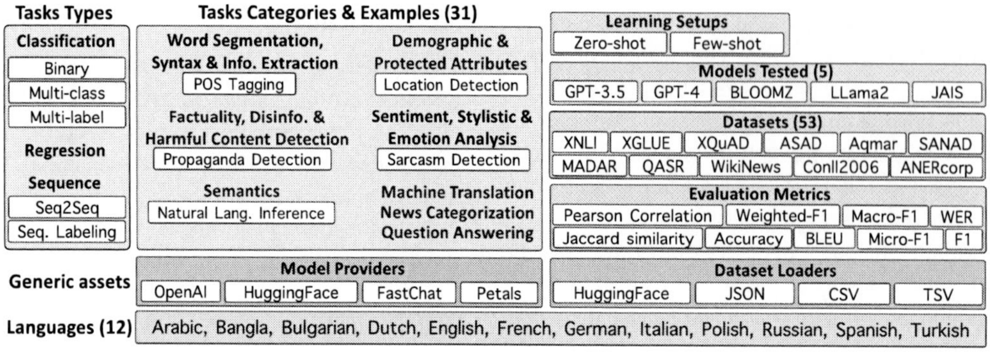

Figure 2: Summary and examples of the 53 datasets, 31 tasks, 4 model providers, 5 tested models and metrics currently implemented and validated in LLMeBench.

k examples (shots) that are both relevant and diverse. We apply the MMR technique on top of embeddings obtained from the multilingual sentence-transformers (Reimers and Gurevych, 2019). However, users also have the flexibility to utilize any custom embedding model.

We have designed a highly efficient process to extract embeddings and compute few-shot examples for each test sample. Specifically, it pre-selects few-shot examples for each test sample during the initial loading stage. This design effectively eliminates the need to apply and compute the MMR score when making API calls, thus enhancing the system's overall efficiency.

The LLMeBench framework includes $\sim$300 designed prompts for zero-shot and few-shot setups that have been validated across a variety of NLP tasks and datasets (see Section 4). This collection serves as a strong starting point for the community and expedite prompt engineering research.

3.4 Caching

One of the significant challenges when accessing APIs is managing timeout issues. The necessity to rerun experiments involving API calls not only requires additional effort but also increases costs. To address this problem, we have developed a caching mechanism, allowing users to bypass making API calls for samples that have already been successfully processed. Specifically, we save all intermediate outputs when processing a data sample, including the generated prompt, the raw model response and the post-processed output. On a re-run, samples that have model responses in the cache do not actually access the API, but rather load the cached response. Furthermore, this caching mechanism plays a vital role in enhancing the post-processing of the models' output, as it can be performed repeatedly without having to call the API. This feature is important, given that different models yield various types of outputs, requiring improved post-processing to align the output accurately with the reference label. To further counter expected timeout and rate limitation issues with APIs, the framework also applies a user-configurable *wait-and-retry* mechanism. This mechanism retries API calls in case of failure, maximizing the chance of receiving a successful response.

3.5 Dataset Auto-Download

The framework comes with support for automatic downloading and caching of publicly available datasets, taking care of extracting and linking them correctly for any `Asset` that requires it. This allows a new user to quickly begin experimenting with and evaluating an existing dataset without the need to manually acquire it first.

3.6 Task Diversity

The framework currently supports and includes a diverse set of tasks, covering a broad spectrum that ranges from word-level tasks to those involving single sentences, sentence pairs, question-answer pairs, and more. The range of tasks covers various NLP research tracks, as can be seen in Figure 2.

3.7 Language-agnostic Framework

The LLMeBench framework is language-agnostic. As of now, tasks for 12 languages have been incorporated, a number that will continuously grow as a result of our ongoing efforts and, ideally, with the support of the community.

3.8 Open-source Framework

We made *LLMeBench* accessible to the community by releasing it as open-source. This will also enable the continued growth and development of the framework within the community.

3.9 Deploying Local Model

For deploying local models, we interface LLMeBench with FastChat framework (Zheng et al., 2023). The latter is an open-source project [5] for serving LLMs with a fast-growing user community. Custom chat templates of popular and new LLMs are rapidly added to the framework. This allows a proper use of instruct-tuned LLMs in inference mode, unlike other popular benchmarking frameworks such Eval-Harness (Gao et al., 2021), which do not use chat templates. This can lead to a mismatch in the expected inputs of instruction tuned models, and put at disadvantage several LLMs, especially the ones with small sizes. Our approach for local deployment solves this issue by relying on FastChat. Huggingface models can be easily deployed in three steps after installing FastChat python package: 1) Running a model controller which plays a role of interfacing between API and model calls. 2) Running a model worker for each loaded model which manages the model in GPU and executes the prompts and returns to responses to the model worker. It is possible to load model worker with vLLM [6] enabling prompt batching for an efficient and fast inference (Kwon et al., 2023). 3) Running an API server which provides a compatible interface with to OpenAI API. The local address and port of the API are set in LLMeBench via `FASTCHAT_*` environment variables.

4 Evaluation of LLMeBench

The framework has already been used across a variety of Arabic NLP tasks and datasets (Abdelali et al., 2024). This involved extensive experimentation using zero- and few-shot learning with state-of-the-art large language models, including GPT-3.5-Turbo, GPT-4, and the 8-bit version of the BLOOMZ 176B model. In Figure 2, we provide a summary of the tasks, datasets, and models that have been implemented and evaluated. Given that our assessment of the framework was based on the current state-of-the-art NLP tasks and datasets, we implemented task- and dataset-specific metrics reported in the literature. Overall, it has been used to evaluate 31 NLP tasks, which were categorized based on ACL tracks, 53 datasets, and different model providers within 2 learning setups. All the task recipes are available within the framework.

5 Related Work

Efforts to assess the performance of LLMs on standard NLP tasks have been underway since the launch of ChatGPT. Notable studies, such as those by Bubeck et al. (2023), Bang et al. (2023), Ahuja et al. (2023), and Hendy et al. (2023), have conducted large-scale experiments considering multilinguality, multimodality, low-resource languages, and a wide range of datasets and tasks.

Such large-scale evaluations require off-the-shelf and easy-to-use solutions to measure the performances of LLMs for a variety of NLP-related tasks. To evaluate OpenAI's models, the company developed the EVALs[7] package, which requires the dataset to be prepared in JSON format using a predefined template. Asai et al. (2023) developed an evaluation framework as a part of their cross-lingual benchmarking effort. This comprehensive framework includes 15 distinct tasks set in a few-shot learning environment across 54 languages. However, this evaluation framework was not publicly available at the time of writing this paper. OpenICL (Wu et al., 2023) is another framework designed specifically for zero-shot or few-shot learning setups. It incorporates various strategies, such as random selection, heuristic methods (including BM25 (Robertson et al., 2009), TopK (Liu et al., 2022), and VoteK (Hongjin et al., 2022)), and a model-based approach, to select few-shot examples. The OpenICL framework is implemented under the assumption that users will utilize HF datasets to load and evaluate models. A prompt is an important part that serves as a bridge between humans and LLMs. To explore the research in this direction Zhu et al. (2023) developed the PromptBench framework for prompt engineering. Eleuther-AI developed LM evaluation Harness (Gao et al., 2021), which includes the implementation of 200 tasks and supports multiple models from the HF hub.

Compared to the aforementioned frameworks (summarized in Table 1), the LLMeBench framework offers customization through custom dataset

[5] https://github.com/lm-sys/FastChat

[6] https://github.com/vllm-project/vllm/

[7] https://github.com/openai/evals

Eval Package	Customization Dataset	Task	Models	ICL (shot) Zero	Few
OpenAI evals[8]	Fixed	✓	Any	✓	✓
LM Harness (Gao et al., 2021)	HF	✓	HF	✓	✓
OpenICL (Wu et al., 2023)	HF	✓	HF, OpenAI	✓	✓
LLMeBench (Ours)	Custom	✓	Any	✓	✓

Table 1: LLMs evaluation frameworks. HF: Hugging Face

loaders, tasks, and models. It also supports both zero- and few-shot prompting. The caching mechanism provided by the LLMeBench framework is a rarity among its counterparts, yet it is crucial for time and cost savings, as well as facilitating efficient post-processing enhancements to model outputs without additional expenses.

6 Conclusions and Future Work

In this paper, we introduce LLMeBench, an open-source framework designed to facilitate the LLM benchmarking process. LLMeBench accelerates evaluation of LLMs using pre-implemented generic datasets, tasks and model providers. In addition, it features a modular design that empowers users to integrate *(i)* new tasks, *(ii)* datasets, and *(iii)* APIs for models. The framework incorporates caching mechanisms that effectively reduce time, costs, and effort associated with task evaluations. Currently, it includes predefined recipes covering 31 standard NLP tasks such as classification, translation, question-answering, and semantic parsing. These recipes can be readily extended to encompass novel NLP tasks, datasets, and LLM models.

In future, we aim to further enhance the framework by integrating a broader array of tasks and languages. By embracing an open-source approach and encouraging active community participation, we anticipate its sustained growth through the incorporation of diverse tasks, enriched datasets, and innovative models. Additional enhancements under consideration encompass integrating cross-validation datasets, and incorporating models featuring varied configurations (such as distinct iterations of BLOOM models). Furthermore, we are actively developing more methods for few-shot selections. Currently, our framework assumes seamless model access via APIs. We are committed to enhancing accessibility by enabling users to effortlessly load and utilize both offline and online models for inference purposes.

Limitations

The LLMeBench is currently limited to API calls, whether they are local or remotely hosted. It also operates under the assumption that the entire dataset can fit into memory, which may not be feasible for very large collections. Implementing iterable loading could be a viable solution to this issue, and is a feature that might be considered for future development. Additionally, many datasets come with cross-validation splits, a functionality that the framework does not currently support.

Ethics Statement

Our framework incorporates publicly available datasets and relies on external models. These models may produce non-factual or potentially harmful content. Therefore, we encourage users to be aware of their interaction with the models.

Acknowledgments

The contributions of M. Hasanain were funded by the NPRP grant 14C-0916-210015, which is provided by the Qatar National Research Fund (a member of Qatar Foundation).

References

Ahmed Abdelali, Hamdy Mubarak, Shammur Absar Chowdhury, Maram Hasanain, Basel Mousi, Sabri Boughorbel, Samir Abdaljalil, Yassine El Kheir, Daniel Izham, Fahim Dalvi, Majd Hawasly, Nizi Nazar, Yousseif Elshahawy, Ahmed Ali, Nadir Durrani, Natasa Milic-Frayling, and Firoj Alam. 2024. LAraBench: Benchmarking Arabic AI with Large Language Models. In *Proceedings of the 18th Conference of the European Chapter of the Association for Computational Linguistics: Volume 1, Long Papers*, Malta. Association for Computational Linguistics.

Kabir Ahuja, Harshita Diddee, Rishav Hada, Millicent Ochieng, Krithika Ramesh, Prachi Jain, Akshay Nambi, Tanuja Ganu, Sameer Segal, Mohamed Ahmed, Kalika Bali, and Sunayana Sitaram. 2023. MEGA: Multilingual evaluation of generative AI. In *Proceedings of the 2023 Conference on Empirical Methods in Natural Language Processing*, pages 4232–4267, Singapore. Association for Computational Linguistics.

Akari Asai, Sneha Kudugunta, Xinyan Velocity Yu, Terra Blevins, Hila Gonen, Machel Reid, Yulia Tsvetkov, Sebastian Ruder, and Hannaneh Hajishirzi. 2023. BUFFET: Benchmarking large language models for few-shot cross-lingual transfer. *arXiv preprint arXiv:2305.14857*.

Yejin Bang, Samuel Cahyawijaya, Nayeon Lee, Wenliang Dai, Dan Su, Bryan Wilie, Holy Lovenia, Ziwei Ji, Tiezheng Yu, Willy Chung, Quyet V. Do, Yan Xu, and Pascale Fung. 2023. A multitask, multilingual, multimodal evaluation of ChatGPT on reasoning, hallucination, and interactivity. In *Proceedings of the 13th International Joint Conference on Natural Language Processing and the 3rd Conference of the Asia-Pacific Chapter of the Association for Computational Linguistics (Volume 1: Long Papers)*, pages 675—-718, Indonesia. Association for Computational Linguistics.

Alexander Borzunov, Dmitry Baranchuk, Tim Dettmers, Maksim Riabinin, Younes Belkada, Artem Chumachenko, Pavel Samygin, and Colin Raffel. 2023. Petals: Collaborative inference and fine-tuning of large models. In *Proceedings of the 61st Annual Meeting of the Association for Computational Linguistics (Volume 3: System Demonstrations)*, pages 558–568, Toronto, Canada. Association for Computational Linguistics.

Sébastien Bubeck, Varun Chandrasekaran, Ronen Eldan, Johannes Gehrke, Eric Horvitz, Ece Kamar, Peter Lee, Yin Tat Lee, Yuanzhi Li, Scott Lundberg, Harsha Nori, Hamid Palangi, Marco Tulio Ribeiro, and Yi Zhang. 2023. Sparks of artificial general intelligence: Early experiments with GPT-4. Technical report, Microsoft Research.

Jaime Carbonell and Jade Goldstein. 1998. The use of mmr, diversity-based reranking for reordering documents and producing summaries. In *Proceedings of the 21st annual international ACM SIGIR conference on Research and development in information retrieval*, pages 335–336.

Yupeng Chang, Xu Wang, Jindong Wang, Yuan Wu, Kaijie Zhu, Hao Chen, Linyi Yang, Xiaoyuan Yi, Cunxiang Wang, Yidong Wang, et al. 2023. A survey on evaluation of large language models. *arXiv preprint arXiv:2307.03109*.

Qingxiu Dong, Lei Li, Damai Dai, Ce Zheng, Zhiyong Wu, Baobao Chang, Xu Sun, Jingjing Xu, Lei Li, and Zhifang Sui. 2023. A survey on in-context learning. *arXiv preprint arXiv:2301.00234*.

Leo Gao, Jonathan Tow, Stella Biderman, Sid Black, Anthony DiPofi, Charles Foster, Laurence Golding, Jeffrey Hsu, Kyle McDonell, Niklas Muennighoff, Jason Phang, Laria Reynolds, Eric Tang, Anish Thite, Ben Wang, Kevin Wang, and Andy Zou. 2021. A framework for few-shot language model evaluation. *Zenodo*.

Amr Hendy, Mohamed Abdelrehim, Amr Sharaf, Vikas Raunak, Mohamed Gabr, Hitokazu Matsushita, Young Jin Kim, Mohamed Afify, and Hany Hassan Awadalla. 2023. How good are GPT models at machine translation? a comprehensive evaluation. *arXiv preprint arXiv:2302.09210*.

SU Hongjin, Jungo Kasai, Chen Henry Wu, Weijia Shi, Tianlu Wang, Jiayi Xin, Rui Zhang, Mari Ostendorf, Luke Zettlemoyer, Noah A Smith, et al. 2022. Selective annotation makes language models better few-shot learners. In *The Eleventh International Conference on Learning Representations*.

Md Tawkat Islam Khondaker, Abdul Waheed, El Moatez Billah Nagoudi, and Muhammad Abdul-Mageed. 2023. GPTAraEval: A comprehensive evaluation of ChatGPT on Arabic NLP. In *Proceedings of the 2023 Conference on Empirical Methods in Natural Language Processing*, pages 220–247, Singapore. Association for Computational Linguistics.

Woosuk Kwon, Zhuohan Li, Siyuan Zhuang, Ying Sheng, Lianmin Zheng, Cody Hao Yu, Joseph E. Gonzalez, Hao Zhang, and Ion Stoica. 2023. Efficient memory management for large language model serving with pagedattention. In *Proceedings of the ACM SIGOPS 29th Symposium on Operating Systems Principles*.

Percy Liang, Rishi Bommasani, Tony Lee, Dimitris Tsipras, Dilara Soylu, Michihiro Yasunaga, Yian Zhang, Deepak Narayanan, Yuhuai Wu, Ananya Kumar, et al. 2022. Holistic evaluation of language models. *arXiv preprint arXiv:2211.09110*.

Jiachang Liu, Dinghan Shen, Yizhe Zhang, William B Dolan, Lawrence Carin, and Weizhu Chen. 2022. What makes good in-context examples for gpt-3? In *Proceedings of Deep Learning Inside Out (DeeLIO 2022): The 3rd Workshop on Knowledge Extraction and Integration for Deep Learning Architectures*, pages 100–114.

OpenAI. 2023. GPT-4 technical report. Technical report, OpenAI.

Alec Radford, Jeffrey Wu, Rewon Child, David Luan, Dario Amodei, Ilya Sutskever, et al. 2019. Language models are unsupervised multitask learners. *OpenAI blog*, 1(8):9.

Nils Reimers and Iryna Gurevych. 2019. Sentence-bert: Sentence embeddings using siamese bert-networks. In *Proceedings of the 2019 Conference on Empirical Methods in Natural Language Processing and the 9th International Joint Conference on Natural Language Processing (EMNLP-IJCNLP)*, pages 3982–3992.

Stephen Robertson, Hugo Zaragoza, et al. 2009. The probabilistic relevance framework: Bm25 and beyond. *Foundations and Trends® in Information Retrieval*, 3(4):333–389.

Teven Le Scao, Angela Fan, Christopher Akiki, Ellie Pavlick, Suzana Ilić, Daniel Hesslow, Roman Castagné, Alexandra Sasha Luccioni, François Yvon, Matthias Gallé, et al. 2022. BLOOM: A 176b-parameter open-access multilingual language model. *arXiv preprint arXiv:2211.05100*.

Neha Sengupta, Sunil Kumar Sahu, Bokang Jia, Satheesh Katipomu, Haonan Li, Fajri Koto, Osama Mohammed Afzal, Samta Kamboj, Onkar Pandit, Rahul Pal, et al. 2023. Jais and jais-chat:

Arabic-centric foundation and instruction-tuned open generative large language models. *arXiv preprint arXiv:2308.16149*.

Aarohi Srivastava, Abhinav Rastogi, Abhishek Rao, Abu Awal Md Shoeb, Abubakar Abid, Adam Fisch, Adam R Brown, Adam Santoro, Aditya Gupta, Adrià Garriga-Alonso, et al. 2023. Beyond the imitation game: Quantifying and extrapolating the capabilities of language models. *Transactions on Machine Learning Research*.

Jason Wei, Xuezhi Wang, Dale Schuurmans, Maarten Bosma, Fei Xia, Ed H Chi, Quoc V Le, Denny Zhou, et al. 2022. Chain-of-thought prompting elicits reasoning in large language models. In *Advances in Neural Information Processing Systems*.

Zhenyu Wu, Yaoxiang Wang, Jiacheng Ye, Zhiyong Wu, Jiangtao Feng, Jingjing Xu, and Yu Qiao. 2023. OpenICL: An open-source framework for in-context learning. In *Proceedings of the 61st Annual Meeting of the Association for Computational Linguistics (Volume 3: System Demonstrations)*, pages 489–498, Toronto, Canada. Association for Computational Linguistics.

Xi Ye, Srinivasan Iyer, Asli Celikyilmaz, Veselin Stoyanov, Greg Durrett, and Ramakanth Pasunuru. 2023. Complementary explanations for effective in-context learning. In *Findings of the Association for Computational Linguistics: ACL 2023*, pages 4469–4484, Toronto, Canada. Association for Computational Linguistics.

Wayne Xin Zhao, Kun Zhou, Junyi Li, Tianyi Tang, Xiaolei Wang, Yupeng Hou, Yingqian Min, Beichen Zhang, Junjie Zhang, Zican Dong, et al. 2023. A survey of large language models. *arXiv preprint arXiv:2303.18223*.

Lianmin Zheng, Wei-Lin Chiang, Ying Sheng, Siyuan Zhuang, Zhanghao Wu, Yonghao Zhuang, Zi Lin, Zhuohan Li, Dacheng Li, Eric Xing, et al. 2023. Judging llm-as-a-judge with mt-bench and chatbot arena. *arXiv preprint arXiv:2306.05685*.

Kaijie Zhu, Jindong Wang, Jiaheng Zhou, Zichen Wang, Hao Chen, Yidong Wang, Linyi Yang, Wei Ye, Neil Zhenqiang Gong, Yue Zhang, et al. 2023. PromptBench: Towards evaluating the robustness of large language models on adversarial prompts. *arXiv preprint arXiv:2306.04528*.

Sig-Networks Toolkit: Signature Networks for Longitudinal Language Modelling

Talia Tseriotou[1*], Ryan Sze-Yin Chan[2*], Adam Tsakalidis[1,2], Iman Munire Bilal[3], Elena Kochkina[1‡], Terry Lyons[2,4], Maria Liakata[1,2,3]
[1]Queen Mary University of London, [2]The Alan Turing Institute,
[3]University of Warwick, [4]University of Oxford
`t.tseriotou@qmul.ac.uk; rchan@turing.ac.uk`

Abstract

We present an open-source, pip installable toolkit, **Sig-Networks**, the first of its kind for longitudinal language modelling. A central focus is the incorporation of Signature-based Neural Network models, which have recently shown success in temporal tasks. We apply and extend published research providing a full suite of signature-based models. Their components can be used as PyTorch building blocks in future architectures. Sig-Networks enables task-agnostic dataset plug-in, seamless pre-processing for sequential data, parameter flexibility, automated tuning across a range of models. We examine signature networks under three different NLP tasks of varying temporal granularity: counselling conversations, rumour stance switch and mood changes in social media threads, showing SOTA performance in all three, and provide guidance for future tasks. We release the Toolkit as a PyTorch package[1] with an introductory video [2], Git repositories for preprocessing[3] and modelling[4] including sample notebooks on the modeled NLP tasks.

1 Introduction

Existing work on temporal and longitudinal modelling has largely focused on models that are task-oriented, including tracking mood changes in users' linguistic content (Tsakalidis et al., 2022b,a), temporal clinical document classification (Ng et al., 2023), suicidal ideation detection on social media (Cao et al., 2019; Sawhney et al., 2021), real-time rumour detection (Liu et al., 2015; Kochkina et al., 2023). Transformer-based models struggle to outperform more traditional RNNs in such tasks, highlighting their limitations in temporal settings (Mullenbach et al., 2018; Yuan et al., 2022). Inspired by the success of models with short- and long-term processing capabilities (Didolkar et al., 2022; Tseriotou et al., 2023) in producing compressed temporal representations, we develop a toolkit that applies Signature Network models (Tseriotou et al., 2023) to various longitudinal tasks. Path signatures are capable of efficient and compressed encoding of sequential data, sequential pooling in neural models, enhancement of short-term dependencies in linguistic timelines and encoding agnostic to task and time irregularities.

We make the following contributions:

- We release an open-source pip installable toolkit for longitudinal NLP tasks, **Sig-Networks**, including examples on several tasks to facilitate usability and reproducibility.
- For data preprocessing for the Signature Networks models (Tseriotou et al., 2023), we introduce another pip installable library `nlpsig` which receives as input streams of textual data and returns streams of embeddings which can be fed into the models we discuss in this paper.
- We showcase SOTA performance on three longitudinal tasks with different levels of temporal granularity, including a new task and dataset – longitudinal rumour stance, based on rumour stance classification (Zubiaga et al., 2016; Kochkina et al., 2018). We highlight best practices for adaptation to new tasks.
- Our toolkit allows for flexible adaptation to new datasets, preprocessing steps, hyperparameter choices, external feature selection and benchmarking across several baselines. We provide the option of flexible building blocks such as Signature Window Network Units (Tseriotou et al., 2023) and their extensions, which can be used as a layer integrated in a new PyTorch model or as a stand-alone model for sequential NLP tasks. We share NLP-based examples via notebooks, where users can easily plug in their own datasets.

* Indicates equal contribution.
‡Work done while at Queen Mary University of London.
[1]`https://pypi.org/project/sig-networks/`
[2]`http://youtu.be/lrjkdfYf8Lo`
[3]`https://github.com/datasig-ac-uk/nlpsig/`
[4]`https://github.com/ttseriotou/sig-networks/`

Proceedings of the 18th Conference of the European Chapter of the Association for Computational Linguistics System Demonstrations, pages 223–237

2 Related Work

Longitudinal NLP modelling has been sporadically explored in tasks like semantic change detection (Bamler and Mandt, 2017; Yao et al., 2018; Tsakalidis and Liakata, 2020; Montariol et al., 2021; Rosin and Radinsky, 2022) or dynamic topic modelling (He et al., 2014; Gou et al., 2018; Dieng et al., 2019; Grootendorst, 2022). Such approaches have limited generalisability as they track the evolution of specific topics over long-periods of time. Social media data have given rise to longitudinal tasks such as mental health monitoring (Sawhney et al., 2021; Tsakalidis et al., 2022a), stance detection and rumour verification (Kochkina et al., 2018; Chen et al., 2018; Kumar and Carley, 2019) requiring more fine-grained temporal modelling . Other tasks, like healthcare patient notes (Ng et al., 2023) and dialogue act classification (Liu et al., 2017; He et al., 2021) are also longitudinal in nature.

Path Signature (Chen, 1958; Lyons, 1998) is a collection of iterated integrals studied in the context of solving differential equations driven by irregular signals. It provides a summary of complex un-parameterised data streams through an infinite graded sequence of important statistics. Thus, it produces a collection of statistics efficiently summarising important information about the path. Signatures are deemed invaluable in machine learning (Levin et al., 2013) as sequential feature transformers (Yang et al., 2016; Xie et al., 2017; Yang et al., 2017; Lyons et al., 2014; Perez Arribas et al., 2018; Morrill et al., 2020), or integrated components of neural models (Bonnier et al., 2019; Liao et al., 2021; Tseriotou et al., 2023). However, they have only been sparsely explored within NLP (Wang et al., 2019, 2021; Biyong et al., 2020), addressing only sequentiality or temporality. Motivated by the wide range of longitudinal NLP tasks and the work by Tseriotou et al. (2023) we present a toolkit for neural sequential path signatures models achieving SOTA performance in a range of such tasks.

Libraries for computing path signatures include `roughpy`, `esig`, `iisignature` (Reizenstein and Graham, 2020), `signatory` (Kidger and Lyons, 2021) and `signax` (see links in Appendix E). Currently, only `signatory` and `signax` offer differentiable computations of the signature and log-signature transforms on GPU (with PyTorch (Paszke et al., 2019) and JAX (Bradbury et al., 2018), respectively).

While the above libraries only perform signature computations, with `signatory` additionally allowing for data stream augmentation through convolutional neural networks, the Sig-Networks library provides users with a complete pipeline for the application of signature-based (Signature Network) models in longitudinal NLP tasks. In particular, Sig-Networks is a pip installable PyTorch library using `signatory` for differentiable computations of signature transforms on GPU, providing a range of off-the shelf models for task-agnostic longitudinal modeling. Furthermore, the pip installable `nlpsig` library simplifies the data preprocessing for Signature Network models, by forming streams of embeddings to be directly fed into the models.

3 Methodological Foundations

3.1 Task Formulation and Background

Longitudinal Task Formulation. We use the following terminology throughout the paper:

- *Data Point*: d_i, is a single piece of information at a given time, i.e. a post, tweet or utterance.
- *Data Stream*: $S^{[t_1,t_m]}$, is a series of chronologically ordered data points $\{d_1,\ldots,d_m\}$ at times $\{t_1,\ldots,t_m\}$, i.e. a timeline or a conversation.

For each d_i, we consider its historical data stream. We divide our models in two categories: (a) *window-* and (b) *unit-based*. In (a) we assume a window of $|w|$ most recent historical data points of d_i, H_i=$\{d_{i-(w-1)},\ldots,d_i\}$, as our modeling sequence. In (b), we follow Tseriotou et al. (2023) to construct n history windows, each of length $|w|$, shifted by k points.[5] The modeling sequence is given by $H_i = \{h_{i_1}, ...,h_{i_{n-1}}, h_{i_n}\}$ with the qth unit (of w posts) defined as h_{i_q}= $\{p_{i-(n-q)k-(w-1)}, p_{i-(n-q)k-(w-2)}, \ldots, p_{i-(n-q)k}\}$.

Path Signatures Preliminaries. In our formulation, the textual data stream is the equivalent of the path P over an interval $[t_1, t_m]$ and the signature $S(P)$ is a pooling layer providing a transformed representation for these sequential data. The signature is a collection of all r iterated integrals along dimensions c: $S(P)_{t_1,t_m} = (1, S(P)^1_{t_1,t_m}, ..., S(P)^c_{t_1,t_m}, S(P)^{1,1}_{t_1,t_m}, S(P)^{1,2}_{t_1,t_m},$

[5]The total number of modeled data points is $k * n + (w - k)$.

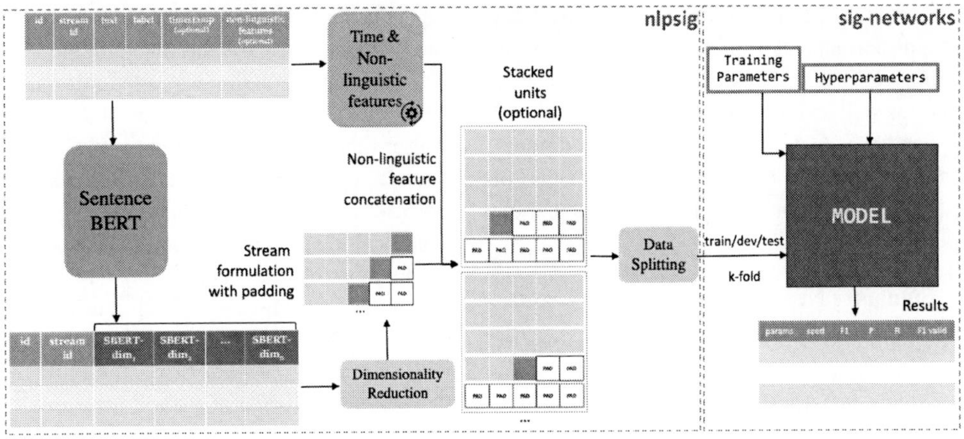

Figure 1: Sig-Networks Tooklit Overview. `nlpsig` library (left side) obtains the input text, label and stream id per data point. The package allows for embedding extraction (i.e. SBERT) and its dimensionality reduction, with optional non-linguistic-feature processing and concatenation. For each data point a stream/window (padded if necessary) is formed including its ordered history. These are shifted and stacked for unit-based models. Data splitting with k-fold option is performed. `sig-networks` library (right side) enables PyTorch implementation for all Sig-Networks family and baseline models with user-specified training and hyper parameter inputs.

... , $S(P)^{c,c}_{t_1,t_m}$, ..., $S(P)^{i_1,i_2,\cdots,i_r}_{t_1,t_m}$, ...). Since the iterated integrals can go up to infinite dimensions, a degree of truncation N (i.e. up to N-folded integrals) is commonly used. A higher N leads to a larger feature space. *Log*-signatures' output feature space increases less rapidly with input dimensions c, and depth N, allowing a more compressed representation. Sig-Networks allows for the selection of the desired N and the implementation of signatures or log-signatures. We use N=3 and log-signatures which achieved the best performance.

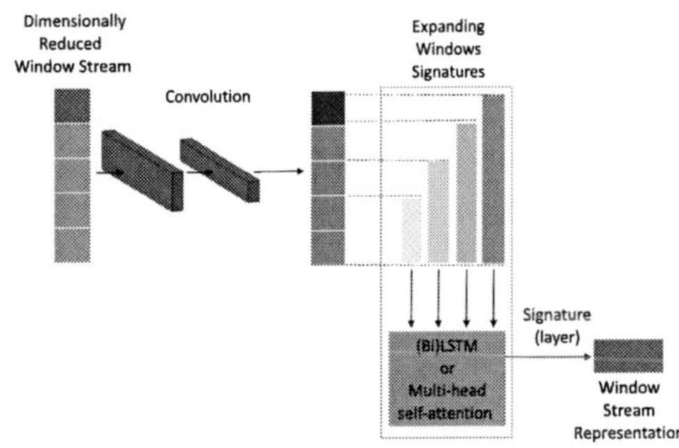

Figure 2: Signature Window Unit and its variations.

3.2 System Overview

Fig. 1 shows the overview of our Sig-Networks toolkit. The system receives a task-agnostic dataset of linguistic data streams. These can optionally include a set of pre-computed linguistic embeddings for each data point (e.g. post), timestamps and non-linguistic external features. Linguistic embeddings can also be computed by the system and then dimensionally reduced using a selected method (§3.3). Timestamps can be processed to produce and normalise time-related features. The data points are then chronologically ordered and padded based on either a *window*- or a *unit-basis*. Data splitting for model training is performed by the relevant module (§4.1), providing a range of options (including k-fold, stratification, user-defined splits). A range of baseline and Signature Network models are available for training (§3.4,4.2,4.3) through user defined parameters, integrating hyperparameter tuning functions for task-based optimal parameter selection.

3.3 Feature Encoding

Each data point is encoded in a high-dimensional space using SentenceBERT (SBERT) (Reimers and Gurevych, 2019) to derive semantically meaningful embeddings. Our toolkit provides different sentence encoding options (§4.1) [6] and multiple options for dimensionality reduction (§4.1). We found UMAP to perform slightly better. Sig-Networks also caters for time-related and external feature incorporation. On the time-related feature front, the

[6]We recommend 384-dim embeddings to facilitate dimensionality reduction required for input to signature transforms.

toolkit provides a range of timestamp-derived features and normalisation methods, which account for temporality in the task according to its characteristics as well as for improved performance (§4.1 & Appendix C). External information and domain-specific features can be either included as part of the stream feature space, c, or concatenated at the output of the model.

3.4 Signature Network Models

The Signature Network model family forms an extension of the work by Tseriotou et al. (2023) on combining signatures with neural networks for longitudinal language modeling. We present a range of models (§5.2) based on the foundational Signature Window Network Unit (SWNU), which models the granular linguistic progression in a stream: it reduces a short input stream via a conv-1d layer operation, applies an LSTM on signatures on locally expanding windows of the stream and produces a stream representation via a signature pooling layer.

SWNU implementation is flexible, allowing selection between LSTM *vs* BiLSTM, convolution-1d layer *vs* convolution neural network (CNN), and the option to stack multiple such units to form a deeper network. Importantly, we also introduce a variant of SWNU ('SW-Attn'), replacing LSTM with a Multi-head self-attention with an add & norm operation and a linear layer (Fig. 2).

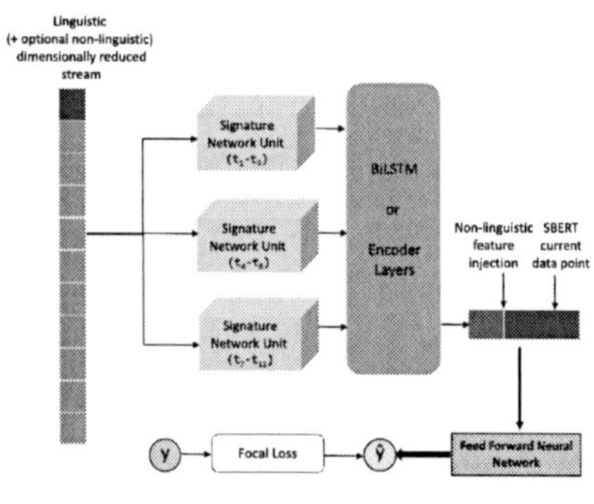

Figure 3: Seq-Sig-Net and its variations using SWNU (yellow, see Fig. 2) on a sample length of 11 points.

Furthermore, the toolkit allows for the flexible use of Seq-Sig-Net (the best performing model by Tseriotou et al. (2023)), which sequentially models SWNU units through a BiLSTM, preserving the local sequential information and capturing long-term dependencies. Further available variants of Seq-Sig-Net include SW-Attn+BiLSTM (replacing SWNU with a SW-Attn unit) and SW-Attn+Encoder (replacing BiLSTM with stacked Encoder layers on top of learnable unit embeddings). The final representation is pooled through a trainable [CLS] token. The number of stacked layers is user defined (see Fig. 3). For all Sig-Network models, we follow the same formulation as Tseriotou et al. (2023), by concatenating the SBERT vectors of the current data point with the learnable stream representation and passing it through a feed-forward network for classification using focal loss (Lin et al., 2017). The system provides flexibility with respect to the number of hidden layers and the optional addition of external features. It also provides separate classes for the signature units so they can be incorporated in new architectures.

4 System Components

As shown in Fig. 1, the toolkit is split up into two pip installable Python libraries. a) **`nlpsig`**: SBERT vector extraction, data pre-processing including dimensionality reduction of SBERT streams and construction of model inputs and b) **`sig-networks`**: PyTorch implementations of our models and functions for model training/evaluation.

4.1 Data Preparation Modules in `nlpsig`

These modules perform data loading and preprocessing. The users can load their temporally sorted dataset, with a minimum of a *stream-id* (identifying the stream that a data point belongs to), *text* and *label* columns. `nlpsig` allows for loading pre-computed embeddings for the data points or calculating them using any pretrained or custom model from the `sentence-transformer` and `transformer` libraries via the `nlpsig.encode_text` modules.[7]

Utilising signatures typically requires dimensionality reduction of the data point embeddings (§3.3). `nlpsig` provides several options via the `nlpsig.DimReduce`[8] class: UMAP (McInnes et al., 2018), Gaussian Random Projections (Bingham and Mannila, 2001; Achlioptas, 2003), PPA-PCA (Mu and Viswanath, 2018), PPA-PCA-PPA (Raunak et al., 2019). The `nlpsig.PrepareData`[9] class is used to process the data and obtain streams of dimension-reduced embeddings as input to the Signature Network family of models (see §3.4).

[7] encode_text
[8] dimensionality_reduction
[9] data_preparation

If the dataset includes timestamps, we automatically compute several time-derived variables with different standardisation options. These variables include but are not limited to chronologically ordered stream indices, time difference between consecutive data points and date as fraction of the year. External non-linguistic features can also be included in the dataset and model. The toolkit provides the flexibility of including these features as part of the path stream and/or concatenated in the output with the SBERT representation of the current data point (see Appendix C). There are wrapper functions in the `sig-networks` package (`sig_networks.obtain_SWNU_input`, `sig_networks.obtain_SeqSigNet_input`) to easily obtain the padded input for each model. Since the `nlpsig` library allows for more flexibility in constructing streams of embeddings, customisation of these wrapper functions is encouraged for different datasets or tasks.

4.2 Training

Through `nlpsig.classification_utils`, the toolkit allows for k-fold cross validation or a single train/test split.[10] Splits can be completely random, stratified (for streams via `split_ids`), or predefined (via `split_indices`). If a subset of the dataset is leveraged for classification (e.g. single-speaker classification in dialogue), the user can define such indices in `path_indices`. For training, the user can select the loss function (cross-entropy, focal loss), a validation metric and specify the early stopping patience. Off the shelf hyperparameter tuning functions are available via grid search.

4.3 Model Modules

Model modules allow for the flexible training of each model. PyTorch classes for the building blocks of our models are provided separately to encourage their novel integration in other systems (e.g. see Appendix G). The toolkit can be used to benchmark datasets using: BERT, feedforward network with(out) historical stream information and BiLSTM. For Sig-Network family models, we provide options for choosing: 1. N, truncation degree, 2. signatures or log-signatures, 3. pooling options in the units, 4. LSTM or BiLSTM in SWNU, 5. dimensionality reduction of Conv-1d or CNN and their dimensions in the unit, 6. combination method of historical signature modelled stream with current SBERT data point and external features, 7. number of encoder layers, 8. path chronological reversion. Importantly, the user can assess their task of interest and define the window size w, number of units n, and shift k (§6.1). After model tuning one can access the trained model object, a set of results for all seeds and hyperparameters, and a set of results for the best hyperparameters.

[10]classification_utils

5 Experiments

5.1 Tasks and Datasets

We demonstrate the applicability of Sig-Networks across three longitudinal sequential classification tasks of different temporal granularity. For all tasks we consider the current data point, its timestamp and its historical stream.

Moments of Change (MoC). Given sequences of users' posts, MoC identification involves the assessment of a user's self-disclosed mood conveyed in each post with respect to the user's recent history as one of 3 classes: *Switches* (IS): sudden mood shift from positive to negative, or vice versa; *Escalations* (IE): gradual mood progression from neutral/positive to more positive, or from neutral/negative to more negative; or *None* (O): no change in mood (Tsakalidis et al., 2022b). The dataset is ***TalkLife MoC***: 18,702 posts (500 user timelines; 1-124 posts each). Annotation was performed on the post-level with access to the entire timeline.

Counselling Dialogue Classification. Given the data stream of utterances during a counselling dialogue between a therapist and a client, the task is to categorise client's utterances into one of 3 classes: *Change*: client seems convinced towards positive behaviour change; *Sustain*: client shows resistance to change; *Neutral*: client shows neither leaning nor resistance towards change. We utilise therapist and client utterances in the stream, while classifying only client utterances. The dataset is ***Anno-MI*** (Wu et al., 2022): 133 motivational interviews (MI), 9,699 utterances (4,817 client utterances), sourced from effective and ineffective MI videos on YouTube & Vimeo. The videos were professionally transcribed and annotated by MI practitioners.

Stance Switch Detection. The Stance Switch Detection task tracks the ratio of support/opposition towards the topic of a conversation at each point in time and captures switches in overall stance. This is a binary classification of each post in a conversation stream into: *Switch*: switch between the total number of oppositions (querying or denying) and supports or vice versa; or *No Switch*: either the absence of a switch or cases where the numbers of supporting and opposing posts are equal. For this task we introduce a new dataset, ***Longitudinal Rumour Stance (LRS)***, a longitudinal version of the RumourEval-2017 dataset (Gorrell et al., 2019). It consists of Twitter conversations around newsworthy events. The source tweet of the conversation conveys a rumourous claim, discussed by tweets in the stream. In 325 conversations 5,568 posts are labelled based on their stance towards the claim in the corresponding source tweet as either *Supporting*, *Denying*, *Questioning* or *Commenting*. We convert conversation structure and labels into a Longitudinal Stance Switch Detection task. Conversations are converted from tree-structured into linear timelines to obtain chronologically ordered lists. Then we convert the original stance labels into *Switch* and *No Switch* categories based on the numbers of supporting tweets versus denying and questioning ones at each point in time.

5.2 Models and Baselines

Using our toolkit, we perform 5-fold cross-validation, repeatedly with 3 seeds (see Appendix A for full details) and compare against the following baselines:

BERT(focal/ce): data point-level (stream-agnostic) BERT (Devlin et al., 2018) fine-tuned using the alpha-weighted focal loss (Lin et al., 2017) or cross-entropy, respectively.
FFN: data point-level Feedforward Network (FFN) operating on SBERT of the current point.
FFN History: stream-level FFN operating on the concatenated SBERT vectors of the current point and the average of its historical stream.
BiLSTM with a single layer operating on a specified number of historical data points.

Our Sig-Networks Family Models are:
SWNU (Tseriotou et al., 2023) uses expanding signature windows fed into an LSTM. We modify the unit to use a BiLSTM and improved padding.
SW-Attn: Same as SWNU but with Multi-head attention instead of an LSTM.
Seq-Sig-Net: Sequential Network of SWNU units using a BiLSTM as in Tseriotou et al. (2023).
SW-Attn+BiLSTM: Seq-Sig-Net with SW-Attn unit instead of SWNU.
SW-Attn+Encoder SW-Attn+BiLSTM with two Encoder layers using unit-level learnable embeddings instead of the BiLSTM .

6 Results and Discussion

6.1 Performance comparison

Signature Network models show top performance, with Seq-Sig-Net achieving SOTA or on-par performance with SWNU across all tasks (see Table 1, detailed in Appendix B). On LRS the best model is Seq-Sig-Net with window length w=20 posts (F1=.678), while on Anno-MI the best model is also Seq-Sig-Net but for w=11 (F1=.525). In TalkLife, Seq-Sig-Net and SWNU both reach top performance (F1=.563). The difference of optimal window length across tasks relates to the characteristics of each dataset (see Table 2 and next paragraph). Additionally, the performance of BiLSTM peaks within the same range of history length, different for each task, denoting the best performing models depend on the temporal granularity of the task. Lastly, SW-Attn+Encoder performs better than SW-Attn+BiLSTM regardless of task and history length, further highlighting the importance of sequential modelling for these tasks.

Seq-Sig-Net outperforms all models across tasks in modeling long-term effects, making it particularly appealing for highly longitudinal tasks; SWNU has the best performance when modeling short linguistic streams. In LRS and TalkLife Sig-Networks outperforms all baselines, for each history length. For Anno-MI, the least longitudinal task due to the short mean/median consecutive sequences of Change/Sustain utterances (see Table 2), we conjecture that most of the performance gain in including historical dialogue information is due to adding more context rather than sequential modelling. This is apparent from the small performance gains of Seq-Sig-Net models compared to FFN History and BERT (focal) versus the much starker performance improvement in the other tasks.

6.2 Time-scale analysis

The degree of temporal granularity across datasets ranges from seconds in Anno-MI, minutes in LRS and hours in TalkLife (Table 2), showing the generalisability of Signature-Networks. TalkLife has an average of 1.58/4.12 consecutive Switches/Escalations and a similar average of such events (1.77/4.03 respectively) in each data stream, meaning that the task benefits from good granularity on short modeling windows. This can be provided by

Model	Anno-MI (3-class)			LRS (2-class)			TalkLife (3-class)		
BERT (focal)	.519			.589			.531		
BERT (ce)	.501			.596			.521		
FFN	.512			.581			.534		
FFN History	.520			.625			.537		
BiLSTM ($w = 5$)	.517			.637			.544		
SWNU ($w = 5$)	.522			.670			**.563**		
SW-Attn ($w = 5$)	.515			.667			.556		
History Length	**11**	**20**	**35**	**11**	**20**	**35**	**11**	**20**	**35**
#units (w=5, k=3)	**3**	**6**	**11**	**3**	**6**	**11**	**3**	**6**	**11**
BiLSTM	.518	.507	.510	.657	.648	.648	.539	.533	.525
SWNU	.522	.512	.493	.671	.654	<u>.673</u>	.550	.537	.539
SW-Attn	.517	.508	.508	.659	.665	.661	.547	.541	.539
Seq-Sig-Net	**.525**	<u>.523</u>	.517	.672	**.678**	.654	**.563**	<u>.561</u>	.559
SW-Attn+BiLSTM	.511	.514	.515	.663	.657	.660	.554	.557	.550
SW-Attn+Encoder	.498	.506	.505	.664	.657	.662	.552	.552	.545

Table 1: Results (macro-average F1) of the Sig-Networks toolkit models on our three tasks for different History Lengths. **Best** and <u>second best</u> scores are highlighted.

both SWNU (window of 5 posts) and a short Seq-Sig-Net of 3 units. Anno-MI presents even shorter sequences of consecutive Change/Sustain intentions (2.21/1.68), but the average number of such events in each conversation is higher (8.86/4.05), therefore benefiting from being less sequential in terms of short-term dependencies but being more sequence dependent on series of windows. Finally, LRS is the most longitudinal task in our experiments showing the highest mean number of consecutive switches (8.52), therefore benefiting from more units in Seq-Sig-Net.

Dataset	Anno-MI		Longitudinal Rumour Stance	TalkLife MoC	
	Change	**Sustain**	**Switch**	**Switch**	**Escalation**
Mean Point Time Diff.	5sec		1hr 26min 40sec	6hr 51min 11sec	
Median Point Time Diff.	3sec		1min 39sec	59min 38sec	
Mean consecutive events	2.21	1.68	8.52	1.58	4.12
Median consecutive events	1	1	4	1	3
Mean no. of events in stream	8.86	4.05	6.45	1.77	4.03
Median no. of events in stream	5	3	0	1	1

Table 2: Dataset Statistics on time and event length.

7 Conclusion

We present the Sig-Networks toolkit, which allows for flexible modeling of longitudinal NLP classification tasks using Signature-based Network models (Tseriotou et al., 2023), proposing improvements and variants. We test our system on three NLP classification tasks of different domains and temporal granularity and show SOTA performance against competitive baselines, while also shedding light into temporal characteristics which affect optimal model selection. The toolkit is made available as a PyTorch package with examples, making it easy to plug-in new datasets for future model extensions.

In the future we are planning to provide further flexibility in the toolkit, by enabling the integration of signature libraries beyond `signatory` for signature computations. This will facilitate its extension to deep learning frameworks beyond PyTorch. Additionally, we would like to allow for the selection of a non-linguistic feature subset to serve as part of the stream and of a different subset to be concatenated with the SBERT representation, rather than having a single processing option for the full set of such features. We also aim to enrich the examples corpus of our repository with additional longitudinal NLP tasks and collaborate with independent contributors on the integration of newly developed signature-based models.

Limitations

While the Sig-Networks library provides sequential models with very competitive performance on longitudinal NLP tasks, it comes with limitations. Firstly, it requires basic knowledge of Python, since it is available as a PyTorch library, and assumes integration in PyTorch systems. In the future, Additionally, its use on classification tasks requires labeled data, which can be expensive to obtain for tasks that require expert annotation. Although our tasks under examination are in English, we believe that this work is extensible to other languages. Since one of the initial steps for obtaining linguistic representations involves the use of a pretrained language model, we expect lower quality for low-resource languages where such pretrained models have poor performance or are non-existent.

Hyperparameter tuning including time feature selection, given that the timestamps are available, is often key in achieving competitive classification performance. We provide guidelines and expect the users to perform a thorough grid search if needed to reach a competitive performance. Lastly, we understand that our data point-level evaluation, which assesses predictions at each point in the stream in silo, can be lacking pattern identification on a stream level. We plan to address stream-level evaluation using the settings from Tsakalidis et al. (2022b) in future work and we encourage users to cross-check performance with stream-level metrics.

Ethics Statement

The current project focuses on providing a toolkit for facilitating research and applications in longitudinal modelling. This is showcased in three tasks, two of which employ existing datasets (TalkLife and AnnoMI) and one is a re-interpretation of an existing public dataset (LRS).

Since the TalkLife dataset involves sensitive user generated social media content, Ethics approval was received from the Institutional Review Board (IRB) of the corresponding ethics board of the University of Warwick prior to engaging in longitudinal modelling with this dataset. Thorough data analysis, data sharing policies to protect sensitive information and data anonymisation were used to address ethical considerations around the nature of such data (Mao et al., 2011; Keküllüoglu et al., 2020). Access to TalkLife's data was obtained through the submission of a project proposal and the approval of the corresponding license by TalkLife[11]. TalkLife data were maintained and experiments were ran through a secure server accessible only by our group members. While we release code examples and results, we do not release any data, labels, models or preprocessing associated with TalkLife data in our git repository.

The AnnoMI dataset is publicly available and is based on transcribed videos of therapy sessions which are enacted.

[11]`https://www.talklife.com/`

The LRS dataset is a re-interpretation of the RumourEval 2017 dataset to reflect switches in stance over time. RumourEval-2017 is a well established dataset for stance and rumour verification. The longitudinal stance extension of the dataset allows studying the changes in public stance over time.

Developing methods for longitudinal modeling is an important research direction for better interpretation of events. Potential risks from the application of our work in being able to identify moments of change in individuals' timelines are akin to those in earlier work on personal event identification from social media and the detection of suicidal ideation. Potential mitigation strategies include restricting access to the code base trained on TalkLife and annotation labels used for evaluation.

Acknowledgements

This work was supported by a UKRI/EPSRC Turing AI Fellowship to Maria Liakata (grant EP/V030302/1), the Alan Turing Institute (grant EP/N510129/1), Baskerville (a national accelerated compute resource under the EPSRC Grant EP/T022221/1), a DeepMind PhD Scholarship, an EPSRC (grant EP/S026347/1), the Data Centric Engineering Programme (under the Lloyd's Register Foundation grant G0095), the Defence and Security Programme (funded by the UK Government), the Office for National Statistics & The Alan Turing Institute (strategic partnership) and by the Hong Kong Innovation and Technology Commission (InnoHK Project CIMDA).

The authors would like to thank Kasra Hosseini and Nathan Simpson for their early contributions to the `nlpsig` library as well as Federico Nanni and the anonymous reviewers for their valuable feedback.

References

Dimitris Achlioptas. 2003. Database-friendly random projections: Johnson-lindenstrauss with binary coins. *Journal of computer and System Sciences*, 66(4):671–687.

Robert Bamler and Stephan Mandt. 2017. Dynamic word embeddings. In *International conference on Machine learning*, pages 380–389. PMLR.

Ella Bingham and Heikki Mannila. 2001. Random projection in dimensionality reduction: applications to image and text data. In *Proceedings of the seventh ACM SIGKDD international conference on Knowledge discovery and data mining*, pages 245–250.

John Pougué Biyong, Bo Wang, Terry Lyons, and Alejo J Nevado-Holgado. 2020. Information extraction from swedish medical prescriptions with sig-transformer encoder. *arXiv preprint arXiv:2010.04897*.

Patric Bonnier, Patrick Kidger, Imanol Perez Arribas, Cristopher Salvi, and Terry Lyons. 2019. Deep signature transforms. *arXiv preprint arXiv:1905.08494*.

James Bradbury, Roy Frostig, Peter Hawkins, Matthew James Johnson, Chris Leary, Dougal Maclaurin, George Necula, Adam Paszke, Jake VanderPlas, Skye Wanderman-Milne, and Qiao Zhang. 2018. JAX: composable transformations of Python+NumPy programs.

Lei Cao, Huijun Zhang, Ling Feng, Zihan Wei, Xin Wang, Ningyun Li, and Xiaohao He. 2019. Latent suicide risk detection on microblog via suicide-oriented word embeddings and layered attention. *arXiv preprint arXiv:1910.12038*.

Kuo-Tsai Chen. 1958. Integration of paths–a faithful representation of paths by noncommutative formal power series. *Transactions of the American Mathematical Society*, 89(2):395–407.

Tong Chen, Xue Li, Hongzhi Yin, and Jun Zhang. 2018. Call attention to rumors: Deep attention based recurrent neural networks for early rumor detection. In *Trends and Applications in Knowledge Discovery and Data Mining: PAKDD 2018 Workshops, BDASC, BDM, ML4Cyber, PAISI, DaMEMO, Melbourne, VIC, Australia, June 3, 2018, Revised Selected Papers 22*, pages 40–52. Springer.

Jacob Devlin, Ming-Wei Chang, Kenton Lee, and Kristina Toutanova. 2018. BERT: Pre-training of deep bidirectional transformers for language understanding. *arXiv preprint arXiv:1810.04805*.

Aniket Didolkar, Kshitij Gupta, Anirudh Goyal, Nitesh Bharadwaj Gundavarapu, Alex M Lamb, Nan Rosemary Ke, and Yoshua Bengio. 2022. Temporal latent bottleneck: Synthesis of fast and slow processing mechanisms in sequence learning. *Advances in Neural Information Processing Systems*, 35:10505–10520.

Adji B Dieng, Francisco JR Ruiz, and David M Blei. 2019. The dynamic embedded topic model. *arXiv preprint arXiv:1907.05545*.

Genevieve Gorrell, Elena Kochkina, Maria Liakata, Ahmet Aker, Arkaitz Zubiaga, Kalina Bontcheva, and Leon Derczynski. 2019. Semeval-2019 task 7: Rumoureval 2019: Determining rumour veracity and support for rumours. In *Proceedings of the 13th International Workshop on Semantic Evaluation: NAACL HLT 2019*, pages 845–854. Association for Computational Linguistics.

Zhinan Gou, Lixin Han, Ling Sun, Jun Zhu, and Hong Yan. 2018. Constructing dynamic topic models based on variational autoencoder and factor graph. *IEEE Access*, 6:53102–53111.

Maarten Grootendorst. 2022. Bertopic: Neural topic modeling with a class-based tf-idf procedure. *arXiv preprint arXiv:2203.05794*.

Yulan He, Chenghua Lin, Wei Gao, and Kam-Fai Wong. 2014. Dynamic joint sentiment-topic model. *ACM Transactions on Intelligent Systems and Technology (TIST)*, 5(1):1–21.

Zihao He, Leili Tavabi, Kristina Lerman, and Mohammad Soleymani. 2021. Speaker turn modeling for dialogue act classification. *arXiv preprint arXiv:2109.05056*.

Dilara Keküllüoglu, Walid Magdy, and Kami Vaniea. 2020. Analysing privacy leakage of life events on twitter. In *12th ACM conference on web science*, pages 287–294.

Patrick Kidger and Terry Lyons. 2021. Signatory: differentiable computations of the signature and logsignature transforms, on both CPU and GPU. In *International Conference on Learning Representations*. `https://github.com/patrick-kidger/signatory`.

Diederik P Kingma and Jimmy Ba. 2014. Adam: A method for stochastic optimization. *arXiv preprint arXiv:1412.6980*.

Elena Kochkina, Tamanna Hossain, Robert L. Logan, Miguel Arana-Catania, Rob Procter, Arkaitz Zubiaga, Sameer Singh, Yulan He, and Maria Liakata. 2023. Evaluating the generalisability of neural rumour verification models. *Information Processing & Management*, 60(1):103116.

Elena Kochkina, Maria Liakata, and Arkaitz Zubiaga. 2018. All-in-one: Multi-task learning for rumour verification. *arXiv preprint arXiv:1806.03713*.

Sumeet Kumar and Kathleen M Carley. 2019. Tree lstms with convolution units to predict stance and rumor veracity in social media conversations. In *Proceedings of the 57th annual meeting of the association for computational linguistics*, pages 5047–5058.

Daniel Levin, Terry Lyons, and Hao Ni. 2013. Learning from the past, predicting the statistics for the future, learning an evolving system. *arXiv preprint arXiv:1309.0260*.

Shujian Liao, Terry Lyons, Weixin Yang, Kevin Schlegel, and Hao Ni. 2021. Logsig-rnn: A novel network for robust and efficient skeleton-based action recognition. *arXiv preprint arXiv:2110.13008*.

Tsung-Yi Lin, Priya Goyal, Ross Girshick, Kaiming He, and Piotr Dollár. 2017. Focal loss for dense object detection. In *Proceedings of the IEEE international conference on computer vision*, pages 2980–2988.

Xiaomo Liu, Armineh Nourbakhsh, Quanzhi Li, Rui Fang, and Sameena Shah. 2015. Real-time rumor debunking on twitter. In *Proceedings of the 24th ACM international on conference on information and knowledge management*, pages 1867–1870.

Yang Liu, Kun Han, Zhao Tan, and Yun Lei. 2017. Using context information for dialog act classification in dnn framework. In *Proceedings of the 2017 Conference on Empirical Methods in Natural Language Processing*, pages 2170–2178.

Terry Lyons, Hao Ni, and Harald Oberhauser. 2014. A feature set for streams and an application to high-frequency financial tick data. In *Proceedings of the 2014 International Conference on Big Data Science and Computing*, pages 1–8.

Terry J Lyons. 1998. Differential equations driven by rough signals. *Revista Matemática Iberoamericana*, 14(2):215–310.

Huina Mao, Xin Shuai, and Apu Kapadia. 2011. Loose tweets: an analysis of privacy leaks on twitter. In *Proceedings of the 10th annual ACM workshop on Privacy in the electronic society*, pages 1–12.

Leland McInnes, John Healy, and James Melville. 2018. Umap: Uniform manifold approximation and projection for dimension reduction. *arXiv preprint arXiv:1802.03426*.

Syrielle Montariol, Matej Martinc, and Lidia Pivovarova. 2021. Scalable and interpretable semantic change detection. In *Proceedings of the 2021 Conference of the North American Chapter of the Association for Computational Linguistics: Human Language Technologies*, pages 4642–4652.

James H Morrill, Andrey Kormilitzin, Alejo J Nevado-Holgado, Sumanth Swaminathan, Samuel D Howison, and Terry J Lyons. 2020. Utilization of the signature method to identify the early onset of sepsis from multivariate physiological time series in critical care monitoring. *Critical Care Medicine*, 48(10):e976–e981.

Jiaqi Mu and Pramod Viswanath. 2018. All-but-the-top: Simple and effective postprocessing for word representations. In *International Conference on Learning Representations*.

James Mullenbach, Sarah Wiegreffe, Jon Duke, Jimeng Sun, and Jacob Eisenstein. 2018. Explainable prediction of medical codes from clinical text. *arXiv preprint arXiv:1802.05695*.

Clarence Boon Liang Ng, Diogo Santos, and Marek Rei. 2023. Modelling temporal document sequences for clinical icd coding. *arXiv preprint arXiv:2302.12666*.

Adam Paszke, Sam Gross, Francisco Massa, Adam Lerer, James Bradbury, Gregory Chanan, Trevor Killeen, Zeming Lin, Natalia Gimelshein, Luca Antiga, et al. 2019. Pytorch: An imperative style, high-performance deep learning library. *Advances in neural information processing systems*, 32.

Imanol Perez Arribas, Guy M Goodwin, John R Geddes, Terry Lyons, and Kate EA Saunders. 2018. A signature-based machine learning model for distinguishing bipolar disorder and borderline personality disorder. *Translational psychiatry*, 8(1):274.

Vikas Raunak, Vivek Gupta, and Florian Metze. 2019. Effective dimensionality reduction for word embeddings. In *Proceedings of the 4th Workshop on Representation Learning for NLP (RepL4NLP-2019)*, pages 235–243.

Nils Reimers and Iryna Gurevych. 2019. Sentence-BERT: Sentence Embeddings using Siamese BERT-Networks. In *Proceedings of the 2019 Conference on Empirical Methods in Natural Language Processing*. Association for Computational Linguistics.

Jeremy Reizenstein and Benjamin Graham. 2020. Algorithm 1004: The iisignature library: Efficient calculation of iterated-integral signatures and log signatures. *ACM Transactions on Mathematical Software (TOMS)*.

Guy D Rosin and Kira Radinsky. 2022. Temporal attention for language models. *arXiv preprint arXiv:2202.02093*.

Ramit Sawhney, Harshit Joshi, Rajiv Shah, and Lucie Flek. 2021. Suicide ideation detection via social and temporal user representations using hyperbolic learning. In *Proceedings of the 2021 Conference of the North American Chapter of the Association for Computational Linguistics: Human Language Technologies*, pages 2176–2190.

Adam Tsakalidis, Jenny Chim, Iman Munire Bilal, Ayah Zirikly, Dana Atzil-Slonim, Federico Nanni, Philip Resnik, Manas Gaur, Kaushik Roy, Becky Inkster, et al. 2022a. Overview of the clpsych 2022 shared task: Capturing moments of change in longitudinal user posts.

Adam Tsakalidis and Maria Liakata. 2020. Sequential modelling of the evolution of word representations for semantic change detection. In *Proceedings of the 2020 Conference on Empirical Methods in Natural Language Processing (EMNLP)*, pages 8485–8497.

Adam Tsakalidis, Federico Nanni, Anthony Hills, Jenny Chim, Jiayu Song, and Maria Liakata. 2022b. Identifying moments of change from longitudinal user text. *arXiv preprint arXiv:2205.05593*.

Talia Tseriotou, Adam Tsakalidis, Peter Foster, Terence Lyons, and Maria Liakata. 2023. Sequential path signature networks for personalised longitudinal language modeling. In *Findings of the Association for Computational Linguistics: ACL 2023*, pages 5016–5031.

Bo Wang, Maria Liakata, Hao Ni, Terry Lyons, Alejo J Nevado-Holgado, and Kate Saunders. 2019. A path signature approach for speech emotion recognition. In *Interspeech 2019*, pages 1661–1665. ISCA.

Bo Wang, Yue Wu, Nemanja Vaci, Maria Liakata, Terry Lyons, and Kate EA Saunders. 2021. Modelling paralinguistic properties in conversational speech to detect bipolar disorder and borderline personality disorder. In *ICASSP 2021-2021 IEEE International Conference on Acoustics, Speech and Signal Processing (ICASSP)*, pages 7243–7247. IEEE.

Thomas Wolf, Lysandre Debut, Victor Sanh, Julien Chaumond, Clement Delangue, Anthony Moi, Pierric Cistac, Tim Rault, Rémi Louf, Morgan Funtowicz, et al. 2020. Transformers: State-of-the-art natural language processing. In *Proceedings of the 2020 Conference on Empirical Methods in Natural Language Processing: System Demonstrations*, pages 38–45.

Zixiu Wu, Simone Balloccu, Vivek Kumar, Rim Helaoui, Ehud Reiter, Diego Reforgiato Recupero, and Daniele Riboni. 2022. Anno-MI: A dataset of expert-annotated counselling dialogues. In *ICASSP 2022-2022 IEEE International Conference on Acoustics, Speech and Signal Processing (ICASSP)*, pages 6177–6181. IEEE.

Zecheng Xie, Zenghui Sun, Lianwen Jin, Hao Ni, and Terry Lyons. 2017. Learning spatial-semantic context with fully convolutional recurrent network for online handwritten chinese text recognition. *IEEE transactions on pattern analysis and machine intelligence*, 40(8):1903–1917.

Weixin Yang, Lianwen Jin, Hao Ni, and Terry Lyons. 2016. Rotation-free online handwritten character recognition using dyadic path signature features, hanging normalization, and deep neural network. In *2016 23rd International Conference on Pattern Recognition (ICPR)*, pages 4083–4088. IEEE.

Weixin Yang, Terry Lyons, Hao Ni, Cordelia Schmid, and Lianwen Jin. 2017. Developing the path signature methodology and its application to landmark-based human action recognition. *arXiv preprint arXiv:1707.03993*.

Zijun Yao, Yifan Sun, Weicong Ding, Nikhil Rao, and Hui Xiong. 2018. Dynamic word embeddings for evolving semantic discovery. In *Proceedings of the eleventh acm international conference on web search and data mining*, pages 673–681.

Zheng Yuan, Chuanqi Tan, and Songfang Huang. 2022. Code synonyms do matter: multiple synonyms matching network for automatic icd coding. *arXiv preprint arXiv:2203.01515*.

Arkaitz Zubiaga, Maria Liakata, Rob Procter, Geraldine Wong Sak Hoi, and Peter Tolmie. 2016. Analysing how people orient to and spread rumours in social media by looking at conversational threads. *PloS one*, 11(3):e0150989.

A Experiment setup details

We train all models using PyTorch (Paszke et al., 2019) and Huggingface Transformers (Wolf et al., 2020) for BERT, using the alpha-weighted focal loss (Lin et al., 2017), except for BERT (ce).

SBERT representations: As noted in §3.3, we use SentenceBERT (SBERT) (Reimers and Gurevych, 2019) to encode each data point to obtain semantically meaningful embeddings. To do this with our toolkit, we used the `nlpsig.SentenceEncoder`[12] class which uses the `sentence-transformers` library. For each dataset, we obtained 384-dimensional embeddings using the "all-MiniLM-L12-v2" model[13].

Model experiment settings: In each of our experiments in §5, we select the best model for each of the 5 folds using the best validation F1 macro-average score on 100 epochs with early stopping (patience set to 3). For training, we use the Adam optimiser (Kingma and Ba, 2014) with weight decay of 0.0001. For all models, we use the alpha-weighted focal loss (Lin et al., 2017) with setting $\gamma = 2$ and alpha of $\sqrt{1/p_t}$ where p_t is the probability of class t in the training data. The exception is for the BERT (ce) baseline model where we used the cross-entropy loss. For BERT, we used batch size of 8 during training due to limited GPU resources available for training on the secure data environment which hosted the TalkLife dataset. For the other models, we used batch size of 64.

For the TalkLife MoC dataset, we use the same train/test splits as in Tsakalidis et al. (2022a,b); Tseriotou et al. (2023). Furthermore, we average the F1 macro-average performance over three random seeds, $(1, 12, 123)$. For Anno-MI and Longitudinal Rumour Stance datasets, we created the five folds using the `nlpsig.Folds` class[14] class (with `random_state=0`). Each fold constructed was used as a test and the rest as the training and validation data. Validation sets were formed on 33% of the train set. When creating the folds, we stratify using the `transcript_id` for Anno-MI and the conversation ID for Rumours to ensure there was no contamination between streams.

For each model, we perform a grid search for hyperparameter selection based on the validation set performance comparing F1 macro-average. For signature window models, prior to hyperparameter search, we performed dimensionality reduction on

[12] https://nlpsig.readthedocs.io/en/latest/encode_text.html

[13] https://huggingface.co/sentence-transformers/all-MiniLM-L12-v2

[14] https://nlpsig.readthedocs.io/en/latest/classification_utils.html

the SBERT embeddings using UMAP (McInnes et al., 2018) with the `umap-learn` Python library. Using the `UMAP`[15] class in the library, we kept all default parameters besides `n_neighbors=50`, `min_dist=0.99` and `metric="cosine"`. In each of the signature window models, we reduced the SBERT embeddings to 15 dimensions. For all models considered, the dropout rate was set to 0.1.

In the rest of this section, we state the hyperparameters choices we had for each model. Note that the full results for each model that we trained (for each hyperparameter configuration and seed) as well as the best hyperparameters for each model and dataset can be found in the GitHub repository for the project in the `examples` folder[16].

SWNU and Seq-Sig-Net: For the signature window networks which used the Signature Window Network Unit (SWNU) (§3.4, 5.2), hyperparameter selection was set through a grid search over the parameters: learning rate $\in [0.0005, 0.0003, 0.0001]$, LSTM hidden dimensions of SWNU $\in [10, 12]$, FFN hidden dimensions $\in [[32, 32], [128, 128], [512, 512]]$ where $[h_1, h_2]$ means a two hidden layer FFN of dimensions h_i in the ith layer. For Seq-Sig-Net, the BiLSTM hidden dimensions $\in [300, 400]$. We took the log-signature transform with depth (degree of truncation) 3. In each model run, the convolution-1d reduced dimensions is equal to the LSTM hidden dimensions (i.e. 10 or 12 here).

SW-Attn and Seq-Sig-Net-Attention models: For the signature window networks which used the Signature Window Attention Unit (§3.4, 5.2) hyperparameter selection was set through a grid search over the following parameters: learning rate $\in [0.0005, 0.0003, 0.0001]$, convolution-1d reduced dimensions $\in [10, 12]$, FFN hidden dimensions $\in [[32, 32], [128, 128], [512, 512]]$. We took the log-signature transform with depth (degree of truncation) 3. While the toolkit allows you to easily stack multiple SW-Attn blocks, i.e. multiple iterations of taking the expanding window signatures and multi-head attention (with add+norm and a linear layer), we only have one block, `num_layer=1`.

For models using SW-Attn units, we must choose the number of attention heads to divide the resulting number of signature channels after taking streaming signatures. For models with conv-1d reduced dimensions set to 10, `output_channels=10`, we set `num_heads=5` since after taking a log-signature of depth 3, the output has dimension 385[17]. For models with `output_channels=12`, we set `num_heads=10` since the number of log-signature channels at depth 3 for a path with 12 channels is 650.

BERT: We fine-tuned the `bert-base-uncased`[18] model on the Huggingface model hub, and used the `transformers` library and Trainer API for training the model. The only hyperparameter we performed a grid-search for was learning rate $\in [0.00005, 0.00001, 0.000001]$[19]. For BERT, we found it was important to use a much lower learning rate than the ones we used for other models due to the larger number of parameters in the model.

FFN models: For models using a Feedforward Network (FFN), either operating on the SBERT embedding of the current point (**FFN**) or operating on a concatenation of the current SBERT embedding with the mean average of its historical stream (**FFN History**), we perform a hyperparameter search over learning rate $\in [0.001, 0.0005, 0.0001]$ and hidden dimensions $\in [[64, 64], [128, 128], [256, 256], [512, 512]]$.

BiLSTM: We apply a single layer BiLSTM on a specified number of historical SBERT embeddings for the data point. We perform a grid search over learning rate $\in [0.001, 0.0005, 0.0001]$ and hidden dimension sizes $[200, 300, 400]$.

B Results

We present class-level performance for each task in Tables 3, 4 and 5.

Model	Neutral(N)			Change(C)			Sustain(S)			Macro-avg		
BERT (focal)	.767			.449			.339			.519		
BERT (ce)	**.784**			.442			.277			.501		
FFN	.764			.424			.347			.512		
FFN History	.761			.449			.351			.520		
BiLSTM (w=5)	.753			.449			.348			.517		
SWNU (w=5)	.762			.447			.356			.522		
SW-Attn (w=5)	.749			.450			.346			.515		
History Length (units)	**11 (n=3)**				**20 (n=6)**				**35 (n=11)**			
	N	**C**	**S**	**Macro-avg**	**N**	**C**	**S**	**Macro-avg**	**N**	**C**	**S**	**Macro-avg**
BiLSTM	.746	.446	**.363**	.518	.754	.446	.322	.507	.755	.446	.329	.510
SWNU	.761	.444	.360	.522	.759	.440	.338	.512	.752	.413	.314	.493
SW-Attn	.759	.450	.341	.517	.754	.438	.333	.508	.749	.446	.330	.508
Seq-Sig-Net	.769	.446	.359	**.525**	.769	**.452**	.347	.523	.763	.446	.342	.517
SW-Attn+BiLSTM	.750	.446	.339	.511	.757	**.452**	.332	.514	.763	.438	.345	.515
SW-Attn+Encoder	.765	.411	.319	.498	.767	.423	.327	.506	.763	.410	.343	.505

Table 3: Class-level F1 scores of the Sig-Networks toolkit models on **Anno-MI** for different History Lengths. **Best** and second best scores are highlighted.

[15] `https://umap-learn.readthedocs.io/en/latest/api.html`

[16] `https://github.com/ttseriotou/sig-networks/tree/main/examples`

[17] `signatory.logsignature_channels(10, 3)` can be used to compute this number.

[18] `https://huggingface.co/bert-base-uncased`

[19] Note in `transformers` (version 4.30.2), the default learning rate is 0.00005

Model	No Switch			Switch			Macro-avg		
BERT (focal)	.724			.454			.589		
BERT (ce)	.720			.472			.596		
FFN	.704			.457			.581		
FFN History	.727			.523			.625		
BiLSTM (w=5)	.730			.545			.637		
SWNU (w=5)	**.761**			.580			.670		
SW-Attn (w=5)	**.761**			.574			.667		
History Length (units)	**11 (n=3)**			**20 (n=6)**			**35 (n=11)**		
	No Switch	**Switch**	**Macro-avg**	**No Switch**	**Switch**	**Macro-avg**	**No Switch**	**Switch**	**Macro-avg**
BiLSTM	.748	.566	.657	.740	.555	.648	.748	.548	.648
SWNU	.759	.584	.671	.736	.571	.654	.759	.587	.673
SW-Attn	.745	.573	.659	.747	.583	.665	.743	.579	.661
Seq-Sig-Net	.760	.584	.672	.754	**.602**	**.678**	.748	.559	.654
SW-Attn+BiLSTM	.742	.584	.663	.741	.573	.657	.750	.570	.660
SW-Attn+Encoder	.746	.581	.664	.742	.572	.657	.756	.569	.662

Table 4: Class-level F1 scores of the Sig-Networks toolkit models on **Longitudinal Rumour Stance** for different History Lengths. **Best** and second best scores are highlighted.

Model	IS				IE				O			Macro-avg
BERT (focal)	.283				.439				.871			.531
BERT (ce)	.229				.431				**.903**			.521
FFN	.281				.432				.890			.534
FFN History	.280				.454				.877			.537
BiLSTM (w=5)	.260				.479				.892			.544
SWNU (w=5)	.301				.494				.894			**.563**
SW-Attn (w=5)	.300				.480				.887			.556
History Length (units)	**11 (n=3)**				**20 (n=6)**				**35 (n=11)**			
	IS	**IE**	**O**	**Macro-avg**	**IS**	**IS**	**O**	**Macro-avg**	**IS**	**IE**	**O**	**Macro-avg**
BiLSTM	.252	.478	.887	.539	.244	.470	.887	.533	.225	.460	.891	.525
SWNU	.292	.471	.887	.550	.275	.448	.888	.537	.270	.457	.889	.539
SW-Attn	.286	.471	.884	.547	.286	.453	.883	.541	.289	.452	.876	.539
Seq-Sig-Net	.301	**.495**	.893	**.563**	**.304**	.487	.891	.561	.303	.480	.894	.559
SW-Attn+BiLSTM	.291	.483	.887	.554	.298	.483	.890	.557	.298	.467	.885	.550
SW-Attn+Encoder	.289	.477	.890	.552	.302	.463	.891	.552	.294	.452	.887	.545

Table 5: Class-level F1 scores of the Sig-Networks toolkit models on **TalkLife MoC** for different History Lengths. **Best** and second best scores are highlighted.

C Time Feature Guidance

As mentioned in §4.1 the toolkit allows for the automatic computation of the following time-derived features if a timestamp column is provided:

- `time_encoding`: date as fraction of the year
- `time_encoding_minute`: time as fraction of minutes, ignoring the date
- `time_diff`: time difference between consecutive data in the stream
- `timeline_index`: index of the data point in the stream

The option to include user-processed time features is available. Optionally, the user can specify a standardisation method for each time feature from the list below:

- `None`: no transformation applied
- `z_score`: transformation by subtracting the mean and dividing by the standard deviation of the data points
- `sum_divide`: transformation by dividing by the sum of the data points
- `minmax`: transformation by subtracting the minimum of data points from the current data point and dividing by the differential of the maximum and minimum of the data points.

The above (normalised) features can be included as part of the path stream in the signature model (*in-path*) and/or concatenated with the SBERT representation of the current data point in the input to the final FFN layers in the model (*in-input*) . During the different task modeling we find particularly important the efficient incorporation of time features. Such decision is task-driven.

For Anno-MI we include the `time_encoding_minute` and `timeline_index` (without transformation) *in-path*. For Longitudinal Rumour Stance we include `time_encoding` normalised with `z_score` and `timeline_index` without normalisation both *in-path* and *in-input*. Finally for TalkLife MoC we use `time_encoding` normalised with `z_score` both *in-path* and *in-input*. Since TalkLife and Longitudinal Rumour Stance are social media datasets they can benefit from the use of *in-input* features that model the temporal semantic component of linguistic representations. We expect *in-input* features to be less beneficial for our specific dialogue task which is semantically stable with conversations being date-agnostic (but not time agnostic). At the same time in the dialogue task of Anno-MI, the use of both the `time_encoding_minute`, which ignores the date, and `timeline_index` *in-path*, allows for modeling both the temporal flow of the conversation and the position (index) of the utterance of interest in the dialogue. While Longitudinal Rumour Stance also benefits from using the `timeline_index` which identifies the position of information with respect to the initial claim, the use of `time_encoding` normalised with `z_score` is more suitable here as it makes use of the date of the comment. In TalkLife only the latter is used, without any index features. Here, since relevant context for each post under consideration occurs in short history windows, the timeline position (index) is irrelevant. By presenting how different time features benefit each task together with the intuition behind the selection process, we encourage users to consider the temporal characteristics of their task in-hand for efficient time feature selection.

D Package Environment

The experiments ran in a Python 3.8.17 environment with the key following libraries: `sig-networks` (0.2.0), `nlpsig` (0.2.2), `torch` (1.9.0), `signatory` (1.2.6.1.9.0), `sentence-transformers` (2.2.2), `transformers` (4.30.2), `accelerate` (0.20.1), `evaluate` (0.4.0), `datasets` (2.14.2), `pandas` (1.5.3), `numpy` (1.24.4), `scikit-learn` (1.3.0), `umap` (0.5.3).

E Path Signature Libraries

Library	Link
roughpy	https://github.com/datasig-ac-uk/RoughPy
esig	https://github.com/datasig-ac-uk/esig
iisignature	https://github.com/bottler/iisignature
signatory	https://github.com/patrick-kidger/signatory
signax	https://github.com/Anh-Tong/signax

F Infrastructure

The experiments with the Anno-MI and Longitudinal Stance datasets were ran on the *Baskerville*, a GPU Tier2 cluster developed and maintained by the University of Birmingham in a collaboration with a number of partners including The Alan Turing Institute. Baskerville provided us access with Nvidia A100 GPUs (40GB and 80GB variants).

The experiments with the TalkLife dataset were ran on *Sanctus*, a Queen Mary University of London maintained server, with a x86_64 processor, 80 CPUs, 384 GB of RAM and 3 Nvidia A30 GPUs.

G Using the model modules

As noted in §4.3, we provide PyTorch modules for each of components of our Sig-Network models to encourage novel integration into other systems. For example, the key building blocks in each of our models are the Signature Window units, SWNU Tseriotou et al. (2023) and SW-Attn, as discussed in §3.4. These can be easily accessed in the toolkit with a few lines of Python code.

For example, in code listings 1 and 2 we can simply load in the SWNU and SW-Attn units and initialise an instance of the module in a few lines. For initialising SWNU in listing 1, we define several arguments: the input channels of our stream, `input_channels=10`, the number of output channels after the convolution-1d layer, `output_channels=5`, whether to take the log-signature or standard signature transformation, `log_signature=False`, the signature depth, `sig_depth=3`, the dimension of the LSTM hidden state(s), `hidden_dim=5`, the pooling strategy to obtain a final stream representation, `pooling="signature"`, to not chronologically reverse the order of the stream, `reverse_path=False`, to use a BiLSTM, `BiLSTM=True`, to use a convolution-1d layer, `augmentation_type="Conv1d"`. The alternative option for `augmentation_type` is to have `augmentation_type="signatory"` which will use the `signatory.Augment` PyTorch module to use a larger convolution neural network (CNN) for which you can specify the hidden dimensions to in the `hidden_dim_aug` argument which is set to `None` in this example. Note that some of these arguments have default values, but we present them all here for more clarity.

```
from sig_networks.swnu import SWNU

# initialise a SWNU object
swnu = SWNU(
    input_channels=10,
    output_channels=5,
    log_signature=False,
    sig_depth=3,
    hidden_dim=5,
    pooling="signature",
    reverse_path=False,
    BiLSTM=True,
    augmentation_type="Conv1d",
)
```

Listing 1: Example initialisation of Signature Window Network Unit object

The SW-Attn unit, called `SWMHAU` in the library, shares many of the same arguments as expected but since we are using Multihead-Attention (MHA) in place of a (Bi)LSTM, we specify the number of attention heads through the `num_heads` argument and specify how many stacks of these layers through the `num_layers` argument. We can also specify the dropout to use in the MHA layer here too.

```
from sig_networks.swmhau import SWMHAU

# initialise a SWMHAU object
swmhau = SWMHAU(
    input_channels=10,
    output_channels=5,
    log_signature=False,
    sig_depth=3,
    num_heads=5,
    num_layers=1,
    dropout_rate=0.1,
    pooling="signature",
    reverse_path=False,
    augmentation_type="Conv1d",
)
```

Listing 2: Example initialisation of SW-Attention unit object

Note that there are variants of these PyTorch modules which do not include the convolution 1d or CNN to project down the stream to a lower dimension before taking expanding window signatures, namely `sig_networks.SWLSTM` and `sig_networks.SWMHA`.

Once these objects have been created, they can simply be called to apply a forward pass of the units, see for example listing 3. These units receive as input a three-dimensional tensor of the batched streams and the resulting output is a two-dimensional tensor of batches of the fixed-length feature representations of the streams.

```
import torch

# create a three-dimensional tensor of 100 batched streams, each with history length w and 10 channels
streams = torch.randn(100, 20, 10)

# pass the streams through the SWNU
# swnu_features and swmhau_features are two-dimensional tensors of shape [batch, signature_channels]
swnu_features = swnu(streams)
swmhau_features = swmhau(streams)
```

Listing 3: Example forward pass of SWNU and SWMHAU objects

For full examples on how these PyTorch modules can be fitted into larger PyTorch networks, please refer to the source code for the Sig-Network family models in the library on GitHub[20].

[20] https://github.com/ttseriotou/sig-networks/tree/main/src/sig_networks

Author Index

Association for Computational Linguistics
209 N. Eighth Street
Stroudsburg, Pennsylvania 18360

CURRAN ASSOCIATES INC.
proceedings.com

ISBN 978-1-7138-9445-2
9 781713 894452